NEVER APOLOGISE
THE COLLECTED WRITINGS

LINDSAY ANDERSON

NEVER APOLOGISE

THE COLLECTED WRITINGS

LINDSAY ANDERSON

Edited By Paul Ryan

Plexus, London

Published by Plexus Publishing Limited
55a Clapham Common Southside
London SW4 9BX
www.plexusbooks.com
First Printing 2004

British Library Cataloguing In Publication Data

Anderson, Lindsay
   Never apologise : the collected writings of Lindsay Anderson
   1.Anderson, Lindsay 2.Motion picture producers and
   directors - Scotland - Biography 3.Dramatists, Scottish -
   20th century - Biography
   I.Title
   791.4'3'023'092

   ISBN 0 85965 317 X

Cover design by Phil Gambrill
Book design by Rebecca Martin
Cover photograph: Lindsay directs *O Lucky Man!*
Frontispiece and back cover: Lindsay Anderson, 1968
Printed and bound in Great Britain by Cromwell Press

CONTENTS

ON CRITICS AND CRITICISM

THE THEATRE

BRITISH CINEMA

Editor's Note

A number of people tried to persuade Lindsay Anderson to collect his critical writings in a single volume, but he always resisted the idea. 'Do you honestly think anyone will want to read this stuff?' he would say, gesturing at one of his many scrapbooks of newspaper and magazine cuttings. So I was surprised to receive a call from him one morning in 1992 suggesting that we meet to discuss the likely contents of such a book. He had been given a commitment from his publishers, Sandra Wake and Terry Porter of Plexus, who had published the scripts of *If. . . .* and *O Lucky Man!* and his book *About John Ford...*, that they would bring the book out in the way he envisaged it. That is to say, a book for the intelligent reader – unburdened with footnotes and academic references. 'And if they're puzzled by a name, Lindsay?' 'They can look it up!'

Over the next few months, Lindsay and I met at regular intervals to discuss the shape and content of the book. We quickly threw out the idea of assembling the pieces chronologically, and I had the difficult task of telling Lindsay that I found his original titles for the book, *Plays, Books and Films* and *The Writings and Memoirs of Lindsay Anderson* a wee bit lack-lustre. 'What's wrong with them?' he said, accusingly. 'Sorry, Lindsay,' I said. Lindsay leant back in his chair, then drawled at me, in a passable imitation of John Wayne, 'Never apologise, it's a sign of weakness.' I recognised the quotation from John Ford's *She Wore a Yellow Ribbon.* 'How about that for a title?' I said, 'Never Apologise.' Lindsay scowled and raised his glasses to his forehead. 'Hmmn,' he said, 'glad I thought of it.'

There were other disagreements, not so swiftly resolved. I sometimes had to fight very hard to include a piece that Lindsay felt was below his current standard. At one point, I conceded that there should be no juvenilia. '*What* juvenilia?' Lindsay thundered, and we stopped work for the day. But the clashes were few, and we found that the pieces fitted fairly comprehensively into the slots he had originally planned: 'British Cinema', 'Theatre', 'American Cinema', 'An International View' and, of course, 'Critics and Criticism'. All that remained was Lindsay's writing on his own career; and this, we knew, had to follow chronology. He had always intended to write his own commentary to these pieces, but I feared he would never even begin it. After all, he had often been urged to write an autobiography, and had even claimed it was under way with various working titles – 'Water Under the Bridge' was one, 'Never Asked Back' another.

It was David Thompson, whose BBC arts documentaries Lindsay much admired, who first suggested that I should sit down with a tape-recorder and cajole Lindsay into dictating the story of his professional life. Lindsay resisted the idea until, one day, he began recounting stories of his childhood and I switched on the tape. We employed a simple technique: a fairly relaxed dialogue touching on all aspects of Lindsay's career. Typically, Lindsay did everything possible to be obstructive. Once, halfway through an anecdote about the Royal Court, he turned on the television and pointed out an actor in an old Hollywood movie. 'Who's that?' he asked. Distracted, I made a stab at recognition: 'Is it Jack Holt?' 'Jack Holt!' Lindsay repeated with exaggerated incredulity, 'Really! Don't you know Walter Abel when you see him?' And so, laboriously, it went on.

At least, it would have gone on were it not for Lindsay's sudden death on 30th August 1994. My intention had been to hand the transcript of our conversations to Lindsay for him to cut out my prompts and questions and to re-cast his own words into his own commentary. Sadly, this could not now happen, and I set about revising the transcript myself. Certain gaps in the record were plugged with notes I had made after our many conversations, and from the transcript of comments Lindsay had made at a retrospective of his films in Cincinatti in 1992. So the 'Commentary' to be found linking the pieces in the 'Anderson on Anderson' section comes from more than one source. If there are any errors of fact, the fault should be laid at my door.

Lindsay's death came as a shock to all of his friends, and it is equally shocking to realise that, in the ten years since he died, so many of those friends have also fallen. Among them: Ben Aris, Ian Bannen, Alan Bates, James Broughton, Constance Chapman, Isabel Dean, John Gielgud, David Gill, Brian Glover, Richard Harris, Jocelyn Herbert, Peter Jeffrey, Margaret Johnstone (Maggie Parker), Kevin Lloyd, Alfred Lynch, Elspeth March, Rosemary Martin, Daniel Massey, Roddy McDowall, Dudley Moore, Bill Owen, Andy Phillips, Bryan Pringle, Karel Reisz, Serge Reggiani, Mary Selway, Ann Sothern, Alexander Walker and Richard Warwick.

Lindsay would have wished to salute them all, perhaps with another of his favourite quotations from *She Wore a Yellow Ribbon:* 'Goodbye is not a word we use in the cavalry'.

Paul Ryan
London, 2004

'If ignorance and passion are the foes of popular morality, it must be confessed that moral indifference is the malady of the cultivated classes. The modern separation of enlightenment and virtue, of thought and conscience, of the intellectual aristocracy from the honest and vulgar crowd, is the greatest danger that can threaten liberty . . .

. . . Our cynics and railers are mere egotists, who stand aloof from the common duty, and in their indolent remoteness are of no service to society against any ill which may attack it. Their cultivation consists in having got rid of feeling. And thus they fall farther and farther away from true humanity, and approach nearer to the demoniacal nature. What was it that Mephistopheles lacked? Not intelligence certainly, but goodness.'

Henri-Frederick Amiel: *Journal* (trans. Mrs Humphrey Ward)

Lindsay Anderson at his desk, 1984.

INTRODUCTION

A Revolutionary Soldier

IF YOU WANT TO MEASURE BRITAIN'S SENSE OF FILM CULTURE, TRY ASKING some young film-goers, on their way into a London cinema, to tell you what they know of Free Cinema. A similar sample on the streets of Paris would have no trouble in giving you chapter and verse on the French *Nouvelle Vague*, but their British counterparts would be unlikely to know what you were talking about. This ignorance of cinema was something which Lindsay Anderson fought against all his life and it became an increasingly lonely battle, not in the least helped by the spread of that most ill-defined of academic disciplines (and Lindsay could never mask his disdain as he pronounced the phrase), 'film and media studies'. When a young film-maker apologised to Lindsay for never having heard of him, claiming that she was probably 'too young', he replied: 'Well, have you heard of Shakespeare?' This was not arrogance, it was Lindsay standing up for every film-maker who had been forgotten by fashion, or left untaught by academia.

Lindsay had a fiery, Celtic soul, but his background – son of a Major General, education at Cheltenham College (later the location for *If. . . .*) and Wadham College, Oxford – meant that he understood completely the world which sought to quench the flames of passion. His poetic term for this world was 'England', by which he meant the cold, southern English, class-ridden cast of mind which has so long dominated British culture. At Oxford, his early interest in film led to his co-founding the quarterly magazine, *Sequence*, an opinionated journal designed to combat the dead hand of English indifference to cinema.

Lindsay's entry into film-making came through documentaries, if only because the industry was closed to tiro directors 50 years ago. From the start he 'challenged the orthodoxy of British Film', rejecting the paternalistic style of the Grierson school, and taking inspiration from the then-neglected films of Humphrey Jennings.

Soon afterwards, with his friends Karel Reisz and Tony Richardson, he founded Free Cinema. It was, he admitted, not so much a movement, nor was it a manifesto for film-makers, but more a way of grouping together often disparate films to get them shown. Although Lindsay once said that the Free Cinema 'manifesto' had been drafted by him 'to give journalists something to write about', it contained in its principal tenets his lifelong credo of artistic and social commitment.

1

No film can be too personal.
The image speaks. Sound amplifies and comments.
Size is irrelevant.
Perfection is not an aim.
An attitude means a style.
A style means an attitude.
Implicit in our attitude is a belief in freedom, in the importance
of people and in the significance of the everyday.

These opinions also informed his writings – after *Sequence*, in the *New Statesman*, *The Observer* and, most memorably, in *Sight and Sound*. It was there, in 1957, that he wrote 'Stand Up! Stand Up!', described by the critic Adrian Turner as 'unquestionably the single most influential piece of British film criticism ever written'. In this article, Lindsay called for seriousness and commitment in writing about film, but he also stated his opposition to the rise of film theory which was at the heart of his dissatisfaction with film study courses: 'It is a matter of fact, not opinion, that the cinema is an art. This does not call for theoretical discussion – unless, of course, you enjoy that kind of intellectual exercise.'

If his critical perceptions helped form his approach to film-making, so did his work in the theatre which was an integral part of his life. For *This Sporting Life*, he employed techniques from London's Royal Court Theatre by spending several days rehearsing scenes between Richard Harris and Rachel Roberts, and then shooting them, as near as he was able, in continuity. The result was a powerful and true portrait of the emotional pain that tears through all strata of life in this country. Its style is much more expressionist than 'social realist', and it stands far above other British films of its time to remain unrelentingly passionate, and resolutely modern.

The same may be said of *If . . . .*, which was the high-water mark of British cinema in the sixties (although, as Lindsay was fond of pointing out, it was an American film, Paramount having stepped in after every British distributor and financier had turned it down). The films that followed, *O Lucky Man!* and *Britannia Hospital*, were less well received but have proved remarkably prescient. If you do not believe me, seek them out again and then, as Lindsay would say, just look around you.

There were many who, unable to meet Lindsay's challenge, sought to discredit him. They characterised him as 'bitter' (forgetting that this adjective is often followed by the word 'truth', and is a precious ingredient of much great art). He could be blunt to the point of cruelty, but this was offset by his fundamental loyalty and generosity of spirit. Despite his often aggressive stance, Lindsay lacked the essential ruthlessness of the careerist and he was fortunate that his small but constant private income allowed him to remain aloof from the desperate financial need that motivates some artists. He was described by many as a romantic revolutionary but he was nothing so commonplace. Like Yeats, for whom he held a passion, and like his beloved John Ford, he was that rare and poetical being, a revolutionary romantic.

II

Lindsay Gordon Anderson was born in Bangalore, India in 1923 where his father, Captain (later Major General) A. V. Anderson was serving with the Royal Engineers. The Anderson family was Scottish and had a strong military tradition. On his mother's side, Lindsay was descended from an English wool merchant who had married into the Scottish Bell whisky family and his only artistic ancestor, as far as he knew, was a Bell who had been 'a painter and a bit mad, a bit wild and a bit drunk'. Lindsay's sense of himself as a Scot grew over the years and allowed him to make sense of his position as an outsider – morally, emotionally and socially – in the English middle-class world into which he was expected to take his place.

His education at Cheltenham College was thoroughly conventional, and his eagerness to volunteer for the 60th Rifles at the end of his time there might suggest that he had accepted the military destiny mapped out for him. In fact, Lindsay often insisted, he put himself forward for officer training only because his country was at war. His time at Oxford, where he began by reading Classics, was interrupted by his wartime military service in the Intelligence Corps, and when he returned he opted to read English.

At that point, Lindsay almost certainly had no clear idea of what it was he wanted to do in life. Since childhood he had had a vague desire to become an actor and he had appeared in school productions at Cheltenham (including one surreal revue which had him portray a party hostess who would drop on all fours and bark like a dog if anyone chanced to mention the weather). But he disliked the experience of amateur dramatics at Oxford, where he appeared in a couple of plays under Kenneth Tynan's direction, and in one directed by Guy Brenton (with whom he would later make the film, *Thursday's Children*). The Oxford University Dramatic Society was, Lindsay once recalled, 'very pseudo-professional and very competitive in a rather unpleasant way'.

His experience of film-going was confined to the standard British and American films of the day, and he had no real knowledge of foreign or classic films. He remembered having seen *Citizen Kane* at Cheltenham but

3

his first 'real creative shock in the cinema', as he put it, came at a post-war screening of John Ford's *My Darling Clementine* at the Odeon, Leicester Square in London. Ford's film alerted Lindsay to the artistic possibilities of cinema and he was enraged to find it consigned by the film critic of *The Times* to 'the graveyard of mediocrity'. Film, which had always been a favourite entertainment for him, became a passion and he was determined that it should be discussed on a critical level appropriate to an art form.

This new interest gave Lindsay a direction and allowed him to find his voice through the critical articles that he began to write for the Oxford-based film magazine, *Sequence*.

He had already written about film for the student magazine, *Isis*, and for *Mercury*, a journal published by and for the armed forces in India. *Sequence* began as the magazine of the Oxford University Film Society which Lindsay had joined to further his film education ('art house' cinemas had not yet come into being and screenings of film classics and foreign-language movies were confined to the film societies). Lindsay's first article for *Sequence* (published in December 1946 under the editorship of Peter Ericsson and John Boud) was, by his own admission, 'a very superficial and ignorant piece' on French film.

One year later the magazine had a new format and an editorial team that comprised Ericson, Lindsay and Penelope Houston. Their first issue was *Sequence 2* and it represented the magazine as it became known. The cover carried a still from *My Darling Clementine* and Ericson wrote an essay on Ford. Lindsay asked his friend Gavin Lambert, whom he had known at Cheltenham, to write a piece on British cinema. 'From the beginning,' Lindsay recalled, '*Sequence* was rather in reaction against what we felt to be an inflated estimation of British films, which took place in a patriotic way at the end of the War when there was a lot of big film-making activity among people like Michael Powell and David Lean at Pinewood. From the first, we drew attention to the lively and dynamic film-making in America, as well as concentrating on, and discovering for ourselves, continental film-makers and film-makers of the past.'

Gavin Lambert's role became increasingly important after the magazine moved to London in 1948, and he co-edited most of the issues with Lindsay and Ericsson. In order to give the impression of a large number of contributors, the editors themselves wrote pseudonymous articles, signing themselves with such fanciful names as 'Alberta Marlow' (the character played by Mary Astor in *Across the Pacific*).

A happy accident allowed Lindsay to meet another important figure in the *Sequence* story when he went to view a print of Hitchcock's film *The Lodger* at the National Film Archive in Aston Clinton. He found that his time on the Movieola had been double-booked with a young man called

Karel Reisz who was writing a book on film editing. The two struck up a friendship and Reisz was invited to join the editorial team of *Sequence* – he and Lindsay co-edited the last issue of the magazine in 1952.

Nothing like *Sequence* exists in Britain today, when even the most serious film periodicals devote endless pages to the 'sociological significance' of the latest product of Hollywood hyperbole. Despite its small circulation and its short life, *Sequence* was enormously influential, and Lindsay had an assured reputation as a trenchant and authoritative figure even before he made his first films.

The *Sequence* years overlapped with certain other important developments in Lindsay's life – not least his first work as a film-maker – but the spirit of the magazine informed all of his creative work and, for better or (occasionally) for worse, his subsequent critical writing. It was in *Sequence*, for example, that Lindsay first coined the term 'Free Cinema', using it as the title for a piece sent to the magazine by Alan Cooke, a film enthusiast who later went on to have a career in television and cinema. Cooke's article – nominally about a group of American and Canadian short films – ended with this trenchant paragraph:

> I prefer to group these films under another heading – Free Cinema –which has the advantage of being inclusive rather than exclusive, of indicating a genre to which we may credit all films which please or illuminate without compromise or self-mutilation. *Muscle Beach* is an example of Free Cinema, and so is *Fireworks*. So (amongst the films discussed elsewhere in this issue) are *Wagonmaster*, *Les Dames du Bois de Bologne*, *Orphée*. All these films, however diverse their intentions, have one achievement in common: an expressive and personal use of the medium. Free Cinema includes the acknowledged successes as well as the *films maudits*, the traditionalist as well as the experimentalist; it constitutes the real avant-garde, the true aristocracy of the cinema.

The signature on the article remained Cooke's, but the voice in that last section is unquestionably Lindsay's. He had, in fact, rewritten the piece to make it, as he himself put it, 'a bit more "important". . . We always did this on *Sequence*; we were always rewriting people's things.' It is easy to see, given Lindsay's definition of Free Cinema in that article, why he should later use the name as the banner under which he and his friends would show their first films, but it is clear, too, that what he was calling on audiences and critics to provide was a personal response to a film.

The first opportunity for Lindsay himself to make films came in 1948 with a chance meeting, at a national convention of British Film Societies, with

Lois Sutcliffe from the Wakefield Film Society in Yorkshire. Her husband was a Wakefield industrialist who wanted an intelligent documentary film made about his company. A short while after first meeting Lindsay, Lois Sutcliffe tracked him down and invited him to make the first of a series of industrial shorts which amounted to his first practical experience of film-making.

These films led to a commission from a local newspaper to make *Wakefield Express* (1952), in which the influence of the documentarist Humphrey Jennings – in particular, of his film *Spare Time* (1939) – is clearly evident. But, as he was to do with other influences, Lindsay absorbed things from Jennings and adapted the essence of Jennings' cinema to meet the needs of his subject and the demands of his own highly individual personality. A style was beginning to take shape. He followed *Wakefield Express* with *Thursday's Children* (1953), co-directed with his Oxford friend Guy Brenton. This remarkable and gentle study of the education of deaf children went on to earn its directors a Hollywood Oscar. It also provided Lindsay with the opportunity to make his first completely personal film, *O Dreamland*, a caustic portrait of a seaside funfair. In its poetic rhythm, its disregard for the linear and for the pretence of 'documentary realism', and its essentially cruel perspective, *O Dreamland* shows affinities with the work of another of Lindsay's heroes, Jean Vigo. Not Vigo the affirmative anarchist and dark poet of *Zéro de Conduite* and *L'Atalante*, but Vigo the savage shoestring surrealist of *À propos de Nice*. It was not by chance that Lindsay, author of that clarion call to social commitment, 'Stand Up! Stand Up!', should be drawn to the work of Vigo, whose own critical writings included the similarly engaged and passionate article 'Towards a Social Cinema'. These two artists looked at the world with similarly unflinching eyes; John Ford may have been Lindsay's father figure but Vigo was the dead brother whose ghost he honoured in all his films.

Other commissions – seven short films for a variety of official bodies in 1955, five episodes of the television series *Robin Hood* (1955-56), and a number of television commercials – helped continue Lindsay's technical development, but his mature style did not manifest itself until 1957 with his documentary portrait of Covent Garden Market, *Every Day Except Christmas*, sponsored by the Ford Motor Company. Working closely with the cameraman Walter Lassally and the sound recordist John Fletcher, Lindsay turned the limitations of their means to marvellous effect, creating a visual portrait of the daily life of the market which is at once poetic and elegiac (a premonitory approach as things turned out – a few years later the market was relocated, far from the centre of London). Here, too, all of Lindsay's influences were blended together: lessons learned from

Vigo, Jennings and Ford are subsumed into a way of conveying feeling and experience that was entirely Lindsay's own. The film ends with a series of 'Fordian' close-ups of market workers, serving no real narrative purpose but possessing great emotional (and, let us admit it, sentimental) power.

In parallel with his progression as a film-maker, Lindsay had continued to develop his skills as a writer and critic. At the suggestion of the film director (later teacher) Thorold Dickinson, Lindsay wrote his first book, *Making a Film*, which was published in 1952. Unlike Reisz's book on film editing, this was not a practical handbook but a careful documentation of the pre-production and production stages of Dickinson's film, *Secret People*. It was conceived by Dickinson and Ernest Lindgren (then head of Britain's National Film Archive) as a complementary volume to Lindgren's classic study of film technique and appreciation, *The Art of Film*. Lindsay was given privileged access to the offices, workshops and sound stages of Ealing Studios and was present throughout the production process, leaving only when the film was being cut together in the editing rooms. He produced a lively account which, if it lacks the stylistic polish of *Picture* (the study by *New Yorker* writer Lillian Ross of John Huston's film *The Red Badge of Courage*), is more informative on the daily business of film-making. He was not required to comment on the film but he was aware of the weaknesses of the material, and realised that, for Dickinson (who had built his reputation with a stylish version of *Gaslight*, the propaganda film *Next of Kin* and a striking adaptation of Pushkin's *The Queen of Spades*), it did not constitute his best work. *Secret People* was neither a commercial nor a critical success, and *Making a Film* fell out of print. But Lindsay's book remains a valuable record of the now-vanished world of the British studio system.

Lindsay himself would have his first chance to work in a real film studio in 1955 when he went to Nettlefold Studios to shoot the episodes for the television series *Robin Hood*. His account of the experience ends with the affirmative sentence: 'A unit is a good thing to be a part of.' He found in his film and theatre work something that would elude him in the field of criticism, a sense of comradeship and unity in which he could thrive. It was a creative and collaborative atmosphere which he sought constantly to generate in his approach to his work.

It was harder to inspire that sort of commitment in the area of film criticism, but Lindsay held to it and – when he moved from the defunct *Sequence* to *Sight and Sound* – he and Gavin Lambert (as well as Karel Reisz and Walter Lassally) wrote unashamedly personal critical reviews of the current cinema. A reader's letter, attacking this subjective style, prompted the most famous of Lindsay's critical essays, 'Stand Up! Stand Up!'

This piece had its genesis in an article which Lindsay had written for

The Observer at the invitation of that newspaper's arts editor, Terence Kilmartin. In 1956, *The Observer* had sponsored an exhibition to celebrate 'Sixty Years of Cinema' and Kilmartin wanted Lindsay, who had briefly been involved with the advisory committee of the exhibition but had dropped out after curatorial disagreements, to write his reaction. Lindsay made it clear that he did not like the exhibition very much, but Kilmartin was undisturbed; he gave Lindsay the impression that a little controversy would be welcome. Lindsay duly wrote a piece, 'The Cinema Is . . . ' which was typeset at the newspaper and sent back to Lindsay in galley form for corrections. But on the Sunday that the article was due to appear, its space was occupied by a large photograph of a member of the British Royal Family visiting the *Observer* exhibition.

'The Cinema Is . . . ' had challenged the patronising and superior tone adopted by shamelessly ignorant reviewers in what passed for criticism in most British newspapers and magazines of the day. 'At least the other arts are protected to some extent by tradition,' Lindsay wrote. 'It is the poor old cinema that gets the bludgeon, that must endure the bad seat and the arrogant heel of the tiro rider out to show his paces.' It was an angry piece, insisting on cinema's right to be taken seriously as an art form which requires all the complexity of approach and response that the term suggests. Attacking one of the exhibition curators, the art critic Lawrence Alloway, Lindsay wrote: 'He believes (roughly) that because the cinema is a popular art, no film can be good if it is not popular. The converse apparently holds too: any film that is popular *must* be good. Another long farewell to Eisenstein. (Mr Alloway presumably employs different criteria when he is lecturing at the Tate Gallery.)' Whether Lindsay was right in his assumption that his article was dropped on the instructions of *The Observer's* editor, David Astor, we may never know, but Astor's vexed voice was certainly one of those raised in the correspondence columns of *Sight and Sound* after Lindsay had developed the central argument of 'The Cinema Is . . . ' into the impassioned polemic of 'Stand Up! Stand Up!'

What sparked Lindsay into writing what amounted to a statement of principle was a letter from J. R. Taylor, student, who would go on, under his full name of John Russell Taylor, to become the film critic and later the art critic of *The Times* and would prove in subsequent years to be one of Lindsay's staunchest supporters. But, in that autumn of 1956, Taylor's letter – calling for a non-partisan, objective aesthetic judgement which considered form without particular regard to content – gave Lindsay all the excuse he needed to pitch the argument contained in 'The Cinema Is . . . ' at a higher level. Lindsay's impassioned response in 'Stand Up! Stand Up!' was a call for critics, film-makers and the public to take sides. It was the kind of exhortation he would repeat throughout his life.

Roger Manvell, then director of the British Film Academy (the organisation which represented Britain's senior film-makers), spoke for many of those who cared deeply about film when, in a letter in the next issue of *Sight and Sound*, he called Lindsay's essay 'by far the most important statement of principle to have been published in your Journal for as long as I can remember.' The impact of 'Stand Up! Stand Up!' led to Lindsay's being compared to such essayists as George Orwell and Cyril Connolly. He was hailed, too, as the film world's answer to F. R. Leavis, the Cambridge don whose critical magazine *Scrutiny* (published from 1932 until 1953) had a discernible influence on the combative, denunciatory style of *Sequence*.

It is amusing to read Lindsay's recommendation of the French film periodicals *Positif* and *Cahiers du Cinéma* in his article on 'French Critical Writing', published in *Sight and Sound* in October 1954, and to move on to an article in the very next issue which attacks these same magazines for their poor critical judgement, and (in the case of *Cahiers*) fundamental solipsism. It might be expected that, as he advanced from critic to film-maker, Lindsay would find common cause with a group of critics – Rivette, Truffaut, Godard, Chabrol and Rohmer – who were moving along the same path. The founders of the French New Wave were, after all, the contemporaries of those who brought Free Cinema into being. But, although he spoke and wrote excellent French and formed many important friendships among the artistic community in France (with among others Alain Resnais, Serge Reggiani, the critic Louis Marcorelles and the poet and critic Jean Quéval), Lindsay disliked the French fondness for theory.

This was not an anti-intellectual stance (despite his occasional protests, Lindsay was himself an intellectual) but it was a reaction against self-regarding intellectual game-playing, which Lindsay found cold and evasive. He admired some, though by no means all, of the New Wave films and it was really through the intervention of the critic David Robinson that Truffaut's first film found itself programmed in the Free Cinema shows at the National Film Theatre. Perhaps Lindsay disliked Truffaut because Truffaut began as the cruellest critic at *Cahiers* and went on to become the softest and most conservative of the New Wave film-makers. His romanticism rarely progressed beyond the adolescent stage and Lindsay might have found Truffaut's charm cloying and insubstantial.

One French film-maker who won Lindsay's unalloyed respect was Jacques Becker, and Lindsay's review of Becker's *Casque d'Or* is a model of the affirmative, committed criticism he was to advocate. Its effect was far-reaching and had much to do with the success of Becker's film in Britain (Simone Signoret won a British Academy Award as Best Actress in 1952) and its eventual revival in Paris cinemas, where it had been poorly

9

received on its initial release. This film is now considered a classic of French cinema but it is important to realise that its reputation was far from assured when Lindsay wrote so convincingly about it.

'Stand Up! Stand Up!' appeared in 1956, the year of the Suez Crisis and of the Hungarian Revolution, the year that John Osborne's *Look Back in Anger* was premiered at the Royal Court, and Colin Wilson expounded his quasi-religious form of existentialism in *The Outsider*. It was the time of the 'Angry Young Man' and the dawn of what would become the New Left. Left-leaning intellectuals had been dismayed at the failure of the 1945 Labour government (ousted by the Conservatives in 1951) and events in Hungary, together with Khrushchev's public denunciation of Stalin, had led to a final disillusionment with Communism for many. Commitment, of a kind that was not blind acceptance of party-political lines, became a watchword.

In 1957, the first issue of *Universities and Left Review* (which would lead to the founding of the *New Left Review*) reprinted 'Stand Up! Stand Up!' as one of two articles devoted to 'Commitment in Criticism'. That same year, the publisher Tom Maschler invited Lindsay and a number of other cultural figures, including John Osborne, Colin Wilson, Kenneth Tynan and Doris Lessing, to contribute essays – each in the form of a 'personal credo' – to a book called *Declaration*. In his introduction to the book, Maschler highlighted the failure of critics to grasp the changes in current British thought and literature and attacked the 'even lower level of journalism' for coining the 'Angry Young Man' label.

Today, these essays hint at the future of their writers as much as they paint a composite portrait of a turbulent moment in British cultural history. Osborne's 'socialist' mask cannot hide his splenetic conservatism, and Tynan's fine, challenging text still leaves room for him to take his place in a redefined establishment culture. Doris Lessing's meditation on the place of the novelist in society, 'The Small Personal Voice', matches Lindsay's 'Get Out and Push!' in its call for artistic commitment and its acceptance of the consequences that that might have for the artist.

Lindsay ended 'Get Out and Push!' with a defiant definition of what he believed an artist – and a critic – should be. After claiming that he would 'fight for the notion of community' represented by the 'good and friendly faces' which featured in *Every Day Except Christmas*, he concluded:

> Fighting means commitment, means believing what you say, and saying what you believe. It will also mean being called sentimental, irresponsible, self-righteous, extremist and out-of-date by those who equate maturity with scepticism, art with amusement, and responsibility with romantic excess. And it must mean a new kind of intellectual and artist,

who is not frightened or scornful of his fellows; who does not see himself as threatened by, and in natural opposition to, the philistine mass; who is eager to make his contribution, and ready to use the mass media to do so. By his nature, the artist will always be in conflict with the false, the narrow-minded and the reactionary: there will always be people who do not understand the relevance of what he is doing: he will always have to fight for his values. But one thing is certain: in the values of humanism, and in their determined application to our society, lies the future. All we have to do is to believe in them.

Thirty years after those words were published, I asked Lindsay if he still stood by them. 'That always makes me a little bit worried now,' he said, 'I don't like to read those bits. Partly perhaps because the positive thing was more feasible at that time, and partly because when one writes like that, or at that age, there is a degree of wishful thinking in it. You don't necessarily believe it but you hope that by saying it you'll encourage people to believe it. In the late 1950s it was briefly possible – particularly if you were relatively young – to believe in a popular leftist front that might work, might transform certain things. That was the side one put oneself on. It was a very liberating period which history handed to the British – or the English – on a plate. I think it was the last opportunity they had to opt for change, if you like, for radicalism. But I'm afraid they turned it down.'

Here is an echo of George Orwell in the attitude to his fellow countrymen, and another of Lindsay's heroes, William Blake. In *The Marriage of Heaven and Hell*, Blake wrote: 'Then I asked: "does a firm perswasion that a thing is so, make it so?"/ He replied: "All poets believe that it does, and in ages of imagination this firm perswasion removed mountains; but many are not capable of a firm perswasion of anything."' Nothing so aptly summarises Lindsay's critical and artistic attitude nor points so sharply to the increased sense of isolation he would feel in later life.

III

The idea of having a series of programmes presented at the National Film Theatre under the title Free Cinema probably came from Karel Reisz, who was the head of programme planning at the NFT from 1952 until 1955. The first selection of Free Cinema films was shown in February 1956. The choice of films for this and the five subsequent programmes was generally attributed to those who comprised 'the Committee of Free Cinema' (that is to say, Lindsay, Karel Reisz, John Fletcher and Walter Lassally); although – as in the case of David Robinson and Truffaut's *Les Mistons* – there were undoubtedly other advisors. Unlike some other movements,

11

Free Cinema was, by its very nature, inclusive rather than exclusive. Nor was it parochial; the six programmes introduced work by Norman McLaren, Georges Franju, Roman Polanski, Walerian Borowczyk, Claude Goretta and Alain Tanner, among others. The Free Cinema screenings of Chabrol's *Le Beau Serge* and Truffaut's *Les Mistons* launched the French New Wave in Britain. Three of Lindsay's own films were shown: *O Dreamland*, *Wakefield Express* and *Every Day Except Christmas*. Lindsay was also the supervising editor on another film shown under the Free Cinema banner, Lorenza Mazzetti's *Together*, showing two deaf-mutes (played by the painter Michael Andrews and the sculptor Eduardo Paolozzi) finding hostility and menace in an everyday, working-class environment. The unhurried style of Lindsay's editing shows his keen understanding of John Ford's slow editorial rhythms, as well as his ability to fit them to the most unlikely material.

Karel Reisz and Tony Richardson were represented by their collaboration on *Momma Don't Allow*, with its inventive use of sound in the portrayal of a London jazz club, and Reisz alone by his closer look at the emerging 'youth culture' with *We Are the Lambeth Boys*. In March 1959, a film selection announcing itself as 'The Last Free Cinema' carried this programme note:

> Some will be glad, others may regret. Ourselves we feel something of each emotion. The strain of making films in this way, outside the system, is enormous, and cannot be supported indefinitely. It is not just a question of finding the money. Each time, when the films have been made, there is the same battle to be fought, for the right to show our work. As the madman said when he hit his head against the brick wall – 'It's nice when you stop . . .' But our feeling is not one of defeat. We have had our victories.
>
> In making these films, and presenting these programmes, we have tried to make a stand for independent, creative film-making in a world where the pressures of conformism and commercialism are becoming more powerful every day. We will not abandon these convictions, nor the attempt to put them into practice . . .
>
> Free Cinema is dead. Long live Free Cinema!

The notion of a socially engaged cinema, as defended by the Free Cinema group and their supporters, was not exactly a new idea. Reference has already been made to Vigo's writings on the subject – and his ideas were carried through his brief career in each of his films. Soviet directors had long addressed social themes, as had a number of British documentarists in the pre-war years, not to mention that informal godfather of Free

Cinema, Humphrey Jennings, in his extraordinary portraits of the British home front during World War Two. Most recent had been the example of the Italian Neo-Realists.

But it would be wrong to judge Free Cinema as a cohesive movement; it was – in the best sense of the term – opportunistic, in that it served as a platform for film-makers whose works might not otherwise be afforded such prominence (and there was a good deal of publicity surrounding the films at the time) or which might not be shown at all. In a 1967 interview, Lindsay said: 'Free Cinema wasn't part of an intellectual movement. If you're trying to describe its meaning in this country, the key word is empirical. Free Cinema came into being for entirely practical reasons.' Karel Reisz, in the same interview, added: 'We made films and wrote manifestos to provide a little publicity for the movement, but the value of these films, if they have one, lies in the films themselves and not in the movement.'

Lindsay was being disingenuous in denying the intellectual content of Free Cinema; his own films kept faith with the ideas he and Gavin Lambert had propagated in *Sequence* and *Sight and Sound*. The leading lights of the New Left – with which Free Cinema was associated – were, quite evidently, intellectuals; even the National Film Theatre itself was, in great part, a legacy of the 'radical bourgeois' intellectualism which inspired the 1951 Festival of Britain and which, today, has its memorial in London's South Bank arts complex.

Most importantly, it was Lindsay's intellect which first earned him the commanding position he held in Britain's cinema community. His analytical ability, and the directness with which he communicated his interpretations and enthusiasms, gave him an exceptional authority. The critic Philip French acknowledged this authority in his obituary of Lindsay for *The Observer*: 'When, in his 1955 *Sight and Sound* essay "The Last Sequence of *On the Waterfront*", he denounced the end of Kazan's picture as fascistic, we all changed our minds about a movie we loved. His unfavourable review of *The Searchers* (1956) put a generation off one of Ford's finest pictures for a decade.'

But if the intellectual impulse which would have given Free Cinema the kind of theoretical basis recognisable to cultural historians was missing, it hardly mattered. The impulse behind Free Cinema was spiritual rather than intellectual, for Lindsay understood how readily theory could descend into dogma. The film critic Alexander Walker was right when he identified the spirit of such documentaries as *Every Day Except Christmas* and *We Are the Lambeth Boys* as one of 'romantic sympathy'. Like Reisz and Richardson, Lindsay did not plunge very deeply into the lives of his working-class subjects, he was concerned primarily with representing them in a way which was affectionate, dignified and non-judgemental.

13

This may seem a soft approach by today's standards, and even then it contrasted sharply with the foreign films in the Free Cinema programmes. Georges Franju's *Le Sang des Bêtes*, for example, took an unflinching view of workers in a Paris abattoir. One of the early sequences of Franju's film showed a white carthorse genuflecting in death as it is 'humanely' executed. The sequence retains its power to shock modern audiences.

But Franju was working in the tradition of French cinema where working-class characters had long been central to features and documentaries, and had been presented as fully-rounded human beings. British-based directors like Lindsay and Reisz were in rebellion against the ignorant stereotypes which were the usual depictions of working-class figures in their homegrown cinema.

Lindsay was keen to make a first feature based on a novel about a hospital casualty department (this was long before such locations became the staple of television drama). He spent a great deal of time on research at Guy's Hospital in London, but Ealing Studios – for whom the film was to be made – found his approach to the subject 'too individualistic' and asked him to add romantic interest to the script. The fact that Ealing would not assign a writer to the project but expected Lindsay to handle the rewriting alone persuaded him that they were not taking it very seriously and, disillusioned, he dropped the idea.

Tony Richardson, who was working as Associate Artistic Director of George Devine's English Stage Company at the Royal Court Theatre, invited Lindsay to direct a Sunday night performance 'without decor' of a play by the poet Kathleen Sully. Lindsay welcomed the chance to broaden his experience of working in drama and so embarked on the third important strand of his career.

The production of Sully's play, *The Waiting of Lester Abbs,* presented on 30 June 1957, was sufficiently well-received for Lindsay to be invited back to the Court at the end of 1958 to direct Willis Hall's *The Long and the Short and the Tall*. Lindsay's cast included many names which would become familiar to British theatre and film audiences in the years ahead such as Alfred Lynch, Robert Shaw and Edward Judd. He had wanted to use a young actor he much admired, Albert Finney, but Finney fell ill and was replaced by another relative unknown, Peter O'Toole. By the time he directed John Arden's *Sergeant Musgrave's Dance* at the Court in late 1959, Lindsay regarded himself as a man of the theatre and described himself in the play's programme as 'ex-critic, ex-film-maker'; he was also now on the Royal Court's staff as an assistant to the Artistic Directors.

At the Royal Court, Lindsay found the artistic radicalism and freedom that he found lacking in the British film industry. George Devine's energy and generosity had attracted a team of writers, actors and directors who were committed to challenging the prevailing mood of London theatre with its emphasis on pleasing, rather than challenging, a predominantly moneyed, middle-class audience. There were really more differences than similarities between such writers as Osborne, Arden and Arnold Wesker but the Royal Court was seen as a broadly socialist theatre which, in truth, it was not. It was, as Lindsay described it, a *social* theatre; that is to say it was concerned with addressing the contemporary social concerns of its audience. Inevitably, social concerns have a political dimension, and to be termed 'political' in Britain in the late 1950s meant being considered 'socialist'.

The Court, for all its attachment to social issues, was not a theatre of 'social realism', certainly not as the term was then understood; the theatrical quality of a work counted above all. *Musgrave* was a case in point. Arden's play, set in a nineteenth-century mining village where a small group of soldiers arrive ostensibly as a recruiting party, was partially inspired by an atrocity committed by British soldiers in Cyprus in 1958. Lindsay was attracted by the dense poetry of Arden's language and by his ability to create a historic parable with contemporary relevance.

The pugnacious pragmatism that Lindsay had displayed in the 'cultural packaging' of Free Cinema was no less evident at the Royal Court. His production of *Musgrave* was poorly received by the London critics and when Lindsay peeked through the curtain just before the start of the second night's performance he saw a near-empty auditorium. Furious at the power of critics to deny the chance for Arden's work to be seen, Lindsay set about contacting a range of theatrical and cultural figures ('all of them,' as he said, 'more important than any critic') and asking for their reactions to the play. The comments he collected gave the lie to the general critical response: 'In years to come,' said Sir Michael Redgrave, 'this play will be "rediscovered" as an important early work by a remarkable playwright. Discover it now.' The poet C. Day-Lewis hailed *Musgrave* as 'Another nail in the coffins of drab comedy and drawing-room unreality,' and the actress Peggy Ashcroft considered it 'the most exciting experience in the theatre since I saw the Berliner Ensemble in *Mother Courage.*' These and other comments were printed on a bold coloured broadsheet which Lindsay and his associates distributed around London's coffee bars, bookshops and university campuses. This 'holding operation', as Arden gratefully called it, succeeded in attracting a new audience for the play, and Redgrave's words have since been proven accurate.

Lindsay worked on one more film in these early Royal Court days, as supervising editor for the documentary *March on Aldermaston*. This was a record of the march, in Easter 1958, from London to the British atomic weapons establishment in Aldermaston organised by members and supporters of the Campaign for Nuclear Disarmament. Lindsay directed some sequences of the film (sharing the task with several others, including Karel Reisz), and he also co-wrote the commentary (with the poet and playwright Christopher Logue) and persuaded Richard Burton to speak it. The Royal Court fielded its own contingent of marchers who chanted: 'William Shakespeare! William Blake! We are marching for your sake!' It was, Lindsay later recalled, 'a liberal gesture, and essentially fun, not at all an occasion of socialist solemnity. We were, after all, there to support life.'

IV

Between 1959 and 1961, Lindsay directed several plays at the Royal Court: Alun Owen's *Progress to the Park*, Harry Cookson's *The Lily White Boys* (in which he finally managed to work with Albert Finney), two one-act plays by Christopher Logue (*Trials by Logue*) and *The Fire Raisers* by Max Frisch. He also made his debut as a West End director with the first production of the Keith Waterhouse-Willis Hall comedy *Billy Liar*, starring Finney in the title role.

Meanwhile, some of Lindsay's Free Cinema associates had begun to make feature films. The mainstream success of Jack Clayton's *Room at the Top* (1958) had opened the door for those interested in subjects that could be described as 'gritty' and 'adult'. Tony Richardson was first through the door, transferring two of Osborne's Royal Court successes to the screen with *Look Back in Anger* (1959) and *The Entertainer* (1960). These were the first productions of a new company Woodfall Films set up by Richardson, Osborne and the producer Harry Salzman. Karel Reisz made his feature debut for Woodfall with an adaptation of the Alan Sillitoe novel *Saturday Night and Sunday Morning*. Reisz's film was notable for its lack of 'star names' (Richard Burton had been cast as a watered-down Jimmy Porter in *Look Back in Anger* and Laurence Olivier had repeated his portrayal of the down-at-heel music-hall comedian in *The Entertainer*); Albert Finney played the amoral factory-worker Arthur Seaton whose opening speech – delivered in voice-over against images of his work on the factory floor – concluded with the famous lines: 'What I'm out for is a good time. All the rest is propaganda.' At last, working-class audiences could see their lives treated with a degree of truth and accuracy never seen before in the British cinema.

Karel Reisz was due to direct the film version of David Storey's novel, *This Sporting Life*, but – keen to gain experience as a producer – he encouraged Lindsay to take it on. Lindsay was always grateful for what he called Reisz's 'grace and insistence' as he had been greatly interested by

Storey's book when it was first published. The film rights had proved too expensive for Woodfall and eventually went to Julian Wintle and Leslie Parkyn of Independent Artists who approached Reisz.

For the leading role of Frank Machin (Arthur Machin in the book, but changed to avoid comparisons with Finney's role in *Saturday Night*), Lindsay first wanted Sean Connery. This was well before Connery became an international star as James Bond, and he was not considered a big enough name. Eventually, he chose the Irish actor Richard Harris to play the Yorkshire miner turned professional rugby player. Rachel Roberts was cast as the sexually repressed widow, Mrs Hammond, with whom he lodges. Although there is a family resemblance between *This Sporting Life* and such earlier films as *Room at the Top*, *Saturday Night and Sunday Morning* and John Schlesinger's *A Kind of Loving*, in that they are all adaptations of novels by Northern English writers set against broadly working-class backgrounds, Lindsay's treatment of the material reflects his and Storey's concern with the deeper implications of human relationships. Just as Reisz had probed working-class life more deeply and critically in his version of *Sillitoe*, so Lindsay had moved beyond the affectionate sentimentality of *Every Day Except Christmas*.

In 1967, Lindsay looked back on his first meeting with Storey and recalled those first impressions:

At that time I still believed, or wanted to believe that things (society) could become 'better'. David, whose father had not been some sort of General, and who had managed to fill out his Slade School Scholarship by battering and being battered, every Saturday during the Season, as a forward in the Leeds Rugby League 'A' team, was not under this misapprehension. Also he was not interested in surface, but in essence; not in what was representative, but in what was exceptional. This made him, and makes him, a very exceptional kind of English writer.

A lot of glib generalisations have been made about the 'Northern' writers who appeared in the late fifties and early sixties. In fact a certain kind of honesty, a certain kind of vitality is all they had in common. David Storey's unique quality – and it is one that I personally value above all others – seems to me a sort of elemental poetry, a passionate reaching-out, and ambition of concept that carries him beyond neatness, completeness, civilised equilibrium. He seeks to penetrate the soul; yet he never forgets the relevance of the social world in which souls meet, conflict and struggle. He labours, often desperately, to balance the ambiguities of our nature, our situation: male and female, tenderness and violence, isolation and love.'

Some have found in this perceptive appreciation of Storey, a portrait of Lindsay himself.

By the time he began shooting *This Sporting Life* in 1962, Lindsay had benefited enormously from his years at the Royal Court. His attention to the details of casting (small parts in the film were taken by, among others, Nicol Williamson, Edward Fox and Glenda Jackson) and the collaborative atmosphere he fostered on set earned him the trust of his actors. In addition there was the time spent – ten days – rehearsing in continuity the scenes between Harris and Roberts, and then shooting of the scenes in sequence. His directorial technique was finely captured by Tom Milne in a 1962 article for *Sight and Sound*. Milne was observing Lindsay directing a scene in which Frank Machin takes Mrs Hammond for a meal in the dining-hall of a high class country hotel:

> Her discomfort in such unfamiliar surroundings is made worse by his boorish behaviour: Watching this sequence and Anderson's patient, quiet, meticulous rehearsal of details of timing and expression, I was impressed by the easy, unforced atmosphere of the playing. Obviously the Jimmy Porter-Arthur Seatonish element in Frank has been kept well in hand, and Mrs Hammond, outwardly elegant and controlled, betrays her unease by the sharpest of detail: this was to be expected. But, even in films like *Saturday Night and Sunday Morning* and *A Taste of Honey*, there is a tendency, probably pressurised for reasons of box-office, not exactly to caricature, but to nudge in the presentation of some of the minor roles. Anderson was rehearsing a shot in which Frank deliberately and irritatingly quibbles over his bill, having it checked and rechecked, finally producing the exact money which he holds ready, and a sixpence which he drops insolently on to the waiter's tray, saying, 'Don't spend it all at once.' Wallas Eaton, as the waiter, is not permitted even the mildest, subtlest of double-takes; simply a weary, superior glance, which is exactly right.

The critical reaction to *This Sporting Life* was almost unanimously positive, and it confirmed Lindsay's reputation as the most artistically mature of the Free Cinema group. Karel Reisz, with typical generosity, called *This Sporting Life* the 'most completely achieved of the "new wave" films, because the most passionately felt and ambitious.' Lindsay's stylistic handling of the narrative – making use of subtle 'jump-cuts', slow-motion techniques and a shifting time-scale – led to his being compared with such European film-makers as Antonioni, Resnais and Godard. Most striking was the complexity with which an adult relationship was portrayed. It is a hallmark of Storey's writing that his characters never speak to illustrate a concept or thesis, they speak to express their feelings or – more often than not – to mask them. They do not say what they are supposed to say; but then neither do we. They confront us with the experience of their lives, and they demand that we respond from nothing less than our experience. As Robert Vas wrote in his *Sight and Sound* review of *This Sporting Life*, 'Here pain is called pain, and the feeling is one of liberation . . . '

But the box-office response was less than satisfactory, and what Walter Lassally, in a 1960 *Sight and Sound* piece, called 'the Dead Hand of apathy, of complacency and convention' soon descended on Lindsay's idea of a committed, social cinema. Richardson cast Albert Finney as *Tom Jones* for Woodfall, the James Bond films attracted huge international audiences, and a 1963 article by the *Evening Standard* critic Alexander Walker (who admired Lindsay's work) was headlined, 'The Year "Kitchen Sink" Went Down the Drain'. Lindsay tried to make a version of *Wuthering Heights* (scripted by Storey and starring Harris as Heathcliffe) but nothing came of it. He went back to the theatre, taking Harris with him for a production of Gogol's *Diary of a Madman* at the Royal Court.

Although Free Cinema was never truly comparable – in scale or impact – to the French New Wave, the legacy of those early films by Lindsay, Karel Reisz and Tony Richardson was a cinema that – for a time – could not easily return to the phoniness of earlier decades, presenting a cosily artificial image of Britain that bore little relation to the lives of the majority of its people.

V

As the stylistic and emotional sophistication of *This Sporting Life* gave way to the flashy 'quirkiness' of such films as *The Knack* which would come to epitomise 'Swinging London', Lindsay confined himself to work in the theatre. In his first season as director at the National Theatre (based then at the Old Vic), Laurence Olivier invited him to direct another Max Frisch play, *Andorra*. At the Royal Court, Lindsay became joint artistic director with Anthony Page and, in 1964, directed a controversial production of Shakespeare's *Julius Caesar* (with a young Anthony Hopkins among the cast). In 1966 he directed Celia Johnson and Tom Courtenay in *The Cherry Orchard* at the Chichester Festival Theatre, and that year he also returned to the cinema with a production for Woodfall Films.

By this time, George Devine – the unyielding spirit behind the Royal Court – was dead. He had been in declining health for some years and had suffered serious heart trouble in 1963. It was to relieve the administrative burden on Devine that Lindsay and Anthony Page had agreed to take over, temporarily, the artistic directorship of the theatre, but Lindsay had resigned his post just before the 1964/65 season opened. Page carried on – with Devine's help – but it became clear that Devine would not be well enough to return to the demands of the theatre's directorship. The news that Devine was to retire had been broken to the press at a press lunch in January 1965. Bill Gaskill – who had left the Court to run the National Theatre with Olivier – later wrote about that lunch and the effects of Lindsay's behaviour at it:

> When George announced his retirement in a farewell speech, it was greeted politely, but with no sense of the importance of the occasion. But Lindsay, whose feeling for the occasion has always been remarkable, leapt to his feet and made an impassioned speech about George. The critics sang 'For He's a Jolly Good Fellow'. I was very moved by Lindsay's speech, and although I had turned down the chance of taking over the Court the previous year, I realised that the continuity of George's work was more important than working at the National Theatre, and I told George I would do it. Olivier sent a telegram: 'The Lord gave and the Lord has taken away.'

Devine's last work at the Royal Court was his performance as the flamboyant Baron Von Epp in Osborne's controversial play *A Patriot for Me* in June 1965. In the last week of the run, he suffered a heart attack. His health never recovered and, in January 1966, he died.

The Woodfall project was to have been a feature film made up of three separate sections, each with a different director. The Free Cinema trio of Lindsay, Tony Richardson and Karel Reisz were to have been the contributing directors, but Reisz found that his subject, a cinema version of David Mercer's television play *A Suitable Case for Treatment*, was going to run to feature length (it was later released as *Morgan*) and he was replaced by Peter Brook. Lindsay's contribution was an adaptation of a short story by Shelagh Delaney, *The White Bus*. Initially, all three segments of the film were to have been adapted from Delaney stories, but Brook and Richardson went for other material and the final result, *Red, White and Zero*, lacked unity. The trilogy was shown once at the National Film Theatre but the distributors, United Artists, were unhappy with it and decided to show each of the constituent films separately at a future date. It was two years before *The White Bus* was given another public showing, on a double-bill with the Czech director Vera Chytilova's *Daisies* at a small cinema in South Kensington. It has never been re-released.

There was a certain aptness about Lindsay's film being shown alongside a Czech feature, as he had only recently visited Czechoslovakia and become friendly with many of the film-makers – Milos Forman, Ivan

Passer and Jan Nemec – who constituted the 'Czech New Wave'. Forman, who gave a memorable account of his first impression of Lindsay ('a man who looked like a docker and spoke like a lord'), invited him onto the set of his film *A Blonde in Love*. It was there that Lindsay observed the cinematographer Miroslav Ondricek at work; when the time came to make *The White Bus*, Lindsay invited Ondricek to Britain as his cameraman. Lindsay's visit to Czechoslovakia resulted in more than professional connections. While there, he met the young actor Vladimir Pucholt who was considered one of the brightest hopes of the new Czech cinema. In fact, Pucholt, gifted actor though he was, yearned to become a doctor but the Czech authorities – mindful of his popularity and of the image he projected – refused him permission to study medicine. With Lindsay's help and financial support, Pucholt was able to take out British citizenship and study medicine in England and is now a paediatrician with a practice in Canada. Shortly after Lindsay's death, Milos Forman paid this tribute: 'Lindsay was for all of us, then young film-makers in a Communist country, a great inspiration as a film-maker, and a towering symbol of an independent free spirit as a man.'

The visual style of *The White Bus* owes a great deal to Ondricek's 'outsider's eye' and the film allowed Lindsay to rehearse many of the ideas he would incorporate into *If . . . .* The break from naturalism and into a barely delineated blend of fantasy and reality would find its full expression two years after *The White Bus*, but the film remains an extraordinary work, un-English in tone but quintessentially English (in the sense that Orwell would have recognised) in content.

While on a theatre engagement in Warsaw, directing Osborne's *Inadmissable Evidence*, with Tadeusz Lomnicki as Bill Maitland, Lindsay was invited to make his next film, *The Singing Lesson* (or *Raz Dwa Trzy*, to give it its Polish title). This was a short documentary about a drama class at the Warsaw Dramatic Academy; it was infused with the spirit of Free Cinema and of Humphrey Jennings (particularly *Listen to Britain*). Along with *The White Bus* it remains the least-seen of Lindsay's mature films (although it had an unheralded screening on BBC television a few days after Lindsay's death).

It was not until 1968 – five years after *This Sporting Life* – that Lindsay returned to feature directing with *If . . . .* In this case, he caught the spirit of the times in a more dramatic way than ever before. This was, after all, the year of 'Prague Spring' and the subsequent Russian invasion of Czechoslovakia, it was the year of the student revolt in Paris, of political assassinations (Martin Luther King, Robert Kennedy) and civil unrest in the United States, of angry protests against the Vietnam war in Europe and America. It was also a time of hope, of the possibility of a new dawning of political awareness and commitment that would be far greater than that called for ten years earlier.

If .... caught the tide of world events without incorporating visual references to the period (of the kind that Godard used in his films at the time and which now make them appear journalistic and dated). 'Although allegorical in form,' wrote David Caute in his book *Sixty-Eight: The Year of the Barricades*, 'Anderson's *If* .... remains the finest film about, or out of, the late sixties.' Structurally, *If* .... owes much to Jean Vigo's school satire *Zéro de Conduite*. Vigo's joyous anarchy gains a harder edge in Lindsay's climactic scene of the English public schoolboys machine-gunning teachers and visitors at a Founder's Day celebration. When the film was screened at the National Film Theatre, Lindsay ran onto the stage and told the audience: 'The rest is up to you!'

Political implications aside, *If* .... was also an immensely personal work for Lindsay in that it drew deeply on his own experiences at Cheltenham College (where most of the location filming took place). The English public school may have represented the snobbery, elitism, and the lack of fundamental human curiosity which Lindsay spent his life attacking, but it was also, to a degree, his land of lost content. It is in childhood and adolescence that we commonly undergo those intense experiences that form us, and there are echoes of that youthful intensity in *If* .... The scene in which the beautiful junior pupil, Bobby Philips (Rupert Webster) watches the senior boy Wallace (Richard Warwick) exercising in the gym – which is photographed in rosy monochrome – is an erotically charged portrayal of nascent homosexual desire, both graceful and romantic. 'No film can be too personal,' indeed.

The 1968 Cannes Film Festival had been one of the casualties of that turbulent year, abandoned in sympathy with the student protests. The following year, *If* .... was awarded the Palme d'Or, and Lindsay was firmly established as a British director of international standing, a film-maker whose name could be mentioned – without apology – in the same breath as those of Buñuel, Antonioni and Resnais. He was 45 years old, and his body of work had been crowned by two masterful feature films.

In the years immediately following *If* .... Lindsay established a new working relationship with David Storey, this time in the theatre. Beginning in 1969 with *In Celebration* and *The Contractor*, and continuing with *Home* (1970), *The Changing Room* (1971), *The Farm* (1973) and *Life Class* (1974), the Storey-Anderson collaboration was one of the most productive in the Royal Court's history. Two filmed records of this period remain: Lindsay's 1974 film version of *In Celebration* which featured the original cast and a minimum of 'opening out' of the play, and the television recording of *Home* – again with the original cast but with Jocelyn

Herbert's beautifully spare decor replaced by a 'naturalistic' setting – proof that Lindsay was not beyond compromise on someone else's behalf, and an act which Jocelyn found hard to forgive. Lindsay considered the film of *In Celebration* the most authentic record, not only of his work at the Royal Court but of what he would call 'the Royal Court style'.

One of the key elements of Lindsay's great success as a stage director was his complicity with actors, and this was born of his own early ambition to become an actor. He was a member of Equity, the actors' union, and made occasional film appearances – in James Broughton's 1952 fantasy *The Pleasure Garden*, which Lindsay also produced, he appeared as an unkempt sculptor obsessed with making his art more 'real' (prefiguring the creative battles he would undertake in years to come). His friend Anthony Page cast him as a Gestapo lawyer in David Mercer's television play *The Parachute*, and later gave him another 'legal' role, as a barrister in the film version of Osborne's *Inadmissable Evidence* (remembering Lindsay's adversarial approach to life, it is perhaps more accurate to say that Page was practising creative 'typecasting'). Lindsay was scathing about the triumphalism that surrounded the Oscar success of *Chariots of Fire,* but he enjoyed appearing in the film opposite John Gielgud as an anti-Semitic Cambridge don, and he remained fond of the film's director, Hugh Hudson. He excelled as figures of authority (Ken Russell cast him as the French War Minister in a TV film about the Dreyfus case) simply because he exuded authority even in repose. In 1966, he even took the stage at the Royal Court, playing a schoolmaster in Donald Howarth's 'production without decor' of the David Cregan play, *Miniatures.*

Lindsay was never 'actorish' in the clichéd, 'camp' sense (he detested the way in which 'camp' valorised the mediocre), but his sense of theatre was always present – that improvised speech at George Devine's retirement party – and there was a subtle element of performance in many of his conversations with his precise use of words and his nuanced reactions. He could expose the banality of another's chosen phrase simply by repeating it, and he had an actor's ability to express everything in a look. This natural gift was, I suspect, carefully cultivated over the years, and it led seasoned professionals to respect and seek to fulfil his demands. Those demands were never that actors should amuse him or astonish him, only that they should compel him to believe them; amusement and astonishment might follow, but always out of this basis of truth in performance. Lindsay was never content – as some directors of his generation were – merely to assemble a cast to 'support' a star performance, and he had a way of directing star names that coaxed and nudged them beyond the bag of tricks and mannerisms that even the most talented star acquires over the years. He described the experience of directing Ralph Richardson in

23

Storey's play *Early Days* at the National Theatre as 'like riding a difficult horse', and David Storey has this recollection of Lindsay directing Gielgud in *Home*:

> 'It isn't possible [said Gielgud] for an actor to sit on stage without moving, Lindsay, for 25 minutes.'
> 'Is it 25 minutes?'
> 'It feels like 25.'
> 'Move, in that case, if you feel like it, John.'
> Until a point had been reached:
> 'It's strange, but once sitting here, I don't feel I want to move again.'
> 'Don't, in that case.'
> 'I shan't.'

The delicacy and discretion of that exchange chimes so closely with Storey's scripted dialogue for *Home* that it demonstrates Lindsay's twin sensitivity to the actor and the text. Lindsay was not one of those ghastly directors who, on the first day of rehearsals, tells the actors to 'trust me' or informs them that 'I am going to take you on a journey'; the trust arose out of mutual respect, they journeyed together, each one finding his or her own route, all of them – finally – treading a collective path.

The theatre was of such vital importance to Lindsay that he could never understand why so many film critics disdained it. When Tom Milne wrote his report on the filming of *This Sporting Life*, he had seen – and was able to quote from – Lindsay's work at the Royal Court. Such cultural breadth, modest though it might seem, is unfortunately the exception rather than the rule for today's film critics.

These pages have concentrated on the first twenty years of Lindsay's working life because they amount to his formation as an artist – a unique artist – of the cinema and theatre. In addition, these years provide a necessary context for the bulk of Lindsay's early criticism. He would never again have the regular platform of *Sequence* and *Sight and Sound* which, under Gavin Lambert, had a lively and informed passion for movies. He became increasingly disenchanted with the British Film Institute, as he would become disenchanted with the British film industry. To watch *O Lucky Man!* (1973) in the 1980s was to recognise the brilliance of its satirical vision, but too few critics recognised it at the time; *Britannia Hospital* (1983) suffered from being released at the time of Britain's jingoistic response to the Falklands War (an ironic reversal of the fortuitious circumstances that attended the release of *If . . . .*). The critical savaging given to this 'last Free Cinema film', as Lindsay often called it, was something from which Lindsay never truly recovered. His vision – and he was, above all else, a visionary artist – had been rejected, and he knew it. There was a continuity in his work which meant that those who rejected *Britannia Hospital* were rejecting the earlier films.

This may seem a harsh point of view but it was the way that Lindsay regarded his work. It did not matter to him that many who admired his films were among those who failed to respond to *Britannia Hospital*: 'How can they not respond and still say they admire my films?' Lindsay once asked.

It is generally assumed that Lindsay hated television. It is true that he was often very rude about it – but what he really hated was the way that television had been so appallingly used. He was not a fan of sports programmes, but he felt that, if the arts could be given the same coverage as sport, in terms of intelligence, generosity of air-time, subject range and lack of exclusivity, television would be making some cultural contribution. His production of Alan Bennett's television play, *The Old Crowd* (1979), was totally misunderstood by the critics, but some things do not play well on television and Lindsay's particular brand of screen comedy needs the community of a cinema audience to be fully appreciated. He was more successful, in television terms, with the American mini-series *Glory! Glory!* (1989), which had a sharper edge than most.

In 1984, his contribution to British Film Year was an outspoken television documentary which gave the lie to David Puttnam's assertion that there had never been an indigenous British film industry by tracing the history of Free Cinema and acknowledging that it was only one of many attempts to establish a proper film culture in Britain. This documentary illustrated something else of great importance which is particularly relevant for this present volume. Although Lindsay often claimed that he was not a critic, particularly in his later years, it was precisely that mixture in him of artist and critic which fuelled the creative dynamic of his personality. Long after he had ceased to write the lengthy articles which established his critical reputation, he maintained a critic's perspective on life. It was this perspective, as much as his highly individual artistic output, which made him an outsider. It also imposed limitations.

In 1975, when Oscar Lewenstein decided to step down as Artistic Director of the Royal Court, Lindsay (who had, together with Anthony Page and Albert Finney, been one of Lewenstein's associate directors) seemed the natural successor. He declined the offer, citing his lack of the necessary administrative ability. In truth, it was the critical edge to his personality which made him uneasy with the pragmatism, even the willingness to compromise, that the post required – the Court was in considerable financial difficulty at the time. In subsequent years, and particularly after the appointment, in 1980, of Max Stafford-Clark as Artistic Director, Lindsay spoke of the Royal Court in the past tense, making it clear that he saw no continuum between the theatre founded by George Devine and that under Stafford-Clark's direction. Stafford-Clark described Lindsay's influence at the Court as 'malign', and even some of Lindsay's supporters found his sniping comments unhelpful. Lindsay the artist might have taken a more sensitive view of a new generation and its preoccupations, but Lindsay the critic could not stop himself from stating what he saw as the bald truth.

The critically combative aspect of his personality was equally evident in personal encounters. 'Have you seen such-and-such?' he would say (naming a current film or play). If you answered 'yes' he would adopt an inscrutable stare and say, 'Well, what did you think of it?' It was pointless trying to sound out his own opinion by admitting or pretending that you had not seen the work in question, for that statement would be met by a look of exasperated dismay and a cry of, 'Well, don't you think you should? I mean, really, don't you care?' Nobody was spared this ritual blood-letting and a half-hearted response could lead to total humiliation.

These teasing games were much more than simply Lindsay's way of keeping himself amused and, for those in the right mood, they could be invigorating. Stephen Frears recalls that he was 'always called upon to give an account of myself' during his regular meetings with Lindsay. 'This was always frightening,' he says, 'but he could provoke you into a sort of moral courage to stand up for what you believed in.' What Lindsay believed in, particularly his unwavering insistence on total commitment, changed little over the years and this highlighted the positive aspect of the critic-artist dichotomy. It gave his work an integrity and a consistency which even his detractors will admit was in constant evidence throughout his career. His youthful arrogance evolved into a patrician authority which earned respect precisely because he was always prepared to stand his ground, no matter how unpopular his opinion might be.

Lindsay was so utterly dismissive of 'film studies' that he was sometimes blind to the contribution he might have made in this field. His irritation with it was in part based upon the dominance of theory (largely literary theory), and in part on the equal dominance of aestheticism – devoid of any social context but often desperately linked to a fashionable, and invariably foreign, school of thought. Lindsay was a moralist, fond of quoting Orwell's comment about Britain being the only great country whose intellectuals were ashamed of their own nationality, and he saw film studies as nothing other than a 'discipline' invented to give jobs to academics.

To this extent, he was opposed to the Leavisite idea that culture should be centred on the universities – culture, he believed, should be centred on and within all areas of life. For Lindsay, no work of art could be worth very much if it did not seek, in however modest a way, to change the world. This is what he sought to do, but he was simply too radical, too subversive for British taste. Paradoxically, this is because he was entirely obsessed with Britain: the popular cinema audience and film-makers seemed more and more to be obsessed with America; the intellectual theorists were obsessed with France; nobody wanted any longer to 'look at Britain'.

Had Lindsay taken an active interest in film education in this country, it would have been another battle, but one which would have earned him keen supporters. His critical style made demands and it might have made demands on the type of films that are discussed in universities. Film studies have not helped create a film culture in Britain, but they might do if those, like Lindsay, who criticised them were to become more involved. Perhaps Lindsay was simply temperamentally unsuited to academic life; he could not bear the inflated egos of academics. When he wrote his 1981 attack on film studies ('A Critical Betrayal') it did not, as he hoped, provoke debate but instead gave rise to a series of indignant replies from the pompous and the self-interested. By the time he made his last film, the autobiographical television documentary, *Is That All There Is?*, it is possible that the younger generation of film enthusiasts might simply have perceived him as a curmudgeonly old eccentric with nothing to say to them. It must have puzzled so many of the young who did not know his films, who had not read his writings.

Lindsay was not an eccentric. He was a visionary poet, a radical presence, a conscience for critics and film-makers alike, and he was the tireless engine that powered the best chance Britain has ever had to create and nurture an intelligent cinema culture. His apparent self-reliance obscured the fact that he often needed support, he needed real encouragement, and he was wounded more than he cared to admit by the negligent treatment he received at the hands of his native film industry. Jean Genet, writing about Giacometti, claimed that 'beauty has no other origin than the particular wound that every man carries within himself'; the wound within Lindsay was caused by his sensitivity to the inequalities and absurdities which existed in the country he so loved and despised. It was caused too, by a very personal paradox: his indifference to being liked was matched by a profound desire to be loved.

In his last years, his health was not good. He collapsed at a film festival in the Czech Republic where he had met President Vaclav Havel (Lindsay was always better appreciated abroad, where his films were constantly shown). He continued to work in the theatre, but – socially – he

seemed permanently tired. The battle, which he fought to the end, was finally exhausting him. In August 1994, he suffered a fatal heart attack while on holiday in France. He was staying at the time with his old friend Lois Smith (formerly Sutcliffe) who had given him his first chance at making films. The wheel had come full circle, and there was a poetry in that: at least one revolution had been achieved.

I once asked Lindsay to define the attitude within his own films, and he replied, 'My films are shot through with suspicion and dislike of institutions and institutional thinking. They appeal to the intelligence, not the intellect. I'm accused of being pessimistic, which is true, but I think the optimistic thing about a work of art is not any hopeful formulation it may end up with, but essentially the vitality of the work itself.'

It is a cliché to describe someone as irreplaceable, but in Lindsay's case the cliché is entirely true. He will not be replaced. His friends cannot believe that he has gone, because there was about him such a sense of *there*ness. He is still there, in the landscapes of so many minds and hearts. For them, at least, Lindsay did not lose that long battle; the availability of his films and this volume of his writings may yet ensure that his spirit has other victories. Lindsay once told David Storey that he would like a line from Yeats' poem 'The Municipal Library Revisited' to be his epitaph: 'A revolutionary soldier kneeling to be blessed.' It fits him well, although, as Storey gently remarked, 'He didn't kneel for very long.' He was certainly – through all adversity – 'a revolutionary soldier'. He placed great emphasis on 'luck', so he would definitely count himself as 'blessed' but nowhere near as blessed as we must count ourselves to have had him in our midst. Let those who neglected him wither into footnotes; future generations will surely Stand Up! Stand Up! for Lindsay.

Paul Ryan
London, 2004

A child of Empire: Lindsay astride a cannon, with native bearer in attendance. India c. 1929.

ANDERSON ON ANDERSON

*Lindsay and his mother, shortly after the family returned
to England from India.*

My Country Right or Wrong?

Sunday Telegraph Magazine, 26 June 1988

PRIMROSES AND FRESH CRUSTY BREAD . . . THE RUGGED GRANDEUR OF HILL
and coastal landscape . . . the soft-spoken dignity of country folk . . .
Rupert Brooke's cosy catalogue of domestic joys. Into what platitudinous
prettiness has English patriotism degenerated! With the hypocrisy, of
course, that goes with complacency. The English still like to think of
themselves as modest, always ready for a self-mocking laugh, essentially
decent. They still believe their justice to be absolute. And, whatever the
evidence to the contrary, English authority is still fair-minded, incorrupt-
ible – mistaken perhaps, but *never* determinedly unjust.

I write 'English' with intention. The cold-blooded Normans of the
south, with their inextinguishable conviction of superiority, have bested
the northern Vikings, and the impetuous Celts. 'England' now stands for
Britain, whether we like it or not. I have not been a kilt-wearing Scot for
some sixty years now: but most of the blood that still courses fretfully
through my veins is Scottish. I have become more aware of this as I have
got older. My boyhood was pure upper-class English. We lived in Surrey.
My prep school was in West Worthing and I went on to Cheltenham
College. I completed my privileged English education at Oxford, with a
good accent and an MA that reassured my mother, even though it was
superior to a BA only because it cost more.

My father, a Scot and soldier, was born in Nassik, North India. My
mother (born in Queenstown, South Africa) was a Bell. I was born in
Bangalore, a child of Empire. Did these antecedents make for an alienation, long unrecognised? Early on, I gave signs of a mysterious appetite
for drama. I went regularly to the cinema with my grandmother, my
brother and my Stonehaven cousins. At Cheltenham, where I was lucky
enough to be among the last survivors of the Classical (Greek and Latin)
side, I made it clear that I was not going to be a regular soldier. Nor
would I take the Civil Service exam: I was thinking of 'going on the
stage'. The War put an end to this foolishness. I mention it only to stress
that, right from the start, my behaviour was not typically English.

I suppose I have always been a dissident. At St Ronan's, my prep
school, I remember that Stead (a friend with hair like pale straw) and I
put up a notice on the Reading Room board which simply said 'I Rebel'.
I don't think this was prompted by anything in particular; I took it down
without much argument when my brother told me not to be an ass. Many
years later I found myself numbered among the Angry Young Men. That

was in the fabulous Sixties, when for a while one could feel oneself in a vanguard of enlightenment, of change. But the conservatism of the English speedily reasserted itself. Harold Wilson, almost single-handedly, discredited the socialist ideal. Social democracy failed, as it always seems to. Mrs Thatcher moved in to save the day.

As Englishness triumphs, I find myself feeling increasingly alien. Whether this is really a matter of racial characteristics I cannot say. But I have learnt to recognise qualities in myself which the English find antipathetic ('tiresome' is the word they would use): a dogmatic quality, for instance; a relish for argument; a compulsive and impatient logic; a preference for the abrasion of principled judgement rather than the ease of non-committal toleration. Very un-English.

The English do not like to think of themselves as philistines. But that, coupled with their insistence on art as a paying proposition, a 'cultural' reassurance to be subsidised by industry, is what they have become. They think seriousness dull; they use the word 'solemn' as a pejorative. Their intellectuals flinch from commitment; hence the repetition of such refinements as 'slightly', 'rather', and 'somewhat'. (Notice, too, how often reviewers will describe original work as 'disturbing', 'unsettling', 'alarming'.) Avowed feeling is suspect; lost altogether is the authority of passion.

Least supportable of all, and most ruinous, has been the inability of the English to abandon the snug refuge of Class. They talk about it, write about it, make television programmes about it – but they cannot struggle free. And let no one imagine that this is an imposition by the privileged. They all like it. It was a Labour government, after all, which in 1945 shrank from the God-given opportunity to create a new system of education, freed from the wastefulness of privilege. We are paying for that now, at the mercy of a 'media' dedicated either to a materialistic conformism for the few, or to the degradation of the many by a vulgarity every day more debased.

I often think of the psychologist's description of a neurotic personality as one obsessed with itself, provoking endless speculation in others. By this definition, England – Britain – has become a neurotic society. 'Right or Wrong' indeed! The blustering American who first proclaimed his patriotism superior to his moral sense is no model for us. Patriotism is agreeable as a sentiment, as a morality it is unacceptable, dangerous. When Elizabeth I proclaimed herself, in Europe's adolescence, 'mere English', it was a proud and touching boast. But we have to grow up. 'Just human' would do for a start.

A Child of Empire

This autobiographical commentary is drawn from the Editor's own interviews with Lindsay Anderson and from notes made available by Lindsay in 1994

MY FATHER, WHO ENDED HIS MILITARY CAREER AS MAJOR-GENERAL Alexander Vass Anderson, was serving in Bangalore at the time of my birth there in 1923. He was then a captain with the Royal Engineers in what was called the British Army in India, not the Indian Army but attached to it. His family was Scottish, from Stonehaven, but he spent most of his life in India. I came to England at a very early age with my brother, who was three years older, and we were brought up in Norwood, in a house which belonged to my grandmother. I am not at all sure that I have any real childhood memories of India; there were many photograph albums at home and it was easy to confuse the photographs with true memories simply through a knowledge of the albums which – for families like ours – gave the feeling of a strong connection with India.

My mother's name was Estelle Bell Gasson, the daughter of an English wool merchant who married a young woman from the Bell Whisky family,

and she was born and raised in South Africa, so I really was a child of the British Empire. My mother came to England with my brother and myself, and she sent my brother to a preparatory school in Yorkshire. He found it a very unpleasant experience and, fortunately as it turned out, he developed ringworm. As a result, he was removed from the school and sent to St Ronan's in Worthing. Later, I followed him there. So

Lindsay's mother was, in Gavin Lambert's words, 'a formidably conservative Bride of Empire, the source of much of his strength, as well as many of his conflicts.'

we were both educated at an upper-class prep school and went on to Cheltenham College. By the time I was twelve years old, I had another brother who was ten years younger than myself. It was around then that my parents divorced. My father was not very keen on his sons, I think; we never saw him again.

At school, I remember, my brother and I were very keen on films. We kept scrap-books with pictures of stars in them. My brother mostly liked Warner Brothers pictures: Cagney, Edward G. Robinson, George Raft; whereas my favourite film stars were Robert Montgomery and Norma Shearer. I think that my favourite film, when young, was *Smilin' Through* with Shearer, Frederic March and Leslie Howard. I acted a bit at school, and would like to say at home that I wanted to go on the stage. This caused great rows, but 'going on the stage' didn't really mean anything in those days because I had never heard of a director and had no idea what a director was. If you went into the theatre, you acted.

Cheltenham was, primarily, a military school preparing boys for examinations to go to Sandhurst and Woolwich. My older brother was keen on the military side, but I had no such ambitions. I developed an early feeling for the Classics – Latin and Greek – but the classical tradition at Cheltenham rather disappeared when the war came. My brother passed out into Woolwich, which was the training college for young officers of the Royal Artillery, the Royal Engineers and the Tank Corps (Sandhurst was for the infantry, and Woolwich considered itself a bit superior). After Woolwich, he opted for the Tank Regiment just as war broke out. Unfortunately they had no tanks, so he became bored and volunteered for the Air Force where he trained in photographic reconnaissance. He wound up flying Spitfire aircraft which were armed with cameras rather than guns.

Meanwhile, I had also come up through Cheltenham. In fact, I had been Head of my House, Cheltondale, although this was largely because the boy who should have been the Head of the House, my friend David McNeill – who was the son of 'Sapper', the creator of *Bulldog Drummond* – left school ahead of time. I don't remember why he left, perhaps it was to go to university. The College Houses tended to take their personality from that of the Housemaster: ours was Ronnie Juckes, whose wife Dolly was rather like the Housemistress in *If* . . . . Cheltondale was a rather pleasant, reasonably civilised, not over-tough House. Of course, the school was pretty philistine, not in an unpleasant way but in a very English way. Any cultural background I received was probably due to my ending up in Upper Sixth Classical studying Latin and Greek, which is a very civilised form of education.

At the end of my time at Cheltenham I sat an exam and was awarded

Lindsay (second left in second row from front) at Cheltenham College.

a scholarship to Oxford. I always remember that, as I was leaving, the Headmaster, Mr Elliott-Smith, addressed the College and declared that 'Anderson has been awarded a minor scholarship at a university.' It struck me at once that he was either being deliberately nasty or else he lacked any sense of theatre. Choosing to say what he did instead of explaining that I had been awarded a Classical Scholarship at Wadham College, Oxford was, consciously or unconsciously, a bit nasty.

When the War broke out, Cheltenham was evacuated for a couple of terms – we went to Shrewsbury because our buildings were commandeered by the War Office. We came back, and were addressed by an officer from the 60th King's Royal Rifle Regiment – the Black Button Regiment. This officer had been sent around the public schools to get advance recruits for the Regiment so that, when the time came for them to go into the Army, they would be officer material in the 60th. That way, the Regiment would have a strand of public schoolboys as officers and not have to accept men from the ranks. So that was how I got into the Army. My brothers and I wound up covering all three branches of the services because, after the War, my younger brother was commissioned into the Navy; sadly he died while on peacetime service in the Pacific.

For myself, I went via Routon to York where I trained in what was then known as the Motorised Infantry and became an officer. No sooner was I commissioned than I received the papers to go and work at Bedford, attached to the Intelligence Corps. I was sitting at a desk in Bedford when

Lindsay in the uniform of the King's Royal Rifles: his wartime service took him back to India with the Intelligence Corps.

the planes went overhead and we realised that they were going to the opening of the Second Front. If I had stayed with my Regiment I would have gone to the Second Front and, most likely, have been killed. As it was, I worked on codes at Bedford and was then sent to India, to the Wireless Experimental Centre in Delhi.

My work in Delhi was a development of the Cryptanalysis Course which I had gone through at Bedford. Our job in the Cryptanalysis Section was concerned with the mathematical breakdown of messages, looking for repetitions of numbers, that sort of thing. I can remember absolutely nothing of it; I can't imagine that I was much good because, although I was intelligent, I was no good at mathematics. Curiously, we were sometimes required to study and decipher messages taken down by the Japanese, even though we had no knowledge of Japanese ourselves.

That went on until the end of the War. One of the things I remember was being drafted, at the end of the War, to look after the Indian Army officers who had been captured and put on trial as traitors to the British. This was because they had been taken by the Japanese and signed documents indicating their opposition to British rule in India. They were exceptionally nice people.

In 1945, I came back from India and went back to Wadham, switching from Classics to English Literature. I was there at the same time as Kenneth Tynan with whom I was associated in a rebellion over the re-formation of the OUDS, the Oxford University Dramatic Society. I also acted for Ken twice – once in a production of *Samson Agonistes* in which I played Menoa, the old father of Samson, and then in *Hamlet* in which I played Horatio. Ken wanted me to play him as an elderly German student so I did it in a sort of Albert Basserman accent. Basserman was a famous German actor who went to Hollywood as a refugee at the beginning of the War. He made a lot of films there and was also in the Powell and Pressburger film, *The Red Shoes*. The part of *Hamlet* in Ken's production was played by Peter Parker who went on to become chairman of British Rail and whose sons, Nathaniel and Oliver, have become successful actors. There were several people in that Oxford *Hamlet* who went on to become professional actors: Robert Hardy, who was known as Tim Hardy in those days; Jack May, who has been in *The Archers* on BBC Radio for many years, and Timothy Bateson, who was, even then, a talented character actor. He went on almost at once to appear in Cavalcanti's film of *Nicholas Nickleby* with Derek Bond.

It was at Oxford that I began, seriously, to write about the cinema. I went to a meeting of the Oxford University Film Society and met, for the first time, Peter Ericsson and John Boud, two undergraduates who wanted to develop the Film Society's own magazine into something more ambitious. John coined the name *Sequence*, and it was eventually published but was not very good. In fact, I wrote a very poor piece about going to Paris and seeing some French films. I really knew nothing, but it was the beginning of the magazine. The first issue which became recognisable as the *Sequence* people remember was *Sequence 2*. So that is how the magazine began, at Oxford. Later, when Peter and I left Oxford to come to London, we brought the magazine with us and published it from the flat I shared with Gavin Lambert (who had been at Cheltenham with me) in Hanover Terrace Mews. From there we established *Sequence* as a quarterly publication, although I doubt that it ever came out regularly every quarter, and we set about creating a personal, authoritative film magazine. I shared the editorship with Peter, and I had already persuaded Gavin to write for us.

We all put up some money and also borrowed from a friend and sympathiser, a photographer called Anthony Panting. Anthony used to phone regularly asking for his money to be returned, but it never was. By comparison to today, it was not an expensive operation because everything was much cheaper then. So we didn't spend a great deal on it, and we would sell it to film societies who would sell it on to their members. I remember a meeting of the London Film Society, at the Scala Cinema in King's Cross, when Olwyn Vaughan, who was the Secretary of the LFS, called out across the foyer: 'Dilys, come and see what these clever children have done.' Dilys Powell was always a good friend and used to mention *Sequence* in her film column for *The Sunday Times*.

Sequence had a very short life, but it built a reputation over a very few years. Of course, things were very different in those days. The number of people who bought *Sequence* was very small and the circulation was prob-

The programme for Kenneth Tynan's Hamlet *signed by the cast, and below the play in performance.*

ably no more than a couple of thousand. But it was read by *interested* people, and this was the time when *Sight and Sound*, published by the British Film Institute, was a real dead duck, a terrible paper. So there was room for a little magazine which may not have sold many copies but which was very refreshing in comparison with the dreary *Sight and Sound*.

When Denis Forman was appointed Head of the British Film Institute, taking over from Oliver Bell and R.W. Dickinson, *Sight and Sound* was transformed, as was the BFI itself. Denis managed to save the Tele-Kinema, which had been built for the 1951 Festival of Britain, from being torn down and it became the beginning of the National Film Theatre. He invited Gavin to come from *Sequence* to the BFI and take over the editorship of *Sight and Sound*, and Gavin revitalised the magazine. Once Gavin had taken over, I began writing for *Sight and Sound* and, for a time, it seemed that the spirit of *Sequence* would be kept alive, but it was not to be.

There have been several attempts to reprint *Sequence*, either in the form of an anthology of selected articles or as a complete bound run of all the issues. None of these attempts has been successful, but the last time a complete reprint seemed possible I wrote an introduction to it.

Sequence

Introduction to a Reprint, 30th March 1991

I HAVE OFTEN ASKED MYSELF WHY I SHOULD FIND IT SO DIFFICULT – ALMOST impossible – to write an introduction to this reprint of *Sequence*, which was published intermittently over a period of five years or so, and went out of business over 40 years ago. The magazine was in many ways a renowned success. However, as the advertising agent we visited in 1950 told us, our chances were those of 'Snowballs in Hell'. He was quite right. After all, we were hoping to attract advertisers (and no periodical that is not subsidised, like *Screen* or *Sight and Sound*, could possibly survive without advertising) to a British quarterly review of cinema that was determinedly uncompromising, specialist and personal, serious and humorous, enthusiastic and well-informed. It is sobering to think that no magazine with these qualities can now hope to survive in Britain. *

Sequence flourished in the late forties and early fifties. It was a fore-runner. Five years after it ceased publication there came Hungary and Suez and the New Left. On the home scene there appeared Free Cinema and the *Universities and Left Review*. The English Stage Company took possession of the Royal Court Theatre and presented *Look Back in Anger*. The Angry Young Men and all they signified were a journalistic invention, yet they marked a change, almost a revolution, in British cultural and social life. The hectic sixties followed, with all their venturesomeness and variety.

It has become fashionable to deride that turbulent decade for its extraordinary mix of 'progressive' politics, of impatience with fossilised structures, of anarchism and flower-power, of drugs, meditation and Pop. We should not forget that the mix had certain ingredients whose loss has proved terribly damaging: most notably vitality and hope. Also a great deal more humour than its critics appreciate, or possess themselves. From the late sixties it was downhill all the way. The seventies substituted profit for experiment. Squabbles in the Labour Party ate away at the Socialist Ideal. The unions became increasingly sectarian, increasingly materialist, until they deserved as well as received their defeat at the hands of Margaret Thatcher.

A reverse continuity can be traced from Britain's New Wave of the late fifties, back to Free Cinema (1956 to 1958) and to *Sequence* in the years after the War. The magazine was not particularly pro-British and certainly not political, but later developments were realist in style and implicitly (not explicitly) left-wing. Greatly to the disapproval of the French-influ-

41

Issue number eleven of Sequence, Summer *1950, containing Lindsay's article on John Ford.*

enced 'intellectuals', they were also closely connected with the theatre, essentially the Royal Court, where John Osborne exploded in 1956, and with writers and actors. The common factor was not theory but intelligence. Tony Richardson was not at first an integral part of the critical movement, but he soon became connected with it. He contributed to *Sight and Sound*, collaborated with Karel Reisz on one of the first Free Cinema documentaries (*Momma Don't Allow*) and was George Devine's close associate in the early days of the English Stage Company at the Royal Court. Together Devine and he discovered Osborne, and Tony directed John's plays and broke into feature production by founding (with John) Woodfall Films and turning *Look Back in Anger* and *The Entertainer* into films.

'No Film Can Be Too Personal'. So ran the initial pronouncement in the first *Free Cinema manifesto*. It could equally well have been the motto of *Sequence*, for the editors were never interested in any judgement that differed from their own. Not that it implied any lack of social interest, for it was this that chiefly motivated the films of the British New Wave. ('Look at Britain' was the title we chose for Free Cinema's series of documentaries – which did not last long). After the Osborne films, Woodfall produced Karel Reisz's phenomenally popular adaptation of Alan Sillitoe's *Saturday Night and Sunday Morning*, which superseded Jack Clayton's *Room at the Top* with unglossy realism and the casting of two unknowns, Albert Finney and Rachel Roberts.

For a time it looked as though new directors, working-class writers and actors would disintegrate the bourgeois Establishment of British cinema. Karel's *Saturday Night and Sunday Morning*, it is sometimes forgotten, derived immediately from his experience as a teacher and his Free Cinema documentary, *We Are the Lambeth Boys*. He produced my *Every Day*

Except Christmas (about Covent Garden Market) and also my first feature film, from David Storey's *This Sporting Life*. Tony made *A Taste of Honey* and *The Loneliness of the Long-Distance Runner*, and his *Tom Jones* (turned down by Balcon and Bryanston) became one of the most popular films, successful both at home and in the United States, ever made in Britain.

It did not last. The Rank Organisation had financed *This Sporting Life*, but it did not do particularly well and John Davis disliked it intensely. Rank, he announced, would in future eschew such squalid and unreal material and return to the manufacture of 'family entertainment'. (It was not long before Rank went out of production altogether.) In 1967 Tony Richardson's *Charge of the Light Brigade*, which combined the radical with the epic, was rejected by critics and public alike. The British cinema returned to its persistently middle-class ethos: themes of criticism and change were not welcomed. In the mid-sixties Ann Jellicoe's moral comedy, *The Knack*, which had started at the Royal Court, was turned by Dick Lester into a crazy, amoral farce (produced by Woodfall, ironically enough). It won the Grand Prix at Cannes and began the vogue for stories of Swingin' London. The vogue proved unsuccessful and in the early seventies the Americans, disillusioned and over-taxed, withdrew with their money to California.

So ended the attempt to revitalise the British cinema which had begun with *Sequence*. Tony Richardson shook the dust of England from his feet and became a resident of Los Angeles, not far from where Gavin Lambert, one of our initial editorial trio, was now living in Santa Monica. In 1973 Karel Reisz made his first American film, *The Gambler*, in New York. John Schlesinger, who had made his debut in 1961 with the North Country *A Kind of Loving*, made *Midnight Cowboy*, also in New York; and Joe Losey, the American exile who had become the favourite of the British critics, won great acclaim with the gracious subtleties of *The Go-Between*. Dick Lester followed *The Knack* with *A Funny Thing Happened on the Way to the Forum*. The British lack of response to films which questioned the *status quo* was clear: 'working-class' subjects were relegated to television, while radical and anarchistic habits were largely discarded. The tradition which had started with *Sequence* came to an end.

So the British 'New Wave' ended. How had it begun? To go back to those first years after the War must require a huge effort of readjustment. It cannot be easy for young or even middle-aged people today to imagine what life was like for the *cinephile* when the British Film Institute was decrepit rather than a profit-seeking bureaucracy; when there was no National Film Theatre and no National Film School; when the idea of owning your

PARTHENON FILMS UNLIMITED
(1942)

Managing Directors : **LINDSAY GORDON ANDERSON** and **GAVIN LAMBERT**

Hollywood Representative
CLAUDINE WEST
(c/o M.G.M. Studios)

Temporary Address
15 SHAFTESBURY AVENUE
PRESTON ROAD
MIDDLESEX
(Wordsworth 3587)

Living in hope: Parthenon Films letterhead featuring Gavin Lambert's aunt, Claudine West, named as Hollywood representative without her knowledge.

own videotaped copies of films by Griffith, Eisenstein, Ford, Renoir, Kurosawa and Ray (to mention no other great names of cinema) would have seemed outlandish fantasy.

During the last war, remember, many new films from Hollywood were never imported. Classics were hard to find. Books about cinema were scarce. There was Rotha's very subjective *The Film Till Now*, erratic histories by Sadoul and Bardeche and Brassillac, and of course those theoretical works by Eisenstein which decorated many intellectual shelves, largely unread and as little understood then as now. Roger Manvell's *Film* was published by Pelican during the War and bought by everyone: it was an excellent 'ABC'. *Sight and Sound* was stodgy, and so was the *Penguin Film Review*, which Manvell edited. Film criticism was rare.

Much the same was true of film-making. There were no television programmes to tell us how films were made, and when their new pictures appeared, film directors were never interviewed. We knew only that celluloid was inflammable, that montage was made with a joiner, a razor blade and sticky tape, and that you mixed sound off film or gramophone records. If you wanted to record synchronised dialogue, you had to enclose the camera in a heavy, sound-proof 'blimp'. If you shot a man at a lathe on the factory floor, or a woman out shopping, both you and they would be distracted by cries from all around (I remember them in a broad Northern accent) of 'Coom on, Clark Gable!' or 'Who d'you think you are – Greta Garbo?'

That was the cinema in 1946, when the Oxford University Film Society produced its magazine. It was edited by two undergraduates, Peter Ericsson from New College and John Boud from Jesus. They were enthusiastic, if ignorant. They promised development. When the next issue appeared, John Boud invented the title *Sequence* and executed a continuity of woodcuts to decorate the cover. This was in December 1946, when I had been flown back from India (where I had struggled as a cryptanalyst at the Wireless Experimental Centre outside Delhi) and joined the Film Society.

That summer I had visited Paris for a week with Gavin Lambert, who had been a school friend in my House at Cheltenham. We had started a film company there, more as a joke than anything else, which we called Parthenon Films. We collaborated on two scripts, one a thriller called *Pursuit* and one an adaptation of *Madam Bovary*, neither of which was produced. Gavin's aunt was Claudine West, who was a scenarist at MGM; she was our Hollywood representative, though I don't think she ever knew it. As a result of our film-going in Paris, I wrote a piece that was published in *Sequence* 1. I would not care to read it now; but it was a beginning.

Next year the Society published *Sequence* 2. This looked more or less as the magazine would look later: on the cover was a still from *My Darling Clementine*. Here was another step forward. By 1947 both Peter Ericsson and I had fallen under the spell of the poet Ford. We had seen *My Darling Clementine* several times, and found it greatly superior – even as we struggled to understand exactly why – to the British films of Lean, Reed and Powell then being hailed and lauded by the press. (The *Times* reviewer consigned *Clementine*, which was set in Tombstone, to 'the graveyard of mediocrity'.) So the first of our relatively long articles on a director, which were to become the centrepiece of the magazine, was devoted to John Ford.

In 1948 *Sequence* came to London and announced in an editorial that it had started its career as a quarterly. The Film Society committee gave Peter and myself permission to remove the magazine from Oxford (they also paid the outstanding bills) and I asked Gavin Lambert to contribute a study of the films of Marcel Carné. The university tradition persisted: Gavin had been at Magdalen for a while, where he had assisted Peter Brook on his first film *A Sentimental Education*. Our co-editor on *Sequence* 3 was Penelope Houston (Somerville) who could write about anything with amazing confidence. On the next issue, Gavin joined Peter and myself to form an editorial trio. Of course we were never really a quarterly, though we did our best to publish regularly. With equal fantasy we announced that we welcomed contributions 'from anyone, on any aspect of the cinema, written from any point of view.' This was never true. *Sequence* was almost entirely written by its editors, with some help from friends. Pseudonyms were taken from characters in films ('Alberta Marlow' was played by Mary Astor in *Across the Pacific*). We were never interested in any judgements or ideas that differed from our own. No one was paid.

John Ford's My Darling Clementine. *Wyatt Earp (Henry Fonda) and his 'Lady Fair' (Cathy Downs) open the dance on the church site.*

Why, you may wonder, did *Sequence* exist? There is surely a great difference between our enthusiasm then, and the ambition that inspires young people 40 years later. We were not careerists. We had no desire to establish ourselves as journalists or even as film-makers. We were certainly not doing it for profit. But it seemed important to say what we thought and felt. Right opinions should be heard. We were, in fact, an odd trio. Gavin wrote scripts for Rank Advertising and worked on his own stories. I had started making publicity films about belt conveyors for Richard Sutcliffe Limited of Horbury, Wakefield. Peter had a mysterious job with the Foreign Office, spoke Swedish and sensibly balanced our enthusiasms. We were each individual, but on fundamentals we did not disagree. We trusted each other.

As publishers we were amateurs. We typed the copy, measured column inches and ems to calculate the size of columns and the number of words on a page. Stills had to be measured (you draw a diagonal across the back) so that blocks could be made. And pictures had to be obtained by fair means or foul. Many were the visits we paid to Wardour Street distributors, purloining stills from filing cabinets, hiding them in briefcases and under sweaters. And many were our friends and sympathisers: Lois Sutcliffe who started me off as a film-maker and sold *Sequence* in Wakefield. The cheerful publicist at MGM who later turned into a woman. Contributors like Satyajit Ray, Douglas Slocombe, Catherine de la Roche. Everyone (listed in our last number) who helped buy blocks for

Sequence 14. Walter Lassally and John Fletcher who helped make up parcels and became fellow film-makers. Stella Paterson and Irene Philips, staunch helpers. Friendly critics: Dilys Powell, George Stonier, Richard Winnington. Alex Jacobs, first encountered at UA, who rode in bicycle races, later helped to publicise Free Cinema and went to Hollywood as a writer where he died of cancer . . .

We had good fun doing *Sequence*: its impertinences still make me laugh. Also Peter's drawings. Most importantly, we took moral relevance for granted: we did not value artistic or stylistic achievements for itself alone. (This was a traditional principle, not to prove long-lasting.) Then in 1950 Gavin moved on, invited by Denis Forman to his revitalised Institute, to edit *Sight and Sound* – from which Michael Balcon did his best to get him fired, because he had dared say rude things about *The Blue Lamp*. Earlier, I had been lucky enough to meet Karel Reisz, when we were double-booked on to the National Film Archive Movieola at Aston Clinton. I was researching Hitchcock and he was viewing *Mata Hari* for his book on film editing; so we watched each other's films. That was a lucky clash, for Karel became a *Sequence* critic and helped me to edit the final number. This, of course, was quite apart from the contribution he later made to Free Cinema, and my debt to him as my producer.

Forty years on, it is probably best to let *Sequence* speak for itself, always supposing it speaks at all. But there are two of its characteristics that perhaps call for comment. In view of developments to come, it may seem surprising that we had so little care for Documentary. But our concentration on feature films, and later on feature film-making, was not simply negative. The British documentarists never seemed to us to be very concerned with the life around us ('The poetry of the Everyday', as the Free Cinema Manifesto put it). John Grierson himself, though a great producer, was more interested in social propaganda than in art. This did not appeal to us.

And anyway, the great period of Griersonian Documentary came to an end with the War. Nothing much was said about post-war Britain by the Shell Film Unit and *Three Dawns to Sydney*. We warmly admired the achievements of Humphrey Jennings, but we had as little sympathy with Grierson and his surviving disciples as they (on the whole) had with us. Arthur Elton reviewed *Every Day Except Christmas* most unfavourably in the Union's journal, remarking on my failure to raise the issue of strikes in Covent Garden and comparing my affection for my characters with Noel Coward's farewell to his ship's crew in *In Which We Serve*. And I remember meeting John Grierson at Beaconsfield, in the tentative pursuit of a job with Group Three. I was received without warmth, but Grierson spoke glowingly of the Group's record. 'We have a director shooting now who may well turn out to be the British René Clair,' he told me. The picture was *Miss Robin Hood*, starring Margaret Rutherford, and the director was John Guillermin.

Equally remarkable, looking ahead to the New Wave, must be the lack of interest *Sequence* showed in the British Cinema generally. By the end of the War, British films were respectable and overpraised. They had made their contribution to the mood of national self-confidence. They reflected the class divisions of the country faithfully enough: working-class comedies to divert the popular audience (George Formby, Gracie Fields, the Crazy Gang), with 'serious' cinema remaining a bourgeois preserve. The industry remained a closed shop. BBC Television still wore the Reithian collar-and-tie, while commercial television did not yet exist. Film-makers were defended by their unfriendly and philistine union. When I wrote of British production as 'The Descending Spiral' and poked fun at Ealing's *Scott of the Antarctic* ('The Frozen Limit', Gavin captioned it) I was referring sarcastically to a piece by George Stonier for *Vogue*, titled 'British Cinema: The Ascending Spiral'. Why should we join in the chorus of praise? It was much more useful, surely, to draw attention to the vision and vitality of American cinema – then much despised. Things would change, of course.

With these attitudes, there was no way that *Sequence* could survive for very long. We had no backing and, at our peak, we only printed 5000 copies. Costs, it is true, were relatively low in those days, but we paid them ourselves and with a loan generously, if inadvisably, made by the photographer Anthony Panting. (How we grew to dread those telephone calls, asking so mildly for payment. In vain.) The magazine was not widely popular. Perhaps it was too 'specialised'. We certainly never had the slightest acknowledgement from, or effect on, the British film industry. We gave some parties, and even film-makers turned up to drink and talk at 19 Hanover Terrace Mews, but I cannot remember that anyone ever asked us back.

Other magazines, other critical tides have flooded in over the last 40 years, mostly proving the rightness of George Orwell when he noted the tendency of English intellectuals to look abroad for their ideas about art. *Sequence*, though, was quite untouched by French influence and the aesthetics of *Cahiers du Cinéma*. We certainly had no time for the *auteur* theory. From the start we knew that the film director was the essential artist of cinema; but we also knew that films have to be written, designed, acted, photographed, edited and given sound. We tried to look for the creative elements.

Inevitably, however, criticism has followed history. Film Appreciation, that horrible 'discipline' which has acquired academic status over these 40 years, still borrows its aesthetics from Europe. Journalists speak popularly with the voice of America. Money talks; and money comes from across the Atlantic. The British have never considered a national cinema (since the War that is) of any importance. No British artist is featured on the wall of portraits displayed outside our Museum of the Moving Image. Every month the covers of British magazines are more regularly devoted to portraits of Kevin Costner, Michelle Pfeiffer, Robert de Niro, Meryl Streep. And each year the prizes awarded to film-makers by Hollywood technicians and artists occupy more space in the British press: Barry Norman is flown to Los Angeles to report on the Oscar ceremony for British television. The tradition of independence and intelligence, of wit and style, which we tried to uphold in *Sequence* has been overwhelmed by the persisting accents of Oxbridge, the bully-boy vulgarities (American accented) of Redbrick, the bloodless theorising of Film Departments.

In 1991 the National Film Theatre (whose new Programme Officer was American) presented a series of programmes under the title 'Images'. Monsieur Raymond Bellour, the visiting British Film Institute 'Research Fellow', introduced his season with a bold pronouncement.

> What is really new is the extraordinary acceleration of the effects of mixing which contaminates every use of the image, which can no longer be understood independently of television or the computer. Thus in the cinema we have entered a new period, a new physics of the image.

Alas there is no *Sequence* around any more to dismiss this stuff with the healthy derision it deserves.

---

* By early 1991 *Time and Tide,* the *Listener, Encounter* had disappeared; the *New Statesman* had combined with *New Society*, and even *Sight and Sound* had amalgamated with the *Monthly Film Bulletin*. (Readers of the new magazine were promised 'the best writing from critics such as Amy Taubin and Jim Hoberman of the *Village Voice*, John Powers of *L.A. Weekly*, John Berger and Anne Billson.' In his first editorial, the editor, in deference to the *Zeitgeist*, assured his readers that *'Sight and Sound* has no interest in nostalgia for the good old things; it wants to start from the bad new things.' His first issue bore this out.)

Starting in Films

Commentary, 1994

LUCK PLAYS A VERY IMPORTANT PART IN THE WORK AND LIFE OF THE ARTIST, particularly the film-maker, and the first piece of luck I had when it came to making films also happened at Oxford. When I came back from India I divided my time between work, the theatre – in productions for the OUDS – and the Film Society. In those days, film societies were the only places that certain classic or foreign films got to be shown outside of the commercial system. The Oxford University Film Society hosted the annual meeting of the Federation of Film Societies. It was at this meeting that I met Lois Sutcliffe who had started the Wakefield Film Society in Yorkshire, and had come along to the meeting with her friend Margaret Hancock from Bradford. Lois was married to Desmond Sutcliffe, who was the Managing Director of Richard Sutcliffe Limited in Wakefield. In those days, Wakefield was surrounded by pits and coal-mines, and Sutcliffe's were the world leaders in underground conveyor systems which were used to bring coal up to the surface. I remember very little about our conversation but there were several of us drinking and talking together, including Peter Ericsson. Naturally, we talked about film but, at the time, I knew nothing about the making of films and certainly had no real ambition to become a film-maker.

After I finished at Oxford, I didn't really know what I was going to do. One day, Lois turned up at my home in Camberley. The snow was falling, I remember, and my mother came to me and said, 'There's a woman here who wants to see you.' I am sure my mother expected the worst, but Lois just came in and said, 'We're going to make a film at the works and I've told them who ought to make it.' I said, 'Who?', and she said, 'You.' I told her she was crazy. I said I had never made a film and knew nothing about it. 'Well,' said Lois, 'you've got to start somewhere.' I have always believed in accepting challenges, and so I went up to Wakefield and started preparing the film, the first film I ever made.

It's important to remember that, back then, there were no film schools. Young or inexperienced people were not taught how to make a film; the only way to learn was by actually making one. All sorts of things that we have now become quite used to did not exist. Tape recording was not fully developed, synchronised recording with a 16mm camera certainly didn't exist. By today's standards the work we did would be considered primitive, although it was no less creative than much of the work that is done now – particularly that done for television. It was primitive from a technical point of view.

The Sutcliffe Film Unit during the shooting of Idlers That Work *(1949). Lindsay seated centre with Lois Sutcliffe second left.*

Anyway, armed with no knowledge whatsoever, I went to Wakefield and made a 40-minute film about the Sutcliffe company. A competition was held at the Sutcliffe Works to come up with a title for the film, and one of the workers suggested *Meet the Pioneers*, which it was duly called. The film was photographed by the local schoolmaster, John Jones, and I was helped by one of Gavin Lambert's friends, Bill Brendon, who worked in the film industry as a third assistant, I think. Lois herself dealt with continuity, and that was the full size of the unit.

I knew nothing about editing. I thought that you had a script where you just wrote down the shots you were going to take and then you joined them all together to make the film. In the end, I suppose I edited the film in about 72 hours at Merton Park. As for the dubbing, I had booked just four hours to dub the entire 40 minutes - music, commentary, everything. Again, I thought that I would speak the commentary and have someone else to change the gramophone records. At the dubbing studio they thought I was totally mad. Knowing what I do now, it was mad; but, as I didn't know anything, it seemed like common sense at the time. And it worked.

Today, it looks very amateurish, but that doesn't matter because it served its purpose. It was shown at the Mechanical Handling Exhibition in Olympia in 1948, and was very well received. *Meet the Pioneers*, like

ALL enquiries about these films should be addressed to the Sales Manager, Richard Sutcliffe, Ltd., Horbury, Wakefield, Yorkshire.

We will be pleased to arrange showings of them, with introductory talks where possible; otherwise to lend copies of the films to those with projection facilities of their own.

TECHNICAL CREDITS

MEET THE PIONEERS (1948). *Production*: Desmond and Lois Sutcliffe. *Direction*: Lindsay Anderson. *Camera*: John Jones, Edward Brendon. *Music*: Len Scott.

IDLERS THAT WORK (1949). *Production*: Richard O'Brien. *Direction*: Lindsay Anderson. *Camera*: George Levy. *Music*: Ralph Vaughan Williams and Aaron Copland.

PRINTED BY THE ALCUIN PRESS, WELWYN GARDEN CITY, HERTS.

Richard Sutcliffe Limited

Presents

MEET THE PIONEERS

and

IDLERS THAT WORK

★

Underground Mining Machinery Exhibition
Earls Court, London   *July*, 1949

The programme for Meet the Pioneers *and* Idlers that Work.

all the films I made for the Sutcliffes, was made without any avant-garde or artistic ambition. I made it as well as I could, but its principal purpose was to promote Richard Sutcliffe Limited.

Again, I was lucky in being asked to do these films because the Sutcliffes saw themselves as a family firm with a style and personality of their own. Before they asked me to make that first film, they had approached a couple of documentary companies and had received treatments that could have been written for any firm which made belt conveyors. It was because these treatments had nothing personal or distinctive about them that they decided to make their own films. Hence the very unorthodox way in which I was invited to make my first film.

Of course, I was aware of the tradition of documentary in Britain which had developed from the Grierson period of the 1930s into the Crown Film Unit during the War. But we were making our films in the post-War period, and the impact of such films as *Coastal Command*, *Listen to Britain* and *Fires Were Started* had lessened. Documentary was on its way out. So I went to work with no pretensions or artistic ambitions, my only concern was with what the Sutcliffes wanted to put onto film, and – as far as possible – what I wanted to put onto film. I make no claims for *Meet the Pioneers* but I think that you can see in it some of my concerns with rhythm and editing, with people, with the importance of putting a human quality across, which have perhaps figured in my later work. But it was in no way self-conscious at the time.

In a shop in Wardour Street I found a camera called the Vinton Battle which cost £100. It looked rather compact, so I suggested we buy it. I didn't know that these cameras were extremely unreliable. The second film we made had to be abandoned because the camera kept jamming. I remember that I was very relieved, after four or five days of shooting, to receive a telegram from the lab that was processing the film: 'ADVISE STOP SHOOTING.' The next film, called *Idlers That Work*, was shot by a chap from Ealing Studios, George Levy, who had been recommended to me by Douglas Slocombe. George brought his own camera, a hand-held Imo 35mm.

I shot the third of the Sutcliffe films, *Three Installations*, with Walter Lassally on camera. Walter and I got to know each other when he came along to help parcel

Fordian compositions from Meet the Pioneers *(1948), Lindsay's entry into film-making.*

up copies of *Sequence*, and he introduced me to a friend of his called John Fletcher. At about this time, the local Wakefield newspaper, the *Wakefield Express*, called the Sutcliffes for advice. 'We keep getting approached by people who want to look around the works,' they said. 'We hear you've got a film man there: is he any good?' The Sutcliffes recommended me, and I enlisted Walter and John to help me make a 33-minute film which was called, simply, *Wakefield Express*. It was made by just the three of us. Walter shot it silent on 16mm and, when I'd cut it, John helped me to put the sound on it, which was all dubbed on afterwards. George Potts, a reporter from the newspaper, came down to London and recorded the commentary in my back bedroom.

By using the device of following a reporter going out in the area to gather stories for the newspaper we were able to take the opportunity of recording something of the way of life in the locality. So the central section is a series of sequences, glimpses of a way of life, which are now of considerable historical interest.

Wakefield Express: *Lindsay filming a children's concert party in the West Riding village of Fitzwilliam, with Walter Lassally behind the 16mm Bolex camera.*

All the documentary films I made were, I hope, personal and subjective. It has always been my ambition to make films which can be described as poetic. The very term 'poetic' implies the subjective, the personal, the emotional; perhaps that is the reason why there are fewer films being made these days which can be described that way.

Later, with the 'short ends' we had left over from *Wakefield Express*, I made an entirely personal film called *O Dreamland*. I was prompted to make it while preparing a film for which I was by no means solely responsible, *Thursday's Children*. A friend from my Oxford days, Guy Brenton, had found a job at the BBC and had been involved with a BBC programme which featured a section on the Royal School for the Deaf in Margate. Guy decided that the school would make a fine subject for a film and he asked me to help him. I agreed and asked Walter to come along and shoot it. Guy had a real interest in disability and he invited me to co-direct the film because I had more experience than he had of film-making. But neither of us was a professional film-maker, really – I wasn't even in the technicians' union, which was essential if you wanted to work in the industry in those days. *Thursday's Children* was neither subsidised nor commissioned; Guy and I put up the money and persuaded a few friends to help out financially.

You would expect that, in a film about the education of deaf children, sound would be of great importance. Unfortunately, we had absolutely no facilities, no provision for synchronised tape or blimped cameras. We shot the film 'wildtrack' most of the time. Towards the end, when we needed sequences of children being taught individually, we went into an adjoining room and shot through the window, having left the tape recorder inside so that it didn't pick up the sound of the camera. This made it impossible to have the sound perfectly synchronised, but we synched it during editing.

In fact, we didn't have enough money to commission the music and put the sound on, so we approached a documentary company called World Wide Pictures, who looked at what we had done and agreed to put the money up. As a result it was billed as 'a World Wide Film', although they were not really responsible for the picture. Armed with the World Wide money, Guy and I finished the film – he dealt with the music track and I dealt with the commentary. Richard Burton was then with the Old Vic company and I went along to his dressing-room and asked him if he would speak the commentary, although we couldn't pay him for it. Richard's agent negotiated an on-screen credit which said: 'Commentary spoken by Richard Burton who gave his services for the children', which was perfectly fine by us.

Thursday's Children remains a very interesting film, especially in relation to other films I have made. Perhaps it might be considered sentimental, but it is impossible to make a film about deaf children without a degree of sentiment or without a certain charm. The deaf have a particular quality. The sense in which they are cut off from the world gives them a greater desire for contact with others in the hearing world. I think it would be difficult to make a bad or unmoving film about the education of deaf children.

Of course, once we had finished the film, nobody wanted to show it. In New York, the British Office of Information – which was devoted to propaganda for Britain – submitted the film to the Hollywood Academy for that year's Oscar race. This was done without my knowledge or Guy's; I don't think we knew at all until we had won it. That was the only way that the film received distribution. It was taken up in America by Republic Films; not a company of great distinction, but beggars can't be choosers. I don't remember if it was ever properly distributed in Britain, but I remember going to see it at the Carlton Cinema in London's West End with Richard Burton's agent. It was shown there in support of Henry King's picture *Untamed* which starred Tyrone Power and Susan Hayward. It may have been shown here and there over the years, but the last time I saw it myself was in a 16mm print, which is a shame because we shot it in 35mm. I often wonder what happened to Guy. He made some other films, I think, but didn't go on to become a professional film-maker. Even so, winning an Oscar for your first effort isn't bad.

The Value of an Oscar

Broadcast on the BBC Home Service, 9 September 1956

FIRST OF ALL I HAVE TO ADMIT IT'S VERY PLEASANT TO GET AN OSCAR. WE ALL know that awards are nonsense – and people are always getting them of whom we intensely disapprove – so I suppose logically we should be quite unmoved if we happen to be given one ourselves. But this doesn't seem to happen. When a friend rang me up one morning to say he'd heard on the eight o'clock news that *Thursday's Children* had won an Academy Award, I was definitely pleased. This is the first value of an Oscar. It fortifies you.

I should, by the way, stress that in my case it was *half* an Oscar. *Thursday's Children*, which was a 25-minute picture about deaf children, was the shared work of Guy Brenton and myself. We wrote it together, and directed and edited it together. It wasn't sponsored by anybody: we made it with our own money, and with money borrowed from friends. Halfway through, World Wide Pictures came in and enabled us to finish it. But there was no guarantee it would ever be shown.

When we were editing the film, we thought it was so good that we couldn't believe we would find it difficult to sell. Perhaps this sounds conceited, but I don't mean good so much because of our work, as because of the children. There is something special about deaf children – something wonderfully expressive, wonderfully alive. We couldn't believe other people wouldn't feel the same. But we were wrong. When the film was finished, we hawked it about in the traditional way, and everyone was very moved, and all the distributors cried, but said of course it wasn't entertainment, and they were very sorry . . . Finally a distribution company – an American one, incidentally – did take on the film, but they still couldn't get any cinemas to show it.

That was how things still stood when we got our Oscar. The next valuable thing it did for us was to get the picture shown. It's true that the gentlemen who book films for Britain's three major circuits couldn't be persuaded to change their minds. But a smaller circuit in the home counties booked it; and we got a showing in the West End, in support of a CinemaScope production starring Susan Hayward and twenty thousand Zulus.

So really it was thanks to the Hollywood Academy that *Thursday's Children* was shown in Britain at all. It's true it never did get on the big circuits – which is the reason why most of you who are listening to this probably never saw it anyway. But it had quite a number of bookings from independent cinemas up and down the country. As a result, it has by now just about covered its cost. Without the Oscar I don't suppose this would have been the case.

What about its effect on us, professionally? I must start speaking for myself alone. Well, undoubtedly an Oscar helps. You get offered work. The curious thing is – at least I found it curious – how rarely these offers seem to have anything to do with the kind of work you've shown yourself to be good at. A sponsor gets in touch with you: he's seen that film you made – the one about blind children (they usually seemed to think it was about blind children) – and he'd found it deeply moving. So he felt you were just the director for this series of half-minute publicity flashes advertising his celebrated brand of Tonic Wine . . .

This sort of thing is gratifying, since it helps you to keep alive. But of course what you're really hoping for is a chance to do something good again. The difficulty here, so far as documentary is concerned, is simple and it's not a difficulty the Hollywood motion picture academy can do anything about. Short film produc-

Thursday's Children: *This oscar-winner co-directed by Lindsay and Guy Brenton featured a class at the Royal School for Deaf Children in Margate.*

tion in this country is utterly uneconomic. That's why we no longer, really, have a documentary movement – just a sponsored film industry.

Let me give you an example. Largely, I suppose, as a result of *Thursday's Children*, I was asked if I would make a film about 'Industrial Rehabilitation'. Now this may sound a bit dry, but in fact those words describe a most important and exciting thing – a nationwide scheme, run by the government, for helping people who've been ill, or had accidents, or who are in any way maladjusted, to find the right kind of work, and get fit to do it. This is a subject of great social significance, and at the same time rich in human interest. The only trouble was that the government didn't have enough money to pay for a film about it. The idea was that the film should be sponsored partly by the appropriate ministry, and partly by a large industrial concern. An admirable example of co-operation between public and private enterprise – but unfortunately the essence of the Industrial Rehabilitation scheme is that it is a public service, which made it difficult to introduce much about private enterprise into the script. As a result, the industrial sponsors backed out; and I didn't make the film. As far as I know, in fact, nobody did. Yet it would have made a good film. It might even have won an Oscar.

The point I am trying to make is that if you work within the system an Academy Award will give you a leg up. Then all the usual conditions, your own ability, and personality, and of course luck, apply once more. If you won your Oscar with a film that was made *outside* the system, it won't make it much easier to repeat the success. In fact it's probably harder because now you know all the difficulties. The problem is to find the opportunity – and the courage – to try to do as well again.

Finding a Style

Commentary, 1994

AT THE TIME OF *THURSDAY'S CHILDREN* I PAID A VISIT TO DREAMLAND, A fun-fair in Margate. It had a strange waxwork exhibition showing 'Torture Through the Ages', featuring effigies of the Rosenbergs being elec-trocuted. I remember a poster which said: 'See the electric chair in which the atom spy Rosenberg was executed' and there was a little hole in the wall through which you could see a police-man laughing. I was very struck by this image and thought that it should be put on film. So I went back to Dreamland with John Fletcher and we just shot a little ten-minute film entirely from my own resources. The film stock, as I mentioned earlier, was left over from *Wakefield Express*, and the film we made, *O Dreamland*, could not have been more different from the lyrical tenderness of *Thursday's Children*. I've always thought of the two films as being comparative, *O Dreamland* being a song of experience as opposed to the song of innocence of *Thursday's Children*.

O Dreamland is a consistently satir-ical film, almost a 'hate film'. It was a quite spontaneous reaction on my part to this phenomenon and to the aspect of the human race that it represented. In a sense, it is also what might be called a piece of Sunday film-making. It was shot on 16mm without synch sound. The sound that was put on later consisted for the most part of the music being played on the jukeboxes throughout Dreamland at the time. It

A Propos de Margate: The amusement park Dreamland, the subject of Lindsay's savagely poetic short, O Dreamland.

remains the kind of film which is within anyone's power to make; I really went about making the film in much the same way as one would go about painting a picture or writing a poem. The emphasis on style and technique which preoccupies modern film schools, and the current requirement of documentary film to be dependent on reportage or the delivery of information, militates against this kind of personal film-making. But I was working in very primitive times, not like today. I've never been very good at doing anything that I don't really believe in or care about, which is not a good basis for being a film director. I don't think of myself as much of a technician, although I think I'm a good editor.

After we shot *O Dreamland* I don't think I did anything with it. I had it in a suitcase for at least six months until I came to make my last film for the Sutcliffes, *Trunk Conveyor*. I took it up to Wakefield and, while we were shooting the Sutcliffe film, I edited it. I suppose it really was the first film I made with no other impetus than my own wish to make it. Of course, there wasn't a lot I could do with it once it was ready for screening. What could anyone do with a 16mm film that was only ten minutes long? It wasn't until I got together with my friends Tony Richardson and Karel Reisz to present the Free Cinema programmes at the National Film Theatre that *O Dreamland* was finally shown. It was actually the first film shown in the first ever Free Cinema programme.

Even then, there was no way of getting a wide distribution for the film because it would have cost too much to clear copyright on the music – which, of course, I had not done – and it was impossible to dispense with the music, as it was an essential part of the film. There was also the fact that the voice used in the 'Torture Through the Ages' sideshow was the voice of the Managing Director of Dreamland. A clip from the film was shown on a television programme and the next day this unfortunate man went into his local golf club to find everyone laughing at him. They had recognised his voice which, naturally, I had not asked permission to use. He wrote a very rude letter to the British Film Institute and refused to allow the film to be shown further.

Commercials and Television

Commentary, 1994

COMMERCIAL TELEVISION STARTED IN BRITAIN IN THE MID-FIFTIES AND I BECAME involved in it quite early through two people I knew from Ealing Studios: Alexander Mackendrick and Sidney Cole. Sandy Mackendrick's wife, Hilary, had a company – it was called H. L. Lloyd, I think – which made commercials, and she asked me to do a commercial for Rowntree's Fruit Gums. After that, I made rather a lot of commercials, all of them character-based. For example, I worked with the actor James Robertson Justice on a series of ads for Cracker Barrel Cheese; he was a good personality although certainly not a technician. Mind you, I really don't think I was ever a very good maker of commercials because I've never been very technological.

I don't know whether the vast change – perhaps you might say improvement – that has taken place in the world of commercials is a particularly good thing. From the public point of view, the rather simple-minded commercials that were made at first were probably rather popular and well-received. But now, of course, commercials are tremendously technical and stylistic, and I often get the impression that they are made for advertising agencies and for other commercial directors, rather than to sell the product. Looking back, I don't have a very high opinion of myself in those days; I was no Ridley Scott. I should have been learning the trade, but I don't think I learnt anything really. I often think it's a pity that I didn't take more advantage of the opportunity.

Some of the crew members I worked with were very experienced. Cameramen like Larry Pizer, for instance, who did a lot of work for Leon Clore for basic rate, and Douglas Slocombe, who did a number of commercials with me. Larry went on to shoot *Isadora* for Karel Reisz and he now lives in America. I suppose that my best-remembered commercials were the series I made for Mackeson Stout with Bernard Miles. For some reason, Bernard was regarded as very difficult – he had just done a series of films for the Egg Marketing Board ('Go to work on an egg') and had apparently been difficult with the director of them. But I knew Bernard and, when I was asked to take over the Mackeson ads, I was sure we would get along very well. We had no problems at all and I think the commercials were very successful and are now remembered rather fondly by a certain generation.

At about the same time that I began making commercials I had the chance, thanks to Sid Cole who was handling the British production end of

By golly: Bernard Miles (right) rehearses with Lindsay for a Mackeson stout commercial written by Bill Naughton, author of Alfie *and* Spring and Port Wine.

Sapphire Films, to direct a few episodes of the TV series *Robin Hood* which starred Richard Greene in the title role. He had had a Hollywood career of sorts but he is probably best remembered now for that television series. We had a number of good actors in the regular cast including, as the Sheriff of Nottingham, Alan Wheatley, who had played the character on the run from the gangsters at the beginning of *Brighton Rock*. In contrast to the commercials, I think I did learn something on the set of *Robin Hood*.

Bernard Miles

For a celebration of Bernard Miles at the Mermaid Theatre, London, 29 January 1991

ONE OF THE BEST, CERTAINLY THE MOST USEFUL, PRESENTS I HAVE EVER BEEN given is the copy of *Roget's Thesaurus* which Bernard Miles handed me to commemorate our collaboration, he as actor and I as director, on the series of Mackeson commercials which we poured onto British television screens a good many years ago. Section 760, paragraph 20, says that synonyms for 'independent', which Bernard has always stubbornly remained, are 'One's own man; Free-spirited; Self-determined, Self-reliant, Self-governing, Self-directing; Autonomous . . . ' All of which things Bernard has always been – and thank God for him in an era of lip service and conformism.

Think again of Bernard, and turn to section 733 ('Cunning'), paragraph 12. 'Crafty; Artful and Wily.' These are followed by 'Canny, Shrewd, Knowing . . . Subtle, Diplomatic, Deep.' Also 'Not to be caught with chaff.' Bernard has always owed his survival to these qualities. 'Lord Miles,' of course, sounds established, but this is far from the truth. To survive is not necessarily to be a part of the establishment.

I first met Bernard Miles as a man of the cinema, a director – which is not, I suppose, how people most often think of him. I think this must have been in the late forties. He had been acting in plays since the early thirties, and in films since 1937. He had stood behind a cartwheel on the stage of the Gate Theatre and at the London Palladium, chewing on a straw and sharing his rustic wisdom with us – rather like an English Will Rogers – and he had performed superbly in *In Which We Serve* and *Great Expectations*. He co-wrote and directed two films, *Tawny Pippit* during the War and *Chance of a Lifetime* after it.

It was *Chance of a Lifetime* that precipitated our meeting. After the War, the British government, in one of their rare efforts to rationalise and support a native cinema, had ordered that any British film of adequate quality and budget must be shown on one of the two principal circuits. The Rank circuit (which had turned it down) was forced to show Bernard's independent production, which showed with great affability the conflict between the managing director of a family business and his workers. Characteristically, this ended in mutual understanding, co-operation and success all round. The film 'failed', of course, partly because the Rank Organisation had no idea how to present it, partly because the industry was happy for the picture not to succeed, and partly because the popular

A performance of 'absolute truth': Bernard Miles as Firs in Lindsay's 1984
production of The Cherry Orchard.

audience was already spoiled by Hollywood's domination of the entertainment market. Bernard was tickled, I think, by the enthusiasm of a
young 'highbrow' for his work. We understood each other very well.

Bernard made no more films, which was a pity. I have always thought
that *Chance of a Lifetime* delightfully expressed his good-humoured common sense, his shrewd understanding of the way human nature works, his
clear-sighted affection that lapses neither into cynicism nor sentimentalism. He has always been a man of the Left, but never a sectarian. He has

always been too wise to be an intellectual. Never a Communist, always a Socialist, of the English kind.

It was Bernard, with his extraordinary truthfulness, who sold eggs to the nation. This led to me being invited to direct those Mackeson commercials, which were written by his good old friend Bill Naughton. At first the advertising agency trembled: Bernard had apparently won himself a reputation for being 'difficult'. Of course, in the event Bernard and Bill and I got on famously. We all, and Bernard particularly, loved talking – or 'yarning' is perhaps the better word. He is tremendously well read in history, tremendously knowledgeable about the lives our fathers lived. Our Mackeson days were full of fun. Early on, Bernard thought it was important he should drink his stout with the proper relish. Each 30-second episode was filmed without a cut, which meant that by the time we had got words and timing and movement absolutely right, many a powerful glassful had been downed. Accent and intonation became authentically blurred. 'It looks good, it tastes good, and by golly . . .' No wonder sales shot up.

I suppose that really the stage has always been Bernard's first and greatest love. He and Josephine, his gracious, wonderfully supportive wife, built their own theatre in their garden in St John's Wood, where the singers they loved came freely to perform the operas they loved. Then Bernard planned and built and ran the Mermaid, that most friendly, least pretentious of theatres. How he persuaded the City Fathers to put up the cash we will never know.

Sadly, I never directed anything at the Mermaid: I was always doing something else, or perhaps Bernard retained the right to choose his actors. And quite right too: that was how he ran his theatre, as a Captain runs the ship. Nothing went on down at Puddle Dock which he did not authorise or supervise. The unique mix of quality and popularity which characterised the Mermaid was typical of the man. Typically, too, it was a family affair. Kept going by that wonderful combination of single-minded zeal (the Puritan word suited him), of cunning and of warmth. There was genius there, no doubt about it.

By great good fortune, when I directed *The Cherry Orchard* in 1984, Bernard was able to join us to play the aged Firs. He arrived at the first rehearsal with a huge, misshapen nose, which he had had specially designed and made for him. It was completely unnecessary, of course. Stripped of all disguise, Bernard incarnated the faithful, wandering, stubborn, old man with absolute truth. It was a joy to have him there, carefully respectful, with that touch of irony that communicated always a healthy, humorous disrespect. There had always been something naughty about Bernard. Perhaps that is one of his secrets. I shouldn't be surprised.

Notes from Sherwood

Sight and Sound, Winter 1956

'WHAT FUN!' PEOPLE EXCLAIM – IT IS ALMOST INVARIABLY THE RESPONSE WHEN I say that I have been directing episodes in the *Robin Hood* series on TV. I know what they mean, of course, but I cannot help wondering what they imagine such a job to be like. Do they think of a merry band of film technicians chasing around in the greenwood? Often they fail to connect it with the idea of a film studio at all. 'Where do you shoot it?' they ask; and are surprised when the answer turns out not to be Sherwood Forest. Nor even Bagshot Heath.

Sapphire Films have been making *Robin Hood* stories for about eighteen months now. The series is presented by Hannah Weinstein, from America, with Sid Cole (from Ealing) as executive producer. Many of the scripts originate in America, but are rewritten in Britain, without any attempt to Americanise speech or attitude. There is a resident band of leading players; a stock company for supporting parts; and a small number of guest artists in each story. To increase speed and economy all the sets are designed from a set of basic components, mounted on wheels, which can be assembled in an infinite variety of combinations – Baronial Halls, Sheriff's Castle, Taverns and Outlaw Headquarters. A main unit shoots in the studio; a second unit (working mainly with doubles) looks after exteriors. Each episode runs for just over 25 minutes, and is shot in five days. Of the 50-odd episodes that have so far been made, I have directed five; and these brief notes are in response to an imperious appeal from the editor of *Sight and Sound* to say something about the experience. The responsibility is hers.

What fun, then? I usually counter this with the word *interesting*. From many points of view. And perhaps, since this is for the readers of *Sight and Sound*, I should start from the point of view of one who has himself done a fair amount of criticising. I will not pretend that this hasn't its comic aspect. I have even felt a certain guilt to be writing severe strictures on de Sica and Zavattini in the evening, while knowing that next day I shall be struggling with a custard pie (or rather wild strawberry cake) routine between Tom the Miller and one of the Sheriff of Nottingham's men-at-arms. This kind of schizophrenia is one of the first things one learns to live with.

The critical, film-appreciative half of one's personality has, however, plenty that it can profitably note. This, after all, is the *inside* of the business that one has been criticising so confidently, from the *outside*, for a number of years. And it is fascinating to see one's own clichés come to life. Film-making is a compound of 'Creative Elements'; also it is the director's medium – provided that the writer has given him the material to work with in the first place. Either you get something from your story or you don't and if you don't, the work is very much harder. In *Secret Mission*, for instance, there was that scene where the Sheriff vainly attempts to persuade the outlaws to desert Robin, with the promise of a pardon. I liked that, and was even inspired to pinch a composition from *Wagonmaster* to go into it. (I doubt, though, whether Ford would have recognised it. The 'nobility' close-ups are harder to get exactly right than you might suppose.) On the other hand, in *Ambush*, I simply could not get myself to believe in Robin's single-handed rescue of Marian and Prince Arthur from Prince John's trap. It just didn't seem probable. It was a difficult sequence to shoot.

A better word than 'fun', and better than 'interesting', is 'experience': this implies both pleasure and interest, and a lot else besides. Technical experience first. Work like this, with its tight discipline of cost and time (you must average about five minutes of screen time a day) must now be the best training for full-scale feature film-making that exists. And when you come from documentary, you discover that there is a great deal of new knowledge to acquire. For instance, I had never before been able to indulge in the luxury of a dolly. My only tracking shots had been made from a conveyor-belt: or by Walter Lassally sitting on a chair, hand-holding the camera, while I pushed. I was therefore ignorant of the acute geometrical problems which even a simple series of camera moves can present. This was something for which Arnheim, Spottiswoode, and Eisenstein had left me unprepared. I learned the hard way, with much scribbling on the backs of envelopes.

But I must not suggest that documentarists are callow innocents, with everything to learn from feature methods and nothing to teach. In high-pressure work like *Robin Hood*, where you frequently have no idea what the set is going to be like until you're on it, the impromptu methods of shooting which are necessary in documentary are very useful. It is more difficult to be impromptu in the studio, to keep that whole, huge, cumbersome machine sensitive and malleable. Studio work is a tougher grind than documentary, more nerve-racking, with more to go wrong and more money being wasted when it does. It is physically exhausting, and terribly hard on the feet. All the more reason, though, to struggle against the temptation (it is very strong) to hug convention; to play safe; to insist on a Mitchell when you could do it quicker and better with a hand-held Arriflex. So many of the rules are bogus: Cocteau's remarks about the futility of conventions (direct reverses, etc.) are absolutely true. Similarly, while many of the distinctions between documentary and feature filming are valid, there are quite a few that are worth contesting.

Technique apart, you learn a great deal about people. Why have so few writers on film-making managed to suggest the human richness of the whole business? Collaboration between artists and technicians: the challenge – and the difficulty – for the director to create a sense of *involvement* for everybody on the floor. How do you make the lonely electrician, up there on his gantry, feel that he is part of the same effort as the camera operator and the star? There is material here for a study far deeper and more valuable than smart Miss Lillian Ross managed to produce from all that snooping round *The Red Badge of Courage*; but of course you would have to care to be able to write it. Consider merely the complications involved in asking the unit to work an extra half-hour on an early night: the director who worries about the sequence, the assistant who worries about the schedule, the art director who wants to start building tomorrow's set, the camera operator who has backache, the electrician who can do with some overtime, the clapper-boy who had a date, and the actor who was called for seven o'clock in the morning and not used till after lunch . . .

Personal impressions apart, it seems appropriate to suggest in these pages that television film-making deserves more attention from critics than it receives. About a series like *Robin Hood*, for instance, most people seem to know little more than that American children have exchanged their Davy Crockett hats for Robin Hood fore-and-afters. Yet the enormous, impressionable audience that sees these films makes them of real importance – and not only in Britain and America. They are shown in Canada and Australia as well. They are even being dubbed for Japan.

Working on the floor at Nettlefold, wondering desperately whether you'll get the next shot before lunchtime, praying that this time the horse will not shift moodily just as Maid Marian is delivering her line (horses are the devil in the studio. But if you always dismount in the second-unit exterior, and walk into the studio shot, the thing just becomes too tame) – in the middle, as I say, of such toil and nervous strain, it is easy to forget or to joke about the vast audience you are working for. And it is true that the audience sometimes gives much less concentration than it gets. (No experience is more sobering than to watch someone watching on TV a film you worked very hard to make.) None the less, the viewing figures are there and the values implicit in what you are doing are being absorbed by not hundreds of thousands, but millions of unreflecting, influenceble minds.

I cannot pretend to be quite objective about *Robin Hood*, and I

Lindsay with the crew, directing an episode in the Robin Hood *series.*

should be interested to read the thoughtful comments of a critic who can be. But I would say without hesitation that here is at least one series which entertains in a good way; which does not take itself too seriously to be humorous; yet is serious enough to insist on a decent moral, to forbid violence and human falsity. Most important, its success proves that the cheapjack policy of so many television producers is as short-sighted as it is socially undesirable. 'It's only TV' is often said as a justification for shoddy workmanship, shoddy scripting, and schedules so cramped as to prevent director and actors even attempting to do more than get the clichés on to celluloid. *Robin Hood* is made for TV, but it is made as cinema. Its success proves that quality can pay.

A last note. Another thing I have learned is to understand why a director like Ford makes so many films – and doesn't much care if the critics say a lot of them are bad. He likes making films. He likes being on the floor. A unit is a good thing to be part of.

Every Day Except Christmas

Commentary, 1994

IN THE FIFTIES, THE BRITISH CINEMA INDUSTRY WAS PRETTY MUCH CLOSED TO young, aspiring film-makers; I think it was even more closed than the American cinema. I was one of a group of friends, among them Tony Richardson (who had already established himself as a theatre director at the Royal Court), Karel Reisz (who was a writer with ambitions to become a film director) and Lorenza Mazetti, a young Italian girl I had met in London and who had made a film called *Together* which I helped her to finish. We were, in a sense, hanging around the peripheries of the film industry. There was certainly no move on the part of the cinema establishment to let young people become professional film-makers and that was what led us to the creation of Free Cinema. It has been described as a movement and, in a way, it was a movement in so far as it was very much guided by our idea of what cinema should be. But it was also a way of getting our films shown and written about. Giving a collective name to what might otherwise be a disparate group of films enabled journalists to write about them. Journalists always seem to need a 'peg', so we created one.

The first Free Cinema programme at the National Film Theatre was made up of my film *O Dreamland*, a film about a jazz club made by Tony and Karel, *Momma Don't Allow*, and Lorenza's film, which I had edited. That first programme was a success and was followed by four or five other Free Cinema programmes. We showed some Polish films, including work by Polanski, and gave the first British screenings of films by Chabrol and Truffaut. Meanwhile, Karel had taken a job with the Ford Motor Company who wanted him to make publicity films for them. Somehow, he managed to persuade them to make a series of films called *Look at Britain* which would feature no advertising, and he asked me to make the first one. It was really a terrifying challenge to be told 'go ahead and make a film about anything you like.' It was a very frightening prospect. I thought I might make a film about long-distance lorry-driving but, in the course of my research, I visited Covent Garden which was then, of course, still the great fruit, vegetable and flower market, and I realised that I had found my subject.

In making a film about Covent Garden market I had no great ambition, no great conception. My 'script' could have been written on the back of an envelope. We were very daring in those days, film was interesting then. Once again, we had to overcome the problem of sound. You could hand-hold an Arriflex camera, but it was impossible to synchronise a tape

Left: Walter Lassally filming Every Day Except Christmas, *his own favourite of the films he made with Lindsay. Right: 'A certain group of Londoners, as they were':
crates loaded onto a porter's protective headgear in* Every Day Except Christmas.

recorder with it. There are some scenes in *Every Day Except Christmas* – as the film we made was eventually called – where we tried to use a tape recorder while we were shooting. If you listen very carefully you can hear the noise of the camera motor on the soundtrack. Otherwise, it was shot strictly non-synch with the sound put on afterwards. In a way, I think that those technical difficulties were probably a good thing. I am not a great believer in tying a film to reality in the shape of synchronised recording of sound and dialogue. It's much better if the film-maker is challenged to be creative in his attitude to the subject.

We were not really influenced by the British documentary tradition, which had been so famous in the then-recent past with films by John Grierson, Basil Wright, Paul Rotha and Harry Watt. We admired Humphrey Jennings, whose name means little these days to people in Britain. Yet he is probably one of the most individual film-makers Britain ever produced. When we put on the first Free Cinema programme, we decided to have a manifesto. We didn't take it too seriously, but nor did we take it completely unseriously. One of the things we said was that 'no film can be too personal.' This may seem a commonplace but in relation to documentary film it is unusual, particularly now in the age of television. Documentary has come to mean information, journalism. A journalistic report on the Gulf War is called a documentary. Our attitude toward doc-

FORD OF BRITAIN are proud
to make a contribution to the programme of
the National Film Theatre

Every

day

except

Christmas

Made for the Ford of Britain Film Library

BOOKING ENQUIRIES
(35 mm. now; 16 mm. later) to

DEPT. RS, FORD MOTOR COMPANY LTD., 88 REGENT STREET, LONDON W.1

Printed in England £.50

The programme for Every Day Except Christmas.

umentary films was very different. It was personal. It was the feeling that, essentially, a documentary film is a portrait of the person who makes it. Today, many people might not agree with this viewpoint.

Every Day Except Christmas is very much a portrait of the English, of a certain group of Londoners, as they were. There was something almost Dickensian about the people in this film, and that has all gone now. So much has changed in the era of technology and television, but there is a very strong evocation in the film of a vanished past. It's also interesting in relation to the class system, which you must always remember when you think of Britain. When the film was finished it was submitted to the committee which chose films for the Venice Film Festival. It was rejected because British documentaries then were supposed to be about all those nice English things like spring or Benjamin Britten. Eventually, we managed to have it sent to Venice as a film made for television – which it was not. To some people's surprise, it won the Grand Prix, and was quite resented for it. The Venice victory was in no way celebrated by the English establishment, which proved that the class system was anything but finished, and still isn't.

Every Day was very much a portrait of people who, until then, had not appeared in British films except as comic relief. Every group or movement has its lesser-known but invaluable members, and Free Cinema was no exception. We had John Fletcher and, each time I see *Every Day*, I realise yet again what a brilliant job John did of the sound-recording. He edited the film with me, and I think that the rhythm and the sound of the film are remarkable. Unfortunately, the *Look at Britain* series collapsed shortly afterwards because the Ford Motor Company withdrew their finances. So I turned to directing plays because I was lucky enough to be invited by Tony Richardson to work at the Royal Court.

Free Cinema

Universities and Left Review, Summer 1957

WHEN PEOPLE ASK YOU WHAT YOU DO, AND YOU TELL THEM YOU WORK IN films, their reaction is predictable. 'Oh! That must be very interesting . . .' They mean it, too. But then go on, and tell them you make documentaries, and you get a different response. The light of interest fades from their eyes and conversation flags. Sometimes they say: 'Wouldn't you like to make real films?'

This sort of standard response is the measure of the failure of British Documentary – a failure for which the responsibility must be shared by many of us. Not by the film-makers alone, but by distributors and exhibitors too. By the politicians who connived at the destruction of the Crown Film Unit; and by the public and the critics who continue to accept a situation in which the production of quality documentaries about Britain is a financial impossibility – and remain content to sit through appalling travelogues and third-rate imported shorts without raising a murmur.

Documentary should not be – it certainly *need* not be – synonymous with dullness. It should be one of the most exciting and stimulating of con-temporary forms. After all, the cinema started with it. Lumière's first films are all admirable documentaries: trains pulling up at stations, workers leaving their factories: still interesting to look at today. But the cinema was soon captured by drama, and with relatively few notable exceptions artists have preferred fiction to the exploration and interpretation of the 'actual', living material. Yet think how rich, fantastic, unexpected and significant 'actual' life can be. Our own documentary movement began to say some-thing in the thirties; and films like *Song of Ceylon*, *Housing Problems*, *Night Mail* still carry their message today. During the war Humphrey Jennings emerged as the British cinema's most eloquent and individual poet: *Listen to Britain*, *Diary for Timothy* and *Fires Were Started* should be compulsory viewing for every British school child. (How many readers of this review have seen them, I wonder?) But in recent years – con-formism, publicity more-or-less disguised, the deadness and the dishonesty of the 'official' vision.

The problem is twofold: creative and economic. British film-makers are not blameless. Energetic and radical in their youth, the surviving members of Grierson's band of pioneers (many of them now established in positions of influence) have abandoned the treatment of contemporary life in their films. This retreat they are apt to rationalise: there are no problems today

73

– or the problems are different – things are more complex – we must think dialectically, internationally, intellectually . . . Yet people still exist, and housing problems, and night mails – as well as Teddy Boys, new schools, automation, strikes and sex crimes. All these are subjects for documentary, and of the right kind: the human kind.

Admittedly the economic problems are formidable. The Conservative Party dissolved the Crown Film Unit in 1952, and since then the official policy is that the country does not sponsor documentaries for home consumption, except in special cases, for specific propagandist or informational purposes. But the present system of distribution and exhibition in the commercial cinema makes the speculative production of documentaries quite impossible: either they are not booked at all, or you get twopence for them. Some kind of sponsorship *has* to be found.

It is in this connection that the movement which we have called *Free Cinema* is significant. Three programmes of these films have so far been shown, all at the National Film Theatre: two of them have been made up of films made in and about Britain, one of films from abroad. They are all relatively modest pictures, in means if not ambition: most of them have been shot on 16 millimetre. (This is the 'substandard' gauge of film, as used on portable projectors as opposed to the standard 35mm film used in normal commercial production.) They have not been made according to any plan or programme: instinct came first, and we discovered our common sympathies after. But all of us want to make films of today, whether the method be realist or poetic, narrative or montage. And we believe that 'objectivity' is no part of the documentary method, that on the contrary the documentarist must formulate his attitude, express his values as firmly and forcefully as any artist. The result has been a group of films on diverse themes: a poetic fable about two deaf mutes in the East End of London; studies of Amusement Park and Jazz Club; Piccadilly on a Saturday Night and Covent Garden all round the clock. These are not intended as picturesque films (although of course they are written about as though they are, very often), nor as simple slices of life. Slices, if you like, but cut with a bias. All of them say something about our society, today.

This programme is presented not as an achievement, but as an aim. We ask you to view it not as critics, nor as a diversion, but in direct relation to a British cinema still obstinately class-bound; still rejecting the stimulus of contemporary life, as well as the responsibility to criticise; still reflecting a metropolitan, Southern English culture which excludes the rich diversity of tradition and personality which is the whole of Britain.

With a 16 millimetre camera, and minimal resources, and no payment for your technicians, you cannot achieve very much – in commercial terms. You cannot make a feature film, and your possibilities of experiment are severely restricted. But you can use your eyes and ears. You can give indications. You can make poetry.

The poetry of this programme is made out of our feelings about Britain, the nation of which we are all a part. Of course these feelings are mixed. There are things to make us sad, and angry; things we must change. But feelings of pride and love are fundamental, and only change inspired by such feelings will be effective.

'We have the Welfare State and the domestic upheavals of the Huggetts . . . Bleak, isn't it?' So someone wrote a letter to *The Observer*, 'explaining' why vital art is no longer possible in this country. This kind of snobbish, self-derisive, pseudo-liberalism is the most pernicious and sapping enemy of faith. We stand against it.

Our aim is first to look at Britain, with honesty and with affection. To relish its eccentricities; attack its abuses; love its people. To use the cinema to express our allegiances, our rejections and our aspirations. This is our commitment.

When you are making a film like *Every Day Except Christmas* – or rather while you are editing it, waiting for a reel to be joined, or reprints to come in from the lab – it is easy to talk about what you are trying to do. But when you have finished, it is difficult. The film speaks for itself, you feel; and if it does not, you have failed, and statements of intention are merely pretentious.

Every Day Except Christmas beat 129 other documentaries to win the Grand Prix at the 1957 Venice Film Festival. As this telegram from Variety *correspondent Gene Moskowitz testifies, the decision was unanimous.*

But perhaps I should say what I was *not* trying to do. I was not trying to make an information film, or an instructional film. And I was *not* trying to make a picturesque film. When John Grierson first defined the word 'documentary', he called it 'the creative interpretation of actuality'. In other words the only vital difference between making a documentary and making a fiction film is that in documentary you are using 'actual' material, not invented situations and actors playing parts. But this actual material still has to be interpreted, worked on creatively, or we are left with nothing but publicity. And if we are to interpret, we must have an attitude, we must have beliefs and values. It is in the light of my belief in human values that I have endeavoured to make this film about Covent Garden market. I hope it makes my commitment plain.

I have been reproached on the one hand for not giving more 'information' about the people in the film; and on the other for not making a more explicit social comment. I have nothing against information films, and no doubt there are some very interesting ones to be made about Covent Garden (statistics, dates, weights, wages, etc.). But this is not the kind of information I wanted to give about these people – and about people in general.

Similarly with social comment. I feel that at the moment in this country it is more important for a progressive artist to make a positive affirmation than an aggressive criticism. (The criticism will be implicit in the affirmation anyway, if it is a genuine one.) In aggressive criticism there is too often a sense of inferiority. The Left in Britain suffers too much from such complexes of opposition. I want to make people – ordinary people, not just Top People – feel their dignity and their importance, so that they can act from these principles. Only on such principles can confident and healthy action be based.

Who pays for these films? One of them was privately financed (*O Dreamland*); *Together, Momma Don't Allow* and *Nice Time* were paid for by the British Film Institute's Experimental Fund; and *Every Day Except Christmas* was commissioned by the Ford Motor Company. There is food for thought here. The Institute's Fund is a remarkable thing, but of course its scope is limited. None of the film-makers who avail themselves of it can be paid anything for his work, and budgets are only adequate for relatively modest productions, generally on 16mm. This is why Ford's sponsorship of *Every Day Except Christmas* is so important. Directors have grown accustomed to think of their sponsors as automatically unreasonable, narrowly utilitarian, and essentially unimaginative: undertaking a subject commissioned by an industrial concern, they are defeated before they start. Yet here is a film made for an industrial sponsor which – whatever its artistic value – has been made completely without interference or pressure, with its director allowed, even encouraged, to express himself as he feels. (It is unthinkable that a film should today be made for a Government department, or for the Central Office of Information, under conditions so liberal and so enlightened.) I am quite conscious of my extraordinary luck in having been able to work like this, and of my debt to Leon Clore of Graphic Films, who undertook the further responsibility of extending the picture from its original 20-minute conception to its final 40-minute length. But – I cannot help wondering – should the existence of films of this kind in Britain have to depend on luck, or on the courage, principle and imagination of an individual producer or industrial sponsor? If so, there will not be many of them.

A number of questions, in fact, present themselves, not merely to film-makers and enthusiasts, but to anyone seriously concerned with present-day realities in our country. And I presume this means all readers of the *Universities and Left Review*. For instance: Why do we not use the cinema; and what are the implications of this neglect? Is it not strange that at a time when so much emphasis is being put on ideals of community, this medium (above all potent in the services of such ideals) should be abandoned to irresponsible commerce? Why does the Left not take a more active and creative interest in an art so popular? And is it not time that artists whose convictions are progressive started to consider a little more seriously their relationship with their audience, the kind of use that can be best made of these mass-media, so that their art be neither exclusive and snobbish, nor stereotyped and propagandist – but vital, illuminating, personal and refreshing.

The Court Style

In *At the Royal Court*, ed. Richard Findlater, 1981

I REMEMBER VERY WELL THE ENGLISH STAGE COMPANY'S FIRST PRODUCTION
at the Royal Court in 1956. Or rather I remember very well the impression it made on me, for strangely enough the impression is much stronger
than my memory of the play, which was *The Mulberry Bush* by Angus
Wilson. At that time I had no professional connection with the English
Stage Company. I was not even a professional of the theatre: I had been a
documentary film-maker for some years, and I had been a film critic (not
a reviewer) in various specialised magazines. I was a friend of Tony
Richardson, who had followed me at Wadham College, Oxford (by
chance, George Devine, Tony Richardson and I were all ex-Wadham men)
and through Tony I was around when preparations were being made for
the opening of the ESC's first season at the Royal Court. It was a confident, hopeful time.

Thus I went to *The Mulberry Bush* as a friend, wholly in sympathy with
what I took to be the aims of the Royal Court enterprise. These went far
beyond the simple encouragement of new work or of new writers that
seems now to be the accepted lore. Indeed, no account of why the theatre
started – at least so far as George Devine and Tony Richardson were concerned – can be complete without some appreciation of the historical context, and of the state of the London theatre and of British cultural morale
generally in the mid-1950s. We were still in the post-War doldrums.
Nothing that was done in the theatre related in any stimulating or significant way to what was happening in Britain or in the rest of the world.
Non-commercial drama was generally 'poetic' drama, represented most
successfully and most reputably by T. S. Eliot and Christopher Fry. The
Royal Court impulse was a 'realist' impulse, and its ambitions extended to
the representation on the London stage of 20th-century European classics,
and even classical revivals. Style, it was understood, was just as important
a part of the theatrical experience as theme or content. George was no sen-
timentalist, and nor was Tony. They had no favourable predisposition
towards writing just because it was 'new'.

The impact on me of *The Mulberry Bush* was above all stylistic, though
not in a formal or decorative way. The play itself had dignity and even a certain pathos because it was, above all, serious. It was a play of ideas, not very
profound and not perhaps particularly original: in its development, it was
even a little silly. But it was seriously written and seriously presented. There
was a blessed absence of that 'desire to divert' (and particularly, of course

Tony Richardson (left) and George Devine.

the desire to divert an English middle-class audience, out for an amusing evening) which had always maddened me in West End theatre. The playing was natural, civilised, unforced. And the presentation was similarly lucid and economic. The settings were realistic, but not fussily or extravagantly naturalistic: they stood out with elegant clarity against a pure, white surround. There was no bowing and scraping to us, the audience; and there was no bullying either. In English culture, where 'serious' is most often used as a mocking epithet, this made the experience a refreshing and even a touching one.

Such were to be the characteristics of what I would call the Royal Court 'style'. It was this style which for so many years made the theatre unique – an achievement much more elusive to definition than the achievement in terms of writers discovered and new plays performed. I think it is also the quality whose loss is most keenly to be regretted.

I had never directed in the professional theatre before I did my first production at the Royal Court in 1957. One day, out of the blue, the Court received a play from Kathleen Sully, an author whom Tony Richardson knew I much admired. He sent me the play, which I read and much liked, and suggested that I should direct it for a Sunday night production without decor. So I did, and it went well enough for me to be invited the next year to direct a play by Willis Hall called *The Disciplines of War*. Always drawn by the emotive power of popular songs, I suggested we retitle the play *The Long and the Short and the Tall*. Again the play went well, and

'The emotive power of songs': It was Lindsay's idea to change the original title of Willis Hall's play The Disciplines of War *to a quote from the lyric of a wartime hit,* Bless 'Em All.

I was invited to become one of the assistants to the artistic directors, together with Bill Gaskill and John Dexter. So my theatrical career began.

Being completely inexperienced in the professional theatre, I did not at first realise what a unique place the Royal Court was. Its freedom from theatrical 'camp' was total. Perhaps this was the strong university influence; certainly it was a reflection of the personality of George Devine. The atmosphere at Sloane Square was never particularly 'intellectual' but it was pretty intelligent and most of us, I am afraid, displayed a rather arrogant intolerance of approaches and standards other than our own. The theatre, it was taken for granted, was always 'about something'. Because our values were anti-establishment, it was generally assumed that the Court could be described as a socialist theatre. This was largely nonsense. It was not even a very intellectual theatre. The tone was far more humanist than intellectual. Liberal, if you like, in its strong rather than its soppy sense. And this commitment inspired all the choices, and was the basis of the style.

Royal Court acting, therefore, tended to be unmannered (not unmannerly), emotionally open, and realistic in class terms. I believe that our production of Alun Owen's first play, *Progress to the Park*, which I directed for a Sunday night in 1960, was the first time that Liverpool accents had been used freely, authentically and un-selfconsciously on the London stage. When we auditioned young actors and actresses in those days we usually had to ask them where they came from and then to repeat their audition pieces, not in the 'acceptable' accents into which they had been drilled at drama school but in the natural accents of their youth. The results were almost always revelatory. (Today, of course, all this will seem simplistic, obvious in the extreme. For some years now the joke has been that middle and upper-class actors are at a disadvantage in the theatre, and must ape a working-class accent if they are to have any hope of employment, which is nonsense, even if in certain quarters there has developed an inverted snobbery, just as odious as the establishment snobbery of the past. But let it not be forgotten that when Albert Finney graduated from RADA, the old *News Chronicle* ran a competition for its readers to select a new name for this brilliant young actor, since 'Albert Finney' was obviously too plebeian to be acceptable in West End lights. And when Tom Courtenay played Konstantin in an Old Vic production of *The Seagull* in 1960, immediately after leaving drama school, more than one critic commented scornfully on the impossibility of an actor in a play by Chekhov speaking with what was plainly a Northern accent.)

In spite of his university education, then, George Devine was not an academic: he was an actor as well as a director, as stimulated by practice as by theory, hierarchic, not afraid of instinct, and anxious to learn. This made him unique in my experience as director of a theatre. He knew about almost everything; he was good at everything, though naturally better at some things than at others; he loved and respected talent, and he was not jealous. He was devoted above all to the service of the theatre – the theatrical experience; not the theatre as a 'vehicle' for ideas, which is in itself a form of philistinism, though rarely recognised as such; and not the theatre as a laboratory for aesthetic experiments. There were quite a lot of plays and writers to whom George simply did not respond, generally on humanist, less often on artistic grounds. But if he did not respond to a writer, he was never afraid to say so – and their work would not be performed at the Royal Court.

The idea of the theatre as a total experience may sound rather obvious. But it is a more subtle idea than it may seem, and examples of it are not so easy to find. The Royal Court was a theatre with a strong tradition of direction: yet it was never a directors' theatre. The text always came first, and writers were to be cherished and encouraged. But they were not to be mollycoddled. There was never any suggestion that a director should *use* a text in order to show off his own prowess or personality; at the same time, particularly in the early days, he was expected to work with his author, guiding him where necessary and where possible, through revisions and rewrites. As the years have passed, of course, this equilibrium has been lost.

As with direction, so with design. A design aesthetic, of expressive simplicity and refined realism, was part of the Royal Court policy from the start. That surround of white net did more than provide continuity to the succession of Royal Court productions. It was also an artistic, even a moral, statement in itself. It did not long survive, alas, as directors of varying principles and personalities succeeded each other; but the principle remained embedded in the consciousness of all. The designer's responsi-

The Royal Court Theatre, Sloane Square, London.

bility was to express and interpret the text. Perhaps even to enhance it. But certainly never to use it, or overpower it. In all, the Royal Court aesthetic had a good deal in common with the Periclean ideal:

> We pursue beauty without extravagance and knowledge without effeminacy.

I hope I have not made the Royal Court seem highfalutin' or artistically self-righteous. We were all too cocky and too disrespectful for that. The real lesson we learned, never to be forgotten, was that seriousness is not the same thing as smugness; and that there is nothing more wearisome than 'camp'. We learned that a theatre dedicated to the service of the playwright is not the same thing as a 'literary' theatre. And we learned that a theatre in which the director was encouraged and expected to provide as personal an interpretation of a text as he is capable of is not the same thing as a 'directors' theatre', in which the director *uses* a text to display his talent and draw attention to himself. The best 'notice' that a director can get is praise for his playwright and praise for his players.

One of the most extraordinary things about the Court style is that it lasted so long – over twenty years. George Devine, to my personal sorrow, never saw a play by David Storey. (I am speaking, of course, only of my own productions at the Royal Court in later years.) But if he had, I'd like to think that he would have responded to their poetry, their realism uncluttered by naturalism, their elegance 'without extravagance'. Their seriousness and their laughter, their vision of society untouched by the crudity of propaganda. And all their splendid actors – surely the most consistent glory of our stage. These are some of the things I mean by the Royal Court 'style'.

Glory Days

Plays and Players, May 1986

I HAVE OFTEN, IN THE COURSE OF A SPASMODIC AND UNEVEN THEATRICAL career, found myself trying to define just what made George Devine's Royal Court such a unique place. I don't mean unique in theatrical history for its extraordinary turnover of original plays, or for its discovery and nourishment of new and original talent. These were certainly phenomenal enough.

My first-ever in theatrical direction, for instance, was a Sunday Night production of *The Waiting of Lester Abbs*, a tragi-comic poetic play by that unique and idiosyncratic writer Kathleen Sully. It had young Ian Bannen in the name-part, with Gladys Spencer as his mother ('These biscuits are rather dull,' I remember her saying with magnificent disdain) and Catherine Willmer as his spiky sister. In the pub scene Fanny Carby led the revellers while Michael Hastings banged the piano. Michael, an early entrant in the Angry Young Man stakes, had made a great hit with

his first play, *Don't Destroy Me,* at the New Lindsey. The critics hailed it as the *Vortex* of its generation. In a fantasy death-cell scene at the end of the play, Alun Owen appeared as the real murderer, with Bob Stephens as the friendly warder. I can't remember exactly what Alfred Burke did. John Dexter, I remember clearly, came on in a scruffy mackintosh as an arresting detective. John, who together with Bill Gaskill was one of the 'Assistants to the Artistic Director' had been detailed by Tony Richardson to look after my inexperience while the Court company was away in Brighton opening *The Good Woman of Setzuan*, with Peggy Ashcroft heading a company that included Esme Percy, Joan Plowright, Rachel Kempson, John Moffat and John

Peter O'Toole sits astride Alfred Lynch, with Ronald Fraser in the background in this scene from The Long and the Short and the Tall.

Serjeant Musgrave's Dance: *Lindsay's biographical note for the programme describes him as 'ex film-maker . . . ex-critic', a sign of his new-found commitment to a theatre career.*

Osborne. (I believe Esme died down there in Brighton. Or was that another occasion?) I'm afraid I sneaked on John (Dexter) when he went to the Derby while I was panicking about how to get all the furniture onto the stage. But somehow it all came out right.

For my first main bill production I was invited by Oscar Lewenstein, who had bought the play in Edinburgh, to direct *The Disciplines of War* by a new writer, Willis Hall. I thought the title was too severe and asked the taciturn Yorkshire author if he'd object to me retitling it *The Long and the Short and the Tall*. 'You're the fucking director,' said Willis, meaning consent.

A highly promising young actor called Albert Finney, whom Oscar had cannily contracted for three plays, was playing Bamforth in *The Long and the Short*, until he came in on the second day of rehearsals looking green. He explained it was because he had drunk too much Pernod the night before, but he turned out to be suffering from acute appendicitis. We postponed the production, but complications set in and I had to replace Albert with another highly promising actor called Peter O'Toole. Opposing him, in more senses than one, was my touchy friend Bob Shaw, playing Sergeant Mitchum. Oscar and George Devine were half inclined to think we should get a 'name' for the Sergeant, and persuaded me that we should all three of us meet Patrick McGoohan in the rackety old pub next to the Court (it is now a 'Brasserie'). Perhaps fortunately, McGoohan spent the time saying what a rotten production the Court was giving of Beckett's *Endgame*; George, who had directed it and was playing Hamm with Jackie McGowran as Clov, was human enough to agree that we should stick with Robert Shaw.

Anthony Page, who was my assistant and knew more about theatre than I did, helped me cast and do a preliminary movement plot for *The Long and the Short and the Tall*. We used to break off from working at night to go into the Upper Circle at the Court and hear Jackie McGowran say: 'You'll have to suffer better than that if you want them to let you go.' I am not sure whether Miriam Brickman had yet graduated from her position as George Devine's secretary (tremendous giggling with Daphne Hunter in the General Office) to become the Court's first Casting Director and patron saint to all actors. Somehow, anyway, I managed to end up with a brilliant and lethal cast of rival ex-RADA contemporaries – Ronnie Fraser, Eddie Judd, Bryan Pringle. David Andrews, who is now a director or executive in TV, had his first professional role as Whining Winnie Whittaker, and Alfie Lynch was a Taffy Evans of wonderful innocence and charm. This in spite of my documentary resolve to cast with regional

Lindsay directs Freda Jackson and Ian Bannen in Serjeant Musgrave's Dance.

Serjeant Musgrave's Dance

WHAT KIND OF A THEATRE?

Every now and then there comes a play which by its originality, its boldness and complete lack of compromise, stands out like a landmark - perhaps a signpost. Such plays are seldom universally welcomed; nor are they likely to win immediate commercial success.

Such a play is SERJEANT MUSGRAVE'S DANCE.

First performed ten days ago, this play had a confused press. But in spite of the criticisms, we believe it will be tragic if it is allowed to slip into obscurity. That is why we are printing this leaflet.

This is not a bid for commercial success. The play is scheduled for a 3½ week run. It will close as advertised on November 14th. But we are optimistic enough, and proud enough of our work to believe that there are enough people alive to the excitement of good theatre to justify a full run of 3½ weeks at the Royal Court.

We agree with Philip Hope-Wallace in finding this play exciting, powerful and fascinating- "a highly original and challenging experiment". If this is what you want from the theatre, come and see it. If on the other hand you believe the theatre is not a place "to make men better" - then you had better stay away.

We add some further comments by other people who have seen SERJEANT MUSGRAVE'S DANCE, and whose opinion we respect, to help you decide -

Two Opinions

Another frightful ordeal. It is time someone reminded our advanced dramatists that the principal function of the theatre is to give pleasure. It is not the principal function of the theatre to strengthen peace, to improve morality, or to establish a good social system. Churches, international associations and political parties already exist for those purposes. It is the duty of the theatre, not to make men better, but to render them harmlessly happy.

Harold Hobson in the Sunday Times.

For the best part of three hours it has worked on my curiosity, and often put that ill-definable theatrical spell on my imagination. I think it is something short of a great play. But wild horses wouldn't have dragged me from my seat before the end... The play is written with an acute sense of language... It gives the actors every chance and Ian Bannen in particular, as the fanatical Serjeant, gives a magnificent performance.

Donald Donnelly, Frank Finlay and notably Alan Dobie bring great conviction to the three other ranks, and Freda Jackson as the sue-wife and Patsy Byrne as the barmaid could hardly do better. Lindsay Anderson produces with great strength and economy in the earlier scenes, which are beautifully set and lighted (decor by Jocelyn Herbert).

...This is a highly original and challenging experiment in drama.

Philip Hope-Wallace in the Manchester Guardian.

What kind of a theatre do you want?

Lindsay created this flyer for Serjeant Musgrave's Dance *to attract audiences.*

authenticity – though I was so touched by the young Welsh actor who had come all the way from Cardiff to audition, that I gave him the understudy. So Peter Gill gained his first foothold in the London theatre. After countless grotesque auditions in a small dressing-room, we found Kenji Takaki, brilliant as the wordless Japanese prisoner, running a lampshade factory in Camden Town.

One evening George Devine gave me two plays to read overnight. One I entirely forget. The other was a dense, dramatic, poetic play called *Serjeant Musgrave's Dance*, which I didn't completely apprehend but found mysteriously impressive. I told George so the next morning. 'Do you think we should do it?' he said. I thought for a brief moment. 'I do.' 'Will you direct it?' Fear clutched me: I was trapped. 'All right,' I said.

Jocelyn Herbert, who had been painting scenery in the Court workshop, designed *Musgrave*, and terrified me by removing realistic, protective walls and furniture, of which there weren't a great deal to start with, at the set-up. Anthony Page introduced me to his Oxford friend Dudley Moore, who recorded a score on the organ of the church at the bottom of Sloane Street. I'm sorry that music has never been used again in any revival of the play I know of: it was terrific. Miriam and I worked at the casting with the habitual Royal Court obsessiveness. I made her cry sometimes, but she was really glad when I wouldn't give in. Frank Finlay, Alan Dobie, Freda Jackson, Donal Donnelly, Patsy Byrne – a cracking lot. I saw a sturdy fellow down at the end of the Circle Bar one afternoon and said to Miriam, 'Who's that? What about him?' Miriam said his name was Colin Blakely. She and George had found him in Belfast, searching out Irish talent for *Cock-A-Doodle Dandy*, then playing at the Court with that stumbling genius Wilfred Lawson. *Musgrave* was the first time I'd worked with Colin: not lately, alas.

I was determined that Ian Bannen should play Musgrave. He tried to escape, running off to the Western Isles, giving the script to the Boulting brothers for their opinion, not answering the phone. The suspense became acute. George would summon Miriam and me to his office and sit at his desk, pumping his pipe and turning over the pages of *Spotlight*, offering suggestions which I could not accept. He became impatient. 'Boy, if I had my way, there's only one actress I'd ever work with. But it's just *not possible*.' But I was unable to give way, and irritated though the professional in George became, the artist, the genius in him respected my obduracy. We landed Ian in the end, thank God.

I have been seduced by such jostling memories from my original intention in this footnote to Royal Court history. What did make

Faces of the Court. Above: designer Jocelyn Herbert, playwright E. A. (Ted) Whitehead (whose Alpha Beta *teamed Rachel Roberts and Albert Finney to powerful effect) and director Bill Gaskill. Below: actor, playwright and director Peter Gill (left) with actor Brian Cox.*

George Devine's theatre such a unique place, unrepeated and unrepeatable? First of all, of course, George himself. He was the only theatre director I have met who seemed never to experience the twinge of jealousy. He loved to recognise talent and he wanted to succeed. He laughed at failure, but his glee was defiant. 'Worse notices than *Live Like Pigs*!' he chortled, coming in with the *Musgrave* reviews under his arm – the critics complaining, almost to a man, of the intolerable boredom of both play and production. George was always there to carry the can; but he gave his artists, his directors particularly, absolute freedom, with only the necessary economic limitations. In other theatres, in the West End and on Broadway, at our own great National Theatre and at the miserable Folger Theatre in Washington, I have found myself resented and reprimanded for not minding my own business where some one or other aspect of a production was concerned. Never at the Court, from that first time I got hold of a big piece of scrap paper, impatiently hand-lettered a 'Coming

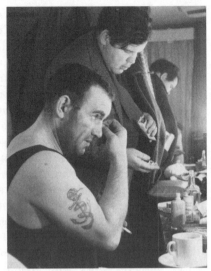

Faces of the Court. Left: Albert Finney making up for his role in Lindsay's production of The Lily White Boys. *Right: Colin Blakely (foreground) and Declan Mulholland preparing to go on stage for Lindsay's production of* The Fire Raisers.

Shortly' poster for *The Long and the Short* and stuck it up at the bar.

For all his great and comforting authority, George was also humble. He searched for and venerated creativity: he loved intelligence. That was the basis of his extraordinary collaboration and friendship with Tony Richardson, without whom also the Court would not have existed or survived. George was socially curious and responsible, not really political. He was a proper liberal – a fighting one – and a wry humanist. Not sentimental and certainly not a Welfare State baby. He was often uncertain of himself, shy, always courageous. I wish I had been grown-up enough to offer him more in return.

In a famous passage, written not long before he died, George described the theatre as 'a religion or a way of life'. Not a 'brothel'. He knew that a theatre – whether it likes it or not – must have, will have a 'recognisable attitude'. Writers and directors and designers and actors, ideally, should choose a theatre whose attitude they approve. 'If you can't find one you like, start one of your own.'

But it is not so easy. To start a theatre you have to have some kind of genius; you also have to have luck. History has to be on your side. In 1956 history was on the side of George and Tony and the Royal Court. Also they had allies of principle, generosity and calibre: Neville Blond and Grenville Poke, Oscar-Lewenstein and Robin Fox, Peggy Ashcroft and

George Harewood.

That was 30 years ago, and the English Stage Company is still at the Royal Court. Everybody likes a birthday, especially the media. But I think we must recognise that today's Royal Court is, no doubt inevitably, a different theatre from the Royal Court I have been remembering. When George Devine left Sloane Square in 1966, Bill Gaskill wielded a new broom and for a spell took the theatre along a somewhat (not completely) different path. Then Anthony Page and I came back and together with Bill revived the old Royal Court spirit for a fine Indian summer which established Edward Bond and David Storey as contrasting major dramatists. Christopher Hampton too, and Ted Whitehead and Donald Howarth and the young David Hare. But the sands were running out: Oscar Lewenstein had a go at running the theatre; then Nicholas Wright and Robert Kidd found themselves o'erparted, whether as torch-bearers of tradition or as innovators.

By 1975 the Royal Court was on the rocks. The English Stage Company had lost its sense of purpose and identity. But by a familiar irony the theatre had now become part of the cultural establishment. The Arts Council, which a few years before had threatened to close the Court if it did not restore free First Night tickets to Hilary Spurling, stepped in and secured the appointment of Stuart Burge as Artistic Director. And Stuart Burge appointed Max Stafford Clark and (yes) Jonathan Miller as his associates. And Stuart Burge went off to direct *Sons and Lovers* for TV and Max slipped into the driving seat. And started *his* theatre. Another story.

But yes . . . we have heard the chimes at midnight a good few times, all those years ago. That we have, that we have, that we have.

Sport, Life and Art

Films and Filming, February 1963 (adapted from an interview with John Russell Taylor)

IN A STRANGE WAY I HAVE NEVER QUITE FELT THAT I CHOSE TO DIRECT *THIS Sporting Life*. It seemed rather to choose me. Though, also strangely, I suppose I must have been one of the first people who ever thought about it as a film subject. This was as a result of reading a paragraph about the book in *The Sunday Times* before it was published. I was intrigued, and ordered a copy.

So much has happened since then that it is difficult to recall exactly what my first impressions were. Certainly I realised at once that this was something much more complex, and much more distinguished, than the story of a footballer's success and disillusion which the advance note had suggested. What struck me at first, I think, was the quality of writing: vivid and immediate, yet also clearly the work of a writer with most subtle psychological perceptions, and a sense of poetry dark, passionate and wholly his own. The central character, Frank Machin, was immediately striking, with an ambiguity of nature, half overbearing, half acutely sensitive, that fascinated me, without my being fully aware that I understood him. The same was true of his tortured, impossible relationship with the woman in the story; a bleak, Northern affair, of powerful, inarticulate emotions frustrated or deformed by puritanism and inhibition. The background rough and hard: no room here for charm or sentimental proletarianism. It was an intimidating subject for a film. I was not sure I would be up to it.

In any case it soon seemed out of reach. There was brisk bidding for the film rights, and the price quickly rose too high for Woodfall who seemed at that time the only company likely to back me as a director. In the end the subject went to Julian Wintle and Leslie Parkyn of Independent Artists, for distribution through the Rank Organisation. I thought that was goodbye. But then Independent Artists offered it to my friend Karel Reisz to direct; and Karel, who was anxious after *Saturday Night and Sunday Morning* to get some experience of production, suggested to me that he should propose me as director instead, with himself producing. Rather impetuously, I agreed. So, to my astonishment, did Independent Artists.

From the start, the film was essentially a collaborative affair. The book was such a personal piece of work that Karel and I both felt that no-one but its author could write the script. We met David Storey and were as impressed by him as we had been by his novel. He had never written for the screen before; and he had some hesitation at the idea of trying to recreate for a strange medium a work which he had already achieved and put behind him. But he did not hesitate for long – for David, who started out originally to be a painter, has an immense appetite (and a gift) for artistic experience. And anyway, as he explained to me at the beginning, he considered the cinema to be the director's medium. I replied maybe so, but I had no wish to dictate the adaptation. What I wanted was a script that had his sanction, and an artistic authority equal to that of the book. I didn't realise how much I was asking.

David Storey (left), author of This Sporting Life, *on location in Wakefield with producer Karel Reisz (centre) and Richard Harris.*

So we set to work, first on a treatment, then, when that was accepted, on a first draft script. David did all the writing, in between frequent and exhaustive consultations with Karel and myself. We went north to Yorkshire and searched for locations together, through the district around Wakefield and Leeds where David had grown up, where he had imagined many of the scenes in the book – and where, incidentally, I had made my first documentaries some twelve years before.

But in spite of this harmony, and much hard work, our first script attempts were not very successful. The book proved difficult to condense without losing the subtlety and complexity which gave it such distinction. I felt that the authority I wanted was not there. And this was where we were joined by another collaborator whose contribution to the picture was to be an essential one. A year or so before I had seen Richard Harris in the play of *The Ginger Man*, in which he gave a superb performance, a much more striking thing than he had ever had a chance to do on the screen; and I had a strong feeling that here was exactly the actor to play Frank Machin in *This Sporting Life*. So we sent a copy of the novel off to Hollywood, where he was filming in *Mutiny on the Bounty*, and asked him if he'd be interested. He replied immediately, with a marvellous letter full of admiration for the book and enthusiasm for the project. Then we posted him the first draft script, and we heard no more.

I began to get anxious. I was still not happy about the script myself, without knowing quite what to do about it; and anyway I felt it would be wrong to go further without a proper consultation with the actor who was going to play such a crucial leading role. So I put a phone call through to Tahiti (not as easy a thing as it sounds, by the way), where Richard was now marooned with *Bounty*, and suggested I should go and see him. He agreed it was essential, so off I flew.

There are many images connected with *This Sporting Life* which will not soon be erased from my memory. One of the most cherished is not from the film at all: it is of being met at five o'clock in the morning at Tahiti airport by Richard Harris, his eighteenth-century seaman's hair down to his shoulders, bursting to tell me what he thought of the script we had sent him. Within ten minutes we were at it; and though neither of us had slept much the night before, we talked and argued right through the day. I quickly realised that he was right. For one reason or another, through all our speculations and discussions, we had lost what was most unique and brilliant in the novel. We were dangerously near, in fact, ending up with just a 'film script'. It was Richard who, with passionate intransigence, brought us back to the book. In the evenings, after his shooting on the *Bounty*, we sat in his bungalow going through the script and his own, heavily annotated copy of the novel, until either he or I would drop off to sleep while the other was talking. And slowly a conception emerged which began to satisfy us. So I came home, and went to see David with the notes which Richard and I had made. He agreed as quickly as I had done, and set to work again with renewed energy. And so in the end we managed between us to produce a script that gave us at least a chance of putting on to film the peculiarly intense, complex and poetic quality of the original.

It is dreadful to be asked what a film is *about*. The film is what it is about. I could turn myself into a critic and try to analyse what we've done; but in fact one discovers what one is doing when one does it. And you discover what you have done when you see it. This can be dangerous, of course, and it's certainly easier for a painter or a writer than for a filmmaker: it's probably one reason why I find scripting so difficult. But to some extent it is necessary. The process of making a film, like the process of making any work of art, should be a process of discovery.

It's easier to say what a film is *not* about. *This Sporting Life* is not a film about sport. Nor is it to be categorised as a 'North Country working-class story'. In fact I wouldn't really call it a story-picture at all. (This is where we went most wrong in our first attempts to script it – in attempting to remove the flashback construction of the first two thirds which

Frank Machin (Richard Harris) lashes out in angry frustration at his landlady and lover Mrs Hammond (Rachel Roberts) in This Sporting Life.

alone made it possible to find the essentially subjective style.) I suppose that the film is primarily a study of temperament. It is a film about a man. A man of extraordinary power and aggressiveness, both temperamental and physical, but at the same time with a great innate sensitiveness and a need for love of which he is at first hardly aware. And this temperament is reflected in a very strange and complicated relationship with a woman – from this aspect you could call the film a love story. And this whole conflict and relationship is seen against a particular social setting. All these things play their part in the picture. The world of Rugby League football, of the kind of people who make up the game, the exploiters and the exploited and the spectators who live vicariously off them, this is the significant background to an intense and tragic relationship between a man and a woman.

People are apt to say that tragedy is impossible today: that the age of Freudian psychology and atomic science has robbed the individual of the dignity and the significance which alone make tragedy possible. Well, flying in the face of fashion, we have tried to make a tragedy. Much as I admire many of the experiments made by the young French directors – and particularly their adventurous breaking away from the outmoded conventions of cinematic 'style' – I think that even in their best work there is apt to be a terrible lack of weight, of substance and human significance.

Their very brilliance seems to trap them in facility and vogueishness. Maybe it's the political and social situation in France that has made it very difficult either for the people who make films to be serious, or for the serious people to make films at all. For all their scorn of artistic conventions, their films do not really *disturb*.

The case of the new British school is rather different. These films have also loosened up in style in a very healthy way, but with a quite different emphasis from the French. Here the first achievement has been the opening up of new-territories, both of subjects and of the social backgrounds in which they are set. This has been a great development – in fact an indispensable one. But it could also be restrictive. It certainly will be restrictive if we make films for too long about 'working-class people', looked at objectively, almost with a documentarist's vision. (Or a sociologist's, which is worse.) Of course, too, it must rule tragedy out; for tragedy is concerned with what is unique, not what is representative. Throughout *This Sporting Life* we were very aware that we were not making a film about anything representative; we were making a film about something unique. We were not making a film about a 'worker', but about an extraordinary (and therefore more deeply significant) man, and about an extraordinary relationship. We were not, in a word, making sociology.

In any conception as ambitious as this, the relationship between actor and director is of course of supreme importance; and fortunately for *This Sporting Life*, the collaboration between Richard Harris and myself which started when we met in Tahiti continued right the way through shooting. I have used the word 'subjective' about the film – naturally enough in relation to a novel written in the first person; and we were determined to capture this quality without recourse to any of the traditional devices of voice-over narration or subjective camera tricks. For me there was the additional difficulty of entering into a temperament very different from my own: for Frank Machin and I had very little in common, and as a result I found the leap into his heart and mind a hard one. This made me continually liable to slip into an *objective* view of scenes that needed to be presented through Machin's own temperament. This would certainly have happened more often, had it not been for Richard's studied understanding, not just of the psychology of the part, but also of its dramatic function (for he is an actor of intense method, as well as intuition). As a result we were able to achieve, working together, what I feel to be a remarkable integration of performance and overall style. Without this degree of collaboration, in fact, the film could not have been made.

If Frank Machin's whole being is the soul of *This Sporting Life*, its heart is in his tormented love story. And here luck was with us again, to give us Rachel Roberts to play the immensely difficult part of Mrs Hammond.

Left: Richard Harris (obscured) watches as Lindsay demonstrates the way he wishes him to play a confrontation scene with Rachel Roberts. Right: the scene as it appeared on screen in This Sporting Life.

This is a woman whose feelings, though fierce, are almost continually suppressed; the relationship deepens without self-explanation, without conventional avowals, through incessant conflict, with all the feelings between or under the lines. It called for an actress of exceptional 'interior' quality, with real wildness within, as well as the capacity for an iron restraint. Fortunately these are precisely the qualities that Rachel brought to the part – and to an extent that makes one marvel that she has done nothing on the screen since *Saturday Night and Sunday Morning*, except for a modest co-feature recently released, *Girl on Approval*. (A familiar story, of course, in the British Cinema, which has a special gift for passing over exceptional talent in favour of the safely second-rate.)

We approached the scenes between Frank and Mrs Hammond with theatrical rather than traditional film method – rehearsing them for ten days before we started, continuing during evenings and weekends during shooting, taking them as far as possible in continuity on the floor. (This self-evidently is the only way to achieve in a film characterisation of the depth and development that are taken for granted in the theatre.) The concentration paid off: I don't think any of us are likely to forget those gruelling, claustrophobic weeks on the tiny kitchen set at Beaconsfield, the whole atmosphere somehow infected with the tense, grinding emotionalism of the situation the actors had to play.

Richard Harris, Karel Reisz and Lindsay on the set of This Sporting Life.

I am asked why I gave up making films five years ago to work in the theatre. The answer (as usually in such cases) is that I didn't give up films: they gave up me. After *Every Day Except Christmas*, which I also only made through the grace and insistence of Karel Reisz, it seemed obvious that enlightened sponsorship of that kind was not going to recur. And a future in 'orthodox' documentary, making milk-and-water propaganda for the COI, or prestige advertising featurettes for oil companies, was too dispiriting to face. Free Cinema failed – even the National Film Theatre became nervous of the programmes, fearing that their official position might be compromised by association with such red-hot socialism. I did a few commercials, half a dozen *Robin Hood*s, and an abortive treatment for a feature film for Ealing. Then, out of the blue, I was asked to do a play at the Royal Court – *The Long and the Short and the Tall*. It was a success, and I enjoyed doing it. I was asked to do more plays. So I stayed in the theatre.

I was not offered the film of *The Long and the Short and the Tall*. At that time in the British cinema no-one who was not already experienced in features could hope to be considered as a feature director. Richard Harris, who played in the film version of *The Long and the Short*, told me recently that he had suggested at the time that the best way to film it was to give it to the original cast and director; but ABPC had said, 'Oh well, you know Anderson, he's very long haired.' But there really has been a revolution since then, starting I suppose with *Look Back in Anger* (which Tony Richardson only directed because John Osborne had the right to insist), but clinched finally by *Saturday Night and Sunday Morning*. Karel's immense success changed the mentality of the producers overnight. Now new directors and unknown actors seemed to be all they were looking for.

I don't think there was any prejudice against me for my disreputable background as a critic. It was just that people who had made documentaries or had directed in the theatre meant nothing to British film producers. They had never heard of them. I have never been aware of any hostility as a result of anything I wrote as a critic, which is surprising when I remember how rude we were to practically everybody in those carefree days.

I don't think anyone in the professional film industry is influenced by criticism; nor is this really surprising. One can imagine criticism so perceptive and illuminating that it can also illuminate for the artist, show him what he has been doing, and tell him truths about himself he did not see. But in practice one seems to know the faults and virtues of what one has done more clearly than the people who criticise it. Perhaps this is because critics judge too much, and interpret too little. When thinking about criticism I always recall the remark by Charlotte Brontë in her introduction to the edition of *Wuthering Heights* published after Emily's death. She talked of the critics who, when the book appeared, had immediately assumed she had written it; and she mentioned one critic who did perceive the essentially original quality of the novel. A true critic, she says, who was able to interpret 'the *Mene Mene Tekel Upharsin* of an original mind'. This, I think, conveys admirably the essential function of the critic. Judgements after all are not so very interesting: they usually tell us more about the judge than about the work. But a critic who can see something new and original (and maybe perplexing to most people as a result), and who has the intelligence and the culture to be able to interpret it, to reveal its true value – this is as valuable as it is rare.

I no longer have ambitions for myself in this direction. In fact I have to admit that the remnants of my critical and polemical past which still survive in people's memories often prove rather embarrassing. Not that I would disown anything I wrote; but after all conditions change and we develop. And to be labelled for life on the strength of people's misinterpretation of an article five or six years old, seems unjust. That ardent piece, '*Stand Up! Stand Up!*' – which I must again stress I don't at all renounce – was anyway never intended as a final declaration on criticism. It was partly a personal statement, and partly an attempt to initiate a debate. I wished to affirm my belief in the dignity of criticism, for the critic should be more than a parasite. He should be a whole man just as much as anyone else; and so of course his moral and social beliefs must affect his judgements. To pretend that one can, or should, eliminate these aspects of oneself in assessing a work of art can only lead to an impoverishment of criticism.

The attempt to initiate a debate failed, of course – largely because people always prefer to smack a label onto one and turn one into a cliché, rather than really to think about and discuss what one has said. The word 'commitment' has become a bore, not because the idea behind it is insignificant or unimportant, but because discussion of it, by Rightists and Leftists alike, has been so lazy and so shallow.

To return to *This Sporting Life*. No doubt I shall be accused, or congratulated, for having deserted the ranks of 'commitment'. Both accusations and congratulations will be misplaced. All works of art have political implications but they have political implications because they are works of art, not *vice versa*. It is a mistake to wish this relationship to be an immediate one, except possibly in a time of revolution. And we in Britain are living far from a time of revolution. If an artist tries to link what may truly be radical about his work with a radical movement in politics, he will quickly come to grief. We do not have a radical movement in politics.

All the same, in spite of the many horrors of the British way of life, I think there are worse places in the world to try and be an artist. It is quite impossible of course, but at least they do not put you to death for it. You can bite the hand that feeds you, with some hope of getting away with it. The artist must always bite the hand that feeds him. He must always aim beyond the limits of tolerance. His duty is to be a monster.

The terrible vice of the English is reasonableness, the pernicious habit of compromise, the gift (and how self-appreciated!) of 'not taking things too seriously'. This is perhaps not a bad recipe for survival; but it is not too good for art. The real danger for the cinema in Britain is not the censor or even the system; it is the danger that people do not want to be challenged or disturbed.

On the other hand, aren't there signs that we are growing up? One cannot help hoping that if a work of art has sufficient charge to it, and emotional truth, people cannot help responding. In our present affluence, at least more good books are being read than ever before; and if D. H. Lawrence were a young writer today, I don't think he would be hounded out of the country. Perhaps, art may win yet. In our case, those of us who have worked together to make *This Sporting Life* will shortly find out for ourselves.

Roberto Gerhard and the Music for *This Sporting Life*

Tempo, December 1981

I first met Roberto Gerhard when I was engaged in the writing of a book, *Making a Film*, about the production of Thorold Dickinson's film, *Secret People*, at Ealing Studios in 1950 or 1951. The scenario of *Secret People* called for a ballet, of undefined Southern European origin, in which one of the principal characters (played by the then unknown Audrey Hepburn) was a principal dancer.

I don't know where Thorold Dickinson had first encountered Roberto. But I remember well Roberto coming to the studio, talking about the theme of the ballet (something quite conventional, I think, about a grape harvest, or something like that) which was choreographed by Andrée Howard. After discussions, Roberto came back and played a theme which captivated everybody. He was given the commission and composed the music for the ballet. I think everybody took the theme to be original; only some years later I recognised it as a traditional folk theme, when I heard it played on the radio in a recording by Segovia. It was the *Cant des Ocells* ('The Song of the Birds'), also made famous by Gerhard's friend Pablo Casals: a beautiful, broad, and romantic melody which, as arranged by Roberto, served its purpose very well.

Some ten years later I directed my first feature film, *This Sporting Life*. This was from a novel by the Yorkshire writer David Storey, a man of powerfully emotional imagination, romantic but not sentimental. These were the qualities I knew I would need in the score for the film. None of the then fashionable film composers seemed to me to have these qualities – the average British 'quality' film score (by, say, Lennox Berkeley or Alan Rawsthorne) would evidence intelligent musicianship, but be lacking in emotion or poetry. Then I thought of Roberto Gerhard. I knew almost nothing of his music except his contribution to *Secret People* – but I knew his style was not sentimentally melodic, while I also knew (if only by intuition) that he had a powerfully romantic sensibility.

I got in touch with Roberto, and he came to see the film at Beaconsfield Studios. He responded to it with great sympathy. His reaction to the film persuaded me that he would be the right composer for it – although he was doubtful about his capacity to deliver in time. (As always, there was a fairly severe schedule which the composer had to conform to.)

I remember visiting Roberto in Cambridge, talking about the score, and

Richard Harris, in This Sporting Life, *scored with 'strong, deep expressiveness'
by Roberto Gerhard.*

even assisting him in throwing various objects down the stairs, in an effort
to produce the right kind of abstract sounds which he felt he needed. I
think he may well have played his proposed score through to me on the
piano, and no doubt we had discussions about it. But of course I could not
fully understand or appreciate it until the recording session, and the time
when it could be played by a full orchestra. For the recording, Roberto
requested that we engage the conductor Jacques-Louis Monod, who knew
his music well, though he had no previous experience in film recording.

When we started to fit the music to the film, there were certain sections
which did not work as well as I had hoped. For the big, violently emotional confrontation of the two principal characters, Roberto had written
a violent, jaggedly emotional music. This seemed simply to duplicate the
dramatic action, and we dropped it. In other areas his music had exactly
the strong, deep expressiveness I was hoping for – without sentimentality,
and without too melodic a basis.

Only in his music for the title sequence of the film did Roberto's
'abstract' (or 'concrete', or whatever other term is most appropriate to
describe his use of apparently random sounds, whether musical or created
by non-musical means) style prove inappropriate. And this led to a disagreement between us which was unhappily never quite resolved. When we

100

played this music over, after the recording session, and set it against the titles of the film, it became immediately apparent that its eccentricity – at least from a wide public point of view – was too bizarre to suit the subject. I remember well one of the dubbing 'mixers' murmuring 'Frank Machin hits Mars,' and I had some sympathy with him. It was obvious that a general audience would be led to expect, not a powerful human story, but some kind of science fiction. Roberto was outraged when I communicated this to him as tactfully as I could. He refused to write a new section – or rather said that if he did he would make it only *more* eccentric and *more* bizarre.

Finally I had to concoct a musical sequence for the titles, using more suitable and suggestive quotations from the score, and linking these by the noise of cheering crowds. This worked extremely well, although of course it made Roberto very angry. I think he refused to come and see the film in London but later (when we were in communication again) he told me that he had seen it in Cambridge, and had been furious.

As a result of this breach, we never collaborated again, although Roberto did send me, some years later, a tape of his Third Symphony, *Collages*, which I wanted to try as the accompaniment to a theatrical production. In the event, I didn't find it suitable, so it wasn't used for this purpose.

I always regretted our falling-out. Roberto Gerhard seemed to me unique among composers of his quality in Britain, for his deep expressiveness (romanticism if you like), which could make his music lyrical without ever being sentimental. His response to *This Sporting Life* was extremely generous and sensitive; and the music he did write proved extremely appropriate and in my opinion enhanced the film greatly. But I didn't think Roberto was a natural collaborator. He was too hot-tempered and self-willed, and he could not accept the fact that, in certain conditions, his word could not be the final one. It was a great pity, since he could so obviously have made a great contribution in the field of music-for-film. I think this is clearly shown by his score for *This Sporting Life*; I don't know anyone else who could have done it half as well.

The Singing Lesson

Commentary, 1994

I CONSIDER MYSELF FORTUNATE TO HAVE BEEN ABLE TO ALTERNATE FILM AND theatre work. It is strange that, whenever I am at a gathering where people are discussing my films, so little mention is made of the work I have done in the theatre. In fact, some of my film work has arisen directly from my work as a theatre director. *The Singing Lesson*, for example, which is a film of mine that few people have seen, came about because I was in Poland to direct the first production there of John Osborne's *Inadmissible Evidence*. It was presented at the Contemporary Theatre in Warsaw during their 1966 season and the leading actor was Tadeusz Lomnicki, who I had met on an earlier visit to Poland. Lomnicki had impressed me some years before with his performance in Wajda's film *A Generation* and we had originally discussed the possibility of my directing him in *Hamlet* before we settled on the Osborne.

During the rehearsal period, I happened to visit an exhibition devoted to the work of the film director Andrzej Munk, who had died in a car crash in 1961. At this exhibition I met the director of the documentary studio in Warsaw and he said, 'Why don't you make a film for us while you're here?' I said that I would love to do something, and asked him what I should take as my subject; he said, 'Anything you like.' This was very generous, but it was also intimidating as I didn't really know Poland. Then one day Joanna Nawroka, my assistant at the theatre, suggested that I come to watch the classes at the Dramatic Academy given by a revered performer in musical theatre, Professor Ludwik Simpolinski. I was a bit lazy and didn't really want to go, but finally I did it to please Joanna. When I watched the fourth-year students at the Academy performing a variety of songs under Professor Simpolinski's tutelage, I was charmed and decided to make my film about the class.

I spoke little or no Polish and the documentary studio arranged for me to have a cameraman who spoke English. He was a very nice fellow but I asked if they could find me someone younger; they could, but they warned me that he could not speak English. Well, that didn't matter to me and, in fact, we got along together very well despite the language problem. His name was Zygmunt Samosiuk. The system in Poland required a script in order to get the money for a film, so Zygmunt urged me to write some sort of one. I made something up, because it is not easy to write a script for a documentary film, and then we just went in and shot the picture. But, obviously, *The Singing Lesson* didn't just happen. These days, with video, there is a great temptation just to shoot what happens, but any documentaries that I have made have always been personal and planned. They are conscious; they may be called theatrical, I don't know.

Those students were an exceptionally nice lot, and very talented. It would not have been possible to make the film in England because the students would never have been so spontaneous, charming and, shall I say, innocent. One of them, Andrzej Seweryn, went on to work with Peter Brook in Paris. But, sadly, a number of people involved in the film have since died – including Zygmunt, I'm afraid. He made a fine, job of the camerawork: it is very well shot and has a lyrical quality which I like very much.

Making that film in Poland gave me a certain freedom of spirit and invention. When you are shooting at home you're rather more conscious of how and where the film will be shown. In Warsaw, I could do exactly as I wished; I didn't have to worry about a lot of boring English people.

While we were shooting in the classroom I decided that it would be a good idea to go outside and shoot in the streets of Warsaw so that the film could be a sort of montage of scenes in the class and the life outside. Perhaps I was thinking of a subtext of innocence and experience. When I had finished, I went back to England, and the

The Singing Lesson. *From top: Lindsay in front of camera, Lindsay in shoe shop, Professor Simpolinski and students in a scene from the film.*

Warsaw studio gave the film to their most experienced editor. She looked at the material and decided it couldn't be put together. This often happened early in my career when I was told that the material could not be edited. I suppose that, in truth, it could not be edited except by the person who had that sensibility in the first place. So I returned to Warsaw to work with another, rather less experienced editor called Barbara Kosidowska. We got on very well and we put the film together without much trouble.

The film's Polish title was *Raz Dwa Trzy* – which means 'One, Two, Three' – and I gave it the English title of *The Singing Lesson*. The English print is very sparsely subtitled because I didn't want the film to be a sort of translation of the songs that were sung in it. I wanted the images to speak for themselves, once we had provided some idea of what each song was about. I feel that we were good collaborators, the editor, the cameraman and I, but the other directors at the documentary studio didn't seem to me particularly friendly. I remember mentioning this to our producer, Mirek Podolski, and he said, 'Of course, they're all hoping this film will be a failure. They don't want somebody in from abroad to make a film and then find everybody saying how good it is.' But none of that oppressed me, because I was enjoying the lightness and freedom of working in a strange but friendly environment, and I was so charmed by the students in that class.

At that time in Poland, when you finished a film, you were required to screen it at the studio in front of all the studio workers. The head of the studio remarked that the people we showed in the street were not smiling. Now the truth is that they weren't smiling for reasons that may have been instinctive or conscious but had nothing to do with me saying to them, 'Look alienated.' But it is an example of the social alienation which was evident in Poland. It comes back, too, to the theme of innocence and experience: the contrast between the students and their world and their attitude towards making music, and the world outside of which they are going to be a part.

The thing that most interests me in the film is the shift between levels of reality: the reality of the classroom, of the students singing; the reality of memory, of wartime (which is the theme of the first song, 'The Coat'). There are many shades and allusions of irony in the film so that the emphasis changes all of the time. It appears very simple but is in many ways quite complex. In some shots you can see a certain gravity about the students as though they know what life is about, or what it is going to be about. It's a shame that the film has not been widely seen outside of Poland, except at one or two festivals; but it was bought not long ago by the BBC, thanks to the efforts of a friend of mine there, so British audiences will have a chance to see it on television.

The White Bus

Commentary, 1994

THE WHITE BUS ORIGINATED AS A SHORT STORY IN A BEAUTIFUL COLLECTION of stories called *Sweetly Sings the Donkey* by Shelagh Delaney. Shelagh's play *A Taste of Honey* had been a big hit at the Royal Court and had been successfully filmed by Tony Richardson. Another associate from the Court, the producer Oscar Lewenstein, had the idea of filming three of Shelagh's stories, each with a different director, and creating a single feature-length film structured as a kind of trilogy. He invited me to participate, along with Tony Richardson and Peter Brook. It was Oscar who suggested that the story I filmed should be 'The White Bus'. Having read it, I met with Shelagh and liked her; so I decided to take it on.

I was very lucky in that Oscar gave me complete freedom. Looking back on things, I now realise that I have only been any good – if I *have* been any good – when making films entirely freely and in my own way. That probably accounts for the fact that I haven't made so very many films; indeed, I'm lucky to have made as many as I have. *The White Bus* was important to me for many reasons, not least because it was the first time I worked with the Czech cameraman Miroslav Ondricek who went

Left: Lindsay directing Penny Ryder and Barry Evans as the young lovers in one of several vignettes from The White Bus. *Right: a foreign eye – Miroslav Ondricek (seated on the ladder), came from Prague to shoot* The White Bus.

on to shoot *If . . . .* and *O Lucky Man!*

I had met Mirek during a visit to Czechoslovakia where I watched him at work with Milos Forman. We became friends, although he spoke no English and I spoke no Czech, and I was looking for the opportunity to work with him; *The White Bus* proved to be just such an opportunity. He accepted my invitation to come to England and, once the tricky formalities of getting permission for him to leave Prague were dealt with, he joined the unit. We quickly found that the language barrier posed no real problem.

Interestingly, *The White Bus* is the one film of mine to be subjected to a detailed filmed record, made by my friend John Fletcher for the British Council. I think it must have been John's idea. The film he made was called *About the White Bus* but, of course, the picture it gives of our making the film is not the whole truth – nothing about the making of a film ever could be. My assistant director, Kip Gowans, actually hated me. He had been an assistant on features, working with John Schlesinger, but once he got out onto the streets of Manchester he didn't know what to do; he was completely lost. The producer, Michael Deeley, a rather sulky-looking chap, later went to America where I don't think he was successful. The art director wasn't much good. But it was great working with Mirek.

The film tells an essentially simple story of a young girl from Salford who has moved to work in London, but returns home for a day to take a sight-seeing bus tour of her home town. Shelagh and I discussed the scripting of the film, and we worked out a kind of script. At one point I suggested that she should play the central role of the girl but she didn't want to, and I am sure she was right to decline. She's quite self-conscious and not an actress. However, she suggested a friend of hers, an actress called Patricia Healey for the role. I had met Patsy and didn't think she would want to play the part but she did, and she was absolutely right. A very talented actress. Some people have remarked that Patsy looks a bit like Shelagh in the film; I suppose their hair was similar, but that wasn't the reason I chose her.

I liked Shelagh very much; we got along well, although, once shooting was under way, she didn't say much. She was there, but she didn't really participate. After a script adjustment, I might say to Shelagh, 'Is that all right?' and she'd say, 'Yes.' I think she felt that the actual making of the film wasn't really her bag. A lot of *The White Bus* was not scripted, and I don't think it could have been really. Take the shot at the beginning of the foundry scene when the characters are walking in silhouette up the gangway; I probably saw the opportunity for that image when we were at the location and told the actors to go up there. Similarly, the scene in the museum of the stuffed animals confronting the human beings: for some reason, Shelagh wouldn't go into the museum, so she never saw the animals or put them in the script. But I saw them when we were going around the museum, and decided to improvise the scene.

There is a sequence in John Fletcher's film which shows Kevin Brownlow editing *The White Bus*. Well, I'm sure that he wouldn't mind my saying that he didn't really understand the film. In a way, it was a bit too straightforward in style – Kevin is rather an Eisenstein man. He would stand at the moviola, I remember, running a sequence and making little cutting gestures, and I would say, 'Look, Kevin, it isn't like that. You can't turn it into *The Battleship Britannia*. It isn't shot like that – you just join the shots together.'

Fortunately, Kevin was also working on his very fine book *The Parade's Gone By*, which was a marvellous and very personal history of Hollywood's silent era. At one point he went off to America to talk to Gloria Swanson or somebody. While he was away, John Fletcher and I took the film and re-cut it.

When Tony Richardson and Peter Brook saw *The White Bus*

Top: *writer Shelagh Delaney returns to Salford to watch location filming of* The White Bus, *adapted from her short story.* Above: *Patricia Healey (who bore a resemblance to Delaney) as the Girl in* The White Bus, *with John Sharp as the Mace Bearer.*

they immediately decided that they should try and make something more remarkable and they jettisoned Shelagh Delaney. The subjects they chose were not good, and when all three films were together under the blanket title *Red, White and Zero* the whole thing made no sense. I certainly don't blame United Artists for not distributing it. But I think that *The White Bus* still stands up on its own and I am sorry that United Artists did not feel capable of distributing it independently of the other two films. They finally made a deal which allowed it to be shown in London – at the Paris Pullman cinema – in support of a Czech feature film called *Daisies*. Unfortunately, the London critics slaughtered *Daisies*, and *The White Bus* didn't do much better. It ran a couple of weeks at the Paris Pullman and hasn't been seen since – except once when it was shown on BBC television at midnight. So not many people have actually seen it and it remains an unknown film.

NEVER APOLOGISE

How *If* . . . . Came About

Unpublished article

APPEARING WHEN IT DID, AT THE END OF A YEAR OF YOUTHFUL DISSIDENCE and revolt, *If* . . . . has often seemed to be a film conceived and made purposely to reflect (even to cash-in on) the revolutionary fever of the late sixties. The truth is quite different. Some time in 1966 I had a telephone call from a friend of mine, Seth Holt, whom I had known first of all as an editor and an associate producer at Ealing Studios, and later as a director in his own right. Seth surprised me by asking if I would be interested in the idea of directing a film with him as producer. He explained that John Howlett, a young writer with whom he had been working, had shown him a script which he had thought was very promising but didn't feel he had the experience to tackle himself. The script was a story of life in an English public school, and John Howlett had written it in collaboration with a friend, David Sherwin, with whom he had shared horrific school experiences at Tonbridge School. They had been working on the script for some years, and in various drafts had submitted it to such people as Nicholas Ray (whose romantic *Rebel Without a Cause* they had much admired) and the British producer Ian Dalrymple (who had told them they both deserved to be beaten). Seth had not felt competent to undertake such a subject as he had not been to public school himself. Of course, I said I would be delighted at the idea of him producing a film for me, and asked him to send me the script.

I remember clearly the excited premonition with which I opened the envelope and extracted a script with the romantically promising title of *Crusaders*. After reading it, though, I found myself disappointed. It was certainly appealing in an anarchic, even poetic way, but I felt there was a naïvety about it, which, though authentically adolescent, made me feel that it could only be directed by the authors themselves. I said as much to Seth, but he asked me at least to take it a step further and meet the writers. So we all met one evening at a pub called The Pillars of Hercules in Greek Street. I liked John and David, and as soon as they realised that I had no wish to 'tone down' their story, they were responsive to my ideas. I agreed to go on discussing the direction a revised script might take. John Howlett was busy working on a script for Seth, so it fell to David Sherwin to undertake the collaboration with me.

I responded to *Crusaders* not just because I approved of its romantic and rebellious spirit, but because there was so much of my own experience that could relate directly to the subject, and not just my experience of school but

108

my experience of society also in the years that had followed. So from the beginning the making of *If . . . .* was a warmly and intimately personal experience.

David Sherwin and I took *Crusaders* to pieces, invented new characters, new incidents and a new structure. We decided early on that we wanted to make a film in 'epic' style – that is to say a film which would do more than simply tell the story of this or that individual, and which would aim consciously at the dignity and importance of a general theme. At that very first meeting at The Pillars of Hercules, I remember, I had started elaborating the idea of an apocalyptic finale; but as the script developed we were consciously determined *not* to appear to be reflecting, in journalistic style, revolutionary student action in France or in America. That was one reason why we were careful to use no contemporary pop music in the picture, and why we eliminated all the fashionable iconography of revolt from the walls of the boys' studies. (The one poster of Che Guevara which can be seen pinned up on the wall of the sweatroom had been pinned up by a boy at the school where we were shooting; I didn't have the heart to take it down.)

Seth Holt did not in the end produce the film. His own director's career suddenly reanimated itself – and anyway I don't think

From top: Lindsay on location for If . . . . *with David Sherwin, who would become a regular collaborator; Chris Menges (the standby cameraman) with Lindsay, Jirina Tvarochova (Czech interpreter) and Ondricek on location for* If . . . . *; Alma Mater: Cheltenham College, Lindsay's old school, and the principal location for* If . . . .

he really liked the direction in which David and I took the script. This was away from naturalism and towards a style which I would certainly claim to be realistic – 'realism' implying a concern with essences rather than with surfaces – and which I would prefer to be thought of as poetic rather than 'fantastic'. We wrote for ourselves, with no thought of pleasing anyone but ourselves – apart, of course, from the millions of film-goers whom we fondly imagined to think and laugh and feel in exactly the way we did; and undoubtedly the imaginative freedom with which we worked was largely responsible for the success of the film, and was due to a great extent to the fact that we were not writing on commission, had no 'development deal', and so felt beholden to nobody, and quite unaffected by any prejudices except our own. In this way *If . . . .* was well and truly in the tradition of 'Free Cinema'.

When we had finished the script, I showed it to my friends Michael Medwin and Albert Finney, who had started their own production company, Memorial Pictures, out of Albert's rewards from *Tom Jones*. They responded enthusiastically and Michael became the producer of – as it then still was – *Crusaders*. It was not until the picture had been shot that it found its eventual title – at the suggestion of my friend Daphne Hunter, then working for Memorial as Michael Medwin's secretary.

I am often asked how we managed to find the actors for *If . . . .* and particularly Malcolm McDowell. The answer is: in a completely orthodox, professional manner. At first I thought that perhaps the script called for boys of exactly the age of the characters. But after some experiment I realised that youth for the screen was a matter of temperament and character rather than of literal years. Miriam Brickman, with whom I had worked at the Royal Court Theatre and who had cast *This Sporting Life* as well as most of the pictures of the British 'New Wave' of the sixties, was our brilliant casting director. It was she who had seen Malcolm McDowell featuring briefly in an episode of the TV series *Dixon of Dock Green*, and she brought him in for audition, together with a crowd of other young men. I remember vividly Malcolm's second audition on the stage of the Shaftesbury Theatre, when he and Christine Noonan improvised with a marvellous, reckless intensity their love-hate scene in the Packhorse Cafe. They cast themselves in an instant.

Other key talents in *If . . . .* brought the blessing of familiarity. Arthur Lowe had given a fine performance in *This Sporting Life*; and I had worked with Mary McLeod and Graham Crowden at the Royal Court. Jocelyn Herbert, most creative and personal of designers, had designed several of my Royal Court productions. And Miroslav Ondricek, whom I had first met shooting for Milos Forman when I visited Prague in the early sixties, had been my cherished collaborator on *The White Bus*. Like most directors, I think, in this uncertain business I have always wanted to continue happy professional relationships.

It was hard to get the money to make *If* . . . . – as it has always been hard to get the money for any British film of originality and risk. The project was turned down, in traditional style, by all the British distributors (even by Granada, then searching for a suitable subject to begin a programme of film production). Eventually Albert and Michael managed to impress Charles Bludhorn, the idiosyncratic head of Paramount Pictures, and we secured the backing of Paramount. It was generally imagined by everyone that our subject was 'too English' to appeal outside the British (possibly even the English) market. In the event, though the picture was enthusiastically received by the British critics, it did only averagely decent business in this country. It was abroad that it made its chief impact, in the United States, in Europe, and even behind the Communist frontiers. If only British distributors could learn the lesson that it is not necessarily by 'international elements' in casting or in script that a film can transcend the limitations of provincialism or parochialism. It is by the vitality of emotional impulse, the urgency of what needs to be said. This is a truth which Americans seem to recognise, alas, much more readily than the English.

School to Screen

The Observer, December 1968

THE LAST SIX WEEKS ARE DEFINITELY THE WORST. THIS ISN'T TO SAY THAT ANY part of making a film is a picnic. One phase of struggle succeeds another, each with its peculiar stress. Those early months of wrestling with the script, with jigsaw pieces that won't fit in, through long walks and exhausting discussions, in search of the necessary amalgam of poetry and narrative, realism and reality. At least then time is your own, and the odd Cornflake will keep you going.

Pressures mount as you step into the market place, to discover what your careful, bold, exciting epic construction looks like from the outside. 'Shapeless', 'no story-line', 'will they care in Wigan?'. There are no parts to offer Julie Christie or Mike Caine. What about Sir Laurence as the Headmaster? Or Sir John, or Sir Michael, Sir Alex or Sir Ralph? Can you shoot it in six weeks?

Then, when by some miracle you have your backing (American, of course), there is the agonising business of searching for technicians, and rediscovering just how subjective and demanding you are when it comes to picking collaborators. After a dozen years in the industry how many have retained enthusiasm? Casting is agony, too (a slip means certain death); but at least you know from experience that you will always find the right actors if you search long and ruthlessly enough. Actors, God bless you!

Shooting is the real war, and so also no fun. The enemies are time – and anyone in the unit whose enthusiasm, energy, loyalty seem less than total. Your demands are impossible, but how can they be less? To make a film is to create a world. Of course, when it's finished it must look easy. 'All things bright and beautiful . . .' God's schedule for the creation of the world probably looked all right on paper; but you can bet he was cursing himself for agreeing to it by the time he got to the fifth day.

You slog through it, with laughter and tears, bad temper and good luck, for your eight (going to ten) or your twelve (going to fifteen) weeks. Then everyone shakes hands, embraces, gets drunk, waves goodbye – and you take a couple of days in bed, and move on to the cutting-room to start another five months' work. At least your unit has shrunk now from 50 or 60 to four or five. You are no longer at the mercy of circumstance. In fact those first eight weeks of editing are perhaps film-making at its purest; an atmosphere of dedication reigns. Then it all begins again. Time reasserts its demands. As the soundtrack, the music, the opticals, the print crowd

Mick Travis (Malcolm McDowell) makes his first appearance in If . . . . *The hat and scarf recall Ivor Novello's entrance in Hitchcock's silent classic,* The Lodger.

upon you, you feel your grasp lessening. You fight to keep control. The publicists, the journalists, the manipulators move in. By the last six weeks you are a defensive, aggressive, paranoid mess. If you'd remembered what it was like, you'd never have started.

If . . . . started over two years ago, when my friend Seth Holt sent me an original script by two young writers, David Sherwin and John Howlett, who had been at public school together, then at Oxford, and had been working on a film about schooldays for five or six years. They called it *Crusaders*, and it was the title that first attracted me, with its overtones of idealism, struggle and the world well lost. 'Charge once more, then, and be dumb . . .' And the personal factor as well. For me, as I suppose for most of the public school educated, the world of school remains one of extraordinary, significant vividness; a world of reality and symbol; of mingled affection and reserve.

Any school – particularly any boarding school – is a microcosm; another inducement for anyone who hankers, as I always do, for that kind of poetry which can claim 'the grandeur of generality'. And from the start, the epic style was what David Sherwin and I aimed at (John Howlett was now working with Seth on another project). The school as paradigm of an

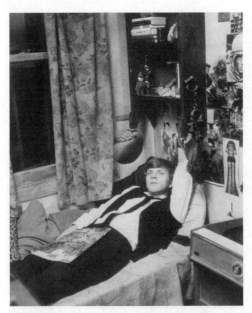

Mick Travis in his study with (behind him) the collaged wall created overnight by Lindsay and Malcolm McDowell.

obstinately hierarchic Britain; of the Western world; of authority and anarchism. Cataclysm seemed always to be the inevitable climax. *Crusaders* had also ended in violence, but on a personal level. We were after something bigger, something that went beyond naturalism, yet with *realism*, an inner logic, that would enable us to progress from an apparently naturalistic start to a violently epic conclusion. (We were not, that is, after an effect-journalism *à la* Godard.) When we wrote it, our conclusion seemed like extremest fantasy. When we shot it, in April and May 1968, it seemed like prophecy.

The style had to be simple, direct, concrete. 'Trendy' was our dirty word; and the more so because our subject was youth. So no pop; no pot; no soft-focus foliage in the foreground and very little use of the zoom lens. We shot some sequences in monochrome because they would have been too expensive, in equipment or in time, to shoot in colour. And anyway colour in films is enhanced, becomes a more positive element, when it is intermittently used. As for nervous quibbles about 'transitions into fantasy', these are unlikely to trouble either the genuinely simple or the properly sophisticated. What child has ever been silly enough to ask, when Cinderella's pumpkin turns into a golden coach, where reality ends and fantasy begins? It is all real.

So what about these last six weeks? Shouldn't they be the easiest? The film is finished, printed, passed by the censor. You have a West End opening date. New York want a print. You should be on top of the world. Instead, you realise you have lost control. Up to now the struggle, however intense, has had a single objective: to clarify and realise your conception. Your audience is present in your mind, but not as a threat. As a *raison d'être*, rather. You have to believe that you have only to make it good: communication must follow.

It is an illusion. Now the film is finished, and you emerge blinking into the light of common day, you realise how little you can be in control of its destiny. Worse, you realise how little reason there is for it to exist at all. The system which permitted (probably by accident) its creation, has no real idea how to use it. How Quixotic it suddenly seems, how doomed to failure, this attempt to straddle a divided culture, to find an audience that is neither *Carry On* nor *New Statesman*, neither ad-mass nor mandarin.

You have only two alternatives. You can retire from the scene, asserting the right of the artist not to be a salesman. Or try, despairingly, to beat the system. You cut the trailer yourself, because the 'professional' job outrages you so deeply. You argue about the advertising. You give interviews – you even solicit them – knowing that neither you nor your work is of interest to the press for what it is, only for what entertainment, high-brow or low, they can be made to provide. You connive at stories that betray the seriousness of your work, the complexity of your intentions – all in the name of publicity. You tell yourself it is all justified if it only helps to get the work seen. Perhaps this is true. But you still feel a wretched loss of dignity, and dread to see your name in the papers.

There is one consolation. By the seventh week it will all be forgotten. Next month's 'balding' bundle of talent will be Karel Reisz; tomorrow's papers will be lining the larder shelves; and Clive Donner and Ken Loach will be meeting Eamonn Andrews. And – who knows? – of the work, something may survive. Perhaps in our anxiety, we underestimate art and even the public. While there are still minds to be moved, imaginations to be stirred, a true film may yet perform its explosive, life-enhancing function. We may yet be revenged.

If . . . . The Colour of Monochrome

Commentary, 1994

IF . . . . CONTINUED MY COLLABORATION WITH MIROSLAV ONDRICEK WHICH had begun with *The White Bus*. Once again, Mirek came from Prague but this time the arrangements were easier to make. Union regulations stipulated that we had to have a stand-by British cameraman, which is how Chris Menges, who was a friend, came to work on the film, but from the point of view of cinematography, it's Mirek's film. His input also added enormously to the interest of the film, helping make it not typically British, despite a subject matter that might lead one to expect a very British, very English film. It is, I think, a young film.

The film also began another important collaboration for me, with the actor Malcolm McDowell. When I first met Malcolm he was a young actor who had done a few things in the theatre and on television. He was a middle-class boy whose father had a pub, I think. He wasn't state educated but went to a minor public school, so the background of the film was not foreign to him. With other characters that was a problem when it came to casting, and it highlights a difficulty that inevitably exists in a class society. The atmosphere of the film had to be, as it is, middle-class or upper-middle-class because it was that kind of school. But when we advertised for people to be in the film, most of the actors who came along for interview turned out to be working-class, and they wouldn't have looked right alongside the real public schoolboys we used for the crowd scenes. Of course, the other problem in casting was that we realised that we ought to have sixteen or seventeen-year-olds. Malcolm must have been about 24 at the time, but I see no disparity when Malcolm is sitting in the Chapel at Cheltenham alongside real boys from the college. In a film of this kind, age is largely a matter of spirit, attitude and feeling, and I don't think that the mature actors who played Mick and his friends, that is to say Malcolm, David Wood and Richard Warwick, seemed particularly old. I am glad to say that *If* . . . . marked the beginning of a real career for Malcolm, and his performance led to his being chosen by Stanley Kubrick for the lead in *A Clockwork Orange*.

The use of monochrome in *If* . . . . has puzzled a number of people, and there have been all sorts of theories about it marking the shift from reality to fantasy. This was not at all the case or the intention. Quite simply, it arose from a technical problem which made it difficult for Mirek, in terms of lighting, to achieve the correct colour quality in the chapel sequence. I suggested that we shoot that scene in monochrome, which we did. Later we shot some other scenes in monochrome, not for technical reasons but merely to give a poetic balance to the film. The results helped us make the film work on a level of imagination beyond naturalism. If you shoot a film entirely in monochrome or entirely in colour you don't disrupt the audience in any way. Whereas in *If . . . .* we found that we were able to use monochrome to give the film's texture something beyond the surface naturalism you might find in a film like, say, *Dead Poets Society* (which, of course, everyone enjoyed and which probably made a lot more money than *If . . . .*).

It is interesting that there are some scenes which seem entirely right within the film but which were not in the original script when we began shooting. For example, the scene immediately after Mick is beaten by Rowntree was one I didn't like. We shot it, but I wasn't happy with it. Then, just before we were due to go into the studio for a week's shooting, I realised what the scene should be. David Sherwin came around to my place and we made a series of collages which Mick could have on his study wall and fire darts into. That scene – Malcolm actually did the firing of the darts himself – solved the transition after the beating. Some people disliked the fact that Mick shakes hands with Rowntree after being beaten, but that is what is done in

From top: shooting in the cramped location of the toilets of Cheltenham College with Ondricek and actor Robin Askwith; Christine Noonan as the girl from the cafe who engages in an erotic fight with Mick before joining the Crusaders; the Headmaster (Peter Jeffrey) opens a draw to allow the 'dead' Chaplain (Geoffrey Chater) to receive the Crusaders' apology for killing him.

those situations. The criticism was that he should be seen as a more overt rebel, but it comes about differently, more interestingly. I felt that his firing darts into the collages broadened the impact and stopped the film being just a school story.

There were other scenes, too, which were called surreal, such as the scene with the chaplain in the drawer. I remember Harold Pinter telling me that he liked *If. . . .* very much but thought I'd made one big mistake by putting the chaplain in the drawer. I said, 'Oh, I'm sorry,' but I thought he was wrong; he's not renowned for his sense of humour, really. It is interesting that a lot of the headmaster's dialogue in that scene was taken from a book written by an ex-housemaster at Eton, so some of the more idiotic things spoken by the headmaster are real.

Emotionally, the film is revolutionary but intellectually, I don't know. I think that it's a film of some subtlety and ambiguity. I wouldn't have thought that, rationally, it seems as though Mick is going to win, since the forces of society are ranged against him at the end. At the time of the film's release, the impact of the student unrest in 1968 was such that the picture was greeted with enthusiasm by the young. In Britain, interestingly enough, it was forbidden to everyone under the age of 18, because it carried an 'X' certificate. But younger people somehow managed to get in to see it. There were some problems with the censor over nudity in the film and cuts were made in various parts of the world, but none of them were really serious, except in Greece, under the Colonels, where the entire last sequence was cut. Obviously that destroyed the film completely. It was shown in 1970 at a British Film Festival in Warsaw but Poland had a reactionary government – a reactionary Communist government, of course – so they didn't buy it, and it was a long time before it was shown there. I met some Poles who had seen it in illegal copies, and they were surprised to discover that the film was shot in colour as these copies had been made in black and white.

We were really enormously lucky in that the film was conceived and worked out before the student revolutions took place, so it came out providentially at just the right time. I think, above all, it is true to the educational experience and the youth experience of David Sherwin and myself; it never pretends to be a documentary about 1968. I remember my friend Louis Marcorelles, a very nice man and a highly respected French critic, coming to see a preview of the film with the documentary director Emile De Antonio. Afterwards I could tell it hadn't gone down very well with De Antonio, and Louis – who was very easily influenced, God bless him – said, 'What a pity you couldn't have real schoolboys and make it more like a documentary,' which was a total misunderstanding of the film.

If . . . . won the Palme d'Or at Cannes in the 1969 Festival, which was very pleasant, but a bit of a fluke, I think. The jury that year was headed by

Triumph: Lindsay displays the Palme D'Or, awarded to If . . . . *at the 1969 Cannes Film Festival, with actress Vanessa Redgrave.*

Luchino Visconti and he wanted the prize to go to *Z* – the film about the assassination of a Greek MP, made by Costa-Gavras. Then there was *Adelen 31*, a sort of socialist film about a strike made by Bo Wideberg. I don't think the jury members could make up their minds between those two films and somebody probably said, 'Why not give it to *If . . . .?*' and that's how we got it. The London Film Festival showed the film and it was nominated for a prize that was given at that time by the British Film Institute. But, just as the British were not interested in financing the film, they were not interested in acknowledging it. The Festival prize went to a film by Straub, *The Little Notebook of Anna Magdalena Bach*. Typical, really.

Notes For A Preface

Preface to the published script of *If . . . .* by Lindsay Anderson and David Sherwin, 1969

ALTHOUGH BOTH DAVID SHERWIN AND I WENT TO (DIFFERENT) ENGLISH PUBLIC Schools, *If . . . .* is not to be taken as an autobiographical film, at least not in a narrow or a literal sense. Of course, there are autobiographical elements in the script. For my part, I well remember Fryer, the tall, distinguished College prefect of Cheltondale in winter term 1936, standing at the door before house prayers and shouting at Hughes Hallett beside me: 'Hallett damn you, stop talking!' And the Reverend So-and-So certainly had those nasty habits of smacking you suddenly on the back of the head, and twist-

Rooftop rebels: Jean Vigo's Zéro de Conduite *inspired the structure of* If . . . ., *and the school dignitaries (top) found an earlier echo in* The White Bus. *But Lindsay's tribute to Vigo's joyous schoolboys (bottom) had a lethal edge.*

ing your nipples, if you were unfortunate enough to land in his Maths set.

But such facile tags as 'the Private Hell of the Public Schools' (*Sunday Graphic*) or 'Hatchet job on the Public School system' (*Sight and Sound*), are misleading. Essentially the Public School milieu of the film provides material for a metaphor. Even the coincidence of its making and release with the worldwide phenomenon of student revolt was fortuitous. The basic tensions, between hierarchy and anarchy, independence and tradition, liberty and law, are always with us. That is why we scrupulously avoided contemporary references (on a journalistic level) which would date the picture; and why it is completely unimportant whether its slang, its manners, or its details of organisation are true to the schools of this year or that. And this is why the film has been understood – recognised – by so many people, of so many ages, and so many countries.

We specially saw *Zéro de Conduite* again, before writing started, to give us courage. And we constantly thought of Brecht, and his definition of the 'epic' style. David referred to Kleist from time to time. John Ford ('old father, old artificer') and Humphrey Jennings (romantic-ironic conservative) were in the bloodstream.

I have been asked very often about the use of colour in the film – or rather the use of monochrome. When Shelagh Delaney and I were working on the script of *The White Bus*, which was also a poetic film, moving freely between naturalism and fantasy, I remember suggesting that it would be nice to have shots here and there, or short sequences, in colour (it was otherwise a black and white film). The idea also appealed to Miroslav Ondricek, and we did it. Almost no one has seen *The White Bus*, but I like the film very much, and I think the idea was successful.

It was this precedent that gave me the assurance – when Mirek said that with our budget (for lamps) and our schedule he could not guarantee consistency of colour for the chapel scenes in *If. . . .* – to say, 'Well, let's shoot them in black and white.' In other words it was not (of course) just a matter of saving time and/or money. The problem of the script seemed to be to arrive at a poetic conclusion, from a naturalistic start. (Like any fairy-story or folk-tale). We felt that variation in the visual surface of the film would help create the necessary atmosphere of poetic license, while preserving a 'straight', quite classic shooting style, without tricks or finger-pointing.

I also think that, in a film dedicated to 'understanding', the jog to consciousness provided by such colour change may well work a kind of healthy *Verfremdungseffect*, an incitement to *thought*, which was part of our aim.

And finally : Why not? Doesn't colour become more expressive, more remarked if drawn attention to in this way? The important thing to realise is that there is no symbolism involved in the choice of sequences filmed in black and white, nothing expressionist or schematic. Only such factors as intuition, pattern and convenience.

This script, as printed here, represents the definitive version of *If. . . .* Unfortunately there is no guarantee that readers will have seen or will be able to see exactly the film we made. It depends where you live. Various versions, differing in various ways from the original, are now circulating through the world. The cuts and modifications demanded by national censorships would indeed provide an interesting footnote to a social history of 1969. In Britain the Board of Film Censors broke precedent by permitting the glimpse of Mrs Kemp's pubic hair as she wanders naked down the

121

dormitory corridor; but as compensation they demanded the substitution at the start of the shower scene, of an alternative take in which the discreet use of towels prevented an equivalently frank look at the boys. Needless to say the film was forbidden to anyone under the age of sixteen.

The American Board of Censors also gave the film an 'X' certificate, but passed it unmutilated. The distributors, however, were not prepared to accept the X-rating outside New York, and cut the picture (again Mrs.Kemp and the showers) for an 'A' rating. Having read about this by chance in *Variety*, we insisted that alternative takes (the same shower scene and a shot of Mrs Kemp from the rear) be substituted.

Plainly, in this third quarter of the twentieth century since Christ, the naked figure is still the object of deepest alarm. Plainly, also, social reaction, puritanism and philistinism are closely linked. Australia cut the film even for its premiere performance at the Sydney festival and Italy refused to allow it to close the festival at Taormina. (The Italian ban was later rescinded as a result of vigorous protests by the Press.)

Eire was alarmed over various sexual references in the scene in Johnny's study; and South African citizens are not allowed to watch Wallace licking his pin-up, or to hear Mick dreaming of walking naked into the sea with her, making love once, and then dying.

The only instance of purely political censorship so far reported (apart from Portugal, where the film cannot be shown at all) seems to be from the Colonels' Athens, where, as far as we can make out, the film has been showing with its final sequence completely excised.

Many people contribute to the making of a film. Many of them get mentioned on no list of credits. For *If* . . . . I would like to record my thanks to Seth Holt who first introduced me to David Sherwin, John Howlett and *Crusaders*; to our patrons, Albert Finney of Memorial and Charles Bluhdorn of Paramount; to Marvin Birdt who stuck his neck out and recommended the script; to my friend Daphne Hunter who suggested the title; people like Peter King and Gerry Lewis and Mort Hoch, who committed themselves to the picture and helped us to get it on the screen; and, of course, David Ashcroft, Headmaster of Cheltenham College, whose liberal understanding and generous help in the creation of a work of art give the lie to facile criticisms of the system of education he believes in. *Floruit, Floret, Floreat!*

I remember also, most gratefully, Pat Moore, for his efficient and effective explosions; Peter Brayham for his fight choreography; Sergeant Instructor Rushforth for his beautiful performance on the bar, and Michael White and Malcolm Miles who helped us out so well on their motor-bikes on the Cheltenham-Tewkesbury road.

Essentially the heroes of *If* . . . . are, without knowing it, old-fashioned boys. They are not anti-heroes, or drop-outs, or Marxist-Leninists or Maoists or readers of Marcuse. Their revolt is inevitable, not because of what they *think*, but because of what they *are*. Mick plays a little at being an intellectual ('Violence and revolution are the only pure acts,' etc.), but when he acts it is instinctively, because of his outraged dignity, his frustrated passion, his vital energy, his sense of fair play if you like. If his story can be said to be 'about' anything, it is about freedom.

In this sense Mick and Johnny and Wallace, and Bobby Phillips and the Girl are traditionalists. It is they, not their conformist elders nor their conformist contemporaries who speak the tongue that Shakespeare spoke ('We must be free or die'). 'England Awake,' Johnny cries in the gym. And Mick : 'We are not cotton-spinners all: Some love

Top: crusaders Johnny (David Wood), Wallace (Richard Warwick) and Mick (Malcolm McDowell) before their rebellion in If .... *Above: Joined by the Girl (Christine Noonan) the Crusaders lead an armed revolt at the school speech day.*

England and her honour yet!' and Wallace, as he lunges, 'Death to tyrants!' They are very, I suppose fatally, romantic. Theirs is still: 'The homely beauty of the good old cause.' Far indeed from filling me with dread, I find the last sequence of the film exhilarating, funny (its violence is so plainly metaphorical), a bit shocking, magnificent (when the Headmaster is shot between the eyes), and finally sad. It doesn't look to me as though Mick can win. The world rallies as it always will, and brings its overwhelming fire-power to bear on the man who says 'No.'

Charge once more then, and be dumb;
Let the victors when they come,
When the Forts of Folly fall,
Find thy body by the wall!

In Celebration

Commentary, 1994

WHEN I WAS EDITING *IF* . . . . I WAS VISITED BY MY FRIEND BILL GASKILL, WHO
had taken over the Royal Court. He asked me if I would direct a play by
David Storey called *In Celebration*. I read the play and could immediately recognise in it David's characteristic writing and preoccupations; it was
very much based on his own family experiences. It seemed to me that the
play was like a novel in certain ways and in need of cutting, so I spoke to
David about this and he agreed to remove one element in the play. Even
then, I remained unsure but I agreed to direct it. Afterwards, of course, I
was very glad I did because it is a very, very good play and doing it was a
great experience for me.

Casting was very important, and I felt it required an authentic
Northern cast. In fact, the most vital thing is to have a good cast and, in
the end, I cast Bill Owen and Constance Chapman – neither of them
Northerners – as the parents in the play. It was the first time that Bill,

*Brian Cox and Alan Bates, as the brothers returning home to Yorkshire for
their parents' wedding anniversary, in Lindsay's production of* In Celebration
at the Royal Court.

who is a Londoner, had played a North Country role, and he has since had one of his greatest successes playing a Yorkshireman in the long-running television series *Last of the Summer Wine*. It was the first time I worked with Alan Bates, although I already knew him socially. He played Andrew, one of three brothers; the others were played by James Bolam, who is from the North-East, and Brian Cox, who is a Scot. Brian played Colin, the youngest brother and the role which corresponds most closely to David himself.

The play was very well received and ran longer than most at the Royal Court – although this was really an accident of scheduling. It ran for three months and that was the end of it. I was

David Storey's own artwork featured on the poster and programme cover for his play In Celebration *(1969) – the first of his stage works to be directed by Lindsay.*

particularly annoyed because there was a play by Arthur Miller, *The Price*, which ran in the West End for a long time, and I thought it characteristic that an English play would only run at the Court and not get a transfer while the Miller play ran for ages. I think that the English rather overestimate Arthur Miller.

O Lucky Man!

Commentary, 1994

I REMEMBER WHEN *O LUCKY MAN!* WAS FIRST SHOWN AT A MAGAZINE PRE-view somewhere in London. A young man, supposedly a critic sent along by *Vogue*, came up to me and said, 'Don't you think it's rather arrogant to expect us to sit through a film as long as this?' I can't remember what I said, but I restrained myself from kicking him. Of course, it isn't a short film and films have tended to get longer in recent years, but *O Lucky Man!* was conceived as an epic – not an epic in the sense of *Ben-Hur*, but in the classical, poetic sense of the term.

After the release of *If* . . . . I was not exactly besieged with offers to make another film, but Malcolm McDowell told me that he'd like us to make another film together. He said he had an idea for a film script based on his own experience. When he first left school, he got a job as sales rep-resentative for a coffee company, and he wanted to make this the basis of his script. I told him to get on with it and he started work. I noticed that it was coming along very slowly so I suggested to Malcolm that he ask David Sherwin to help him write it. David and Malcolm eventually showed me a script called *Coffee Man* which was a bit like an Ealing com-edy. I thought it was fine, but not very ambitious. Soon afterwards, Malcolm went off to make *A Clockwork Orange* for Kubrick and I found myself developing his script with David Sherwin.

Interestingly, Kubrick had been very influenced by *If* . . . . and, after the expense of *2001,* he wanted to show that he could make a film cheaply and quickly. He contacted Michael Medwin and asked if he could see the budget schedule and other relevant details on *If* . . . . , and Michael was delighted to get everything ready for him. Kubrick was invited up to the Memorial Films office to view all the material, but he insisted that it should be sent to his home, which it never was, so he didn't get to see our schedule. Malcolm told me that, after just one day's shooting on *Clockwork Orange*, both he and Kubrick realised that they couldn't pos-sibly make the film in six weeks as was planned. I think that at the end of that first day they had perhaps got one shot done, if that. The assistant director, a nice fellow called Derek Cracknell, managed to get himself fired after a day or two, but Malcolm had got to know him and liked him. He eventually became our assistant on *O Lucky Man!*

This was a time of great confidence and we were able to work on the script without reference to a studio or distributor. I think Malcolm and I put up some money for David Sherwin to live on while he was writing the script, and it was not until the script was finished that we attempted to raise the money to make the film. We knew that *Coffee Man* wouldn't do as the film's title. In developing the script, I had introduced the epic quality, the musical element and the important role that luck plays in life. So, one day, Malcolm came to me, very excitedly, and said, 'Your new film is going to be called *Lucky Man*.' I thought for a moment and then said, '*O Lucky Man!*'

At one point, while David Sherwin and I were working on the script, I said to David, 'Graham Crowden could play this part,' and David said, 'No he can't, we've already decided he was going to play another character.' I said, 'Well, he can play both parts.'

From that came the idea that many of the roles in the film could be played by the same actor. So an actor might play two, three or four parts. Wallas Eaton probably played five or six parts. Many of these 'doublings' were not even noticed by audiences. This use of the same actors throughout the film became part of the creative conception of the film, as did various themes such as Zen Buddhism, which is very strongly apparent at the end of the film in the scene between Malcolm and myself.

I played the part of the Film Director in that last sequence,

From top: Mick Travis – businessman. Malcolm McDowell with Warren Clarke as the chauffeur in O Lucky Man! *; Lindsay on set with Alan Price, whose music was intrinsic to the plot and structure; On the roof with Helen Mirren as Patricia, the businessman's daughter who seduces Mick.*

127

not because I think of myself as an actor but because it seemed somehow right that I should figure in it. *O Lucky Man!* is, in a sense, a film about how we should live. Mick starts out in the first half of the film in search of status, gain and profit and is sent to prison; then he tries to lead a Good Life and that is equally disastrous. The end is a sort of ironic evocation, I suppose, of the Zen attitude to living, which is to live life and accept it and to smile the right kind of smile but not to ask why. In that way, I suppose the film is open-ended. I do think it is important for a work of art to be open-ended so that an audience can make up its own mind, not going out feeling that its mind has been made up for it. As one gets older one probably becomes less radical, I'm not sure, but I have never been a socialist; I've never understood how people think that socialism could work because I have always believed in original sin.

Alan Price was an obvious choice for the film's music. He had composed and played music for some of my theatrical productions, so we knew each other very well. He had begun performing frequently with his friend Georgie Fame, and I thought it might be interesting to make a documentary about them. In the end, I began to doubt that anyone would finance such a film, but the idea of Alan as a composer and leader of a small group inserted itself into the conception of *O Lucky Man!* So Alan became a character in the film, as well as the composer of the film's score, and his presence radically affected the development of the script. In a way, Alan's presence in the film might be related to the way Brecht used music in his plays.

In a way, too, the film is best summed up by Alan's music and his song 'Changes'. I really believe that Alan did a wonderful job. Many of the ideas, and the whole idea at the end, came from Alan's music. I don't know anybody else who could have written it – John Lennon perhaps, but Lennon was, in a way, more bitter and more sentimental. Alan's music has the right combination of irony and lyricism that the film demanded. The music is totally organic to the film and the ending, with the singing of 'Round and round/and round and round we go/Round the world in circles turning/earning what we can/while others dance away' becoming a central motif.

Stripping the Veils Away

The Times, 21 April 1973

DAVID ROBINSON: THE ORIGINAL STORY OF *O LUCKY MAN!* IS BY MALCOLM McDowell, who's also the leading actor . . .
Anderson: Yes, after we'd finished *If* . . . . he didn't get very much work – he'd lost his television contacts, and the film had not yet made an impact – so he started to work on this idea, which he had even before *If* . . . . when he was acting at Stratford. The story was based on his early adventures as a coffee salesman. The first 15 or 20 pages seemed to me quite lively, but it was not making very quick progress, so I suggested he get together with David Sherwin. It's easier if you have a writer to work with, and we'd all collaborated happily already.

After a time he and David brought me what they'd done, and I was sufficiently interested to be stimulated. I felt the whole approach sympathetic and that inside it was the potential of something of more weight and resonance than a genre comedy – which is what they were writing and which is now, I suppose, the first 20 or 30 minutes of our film.

As it now stands, the form of the film is a very traditional one – the epic and moral form which you can trace from Shakespeare, from *Pilgrim's Progress*, from *Gulliver's Travels*, from *Tom Jones*; with the hero journeying through a lot of adventures and encountering a lot of characters – 'humours' if you like. It's a form which hasn't been attempted very much recently – middle-class artists lack the confidence for it.
Robinson: The musical element is very important and very integral to the form, of course. How, technically, were the songs integrated so exactly?
Anderson: Well, that is a tribute to Alan Price's intuition as well as the care we took in preparing the whole thing. The place of each song was specified in the script – sometimes in a Brechtian way, as 'Song of . . . ' Then I wrote a paragraph of what I thought the song should be about.

Alan then took this and interpreted or readjusted the idea to the song in terms of his feelings and attitudes – which were sufficiently different from mine to be creative, and sufficiently the same for it to work.
Robinson: Alan Price provides the Chorus; but at the same time he's a very positive presence in the film – sometimes even appearing as a parallel and complementary character of the hero, Mick.
Anderson: That aspect of the film grew quite instinctively and not by design. It's true that because the songs are a Chorus and express the ironic attitude of the film quite directly, the persona which Alan presents takes on an air of *knowledgeableness*. And also because he obviously stands

'Brothers!' Mick's hapless exhortation of the tramps was lifted from Maxim Gorki's play, The Lower Depths.

apart from the action – even in the little bit of the story that he's involved in the character still stands apart – he remains slightly enigmatic. You feel perhaps that he has attained that attitude to life that it takes the hero, Mick, the whole story to get to. Mick encounters him about half-way in his progress through illusion; and it is an encounter that perhaps gives you some foretaste of the position Mick is going to arrive at after many trials and tribulations. There's this funny double thing, that he doesn't play a real function as a character apart from his function as a Chorus; and yet you feel the character there.

I think interestingly that the character of Alan in the film is as near as the film gets to any kind of sentimentalism, because it's the nearest it gets to a straight portrayal of wisdom – not wisdom, exactly, but a portrayal of somebody who knows what life is about. Perhaps it reflects a little of my feeling of the instinctive realism of what the Americans would call 'The People' – in the sense you get at the end of *The Grapes of Wrath*. In this country we're rather shy of making such affirmations, and we're also rather classbound. But in a sense it is a statement, a very oblique statement or suggestion about our class situation.

Robinson: The central character, Mick, has come on from *If . . . .* some of

130

the audience will already know him.

Anderson: Well he has and he hasn't. Of course we have called him Mick Travis, because to all of us in some way, naturally, *If . . . .* was a shared experience that we look back on with pleasure. But Mick in this film is not by any means the Mick Travis of *If . . . .* I don't think that *that* Mick Travis would ever have cared if he was going to earn £12, £25, or £100 a week, or not for long. He wouldn't base his life on the idea of success. But Mick at the beginning of *O Lucky Man!* is a young man who is thinking in naive, energetic and quite likeable terms of succeeding. And indeed that carries him through the whole long first section of the story. At the end, where he's come a cropper, he says to the judge: 'I did my best to be successful.' And the judge says: '*And you failed.*' Really, in a way Mick is sent to prison for failing.

I do think, too, it's quite a different performance. For me the extraordinary quality of Malcolm McDowell's performance in this film is to ring so many changes on innocence. And to keep a character who is most of the time reacting, continuously dynamic and interesting.

Robinson: So one must not think of it as the Out in the World to *If . . . .* ?

Anderson: No. There are of course allusions and references to *If . . . .* but your understanding and enjoyment is not in any way affected by not knowing the other film. For people who know it, you just provide an additional stimulus and point of reference. In the interrogation the first interrogator says to him, 'Was your headmaster correct to expel you from school?' and of course if you've seen *If . . . .* that's a comic idea, because we imagine that we have seen him, or another Mick Travis – perhaps his cousin, I'm not sure – shoot his headmaster through the forehead at the end of the film, so the idea that the headmaster subsequently expelled him . . . !

The end of *If . . . .* is romantic, because for me it has the feeling of the romantic hero at bay. If you really look at the last scene of *If . . . .* you can't really think that Mick is triumphant. *O Lucky Man!* is not a romantic film. It does have sentiment, and I think it does have poetry. But I don't think it is romantic. Perhaps I have finally purged myself of romanticism, which is sad in a way, because romanticism can be very sweet.

If . . . . is a realistic film though, and I think that this is a realistic film. According to the definition that was so well provided by Brecht: 'Realism is not a matter of showing real things, but of showing how things really are.'

Robinson: How do you see the acting style in terms of this realism?

Anderson: I've aimed at a realistic style of acting as opposed to a naturalistic style, which is more what is commonly thought of as film acting. I think that in their own convention the people in this film are very real – very eccentric and very extreme, but I hope they carry total conviction. It is a very particular style. Because you can never afford to fall into naturalism. It must always be *natural* but not *naturalistic*. Just as the style of the film has to be a compressed one, has to be a tense and worked style, so the acting can never be just behaviour.

I think this presented the biggest challenge to Malcolm, because everyone else was playing not caricatures but sharply defined characters, almost, as I've said, 'humours'. He was playing someone that was the centre of the film, and yet with whom the audience must be able to identify, so that he could not be bizarre or caricatured at all. And yet it was obvious that he could never afford to fall back on mere behaviour. When he did, it never rang true, and we had to stop and start again. He had in a way to wind himself up. It's the kind of part which has to create its own dynamic, because it doesn't come from anything else. In that way it is a very stylish performance, though with the kind of style that hardly shows, unless you are conscious of what to look for.

Robinson: I suppose the acting style is initially formed in the way the script is written.

Anderson: Yes: because the writing is also extremely spare – the kind of writing where every line is charged. In the same way the characters have to present themselves completely the moment they appear. There's no time to explore or reveal layers in the psychological sense. That calls for a very special kind of acting. And maybe the theatrical experience of most of the cast is valuable in that respect.

Robinson: It is, overall, a style that relates distinctly to *If . . . .* and *The White Bus*; but I can't relate it directly to anything you've done on the stage – unless we go back to *Serjeant Musgrave's Dance* – or *The Lillywhite Boys* perhaps.

Anderson: It's quite true, and one of the very strange things I find that's happened to me in the last five years. The plays that I've done have become more and more naturalistic, in a very refined way, I think – because the naturalism of *The Changing Room* is a very refined and poetic naturalism – whereas the films, leading up to *O Lucky Man!*, have become much less like what people expect to get from cinema.

I don't quite know how this has happened. Except that naturalism in the cinema seems somehow to be too small and overexplored and in the end not eloquent enough to make the kind of comment that makes it worth making a film. I've never felt that it was enough to put on the screen just behaviour, or things that approximate to journalism. In a way it's too easy; and it's all been done. Whereas the challenge of the cinema is to use this fantastic medium to go beyond the easy naturalism and get back to the expressiveness and variety and the sense of style that there was in the silent cinema, and to use the additional things offered by sound and colour to strengthen that eloquence, rather than just make the whole thing more naturalistic.

Robinson: You've chosen, of course, to work in a comic idiom; and you've used actors like Arthur Lowe and Dandy Nichols who often work in the most popular areas of comedy.

Anderson: Yes. I think the popular tradition of comedy is tremendously strong and tremendously good. The kind of thing you get from *Till Death Us Do Part* and *Dad's Army*, at its best, is really much better than most of what is being given to us by the serious and experimental theatre. I think we should draw on these strengths and these traditions to make things that are entertaining to everybody and acceptable to everybody, and at the same time can reflect some of the important and stirring elements in being alive at the moment.

In saying that it isn't enough just to be journalistic and naturalistic – for instance to make a film about conditions or about people being poor in the serious, sentimental way which would perhaps have been acceptable 20 years ago – I think that now we're so deluged by information and preaching by the media on these subjects that everybody's sick to death of them. There's such a multitude of horrors that the only possible way to make a comment is through laughter and comedy. I don't think that we can make serious films about the hydrogen bomb any more. *Dr Strangelove* started as a serious film, and

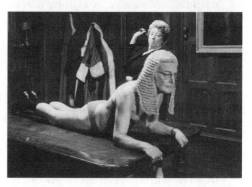

From top: Miroslav Ondricek (second left) with Lindsay and (far left) actor/producer Michael Medwin on the set of O Lucky Man!; *Arthur Lowe appears as the Zingaran President, Dr Munda, with his 'home secretary' Madame Paillard (Rachel Roberts); having allowed the jury at Mick's trial to retire, the Judge (Anthony Nicholls) submits to a beating from the Lady Usher (Mona Washbourne).*

133

Kubrick found it turned itself into a comedy. The follies you read about every day when you open the paper are so absurd that the only way to comment on them is through laughing at them, because if you try to be serious about them, they dwarf you.

When you start a film like *O Lucky Man!* and when you work on the script, the events in it seem rather extraordinary and preposterous. You ask yourself if you will get away with it, because the journey of the hero is so packed with bizarre and outrageous incidents. But of course as you make it and finish it, you look around, you open your morning paper or watch television and you find that, in fact, the events which are reported quite seriously are even more fantastic and more outrageous than anything you have in the film.

So that now I know that if by some frightful mischance we had to go back and remake the picture because Denham Laboratories blew up, we couldn't just remake that same script.

Though I suppose the truth is that art doesn't quite work like that; and when you isolate something, and put it on the screen, it always seems more shocking than when you read about it in the newspaper, simply because you isolate it and force people to look at it. Whereas normally we stumble through life so bemused and so assaulted by the barrage of news, the barrage of hideous events, that veils drop mercifully between us and reality. One of the functions and privileges (I suppose) of the artist is to strip the veils away. And if he can do it without being too self-righteous and without being too depressing and morbid; and if he can do it with healthy laughter, so much the better.

Robinson: Do you remember an idea you had over fifteen years ago of doing a film called *News of the World*, in which you would have restaged some of the bizarre events from the Sunday paper crime reports?

Anderson: I'd forgotten about that. That's the obsession, you see, that's finally come out in this film. *O Lucky Man!* is that film, in a way, transmuted to a different key. I can see looking back that it corresponds to a kind of obsession of an analysing and synthesising temperament – boring words I'm using. It corresponds to the kind of fascination of a film-maker like Humphrey Jennings, who in his best work is concerned with building the pattern out of the fragments. I think that the obsession with trying to find the unity out of the endless variety of life is part of the idea of this film.

Inevitably I expect my progressive friends to attack me. I was attacked – what, seven years ago – for 'ceasing to lead the movement'. In the first part of the film you have the orthodox attack on institutions, on capitalism, on power, with which I totally agree. But when our hero adopts the philosophy of humanism, you see that in fact that attachment is also revealed in our story as being an illusion. Really the Salvation Army man in the film is quite right, when he sees The Old Adam in Malcolm's humanism.

The poor people are just as beastly to their fellow men as the rich people. And I don't think the tone of the film is such to say that they're beastly to them only because they're poor. They're beastly to them because they're human beings. When Mick is thrown over the edge of a dump by the down-and-outs he's tried to help, and looks up and sees them all there, it's just man's inhumanity to man, isn't it? I think that's something that the socialist will regard as extremely reactionary.

It's not a coincidence that he walks in front of a fence on which is written 'REVOLUTION IS THE OPIUM OF THE INTELLECTUALS'. What I like about the film is that it has that irony. It hasn't just got the simple irony of being nasty about rich people. It's nasty about poor people as well. It's nasty about people. And it's really much wiser to be nasty about people because sometimes there are nice people and that's a pleasant surprise. But it's much better to be prepared. Don't you think?

But let me ask you a question. How do you interpret the final climactic scene of the film between Mick and myself, playing the director?

Robinson: When Mick, having gone through all his adventures and misadventures, goes for an audition? You tell him to smile; he says he cannot smile without a reason, and when he persists you take the script and hit him over the head whereupon he does break into a wide, joyful smile. I think I didn't interpret it. I just saw it as Mick coming through all the fires and finding that life still demands.

Anderson: I don't think you can say, 'I don't feel anything,' or 'I don't feel the need to interpret.' You're not being a critic. You have to tell yourself something, come to terms with that moment. Do you, for instance, see it as obedience on his part? It could be interpreted like this; and there are people, it seems, who interpret it as his obediently giving the smile that gets the part and my being just another of the disasters of life. Now this is not in any way my feeling.

It's not at all about a young actor who's going to get a part. It's about life. Actually this is the paradox that people find difficult to accept: that he is hit over the head and experiences, in traditional Zen terms, his moment of illumination. And he doesn't look at us – into the camera – and see clearly, in obedience to the fact that he has been hit on the head and told to, but because that moment suddenly brought to him the awareness of the correct way of relating to his experience, to everything that has happened to him and will happen to him. Well, that's if you want to give that type of interpretation. I hesitate to, because I want people to make their own.

There is, of course, an interesting pointer, way back in the film, when he has set out on his first job of selling coffee, and we hear over his car radio this little talk about Zen and about living in the moment and about how illumination may come suddenly.

Robinson: I failed to make that connection.

Anderson: Well you've only seen the film twice.

Robinson: A lot of people will only see it once, and are likely to miss the point like me . . .

Anderson: All right. They can read it any way they like. I'm just telling you how I see it, and your answer is not 'How interesting!' but 'A lot of people won't see that.' What do you expect me to say to that?

Robinson: I'm saying it because I, seeing this film, failed to make the relation I should have made.

Anderson: Well you're lazy. You've just stepped over that bit, without bothering to work it out. That's not good enough in your job, which is to help people see a film in the right perspective, not just sit back and tell me that they're not going to understand it. That's fair, actually, you know. That's what gives the critic his dignity, as an interpreter.

In fact, of course, the film is conceived on an epic scale, and the working is very close. I hope that every foot is packed, is tense. There is not a moment of the film that isn't very carefully considered, that doesn't put things under a very intense microscope. I know that I'm not capable of the large, relaxed gesture.

But in fact when you say people won't see this or won't see that, I don't actually mind. Because the film is full of a number of things. It is entertaining, it's got lovely music, it's got a lot of jokes and it's got a lot of adventures. And I'm very happy for people to take what they will from it. If you ask me what there is in it to be taken, I will tell you. It may be that other people will take different things. Perhaps they'll just have a good time. That doesn't matter. That's good. You can't engage your audience purely intellectually because that's not what they're there for. They're there to feel, to laugh and to enjoy themselves.

The Old Crowd

Introduction to the published script of the play, in *The Writer in Disguise* by Alan Bennett, 1985.

THE ENGLISH ARE PROUD OF THEIR SENSE OF HUMOUR: IT IS WHAT DISTIN-guishes them from foreigners. And the mark of a sense of humour, we all know, is the ability to laugh at oneself. The English like to think they like to laugh at themselves. This may have been true once, when there was no apprehension that the Sun might one day Set. But it is not true today.

This is one truth I have learned from the experience of *The Old Crowd*. Another, less disputable, is that television is the most conformist of the media, a powerful and pernicious stifler of originality, a bastion of the sta-tus quo. I am not thinking in strictly 'social' terms: another connection which *The Old Crowd* made clear was that between social and artistic con-formism. The almost universally apoplectic reception it received from the television critics – it was significant that the only one who understood and appreciated it was American – reminds us that the press, whether profess-edly Left or Right, is essentially an establishment body. The highest ambi-tion of a *Time Out* writer in the 1980s will be to get regular employment on *The Sunday Times* or *The Observer*. Protest is a commodity. The good ship Britannia is waterlogged in a shark-infested sea. Don't rock the boat!

Another national characteristic: the Anglo-Saxons do not favour art that claims relevance to *actuality*. By which I mean relevance to the con-temporary social or political situation, whether at home or out in the world. This explains the fashionable predilection for the plays of Harold Pinter or Tom Stoppard (two authors who flatter their audiences without disturbing them), for the non-disruptive humour of *Monty Python* or *Not the Nine O'Clock News* (facetiousness masquerading as satire), for the novels of Anthony Powell or Martin Amis, the television plays of Dennis Potter. The English conception of 'committed' art is naif, essentially because the English intellectuals shrink from the abrasion of reality. They claim to find significance 'boring' in order to disguise their fear of ideas.

These, as I say, are some ideas brought home to me by the experience of *The Old Crowd* – such a rich experience, even though it was a mere TV play, written and made with a great deal of thought, fun and care. Shown once and savaged by the press with a humourless hostility as astonishing as it was suggestive. How on earth did it come to be made at all?

The responsibility must be shouldered first by Stephen Frears; and I shall always be grateful to him for it. Stephen had already directed, with great success, a number of plays written for television by Alan Bennett.

137

The Old Crowd: *cast members Peter Bennett, Jill Bennett and Isabel Dean in rehearsal with Lindsay for his Bunuelian vision of an Alan Bennett script.*

When London Weekend Television invited him to make another series of six, he decided that he would only direct some of them himself. The rest he would produce. He paid me the compliment of inviting me to take one on, and sent me three scripts to choose from. I had always admired Alan's writing, for its rare combination of wit and feeling, the way it so precisely catches the poignancy as well as the comedy of existence, which we habitually express in the banal or grotesque clichés of everyday conversation. Also, sometimes hidden beneath the surface triviality of his style, I sense strong currents of sadness and disturbance.

I liked one of these plays particularly. It happened to be the one furthest from completion. It presented the situation of a moneyed, middle-aged couple who had moved into a London house and were giving a house-warming party for a group of their oldest and best friends. Their only problem was the loss of their furniture, misrouted on the road from Horsham and ending up in remote Carlisle. They decided to hold their party all the same, with dinner provided by caterers and served by two ambiguous waiters, who may (or may not) be out-of-work actors, As far as I remember, the piece did not have a clearly defined ending. It was called *The Old Crowd*.

This script appealed to me because it was bizarre as well as comic. Its situation struck me as more poetic than anecdotal, very apt to imagine certain obsessive aspects of contemporary English life: strain, menace, disintegration. And it was unfinished, which meant that there was still room in it for a director to make a creative contribution. All the same, I found that I did not call Stephen back or take the matter further. Partly this was due to an instinctive reluctance (not in the end unjustified) to enter the alien and wasteful world of television in which one may labour long over a work that will only ever be shown once. Partly it was sheer laziness, a weariness at the thought of starting once again the long travail, the inevitable frictions and painful expense of spirit which is inseparable from any creative, collaborative undertaking. But mostly I drew back because I knew that television was traditionally and emphatically a writer's rather than a director's medium. This was a series of 'Six Plays by Alan Bennett': the directors would be required simply to stage them. My formation in cinema would, I knew, impel me in quite another direction. The stage belongs to the writers and actors: I have never cared for 'Director's Theatre'. But the cinema at its best and purest belongs to the director. Television drama is a bastard form. I could only approach it as I would approach the making of a film – personally and subjectively. And that, I felt, might well (and reasonably) be unacceptable. This was essentially why I did not call Stephen back.

He, thank goodness, called me. I told him I liked *The Old Crowd*, and that if it was a film I was being asked to undertake, I would certainly have enjoyed working on it with the author. But a collaboration for television would only work if that was truly what our relationship could be – as long, in other words, as we could both feel we were making something we could both sign. I didn't want to start anything I felt might not be harmoniously finished. And such harmony is rare.

Stephen understood what I was talking about: directors usually make the most understanding producers. He said he would talk to Alan Bennett. The next day he reported that there was no problem: Alan would be happy to collaborate. So he came round and we started work.

As is the case with every successful collaboration, it would be impossible to separate contributions: at least I could not. Alan's original script provided, of course, the starting point and the basis, the characters and the dialogue. I must take responsibility for the disruptive elements that eventually made our work so resented. I felt that I had never seen anything in television drama quite so exciting, quite so amusing or *real* as those occasional glimpses of sound equipment, even of whole camera crews which would suddenly flash before one's eyes when television plays had to be recorded 'live'. Without quite knowing why, I suggested that we incorporate a series of such glimpses as a developing theme. The idea intrigued

Alan and he agreed. Hence the repeated appearances of the camera and crew, observing the dramatic action with detached concentration, extending even to a shot in the gallery with multiple images on the monitors and Stephen Frears in the role of the director, picking his shots while The Old Crowd line up to sing 'Goodnight Ladies'.

('Alienation' is the Brechtian term – a translation of his *Verfremdungseffekt* – usually applied to such a style, but I have always thought this a heavy word and not a very accurate one. The real purpose of such devices, which can include songs, titles between scenes, etc., is not to *alienate* the audience from the drama, but rather to focus their attention on its essential – not its superficial or naturalistic – import. Of course this is almost impossible to achieve with an audience either too unsophisticated to understand the language of art, or too wedded to the aesthetic and social status quo to accept anything that hints at the subversive. For some reason, Anglo-Saxons cannot bear the idea of being taught anything: teaching implies learning, which implies development, change, growing-up. Hence their violent resistance to Brecht, whom Bernard Levin once credited with the intelligence of a six-year-old child – until his work could be safely enshrined as an elaborate but meaningless art object at the National Theatre.)

Probably the most anarchic ideas in *The Old Crowd* were mine – the homage to Buñuel under the dinner table – the sexual savagery behind the TV set . . . but I never felt these developments were inorganic to Alan's original conception, and nor did he. Anyway, the script as he had originally imagined it always seemed to me to carry mysterious suggestions of catastrophe and threat. Our work merely continued along these lines. We had some arguments, of course, as good collaborators must. I would object to some of the jokes with which Alan, being so good at them, would compulsively pepper his dialogue. And he would check me when my inventions became indulgent. He wanted the Lady Entertainer to sing 'Pedro the Fisherman', which I thought too jokey: we settled on 'Because' and 'We'll Gather Lilacs'. I wanted The Old Crowd to sing 'My Old Kentucky Home'; Alan disliked the Fordian echo and specified 'Goodnight Ladies', which was, of course, the perfect choice. Fortunately both Alan and Stephen were so highly regarded by London Weekend that we were able to develop our script with complete imaginative freedom. Which is the only enjoyable way to work.

I would think that the 'cinematic' as opposed to the 'TV-literary' style of *The Old Crowd* would make it difficult to read. Many sequences are not dialogued at all, depending entirely on the expressiveness of the action and the performers. We were tremendously lucky in our cast. Diana Parry, the very experienced and long-suffering Casting Director at London

Weekend, clearly thought my prejudices were as unreasonable as my ambitions were high, but by great good fortune many friends and colleagues with whom I had worked before in film and theatre were free and even eager to take part. My preference for working with actors with whom I have already collaborated happily and successfully always seems to astonish journalists. I find this strange. There is certainly nothing new about it either in theatre or in film tradition. The players in *The Old Crowd* mostly know each other and knew me from films like *This Sporting Life*, *If . . . .* and *O Lucky Man!* (Rachel Roberts, Peter Jeffrey, Philip Stone), as well as from the Royal Court in the great old days and, more recently, from the Lyric Theatre Company (Jill Bennett, Frank Grimes, Valentine Dyall, Jane Ottaway). I'd known Peter Bennett ever since I'd directed him as one of the Merry Men in the classic TV *Robin Hood* series; and I had known Isabel Dean so long as a friend that it felt as though we had worked together. So The Old Crowd were not strangers to me or to each other, and this helped a lot. Elspeth March as the magnificent Totty, Cathleen Nesbitt (repeatedly insisting that she had no idea what was going on, which no doubt helped her to perform with such contained acerbity), Adèle Leigh as the sweet-voiced Lady Entertainer, and David King as her accompanist – all these were cast in the usual way, from memory, suggestion and inspiration. Jenny Quayle and Martyn Jacobs, the 'Children', were chosen from the many talented young people whom Diana Parry produced from her long lists. Like latecomers to a party, they at first found the convivial, allusive atmosphere strange; but after three weeks' rehearsal they were one of a seamless company.

I have emphasised the closeness and the particularity of the players in *The Old Crowd*, because I think the importance of the 'chemistry' of a well-chosen cast often passes unremarked, even unperceived by critics and public alike. So how much more by the reader of a script. It is the actors, after all, who give the human feature and personality to the *idea* of the character which is all that the writer can provide. You can tell a director's personality by the actors he likes to work with – or by whether he likes to work with actors at all. (Many don't; as many don't too much care whom.) It is a human choice, not just a question of ability, nor just a question of physical rightness. What does he see in her? What does she see in him? These questions can never be answered. But they are all-important.

Nor will readers of *The Old Crowd* be able to hear the witty and emotive music written for it by George Fenton; and how can the arrival of Totty resonate fully without the broad Elgarian theme which elevates her to mythical status? They will not see the spacious and atmospheric decor provided by Jim Weatherup, nor the images lit and composed by John Fyfe and his cameramen. The script really is a blueprint, and less easy to visualise, even to the expert, than the plans for a house, an aeroplane or a food-mixer.

I used to think that I was a reasonably fast, at any rate not a wastefully slow worker; but shooting *The Old Crowd* took much longer than I anticipated, the result, unarguably, of my way of working: it certainly was not due in any way to the technicians of London Weekend. The crew operated, in fact, with extraordinary commitment – somewhat mystified, but intrigued, amused and buoyed up by a feeling that they were taking part in something extraordinary. To some extent, I'm sure, this was because I spent most of my time on the floor (cinema-style) in contact with actors and technicians, while Stephen Frears was in the control room, calling the shots. The chilling effect of reducing the director during shooting to a depersonalised voice, usually communicating with his actors only through the ear-phoned floor manager, is something I dislike intensely. And I have no doubt that the sense of communal enterprise that resulted from having the director on the floor was largely responsible for the technicians' readiness to extend our last day's shooting to four o'clock in the morning. And the actors too. Expensive, of course.

The Old Crowd took a long time to edit. There were two reasons for this. First, a strike of Production Secretaries (I think) meant that nothing we shot could be 'time coded'. In other words, no shots could be numbered or catalogued for identification. This naturally slowed the process; but at least I could take the tapes home with me and play them until I was familiar with the coverage and variations between takes. We spent some days in Wardour Street doing 'off-line' editing. Where or how this term originates I could never discover: it meant doing a preliminary edit from a transfer of the material before making a final cut version from the original tapes. (Of course you do not 'cut' tape as you do film. You transfer the exact section you want from any shot to a 'master' tape, and so build up, shot by shot, your edited version. It is not easy to explain.) For some reason, also connected with the union, this process had to be kept secret. So when we finally came to edit the final version from the original tapes at London Weekend, my first edit had to be kept on a video machine in an office some distance away from the editing suite. Whenever I needed to refer to it, I had to run down the passage, hurriedly check the off-line version and then run back. Andrew Vere, who did the original cut with me, had to receive a credit as 'Special Assistant to the Director'. Anything more accurate, I was told, would have precipitated another strike.

This whole process took nearly a year. Not of continuous work, of course. The London Weekend editors were busy on weekly sit-coms, the Sports Reports and Current Affairs. It was not until a show date was set that I was given enough continuous time to finish the work in a few concentrated days. The technological potential of video is probably limitless;

The Old Crowd: *Two actors from Lindsay's 'stock company' who were also among his closest friends, Frank Grimes and Jill Bennett.*

but the elaboration of equipment and the expense of using it impose huge limitations. And I shall always prefer a medium whose material I can touch, inspect against the light, run through my hand.

I was in Sri Lanka when *The Old Crowd* was shown on ITV, nearly a year after we had shot it. I was returning from a theatrical production in Australia with Rachel Roberts, and had mistaken the day of the Singapore Airlines departure for London. When I returned to my hosts, they showed me a clipping from *The Observer* which their friend Arthur C. Clarke, the famous science fiction writer, had sent over to them. It was a review of *The Old Crowd*, as scathing as it was shallow, by their popular television critic Clive James. Its tone did not surprise me. On the cutting Arthur Clarke had written 'Poor Lindsay!' Why doesn't he write 'Poor Clive James!' I wondered.

I really was not surprised. Indeed Alan Bennett recalls that I had warned him that we'd be told that I had ruined his work, and this certainly came true. But it would have been hard to anticipate the barrage of outrage that rained down on *The Old Crowd*, reminiscent of famous philistine explosions of long ago, hardly to be expected in this age of enlightenment. Indeed, speaking personally, the reception of this piece signalled the end of the acceptance which had seemed to make the sixties and early seventies at least a time of promise. The mood had changed: geniality and intelligence were out: the cat calls came as from a single voice. 'Rubbish!' (*Sunday Telegraph*). 'Tosh' (*Observer*). Meaningless' (*Sunday Express*). 'Inexplicable' (*Daily Telegraph*). 'Nonsensical farrago' (*Spectator*). 'Raucous travesty' (*New Statesman*). *The Guardian*, the self-proclaiming defender of cultural as well as political liberality, seemed particularly incensed. Their television critic had remained comparatively calm, noting only that the piece 'wasn't funny' and mourning that Alan Bennett's absolutely unique 'talent' had been 'crowded out'. But *The Guardian*'s literary editor, Richard Gott, was so infuriated – perhaps particularly because a few days earlier his paper had devoted a whole page to a friendly account by Tom Sutcliffe of the shooting of *The Old Crowd* – that he wrote a special article, putting his feelings on record. 'Miserably slender . . . insufferably pretentious . . . drivel . . . what does it all mean?' Gott's 'towering rage' (his phrase) provoked a series of letters on *The Guardian*'s correspondence page which mostly echoed his indignation – 'Surely an hour-long TV programme costing £250,000 cannot help in these days of pay restraint!' (K. A. Spencer, Hull) – and culminated in finely rhetorical protests from Lady Gaitskell ('Disgraceful expense . . . an intellectual and artistic "confidence trick" . . . laced with snippets of sly, obscure pornography') and the veteran documentary director and film historian Paul Rotha ('A pretentious load of old cabbage').

Much of the criticism of *The Old Crowd* was interesting for the way it exemplified that old, unchanging philistinism which is insulted by any suggestion that an original work may deserve or require effort for appreciation, and which almost congratulates itself on its cultural ignorance. Two critics in the 'quality press' imagined that the piece was derived from or influenced by Pinter: 'just a protracted send-up of the works of Harold Pinter' (*Sunday Telegraph*), 'full-length parody of a Harold Pinter play' (*Spectator*). The *Daily Express*, on the other hand, thought it was done 'in the manner of the French cinema'. *Time Out* found it 'a mosaic of concerns rooted in Brecht's dramatic theory' (and failing because it was not Marxist). The *Evening News* described it as 'a piece of surrealism'. Richard Gott quoted a friend who thought that Frank Grimes 'biting' Jill Bennett's toe was 'just silly', and the *Evening News* critic asked, 'What was the point of that disreputable and surly waiter getting under the table and cutting off the toes of Jill Bennett's stockings *without her objecting*?' (my italics). Really there are still a surprising number of clean-limbed English gentlemen around, who cannot tell a suck from a bite – and are charmingly perplexed when confronted by the perverse pleasures of Rough Trade.

Behind, or beneath, this dismissive indignation, there certainly smouldered something much more interesting. A sense of affront and a defensiveness only intermittently acknowledged. *The Guardian*'s literary editor (who probably thinks of himself as an anti-establishment man) had to rationalise his bourgeois resentment with a disingenuousness typically 'liberal'. 'Perhaps it was about the emptiness that lies at the heart of bourgeois society – in itself an excellent *though threadbare* theme.' My italics again: for a theme cannot be 'threadbare' and 'excellent' at the same time. And a *Guardian* writer who thinks that 'bourgeois emptiness' is neither a valid nor a present subject must be capable of self-deception indeed. Elsewhere Gott fell back on the reactions of anonymous colleagues – 'Alan Bennett's observation of middle-class manners and speech really isn't that accurate' and 'poking fun at the middle classes is not enough any more.' Others were more honest. In the *Daily Express* James Murray protested at 'the brutal pillory of a class the audience were invited to despise'. *The Sunday Telegraph's* commentator on economic affairs took up the cause of the 'long-suffering middle classes' and justified the status quo by quoting a new Nuffield study ('published in last week's *New Society*') which discredited the idea of a 'crumbling middle class'. *The Observer* critic managed another facing-both-ways jeer at Anderson's presumed conviction that 'Bourgeois Society is crumbling'. The determination to discredit a subversive voice was unmistakable. It was certainly significant, as I have said, that the only intelligent, restrained response to *The Old Crowd* came from the American writer Herbert Kretzmer, at that time reviewing TV for the *Daily Mail*. 'An unsettling production,' he called it, 'which said more about the state of Britain than a dozen hectoring *Panorama*s' and which 'reflected with superb skill and timing, our current mood of impotent rage and resigned despair . . . none of us, in other words, can look forward to relief and respite.' Precisely (and regrettably) so.

'These days you're on your own,' says Rufus grimly to George and Betty and Pauline: 'Wartime.' It does not seem such an extravagant comment on Britain in the eighties, where seven hundred 'pickets' mass daily against policemen with truncheons and riot shields to prevent one man going to work – emotion on both sides inflamed by omnipresent television cameras . . . In which the robbing, battering and raping of old ladies as they totter home through inner city streets, their pensions in their purses, has become commonplace . . . In which masked sexual criminals terrorise whole counties . . . In which ambulances fail to arrive, trains fail to run, 'essential services' prove a luxury. Our Old Crowd are keeping their eyes closed and their little flags flying in a country which presents a reality no more distorted than a cartoon by Rowlandson, a horror comic by Kafka, a satirical extravaganza by Buñuel. (I am talking of genre, of course, not of achievement.) Resolute, however, remains the resolution not to see, *not* to acknowledge, *not* to act. I am reminded of a notice some ten years ago of O *Lucky Man!* in the intellectual review *Encounter*, in which an academic from Oxford, John Weightman, dismissed the film because an England in which nuclear power stations exploded, policemen were corrupt and an industrial giant was shown to be in profitable league with a reactionary African government 'doesn't seem to be in England at all'. ('It hasn't settled for a coherent stylisation . . . uninterestingly cynical.') Truly there are none so blind as those who choose not to see.

One stylistic feature of *The Old Crowd* that was not approved by Herbert Kretzmer – though it did not provoke him to the scorn and outrage of his English colleagues – was our intermittent cutaways to the studio, camera, etc. He felt that these intrusions of studio reality into the reality of the dramatic situation let the audience, so to speak, off the hook. 'It's only television,' they could think, and therefore evade uncomfortable implications. My own feeling is exactly the opposite. As long as the world of the drama remains an enclosed one, a self-contained fiction, the audience can regard it as 'only a play'. And I find the interplay or clash of 'realities' stimulating rather than anodyne. Perhaps this is a matter of temperament. And anyway, one would be optimistic indeed to imagine that one could make a contemporary audience *think* with a television or any other kind of play.

Yet the English critics continue to defend the cause of naturalism with vehemence, even with fury. They dealt with the reality-juggling in *The Old Crowd* either by professing befuddlement, or by contemptuous dismissal. 'Any trainee director doing that sort of thing would have been immediately sent back to training school' *(Evening News)*. 'Possibly a rather desperate reminder that this was a TV piece, since nearly everything particularly acting and direction – wore a decidedly stagey air' *(Telegraph)*. 'Stale old device . . . this tedious alienating technique . . . this drab device' *(New Statesman)*.

Just why, one cannot help asking, this insistence that naturalism is the only valid style in TV or cinema? Why this demand that the fiction remain enclosed, this assumption that any reminder of the author's presence is a callow solecism, 'obvious', 'tedious', 'old hat'? (Except perhaps when excused by a foreign accent – Pirandello, Brecht, Buñuel . . .). The *Observer* critic begged the whole question in familiar, cocksure style: 'By such means a few television directors built short-lived reputations back in the fifties. Nowadays the tyro director is expected to get over that sort of thing in training school. Like good directors in any medium, the good TV directors . . . rarely draw attention to technique.' Critically this is very primitive thinking: as no one should need reminding, technique and style are two very different things (the technique of *The Old Crowd* is in fact very simple). But the prejudice behind the bluster is significant.

In an important sense, a naturalistic work accepts the world as it is. That is to say, it can only criticise or expostulate in terms of the status quo.

A dissident or subversive vision demands a style that rejects the terms in which the conforming world presents itself: this is the only way it can offer a version of reality in essentially different, critical terms. The dissenting artist must hack away the props which hold up the status quo, in style as well as theme. So, if in the middle of an apparently 'real' conversation between a group of confident characters the camera pans away to show *another* camera and technicians (are they technicians or are they actors?) observing them, their reality and confidence is called in question. The effect – like any sudden deflation – may also be comic.

Of course anyone watching and identifying with the characters rather than with the dissenting author will likely find this procedure disturbing. They may resent it to the point of outrage. If they are artistically naif, and if it has never occurred to them that the world can be seen in any perspective other than theirs – then they may really find the whole thing 'incomprehensible', 'meaningless', 'gratuitous'. The dismissive epithets are legion: here are a few more. 'Solemn', 'humourless', 'self-conscious', 'self-congratulatory', 'pretentious', 'undergraduate', etc., etc. None of these, as commonly used by critics, signifies anything at all except a determination to discredit the work. And the critics who are likely to be most venomous are those who habitually pass for 'satirical' or 'non-conformist'. The *Observer* critic, Clive James (TV Critic of the Year in 1978 and runner-up in 1979, chat show presenter and highbrow reviewer), is a splendid representative of such licensed jesters of conformity, read because they are 'amusing', not because their perceptions are either useful or correct.

To be amusing is not necessarily to be humorous. *The Old Crowd* is, of course, a comedy (however 'disturbing') and, of course, there is a comic ambiguity about its stylistic departures from the norm: they are tongue-in-cheek as well as significant. I only wish that it could be seen as well as read. Perhaps one day it will be.

We almost made a film of it. In 1979 I was asked by Jorn Donner, the Finnish director then in charge of the Swedish Film Institute, to make a film for him. Neither Alan Bennett nor I felt that we had exhausted the potential of *The Old Crowd*, so I suggested a new, expanded film version. The idea was accepted. Alan and I worked on a script: we found it would be possible to use a set already standing in the Film Institute studio: a young Polish cameraman agreed to come from Warsaw to shoot it. Then, a few weeks before we were due to shoot, the project collapsed. Donner had miscalculated his finances and neglected to secure the approval of his board. And the unions objected.

It was a big disappointment. But of course the script is still there. And The Old Crowd are still around, or most of them. Any offers?

147

Britannia Hospital

Commentary, 1994

BRITANNIA HOSPITAL WAS INSPIRED BY A NEWS STORY IN THE *DAILY MIRROR* about a strike of hospital workers in London's Charing Cross Hospital. They were opposed to the admission to a State hospital of private, fee-paying patients. Doctrinaire Leftists in Britain are ideologically and sentimentally against anything of this kind being allowed within the framework of the National Health Service. This gives rise to many ironies – for instance, the fact that at least one large and influential union has taken out private medical insurance for its members, assuring them of priority treatment. This action caused a great deal of anger among orthodox Leftists who felt that no union member or representative should ever be treated by a doctor who was not working for the NHS.

The *Daily Mirror* carried a front-page photograph of a stout, benevolent-looking matron clutching a large handbag and pointing up at the tower-block hospital. This was Esther Brookstone – affectionately known as 'Granny' Brookstone – and she was the union official who was leading her members in righteous strike action. She inspired the character played by Joan Plowright in *Britannia Hospital*. Granny Brookstone and her col-

Britannia Hospital: *Leonard Rossiter (foreground) had played a small role in* This Sporting Life *but had since become a major star of British television.*

leagues instituted a boycott of the hospital with pickets on the gates refusing to admit supplies. All this led to farcical or tragic scenes with doctors and nurses on one side and pickets stopping ambulances on the other. This gave me the idea of a comedy based on the kind of irony which is all too common, not just in the NHS but in many aspects of semi-socialist Britain.

My initial idea was not particularly developed, of course. I just had visions, rather more extreme than we finally had in the film: union members breaking into the hospital and throwing private patients out of the windows; Arab sheiks in their beds, with their life-support machines attached, drifting down in slow motion from the 50th floor. The script is credited to David Sherwin who worked on the idea I gave him, but David was not party to these early fantasies. In fact, he wasn't at all sympathetic to the idea and has told me many times since that he never really understood it until he saw the finished film. Before passing the idea to David I had tried to have it developed by writers I had never worked with before, but that didn't work out, so I was driven back to David.

David and I have a peculiar working relationship. We are very good friends, but he isn't someone who finds writing particularly easy. So there is a great deal of my shouting at him and his being reduced to a state of neurotic impotence, and then my being forced to find a solution which we can then elaborate together. Our relationship does not conform to any norm of screenwriting that may be regarded as characteristic of professional cinema. We hammer out a script together, and the developments in the script are done in partnership. In the end, there is no real distinction to be made between the contributions made by David and myself. One might say, in the case of *Britannia Hospital*, that the original idea was mine, and the general plot development was my province, whereas a lot of the characterisation and dialogue were David's; but, even there, it is hard to make any rigid distinctions.

Of course, once the idea had been worked out, nobody wanted to finance it. We originally called it *Memorial Hospital* and offered it to Michael Medwin at Memorial Films. Michael was quite unable to do anything with it, but I was lucky to have it taken on by a producer named Clive Parsons. Clive was very keen and worked like a beaver to get the money for the film. I finally managed to get a development deal, by complex and quite amusing methods, from Twentieth-Century Fox in Hollywood. I happened to be in Los Angeles and had been asked to talk to Sandy Lieberson, a friend who was briefly in charge of production at Fox, about another project which was not mine; it may have been one of Michael's. Sandy and I fell to chatting about what I was currently working on, and I said, 'Look, Sandy, you're not going to be here for very much longer' – I knew he was going to leave in a few months' time – 'why don't you put *Britannia Hospital* down as a project for development by Fox? At least that will give David Sherwin enough money to write it. Then we can send it back to Fox who will immediately reject it, but we'll have the script written.'

To his eternal credit, Sandy agreed. The script development cost nothing, really, and Fox did indeed reject it when they finally read it. But that was all right, because the script now existed and could be passed to Clive Parsons. I've always been grateful to Sandy for his help, but I don't think he likes to be reminded of the episode. Clive, God bless him, managed to raise the production money from the large British company, EMI. Unfortunately, they lost their money and I am sorry about that. But when a film loses money nobody sleeps any the less soundly.

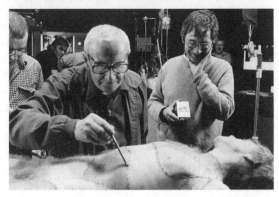

Top: a Laugh Riot: Britannia Hospital. *Above: Lindsay prods a prone McDowell, watched by an amused David Sherwin.*

Britannia Hospital is certainly a more desperate film than the others I have made, but I see it as an absolutely logical development of my earlier work. For example, in its own way it relates to the attitude of *O Dreamland*. People sometimes talk of *If . . . .* , *O Lucky Man!* and *Britannia Hospital* as a 'trilogy', but they are not a trilogy in the strict sense of the word. They are simply three films which I have directed, on which David Sherwin was the screenwriter, and in which Malcolm McDowell has more or less leading roles. Obviously, the films have a lot in common but I tend to think of them as a philosophical sequence. A lot of the ideas dealt with in the three films are similar, but I hope that all three show a development in the maturity of those ideas. I hope, too, that they are seen as different.

I don't know why we decided to use many of the same characters in each of the three films, except that one becomes fond of characters – and certainly fond of the actors – and you want to use them again. Much of this has to do with the actors and with the sense one has of a company, a repertory company if you like. This sense was most marked in O Lucky Man! in which some actors played two, three or more roles each. I think that there is an added humour, even a certain added richness, in having characters recurring, although it is an important principle to me that it is not necessary to have seen the films preceding it to appreciate Britannia Hospital.

Obviously, Britannia Hospital relates to If . . . . and O Lucky Man! through the presence of Malcolm McDowell playing Mick Travis. But it also shows a development of thought and feeling from the earlier aggressive idealism to a very bleak picture of human nature and the possibilities confronting humanity. Travis has declined, he has become corrupted; he is now a journalist working for the media. He is a principal character rather than the principal character. Clearly Mick Travis is not the same character in all three films, and in O Lucky Man! he is anyway two different characters, and they are not characters in the psychological sense. These ambiguities may be amusing, enlightening or stimulating. I think they add an extra layer of significance to the enjoyment of a film, no more than that.

It is nice, for instance, that Biles is a character in all three films and is, each time, played by Brian Pettifer. Actually, something occurred to me only when we had finished shooting Britannia Hospital. I realised that, in the kitchen scene, Biles is confronted by Keating, the truculent and aggressive union leader. Now you can, if you wish remember that these two characters, Biles and Keating, were at school together in If. . . . and that it was Keating (played in both films by the same actor, Robin Askwith) who had put Biles head-first into the lavatory. When they meet again in the kitchen of Britannia Hospital, the confrontation is less violent, but equally edged. You can see this development again in the character of Professor Millar, played in Britannia Hospital as he was in O Lucky Man! by Graham Crowden (who was also in If . . . . , as the History Master).

I think it is a very well-acted film. Particularly so because the style of acting demanded by the film is not one which you would expect, conventionally, in the cinema. Actors going into a film take it for granted that they will be acting in an intimate and naturalistic way and, of course, the acting in Britannia Hospital is the opposite of that. It is caricature, very strongly outlined, but with an essential reality. If that is successful in the film it is, in no small degree, due to the cast and their familiarity with the style. I had worked before with nearly everybody in Britannia Hospital in either film or theatre. Once again, Alan Price provided the music but Mirek Ondricek – who had shot If . . . and O Lucky Man! – was unavailable. He was shooting a film in America for George Roy Hill, but I was very fortunate and wise to ask Mike Fash, who had done some work for me at the BBC, to shoot *Britannia Hospital*. He was a great help and later shot *The Whales of August* and *Glory! Glory!*

We also had a degree of rehearsal. This is always difficult in the case of a film, especially if you have a large cast. In our case, we had a huge cast – something like 80 or 90 speaking roles of various sizes. We rehearsed over a period of a couple of weeks before we began shooting. We started, without being too theoretical, with discussions of style in an attempt to achieve a common acceptance of a caricatural style. It is interesting that the word caricature is so often used in a purely pejorative sense as though acting and dramatic art by its nature ought to be naturalistic and psychological, which is, of course, nonsense and not in the least traditional. I think it would be wrong to call these films 'epic' in the Brechtian sense as opposed to 'naturalistic' in the bourgeois sense. But we did work on the acting, although, once you start shooting you don't have much time to rehearse, simply because you are trying to get the thing shot. Yet if you don't rehearse before you start you inevitably end up with more or less stereotyped performances; there isn't time for anything else.

There were a few scenes which David Sherwin found difficult, if not impossible, to write and we sought contributions from the actors. But that was before we went into production. Quite honestly, I will take help and suggestions from anyone. There was little, if any, improvisation. When you work naturalistically, it's possible for actors to improvise lines, scenes or situations, but it was almost impossible to improvise in a film which was so stylised. If a scene is a bit weak and you have an intelligent actor like Graham Crowden, you can work on it. There were one or two bits we thought were a bit weak when we came to them and we rapidly improvised or worked on sections to make them stronger. But that was improvisation in its broadest sense.

The scenes featuring the two characters in the van are not as strongly or as clearly written and developed as they ought to have been. On the other hand, you have statements from them in their first scene which are fairly indicative of their attitudes. For instance, one of them is saying that he's been making a programme about the starving children of India with obviously no concern whatever, and the other one has been seeing South American-banana-growers blowing themselves to bits. They aren't at all interested in what they're doing, only in getting high and watching rubbish on television.

Malcolm McDowell's character may be perceived at first as the sympathetic hero, someone for the audience to identify with, just because it's Malcolm and he is once again playing someone called Mick Travis. But the way he plays his first scene on the roof and the things he says are totally opportunistic and unpleasant, and quite characteristic of a totally unin-

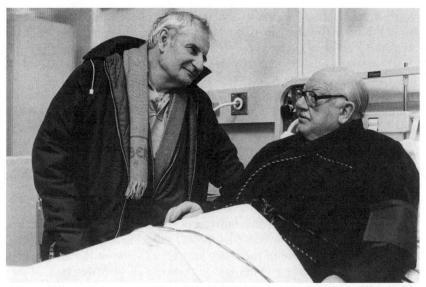

Arthur Lowe (right) made an uncredited appearance in Britannia Hospital *and died before the film was released. 'Some people expected me to cut Arthur's scene,' Lindsay recalled, 'but he would have hated that; he was a real pro.'*

volved media person. He has moved away from Britain, and he says at the beginning, 'I got out just in time.' He's sold out and his ideals have gone out of the window. As a result he is probably very successful. I think that if you want to look at the 'trilogy' as the progress of Mick Travis it's rather sad. I am afraid he has ended up with a kind of corrupt success like many people in this world. I don't see anything particularly likeable about him, unless you're looking for a hero and think it must be him because it's Malcolm, it's Mick. That, presumably, is why people are surprised when he gets his head pulled off. But he's just a shit, that's all; there are a lot of them about. He probably deserves to have his head cut off.

I don't think that there is a character in *Britannia Hospital* with whom you can sentimentally identify, but I think that all the characters – by virtue of their absurdity and vitality (and one might say their integrity, because they are all absolutely true to themselves) – are, in a peculiar way, likeable. Some of their attitudes and actions are reprehensible, but I hope that being in their company for a couple of hours is more pleasant than unpleasant. To that extent, it's a sentimental film.

Of course, *Britannia Hospital* is not really a film about the National Health Service, any more than it is really a film about a hospital. There isn't a great deal about the hospital as a hospital in it, there is much more about the hospital as an institution. One of the things that happened as we worked on the film was that it became more about British society and, indeed, Western society in general. I think – hope – that *Britannia Hospital* is in many ways an extremely violent film, but that the comic accent and viewpoint is maintained so that the violence never gets out of hand or becomes too naturalistic.

For instance, the scene in which the armed police beat up the demonstrators would have been very easy to make a great deal more violent, in a newsreel style, than it is. But it is sufficiently violent to stand for the conflict which it represents between establishment and dissidents. To prevent it from becoming too much like a newsreel, there is no sound on that sequence except for the noise of the band playing the National Anthem. To that degree, it is abstracted.

But I don't believe it is possible to take on this kind of subject, and to maintain the seriousness which must be at the basis of the comedy, unless you are prepared to go beyond what people expect in a comedy or a diversion. I suppose that one of the film's principles is that of the unexpected; so, if people are sitting comfortably thinking they're seeing a Monty Python-type picture, something must suddenly occur which they would not expect to find, and indeed wouldn't find, in a Monty Python movie.

Of course, I know that there are people who are very disturbed by the sight of blood, and there is a large amount of blood in the film. But I hope the blood is sufficiently extravagant in its use for it to be ludicrous. It is supposed to be funny. I wanted a real anarchic quality in *Britannia Hospital* and you can't have that without being, to some degree, disturbing. I'm afraid that, once again, I was attempting to make people think. Satire is always aimed towards the intellect, which is probably why it is not popular and never has been. Some satirical poems have certainly survived but we must remember what the American director and playwright George S. Kaufman once said: 'Satire is what closes on Saturday night.' The popular audience doesn't want it; the popular audience wants to be reassured and not to be reminded of all the awful things that are happening or that may happen unless human beings behave intelligently.

There is also a tendency to talk about satire today as if it were a cheeky but respectable type of humour. In fact, one of the chief reasons why satire is not traditionally popular is because it is disturbing and, fundamentally, questioning. What is particularly disturbing for *me* today, in the age of television, is that we have less and less of this kind of humour. I think that this was one of the reasons why *Britannia Hospital* was very strongly and widely resented in Britain – to a degree that surprised me, but I am always taken by surprise by these things. The critical reception, apart from one or two supportive dissident voices, was extremely hostile and defensive, and I must admit that I was surprised that people retreated so rapidly into conformism.

The film was generally well received everywhere but in Britain. Now, some say the reason it was disliked in Britain was because it was anti-British and was released, quite by chance, at the time of the Falklands War, but I don't believe that was the reason. The film is not anti-British, it's just a film about human beings. It was enjoyed in Hungary, where they seem to like the films I make. The critics in New York were sympathetic and intelligent, and one of the letters I received about the film, and which I very much appreciated, came from Andrzej Wajda in Poland. He said it was the best Polish film he had seen for a number of years. He also said that it reminded him of the kind of film made in Poland under censorship. In those days, Polish film-makers would put in as many critical and dubious elements as possible because they knew the censor would cut some of them out. They had not been cut out of *Britannia Hospital*, which remained full of targets. I suppose that's what happens when many years go by without giving one the chance to make a film, so that when you do make a film you put into it everything you can and everything you feel and think. Perhaps Wajda was right in finding it too full in that way.

Perhaps, as a piece of film-making, it asks too much. After all, here is a film which begins with a dying man being driven to hospital but the ambulance is stopped because the union pickets won't let it through. Then, when he finally gets in, the porters go off to play cards and have a cup of tea. Well, you have to be quite sophisticated to laugh at that, and the popular audience doesn't laugh at it. They probably don't think it's funny. I think it's funny, so perhaps there is something wrong with me.

One of the chief problems is that the film demands, or at least invites, thought; and that is a risky thing to demand in any medium, but particularly in the cinema. In other words, *Britannia Hospital* is a serious film. Of course, one hopes to have it both ways. One tries to produce an entertainment that will be diverting in the manner of a strip cartoon, as well as something serious, inviting serious thought. Whether I succeeded or not is not for me to say. Whether *Britannia Hospital* can be enjoyed on a *Tom and Jerry* level, I don't know, but I hope so. There are certain allusions to other films of mine, but it doesn't matter if you don't pick them up. It doesn't matter if you know that Mick, as he says, originated in Britain and, like a large number of Brits, emigrated to America, the land of opportunity, to become both successful and ruthless. He says that he sold coffee, but if you've never seen or heard of *O Lucky Man!* it doesn't matter very much.

Unfortunately, critics are very good at dismissing things. There are lots of words they can use to do so: words like 'obvious' or 'boring' or 'banal'. I think back to all the words that were used about Brecht when his company first came to Britain in 1956 and was dismissed by the bourgeois press. When you deal with moral problems you will very often find them dismissed as 'banal' by people who don't want to face moral questions; that is their way of evading them.

For instance, a critic in *The Times* (not David Robinson, who is a very respectable film critic, but a hack who was substituting for him when *Britannia Hospital* came out) said that he found the film declined into, to use his phrase, 'the old humanistic huff and puff'. It is very interesting that we can dismiss the basic moral challenges of our time in that way. It also shows a lack of attention and of analytical power because of its response to the final speech by Professor Millar. The speech begins in an extremely sane way as a fundamental analysis of human beings' attitudes to one another. In that sense, it takes the humane and intelligent point of view. But then you have another about-face when Millar, who is obviously mad, reveals his insanity by showing that he imagines that everyone can be cured by the invention of an artificial brain. So you are confronted with the fact that the man who seems to have turned into the purveyor of wisdom reveals that he is madder than anyone.

I have no idea how the ending came about, but the whole thing grew. The very last speech is taken from *Hamlet* and was prompted not only by its being one of the great passages of dramatic literature but by the fact that my last work before starting the film was a production of *Hamlet* with Frank Grimes, who speaks the speech in *Britannia Hospital*. It is, if you like, another aspect of organic development. So many things which are part of your experience, thought and feeling come together to make this invention, this pattern, which you hope will be significant. The film's final implication is that the ills and mistakes of humankind cannot be cured by the application of pure intelligence, although Millar believes they can, but there must be some moral answer to the problems that confront us.

The film gives no answer, which again goes to prove how mistaken I was in encouraging people to think. The end of the film is a very direct challenge to the audience and is probably bleak in its implications. But I feel that if I am going to make a film it must have something to say, some challenge to thought or feeling which is of our time and that one need not be ashamed of making. To some degree, movies have abandoned seriousness – I don't mean on the sentimental level of Spielberg, but there is a retreat into fashionable aesthetics and the contemporary point of view that movies are about movies.

I recall Robert Benton, the American writer-director, being quoted in an interview about his film, *Still of the Night*. Bob is an extremely intelligent chap and a good film-maker, but one gets trapped by journalists, and Bob found himself taking a defensive position, quite unnecessarily, because he had made an entertainment. He was quoted as saying, 'It's just a movie. There are some movies that are not about anything more than the 90 minutes they take you to see them. They have no redeeming social value . . .

they're not works of high art, or even works of low art for that matter. They are essentially about the act of watching a movie.' Now Bob has no need to speak defensively about 'redeeming social value', he's not that much of a puritan, and a film doesn't have to be 'about the act of watching a movie'. *Still of the Night* isn't about the act of watching a movie, it is a movie to be enjoyed. But it is not very fashionable to say that today, which is a great pity.

If you make a political film, it doesn't mean you have to conform to the policy of any established political movement. I don't think a political film can do that. It has to provoke its audience into making political judgements. In *Britannia Hospital* I was not *making* those kinds of political judgements. The degree to which you can say that the film is anarchic is in its essential criticism of *all* establishments. It is equally critical of institutions of the Right and of the Left, but it is in favour of intelligence, and this is perhaps old-fashioned. I would call it a humanistic film because the human race, the human phenomenon, is put at the centre and it is not helped out by any political philosophy or by any spiritual aid or crutch. In that way, it is not a religious film. In the end, you are left with the implication that, unless the human race is capable of developing a moral intelligence, it is likely to destroy itself. Here again we can relate to Brecht in that it is an attempt to stimulate its *audience* into finding a solution. Alas, most audiences don't want to come out of a cinema and think about what they've seen. My hope had been that the film would be sufficiently funny or extravagant, in a comic way, to carry a popular audience along with it, but I was wrong.

When *Britannia Hospital* was rejected, it seemed to be rejected primarily because it offered an unsparing and highly realistic, satirical criticism of society. I remember particularly Margaret Hinxman, a very nice lady, coming out of a preview, tottering and looking pale, and saying, 'Oh, you haven't left us any hope.' I recognised this desperate middle-class craving to cling to some – even fictitious – idea of hope rather than being invigorated by the *truth*. This is a real symptom of decline and decadence, if the truth is regarded as something 'depressing'.

I can see that, to the extent that my films reflect a point of view, they have become more anarchic and even pessimistic (a word I don't like, as I don't like the word 'optimistic'). But from any theoretical or social point of view, my films are anarchic, in the sense that they put the ultimate responsibility on the individual. It's difficult to be objective about one's own work, but I think that they are clearly shot through with suspicion of institutions and a dislike of institutional thinking. Their appeal, a somewhat desperate one, is to the intelligence – not the intellect, but the intelligence. From a certain point of view they are certainly pessimistic, but I think that the optimistic quality in a work of art is not any hopeful formulation it might contain, but is essentially the vitality of the work itself.

157

Wham! in China!

Editor's Note

Music played an important role in Lindsay Anderson's career. His own tastes were eclectic, and he took great pleasure in pop music, but the videos he made for the singer Carmel were among his least likely collaborations. Even less likely was his commission to direct a film about the pop duo Wham! on their 'epoch-making visit to China' (as Lindsay described it to Gavin Lambert). The final result, Wham! in China: Foreign Skies, featuring twelve of the band's songs and billed as 'A Lindsay Anderson Film', premiered at Wembley Stadium in June 1986, before 72,000 fans.

Except that it wasn't Lindsay's film. His version, a documentary called If You Were There, featuring only four songs, was rejected by the 'Whammies', as Lindsay scornfully called them, and he was fired. He admitted he took the job 'in a spirit of curiosity. Curiosity about China and curiosity about the odd confrontation of China and Wham! – and even curiosity (though not very great) about Wham! itself.' It was also because Michael assured him he 'didn't want a routine, teeny-bopper promotional film, but hoped for something more in the nature of a satirical documentary.' But of course, he did want a promotional film.

As Lindsay resignedly told me, 'If you tell an insecure, egotistical 21-year-old that he is a genius, what on earth can you expect?' His cut of the film still exists, and it remains in the gift of George Michael to give a screening to what is now 'an historical document'. In November 1985, shortly after his removal from the project, Lindsay wrote the following open letter.

To Whom It May Interest Or Concern

HAVING RECEIVED A FEW DAYS AGO MY VHS TAPES OF *IF YOU WERE THERE* – which is the title I finally gave to our documentary film about the visit of Wham! to China – and having agreed yesterday with my agent on the terms of my contract to make the film –which I hope will shortly be signed – I feel the time has come for me to outline, for anyone who may still be interested, the history of this enterprise since shooting finished and we all returned from China.

In brief: after an apparently very successful showing of the cutting copy of the film some three weeks ago, with a rough dub of the soundtrack, I was informed through my agent (this was about ten days after the showing) that I was replaced as director of the film, which was to be recut in some unspecified way. Possessing no legal rights in the film, I was of course in no position to contest this decision. I gathered that an associate of Jazz Summers was being flown in from Los Angeles to supervise the recutting of material. His name is Strath Hamilton and he is an Australian, apparently experienced in the making of commercials and video promos. I felt almost sorry for him, particularly since the editor, Peter West, and his assistant, together with the sound editor, Tim Arrowsmith, and *his* assistant, all resigned. Or rather hung on until their paychecks were brought up to date, then quit the cutting rooms.

Such was the climax of some five months work on editing. I need hardly describe the magnitude of the task, or the concentration and skill necessary to achieve a shaped, cohesive and rhythmic whole out of the miles and miles of material – some of it excellent, much of it unusable – which was the product of those hectic days of filming in Peking and Canton.

During those months, the work in progress was seen and each time approved by Wham!'s two managers, Jazz Summers and Simon Napier-Bell. So struck, indeed, was this dynamic duo by the punch and vividness of our first cut of about half the material, which ran just over an hour, that they asked enthusiastically whether the completed film might run to ninety minutes. I replied that I thought it could, and that was the length we had in mind as we continued to edit the material. (I'm sure I don't need to add that we never had any inclination to stretch the material beyond what seemed to be its natural length.) Several sequences, in fact, were dropped completely (including the notorious Football Match and the interview with George Michael on a Canton hotel massage table, in which he gave out with his ideas on China, the Chinese people, their system of government etc., etc.)

George Michael himself – 'the man who signs the cheques' as Jazz Summers put it – did not visit the cutting room, although he was supposed to be providing additional music for the picture. After our return from China, two days additional shooting were done at Shepperton Studios, shot by a three camera team under Peter McKay. I was never exactly sure – since I was never consulted or given any information – of the purpose of these extra days of shooting. I *think* it was something to do with providing versions of the songs mimed to the soundtracks from the Hong Kong concerts. In any case, they did provide a number of useful inserts. After this George Michael unfortunately viewed four or five hours of rushes, preparatory to his working with a video director on the video promo of 'Freedom'. Being completely ignorant of film making, he became quickly discouraged and even despairing of the quality of the film material. Talking with his usual disarming frankness, he later gave interviews to the press in which he expressed his disappointment and scepticism about the film and said it would very likely never appear. I became alarmed about this, but was vehemently assured by Martin Lewis (who was in the U.S. during our editing period, himself both directing and producing a film about Julian Lennon) and Jazz Summers . . . So much for the authority of 'Producers'.

As cutting proceeded, showings were regularly scheduled at which Wham!, or at least George Michael, were to appear. First George was exhausted after his China experience; then he was preparing for his American tour; then he was delayed in the U.S. to relax after his tour and to have dinner with Brooke Shields; then he decided (still without having seen anything) that he would *not* after all write any music for the film; then he got the time wrong or was delayed by traffic . . . On three occasions I wrote to George Michael to let him know of our progress and to hope that he would involve himself creatively with the formation of the film. (I had to write because I was not allowed to know his telephone number.) None of my letters were acknowledged or received an answer.

By late September the film had acquired its final shape. It was/is constructed in episodes, each preceded by a title, all without commentary. The concerts in Peking and Canton, which constituted the latter half of the film (with some documentary intercutting) featured four numbers, with 'Go-Go' as a finale. I would describe the tone of the film roughly as 'humorous – lyric – ironic'. Of course I am not in a position to be objective, but I can certainly say that I'm proud of what was achieved in a style of pure montage – no commentary, much freshness of observation, a musical rhythm throughout. A picture that could certainly appeal to a wider audience than the familiar Wham! teenies.

Dubbing (as we call it here: 'mixing' in the U.S.) was set for late October. This had to be postponed because the composer selected by Jazz Summers to supply additional music was not free until November. Amid great apprehension, Wham! – both George and Andrew – finally appeared at a screening in mid-October. A few friendly 'outsiders' had also been invited to provide an atmosphere of 'audience'. Everyone enjoyed the screening and applauded happily at the end. WHAM! hung around for forty-five minutes afterwards, drinking wine and smiling broadly. And none more broadly than Jazz Summers and Simon Napier-Bell.

Seemingly what happened was this: George, Andrew, Simon and Jazz all had dinner some nights later. Alcohol was consumed. George expressed his disapproval of the film, or at least his feeling of its unfitness for purpose. (The only specific objection I have heard is that the cutting of the numbers was insufficiently 'modern'. This I take to mean that they don't look like a video – but then of course documentary material can never look like a video). The decision was made, after (I suspect) some in-fighting between the managers, to 'get rid of Anderson'. George disappeared, either to finish working on his new single or to have a holiday, Andrew went to race cars on the Continent, Simon Napier-Bell took off for the West Indies – and it was left to Jazz Summers to mastermind the transformation of Wham! in China! into an acceptable piece of pop promotion. Strath Hamilton and a new editing crew were the answer. Plus, of course, the expenditure of another million dollars or so. Someone should write a book about it.

None of this, I suppose, is exactly astonishing. In fact, when I first took on the assignment I warned myself not to get too 'involved', since such projects so often – even usually – end by conflict between creators and exploiters. And in such situations the exploiters must always win. I must admit though, that I was not prepared for the incredible waste, silliness, lack of conscience, ignorance, lack of grace, lack of scruple, egoism, weakness, duplicity and hypocrisy which have characterised the whole operation. Nor did I quite realise that however cool I might be during the shooting of the picture, I could not resist total and creative involvement once it came to the editing. I am not going to claim that the loss of Wham! in China! is a creative catastrophe on the scale of Von Stroheim's *Greed*: but I do think that between them the Whammies have destroyed or suppressed an enjoyable, informative, entertaining and even at times beautiful film.

And fortunately *If You Were There . . .* has not been completely lost. Before we picked up our carrier-bags and stole away from the cutting rooms, we were able to make a transfer on one-inch tape of the cutting copy of the film, together with the dubbed track, putting in titles and opticals where planned. A VHS version of this was taken back to New York by Lee Rolontz, who had brilliantly organised the whole editing operation in London – and no doubt Martin Lewis at Springtime will be in possession of a copy. In Britain Nomis (Simon spelt *backwards* if you hadn't noticed) are in possession of the one-inch tape and also VHS tapes.

It only remains for me to say sorry – and thank you. Film making has always been a risky business – especially for artists – and never more so than in this age of Video.

Better luck next time!

LINDSAY ANDERSON
London, November 1985

The Whales of August

Commentary, 1994

The Whales of August was made as a result of the admiration, the devotion of its producer Mike Kaplan, for Lillian Gish. Mike had known Lillian for a long time and he wanted to produce a film which would give her the opportunity, late in life, to play something beyond the minor roles she played in Hollywood films towards the end of her career. He wanted also to give audiences the chance to see just what her great qualities and characteristics were. He saw a play called *The Whales of August* by David Berry and thought this would provide ample opportunity to work with Lillian. In the mid-1970s, Mike invited Lillian to see the play and afterwards she said, 'Yes, I'll play that part if you can set up the film,' and left it at that.

Mike set out to raise the money and it was a long while before he was at all successful. In the 1980s it proved possible to finance a film which might get its money back through television and video sales. Mike asked David Berry to write a film script of his play, and Mike worked on it with him. Finally, he asked me if I would direct it. Of course, I said yes at once, although I didn't really believe that Mike would get the money for the film. But the opportunity of making a film with Lillian Gish was quite amazing when one considers that she was D. W. Griffith's favourite actress. To my surprise Mike did get the money from a company called Alive Films, which was then operating in Hollywood. Once the money was in place, Mike approached Bette Davis – who had already turned down the part of Lillian's sister in the film – and she agreed. Then Mike came back to me and we went to see Lillian.

We never really knew exactly how old Lillian was, but she must have been in her late eighties or early nineties. She was not at all sure that she was able to do the film and, frankly, neither was I. Mike and I discussed it and, in the end, agreed that we should have a go. It was an extraordinary script with a part for Bette Davis which she could play better than anyone else. For other characters in the film we approached other screen veterans: Anne Sothern, Vincent Price and Harry Carey Junior, the son of Harry Carey the early Western star. I knew Vincent socially, and he was delighted to have the opportunity to escape from the comic horror roles he had become well-known for playing. He was a very sensitive actor and a highly cultivated man with a marvellous sense of humour. When his wife – the Australian actress Coral Browne – saw the proposed cast list for *The Whales of August* she suggested that the production company be renamed *Barely* Alive Films. Harry Carey was an old friend. He had never become

The Whales of August: *cast and crew on location in Maine. Seated, front row, left to right: Ann Sothern, Lillian Gish, Bette Davis and Vincent Price; Frank Grimes (behind Gish) and Harry Carey (next to Price). Producer Mike Kaplan behind Price and Lindsay seated with clapper board.*

the big star that his father was, but he had a very distinguished career working as part of John Ford's 'stock company'. He's very modest; on his first day of shooting, he took one look at Bette Davis and Lillian Gish and said that he would be more comfortable filming with horses. I said, 'Oh, come on, they're just people,' and he got over it.

I was not entirely satisfied with David Berry's script because I don't think he had really made up his mind about how the film should end. In the script that I was given, the two sisters parted, although there was an implication that they had reached some understanding of each other. I thought that was foolish really and that it didn't make sense to part the two women at the end. The idea that the sister played by Lillian Gish was going to go and find her own life was reminiscent of *Kramer vs Kramer,* and the American idea of women finding their own way. It seemed ridiculous in that situation. I thought that the only possible conclusion was that the two sisters should learn to live together and should, to a degree, learn how to understand each other. So, together with my assistant, I rewrote the ending before we started shooting. In my version they stayed together and it seemed much stronger. I made it a condition that this change had to be accepted otherwise I wouldn't do it, and the author accepted.

163

David Berry had written the script in Maine, and we decided to shoot the film there. Unfortunately, his own house was not ideal, but we were extraordinarily lucky. We took a boat up to Portland and sailed around the islands where we spotted a house on a promontory. We knew at once we had our location. I was with Mike Kaplan and the production manager and, I think, Mike Fash, who was to shoot the picture. I was lucky again to get Mike, who had worked with me on *Britannia Hospital* but had since emigrated to Connecticut. My friend Jocelyn Herbert came from Britain to be art director, together with some people brought from Hollywood by Alive Films, but who were almost all pretty disastrous. It was a curious unit in that it was half British and half American, also it was filmed in Maine which is very different from the rest of America. It was edited in London and the music was composed by Alan Price, with whom I had worked so often.

I think that actors are actors whatever their nationality, and they all respond imaginatively and emotionally. Of course, we were working with senior artists so we couldn't film long hours, but they were all, naturally, very fine professionals. I'm very glad that Lillian had the chance to make that film so late in her life and her career. It proved to be her last. I don't know if Bette completed another film; she had been very ill and, I suppose, had always had a difficult temperament. I've always said that Bette was, in some way, possessed of the devil. Lillian was possessed of an angel, bearing in mind that angels are not in any way soppy – Lillian certainly wasn't soppy. Anne Sothern was a very good actress and pleasing to work with, and she got along well with Bette. But Bette resented Lillian – nonsense really. Bette probably never really liked sharing the limelight, that was all part of her being a star. We had our bumpy moments.

The film was best received in Japan. I think that is because the Japanese have a certain reverence for age, and they're not frightened of it. Perhaps in the United States, and in Britain too, people are a bit scared of age. We made the film out of immense admiration for Lillian Gish and Bette Davis and we thought that people would be happy to see them act. What perhaps we did not realise was that many people would rather sit at home and watch *Now Voyager* on television than see Bette Davis at the end of her career giving a splendid performance. However, that is all irrelevant and the important thing is that we made the film. I'm very happy we did, because filming David Berry's play with those very fine artists was a great experience.

Lillian and Bette: Bette and Lillian

Unpublished article written for *The Sunday Times*, May 1988

BETTE ARRIVED FIRST. WE WERE AN HOUR OR AN HOUR-AND-A-HALF OUT OF Portland, across the usually smooth waters of Casco Bay, by the ferries which made the stopping trip round the islands three or four times a day, or forty minutes by water taxi, piloted by skilful young Coley, whose passengers were limited to four or five. But the vessel which brought Bette Davis over from the mainland I had never seen before. It looked very large, almost threatening, wide, white, high in the water, like a miniature ocean-going liner. I realised that the Production, terrorised and cringing, as always in America at the presence of a star, had felt the need to provide some special vehicle to carry Miss Davis over to Cliff Island for the shooting.

They had forgotten the tides. The water was low and Bette's vessel was too large, too high in the water, to berth comfortably at the jetty. The gangway would not stretch down to the landing stage. The tiny potent figure in the smart black dress, the tiny hat perched on an exuberant hair-do, stood waiting impatiently on the deck. The producer, who had been to meet her at the airport, dithered at a safe distance. Everyone was indecisive, intimidated. 'Come on!' I called. 'You'll have to lift her down.' Hands reached forward and Bette found herself sitting on the edge of the deck, incredibly thin legs dangling into space. 'Lift me down,' she commanded. She was swung out and down: Mike Fash pushed forward to grab her as she descended. Unperturbed, she talked.

'My God – would you believe it? I just knew that was going to happen . . . On the plane from New York . . . And I haven't seen him for fourteen years . . . Gary Merrill! I got on the plane and looked around – and there the bastard was! Would you believe it?'

She cackled and tottered, still talking, as her feet touched the landing stage. 'Hold on!' I urged her. She clutched the framework of the jetty.

'I just knew that would happen . . . the first time I've been back since we lived up here . . . I told him to come forward and sit with me, but he wouldn't. He looked pretty good . . . '

She ran on. Did I give her a welcome embrace? I can't remember; if I did, she took no notice. Mike came forward and smiled his charming, efficacious smile. 'Good morning, Miss Davis, I'm Mike Fash, your cameraman.' Bette showed interest. 'Hello, Mike.' She was susceptible. One up to us.

Lillian arrived the next day, quite differently. She had been somewhere out West, attending a festival in honour of her beloved sister Dorothy, with whom she had made her first movie so many years ago and with whom she

Top: legendary ladies – Lillian Gish and Bette Davis on the set of The Whales of August. Above: Gish and Davis in character: 'Lillian's reputation is angelic, Bette's is devilish. It did not take long for both to prove justified . . .'

played in one of Griffith's greatest successes, *Orphans of the Storm*. (Dorothy sparkled in comedy, while Lillian's gift was for courageous pathos. She was a star in Britain and played a silent Nell Gwynn for Herbert Wilcox. She and Lillian both had great stage successes in *Life With Father*. She died in 1968.) This time there was no cabin cruiser. Lillian came out of Portland by water taxi. She wore a useful mackintosh coat, a white scarf round her face and a man's cap on top of it. Her little boat did not ride high in the water, so there was no trouble at the landing. There was a wheelchair waiting in which she could be carried up the quite steep gangway to the jetty, but she preferred to walk. With her two sticks and Jim, her friend and manager, to support her from behind, she managed it without difficulty. A knot of admirers applauded respectfully. Lillian waved.

We drove to her bungalow. Looking out over the bay, with its lovely view of water, sky and wooded islands, Lillian remarked, 'We shouldn't really be paid for enjoying all this beauty.'

One of the endless fascinations of this extraordinary partnership (confrontation?) of stars was their absolute difference in everything except God-given talent, and life-acquired professionalism. Lillian's reputation is angelic. Bette's is devilish. It did not take long for both to prove justified – provided one remembers that there is nothing soppy about an angel; and that devilry can have its own peculiar charm.

Angels are strong. The road from the Biograph Studio in New York, where 72 years before the Gish sisters had run round in terror while D. W. Griffith fired blank revolver shots at them, to our cramped and crowded living-room set on Cliff Island, is not one that could be travelled by a moral or psychological weakling. Lillian had worked continuously, as Griffith's, then MGM's biggest star – till Louis B. Mayer demanded that she provide him (or let him manufacture) a 'scandal' with which he could tart up her image. So she turned her back on Hollywood and went back to the theatre, where she played Chekhov, Shakespeare (Gielgud's Ophelia) and any number of moderns. She made films, too. She had never retired.

Nor had Bette, since George Arliss picked her out of a crowd of *ingénues*, to play opposite him in an early talkie. Her years of struggle and triumph at Warner Brothers still provide television with a unique succession of romantic dramas: her Margo Channing in *All About Eve* has entered into contemporary myth; so have the memorable grotesqueries of *Baby Jane* and *Hush, Hush Sweet Charlotte*. She fought and defeated a hysterectomy, a stroke and a vengeful daughter.

Neither of these two ladies had ever made concessions.

When we shot *The Whales of August*, Lillian's principles were exactly those with which she had performed in *The Birth of a Nation* or *The Wind*. Her job was to serve the director, and the script. This did not oblige her to transgress her standards of artistry or taste. If she did not like a line of dialogue, she would change it or cut it out – always with her director's permission, firmly requested and readily granted. She did not like to be shot from a low angle, and she liked the camera to see into her heart through her eyes.

I was particularly happy with one set-up. Lillian was preparing for an evening visitor: the camera followed her round her room, setting out her clothes, taking from her dressing-table drawer an old telegram of wartime loss, sitting to read and remember as she gazed through the window at the Atlantic waves rolling in . . . I sensed that Lillian was not entirely pleased; I asked her why. She pointed out that she ended the shot in profile; for her, feeling was exposed through the eyes. 'But it's a lovely, expressive image,' I said. Struck by a sudden inspiration I added: 'Remember Whistler's *Mother*.' 'Ah, yes,' said Lillian. 'But think of the '*Mona Lisa*.' She had me there. (But we did not change the set-up.)

Bette's method of conveying reservation was cruder. 'Rubbish' or 'ridiculous idea' would be her usual comment on a directorial suggestion. (I noticed, though, that when it came to the take, the suggestion was generally used.) Contest rather than collaboration seemed for her to be the essence of the actress-director relationship. 'That's twice I've given in to him today,' she would announce to the unit, on accepting an idea. 'I must be slipping.' She liked to give directions herself, to push the furniture around, to bully some humble (generally inept) member of the crew. Only once was I driven to snap. 'You're not taking over the picture, Bette,' I heard myself say. She stiffened in outrage and walked off the set. Both she and I called for the wretched producer. It was quite exciting, like old Hollywood.

For all her trials and conflicts with Warner Brothers, Bette had no relish for the freedom of location shooting. She yearned continually for Burbank. 'We should be doing this in the studio,' she would grumble, remembering fondly those days of *Old Acquaintance*, *The Letter*, *Now Voyager*. She longed for those big staircases, the arcs, the backdrops: she didn't notice the lovely, changing seascapes which we would see through our windows. No use pointing out that if we had been in the studio, we wouldn't have been making *The Whales of August*. 'So much the better,' she would certainly have replied.

Lilian had no such nostalgic thoughts. After all, she had lain for hours on a real ice floe, not in the studio tank, while Griffith shot her drifting towards the falls, her long hair, her little hand trailing in the icy water. She had never cut her hair – an unnecessary extravagance when she and Dorothy were young and poor. And to this day the joints in her hand will ache when the weather is damp, remembering the freezing river of *Way Down East*.

Shrewd as well as innocent, Lillian likes to repeat her mother's advice as to how most sensibly to get through life. 'You can get on in life by being rude to people,' she would say. 'But you'll find things a great deal easier if you treat people well, with kindness and courtesy.' And that's how she does it. Bette's mother, on the other hand, surely gave her daughter no such counsel. Bette's impulse is to treat the world with hostility. She can be fearfully rude, often cruelly so. The sad thing is that this can make a splendid spectacle. Journalists love it, calling it 'feisty'. Chat show hosts grow fat on it. Whether this encourages Bette to be horrid I can't say. Probably she needs no encouragement.

I realise that in telling these tales I am myself playing the media game. In a good cause, I tell myself. Here are two great artists, not in conflict, but performing with a unique ripeness of talent, a classic simplicity and truth. It is a kind of acting not now fashionable. Hollywood Academy members in 1988 gave their nominations to Cher and Holly Hunter. Here in *The Whales of August* they had the Duse and Bernhardt of the movies side by side, no holds barred. 'Ah, did you once see Shelley plain . . . ?' Well, here they are. We can forget the rest.

Bette Davis

Obituary for *The Guardian*, 11 October 1989

DIRECTING BETTE DAVIS WAS LIKE PLAYING WITH A VERY SHARP KNIFE. SHE met the world like an enemy: to collaborate was to concede. She had the charm of vitality, but there was the threat of cruelty there as well. Even if she wasn't offensive, she conveyed the fact that at any moment she might be.

Americans and journalists like this kind of thing, which they call 'feisty'. It works well on chat shows, and it makes good copy. But in Bette's case it was not fun. It was destructive and often ugly. Lillian Gish, who believes in treating the world with courtesy, could not understand why Bette should be nasty to her. 'She's very unhappy,' I would say, though I knew this was not the reason, or not the whole reason.

Had she always been like this? Those who had known her in the old days usually said: Yes – but she had got worse. Her painful illnesses, obstinately endured, were no doubt partly to blame. She had fought many battles in her long career; and perhaps it had become a habit, even when there were no longer any battles that needed fighting.

By the time she came to make *The Whales of August*, she was no longer quite the mistress of the sharp-edged technique which powered her great performances. She could not admit her lapses, so one had to be tactful when another take was necessary. She took no pleasure in our glorious location and would have been happier (or so she said) on a sound stage at Burbank. She was shrewd rather than wise.

And yet . . . Bette trailed clouds of glory; her courage was splendid, her integrity total. She never made pain or fatigue an excuse for postponing a shot. Her scenes were completed a day or two before shooting ended; but she lingered on and would come and sit with us on the set. She even became friendly to Lillian. And she was the last of the team to leave Cliff Island.

Lindsay on location for
The Whales of August *with Bette Davis.*

Glory! Glory!

Commentary, 1994

GLORY! GLORY! WAS MADE IN TORONTO FOR HOME BOX OFFICE AND ORION Films. It was shot as a full-length feature film but shown on television as a three-hour mini-series. In fact, although it was made on celluloid, it was transferred for editing onto video and no theatrical copy exists as far as I know. It was shot in Toronto because of various deals which I don't really understand, but which made it cheaper to make in Canada than in the United States. The three principal actors, Ellen Greene, Richard Thomas and James Whitmore, were Americans and were chosen by the film's producer, Bonny Dore, who originated the project. The original plan was for Stan Daniels, who wrote the script, to direct, but HBO insisted on an experienced director. They further stipulated that a director be found who was not a routine television director but somehow 'special'. So Bonny, who had never heard of me, contacted my then agent in Hollywood and sent me Stan Daniels' script.

The script arrived out of the blue on my desk in London and, as it happened, it arrived at a fortunate time. I was due to direct a play in London with Rex Harrison, but Rex was costing so much that the producer wasn't going to give percentages until his investment paid off. I got fed up with the situation and withdrew. So I wasn't doing anything. Stan Daniels' script was at that time called *Sister Ruth*, and I thought it was very well written. Now sometimes in Britain you hear from an agent in California who says, 'They want you there tomorrow,' and that is what happened. I said, 'Yes, okay,' and I realised that I was being asked to sell a project about which I knew very little.

In Hollywood I behaved as though I knew all about the project; it was going to be a colossal success, I said, and I was very much looking forward to doing it. As a result of this, they took it on. The next day, someone from Home Box Office rang up and said, 'I'm glad we're going ahead but how are we going to sell it?' I said, 'I don't know – this is your project. Presumably you have some idea of what you're going to do with it.' You will have to excuse my repeating his language, but he went on, 'I want you to show me one thing: the first time this girl comes on and sings, I want you to guarantee to me that every man watching that television programme is going to cream his pants.' I wondered quite what to say. 'Oh yes,' I said finally. 'Certainly, I get the idea.' So we went ahead.

I went to Toronto. Apart from the three leads, the rest of the cast were Canadian. I insisted that they should get hold of my friend and collabora-

Glory! Glory!: *James Whitmore, Ellen Greene and Richard Thomas in Lindsay's satirical view of television evangelism.*

tor Mike Fash who had already shot *Britannia Hospital* and *The Whales of August*. Fortunately, Mike was available and able to come up to join us, otherwise I doubt that I would have been able to shoot as fast as we did. We shot a three-and-a-quarter hour film in 35 days largely due to Mike's skill and dynamism. We went through various traumas, oppressed by an idiotic schedule which had no relevance to the job; but I liked the script and I liked working in Canada. It was good to work with the actors: James Whitmore was tremendously good – a very amiable curmudgeon whom I liked and admired; Richard Thomas, too, was very intelligent and hard-working.

The film was shown on HBO and later in Britain, and although it was successful I have never been asked to do another film for HBO. One of the mottos of my autobiography, if I ever write one, will be 'never asked back'. I'm very naive about these things because I really don't understand why that should be the case when something has done very well. *Glory! Glory!* remains of genuine interest because the phenomenon on which it's based – the American TV evangelist – is a very interesting and significant one. Of course, the film is never as unpleasant as the evangelists are in reality. In the end, there is something likeable about it. It has a satirical slant but is not in any way sour.

171

35 Days in Toronto

Interview with Gerald Pratley, *Sight and Sound*, Spring 1989.

ANDERSON: I HAVE DONE HARDLY ANYTHING FOR TELEVISION BEFORE *GLORY!* *Glory!*, except for one play, what they call a television play, *The Old Crowd* (1978), from a script by Alan Bennett. I had a very good time working on that with Alan, but it was received with great hostility by almost all the critics and I was labelled 'the only man who had ever made Alan Bennett unfunny'. I think that was because we really went out on a limb and made a film which was satirical and a bit surreal, in places a kind of *homage* to Buñuel, and that isn't at all the kind of thing people expect to see on television. It was really gratifying that it created such a stir and was so disliked, though when it was shown again recently nobody took any notice of it at all.

The only result, unfortunately, was that I wasn't invited to do anything else for television in Britain. So when this invitation arrived from America I was particularly intrigued, because the script had a kind of satirical energy and edge to it which seemed unusual for television, and quite close to many contemporary issues, I am happy to say, notably in its satirical view of TV evangelism. It's interesting that the script was not written as a result of the revelations of the last year or two, but had been under way long before that. I think the producer, Bonny Dore, got the idea after doing research on Oral Roberts. She got hold of a Canadian writer, Stan Daniels, who is experienced and very good – he has worked on *The Mary Tyler Moore Show* – and he did a script which was more intelligent and hard-hitting than you might expect. The reason, I think, is that *Glory! Glory!* has been taken on by Home Box Office, American cable, rather than a network, and HBO are anxious to produce the kind of work that can't be seen on network. They are happy that we should be a bit trenchant or outrageous, and there has never been any suggestion that the edge of the film should be blunted.

I had been going to do *The Admirable Crichton* in the West End, but my negotiations with the producer fell through. So I was at a loose end when this offer arrived out of the blue. It had to be undertaken quite soon, so there wasn't any of that tiresome business of having to work for ages on the script and argue over it with the producers or the sponsors. I thought, 'Well, it's time I had a go. Maybe it's time I sold out!' I haven't sold out yet, and I'm getting tired of being labelled as someone of great and rather boring integrity – so let's have a go. And that's how I got into it, and came to Toronto to film it.

35 days in Toronto: Richard Thomas (left) waits as Lindsay discusses a point with James Whitmore (seated) on the Canadian set of Glory! Glory!

Pratley: I understand that HBO wanted you to shoot this three-and-a quarter-hour film in 35 days, which on the face of it seems an impossibility. How did you cope with that?

Anderson: I didn't have any preconceived plan; in fact, I was extremely doubtful that I would be able to do it. The only wise precaution I took was to ask Mike Fash to join me. I worked with him on *Britannia Hospital* and *The Whales of August*, and he has now emigrated to America and has also done a lot of work in Toronto. He knows people here, he knows technicians, he was able to pick a very good crew, and I insisted that he should be the cameraman. If they hadn't got Mike, I might well not have done it, because I would never have been able to shoot in 35 days. I am not a very slow director, but I'm not a lightning one either. However, I was very lucky: our unit was extremely good: we had an excellent first assistant and on the floor the organisation was first class.

Pratley: Did you have a say in the casting?

Anderson: Yes, as far as the leading parts went, in a limited way because I came into the project late. Bonny Dore had had some trouble getting the film financed and HBO were dubious about the subject. They finally said

173

that they wanted a director who was not from television, and I suppose that's how someone hit on me. When I went out to Los Angeles, I quickly realised that not only I was on test but, in a way, the whole subject, and I had to convince Home Box Office that I could make this film and be the right person to do so. I'm quite good at putting on an act of confidence, which more or less is what I did, and somehow they said OK.

By that time, however, there had been a great deal of research done on the actors. Fortunately, when I heard the name of Richard Thomas as a possibility, I immediately said, 'He will be excellent,' and the same with James Whitmore. Ellen Greene I only knew from the film *Little Shop of Horrors*; I saw four short-listed actresses and chose her. In Canada I participated in the casting with Karen Hazzard, the Toronto casting director, who produced lots of actors, made some very good selections. There was certainly nobody cast whom I didn't approve of.

We are only in Toronto because of the complex financial reasons – which are far beyond me – that make it cheaper to film here than in the States. The picture is supposed to take place in Texas, but there is some complicated tax-shelter arrangement here. If you employ a certain percentage of Canadian talent, the film qualifies for a tax rebate or something of that kind from the Canadian government. That's why we ended up in Toronto, with at least ten producers.

It was a situation that makes for complications. As is traditional, however, the producers didn't really contribute anything beyond having made the original deal. As long as we kept on schedule, there wasn't any interference with the way I was doing the film, nor did I find it necessary to depart from the script. The elements in the script were sufficiently attractive and the actors sufficiently sympathetic and stimulating for us to be able to steam ahead. It's still something of a miracle that we managed to get through the picture in 35 days. The additional requirement, which was that the director's cut should be accomplished in three weeks, turned out to be a total fantasy. In fact, we have done it in about six weeks – which, in itself, is quite ridiculous.

This has been another new experience for me. The picture was shot on film and transferred to tape, and we have been editing it on a system called Ediflex. This is much too complex for me to describe or understand, but it has enabled us to get through the editing faster than if it had been on film. There again, I have had the advantage of an absolutely first-class editor, Ruth Foster, an American young woman who was one of the first really to get into the complexities of Ediflex editing. She had a terrific initiation when she had to edit the Paul Simon African concert, which I understand was extraordinarily complicated. She has now got through *Glory! Glory!* marvellously – the only problem being that she was quite considerably pregnant when we started the work, which has meant another race against time.

Pratley: Have you found it difficult to adjust to computerised editing procedures?

Anderson: Not exactly, because I don't mind working with a technology that I don't fully understand provided the creative part of it is familiar. Editing on this machine is not so very different from the traditional system. Except that there are some things you can do much more quickly and some things that drive you almost mad with impatience. All the same, I think the ability to handle film and to take the strips out and hang them in a bin and look at them is invaluable. It's much more difficult to have to do everything on a video screen and carry it all in your head. So this is not something I particularly want to do again, although there is always the stimulus of a new experience.

Pratley: There is a great admiration in North America for British films which are said to be made for television, whereas the American made-for-TV film only has a reputation for cutting corners.

Anderson: In Britain, Channel 4 has helped to finance films and then has the right to show them, either before or after their cinema screenings. But the films have not exactly been made for television – they have been made for Channel 4, if you like, and that is a different thing. Though if you take *My Beautiful Laundrette*, the interesting thing is that it *was* made for television and was shown in cinemas really quite by chance and at first somewhat to the alarm of the director, Stephen Frears, because he said, 'Well, I only made it for television.' I think the real difference is the kind of subject liable to be financed by Channel 4, which leads to some of the new British films being a bit lacking in the ambition one associates with a cinema film. There is a certain restriction of imagination or idea, rather than the feeling that if you make a film financed by television you have to restrict it in terms of technique or style.

Glory! Glory! is somewhat different. Plainly, although the spread of the story is quite great, it's not possible in 35 days to give it the kind of wit you would have in a movie. If we were making it as a movie, we would certainly have had at least a week or ten days in Texas to shoot some locations. Here we have had one day shooting at York University and that has been our exteriors. My approach to it has been completely pragmatic – to get the script on film as inventively and expressively as possible. When you take on a subject like this, I don't think you indulge too much in theory.

Pratley: How far did the schedule force you into different procedures from those you followed on *The Whales of August*?

Anderson: If we had been making *The Whales of August* for television, I imagine it would have been done on a four-week budget, and it wouldn't

Ill-met by moonlight: Lindsay directing Ellen Greene with Richard Thomas (foreground) for a studio 'exterior' shot on Glory! Glory!

have been shot in Maine but in a studio with a few exteriors. It would have been a different kind of film and it would have been much diminished. I think the fact that we were making a movie creates a psychological difference. I know that some of the American technicians on *The Whales of August* expected us to shoot it like a television movie. They just expected us to give it an overall lighting and then go in to shoot all the sequences. But, of course, we didn't. We shot it with the care that goes with making a movie. But that is true of this film also, and how you have to look at it, if you like, is that the restrictions or economies are present in the script.

I've had the producer say to me once or twice, 'Oh, it looks a bit claustrophobic,' and I have to say to her, 'Well, since you gave me one day to shoot exteriors, and since we never had a particularly convincing exterior location for the headquarters of this evangelist movement, what more do you expect?' But, of course, the trouble is that the better the film turns out, the more they begin to judge it as though it was *Gone with the Wind*. I have to repeat '35 days' and, of course, they forget about that. At the beginning I said to Jamie Paul Rock, a very fine first assistant, 'Look, do you think we can possibly do this?' He said, 'Yes, I think we can, with style and humour.' I thought, well, I've got a good chap there, and I think we did it with style and humour.

Jamie Paul Rock, interestingly enough, is American by birth, and perhaps that accounts for some of his energy. I have found that the Canadians I have worked with have mostly been very agreeable, but there is a strange conformism and acceptance of things – certainly a lack of radicalism which I hadn't expected. I had probably thought they would be more like the Australians, but Canadians aren't like Australians, and they're not really like Americans either. They seem to be oddly satisfied with the way things are.

Pratley: When you are filming overseas, do you keep in touch with what is going on in the world, or in the film world? Is that important to you?

Anderson: It's absolutely unimportant: I don't keep in touch. Occasionally I look at the British papers on a news-stand and I even think of buying one. But when I look at them, I see they are just the same trendy, devitalised rubbish as when I left. When you leave home, and you are away even for a month, you somehow expect great changes to have taken place, and it's so dispiriting to read *The Guardian* or *The Independent* or *The Times* and to see that nothing has changed. It's nice just not to have one's nose rubbed in it every day of the week. As far as I'm concerned, there is nothing to keep in touch with, and it's a nice change to see only the Canadian papers, which contain practically nothing, and indeed to be cut off from all the media nonsense.

Pratley: How important is it for you to know what other film-makers are doing?

Anderson: Not important at all! It's interesting on a personal level to read that my friend Karel Reisz may be directing a script by Arthur Miller in America. But I have to admit that as one gets older one is less interested in other people's work, and I don't really go to see films much. I often feel that I would like to see something, but the business of getting to a cinema and going in and seeing it is so tiresome. Somehow, I do think that after a certain length of time one begins to feel one has seen everything already. It's rare to get stimulus from anything that is being made contemporarily. And that's because one is more concerned with what one is doing oneself: when you are making a film, that's the only film that really exists. If I go and see a movie while I am making a film, I often feel that I'm watching the wrong movie. So, maybe when I get back and have had a bit of a rest, I might venture out and see something. On the other hand, I might stay at home and put my video library in order.

Pratley: Do you rent films on video?

Anderson: I've hired two or three films to have a look at here. At home, I don't think I have ever hired a video. I enjoy recording films on video from the current television programmes – the classic films, that is. But going to

see films in the cinema is generally rather a gruesome experience. I have
the impression that they are a bit better in Canada, but in Britain cinemas
are depressing places to visit. The exhibition side of the industry is quite
largely responsible for the wholesale decline of British cinema, which is
just symptomatic of the whole national spirit. But I mustn't go on saying
things like that, because it makes me unpopular!

Pratley: You started doing documentaries, you have directed features, you
have filmed plays, a rock concert, commercials, you even did a music
video, you've worked in the theatre, and now you have done television in
the American sense, what they call a mini-series. Looking at all this, you
must feel a certain amount of satisfaction.

Anderson: I am more conscious of the fact that critics, journalists and producers find it difficult to pigeonhole one if one has done such a variety of
things and in different styles. The essence of media success, as you know, is
to be pigeonholed, and if I am put in any slot it is as a result of *If . . . .* , *O
Lucky Man!* and *Britannia Hospital* as a difficult, ironic, satirical and not
exactly popular commentator on the ways of the world. That means I
have never felt precisely accepted as a contemporary director, chiefly
because people don't quite know how to define what I do or what I have
done.

None of that matters a great deal, of course, except that with a general
reputation for being difficult, which actually means being demanding, one
finds oneself not the first choice on many people's lists. It may be significant that the last two things I have done have been in America. Not characteristically American, not Hollywood productions, but not British either.
I don't think I would ever have been invited in Britain to direct something
like *Glory! Glory!* To me it has been a stimulating experience, an extremely exhausting one, and I am looking forward to completing it. What will
happen next – I haven't the slightest idea.

I'm surprised, however, that I have made as many films as I have. I
never thought that I was particularly difficult and I've always had a feeling that I could do many different kinds of films, but I can see how I certainly have typed or seemed to type myself. I also realise, looking back on
things, that I have always been lacking in career dynamics. That's due to
a certain laziness that is within me. I'm not lazy when I'm actually working, but I'm like many people who are very obsessive when they work.
When they have finished a job they become extremely lazy and don't want
to do anything, because they remember how awful it was.

Really, considering the kinds of demands I have made and the kinds of
films I have managed to complete, I think it is quite extraordinary that I
have made as many as I have. I count them up sometimes – I can't remember how many there are – and I'm certainly pleased, after a rather choosy

career, to end up with an American mini-series. At least it shows that I have had it in me to make, I hope, a popular film. I've always thought the films I've made are going to be popular, but they almost never turn out to be. This one, which I've had great doubts about, I've been told by one or two people is going to be popular. So I hope they are right: it would be a good way to bring an erratic career to an end.

Journalist and critics seem to expect every film-maker to make two a year. But in fact, while *needing*, if you like, to make films of a certain personal quality, I have also very much enjoyed working in the theatre. Film people hardly acknowledge the existence of the theatre. They don't go to it, they know very little about it, so that side of my career is generally not at all marked by film writers. I only wish that some of the productions I have done could have been recorded. It's sad that experiences and achievements of that kind vanish into thin air, and we are left with the often extremely inaccurate accounts of writers and critics. However, there they are – they have mostly gone, but they have represented a considerable part of my life and one that I am proud of.

The Long Night of the Russian Canapé

Independent on Sunday, 25 November 1990

'GIVE ME DOLLARS' – THIS IS WHAT THE WHITE-COATED MAN BEHIND THE BAR at the Rus Hotel in Kiev said to our Intourist entertainments representative when he asked for a cup of coffee. Konstantin, bright and energetic in brown leather jacket and with well-trimmed moustache, was furious. 'What right has he got,' he fumed, 'to ask me for dollars? He should be serving coffee for roubles.' But it did no good: if you only had roubles – no coffee.

This business of currency was to overshadow the whole visit. I had flown out to the Soviet Union to be with my friend Malcolm McDowell and his girlfriend Kelly. Pippa Markham, Malcolm's agent, and her designer husband Michael Vail had also come along to help Malcolm introduce a retrospective programme of his films in Moscow, Leningrad and Kiev. Just why Malcolm was doing this tour, no one had any idea. One of the new wave of Westerners breaking the old barriers, he was filming at Mosfilm in *The Man Who Shot the Tsar* – a Russian picture with a Russian script, cameraman and director. Malcolm plays the Bolshevik in command of the detachment who guarded the Tsar and his family and eventually slaughtered them. The film is being shot in two versions, English and Russian. Some mysterious services are being provided from London by a company which calls itself Spectator Entertainments, in return for Western distribution rights. Spectator is being run by an enterprising Latvian businessman, Ben Brahm, whose previous experience has been in computers. Nothing much changes in the cinema.

At Moscow Airport we were met by Konstantin of Intourist and by Lorka, who would be our guide and interpreter. Both spoke excellent English. Lorka told us that he was translating *The Odessa File* with his grandmother: he would do the beginning and the end, and she would do the middle. Frederick Forsyth was selling well in Russia.

To Mosfilm, where Malcolm was finishing the first half of his shooting. It was night when we arrived. The studio was large and sprawling and we stumbled in the dark. The cavernous stage was reassuringly like a stage anywhere; Malcolm was cheerful as ever. He had a silent shot to do: the Tsar-slayer returns after the burial of his royal victims and looks round at the cellar which had been their last prison. The set was drab and atmospheric. The camera was hand-held by the cameraman, with a focus puller walking beside him. The director was in attendance, of course, but there

Old pals' act: in 1990, Lindsay travelled to Russia with Malcolm McDowell, who was honoured with a film retrospective in Moscow, Leningrad and Kiev.

was no continuity girl. When the assistant called for silence and a shot, distant voices continued to sing and there was banging somewhere. No one seemed surprised.

Always an anarchic presence, Malcolm had been having a good time. He liked the Slavs. He had started on location, some 40 miles out of Moscow, where everything was scarce. In the capital the story was the same, except that as a visiting star on expenses he was decently looked after and lent the director's quite spacious flat (not luxurious by our standards). Mosfilm was dirty and shabby, with peeling walls; there was a new camera assistant every day; and there was never silence for shooting. Still, Malcolm enjoyed it because the project was a serious one. Other visitors from the West had not felt quite the same, but then Malcolm has never been worried about protocol.

The next day there was a press conference. We were taken to the Film Makers' Union and sat at the top of a square of tables. On the walls were rows of portrait photographs of classic directors from Eisenstein to Bondarchuk, but it was obvious their day had passed. It soon became clear that stars were as much admired here as in the West. The questions were instantly forgettable: I closed my eyes.

We tried to do the usual things. Pippa wanted to walk across Red Square, but it was closed (someone was making a film), so we were not able to see Lenin, now solitary in his mausoleum. The popular, arcaded store, Gum, was crowded, but mostly empty of goods. People queued for fruit and vegetables, and had their names taken in case something turned up.

We visited Chekhov's Moscow house, which we looked round in felt overshoes. It was spick and span and empty. The nice old lady who sold tickets dug around and produced mini-portfolios of Lermontov's Moscow and Literary Moscow, all captioned in Russian. There were no postcards. Moscow also has a Mayakovsky Museum, which Michael was anxious to inspect. We were to be shown round by an English-speaking guide for whom we waited, but she failed to turn up. So we went round ourselves. Designed in chaotic, largely incomprehensible style, the exhibition is built around a circular ramp which takes you up to a little room at the top – a desk, a bookshelf, a window, a bed . . . This is the very place, it seems, where the poet-propagandist-actor-playwright shot himself. His last letter is displayed. Though in the middle of Moscow, the place was practically deserted. No pictures or postcards either.

These jaunts, of course, had to be paid for. We trouped up on the stage at two openings, were presented with flowers and spoke to large friendly audiences. Malcolm, whose lightly sketched face looked down from hoardings all over Moscow, said how happy he was to be making a film in Russia, how happy he was to be working with Karen Shakanarov and made the usual thank-yous before introducing his first film: *If . . . .* I explained that Britain is a class society, with a class system of education. Parents pay for their children to go to college. The Russians listened respectfully but without enthusiasm; they had heard all this before. The programmes never included *Clockwork Orange*, which was what they really wanted to see, because Stanley Kubrick, for some reason, would not allow it to be shown.

I was never quite sure what films actually were shown: we never saw any, since we were always hauled off to some reception, where the Russians enjoyed vodka, wine and substantial canapes. I just had time, generally, to see the large audiences mutely watching the introductory shots. In Moscow, as the credits of *If . . . .* began to roll, against Miroslav Ondricek's lyrical vista of Cheltenham College, I heard the translator's voice begin to fight with the soundtrack and was glad to be led away to the large Russian Hotel for the reception. We crossed a dance floor where middle-aged couples were laughingly doing the Twist. In the reception room, where tables groaned, I was relieved to find vodka and wine among the canapés; the alcohol would certainly not have been there three years ago. It was the drink that chiefly interested the Russians, who kept to themselves, talking and laughing loudly.

Mike was lucky enough to meet Vassily Pichul, the director of *Little Vera*, which he much admired. Pichul has just made his second feature, this time financed by a young private banker. *Little Vera* had been backed by Mosfilm; now the private bankers are beginning to sponsor production. In 10 years' time, Pichul says, they will be Moscow's millionaires. He sniffed at the mention of Eisenstein and Pudovkin. 'Marxists,' he said.

Outside the hotel was Moscow's own Cardboard City, where the paupers and the dispossessed were sheltering, Western fashion, in their cartons and boxes. Konstantin suggested that the uneaten food should be taken out to them, but it wasn't.

Then to Leningrad, where we saw the Summer Palace of Catherine the Great. We ate lunch at the café which had been frequented by Pushkin (no beer or wine), but only one incident there was heart-warming, like in the old days. Pippa and Michael said they wanted to go to the theatre: it didn't matter to what, just to see what it looked and sounded like. At first the response was perfectly agreeable: of course, why not? We'll let you know . . . then, in typical Russian style, complications became evident: we're not quite sure, the tickets are being attended to, we'll let you know . . . Finally it became obvious that, for some mysterious reason, seats could not be booked: the visit would not take place. Hearing this, our driver offered to take us to the Kirov; we would get in, he was sure.

We arrived at the theatre and our driver plunged into the crowd. Somehow he got himself taken to the house manager. A few minutes later, he emerged and beckoned us in. We were greeted with smiles and asked politely about our work: Pippa was an agent, Mike a theatrical designer and I had recently been directing at the National Theatre, which was almost true. Without fuss we were told we could buy tickets (the equivalent of £1 for the three of us) and escorted into the beautiful nineteenth-century theatre where we sat in armchairs and watched the first two acts of a well-sung, monumental *Prince Igor*.

I tried to imagine a London taxi-driver being well received at Covent Garden. How long will such civilised manners continue to exist in Leningrad? Free Soviet citizens can look forward to capitalism now – to independence, unemployment, the homelessness and high prices which will accompany free speech. And a craving for hard currency.

Is That All There Is?

From a letter to Paul Ryan, 27 January 1993

QUITE A LOT OF PEOPLE HAVE SEEN [*IS THAT ALL THERE IS?*] BUT VERY FEW have said anything more than that it is 'tremendously funny' or 'frightfully good'. Neither of which leaves one much the wiser. But although there's a lot of humour in it, I suppose (and hope), I'm really glad you got more out of it than that. That the only guarantee of survival just now, for instance, is a willingness to conform. I realise more and more that an unwillingness (or an inability) to conform can only militate against one's chances of success (unfortunately!).

You're quite right in supposing that there'll be many people who think of that film, or of my position generally, as being 'without hope'. But 'hope' in that sense only implies some facile anodyne . . . It's interesting, though, isn't it, that so much of what has happened in the last couple of years seems to conform exactly to the spirit of that film [*Britannia Hospital*]. Which certainly doesn't mean that it would be any better

The great dictator: Lindsay delighted in writing postcards, but dictated his letters to his long-serving secretary, Kathy Burke, who played a key role in assembling Lindsay's archive after his sudden death in 1994.

accepted now than it was when it was first disastrously shown. Wasn't it Eliot who wrote that 'human kind cannot bear very much reality'? And I remember an article that Gavin Lambert wrote a long time ago in *Sight and Sound*, whose title was a quotation from *Sunset Boulevard*. He called his piece 'Who Wants Truth?' I must really look that piece out: I've thought of it often recently.

Your remark about how it is now fashionable to be 'shocking' reminded me of the charity preview I went to on Sunday to see *Dracula*. Very 'shocking' and full of technological marvels – but narratively not at all gripping or frightening. But the film has been a huge success, I believe, in the US – and no doubt will repeat its success here. I don't know whether age has something to do with it – no doubt it has – but it did make one sigh for the good old days of (say) *Manhattan Melodrama* or *Tobacco Road*. Yes, people today do seem to need art which reassures them – or which shocks them without any real penetration. Anyway, I do really thank you for feeling that *Is That All There Is?* can be seen as a vindication of my work to date. I did try to make something which would be affectionate and humane as well as realistic and caustic . . .

God knows if or when [*Is That All There Is?*] will find an audience – the BBC are not good at letting one know when or how a film of this kind will be shown. Still, it exists, and I suppose that's all that matters.

Lindsay Anderson died on 30th August 1994 during a visit to France. He was 71 years old. *Is That All There Is?* finally received its first screening on BBC Television one week later.

Lindsay with his scrapbooks in the kitchen of his Finchley Road flat.

ON CRITICS AND CRITICISM

Lindsay at the start of his commercial film career.

Angles of Approach

Sequence 2, Winter 1947

To MOST PEOPLE, WE MAY AS WELL ADMIT AT ONCE, THE SUBJECT WILL NOT
seem one of any importance – hardly, even, of any meaning. Our more for-
ward-looking critics are always telling us how public taste is improving,
how the film-going masses are no longer content with the traditional
puerilities of Hollywood and Elstree. It is probably true that an intelligent,
artistically good film can hope for a larger public than it could ten years
ago, but the improvement in taste is an exceedingly gradual one. There has
been no revolution. Most people still demand nothing more from the cinema than that it should provide them with light entertainment; people
who would never think of wasting an evening over a novel by Cronin or
James Hilton will cheerfully swallow a *Random Harvest* or a *Seventh Veil*.
I do not deny that it is far easier – even pleasanter – to sit and watch Ann
Todd and James Mason for 90 minutes than to sit and read *We Are Not
Remembered*, say, or *Green Citadel*, but to approve of one and disapprove
of the other does imply an approach to the cinema that is different in kind
from the approach to literature.

We may regard people who go to the cinema of set purpose 'to be entertained' (or rather '*only* to be entertained') as misguided, but there is not
much we can say to them. They do not, most of them, deny the value of
film as an art; they are just not interested in it. We can only point out to
them the absurdity of scorning the second-rate in one medium, and lapping it up in another. Better, really, that they should leave the cinema alone
altogether than that they should allow themselves to be diverted by *A
Matter of Life and Death*, but confess themselves too lazy to cope with
Ivan the Terrible. However, so long as they admit that they go to the films
simply to gratify an appetite for the meretricious, they do little positive
harm, the loss is chiefly theirs.

As Virginia Woolf once pointed out, it is not the low-brow, but the middle-brow who is the real enemy of the good. In cinematic terms, it is not
the factory-worker who queues for an hour to see *Duel in the Sun* who
needs most urgently the light of the gospel, but the lady-critic who writes
of *La Symphonic Pastorale* as 'morbid, and not my kind of morbid either,'
and who trots off home to curl up in front of the fire with the new Rumer
Godden; or the socially conscious cinemane who sits, dutifully enraptured,
through *Children on Trial*, and leaves halfway through *Zéro de Conduite*
because he finds it strange, silly and irresponsible.

Writing recently in *Vogue* G. W. Stonier ('William Whitebait' of the *New*

Statesman) has attributed the recent renaissance of the British film to, amongst other things, the influence of an enlightened minority of film-goers. 'Minorities', he writes, 'always have, and always will lead every movement in art, entertainment, politics or religion.' True enough; unfortunately this particular minority is, comparatively, a very small one. As a result, it can afford far less than most minorities to allow its ranks to be split, its influence to be weakened by heresies and critical blind-spots. One or two of these heresies I will now proceed to examine, and if possible to discredit.

I have quoted Virginia Woolf on 'middle-brows'. Appropriately enough, one of the most prevalent – and pernicious – of current cinematic heresies might itself well be described as 'middle-brow'. The term perhaps demands definition: from the cinema the low-brow demands diversion, nothing more. The middle-brow, however, is on the highroad to Art and Culture. He is aware, just, of what we may call fundamentals, and he thinks that a good film should show itself aware of them too. But he is incapacitated by a dislike of reality – reality plain, that is; what he likes, what he rapturously accepts, is reality romanticised. It is the prevalence of this trait that is largely responsible for the present highly inflated reputation of the British cinema. Hear Mrs. Woolf address her low-brow friends: 'Why . . . are you so damnably modest? Do you think that a description of your lives, as they are, is too sordid and too mean to be beautiful? Is that why you prefer the middle-brow version of what they have the impudence to call real humanity? – this mixture of geniality and sentiment stuck together with a sticky slime of calves-foot jelly?' 'A mixture of geniality and sentiment' (sentimentality would perhaps be even nearer the mark) '. . . a sticky slime of calves-foot jelly.' Could any phrases describe more aptly the atmosphere of those great popular and 'artistic' successes of war-time – successes like *In Which We Serve, The Gentle Sex, The Captive Heart*? I do not want to suggest that these films are worthless; they all have redeeming features, some many, some few. But in almost every case fidelity to background, good acting, or sensitive direction palliated rather than atoned for sentimental falsification of character and atmosphere. 'The point about these films,' Mr Stonier writes in his *Vogue* article, 'The Coming Heyday of British Films', 'is not merely that they give a true picture of life, but that in doing so they rouse and satisfy. They represent, in fact, as syrupy fiction cannot, an attitude to living and to the art of the cinema, their drama is not pre-determined . . .' And this, if you please, of a list which includes *In Which We Serve*, most handsome of mock-heroic fakes, and *The Way to the Stars*. Has Mr Stonier ever analysed the plot of *The Way to the Stars*? If he does, he will find it the epitome of all the popular West End comedy-drama successes of the last ten years – young lovers, comic background characters, misunderstandings, happy ending and all. Certainly the RAF background is well observed and realistically done; but the story that unrolls before it contains all the ingredients of a romance by Berta Ruck or Ethel M. Dell, and is as expertly contrived. I can, in fact, think of no two epithets that describe it better than 'syrupy' and 'pre-determined'.

Much the same arguments can be brought against the other films in Mr Stonier's familiar list. The truth is, that though British films have improved, not many of them have had enough imagination or integrity to achieve anything approaching artistic success. It is important that we should not try to delude ourselves or each other as to their real value; complacency is no friend to progress, and at the moment we are much too complacent about our films. This is how one London critic described *Odd Man Out*: 'It is more than a milestone. It is a terminus. And if films are hereafter to go forward they must do so by the blazing of fresh trails in virgin technical-country whose fringes we have touched, but not yet trodden.'

But here we are touching on other heresies. Middle-browism is by no means confined to the British cinema (e.g. *Mrs Miniver*, *The Best Years of Our Lives*), and anyway Mr Stonier is no middle-brow. In his article for *Vogue* he seems (not, perhaps, surprisingly) to have fallen victim to the fashionable cult of artistic patriotism. At its best this leads merely to overpraise of the second-rate; at its worst it equates the critic with the economist and turns him into a sort of voluntary blurb-writer for the national product. This does not mean that good foreign films are denied praise. The critical reasoning goes more like this: if it's foreign and good, then it's good; if it's British and good, then (as in the case of *Odd Man Out*) it's the World's Best. From here it is only a step to the conviction that if a film is British and bad, then its success, abroad if not at home, is still desirable. Dr H. H. Wollenberg, for instance, one of our most earnest writers on the cinema, analyses in *Sight and Sound* 'the factors responsible for the fine reputation of the British film'. He starts with a commendable if optimistic, anti-commercial broadside: 'One is so tired of that unceasing procession of glaring posters and publicity stunts announcing the smashing world success, the record-shattering box office sensation . . . they have long ago become meaningless, and even the least discerning film-goer has probably ceased to pay much attention to these outpourings of certain publicity factories.' After this, it is something of a surprise to find Dr Wollenberg quoting with approval dispatches like the following: 'A correspondent from Buenos Aires . . . tells me that British films, during the last year, have enjoyed a great success. *The Seventh Veil* had entered the 25th, *Madonna of the Seven Moons* the tenth week of their first runs, and *The Man in Grey*, just released, is expected to contribute to the singular popularity of the British film. And from Cuba, my Havana correspondent writes that, among others, *The Seventh Veil* and *Madonna of the Seven Moons* had "triumphant"

L'Eternel Retour *(1943). Nathalie (Madeleine Sologne) and Patrice (Jean Marais).*

runs in the most prominent cinema, "America".' And from Germany Dr Wollenberg quotes with glee the dispiriting information that *'The Man in Grey*, too, had a long run. Running at present after a gala premiere, is *The Wicked Lady.*' From these rather revolting facts (though to a British economist, admittedly, cheerful) Dr Wollenberg draws the ludicrous conclusion that 'the British film effort appears to be on the way to contribute largely to what is the very mission of the cinema at large.' This sort of complete abandonment of critical standards is not likely to contribute to anything except the financial betterment of 'certain publicity factories', into whose hands Dr Wollenberg is so guilelessly playing.

Or, if the trouble is not 'economic', it is 'sociological', or simply priggish. There is a joyless conviction about that, to be good, a film must be what is called 'serious'. 'It is disturbing,' we read in a publication from the Newcastle Film Society, 'when the serious critics all combine to praise films like *The Glass Key* or *Double Indemnity*, which appear to be empty of dramatic conflict, social significance or intellectual stimulation.' Setting aside the obvious, but irrelevant, rejoinder that few phenomena could be more socially significant than the contemporary American cycle of crime films, we may note the fallacy that invalidates such criticism – the fallacy that art in general, films in particular, must justify themselves by fulfilling some utilitarian social function. Nothing, in the end, is allowed to be simply what it is: if a good film is praised, it is for being what it is not; if it is condemned, it is for not being what it never set out to be. Typical judgments that result from this sort of attitude are that *Caesar and Cleopatra* is a 'better' film than, say, *Meet Me in St Louis* because it is of 'intellectual interest' or that it is a bad film because it cost so much money; that *Theirs is the Glory* cannot be a bad film because of its subject; that, for the same reason *The Maltese Falcon* cannot be good; that *L'Eternel Retour* is Nordic and pro-Nazi. And so on . . .

Almost all these misjudgements may be attributed to the primary vice of allowing outside considerations – irrelevancies – to load the balance when the merits of a film are being weighed. It is the critic's first duty (and in this sense we are all critics) to perceive the object of a film and to judge its success in achieving that object. This does not mean accepting every film at its own valuation; it means allowing every film to justify itself by its own standards, not by our preconceptions. Of course, the doubt may arise as to the validity of those standards. 'It is well done,' we may say, 'but is it worth doing?' Here it is not possible to dogmatise: but it is as well to remember that all sorts of different things are worth doing, and many of them perhaps things we have never thought of, things that fit in with no pre-conceived ideas of our own.

The first duty of the artist is not to interpret, nor to propagandise, but to create. And to appreciate that a genuinely creative work of art involves the willingness to jettison our own prejudices and viewpoints, and to accept those of the artist. If you expect all films about children at school to be realistic in style and psychological or sociological in approach, you will not be able to get much enjoyment from a fantastic, satirical master-piece like *Zéro de Conduite*. If you have forgotten that poetry, visual as well as verbal, is its own justification, you will call *L'Atalante* sordid and obscure and join the critic of *The Times* in condemning *My Darling Clementine* to 'the graveyard of mediocrity'. Of course, by accepting other people's standards ready-made, one escapes the tiresome duty of having to think, feel and see for oneself. And one escapes a considerable amount of irritation. For there is nothing more sheerly irritating than to see second-rate stuff hailed as first-rate, good ideas spoiled by bad treatment. In the cinema the spirit of delight comes less frequently perhaps than in any other art; it is certainly less accessible. Also it has to be paid for.

What is comes to is this: if we are fully to enjoy (which involves fully understanding) Ford, Vigo, Cocteau, Eisenstein and the rest, we must pay for our enjoyment by many a tortured hour spent squirming, yawning and cursing at Welles, Powell and Pressburger, Sam Wood . . . (there's no end to that list). If you *enjoy L'Eternel Retour*, you may enjoy also *King Kong*, but not *Black Narcissus*. If you enjoy *Black Narcissus* you cannot enjoy *L'Eternel Retour*. (If you think you enjoyed both, you are wrong.) There is ultimately, only one angle of approach; it will cover all that is good, but it cannot be broadened to include the second-rate. 'Prove all things: hold fast that which is good.' The rest, whether British or Russian or French, whether aesthetically or sociologically or politically well intentioned or not, whether feted by the Sunday papers or awarded the *Daily Mail* trophy for the greatest artistic achievement of all time, may confidently be consigned to the rubbish-heap, to limbo, to the outer darkness.

Creative Elements

Sequence 5, Autumn 1948

IT IS, AS EVERYONE IS AGREED, ALMOST IMPOSSIBLE TO KNOW WHO PRECISELY is responsible for the excellence of any particular film. The number of people concerned is so large, the techniques are so varied and so complex, external considerations so influential and so obscure . . . It is not surprising if many critics seem to give up the struggle, and to resolve to treat films on the whole as isolated phenomena, conjured up out of nowhere by a director and some actors, and to judge them in general terms. Since their chief interests often lie in other fields of art – literature or the theatre – the result is a predominantly literary approach to films even by people who now and then use terms like 'cinematic' and 'filmic'; technique is, for the most part, taken for granted, except as a useful weapon for the ignorant to flourish in the face of something they cannot understand.

An exception must be made of that aspect of film technique known as 'direction'. For a long time neglected by all save the cognoscenti, the director has at last come into his own. Critics who wish to qualify as 'serious' mention directors frequently, usually after comments on the story and the acting, and in combination with some approving but colourless adverb – as if conscious of their importance but mystified as to their exact position in the scheme of things. A critic in a London weekly thus describes *The First Gentleman* as 'unconvincing', 'unreal and, alas, boring', but timidly pronounces: 'The direction by Cavalcanti is good.' Miss Graham is on the right track, but has evidently not advanced very far along it; competent criticism – merely a syllogism, after all, for full appreciation – demands the capacity to analyse, to comprehend 'what' through 'how'.

It should not be necessary to emphasise that analysis is not the enemy of intuition; intuitive appreciation is valuable but uncertain. Centuries of literary criticism have accustomed us to analysis of plot and character: by its means we accept exposure of falseness or sentimentality. It is less generally realised that other aspects of a film besides its script may have their clichés. Knowledge, anyway, never lessens enjoyment of the good, however it may affect our attitude towards the indifferent and incompetent. We generally enjoy more keenly when we know as exactly as possible what we are enjoying, and why.

A studio-made film is a co-operative venture, necessitating many more or less creative workers. (By 'creative' I mean any skill not specifically definable; the clapper-boy, whose function can be exactly specified, is not creative, while the cameraman is, or should be.) The merits and defects of

194

any film may thus be the joint or individual responsibility of many people – the producer, the actors, the designer, the composer, the sound-recordist, the editor, the director, the cameraman, or the scriptwriter. Of these it is rare that all can be described as creative workers. In a routine commercial production the 'technicians' are concerned simply to make visible and audible the scriptwriter's conception – while he (usually in the plural) has done what was demanded of him by the producer; and the producer's demands were dictated by the receipts of his last-but-one-picture. But 'live' film, a work of art as well as competence, each element contributes to the worth of the whole. (The critic, if only to perform the elementary duty of giving credit where it is due, should be capable of isolating and evaluating each contribution; even the amateur will find that this ability adds to his understanding and enjoyment.)

In one sense the most responsible member of any film unit is the producer, as is demonstrated by the large salary he usually commands. The producer controls the budget, and money is power. There is no reason to suppose that what Capra wrote of Hollywood in 1939 is much less true today: 'I would say that 80 per cent of the directors today shoot scenes exactly as they are told to shoot them, without any changes whatsoever, and that 90 per cent of them have no voice in the story or the editing.' No doubt these figures account for the many otherwise inexplicable lapses of notable directors. It is not surprising that, in America especially, the ambition of most is to produce, or at least co-produce, their own films: unfortunately the policy is not always justified by results. Given their heads, Capra, Ford, George Stevens produce *It's a Wonderful Life*, *The Fugitive*, *I Remember Mama*; in Britain, Launder and Gilliat, Powell and Pressburger emerge from Independent Producers with *Captain Boycott* and *A Matter of Life and Death*.

Like the theatre impresario, the producer undoubtedly has a creative function. To bring together artists and technicians who are sympathetic and will therefore combine well; to present them with a congenial and worthwhile subject; to supervise production with efficiency, tact, taste, understanding – these are tasks which demand a rare and valuable ability. The great names of Hollywood – Thalberg, de Mille, Zanuck, Goldwyn – have been showmen and organisers of genius, but rarely men of culture. Zanuck's personal supervision has ranged from *The Grapes of Wrath* to *Forever Amber*; in Britain, the productions of men like Korda, Balcon, Del Giudice, give evidence of certain standards, but they are not sufficiently firm to preclude disappointing errors and failures; in France one has learned to expect high standards from André Paulvé (producer of *Les Visiteurs du Soir*, *Les Enfants du Paradis*, *L'Eternel Retour*). Significantly

M. Paulvé is reported to be giving up producing as an unrewarding job; such is at present likely to be the fate of any Diaghilev of the cinema.

Without external evidence the producer's contribution to a film cannot be estimated; other elements – acting, music and design, for instance – speak for themselves. Of these three in particular, acting is the most vital. The excellence of its Berlioz could not make *La Symphonic Fantastique* a tolerable film; Duvivier's *Anna Karenina* remained a bore for all the sumptuous accuracy of its settings. But greatness of performance has redeemed many otherwise unremarkable pieces – witness the earlier *Anna Karenina* and, indeed, almost every film made by Garbo in America. For the success of a dramatic film, good acting is indispensable, and in this sense (and no other) it is true that the French cinema is, in Miss Powell's words, 'essentially a cinema of actors'. Specialised experiments apart, all good cinema flourishes on good acting; even the frequently mocked star system has produced many players of great and lasting talent. American ensemble playing is less often remarked upon than French, though films like *The Front Page*, *The Maltese Falcon*, *Roxie Hart*, *Crossfire*, owe much of their success to their high standards of performance. Screen acting is a varied and subtle art, with room for the stylised magnificence of Cherkassov's Ivan, the larger-than-life ebullience of Brasseur and Reggiani, the intimate naturalism of Fonda and Jane Darwell, and the anonymous players of *Espoir*.

The composer and the designer have contributions to make that are equally subtle and varied – though not in every case essential. In scrupulously realistic productions, impressive work may be achieved without either a musical score or studio-made sets. Among recent films, *Le Corbeau* and *Gentleman's Agreement* have no music (the intrusive uprush of Newman's strings at the fade-out of the latter only emphasises the falsity of the 'solution') and thrillers like *The Naked City*, *Kiss of Death*, authentic pieces like *Farrebique*, *Sciuscia*, *Fires Were Started*, needed no art-direction. While location shooting may impose limitations, these are less detrimental than inadequate studio settings – which is no doubt a major reason for the present popularity of location work. It is not a justification of most backcloths, back projection, false perspective and so on, that they pass unnoticed by the majority of film-goers; even when they are not positively destructive of atmosphere, they are generally negative in function, supporting the action but contributing nothing to it.

But it is to films which aim rather to create their own world than faithfully to reflect actuality, that the designer and composer can make their most valuable contributions. Variations in style are of course infinite; good designs vary from the ruthless expressionism of *Caligari* to the magical re-creation of period accomplished by Meerson in *La Kermesse Heroique*, from the gothic extravagances of Laurence Irving's *Uncle Silas* to the affectionate near-realism of Minnelli's designs for his own *Meet Me in St Louis*. Music similarly – from Prokofiev's elaborate symphonic scores for *Alexander Nevsky* and *Ivan the Terrible*, or the almost balletic commentary to Clair's early comedies, to the looser but also finely calculated use of popular and traditional music to point the pathos, the charm and the tragedy of films as diverse as *Douce* and *The Ox-Bow Incident*, *Zéro de Conduite* and *The Grapes of Wrath*. Misused, these arts can of course harm as much as they assist. We are all familiar with the standardised interiors, the shoddily unconvincing exteriors of the routine commercial production from any country. The intimacy with which sound and visual are wedded in a film makes music even more potent to falsify and cor-

Creative Element: cameraman Greg Toland's compositions for Wyler's Little Foxes *and Welles'* Citizen Kane.

rupt – a soundtrack drenched with cheap music can degrade sentiment to sentimentality, sincere gesture to pretentious flourish. Stripped of Hageman's ponderous symphonic clichés the first ten minutes of *The Fugitive* might turn out to be impressive, perhaps even moving. But as they are . . .

At their best, by precise evocation of mood and atmosphere, a designer and a composer in sympathy with their subject can incalculably reinforce the total effect. Yet it is possible (though it may be undesirable) to draw a distinction between their work and that of the remaining artists on our list. The sound recordist has most in common with them, for in a sense his work also is *applied*; and we cannot without external evidence know how much of the natural soundtrack springs from him, how much from the director or writer. Similarly with the editor; we know that the rhythm of a film is of primary importance, depending on the exact timing of each shot, the precise moment of cut, and length of fade or dissolve; but the ultimate responsibility for shape, and therefore for rhythm, is the director's. As far as criticism goes, then, we are left with three men whose work must be appraised, three men whose contributions are vital, interdependent. For here we approach the holy of holies, the inextricable Trinity of the film: scriptwriter, cameraman and director.

From another point of view, this resolves itself into the familiar question – form (or style) and content. To what extent can we separate the thing said from the way of saying it? At least in the other arts we are dealing with facets of the same personality; in the cinema we have a varying number of artists – each perhaps with a slightly different conception of the work they are combining to create.

Superficially it might seem possible to isolate the contribution of the scriptwriter; at least one can listen to dialogue, examine construction and motivation. And it is true that a script's limitations in these respects are the limitations of a film. From a script which raises controversial issues and then evades them, which cheats its way out of an emotional problem, which falsifies character, no director on earth can make a wholly satisfactory film. But a film script is not a play or a novel; a scriptwriter has to visualise, to conceive his story in terms of picture rather than dialogue, and somehow to indicate on paper its pictorial quality and rhythm. Hitchcock has often been reported as saying that all the important work on his films is done on the script – but even Hitchcock is careful to direct his own films.

For it is under the director's guidance that the film is created, transformed from the inadequately expressed idea of the script to a living sequence of sound and images. And for the appearance of every image he is dependent on the cameraman. It would be simpler if we could regard the cameraman as a 'technician who merely complies with the director's demands; but, to demand specific effects, a director must be a cameraman himself, which is rare. It is not, perhaps, generally appreciated that composition, lighting and movement are very often the cameraman's responsibility, and yet these are amongst the chief means of expression in the cinema. A good cameraman can make a dull director's work seem interesting – compare *Pursued*, photographed by Wong Howe, with any other of Raoul Walsh's recent films (*Desperate Journey, Cheyenne*). A great cameraman, like Tisse or Toland, will make the photography an integral, conceptual part of the film: Toland's achievement is particularly astonishing, varying from *The Grapes of Wrath* and *The Long Voyage Home*, to *The Little Foxes* and *The Best Years of Our Lives*. If the script of the latter film had been worthy of the direction and the beautifully judged camera work, it would have deserved its awards.

Good films, the purest and the best, speak through camera work – composition and flow of images – as much as through the words spoken by the characters or the 'literary' significance of the plot. Style and content fuse to form something new, something individual, a whole greater than its parts. A synopsis of *L'Atalante* means as little as one of a lyric poem; on paper *My Darling Clementine* is just another western. But as they unfold upon the screen, with grace of movement, freshness of vision, they are found to possess a magic power to excite, to enchant, to revive. To describe this as 'formal beauty' is inadequate and misleading, for the phrase implies the frigid, sterile formality of a work like *Day of Wrath*, rather than the living poetry which is the result when even a commonplace story is given shape and meaning by an expressive camera, sympathetic music and design, skilled actors, and above all by creative direction – direction which gathers all these elements together, and gives them unity and life.

So, in this gathering together, this fusion, there must be a central figure, one man conscious of the relative significance of every shot, the shape and flow of every sequence. But he cannot stand alone; he stands with, dependent on, his author and his cameraman. No doubt in an ideal world the same man would fulfil each function, but it is no use writing criticism for an ideal world. Eisenstein himself wrote and designed all his productions – Vigo wrote his own scripts; so do Clair, Sturges, Welles, Chaplin; Renoir and Grémillon sometimes; Ford and Carné never. But it is not surprising that the cinema is full of famous partnerships – Carné and Prévert; Eisenstein and Tisse; Ford with Johnson and Nichols; Ford and Sturges with their favourite actors; Carné with Traunei the designer.

It is a complex series of relationships, susceptible to so many changes of emphasis that all generalisations are sooner or later falsified. But one constant truth emerges – that the evolution of a whole and consistent film demands a rare, almost miraculous fusion of many and various creative elements. Inevitably, perhaps, some critics, soured by prolonged exposure to the second-rate, sell out at last; and proclaim with the loud, self-assuring accents of those who resign from an honourable but fatiguing struggle, that the film is not an art. Only one answer is necessary – that it has been done. It is by their instinctive appreciation of what the critic distils by careful analysis, that the few great men of the cinema have made those rare and treasured works which are to the cinemane (as her quotations to Virginia Woolf), 'text after text to be hung upon the wall, title after title to be laid upon the heart like an amulet against disaster.' Their existence alone entitles film to its present, indisputable position among the arts.

The Director's Cinema?

Sequence 12, Autumn 1950

'THE OTHER DAY I SAW TWO REELS OF A PICTURE, ALL I COULD STAND: AND while watching it I wondered what you would say of it, of a film of such cheap and vulgar behaviour, of direction which allowed a cute little leading lady to make cute little faces at the hero behind his back, of crude little scenes of nothing but interminable bickering, of comedy so drab and hackneyed . . . And just as I was preparing to drop you a line the next day and cite this as an example of what happens to a director when he has a shabby script, I discovered in your article on Ford that you treated *She Wore a Yellow Ribbon* seriously and with respect . . .'

It is always gratifying to find that anything one has written has aroused comment, provoked disagreement; and so, although I had imagined that other judgements in that article (*'They Were Expendable* and John Ford', published in *Sequence 11*) were more controversial than a parenthetical reference to *She Wore a Yellow Ribbon* as a 'pot boiler . . . with much of the old sweep and strength of sentiment', I was nevertheless glad to receive this outraged cry from a friend, a knowledgeable man, of some celebrity and experience in the making of films.

I was particularly interested because, by the time that letter arrived, I had seen the film in question a few more times, and had formed an estimate of it which would have provoked my correspondent to even louder, more incredulous cries. My first reactions indeed had not been so very different from his; 'a sprawling epic of the Frontier', I had written (elsewhere, fortunately), '. . . with distressing frequency feeling lapses into sentimentality, characterisation into banality, and humour into tedious horseplay. The standard of performance is very uneven: the young people are featureless and scarcely competent; Victor McLaglan is given every encouragement to overplay, and though John Wayne is a solid, engagingly simple Brittles, his is not the most interesting of personalities.'

Now let me thrust my right hand – the hand that wrote that review – into the fire. *She Wore a Yellow Ribbon* is a fine film, full of vigour and enjoyment. Its faults, which admittedly prevent it achieving that perfection of finish which distinguishes Ford's best films, should not blind one to this first and essential truth. Its story, rambling and carelessly constructed, is set on the Southern Frontier in the seventies, at a time of continuous friction between the American Cavalry and the resentful, mutinous Indian tribes. Its hero is an elderly Cavalry officer, Captain Nathan Brittles, whose last patrol is brought to failure by the insistence of his commanding officer that he escort on it two women leaving the fort for the winter: their presence slows down the column and fatally enables the Indians to attack and burn the stage post, and to rise in revolt. Only by the exercise of personal, and strictly unorthodox initiative, does Brittles avert the possibility of a serious rising. Then, his task accomplished, he rides away to the West and to retirement – to find himself recalled with honour, as chief of Civilian Scouts.

To accuse the film of roughness is perfectly just. The narrative proceeds with amplitude, and without perceptible effort to build to a dramatic climax; the continuity is not all it should be; the romantic element is entirely conventional. There are passages in it which may be guaranteed to shift the hyper-sensitive uneasily in their seats – studio sunsets which suffuse the entire screen with a glow of vivid orange, at least one sequence of the crudest knockabout, and an ending as chock-a-block with false conclusions as a Beethoven symphony. One is not surprised to hear the professional film-maker react with such vehemence against its defects.

Under certain circumstances, though, carelessness in the composition of a work of art ceases to be of great importance: when it is compensated by energy and feeling – by sweep, in fact, and strength of sentiment. It is perhaps misleading to describe *She Wore a Yellow Ribbon* as having much of Ford's 'old' sweep. For its largeness covers comparatively little action; compared with *Drums Along the Mohawk*, for instance, its theme is the merest incident; and as a result its spread, its mass, seems correspondingly the greater. It is a picture painted with a bold, even a reckless brush, with a disregard for detail which shows the self-confidence of an artist who makes his pictures as they please him, trusting his ability well enough not to exert himself overmuch in the task of making it all clear to the less quick-witted amongst his audiences.

Which is not to say that the detail is not there – when it pleases Ford to insert it. But it pleases him to insert it to fill in the background of his picture, to make it spring emotionally to life, rather than for the sake of clarifying the development of its story, or of rendering it palatable to those whose tastes may lie primarily in other directions. From beginning to end the film has that sense of material well-loved and lived in, like an old suit of clothes, a bit shapeless by now but still with many years of good wear ahead of it. You can take it all simply as an adventure of the wide open spaces – an aspect of the film splendidly evoked by the commentator's 'feathered bonnets against the Western sky' – but it is an adventure which owes a great deal of its excitement, and all its peculiar magic to the love and knowledge which have gone into the recreation of its vanished world.

201

She Wore a Yellow Ribbon *(1949). Captain Brittles (Wayne) and Sergeant Quincannon (McLaglen).*

The backgrounds, fort and plain, are scrupulously presented: the one with its familiar routines and reassuring hierarchies, the other with its perpetual stimulus of beauty and danger. And against these the ethos of the United States Cavalry of the period is fondly and faithfully revived. There is romantic emphasis of course on gallant uniforms and (on the soundtrack) swinging choruses, but these are no musical comedy soldiers. They are rowdy, courageous campaigners, faithful servers of their flag. This tradition of service, a familiar Ford theme, is personified in the film's hero, the grey-haired Nathan Brittles, who has spent his life in and for the Cavalry, lost a wife and daughter to it, and now faces with reluctance the prospect of a lonely retirement and with what sympathy and friendly humour do Ford and Wayne bring this delightful character to life. Around Brittles are grouped figures of similar authenticity: his Colonel's brisk and kindly wife; a cautious, wide-awake Southern sergeant, lately a Captain in the Confederate forces; a roystering Irish sergeant, whose full-blooded humour has real character behind it, until it goes overboard in a final, music-hall turn of a bar-room brawl. Compared with these, it is true, the youthful triangle is not much more than adequate but they have no reason to be anything more. It is not their film.

To those who accuse *She Wore a Yellow Ribbon* of sentimentality there is no answer, for the distinction between true sympathy and mawkish weakness is one that we have to make for ourselves. It is rash, though, to avert one's eyes on principle from a scene in which an elderly man sits quietly before his wife's grave and talks to her, or accepts, with an audible snuffle of emotion, a farewell token from his troop. Presented without self-consciousness, with no forcing of the pitch, these scenes have a genuine tenderness; and so has the ceremonial meeting of Brittles with his old Indian friend, Pony-That-Walks; and the efforts of the Colonel's wife and the Irish sergeant to comfort the little boy and girl found cowering, too frightened to speak, in the burned-out stockade. As was not the case with Ford's previous patrol across this territory (*Fort Apache*) such intimacies balance the more spectacular panoramas, and give the film emotion as well as excitement, depth as well as sweep.

> Nobody, in all truth, admires Ford more than I do – when he is provided with the strength and support of a script . . . But how could you have sat through *She Wore a Yellow Ribbon*? What would you have said of it if you hadn't known that Ford had directed it?

I have allowed myself to dwell on this film, not merely for the pleasure it gives me to write about it, but because it seems to me that from these utterly different responses to it, some interesting critical implications may be drawn. A disputed problem, for instance, on which it may throw some light is the currently popular one on writer *versus* director: to what extent, that is, can the achievement of a director be estimated and praised independently from that of the writer who has furnished him with a script? Can, in fact, a director like John Ford be considered an artist at all?

Let me quote again from my correspondent, advancing from *She Wore a Yellow Ribbon* to attack the whole basis of that article on Ford:

> While a good many of the things you say about Ford are unquestionably true, I feel that the whole spirit of your article – and of your editorial policy generally – is that of a cult, a cult dedicated to the worship of the director to the exclusion of all other contributors to the making of a film. I can only attribute this to a stubborn blindness to the actual processes of making a picture; it is only the non-professionals who carry this adulation to such lengths.
>
> Take *The Grapes of Wrath*: Ford worked on a script by Nunnally Johnson, who in turn was working with material from John Steinbeck. Who but an incredibly vain or fatuous person could feel for one second that he had more than a faintly contributory interest in a third reworking of someone else's book? *The Grapes of Wrath* is a novel by John Steinbeck; he and his creation are the sum and substance of the film of that name.

What, one wonders, will be said to this by all those film society secretaries, busy at this time of the year with their programme notes for next season's showing of 'John Ford's *The Grapes of Wrath*'? But worse follows:

> The contribution of the director, in my opinion, is the least to be proud of. He does not contribute the story and plot, he doesn't provide a character, he doesn't write a line of dialogue, which I should say are the salient elements of a film. His contribution to the photography is again collaborative, to varying degrees, and the photography is the only element allowing for creative development . . .
>
> In other words, the margin within which a director can operate and exercise his own invention and creative ability seems to me too small to warrant the almost entire credit which *Sequence* and other similar magazines give to him.

This represents a challenge; and, as a challenge should be, it is couched in strong words. But my correspondent is by no means alone in his protest – a familiar one from screenwriters of many generations. Recently, for instance, the same dispute has been given an airing in *Sight and Sound*, this time in a clash between a British director (Thorold Dickinson) and a Hollywood writer (Howard Koch). The trouble started with Mr Dickinson's article, 'The Filmwright and the Audience', expressly a plea for the recognition of the director as the true creator of a film, the filmwright:

> There are so many departments in sound film, and so many more in the colour film, that nowadays there is a genuine tendency to believe that one man can no longer govern the job. My contention is that we must find and encourage the one man who *can* govern the job. For, excepting those film makers who hunt in pairs, the sound film is as much a one-man job as any other art.

Mr Dickinson is prepared, of course, to admit the existence of the filmwright's collaborators, and to a certain extent he will tolerate them. Film direction is an exhausting business and in the preparation of a picture it is as well for the director to have skilled assistance – particularly in the matter of dialogue writing, which is a gift as special as direction'. In this aesthetic of film, indeed, the writer figures chiefly as a dialoguist, and is encouraged to keep his ambitions humble:

> The creative writer seldom has the patience to master the elements of cinema to the full . . . There is no doubt that a writer is more interested in the speaking of his dialogue, which is a direct expression of his talent, than he is in any interpretation which the director may give to his descriptions of visual action . . . Undoubtedly the screenwriter is frustrated in

every element of his work except in the direct use of his dialogue.

It would have been surprising if assumptions as bold as these had met with no challenge, and sure enough they did (though some dispiriting inferences might be drawn from the fact that no writer in this country was interested, or competent to defend his *métier*). At all events, it was from Howard Koch, in Hollywood, that the expostulation came:

> It seems to me a strange notion that the visual and the auditory can be so neatly separated, or that the playwright will be able to function in such an isolated role. Does Mr Dickinson really believe that a writer creates only by ear?

Granted that a film may be defined as 'experience re-created for the screen', to Mr Koch the important question remains – 'who conceives this experience in its essential dramatic terms?' And promptly comes the not-unexpected answer:

> It seems incontrovertible to me that the writer is the primary creative source. He puts down on paper the significant symbol, visual as well as auditory, through which character is revealed in a progressive series of definitive tensions. It is the writer's imagination that first previews – however inchoately and incompletely – the substance of what eventually appears on the screen.

Before plunging to the rescue of *our* time-honoured 'primary creative source', it is as well, I think, for us to make a fundamental admission. There is no doubt that by the majority of critics, the film-appreciative amateurs, the screenwriter is unjustly and often ludicrously neglected. Week by week the patently collaborative productions which appear on our screens are talked about and written about as though the director alone were responsible for their merits, or their defects. It is not a matter of deliberate subordination of script to direction. Critics react and write in this way automatically; no alternative approach has suggested itself to them.

Examples of this habit present themselves almost whenever film criticism is read, but a few instances may be of value. For example, Mr Koch himself might have raised his eyebrows to read in the *Daily Telegraph* a three-column attack on his screenplay for *Mission to Moscow* which never got around to mentioning his name, or even to suggesting that any individual was responsible for the preparation of the script. ('Warner Bros . . . chose to treat one of the great crises in the history of mankind after the old scenario formula . . .') Likewise, a relatively literate review of *The State of the Union* in the *Manchester Guardian* represents the film as the sole, unaided work of its director: 'another of those moral lectures by Mr Frank Capra, which may be oversimplified but are certainly presented with force and good humour. This time his text is the same . . . In the end Mr Capra withdraws Mr Tracy's candidature.' (The film was, in fact, adapted by Anthony Veiller from a successful Broadway comedy by Howard Lindsay and Russel Crouse.) Even so distinguished a writer as Charles Spaak fared no better when his adaptation of *The Idiot* was shown in London; thus, the *Evening Standard* reviewer: 'In *L'Idiot* the French have successfully brought to the screen the sincerity, the passion and the pathos of Dostoevsky. Director Georges Lampin has not spared us a single element of the deep suffering and bewildering frustration that dominates this great novel . . .'

The ignorance which is revealed by statements such as these is not pardonable. The methods commonly practised in the making of a film are not secret. By now, presumably, every critic has by heart that statement of Frank Capra's on the position of the Hollywood director in 1939 ('I would say that 80 per cent of the directors today shoot scenes exactly as they are told to shoot them without any changes whatever, and that 90 per cent of them have no voice in the story or editing . . .'). And even where the director is a man of privilege, it is common knowledge that he will be shooting from a script to which the writer has contributed considerably more than a mere story outline with dialogue. An experienced screenwriter has to go through years reading scholarly comments on 'directional touches' in his pictures which were set down in detail in his scripts.

But this attitude is only partially the result of ignorance. A powerful element in it is an inadequate appreciation of the traditional high-brow aesthetic of the cinema as the director's medium. Swallowed whole, without the necessary mastication of analysis or forethought, this is naturally apt to appear in print in half-digested lumps. And then also, it complicates things so to delve further into the matter. Apart from the labour involved, and the bore of having to fit all those names elegantly into a single review, there is the question of how much one's readers will actually take. Neither in this country nor anywhere else is there much of a public for expert film analysis; it is no wonder if even our two or three responsible press critics seem often to be performing as journalists rather than engaged in the serious business of criticism.

None the less, the problem and the obligation remains – part of the job. Mr Koch puts it with the bitterness born of experience when he writes:

From some future perspective, I feel certain it will seem a strange phenomenon in the history of the cinema that, for a period, its leading critics assembled in New York to evaluate the contributions of stars, directors and producing companies, without any recognition of the basic creative work on which the others rest. And a few offices down the hall, the reverse process is taking place – the Drama Critics' Circle are granting their award to the author of the season's best play!

In Mr Koch's case there is this strength; and there is also weakness. Partly this weakness springs from the extreme professionalism of his approach. There are advantages in being an 'engaged' as opposed to an entirely detached critic: the professional is familiar with the raw materials of his art, less likely to make the elementary howlers to which the non-professional is prone, more disposed to fit his theories to the facts instead of vice-versa. But he also runs his risks. It is possible for a critic to sit too close to the screen. Mr Koch is obviously caught up in the Hollywood picture-making machine, and finds it difficult to look in any other direction. 'These are the facts of life,' he writes, 'at least in Hollywood' – and it is with the facts of Hollywood life that he is primarily concerned. As a result his attack on the critical treatment of the standard Hollywood product is convincing enough, but his generalisations tend to run astray.

Mr Koch's general reflections on the art of the film (and, for that matter, those of my correspondent) suffer also from being angled too exclusively from the viewpoint of the professional writer. He writes, as he states, 'as an American playwright', and as such it is evident that he is thinking really in terms of literature and the theatre. To him ideas are expressed in the cinema through words and through acting first, and secondly through such visual symbols as can be specified directly in the script (and which are therefore often described as 'literary'). The films which he, and people like him, most admire are those in which the director's function approximates closely enough to that of a stage director – in whose power it is also to 'enrich' the dramatists' original. 'The play, in both cases, is conceived and written in terms of visual action and dialogue which actors perform under the guidance of a director.' This anti-traditional view puts the film director severely in his place, demanding of him technical capacity, sensibility to the ideas and characters provided for him by his author, but no independent response to his material, no desire to present it in the light of his own imagination, illuminated by it, or transformed.

This point of view ('this misconceived parallel of theatre and film') is directly opposed by Thorold Dickinson. Now Mr Dickinson is also a practising film-maker – or filmwright, as he would prefer to be called –

and as such his view also is slanted from his personal, practical approach to the cinema. His cavalier dismissal of the screenwriter is obviously the result of his need, in the preparation of his scripts, of the assistance of a professional dialoguist. This leads him generally to underrate the craft of the scenario writer, since on his own pictures he prefers to do the rest of the job himself.

When it comes, though, to talking in general terms, Mr Dickinson shows himself truly and firstly a man of the cinema. His emphasis on the expressive potentialities of film technique is the result of a proper realisation that what a film says should be inseparable from the way it says it. This striving towards integrity in the creative process is the reverse of Mr Koch's attitude, who is more concerned to preserve the integrity of his script than to see it assimilated into a new thing, an original film. In view of which, one is not surprised to hear that when he 'tries to imagine motion picture direction on its highest and most creative level', Mr Koch 'invariably thinks of William Wyler' – indeed a perfect example of the director of this class, who seeks with honesty, artistry and technical skill of the very highest order to make his films a true and perhaps enriched realisation of their authors' intentions. What Wyler does not attempt to do – the declaration is his own – is to use the cinema to express his own feelings or his own ideas; and as a result there is about them a certain impersonality which marks them as the work of a brilliant craftsman rather than a serious artist.

The same may be said, with varying degrees of emphasis, of three of the other four directors whom Mr Koch singles out for particular approbation – Max Ophuls, Mark Robson, Joseph Mankiewicz and Rudolph Maté – of whom only one can be said to make films recognisably his own, linked by their consistent values as well as by their common elegances of style. It is, indeed, in his apparent incapacity to distinguish between Ophuls and the other directors whom he mentions that Mr Koch betrays his fundamental insensibility to cinema. He looks forward to the time when 'the motion picture will mature, and all its collaborating talents will gain satisfaction and significance by the shift in emphasis from the gloss of its wrapping to the integrity of its content.' The antithesis is naive. A film, like any other work of art, gains in quality in proportion as its literary content (that part of it which can be expressed in words) becomes identified with its manner of treatment. It is this fact which film writers seem unable to appreciate, so that they are apt to indulge in such dreamy fantasies as that put forth by Margaret Kennedy in her little book *The Mechanised Muse*, in which she opines that 'if screen poetry should ever reach the heights destined for it, perhaps the supremacy of directorship may turn out to have been a passing phase.' She continues wildly: 'or perhaps some director may desert the arena for the Ivory Tower. He may decide that his art is creative rather than executive. Retaining all his prestige and decisive authority, he may toss his megaphone to some trusted subordinate and quit the hurly-burly of the floor. In his office he will build a sanctuary where he can be vacant and pensive . . .' 'Vacant' is the word. One may as well imagine a painter conceiving an idea for a picture in his mind's eye, sketching it on a piece of paper with notes on the imagined colours – and then handing it over to 'some trusted subordinate' to execute in paint.

To revert to Mr Koch's antithesis: it is safe to say, of a film in which form and content can be so easily distinguished, that its level *as art* will not be very high.

'What would you have said of *She Wore a Yellow Ribbon* if you hadn't known that Ford had directed it?' The question is unanswerable, although I like to think that internal evidence would have established the film's authorship as certainly and almost as instantly as his name upon the credits. The subject in fact is one to which this particular director has responded with deep and evident sympathy; and as a result, the film has become – unmistakably – his. For this reason it is pardonable for a critic to discuss it without focusing much on James Warner Bellah, who provided the original story, or on Frank Nugent and Lawrence Stallings, who worked it into script form.

It is interesting to find this confirmed in an article by Nugent on Ford, published in the *Saturday Evening Post*: 'Ford never has formally surrendered to the talkies. His writers are under standing orders to keep dialogue to an "irreducible minimum". Ford usually manages to trim the "irreducible" still more. He always works with his writers on a script, but never lets them forget who holds the whip hand.' Contrast this with Wyler (by Koch): 'In the preparation period he never tells a writer what to write – he has too much respect for the creative process . . .'

Of course, there can be no final judgement in this controversy. 'To generalise,' said Blake, 'is to be an idiot;' and it would certainly be idiotic to suppose that any strict generalisations can be evolved on a subject as complex and shifting as the creative responsibility for a film. A good film must draw its original inspiration from a script but it may grow to full creative life through various patterns and degrees of collaboration. And the fact remains that (granted, on his part, the inclination and the capacity) the man most in a position to guide and regulate the expressive resources of the cinema is the director. To that extent it remains, and will remain, the director's medium.

The Film Artist – Freedom and Responsibility!

Unpublished article written for the Russian review, *Iskustvo Kino*, 1959

WITH MANY OF THE THINGS THAT GRIGORY KOZINTSEV SAYS IN HIS ARTICLE, 'Deep Screen', I am in complete agreement. In fact, I cannot imagine that anyone that claims to work as an artist in this most challenging, and difficult, and wonderful medium can think otherwise. Kozintsev believes in the cinema – not just in certain films, classics or prizewinners – and so do I. He is disappointed and dismayed by the number of pretentious, untalented people who claim to be artists, but whose chief skill seems to be the management of a successful career – and so am I. Yet here perhaps we are unreasonable. In any medium the number of true creators is always small. Think of the number of mediocre painters, poets, writers there are: we should not be surprised if the proportion of outstanding film artists is even lower.

Because the material difficulties of film-making are so great, the price of failure so high, the great majority of film-makers are always bound to be second-rate, exploiting the discoveries of artists greater than themselves, often degrading them and compromising them. After all, how many of the great innovators enjoyed peaceful, successful careers? Griffith – Eisenstein – Vigo – Welles . . . Tragedy is a part of the lives of all these men: yet all of them have influenced the work of countless others. Security and success is not likely to be the reward of those who dare to be truly original.

I agree that the essence of every great work of art – or let us say of every *good* work of art, since greatness is too exceptional to generalise about – is likely to be its contemporary quality. If a film is true to its time, it will be true to all time. Whereas if an artist deliberately evades the problems of his own time in order to concentrate on 'eternal' values, he will most likely produce work that has no real depth or significance, because it has no roots. The problem then arises: how is this contemporary quality to be achieved? What exactly are the problems particular to our time, and what should be the artist's approach to them? In Kozintsev's own words, how can we 'focus all the force of cinema art on defending man and mankind, progress and peace'? He believes that one useful way towards this is for artists to discuss these problems together. This is where I am afraid I become sceptical.

My first objection is a quite practical one, and it arises from the enormous difficulty of working seriously in the capitalist, entertainment industries of the West. I know that these difficulties are understood – at least theoretically – by our Russian colleagues. And I know too that Soviet film-makers have had, and presumably still have today, their own considerable problems. Yet I find that in practice they are often strangely innocent and optimistic about the situation in countries like Italy, France, America and Britain. Frequently in Russia I have been asked my opinion of various British films, and who I consider to be the 'best' directors of British feature pictures. And when I give my answer in terms of almost unqualified disapproval; when I am unable to name any of the well-known British directors with much enthusiasm – I am regarded as a 'cynic', an eccentric, an unreasonable perfectionist or perhaps merely a conceited idiot.

Yet surely the explanation is a simple enough one? Of course, I agree that certain British directors are capable of good technical work; that some British comedies have charm (though more, I suspect, for foreigners than for intelligent Britons); and that Alec Guinness is a very talented actor. But I am too conscious of the compromises on which all this work is based, of the great opportunities missed, of the magnificent subjects which our system will not allow us to tackle, to be able to praise films and artists of this kind. It is the same with Olivier's Shakespeare films. I think that *Henry V* is a good film; that *Hamlet* is a bad film; and I have not seen *Richard III*. But in relation to the present situation in Britain all these films, good or bad, are perfectly meaningless. Shakespeare has today become merely a respectable evasion of the present. His plays are performed without any feeling for their significance for today. The vast majority of British people do not understand them and care nothing for them. Perhaps they could be helped to do so, by presenting them in a different way, specially calculated for the present-day audience, but that is not the ambition of Olivier. And this is why – though this will probably seem shocking to many of my Russian friends – Laurence Olivier's failure to find finance for his film of *Macbeth* leaves me completely indifferent.

Now unfortunately these are not problems that can be solved or even illuminated by discussion between film-makers at a round table. As Bernard Shaw pointed out in *Major Barbara*, you have got to make men's bellies full before you start trying to make them good. Similarly, film-makers must be given cameras and film stock and money before discussion of their responsibilities as artists can have any meaning. We can only really learn our capacities and our potentialities in practice – by working. Eisenstein, as we all know, had no idea that he was going to make *The*

Battleship Potemkin when he started his film on the revolution of 1905. And his theories of 'cinema idiom', his revolutionary conception of film, came from his film-making, not *vice versa*.

Even setting aside these films that are not being made, and these artists who have no opportunity of working, it will be hardly profitable to discuss these problems with the kind of directors who are able to flourish in corrupt systems. If Carol Reed, David Lean, J. Lee Thompson, Ronald Neame and all the others were the sort of men who were able to see their work in this perspective – they would not be where they are today. Neame's version of *The Horse's Mouth* is not such a disappointing betrayal of a splendid novel because of any misunderstanding on his part that can be corrected. It reflects faithfully and irremediably his mediocre talent and imagination. No discussion will change that.

My second reservation is less personal, more general. It arises from the use of the word 'realism'. I think that Kozintsev is quite correct when he points out how much 'realist' film-making today is in fact just as mannered as a style based on eighteenth-century prints or employing baroque flourishes of style. Much of the work of the American actors' studio seems to me to fall into this category, where, in the name of intense psychological truth, a manner of acting has evolved (you see it in most of the films of Kazan) whose naturalism is egotistical and superficial rather than generous and deep. This is always liable to happen when talented people work without complete honesty – and I mean honesty to themselves as well as honesty to the rest of the world.

Even an excellent film like *The Cranes Are Flying* is to some extent spoiled by weaknesses in the scenario which all the brilliant technique in the world cannot completely atone for

'Realism', as Kozintsev implies, can only imply a valid relationship to contemporary reality – not any specific style or manner. This is precisely why it is such a dangerous term to use. For it means that each new work has to be considered separately, for its special, unique way of expressing its special, unique aspect of the truth. Unfortunately there are few critics – and fewer businessmen on our side, officials on yours – who are capable of doing this. And instead they fall back on terms like 'realism' (or 'socialist realism') which they use without true understanding in order to attack what is new and perhaps genuinely expressive. Art is more often disturbing than soothing, and we must not fall into the error of expecting artists to give us what we already imagine, in terms that are familiar and comfortable, or to be content to tell us what we already know.

I think this is no less a tendency in Russia than anywhere else in the world. I think of a little film like the Polish *Dom*, by Borowczyk and

Lenica. I have heard this film discussed in Moscow in much the same way as I have heard it discussed in London: with hostility, and a lack of comprehension which the speakers seem to be proud rather than ashamed of. And why? Because these young artists have used a strange, allusive, disturbing style to express their message. But perhaps their message could only be expressed in that way. In fact *Dom*, with its images of insecurity and unease, its evocation of a world in which the individual and human society as a whole are menaced by science misapplied and the ever-present threat of bombardment, seems to me to illustrate perfectly the truth of Kozintsev's remark: 'an artist is always like a seismograph, registering the inner shocks of his epoch.' And I have seen no example of work by short and documentary film-makers in Russia which would justify them in complacency about the creative work of others.

Soviet cinematography began in a period of colossal social upheaval and struggle, when national emotions were clear, simple and intense. In such revolutionary conditions the task of the artist is comparatively simple. It is when the revolution has been achieved, when some sort of stability has been won, when the old complexities of human existence return – it is then that the artist's function becomes harder. The tradition of the Soviet cinema has been largely simple, epic, affirmative. But conditions have changed; and as new 'complexities and depths' have to be explored, it is wrong to imagine that the style and artistic philosophy that were created out of different conditions will be adequate to the task.

The criticism has been made of my films here – and the films of my friends that I have brought with me – that 'they only show what is: they should show what *ought to be* – and how this can be achieved.'

First, let me say that I disagree that the Free Cinema films only show what 'is' – in superficial, reportage terms. Or at least let me agree that they have failed if implicit in every shot is not an attitude, a scale of values, an indication of what 'ought to be'. But it is impossible to express every truth in clear, precise words. This is to degrade art to the level of poster-propaganda. In a work of art of the best kind, it is the style itself that is expressive. A film must not be a suite of banal, predictable images to carry words or dialogue more suitable to a pamphlet or a newspaper article.

Nor does a film become necessarily more creative if it is technically perfect, photographed in delicate or exotic colours, using the latest systems of wide-screen panoramic screen and stereophonic sound. Films of this kind are a sort of drug: they blunt the sensibilities of critics and audiences, who quickly become (it seems to me) incapable of responding to work that is made with genuine vision and feeling. I have been told that the 16mm films made by Free Cinema are too 'amateurish' to mean much in Russia.

Such critics forget that a modest pencil sketch by a creative artist, made on poor paper perhaps, and faded and torn, still has more value and importance than a huge, conventional oil painting made by some timid and conformist academician. I even think that Russian film-makers might benefit from having less money to spend on their films, smaller crowds, fewer extravagant crane-shots and more modest apparatus. Then they might be forced to find the means to express themselves with greater urgency, spontaneity and feeling. And especially this seems to me to be true of documentary, where the artistic level is too often that of the picture postcard or the 'effective', empty magazine-illustrations.

It is not the business of the artist to provide solutions in a political or economic sense. He should rather express truths in such a way that – where political problems are relevant – the correct solutions will follow inevitably. Of course situations may arise in which it is the duty and the privilege of the artist to help the cause in which he believes by direct propaganda. But this is not his normal, or most valuable function. The artist can reveal aspects of the truth that cannot be shown in any other way. Sometimes these aspects may be unexpected. Sometimes they will be unwelcome. But they must be respected if we really value art, and are not just paying conventional lip-service to it. And this respect means that we must be prepared to find that a truly original artist will speak to us in a language, a style that is unfamiliar. Painters like Cézanne and Van Gogh and Manet at first seemed to be using incomprehensible modes of communication. Meyerhold and Mayakovsky were no common favourites. Vigo and Buñuel are now great names of the cinema: 25 years ago there were plenty of people who thought them worthless eccentrics. From such examples artists should learn courage, and critics humility.

Freedom and responsibility are not contradictory conceptions. They are complementary. Artists must be both free and responsible: but before they can be truly responsible, they must be free. Of course, the innovator, the original creator will seem irresponsible to many people. Nor will all artists ever agree about the best way of creating, the best way of 'defending man and mankind, progress and peace'. If we are honest, we will often have to admit: we do not like each other's films.

In harmony and a common purpose there is strength: but we are lucky if we find ourselves in such a situation. If we do not, there is no need to be discouraged or unduly dismayed. Disagreement and conflict – on the creative plane at least – can be fertile too. What we want is not a world in which we all agree; but a world in which we can disagree as much as we like – in safety.

The Cinema Is . . .

Unpublished article written for *The Observer*, 1954

A QUESTION I ASK MYSELF QUITE OFTEN IS: WHY IS SO MUCH NONSENSE talked about the cinema?

It is true that anybody concerned actively with any of the arts is liable to feel the same. I have yet to meet a practising painter, or sculptor, or poet, who has much respect for his critics. I am reminded of the talented novelist I met last week, and asked what she thought of her notices. She replied that she and her thirteen-year-old son saved them to read together. 'And we have a jolly good laugh,' she said.

But I persist in believing that film people get the worst of it. Other critics may be wrong; but at least they rarely boast of their ignorance. Films seem to make them aggressive: they want to attack, not merely the craftsmen, but the art itself.

'The cinema is . . .' 'The cinema is not . . .' How one's heart has learned to sink at paragraphs which begin like this. The cinema, it is clear, is anybody's game. But the peculiar thing is not so much that the generalisations are made, as the kind of superior, denigrating attitude which so often informs them.

'Some people consider the film as an art. Others less daring, like myself, would classify it as a craft, capable, on rare occasions, of producing a work of some significance.'

So much for old Eisenstein! It is true that Mr Kenneth Pearson went on to inform the readers of *The Sunday Times* of the precise basis of his aesthetic. 'My own definition of a great art chooses for its criterion the number of agents between the inspiration and the audience: the fewer, the higher.' Which brings a string quartet automatically nearer greatness than a choral symphony, and makes *Symphonic Variations* a finer ballet than *Swan Lake*.

At least the other arts are protected to some extent by tradition. It is the poor old cinema that gets the bludgeon, that must endure the bad seat and the arrogant heel of the tyro rider out to show his paces.

Like any of the popular arts – by now this should go without saying – the cinema produces an immense, over-publicised quantity of rubbish by comparison with its output of serious work. Socially this rubbish may be significant: aesthetically it is not. It is the same with literature, with music, with architecture and the graphic arts. A reputable novel reviewer does not bother with popular romances, cheap thrillers and magazine fiction: he restricts himself to what is in fact a minority selection. Mr Peter

Heyworth does not analyse, week after week, the merits of the Top Ten.

Film critics, unfortunately, are expected to do the very reverse. Minority work must pass unremarked, or be squeezed into half an inch at the end of the column; while the latest soap-opera is dealt with at length. No wonder facetiousness takes over as the level goes down. Those desperate generalisations become almost understandable.

Poor film critics then . . . Yet the strange thing (the really pathetic thing) is the adjustment they make with their predicament. They come to prefer that level, and seek to keep their readers on it too. Even readers as progressive and enlightened as you.

'I have never understood the taste for violence and squalor in the cinema. We know that dreadful things go on all around us; we know that life is grim, and we deplore it; but I can see no merit in bringing the misery into our recreation.'

How many Sunday morning eyebrows were raised, I wonder, when these words appeared in *The Observer* just a few weeks ago. I would like to think a million; but I doubt it. Yet a poetry reviewer who rejected Dylan Thomas for Wilhelmina Stitch would have a short run for his money.

In using a word like 'serious' in connection with the cinema, I am conscious of taking a risk. So many people nowadays – and presumably among the readers of this article – equate seriousness with dullness. What they cry out for is 'fun'. And here again the cinema gets into trouble; for films can be so funny that they are resented when they are anything else. If you imagine this is a purely popular viewpoint, you are wrong. This is how a recent third-rate Hollywood extravaganza was reviewed in *The Times*:

'This is the cinema as the cinema should rightly be, not concerned with the psychology of drug addicts and prostitutes, but, in its choice of subject and treatment, warm, vague, extravagant and sentimental.'

What a thin, 'camp' kind of enjoyment is suggested here, how patronising, and how damaging too. It requires only an extension of his attitude to reach the familiar jokes about film societies which show *Potemkin* and *Caligari* to young audiences in schoolrooms and village halls.

This *Times* notice brings us, indeed, to a new pervision, only quite lately fashionable. This involves not dismissing the cinema, but rather reserving praise for its most meretricious aspects. One of the leaders of this cult, Mr Lawrence Alloway, is responsible for that half of the last room at the *Observer* Exhibition which trumpets the achievements of the American commercialised cinema. He believes (roughly) that because the cinema is a popular art, no film can be good if it is not popular. The converse apparently holds too: any film that is popular *must* be good. Another long farewell to Eisenstein. (Mr Alloway presumably employs different criteria when he is lecturing at the Tate Gallery.)

Of course it depends finally what you mean by 'the cinema'. When described recently as the 'Arabian Nights' Entertainment' of our time, this was only a very partial truth. The cinema of Goldwyn, Rank, Selznick, Valentino and Dors may, I suppose, be so described. You may call it opiate. But there are finer connotations. The cinema of Vigo and Chaplin, of Dovchenko, Renoir and our own Humphrey Jennings has nothing much to do with bread and circuses. A lot of people may be unfamiliar with it: that does not make it any less real.

The cinema can be exotic, but not necessarily. There is certainly nothing remote about it, in the sense of being unrelated to the business of living. If this impression exists, it is only because of the present economic organisation of the film industry. A disappointing aspect of the 'Sixty Years of Cinema' exhibition is its final endorsement of this conception of the cinema: as something mysterious, extravagant, divorced from the human realities of our time. It is right that the survey should end with creation, with the making of a film. But what is the true significance of that elaborate replica, bloodless and orthodox, of a commercial production machine? Round the large studio camera stands a group of wax figures. Their stiffness does not suggest creative tension. In front of the camera sits another dummy, in RAF uniform. A British war film is being made.

But this is not 'the cinema'.

But what is?

The cinema is, firstly, flesh and blood, for all its apparatus. And after all, you can make a film for £100, by yourself if you want to. More easily if there are two of you; and better still if there are three. A 16-millimetre camera, which you can hold in your hand, will record expressions as subtle, decors as remarkable as any studio camera weighing half a ton. Film-making is never easy: but it is possible.

All this is not to deny the validity of the cinema of vast apparatus: it simply depends on who controls it. The cinema is a war party of Apaches whooping murderously after the Lordesville stage; and it is also Jean Vigo killing himself to finish *L'Atalante*. Nothing is too grand for it, and nothing too humble: it is its scope which matters, not its limitations. And we have hardly begun to use it yet.

'What is the cinema?' The question is pointless.

The cinema *is*.

Stand Up! Stand Up!

Sight and Sound, Autumn 1956

'It is beginning to dawn upon us all that what is needed most today is a criticism of criticism . . . For it is the critic, rather than the work of art, who should be put for a while upon the dissecting table.' – *Ernest Newman*

'It has for some time seemed to me that a criticism which has at heart the interest of liberalism might find its most useful work not in confirming liberalism in its sense of general rightness, but rather in putting under some degree of pressure the liberal ideas and assumptions of the present time.' – *Lionel Trilling in* The Liberal Imagination

'Stand up, stand up for Jesus!' – *George Duffield*

IT IS MUCH EASIER TO WRITE REVIEWS OF FILMS THAN TO FORMULATE THE principles from which such reviews should be written. And nowadays, when we are all nervous of fundamentals, it is comparatively easy to get away with critical writing that is vaguely based on the accepted standards of the time. See what the artist is trying to do; estimate the success of his attempt; relate the whole thing loosely to the commonplace assumptions of contemporary 'liberal' feeling. This, I suppose, sums up the critical method of most of us, with emphasis falling rather heavily on the words 'loosely', 'commonplace' and 'assumptions'. But at last the time comes when such a method seems insufficient, and we feel the need to examine the problems more closely. I am grateful to Mr J. R. Taylor for the letter which is printed in the Correspondence columns of this issue, and which I have been invited to answer here; his objections reinforce the feeling I already have that this examination is overdue in the case of film criticism no less than in the fields of Mr Newman and Mr Trilling.

I am happy that Mr Taylor should have sensed an 'implicit standard of judgement' in my writing on films, even if he is made suspicious by the fact. But many of his deductions from my assumed partiality for the 'simple, warm and human' hardly seem to follow. When an inexpressive, conventional pseudo-style is generally in favour, with all the emphasis on technical display, one may very well develop a 'weakness for the just-competent and the unpolished'. But of course it still depends *what* is unpolished.

This in no way involves a 'distrust of films which demand a sophisticated and civilised response'. And I have yet to meet Mr Taylor's 'committed' critic who thinks that a newsreel is 'the height of cinematic art'. (He sounds a simple-minded sort of chap.)

But in raising this issue of commitment, Mr Taylor is certainly on to something. Some confusions persist: it is untrue that a committed critic necessarily ends up despising style and becoming an inverted aesthetic snob. On the other hand a critic's moral or social convictions *may* lead him to reject work that is found entertaining by people who do not share them. This proves nothing. The essence of the matter is in the importance we attach to our principles, and the extent to which we think they are relevant to our enjoyment of art. Mr Taylor's position here is entirely clear. He believes that we can ask no more than that an artist's work be 'a true reflection of a point of view' – without regard to what that point of view may be. 'Moral judgements should be presented as what they are – personal, subjective tastes.'

In this sentence I think Mr Taylor expresses, or at least reflects, the majority view at the moment. It is a view to which I am absolutely opposed, and which I think must be opposed. It is with this aspect of criticism, therefore, that I shall concern myself in this essay – it being understood (I hope) that I am not thereby dismissing 'aesthetic' problems. Style is important also (only not exclusively); and in the best art, anyway, style and commitment are inseparable.

Instead of starting with any theoretical discussion about the nature of criticism, it may be useful to clear the ground by considering some aspects of its practice at the moment. What basic assumptions, what attitudes do we find common in the writing of present-day critics? A first important point is that the cinema has at least achieved respectability.

Thirty years ago it was only a minority who took films seriously: but in their seriousness was passion. They had the inspiration of knowing they were pioneers. The founders and members of the Film Society, the writers and readers of *Close-Up* – these revered the cinema and were burningly aware of its possibilities. It was stimulating rather than discouraging to them that the general attitude of the cultured was contemptuous and undiscerning: names like Griffith, Eisenstein, Pudovkin, Gance, Flaherty and Pabst were good enough to fight for. Today you might imagine that the fight had been won. We already have our National Film Theatre, while the National Theatre remains merely a broken promise: the health of the British film industry is discussed frequently, and with concern, in the House of Commons; and the posh papers (to borrow John Osborne's useful phrase) devote space to it, send representatives to its festivals, and honour its golden jubilee with ambitious exhibitions. Yet this wider accept-ance seems only to have been won at the price of diluting that original enthusiasm; a great deal of the old seriousness has been lost. It could even be maintained that the significance of the cinema – or rather the acknowl-edgement of its significance – has actually been reduced. It is of course inevitable that the majority of films made for popular entertainment in a capitalist society, where the general educational level is low and popular culture increasingly corrupt, should be of poor artistic quality; nor is it surprising if people whose only experience of the cinema is through such films form a low opinion of it. What is surprising, however, and perhaps significant as well, is a tendency among critics – that is to say among the articulate representatives of the educated minority – to subscribe to this opinion themselves, and even to encourage it.

A particularly striking example of this tendency is the habit of certain writers – and they seem to be growing more rather than less – of turning on the cinema and declaring that it is 'not an art'. Now I do not intend to pursue this as a serious argument; I simply want to draw attention to the phenomenon of its repeated expression. The classic instance, I suppose appeared in Miss C. A. Lejeune's column in *The Observer* just nine years ago; and it is worth quoting as the openly professed philosophy of a crit-ic who occupies a leading position in her profession. The article was head-ed 'Taking the Plunge'.

> A few weeks ago I hinted that I was on the brink of giving up the pre-tence that films were an art, and settling for the conviction that 'most of them are just vulgar and illiterate rubbish, and the rest are good entertainment provided for the relaxation of people whose brains are not at the moment up to anything tougher.' At the time of writing I was not prepared to take the full plunge. Today I am. Today I am ready to declare categorically that films are not an art; and I feel very much the better for it . . .

In case I may be judged unfair in quoting an article printed in 1947, I should add that Miss Lejeune has given us evidence that her views remain the same. In fact when this year her newspaper backed an exhibition of 'Sixty Years of Cinema', her contribution to the catalogue included the statement, 'Too much highflown nonsense is talked about art and culture in relation to films.' (She went on to advise her readers: 'Cherish the little things; a dance, a tune, a face, a movement of water, a ripple in the corn. . .')Miss Lejeune is not alone in taking this attitude. To a remarkable extent, in fact, deni-gration of the cinema, denial of its importance and its significance, has become common among those who write about it professionally. Consider the tone of a recent column of criticism in *The Sunday Times* by Mr Kenneth Pearson.

> Some people consider the film as an art. Others less daring, like myself, would classify it as a craft, capable, on rare occasions, of producing a work of some significance . . .

It is not as if Mr Pearson were here initiating a real discussion: he is simply leading in to a review of *Trapeze*. What is significant is that such sentiments should be felt to provide an acceptable journalistic opening to a column of cultured film criticism. Mr Pearson can only write like this because he senses that it is safely fashionable to do so.

Exactly the same fashion is reflected in a recent notice (of *The Rains of Ranchipur*) from *The Times*: 'This is the cinema as the cinema should rightly be, not concerned with the psychology of drug addicts and prostitutes, but, in its choice of subject and treatment, warm, vague, extravagant and sentimental.'

To reserve your enthusiasm for the more meretricious productions of the cinema is only another way of denying its claim to the same attention as literature, music, painting or any other of the arts. (It is impossible, for instance, to imagine a reputable dramatic critic writing in this way.) But what is the reason for such denial? Is it to be ascribed to simple, good-old-English philistinism? It is difficult to know what other term to apply to the following observation by the critic of *The Observer*: 'I have never understood the taste for violence and squalor in the cinema. We know that dreadful things go on all around us; we know that life is grim and we deplore it; but I can see no merit in bringing the misery into our recreation.'

The simple term 'philistinism' is not however quite enough. For this is a word that can cover a number of attitudes. It can be impatient and actionful, like Goering reaching for his revolver – and there are times, when culture has become snobbish and claustrophobic, when this may be useful. (One can remember the occasion – and how long ago it seems – when even Sir Herbert Read was driven to cry 'To Hell with Culture!') But there is another kind of philistinism, timorous rather than pugnacious, which shrinks from art because art presents a challenge. This can be an even more insidious enemy, because it often disguises itself with the apparatus of culture, professing the very values which it is in the act of destroying. 'Do not misunderstand me, please,' writes Miss Lejeune, having just declared that a film is nothing but 'bits of celluloid and wire', 'I am not intending to belittle the screen.' And I do not suppose that this is the conscious intention of the other critics I have quoted, either. But it is what they are doing.

'It was a fine day, and I must have been three or four, when Nanny popped me into a charabanc and took me off to Blackpool to see my first film . . .' Such were the opening words of the introduction, by Mr Richard Buckle, of the catalogue to *The Observer's* recent exhibition, 'Sixty Years of Cinema'. By the time this essay appears, the exhibition will have closed; and perhaps it may be thought that it would be better to let the whole business slide into oblivion. If I disagree, it is not for the pleasure of being wise after the event, but because 'Sixty Years of Cinema' was an event of great (if unhappy) significance and closely relevant to my theme. Here was an ambitious exhibition, visited by well over 200,000 people, backed with all the prestige of a great liberal newspaper, and sponsored as well by the British Film Institute and the Cinematheque Française. The idea of the cinema expressed in it is therefore of considerable importance, both for its direct impression on all those virgin minds (innocent of any previous experience of the mysteries of film appreciation), and for the evidence it provides of the satisfactions sought today by enlightened people from the art of the film.

After some reminiscences of his early film-going days ('The Babylonian orgy in *Intolerance* set a standard for parties which I have aspired to ever since . . .'), Mr Buckle continued his introduction as follows:

> The pleasure many people said they had from the Diaghilev exhibition, which I drifted into organising almost by accident, made me think that here and now we might invent a new kind of exhibition, a show where people had fun (whether they wanted instruction or not), and were carried out of themselves, as they are in the theatre. By a happy chance the editor of *The Observer* is as eager as I am to give opportunities to artists, and fun to people in general.

Of particular interest here is the careful profession of amateurism. 'The Diaghilev Exhibition, which I *drifted into organising almost by accident . . .* ' Thus Mr Buckle avoids from the start any possible accusation of being over-serious: the implied assumption is that if you are serious, you are probably also boring. It is no coincidence that the word 'fun' appears twice before the end of the paragraph. Just as in this context, words like 'instruction', 'culture', even 'art' acquire connotations of pretentiousness and gloomy didacticism, so the idea of pleasure dwindles into that of 'fun'. But what a pinched, jejune notion of pleasure this is, that exercises only the most superficial faculties, and affects a kind of modish infantilism to justify its retreat from the responsibilities of being an adult.

Granted this basic attitude, it was inevitable that the exhibition should take the form it did: an orthodox, unadventurous choice of stills, selected on conventional academic and chronological principles, disposed in a series of sophisticated decors, which tended to 'kill' rather than to set off the material on display. A detailed criticism of the exhibition would take too long, and anyway be out of place: a few instances should suffice to convey the general effect. Thus, the American cinema of the twenties was represented by (I quote from the catalogue) 'an amusing photomontage of Hollywood stars at home, seen through the arches of a Spanish-colonial colonnade.' Somewhat naturally the diminutive stills from *Greed*, *The Big Parade*, and perhaps *Sunrise* and *A Woman of Paris*, set against this background, told nothing of the creative achievements of the early American cinema, beyond the fact that the actors in it wore old-fashioned costumes. In the rooms that followed, rows of stills from German, Russian and French films similarly expressed nothing of what those cinemas represent, either in human or aesthetic terms. The British room was got up in a picturesque dock-side setting (the sort of urban, working-class decor that is rarely featured in British story-films), and in the haphazard selection of stills, displayed as though the work of pavement artists (!), no distinction was made as to genre, purpose, or quality. The early days of American sound films were symbolised by a huge perspective model of the New York skyline; while Hollywood production of the last twenty years was represented by further batches of stills lost in a mannered, painter's impression of the United States. ('Mr Leonard Rosoman,' wrote Mr Buckle, 'who has never been to America, has conjured up . . . a flowing pageant of landscape and figures which is just *my* idea, anyway, of what life is like in that mysterious continent.')

As I have said, all this was inevitable. *Not*, however, because of the necessity to 'popularise' a subject which otherwise would have been dry and inaccessible to an audience of ordinary people. To believe this is to reveal a complete misunderstanding, and a fundamental lack of sympathy towards the essential achievements of the cinema during its 60 years of life. Further it is to reject its potentialities. Nor is it simply a question of being unable to represent motion pictures satisfactorily by still photographs. That stills can be used creatively, to make a significant statement – and at the same time an attractive one – has been shown by Edward Steichen in his fine exhibition, 'The Family of Man'. But Mr Steichen did not start off with Nanny, in pursuit of fun. He proved instead the deeper pleasure that can be drawn from a skilful and sincere expression of faith, of belief. Mr Buckle, with his 'Hall of Glamour', where portraits of Marilyn Monroe and Rita Hayworth confronted Tony Curtis, Alan Ladd and Lex Barker, like photographs in a Charing Cross Road outfitter's window, proved nothing except the truth of Joubert's *pensée*: 'Nothing shrivels up man so much as trivial pleasure.'[*]

Only one room in 'Sixty Years of Cinema' achieved a real expressiveness, a suggestive power beyond the conscious intentions of its designers. For I do not suppose that either Mr Buckle or Mr John Piper intended their 'Shadow Theatre' to evoke so disturbingly an atmosphere of cultural decay: if, indeed, they had consciously worked to this end, the symbolism of the *mise-en-scène* could not have been more potent. Fittingly, it was the last feature in the exhibition (after the Hall of Glamour). Passing between a powerful projector-lamp on your left, and a white screen on your right, you found yourself in a dark, empty-seeming hall. As your eyes grew accustomed to the gloom, you became aware of twisting, gilt rococo pillars, a chequered sham-marble floor, and, round the walls, a number of recesses in which stood anonymous, decomposing statues, limbs and faces crumbled as if with age. In the middle of the floor, on a group of spindly gilt chairs, people were sitting, silent, apparently without thought or feeling, staring listlessly at the other side of that white screen behind which you passed to enter the room, and on which is thrown the silhouette of every passer-by. A slow movement from one of the watchers attracts your attention. You see that it is a woman, and that she is raising a cup to her lips. You look round, and there, in the corner, you perceive it – an Espresso Coffee Bar. It is like a scene from *L'Age d'Or*.

There is one other feature that must not be overlooked – though if your eyesight is not sharp, it very well may be. In the darkest corner of the room there is a shelf. On this rests a large book. Peering at a typewritten notice on the wall, you learn that this contains stills from the 25 best films ever made. But there is no light by which to see them.

It is a matter of fact, not of opinion, that the cinema is an art. This does not call for theoretical discussion – unless, of course, you enjoy that kind of intellectual exercise. If it is simply the truth we are after, the question has already been answered, empirically. If *L'Atalante*, *Strike*, *Rashomon* and *Louisiana Story* are not works of art, then there is no way of describing them. And if Griffith, Renoir, Jennings and de Sica are not artists, we will have to invent a new word for them.

The importance of the cinema as a cultural and propagandist force is a matter of fact also. Everyone who has seen more than half a dozen films with his eyes open knows that if the cinema does not create the significant social movements of our time, it intimately reflects them. And that it provides a reflection just as intimate – and just as significant – of social stagnation. A further point worth emphasising is that the cinema makes its appeal above all to the youthful; that is to say, above all to those whose minds are unformed, and open to impression.

These facts alone are enough to condemn the thoughtless denigration of the cinema, of which I have given a number of fashionable examples. The consistent impression created by such writing is that films provide at worst a vulgar means of escapism or wish-fulfilment (Bread-and-Circuses), and at best an amusing, rather exotic diversion ('The Arabian Nights' Entertainments of our time'). To apply to them serious standards of criticism, aesthetic or social, is to indulge in 'highflown nonsense' and to prove oneself a glum, humourless and boring person.

Leaving aside for a moment the graver implications of such an attitude, we may remark that at the least it is damaging, tolerating the shoddy and the third-rate, and muffling work of importance by a flippant or purely sentimental response. It is impossible to praise things that are bad without injuring things that are good. By celebrating the merits of the trivial and the meretricious, or by being lengthily funny at its expense, we lower the prestige of the cinema, and, indirectly, make it more difficult for anybody to make a good film.

Granted, however, that this is not the way to write about the cinema, the basic critical problems still remain. And amongst them – most urgently perhaps – the one which has precipitated this essay. To what extent must we aspire to objectivity, like a sensitive but impersonal reagent; and to what extent must we involve our own convictions, moral as well as aesthetic, social as well as moral? 'Sixty Years of Cinema' was a perfect example of the attitude which rejects any such notion of involvement, in favour of an academic objectivity, lightened with decorative touches and a few, purely frivolous, personal indulgences. In this it reflected current fashion with complete fidelity (at least I can call to mind no criticism levelled at the exhibition for lack of conception or point of view). So widely accepted, in fact, is this approach, so literally does it go without saying, that it is difficult to find any explicit statement of the 'uncommitted' position. Some twenty years ago, however, there was a declaration by Alistair Cooke which so exactly performs this function that it is still relevant today. It is a 'Critic's Testament', delivered by Mr Cooke when he started reviewing films for the BBC, in 1935.

> As a critic I am without politics and without class. For a film hero I am prepared to take John Barrymore, George Robey, a Battleship, Mickey Mouse, or an Italian Straw Hat. I hope that everyone who wants to make a lot of money in films will make it, that every girl who aches to become a star overnight will become one . . . My malice extends only to those who have a dull talent . . .

Mr Cooke was aware that he might run up against certain problems as a film critic. 'A month ago I had an earnest letter asking me rather gravely what I was going to do about politics . . . Even in the story-film . . . there

225

is constantly an implication it is impossible to overlook. I mean a political, a social one.' These implications, however (although 'impossible to overlook'), he refused to face. 'As a critic I have no politics.' The rejection of moral as well as social responsibilities was absolutely specific:

> However much I want in private to rage or protest or moralise, these actions [i.e., war films, etc.] have nothing to do with critics. As a moralist I could be shocked. As an educationalist I might lament that the subject was not elevating. As a businessman I might feel glum that the seduction was clumsy and therefore bad box-office. But I am not a moralist, an educator, a businessman. I am merely a critic and I have to try and decide whether Miss Harlow's smiles and pouts were performed expertly enough to entice Mr Gable away . . . So if a film comes from Elstree and is full of propaganda for, let's say, social slavery, it is not for me to say that such propaganda is socially shocking.

It is fascinating to find Mr Cooke in 1935, expressing both the essential attitude and the characteristic tone of a number of critics today. There is the claim to a liberal standpoint, 'without politics and without class', that tolerantly estimates every work on its own merits. Immediately, however, the liberalism is negated by a sort of facetious self-parody: 'I hope that everyone who wants to make a lot of money in films will make it . . .' Taken seriously, this would imply abandonment of any standards at all. But of course its purpose is exactly to ensure that the writer is *not* taken seriously; to prove that he does not take himself too seriously either. Scorn of 'highbrow nonsense about art and culture' is only round the corner from here, and so is the pursuit of 'fun'. It is the 'dull' talent that the critic really disapproves of: he wants to be entertained.

The problems of commitment are directly stated, but only apparently faced. From the first, the question is begged by the use of phrases which make Mr Cooke's correspondent seem just an old fuddy-duddy – 'an earnest letter', 'rather gravely'. . . The denial of the critic's moral responsibility is specific; but only at the cost of sacrificing his dignity. 'I am *merely* a critic.' And facetiousness lends its defensive aid once more with the joke about Miss Harlow's smiles and pouts. The instance of a propagandist film for 'social slavery' from Elstree is similarly dishonest: the case of an antisemitic film from Nazi Germany would have been more awkward.

The examples of criticism I have quoted in the foregoing pages all derive from assumptions similar to these: the holding of liberal, or humane values; the proviso that these must not be taken too far; the adoption of a tone which enables the writer to evade through humour. The fundamental issues are balked. Just as Mr Cooke uses an example which he knows his audience will think absurd, Mr Taylor in his letter demands fair treatment for a film 'glorifying the good side of war'. (It is the film that glorifies the bad side of war that presents him with a challenge.) It is true that Mr Taylor presents the slightly different case of the critic who has a further reason for rejecting moral issues as irrelevant – in favour of what he calls 'nonpartisan aesthetic judgement'. In other words, he believes that a critic's function must be restricted to an examination of the aesthetic form of the film under discussion.

I hope I will be pardoned if I say that I find this distinction between form and content somewhat naïf. It is the essence of poetry (in any medium) that the thing said cannot be critically distinguished from the way of saying it. Perhaps we see here the pernicious influence of a school of 'Film Appreciation' which analyses every film according to certain textbook conceptions of technique, and which is as insensitive to meaning as it is to subtleties of individual style. In fact, since these aesthetic principles are never precisely formulated, and since close analysis of statement or implication is considered irrelevant, criticism has no alternative but to fall back on an entirely subjective kind of 'impressionism'. Hence the extreme overuse of terms like 'moving', 'deeply moving', 'strangely unmoving', etc. Particularly striking in this connection is a recent pronouncement of critical method by Kenneth Tynan, the best of our contemporary theatre critics. 'What counts,' says Mr Tynan, 'is not their [i.e., theatre critics'] opinion, but the art with which it is expressed . . . The subtlest and best-informed of men will still be a bad critic if his style is bad. It is irrelevant whether his opinion is "right" or "wrong".' In other words, in criticism as in art, it is showmanship that counts.

Effect, then, is more important than meaning. From this position it is only a step to a conception of art that actually rejects significance. Some time ago an article of mine was published in *Sight and Sound* which closely examined the social implications of *On the Waterfront*. I was amazed, not by the number of people who disagreed with me, but by the number of people who thought that this sort of thing was *somehow beyond the function of criticism*. Most significant was a comment on the article which appeared in *The Times*:

> Films are the folklore, the character and aspirations of the nations made visible, yet it would be unwise to search too keenly in every scene of boy-meets-girl for political or any other symbolism . . . People like Mr Anderson perform a valuable service when they draw attention to hidden significances and covert propaganda, but the normal person will go on regarding the screen with the unseeing gaze Watson fixed on the bowler – and perhaps be none the worse for it.

Analytical criticism, it is here implied, is unwise, abnormal – even when it exposes covert propaganda. The logically following epithet, I fear, is 'subversive'.

It is over ten years now since we (the junior officers) nailed a red flag to the roof of the mess at the foot of Annan Parbat, to celebrate the glorious news from home. (I mean, of course, the result of the 1945 election.) The colonel did not approve, but even he seemed to feel that a new era might be upon us; and no disciplinary action was taken.

It is also over ten years since Humphrey Jennings, in a film made for the British government, linked the lives of a farmer and an engine driver, an RAF pilot, a coal miner, and a baby called Timothy. It is as beautiful a film today as it was then, but it has gained sadness; for the questions it asked about the future do not seem to be getting the hoped for answers. From one point of view this is paradoxical. We have had our social revolution; we have a fine system of social security; and our technological achievements are something to be proud of. How then to explain the prevalence of cynicism, the baffled idealism and the emotional fatigue? Why are so many young voices resentful and defeatist rather than pugnacious and affirming?

> I suppose people of our generation aren't able to die for good causes any longer. We had all that done for us, in the thirties and forties, when we were still kids. There aren't any good, brave causes left. If the big bang does come and we all get killed off, it won't be in aid of the old-fashioned, grand design. It'll just be for the Brave New-nothing-very-much-thank you. About as pointless and inglorious as stepping in front of a bus.

Most critics have attempted to write off John Osborne's hero (this is a quotation from *Look Back in Anger*) as a negligible, bad-mannered young bounder, 'racked with uncertainty and rotten with self-pity'. Predictably, they have shirked the task of analysing his bounderishness: the writer in the *Times Literary Supplement*, from whom I have taken this comment, can find no virtue either in Jimmy Porter or the play, even though he admits that 'there is something about this nagging young man which audiences recognise as giving him some vital connection with the social system'. As to what this 'something' is, we are not enlightened; characteristically this is the end, not the beginning, of the examination of the play.

In so far as Jimmy Porter's grievances are social at all (and it should be realised that the play is primarily the study of a temperament), they are not material grievances. The young people who respond so unmistakably to *Look Back in Anger* are responding to its outspoken attacks on certain venerable sacred cows, and also to its bitter impatience with the moral vacuum in which, they feel, public life – and cultural life – is today being conducted. The class resentment is only part of it. If there 'aren't any good, brave causes left' (or if that is the feeling in the air), the fault is not so much that of the Right, the Tory element in politics and art, as of the Left, the progressives, the liberals in the broadest sense of that long-suffering word. The manner in which the British political Left has muffed its chance to capture the imagination and allegiance of the nation is too obvious to need dwelling on: from the peaceful revolution of '45 to 'You Can Trust Mr Attlee', and Mr Gaitskell in pin-stripe trousers helping with the family washing-up, the descent has been sure, steady and well-publicised. Less easily – or at least less often – remarked has been the steady draining away of vitality from what we may call the cultural Left, its increasing modishness, and its more and more marked aversion from emotional simplicity or moral commitment.

'We are all existentialists nowadays, at least in the same vague, popular sense that it was ever true to say we were all socialists.' This is the prevailing tone – over-allusive, fatigued, intellectually snobbish – of the *New Statesman* intellectual of today; while the indefatigable Mr Kingsley Martin, on the front page, continues to chastise the Labour Party for its lack of realism, and to warn it that it may 'drift further and further away from the realities of working-class life'. [**] We cannot but smile at such wild discrepancies, but really this sort of thing is sad rather than funny; and particularly because, of the two remarks, it is the second that is outdated. (The contemporary liberal intellectual is far less diverted by the realities of working-class life than by the variations between 'U' and 'Non-U' usage.)

A particularly pregnant example of the kind of debilitation I am describing is offered by the recent (18 August 1956) review in the *New Statesman* of the 'Family of Man' exhibition. 'What strikes one most,' writes Mr John Raymond 'about this amazing cross-section of men and women is its unity – a unity of fear'. Affirmation and the pursuit of happiness (which are the theme of the exhibition) being out of fashion, Mr Raymond stands to make a distinctly smarter impression if he jettisons Mr Steichen's statement, and substitutes something more up-to-the-minute of his own. The crucial passage in this argument so perfectly crystallises its pseudo-liberal attitude that readers must bear with me while I quote it in full.

What is Mr Steichen's message? 'All men are created equal'; 'No man is an island entire of himself'; 'Where there is neither Greek nor Jew, circumcision nor uncircumcision'; 'We must love one another or die'? Judging by the Bomb that ends the whole affair, Auden's discarded line appears to be the text that the sponsors are bent on hammering home. If only Timbuctoo can learn to love Old Trafford, the lion will lie down with the lamb, our bombs can be beaten into atomic ploughshares and Walt Whitman's 'new city of friends' can be turned into a reality. Such a jejune motif does poor justice to the riches of this collection, even when eked out by the trite international maxims that stud the walls – 'The world of man dances in laughter and tears' (Kabir); 'Clasp the hands and know the thoughts of men in other lands' (Masefield); 'Eat bread and salt and speak the truth' (Russia) . . .

Such accomplished perversity demands analysis if its subtleties are to be fully appreciated. Confronted by the tremendous issues raised by this exhibition, the enlightened Mr Raymond is at no loss for a protective shield of sophisticated cross-references. His piece is headed 'All The Conspirators' – a quotation from *Julius Caesar* which is wholly inapposite, but has the merit of connoting Shakespeare and (more important) the first novel of Christopher Isherwood. The reference to Auden settles us even more firmly within the charmed circle: this gospel is limited not just to the (comparatively large) number of people who can pick out Auden's line from the group of quotations listed at the beginning of the paragraph, but to the selecter elite who are aware that Auden has omitted the line from the latest edition of his short poems. His position of cultural superiority thus established – Walt Whitman is another OK reference, and may safely be patronised – Mr Raymond can proceed confidently to dismiss as a 'jejune motif' such poetic conceptions as the lion lying down with the lamb; the sword beaten into the ploughshare; and Whitman's 'New city of friends'. This is the point where the hard work of writing a criticism of the exhibition is smoothly side-stepped; instead of pointing out where Mr Steichen fails to measure up *poetically* to the texts he has chosen, Raymond dismisses the texts themselves, and with them an inspiration which has long found a place in the hearts of men, and still does today. The slickness with which this dismissal is effected is alarming, because it shows Raymond's sense that he is writing with, not against the current. It needs only the word bomb with a capital 'B', and the facetious jingle of Timbuctoo and Old Trafford, to discredit the positive ideal of human brotherhood which is the essential inspiration of the whole exhibition.

I have given care to an examination of this passage, not because in itself Mr Raymond's reaction to 'The Family of Man' is very important, but because of his ability skilfully to express the social and cultural attitudes of his class and time. The really shocking thing about such a piece is that nobody is shocked by it. (The only comment it aroused among readers of the *New Statesman* was a letter pointing out a quotation from Schiller had been wrongly attributed to Goethe.) The commitments, in fact, of the liberal intellectuals are now so taken for granted that they have ceased to have any force whatever; and to speak out for them is to run the risk of appearing simple. Mr Raymond can end his review with a pessimistic quotation from Lord Russell – 'Brief and powerless is Man's life' – without fear of arousing the slightest protest from the readers of a radical left-wing periodical. His style, though intellectually more pretentious, echoes the uncommitted Mr Cooke twenty years before him: sceptical, amused, implicitly mistrustful of affirmation, even while continuing to pay indulgent lip-service to it.

Readers of *Sight and Sound* will probably by now be feeling that I have strayed far from my subject: indeed, if they take it for granted that 'non-partisan aesthetic judgement' is the sole province of a critic, they are bound to do so. But my whole point is that criticism (film criticism included) cannot exist in a vacuum; and that writers who insist that their functions are so restricted are merely indulging in a voluntary self-emasculation. 'I am not a moralist . . .' insisted Mr Cooke, 'I am merely a critic.' Why should anyone be content to be a mere critic? 'I have little or no idea where I am going,' wrote Mr Tynan on becoming dramatic critic of *The Observer*, '. . . I see myself predominantly as a lock. If the key, which is the work of art, fits snugly into my mechanism of bias and preference, I click and rejoice; if not, I am helpless.' But one searches in vain for some basis for this critical philosophy of passivity and self-restriction. A critic has his special gift, but is he any less a man than the rest of us? The moral faculty and the intellectual faculty are essential instruments to him. They are certainly no less important than the ability to write vivid and evocative reportage.

I have discussed quite extensively in this essay what seems to me the prevalent tone of contemporary liberal writing. I am not of course using the word 'liberal' in any political sense, but rather as applied to the general humanism that makes liberals of practically all of us today (nominally at least). Everyone believes in social and artistic liberty, even if we differ about the means of achieving them; everyone believes in the importance of the individual, in freedom of speech, assembly and worship, in tolerance and mutual aid. The fact that it is almost impossible to express these beliefs except in terms of platitude does not in itself discredit them. That affirmation should have become the prerogative of politicians and blurb-writers is shameful. But this only means that belief has to be rescued, not that it must be abandoned.

Our ideals – moral, social and poetic – must be defended, with intelligence as well as emotion; and also with intransigence. To look back (and around) in anger may be a necessary beginning, but as Jimmy Porter himself demands, 'The voice that cries out doesn't have to be a weakling's, does it?' That is why I have evoked that image of the red flag over an officers' mess near Delhi – not to suggest that I necessarily see our only answer in communism. Nor does the fact that I have quoted Duffield's hymn in the title of this essay imply that I am pinning my hopes to a Christian revival. I do not believe that humanism is exhausted; nor that we are without rebels capable of defending its cause. This is a responsibility to accept. (But responsibility is not conformism.)

The cinema is not apart from all this; nor is it something to be denigrated or patronised. It is a vital and significant medium, and all of us who concern ourselves with it automatically take on an equivalent responsibility. And in so far as film criticism is being written here and now, and deals with an art intimately related to the society in which we live, it cannot escape its wider commitments. Essentially, in fact, there is no such thing as uncommitted criticism, anymore than there is such a thing as insignificant art. It is merely a question of the openness with which our commitments are stated. I do not believe that we should keep quiet about them.

---

*This Hall of Glamour was introduced after the exhibition had already been open for seven or eight weeks presumably in an attemtpt to increase its popular appeal. Symbolically, a display of scenes from All Quiet on the Western Front, The Road to Life, Partie de Campagne and My Darling Clementine had to be taken down in order to accommodate it. It was at about the same time that the exhibition posters were changed, and a new slogan adopted: 'From Valentino to Dors'.

**Both these quotations are taken from the same issue of the New Statesman, December 1955.

Get Out and Push!

In *Declaration*, edited by Tom Maschler, 1957

> 'O for a single hour of that Dundee,
> Who on that day the word of onset gave!'

LET'S FACE IT; COMING BACK TO BRITAIN IS ALWAYS SOMETHING OF AN ordeal. It ought not to be, but it is. And you don't have to be a snob to feel it. It isn't just the food, the sauce bottles on the café tables, and the chips with everything. It isn't just saying goodbye to wine, goodbye to sunshine. After all, there are things that matter even more than these; and returning from the Continent, today in 1957, we feel these strongly too. A certain, civilised (as opposed to cultured) quality in everyday life: a certain humour: an atmosphere of tolerance, decency and relaxation. A solidity, even a warmth. We have come home. But the price we pay is high.

For coming back to Britain is also, in many respects, like going back to the nursery. The outside world, the dangerous world, is shut away: its sounds are muffled. Cretonne curtains are drawn, with a pretty pattern on them of the Queen and her fairy-tale Prince, riding to Westminster in a golden coach. Nanny lights the fire, and sits herself down with a nice cup of tea and yesterday's *Daily Express*; but she keeps half an eye on us too, as we bring out our trophies from abroad, the books and pictures we have managed to get past the customs. (Nanny has a pair of scissors handy, to cut out anything it wouldn't be right for children to see.) The clock ticks on. The servants are all downstairs, watching TV. Mummy and Daddy have gone to the new Noel Coward at the Globe. Sometimes there is a bang from the street outside – a backfire, says Nanny. Sometimes there's a scream from the cellar – Nanny's lips tighten, but she doesn't say anything . . . Is it to be wondered at that, from time to time, a window is found open, and the family is diminished by one? We hear of him later sometimes, living in a penthouse in New York, or a *dacha* near Moscow. If he does really well, he is invited home, years later, and given tea in the drawing room, and we are told to call him Professor.

It is a cosy enough fantasy, if you like that sort of thing. But unfortunately fantasy tends to become confused with reality, when enough people surrender to it: and this is what seems to have happened here. The only trouble is, we are not alone in the world. We are not even as far away from the rest of it as we used to be. Sometimes the old house trembles, when one of those backfires goes off particularly hard; but if you suggest a bit of rebuilding, you are looked at as though you've said something disgusting. Why is this? I ask myself. Do people doubt that we have the capacity to re-shape, re-invigorate, to adapt ourselves to the changed conditions of our time? Certainly far too many of us, and particularly those who speak with any kind of authority, seem to be anxiously obsessed about the 'Greatness' of Britain – and to be able to conceive it only in terms of the past. One remembers those nostalgic headlines in the *Daily Sketch*: EDEN GETS TOUGH. SAYS 'HANDS OFF OUR CANAL.' IT'S GREAT BRITAIN AGAIN!

I work in the cinema, which gives me a further reason for despondency when I return to Britain. Admittedly this is a difficult enough medium to work in anywhere, but in few other parts of the world is so little significant use made of it. My most recent visit to the Continent was to the Tenth International Film Festival at Cannes. We saw films from some 35 countries, from East and West, Right and Left. And really, after a winter in London, it was astonishing to find the amount of responsible, meaningful work being done by film-makers in the world outside: humanism breaking through, in Russian pictures as well as American, in films which cost practically nothing from Ceylon as well as in the big-budget affairs from France, Italy and Japan. Prizes went to Poland, Sweden, France, America, Russia, Rumania, Japan, Yugoslavia . . . Britain did not figure in the list. It is six years since a British feature won a prize at Cannes. And this is not the result of political or economic intrigue: it is a fair reflection of the way our films have fallen out of the running. The cinema reflects, much more immediately than most of the arts, the climate and spirit of a nation. Abroad particularly, where one gains that extra measure of objectivity, it is alarming to see what we produce, what we put up with.

What sort of cinema have we got in Britain? First of all it is necessary to point out that it is an *English* cinema (and Southern English at that), metropolitan in attitude, and entirely middle-class. This combination gives it, to be fair, a few quite amiable qualities: a tolerance, a kind of benignity, a lack of pomposity, an easy-going good nature. But a resolution never to be discovered taking things too seriously can soon become a vice rather than a virtue, particularly when the ship is in danger of going down. To counterbalance the rather tepid humanism of our cinema, it must also be said that it is snobbish, anti-intelligent, emotionally inhibited, wilfully blind to the conditions and problems of the present, dedicated to an out-of-date, exhausted national ideal.

These are all quite familiar middle-class – or more precisely upper-middle-class – characteristics. Now I know that to many people, mention of 'class' always seems to be in bad taste. We are supposed to have risen above all that sort of thing. But we haven't. The grim truth is that we still live in one of the most class-conscious societies in the world, and I see nothing to be gained from the pretence that this is no longer so. The only way, in fact, we can usefully communicate with each other is by being honest about our backgrounds and our inherited prejudices. (This is not the same thing as saying we should hang on to them.) So I state here that I am fully qualified to talk about upper-middle-class characteristics, because that is the class into which I was born. My father was an Army officer, and my mother the daughter of a wool-merchant. I was educated at a preparatory school on the South Coast, and at a West Country public school. (*Floruit, floret, floreat . . .*) Thus, though I dislike as much as anyone the smarty left-wing dismissal of all sentiments of patriotism or fair-play as public school juvenilia, I need no prompting to admit that most of these characteristics we are discussing stem directly from our upper-class system of education.

The snobbery of our films is not aristocratic. In British films the aristocracy is generally represented by Mr A. E. Matthews, and is treated, though respectfully, as a fine old figure of fun. Similarly, the functions of working-class characters are chiefly comic, where they are not villainous. They make excellent servants, good tradesmen, and first-class soldiers. On the march, in slit trenches, below decks, they crack their funny Cockney jokes or think about the mountains of Wales. They die well, often with a last, mumbled message on their lips to the girl they left behind them in the Old Kent Road, but it is up there on the Bridge that the game is really played, as the officers raise binoculars repeatedly to their eyes, converse in clipped monosyllables (the British cinema has never recovered from Noel Coward as Captain 'D'), and win the battles. A young actor with a regional or a Cockney accent had better lose it quick: for with it he will never be able to wear gold braid round his sleeve – and then where are his chances of stardom?

Most people are innocently unaware of the way this kind of snobbery restricts our cinema, as it does our theatre too. I suppose this is because it is so very English in its tone, and therefore whimsical, indulgent and unselfconscious, never violent and seldom aggressive; never imagining that it could arouse resentment; sublimely convinced that it reflects the natural order of things. There are elements of truth, even, in its stereotypes; but their untruth is far greater. It is, up to a point, reasonable to show British as, on the whole, more equable than Italians: but it is merely libellous to insist that our emotions are so bottled up that they have ceased to exist at all. You know the sort of thing. Mrs Huggett, the policeman's wife, is told of her husband's death in the course of duty. (He has been knifed while attempting to arrest a Teddy Boy for dancing rock-and-roll on the pavement at the Elephant and Castle.) There is a pause, pregnant with noth-

235

ing. Then Mrs Huggett speaks, quiet and controlled: 'I'll just put these flowers in water.' Polite critical applause for another piece of truly British understatement. English film-makers, to quote Roy Campbell, use the snaffle and the bit all right – but where's the bloody horse? (The horse, naturally, is out in the stable, round at the back of the house. And that's where we've been told not to go.)

The number of British films that have ever made a genuine try at a story in a popular milieu, with working-class characters all through, can be counted on the fingers of one hand; and they have become rarer, not more frequent, since the War. Carol Reed's film of *The Stars Look Down*, made in 1939, looks somewhat factitious today; but compared with his *A Kid for Two Farthings* two years ago, it is a triumph of neo-realism. The real objection, though, is not so much that 'popular' subjects are falsified, as that they are not made at all. Quite recently a friend of mine took a story to a distributor to find out if he would agree to handle the film if it were made. (It is these middlemen, incidentally, who decide what reaches the screen in Britain, not the producer or the public.) The reaction was illuminating. It was a story of working-class people, and it opened in a garage yard, with the men sitting in the sun, eating their lunch-hour sandwiches. One of them, a boy of sixteen, has a cold and needs to wipe his nose. 'For pity's sake, get your snot rag out,' grumbles one of his mates. The distributor's decision was unequivocal, and its grounds clearly expressed. 'It starts on that social level, and it never rises above it. Audiences just don't want to see that sort of thing.' And this is why – even if the talent to make them were around – equivalents of *Marty* and *The Grapes of Wrath*, *Two Pennyworth of Hope* and *The Childhood of Maxim Gorky* cannot be produced in this England.

This virtual rejection of three-quarters of the population of this country represents more than a ridiculous impoverishment of the cinema. It is characteristic of a flight from contemporary reality by a whole, influential section of the community. And, which is worse, by reason of their control of the cinema, they succeed in imposing their distorted view of the present on their massive and impressionable audience. According to the testimony of our film-makers (the oath is administered by the Censor), Britain is a country without problems, in which no essential changes have occurred for the last 50 years, and which still remains the centre of an Empire on which the sun will never have the bad manners to set. Nothing is more significant of this determination to go on living in the past than the succession of war films which British studios have been turning out for the last four or five years, and which shows no sign of coming to an end. Now, of course there are many different ways of making films about war. You can make a film like *All Quiet on the Western Front*, which is an outcry against the whole abomination. Our war films are not like that. Or, like the Poles in the last few years, you can keep returning to the War because you are obsessed by it; because it crystallised a conflict, an essential aspiration; because it evokes ghosts that have to be exorcised. But when the Poles showed *Kanal* at Cannes, they prefaced it with an announcement. 'This film,' they said, 'is not made as an exciting entertainment. It is made as a reminder of what occurred, and as a warning, that such things should not be allowed to happen again.' We do not make war films like this either. These stories continue to be made in Britain firstly because they are profitable. Secondly, because the world of the services is one which perpetuates the traditional social set-up of the country, its distinctions of class and privilege. And thirdly, because by escaping into war, we can evade the complex uncertainties of the present, and the challenge of the future. Back there, chasing the *Graf Spee* again in the *Battle of the River Plate*, tapping our feet to the March of *The Dam Busters,* we can make believe that our issues are simple ones – it's *Great* Britain again!

In 1945, it is often said, we had our revolution. It is true we had something; though for a revolution it was a little incomplete. According to the British cinema, however, nothing happened at all. The nationalisation of the coal fields; the Health Service; nationalised railways; compulsory secondary education – events like these, which cry out to be interpreted in human terms, have produced no films. Nor have many of the problems which have bothered us in the last ten years: strikes; Teddy Boys; nuclear tests; the loyalties of scientists; the insolence of bureaucracy . . . The presence of American troops among us has gone practically unremarked; so have the miners from Italy and the refugees from Hungary. It is only with reference to facts such as these, that criticism of British films can now have any relevance; for, on the present level, aesthetic discussion can hardly be more than a game. What we need to consider is the image of ourselves that our cinema is bent on creating, and whether we, as a nation, should continue to accept that image. Further, we must question the significance, and the justice, of the use those in political and financial control of us are content to make of this powerful, essentially democratic medium.

The cinema is an industry. This is a statement which no-one is likely to contest. It is also an art – and most people will allow that too. But it is something else as well: it is a means of communication, of making connections. Now this makes it peculiarly relevant to a problem of the most urgent importance to us – and it is admitted to be so by both of our effective political parties. I mean the problem of community – the need for a sense of belonging together – of being prepared to make sacrifices for the common good. Naturally, it is only in difficult times that we hear these principles invoked by politicians. Then: 'All hands to the pumps!' they

237

call. But it is no use expecting to find the deck hands running unless they have been made to feel, earlier in the voyage, that the ship is theirs, and worth their trouble to save. That they are a part of it. One of the most powerful ways of helping people feel this is by making films. There was a time when this was understood in this country, at least by a few. In the thirties the British documentary movement, led by John Grierson, built up a tradition of good, social-democratic film-making. And when the war came, and the GPO Unit could be transformed directly into the Crown Film Unit, the nation was very happy to reap the benefit. During a war it is useful to be able to appeal to national democratic sentiments. ('Your courage, your hard work, your cheerfulness will bring Us victory!' as that unfortunate poster put it.) But after a war, when the slogan is 'Back to Business as Usual!' democratic sentiments are apt to seem unnecessary, and such appeals are discontinued. It is true that Crown continued to function for a time, making films about health, about education, about the national economy; but this was under the Labour Government. With the return of the Tories, in 1951, the unit was disbanded. It had become a luxury. And today it is practically impossible to make films of this kind in Britain. There is no money for them (except in rare and special cases) from the Treasury. They are not wanted by the men who book for the circuit cinemas. Their speculative production is out of the question. Who are the losers by this situation – the businessmen? Or the community?

'It is vitally important that words like Duty and Service should come back into fashion . . .' So Lord Hailsham told the nation in a recent political broadcast. But questions prompt themselves: Duty to whom, and why? Service to what ideal? One is again reminded of that wartime poster. And when Mr Macmillan, making his first broadcast as Prime Minister, talks about 'dreary equality', we recognise the concept of society that inspires him. We are back with the hierarchy, the self-idealised elite of class and wealth, the docile middle classes, and the industrious, devoted army of workers. 'All things Bright and Beautiful . . .' 'The Rich Man in his Castle, the Poor Man at his Gate . . .' 'Wider still and wider, Shall thy Bounds be set . . .' These are the songs Mr Macmillan will lead us in, with additional verses by Sir Arthur Bryant and A. L. Rowse, and *The Times* to lead the admonitory choruses: 'All this is part of a deplorable flight from responsibility which has sapped so much of the effectiveness both of our national life and our international position. Other nations do not realise that it is easier for us to blame ourselves, and that while we are generally masters of understatement, this does not apply where our conscience is concerned.'
Fine words . . . They come from that celebrated leader – 'Escapers' Club', it was headed – in which *The Times* rebuked those who suggested

that Nasser's seizure of Suez was being injudiciously handled by the government ('a deplorable flight from responsibility'). It was a call to greatness indeed. It ended: 'Doubtless it is good to have a flourishing tourist trade, to win Test matches, and be regaled by photographs of Miss Diana Dors being pushed into a swimming pool. But nations do not live by circuses alone. The people, in their silent way, know this better than the critics. They still want Britain great.'

A classic expression, this, of the Tory mentality, proudly bunkered to the last. Images of tourism, sport and a corrupt entertainment industry are lumped together as symbolising popular culture, and dismissed. And what is the alternative by which the People (in their respectfully silent way) are to be inspired? The attack on Egypt provided the answer.

But it won't do. By now, surely, even *The Times* must have gathered that this kind of antique notion of greatness is simply out of date. Fundamentally, our problems today are all problems of adjustment: we have somehow to evolve new social relationships within the nation, and a new relationship altogether with the world outside. Britain – an industrial, imperialist country that has lost its economic superiority and its empire, has yet to find, or to accept, its new identity. The irresolution expresses itself widely, and in many different ways: in discontent or opportunism among young people, in nostalgic complaints and futile bombast from the established Right, and in a weary shrugging of the shoulders from those who were Pink, or even Red, twenty years ago. But the real question remains unanswered. If 'Land of Hope and Glory' is to be decently shelved, what song are we to sing?

In literal as well as metaphorical terms, the answer of the Left is so far inadequate. I have rarely heard a more depressing sound than the singing of those few, indomitable, old-fashioned Leftists who raised their voices in chorus at the end of the Suez demonstration in Trafalgar Square:

> 'Let cowards flinch and traitors sneer –
> We'll keep the Red Flag flying here . . .'

It was more of a moan than a song; and no wonder. For how can a tired old vision like this expect to win new allegiances today?

I am not going to say that the British Labour movement is as out of touch with the present as the Tories. Their stake is in the future, and they are under no such temptation to romanticise the past. But their failure of imagination has been hardly less disastrous. The old, moral inspiration of radicalism has dribbled away, and its loss has certainly not been made good by Fabian intellectualism. The trade unions are as capable of philistine, narrowly sectional actions as the Tories – perhaps even more so. The

239

internationalism of the Left was not strong enough to extend open and unqualified help even to the Hungarian miners; and in place of a forthright appeal to the common sense and conscience of the nation, the Labour Party descended at the last General Election to a campaign frankly bourgeois and paternalistic in its inspiration: the chintz armchair – the Premier and his Pipe –'You can trust Mr Attlee!' They deserved to lose.

We have a thousand problems to resolve in this country, but the essential one is this: What kind of Britain do we want? What ideal are we going to set ourselves in our re-ordering of society? What truths do *we* hold to be self-evident? These are not abstract questions, nor even political questions in any professional sense: their answers will affect the lives and work of all of us who do not regard ourselves as predestined outsiders. At least the Tory position is frank, with its rejection of equality as a 'dreary' ideal, and its determination to return to the old way of a privileged society and a capitalist economy. It is socialism which has yet to present its solution dynamically, to shake off its complexes of inferiority and opposition, to speak with confidence, and from the heart. We are still between Arnold's two worlds, one dead, the other powerless to be born: and the frustrated exasperation that inevitably results, particularly among the young and ardent, has been one of the most significant phenomena of recent years: 'There aren't any good, brave causes left. If the big bang does come, and we all get killed off, it won't be in aid of the old-fashioned, grand design. It'll just be for the Brave New-nothing-very-much-thank-you . . .'

It was at this point in *Look Back in Anger* that a friend of mine wanted to jump to his feet and call out: 'What about Suez?' I knew what he meant, but it would have been a silly thing to do. John Osborne could, of course, have made Jimmy Porter a resolute and positive Leftist, but in that case he would have written a different play – and, things being what they are, probably a less interesting one. It would also be a great deal too facile to dismiss Jimmy Porter's angry point of view as merely the rationalisation of his neurosis: this is what most of the elder critics attempted to do, in their reluctance, or their inability, to interpret the portents. ('A young man at the centre of the stage, self-pitying, attitudinising, talks at length, cheaply, violently, foolishly . . .' – Mr J. C. Trewin.) But the public came; and largely a young public. What did they see? Not merely, it is obvious, the hysterical boor which is all the central character could seem to the middle-aged, unperceptive eye; but a tremendously forceful expression of their own disgust with contemporary hypocrisies, and at the same time a reflection of their own sense of confusion and lack of focus. This was the heartening thing: that here at last was a young writer, using the language of today, giving passionate expression to his uncertainty and his frustrated idealism – and being received by his contemporaries, at least, with understanding and enthusiasm.

It is not really Osborne's anger that is significant, so much as the com-plement of it: his baffled aspiration, his insistent plea for a human com-mitment. These are qualities that have been out of fashion for a long time. Indeed it is ironic to find Osborne's name linked journalistically (as an 'angry young man') with two other writers who are fashionable precisely because they express the directly opposite attitude to his own. Both Kingsley Amis and John Wain have a certain satirical view of society which gives them a remote affinity to Jimmy Porter; but basically they are both of them anti-idealist, anti-emotional, and tepid or evasive about their social commitments. It is because they are so depressingly representative in all this of what we may call the Liberal establishment, that I think it is worthwhile considering one or two of their characteristic statements in some detail.

Amis has perhaps been the most honest. In an extremely illuminating pamphlet issued by the Fabian Society (*Socialism and the Intellectuals*), he has done his best to define his position. He is discussing what he calls 'a quality as characteristic of the fifties intellectual as of his predecessor in the thirties':

> Romanticism in a political context I would define as an irrational capac-ity to become inflamed by interests and causes that are not one's own, that are outside oneself. If this sounds hostile or bad-tempered, I had better say at once that I see myself as a sufferer from political romanti-cism just as much as the next man. Anyway, by his station in society the member of the intelligentsia really has no political interests to defend, except the very general one (the one he most often forgets) of not find-ing himself bossed around by a totalitarian government . . . Furthermore he belongs to no social group which might lend him sta-bility; his only group is the intelligentsia itself, where stability is associ-ated mainly with alcoholic coma. In these circumstances our intellectu-al shops around for a group and for a cause to get excited for.

In a passage like this, most of Amis' attitudes are clearly illustrated: they are unattractive, but they are fashionable. They are also expressed with astonishing poverty of thought and looseness of language. Consider this 'definition' of political romanticism: 'irrational' in the first sentence is sim-ply question-begging, and phrases like 'not one's own' and 'outside one-self' are meaningless as they stand. (Where exactly *do* our interests end, and our causes become the responsibility of others?) All the statement amounts to, in fact, is an instinctive reaction against any kind of political idealism. This is made explicit later in the essay, in similar terms of jocu-lar cynicism: 'I think the best and most trustworthy political motive is self-interest. I share a widespread suspicion of the professional espouser of causes, the do-gooder, the archetypal social worker who knows better than I do what is good for me . . .' This is not argument, but backchat. There is no logic in the writing; but there is self-revelation.

Amis reveals himself as a coward, too scared to take up any stand at all. Antagonistic to principles, he equates them with 'romanticism' – a word with good, pejorative overtones that he takes no trouble to define. At the same time he is careful to claim that he is himself a romantic, thus covering himself both ways. His humour is consistently derisive, of his own pretensions to seriousness as well as everyone else's: he will rather pose as a philistine than run the risk of being despised as an intellectual – witness his meaningless crack about the 'alcoholic coma' of the intelligentsia. He can use no simple, emotional terms without apologising for them ('Hopes and aspirations, to coin a phrase . . .'). He refuses to make his own position plain, referring throughout his pamphlet to 'our intellectual', 'your intellectual', 'our contemporary romantic', never explaining in what relationship he himself stands to this shadowy figure. And finally it is clear that he can only conceive of a cause in negative terms – in terms of war, or poverty or 'the rise of Fascism and so on . . .' (his own phrase). Socialism as a positive ideal, involving definable human values, apparently means nothing to him: his only real concern is not to be caught out, not to expose himself through naïf enthusiasm to the ridicule of the sophisticated, not to commit himself. One can only wonder why he continues to vote Left: through a lingering, irrational, shame-faced humanism, I suppose.

This humanism does not appear to be shared by John Wain, a writer whose name has been closely linked with Amis, and who has achieved a roughly equivalent celebrity in the same fashionable literary columns. As a result, when Wain explains his attitude to the contemporary situation, we find him implicitly far further to the right. I take this quotation from an article by him, 'How it Strikes a Contemporary', from the *Twentieth Century* (the piece is carefully sub-headed 'A Young Man Who is Not Angry'). The discussion is on education.

> Obviously the greatest single factor in keeping England a class-bound society is the fact that education is conducted along lines dictated by considerations of class. If you want to move towards a classless society, reorganise education. If you don't, leave it as it is. And the answer of the English people has always been quite unambiguous. They *don't* want a classless society. Only a few people here and there, mainly among intelligentsia, certainly not 'normal' English folk, have ever wanted such a thing. Therefore, they don't want to reorganise education. The public schools remain, as part of a system of rewards. If you are 'successful', i.e. make money, one of the ways in which your suc-

cess is rewarded is the power to send to your children to expensive schools, where they will receive . . . the unalterable marks of membership of the governing class. Who am I to try to interfere with anything so deep-rooted?

The attitude is essentially the same, with certain modifications. The disavowal of responsibility is complete and specific – though quite unargued. One might, after all, just as sensibly ask who is John Wain that he does *not* try to interfere with something so deep-rooted? It should all depend, of course, on what John Wain himself believes; but this we are not told. At least not in so many words. It is plain, however, where his sympathies lie, if only from the 'unambiguous' testimony which he cites so confidently on behalf of the English people ('English' is used for 'British' throughout the article); but just where this unmistakable answer has been given is not divulged. Notice again, too, the inferred denigration of the 'intelligentsia' – the cranky reformists – as opposed to 'normal' English *folk*.

Like Amis, Wain writes with a pretence of logical argument, but in fact he is doing little more than stating his preferences. They are conservative. Setting out, for instance, to justify 'The Establishment', he uses the odd reasoning that it deserves preservation because it has escaped the corruption which has vitiated popular culture and which therefore presumably disqualifies the people as a whole ('normal' English folk?) from serious regard. 'The life of a judge, a bishop, a professor, or a cabinet minister is substantially the same now as it was then [in the 1850s!]. It follows that the traditionally English attitudes have survived best among these people. And this is no light matter.' What these traditionally English attitudes are, and how much they are worth, we are not informed; nor is there any suggestion that this privileged minority has any responsibility to other sections of the community. 'The working class have been robbed of their traditional way of life and, *until they have time to build up another*, they will be at the mercy of anything contemptuously thrown in their direction by the entertainment industry and the cheap press.' The italics are mine. The suggestion is thus that, until the working class has independently managed to accomplish this remarkable feat, we had better continue to side with 'the only people who have managed to get into any sort of relationship with the past . . . the property-owning aristocracy and *bourgeoisie* . . .' And this will involve, naturally, continued veneration for Eton and Winchester which, 'whatever else they may be and do, stand out as institutions with a conspicuously *national* flavour.'

The effect of such patent snobbery masquerading as reasoned argument is comic: but the spirit behind it is not. Writing like this is neither intellectually sharp nor morally sound; its statement amounts to little more in

the end than a rationalised rejection of principle, a rejection of responsibility, and a disingenuous justification of the *status quo*. Amis's human
impulses are genuine; even if he cannot really bring himself to trust them,
he does not altogether abandon them either. Wain is talking already like
an empty-headed, avuncular Tory:

> That is why intelligence is the most crying need in English life today.
> And that intelligence must be directed towards the recovery of a
> national character, a 'way of life' that will revive national pride, in the
> best sense – the sort of pride that makes it impossible to stoop to mean-
> ness or bullying.

At this rate he will soon be writing speeches for the Queen.

I have already stressed that what is important about Amis and Wain – in
this context at least – is what they represent, the light their social and
moral attitudes throw on the culture that has produced them, and made
celebrities of them. I want to make this point clear, because otherwise I
shall certainly be accused of personal malice. But ideas here are more
interesting than personalities; and it is fascinating to see how completely,
from the quotation of these two passages, the gaunt spirit of British 'liberalism' is conjured up.

I put 'liberalism' in inverted commas, because the genuinely liberal
spirit is one which I respect, indeed do my best to express. But there is
not much of it around in Britain at the moment. What we have in its place
is a weak-limbed caricature, featuring only its most pallid virtues. This
kind of liberal will commit himself to nothing more specific, or more
dynamic, than a vague notion of 'decency'. He is on the humane side. He
opposes the death penalty; he disapproves of our action in Suez. But his
reactions are all *against*: his faiths are all negative. Tolerance is the most
positive virtue he can accept, and for a political ideal he can find nothing
more inspiring than the ambition 'not to find himself bossed around by a
totalitarian government' – though this can hardly be more than a pious
hope on his part, since he is mistrustful of political programmes, and does
not really believe in the efficacy of political action. Politically, in fact, he
exists in a vacuum, as Amis admits (though he implies, wrongly, that this
is the inevitable position of a 'member of the intelligentsia', instead of
simply a sad self-portrait). He is prepared to dislike, or deplore, particular phenomena in our society, as John Wain dislikes the entertainment
industry and the cheap press, but he is not prepared to make connections
between abuses and the system which produces them. His paper is *The
Observer*.

The broad division of this country between Conservative and Labour (with a floating vote of 'liberals') is not a division between good and bad, right and wrong (and this naturally goes for the 'liberals' too, with whom this paper belongs). We believe that the two great political parties represent sections of the community that are of equally great merit; that there is equal value in the basic attitude, conservative and radical, which each represents.

At first sight this quotation from an *Observer* editorial (for New Year, 1957) might appear to be an affirmation of a principle, a statement of mature liberalism. That is obviously what was meant. But where (again) is the bloody horse? In fact, affirmations of this kind amount to nothing more than a refusal to take the responsibility of analysing the situation in which we find ourselves today, and of agreeing on a consistent policy by which to deal with it. Effects remain unrelated to causes, and *The Observer*, which has consistently opposed Tory policy on such crucial issues as the death penalty, Cyprus and Suez, still continues to speak of the Right in benevolent general terms, and to find 'equal value' in its 'basic attitude'. This is not the maturity of liberalism, but its decay. All points of view are *not* equally right, and to suppose that it is somehow narrow-minded to opt for one consistent line of action rather than for all policies simultaneously is the shortest way to render oneself politically ineffective. With nothing to guide them but their kind hearts and their good intentions, liberals of this persuasion will probably be found on the progressive side of the barricades – but when the fight is already lost. They may charge the mounted police in Whitehall – but it will be at a demonstration that ought never to have been necessary. They will be conscientious objectors to wars which they have been too fair-minded to prevent.

There is no need to be an economist, or a political theorist, to understand that the world has changed, and that attitudes which sufficed a hundred years ago are not adequate today. Industrialism and mass education have transformed society, and crowded it to a point where everything impinges on, and affects, everything else. We can no longer afford the luxury of *laissez-faire*, and if we try, we are going to find that it is the most pernicious elements that come out on top. I have not got these ideas out of a book, nor from listening to the wireless, but from personal experience. I have learned that it is impossible to work in the cinema, or usefully to discuss it, without reference to the system within which films are produced; and once that reference is made, it is impossible not to consider the basis of the system, the way it has grown, the motives which sustain it and the interests that it serves. The kind of cinema it produces, and the kind of cinema it suppresses. And such considerations lead me inevitably to a political position. They do not make me a politician, nor a propagandist; but they give me direction. Naturally, they affect the way I look at things.

All this is extremely simple; and I am rather amazed that it should need to be said. But it is not only the 'liberals' who refuse to make these primary connections. We find them equally shunned by intellectuals all along the Left, to whom art remains a diversion or an 'aesthetic experience', and Brecht is a bore. It is this, perhaps, as much as anything, which explains the deadness, the triviality, and ultimately the complete irrelevance of practically all the publicised art-work in this country at the moment. And in particular, of course, this applies to those channels of criticism and discussion, those disseminators of thought, the weekend reviews, the 'serious Sundays', and the critical programmes of the BBC. Right or Left here make no odds: it is a coterie world, perfectly directionless, a world of word-spinning and self-display, and it exists in a political limbo. (This is almost inevitable since the same people write in all the magazines.) From time to time gestures are made, allusions struck, which might seem to impinge on the outside world; but the only essential references are to other works of art, wine, or the personal foibles of the author. Ideas here have become totally dissociated from communal life, and the only audience considered worth addressing is the cultivated, 'liberal' few, who are flattered rather than discouraged by the implication that they belong to a minority.

> *The Rest is Silence* is a maddening novel, like a joke parcel, you go on unwrapping and find there is nothing really there . . . it leaves you feeling as if you have been turning over the pages of one of those unreadable magazines which you find in the lounges of Swiss hotels.

> We are all existentialists nowadays, at least in the same vague, popular sense it was ever true to say we were all socialists . . .

> It was a great performance, but can I add – after being allowed to embrace Mme Feuillère figuratively and with infinite respect – that it was not the greatest conceivable performance? . . . ! am almost sure I heard, with my own ears,
>   *Soleil, je te viens voir pour la dernier fois.*
> Is it possible that Mme Feuillère could have missed one of the most beautiful mutes in French literature? I prefer to think I had a momentary black-out . . .

It is surely preposterous that our leading radical weekly should address its readers in terms like these – for all three quotations are from the *New Statesman*, and one of them is parody. They illustrate perfectly what

George Orwell, writing of the left-wing intelligentsia in *England Their England*, described as their 'severance from the common culture of the country'; and they illustrate too (in their manner as much as their matter) how the cultural climate of the Left remains that of the status quo. This languid, over-sophisticated, salon voice is not one that could ever, conceivably, touch the conscience or inspire the heart to make new affirmations.

Some people may feel that this is unimportant; that culture and politics are unrelated. It is not, and they aren't. A socialism that cannot express itself in emotional, human, poetic terms is one that will never capture the imagination of the people – who are poets even if they don't know it. And conversely, artists and intellectuals who despise the people, imagine themselves superior to them, and think it clever to talk about the 'Ad-Mass', are both cutting themselves off from necessary experience, and shirking their responsibilities. Britain must be one of the few countries in the world where intellectuals are content to accept the bourgeois view of themselves as trivial *décorateurs*, or as irresponsible and anti-social outsiders. Or where artists insist on confining themselves to the manufacture of entertainment (more or less high-class) or to onanism, and lash out in angry fear when anybody suggests that their range might be extended if they could relate their work to the world outside themselves, or at least consider their art in relation to their fellow men. One knows that this raises complex problems, and nobody wants to impose a Zhdanovite socialist-realism here (the notion is more ludicrous than sinister); but it would do us no harm to at least start thinking about these things. Yet here, in 1957, is the reaction of an English poet to the suggestion that his work is likely to be impoverished if he continues to deny the relevance to it of the ideas of our time:

> Do these writers in any way justify the Soviet use of tanks and firing squads in Hungary? If they do not, it is strange that they fail to conclude that ideology is not necessarily a good thing. If they do, perhaps you will forgive a certain committedness in the expression if I say that their attitude seems to me to typify not 'the impassioned imaginative core' of our society, but a rapidly shrinking clique of intellectual and moral lepers.

What is the significance of this hysterical refusal to take part in contemporary existence, to face its challenge and its risks? You would think our poets were sick, and perhaps they are – sick with the incurable, paralysing disease of mediocrity.

No doubt about it: we need a new intelligentsia just as much today as we did in 1941, when *England Their England* was written. It is depressing indeed to find how little things have changed. A young writer like Amis will criticise Orwell (amongst other things, for encouraging 'political quietism'!), but he apparently fails to perceive how he, and his own generation, conform to the pattern of snobbishness and pusillanimity which Orwell exposed. The hope that the War might destroy these barriers, these inhibitions, has been proved vain: that sense of comradeship and mutual aid has vanished as though it had never been. To Amis himself now, any kind of direct relationship with working people seems to imply unthinkable embarrassment, and he can only deal with it in facetious terms: 'I cannot see myself explaining, to an audience of dockers, say, just why homosexual relations between consenting adults should be freed from legal penalty.' I suppose this is meant to be funny; but what a disagreeable ignorance of what working-class people are really like. He ought to try the experiment he describes. He might be surprised to find that his own enlightenment is not so very much superior to that of the working men – he might even get a good poem out of it.

We need, as I say, a new intelligentsia: and if we are not very careful, we are going to get one, though not of a kind that will do us much good.

> I would hardly count the Hungarian oppression or the Suez crisis as matters of supreme importance. They may involve 'human freedom', but after all, human freedom means a great deal more than political freedom, and I have always felt rather contemptuous of the sort of writer who allows himself to be swept into some political movement. It means he has committed himself too easily, too superficially.

I have nothing against transcendentalism as such, or against religious faith: but I certainly mistrust it when it can achieve expression only in terms as egotistical, confused and anti-human in implication as Colin Wilson's doctrine of the neo-Superman. He is right to despise the 'liberal' intellectuals for their sapless spineless triviality; but if they are merely rationalising their own sense of defeat, he in his turn is only rationalising his ambition, his conviction of superiority and his yearning for power. This is the swing-back of the pendulum with a vengeance – and nothing could be more ironic than the immediacy with which the liberal establishment collapsed under the first rude shove from the Outsider's elbow. Toynbee and Connolly went down on their knees, and within a week he was famous. A movement had been created. Significantly, the platform for the opinions I am quoting was given to Wilson by John Lehmann's post-post-Bloomsbury *London Magazine* (the review, it will be remembered, that Mr T. S. Eliot told us we had a moral obligation to buy).

The writer is not merely to be blamed for standing apart in matters like the Hungarian revolution, and Rosenberg trial. If he is absolutely honest and really serious about the problems of his time, it is imperative that he stand apart. Any other attitude would open him to a charge of immaturity, jejeune [sic] silliness. . .

Again, it is not Wilson himself who matters, but the thought that we live in a society where the expression of a philosophy so immature, so jejune (and so, if I may say so, *jeune*) can elevate a young writer to instant celebrity. Is it really necessary to point out that even if human freedom, at its most metaphysical, means 'a great deal more than political freedom', the two notions are not entirely separable? That a commitment to political principles need not necessarily be any more easy or superficial than a discipleship to Nietzsche or Shaw; and that to perceive the relationship between economic and human problems does not make a man a 'mere political jumping-jack' – another Wilsonian synonym for the man of social conscience.

Between the irresponsibility of this new authoritarianism, and the irresponsibility of the liberal sham, we have got to find our way: and perhaps the prospect is not as desperate as it looks. For at least certain myths, which have dominated and retarded us for far too long, have been lately exploded. The myth of the imperialist, hierarchic society has foundered at Suez and can never be raised again; and the myth of Russian-Communist infallibility, which for so many years absolved our left-wing intellectuals from the duty of thinking for themselves, has gone with the Twentieth Party Conference and the Russian action in Hungary. Are we to feel lost and deserted as a result? Or are we going to be capable of at last accepting our responsibilities to the present, and of finding political maturity? I started this essay with a despondent fantasy of the domestic scene. But it is not obligatory that the British intellectual should surrender to the pressures which would keep him, patronised and ineffective, in the nursery; nor is his only solution to escape. He could stay at home, grow up, and take over his inheritance.

If we are to do this, one of the first things we will have to learn is to talk to each other. This may seem an odd thing to say, when there is so evidently too much talk already; but I mean talk that relates to actuality, not just the incessant chasing of ideas round a wall of death. Useful controversy is something that is almost impossible to achieve at the moment: discussion has become a game, in which there is general agreement that we should lay off personalities, that dog should not examine dog too closely, and speaking should not be frank. The result is a thick and airless atmosphere of common-room theorising, in which to be too outspoken or specific is to be judged guilty of bad taste, or exhibitionism. The critical reception of *Look Back in Anger* was a good instance of this: of all the critics who attacked the play, how many were prepared to examine its implications with any degree of care? Another characteristic example of evasive action came from *The Times* not long ago – this time with reference to an article written by myself (on themes somewhat similar to those I have developed here):

> [the article] certainly hits hard at those critics and that school of criticism Mr Anderson feels to be too recumbent, but it nevertheless gives the impression that it is an artificial exercise carried out for the purpose of testing the reactions of others, an elaborate trailing of the coat . . .

So your sincerity is doubted, or your integrity is accused; or you are patronised, or written off as an angry young man. And the embarrassing issues can continue to be evaded. Doubtless – it will be interesting to see – similar tactics will be used against this book. But I have a feeling they will be ineffective.

I have a feeling – and I hope it is more than a hope – that it is no longer seriousness that is felt to be a bore (particularly among younger people), so much as obsessional flippancy and the weary cult of the 'amusing'. When the *Universities and Left Review* appeared, in the spring of 1957, it was reviewed neither in the *New Statesman*, *The Observer*, *The Sunday Times*, nor *The Times*. Yet it sold out its first edition, reprinted, and sold out again. I take this as a portent. Perhaps people are beginning to understand that we can no longer afford the luxury of scepticism, that we must start again believing in belief. 'Only connect . . .' said Forster, a long time ago; and it was a marvellously wise thing to say. But then, more recently, he told us that he did not believe in belief. Perhaps it is that that has muffled him. 'We had far better put our industry into being clever than into being good,' wrote V. S. Pritchett the other day in the *New Statesman*. The antithesis is not so much false, as old-fashioned.

Of course Lord Hailsham is right, and we must start being able to use words like duty, service, obligation and hope again without blushing – and community, and conscience, and love. But it is more than just a matter of bringing such terms back into fashion by using them in a party political broadcast. It is going to take a revolution to make these words clean, to revitalise the ideals they stand for, after their long debasement at the hands of journalists, politicians and copy-writers. And only a revolution of this kind can save us.

I may seem to have come a long way from the cinema: but the connections are direct. In our country today, if you take a camera and lights into a factory, or a coal mine, or a market, there is always a time to go through in which the cry is 'J. Arthur Rank's here again!' 'Come on Clark Gable!' or 'Send for Diana Dors!' And this is not because the British are hopelessly self-conscious, or unimaginative, or facetious. It is because the cinema, as it is at present, can mean nothing to them except in terms of commercial parody. I want a Britain in which the cinema can be respected and understood by everybody, as an essential part of the creative life of the community. And if I have made a 40 minute film about the people of Covent Garden, I do not want to be told that I must cut it to eighteen minutes if I want British audiences to see it – because American feature films are running long this year. Those good and friendly faces deserve a place of pride on the screens of their country; and I will fight for the notion of community which will give it to them.

Fighting means commitment, means believing what you say, and saying what you believe. It will also mean being called sentimental, irresponsible, self-righteous, extremist and out-of-date by those who equate maturity with scepticism, art with amusement, and responsibility with romantic excess. And it must mean a new kind of intellectual and artist, who is not frightened or scornful of his fellows; who does not see himself as threatened by, and in natural opposition to, the philistine mass; who is eager to make his contribution, and ready to use the mass media to do so. By his nature, the artist will always be in conflict with the false, the narrow-minded and the reactionary: there will always be people who do not understand the relevance of what he is doing: he will always have to fight for his values. But one thing is certain: in the values of humanism, and in their determined application to our society, lies the future. All we have to do is believe in them.

French Critical Writing

Sight and Sound, October-December 1954

ONE OF THE MOST DELIGHTFUL FEATURES ABOUT A VISIT TO FRANCE – APART from food, sunshine, etc. – is that civilised attitude towards living that finds its most obvious expression in the way people talk about the arts. At a theatrical festival at Angers this summer, I asked a young Frenchman, not in the least an intellectual, if he was going to see the *Hamlet* which featured among the revivals more familiar to a French audience. He seemed surprised. *'Evidemment, on va voir* Hamlet . . .'

'Evidemment . . .' The little word evokes a world picture wholly different, and considerably more sympathetic than its British equivalent, in which the arts tend to be tolerated, or patronised, where not positively mistrusted. Amongst professionals the gap is just as wide. Compared with the French we have the air of a nation of amateurs, in film criticism no less than in any other cultural activity. Readers of *Sight and Sound* will probably remember that illuminating quiz on professional attitudes to which half a dozen or so of our leading film critics contributed some issues back. 'I consider it undesirable for a critic, whose job is to appraise the finished product, to become immersed in the technical mumbo-jumbo of the studio. It is his job to eat the pudding, not to meddle in the kitchen.' 'I have always believed that critics can serve their function most usefully by standing as far as possible aside from the commercial and technical trees to look at the wood on the screen.' An unfortunate metaphor, this last one, but certainly revealing: imagine a music critic who scorned acquaintanceship with the 'trees' of harmony and orchestration on the grounds that such knowledge would obscure his appreciation of a symphonic 'wood'.

This proud affirmation of the value of ignorance is at least one vice from which French critics are wholly immune. They are lucky, of course; secure in their cultural tradition, they are under no pressure to write down to their public, to dress up their criticism in the specious gladrags of journalism, careful to avoid any suggestion of the esoteric or the specialised.

All this is not quite to suggest that it would be worthwhile subscribing in Britain to the *Figaro Littéraire* for the sake of M. Claude Mauriac's weekly contribution; or, indeed, to any of the French weeklies or dailies. French readers in search of informed writing on the cinema are more fortunate than British, but such criticism is rarely important enough to deserve export, however relatively superior. But there are a number of specialised publications which are well worth attention: for instance, the admirable collection of monographs published under the title *7e Art* by the Editions du Cerf, under the direction of Jean Quéval and Jean-Louis Tallenay.

Admirably produced, and very well illustrated, these little books show a standard of specialised knowledge and gusto quite beyond anything one can imagine being done in this country. Jean Queval's book on Marcel Carné was noticed in *Sight And Sound* on its publication three years ago. Since then, the collection has expanded in five parallel series: on individual films (Georges Charensol on *Belles de Nuit*); on individual directors (Quéval's *Carné* is to be followed by a *Jean Renoir* from André Bazin); on problems (*Le Cinéma a-t-il une âme?* by Henri Age, and *Le Cinéma et le Sacré* by Agel and Amedée Ayfre). A technical series is to be opened by a book on the art of the cameraman; and a general group includes a study of the Western; *Seven Years of French Cinema* (1945-53); a review of world production in 1953; and a survey of the French cinema from its beginnings to 1945.

Some of these books are better than others; none is without value. Perhaps the least successful is the review of 1953, the work of six critics (including our own Gavin Lambert, whose appreciations of *Cinerama* and *Limelight* are reprinted from *Sight and Sound*); a formidable spread of territory is covered – American, British, French, Italian, Russian, Spanish production, special chapters on animated cinema, on short production, on Trnka and Grimault – but there is lacking the harmony between contributors which is needed to give such a survey, particularly one presented from an assessor's rather than a cataloguist's viewpoint, the consistency it needs. Not surprisingly, the books on the French cinema are distinctly more successful; but so is J. L. Rieupeyrout's monograph on the Western. Written from a historical rather than an aesthetic viewpoint, this covers the development of the genre as well as the relation of Hollywood's picture of the West to the actual history of the Frontier. Here surely is the basis for a wonderful series of programmes at the National Film Theatre. I recommend the book very strongly, and indeed the whole collection.

I have not left myself much space for two periodicals which deserve recommendation: *Cahiers du Cinéma* and *Positif*. The latter, and junior of these, has developed prodigiously from a young provincial review, published in Lyons, to a lively, uncompromising specialist bi-monthly. Special numbers have recently appeared devoted to Vigo (a fine piece of editing) and the Mexican cinema. 'Aspects of the American Cinema' and 'French Cinema Since the War' are shortly promised, and should be well worth acquiring. *Cahiers du Cinéma* (the inheritor of the proud tradition of Jean-Georges Auriol's *Revue du Cinéma*) is equally uncompromising, and rather more luxuriously produced. Two of France's best critics, the sympathetic Jacques Doniol-Valcroze and the exhaustive André Bazin, are its editors, and contribute regularly to its pages. (One regrets that the name of Jean Quéval no longer appears in *Cahiers*; their team is not so strong that they can afford to drop this perceptive and unhysterical critic.) Amongst valuable features which have lately appeared in the magazine, perhaps the most remarkable are a series of tape-recorded interviews with Renoir, Becker and Buñuel. These are excellently done, authentically and amiably self-revealing; without over-statement, they can be described as important.

I have stressed in this note the enlivening qualities of French writing on the cinema; I have not emphasised its more irritating aspects. These certainly exist. Though the French are commonly assumed to think more lucidly, more logically than us, there is little evidence in their film criticism to support the theory. Much of the reviewing in both *Cahiers* and *Positif* tends unhappily towards the dithyrambic; the younger critics especially seem short on analytical capacity, anxious to establish themselves as littérateurs. In *Cahiers* in particular this seems to have led to a perverse cultivation of the meretricious. One quotation must suffice: '*La gentillesse est le signe des grands cinéastes; de cette vérité prenhière, Otto Preminger offre d'entrée la vivante confirmation.*' The adulation of directors like Howard Hawks, Preminger, Hitchcock, even Robert Wise seriously vitiates much of the writing in *Cahiers*; an examination of the attitude behind it would be worth attempting. But let me end on the note of commendation: both these magazines offer informed and stimulating writing on the cinema. They will often annoy: they are seldom dull.

Positif and *Cahiers du Cinéma*

Sight and Sound, January-March 1955

THE FRENCH AGAIN. EACH OF THESE ISSUES MAKES A SPECIAL EFFORT, *POSITIF* in the name of the American cinema generally, *Cahiers du Cinéma* in peculiar homage to Alfred Hitchcock; it is rather disappointing to have to record that they are respectively rather inadequate and inexcusably bad. For the light they throw on certain vices endemic in French criticism, however, they merit attention.

Positif first, because it is better. A survey of the American social film: an interview with Paul Strand and a long appreciation of *Salt of the Earth*: Zinnemann and Dassin: and a very justifiable smack at *Cahiers du Cinéma* in the shape of a deflation of half a dozen of their pet 'cult' directors (Hawks, Ray, Preminger, etc). Much of this is sympathetic; but one regrets the almost complete absence of humour among these young critics (with the attendant absence of a sense of proportion) and – which is more serious – a consistent inaccuracy and an ignorance of the way films come into being that is only partially concealed by the self-confidence of the writing. A basic weakness in most French writing on the cinema of this kind seems to be this extraordinary unawareness of the fact that films have to be written before they can be directed; that comparatively few American directors have actually *conceived* the films they have made; that there are such people as producers, who often assign directors to subjects which do not necessarily suit them, but who at their best can exercise considerable creative influence on their pictures. *Julius Caesar* obviously reflects the personality of John Houseman as much as that of Mankiewicz; yet the critics of *Positif* do not even acknowledge his existence. (*'En adaptant* Jules César, *Mankiewicz a choisi la mauvaise formule . . .'* The following total comment on the film is also unhappily typical: *'Ça et la, Marlon Brando sauvait la texte de Shakespeare.'*)

Analytical criticism, discussion of a film-maker's personality, is impossible if a good half of the constituent elements of each film is simply ignored. *'En adaptant* Les Raisins de la Colère, *John Ford a dulcoré le roman de Steinbeck . . .'* Any estimate of Ford which starts with a confusion as elementary as that is not likely to go far. Similarly, the importance of Laszlo Benedek, honourable and skillful director though he is, is absurdly exaggerated when one assigns to him the entire creative responsibility for *Death of a Salesman*.

All the same, there is much more to be said for *Positif* than for the latest number of *Cahiers du Cinéma*. This magazine seems now to have been almost completely taken over by the covey of bright young things whose eccentric enthusiasms, paraded so generously in recent issues, have already sadly impaired its reputation. Here they are more vociferous and preposterous than ever. To the accompaniment of a ceremonial tattoo of mutual back-slapping, Hitchcock is hoisted into the Pantheon – up there with Murnau, Renoir and Howard Hawks. 'Depuis Le Fleuve, Monkey Business et Under Capricorn, le cinéma est entré dans ce que nous pouvons appeler "la phase de l'intelligence".' Can absurdity go further? The answer is, Yes. In the course of this issue Hitchcock is compared with Dostoevsky, Faulkner, Bernanos, Nietzche, Rousseau, Hardy, Richardson, Poe (a 'classical' poet, apparently), Meredith, Homer, Aeschylus, Corneille, Balzac and Shakespeare. More marvellous still, all this is done on the strength of a handful of Hitchcock's American films, most notably Under Capricorn, I Confess and Strangers on a Train. For those who can view with equanimity this degradation of a fine magazine, there is some amusement to be found in all this, particularly in Hitchcock's own, plainly gleeful reaction to these fantastic accolades. ('"Is it true that you don't really like your American films?" He smiled as he shook my hand. "Not really."') But, strange as it may seem, all this admiration for Hitchcock does not inspire in these critics the slightest interest in his work as a whole; there is not a word in the whole issue on his British films.

Or perhaps it is not so strange. One is driven to the conclusion, paradoxically, that these critics are not really interested in Hitchcock at all. They are above all interested in themselves. While the writing in Positif, though rather uncommunicative of enjoyment, is at least honest, the majority of this group of critics now occupying Cahiers remind one of that grim remark attributed to Cyril Connolly when encompassed by enthusiasts at some highly charged literary gathering. 'It's us they want to see,' he said, turning to a fellow-victim, 'but it's themselves they want to talk about.'

Catholicism and the Cinema

Review of *Dieu au Cinéma* by Amedée Ayfre, in *Sight and Sound*, January 1954

THE CHARACTERISTICS OF CATHOLIC WRITING ON THE CINEMA HAVE NOT PERhaps been such as greatly to encourage one to a perusal of a book entitled *Dieu au Cinéma*, written from an avowedly Catholic standpoint. One distrusts the – to a Protestant eye – apparent casuistry with which some Catholic writers seem able to justify, or at least condone, work not merely unsatisfactory from an aesthetic point of view, but sometimes morally pernicious, simply because it serves as effective propaganda for their Church. Thus, opening this book at random, and lighting upon a still of Céleste Holm and Loretta Young, impeccably nunned, grinning away tenderly behind a wire fence (*Come to the Stable*), one fears the worst. A glance at the caption, however, persuades us to think again: 'No, these women have not attained the fullness of joy of a Francis of Assisi, the simplicity of "Little Flowers". They have never emerged from a world of fairy tales and Father Christmas.'

It is at once apparent that M. Ayfre is anything but an apologist for second-and third-rate Catholic cinéastes; he comments without fear or favour, with a pleasant irony and a conspicuous honesty. About, for instance, the 'resolution' of *Angels with Dirty Faces* (in which gangster James Cagney pretends to die a coward's death in order to discourage his youthful admirers from following his example) he writes: 'An admirable lie perhaps, from a dramatic point of view, and cinematically extremely well realised . . . but a lie none the less, of which moreover one at once gets the aftertaste of dishonesty and jesuitism, when the priest replies "yes" to the boys' anxious question as to whether the gangster died a coward.' M. Ayfre has no patience to spare for Father Crosby and Sister Ingrid, for Hollywood religiosity in general, or for anything aesthetically second-rate.

'Aesthetic' is the key word. For while the title of his book might lead us to expect simply an analysis and an evaluation of the various representations of religion by the cinema, M. Ayfre's purpose is more complex. The object of his enquiry is rather to study the expression of religious views in films from a strictly aesthetic point of view, and to seek to establish, if possible, some relationship between the degree of success with which kinds of religious feeling have been communicated, and the various aesthetic means of their realisation.

For this ambitious task, the author is well equipped. He is a graduate of the Sorbonne, and a member of the Institute of *Filmologie*. This latter qualification is somewhat ominous, for M. Cohen Séat – the inventor of the whole mysterious science of Filmologie – is none other than that formidable pedant who managed to write an entire book on the cinema without mentioning the title of a single film. Such, fortunately, is not the approach of M. Ayfre. He has evidently seen and enjoyed a lot of films; he knows well the historical background of his subject; and he is quite exceptionally responsive to the art of the cinema in practice.

It must be admitted that his book is of a fair density. Dividing the possible approaches to religion into four main categories – *Dans et par l'histoire*; *Dans et par la vie sociale*; *Dans et par la psychologie*; *Dans la perspective phenomenologique* – M. Ayfre equates each of the last three with a national school of cinema – respectively the American, the French and the Italian neo-realist. Arguing with ingenuity and considerable penetration, he seeks to clarify the three-fold relationship between the religious values explicit in a number of particular films; the intellectual standpoint of the artists concerned; and the aesthetic means (the 'film form') employed to give expression to those values and that standpoint. Thus, in his first category, he defines interestingly the conflict between the spiritual grandeur which it is the purpose of these films to portray, and the material grandiosity with which they are almost invariably realised.

In the American school he adduces an ingenious relationship between the absence of 'tension' evident in these films (i.e. their denial of any transcendental values, symbolised by their refusal to portray the clergy in the performance of their sacramental functions; and their consistent reliance on the comfortable stereotype in place of the fallible human being), and the flat, assured academicism of their style. The French school he divides into films dominated by the actor (*Monsieur Vincent*), and films dominated by the director (principally Bresson); and the work of Rossellini and de Sica provides a starting point for an investigation of the 'phenomenological' approach – that in which the artist accepts the world as he finds it, 'setting us face to face with a human event considered in the round, and abstaining from analysing it, breaking it into fragments.' The pursuit of these main lines of argument is varied by many lively discussions *en route*.

The game of aesthetic philosophy is one to which one either is, or is not, partial. M. Ayfre, who clearly relishes it, plays it with skill and general reasonableness, even if he does get led away here and there into thickets of abstraction extremely difficult to penetrate. Some of his classifications seem arbitrary. It is cheating, surely, to include *Monsieur Vincent* under 'La Psychologie' (just because it is French) instead of under 'Dans et par l'histoire'. Often, too, it is difficult to feel that his inclusion of certain films in the enquiry is justified at all. Is the humane idealism of *The Grapes of Wrath* really any more 'religious' than that of *The Ox-Bow Incident* or

The Childhood of Maxim Gorki? And the whole section on the Italian cinema – with the exception of the revolting *Cielo Sulla Palude*, which M. Ayfre strangely approves of, and whose relevance is admittedly direct – seems something of a sidetrack.

Even those, however, whose approach to the cinema is more pragmatical, will find a lot in this book to interest and to stimulate. M. Ayfre, as I have said, looks at films with an acute and searching eye; he is sensitive to film style as are few writers on the cinema, he can analyse the creative influences on a film of camerawork, script, découpage and acting with a justice that is always illuminating. One may well disagree with some of his judgements, just as one may find the more theoretical turns of his arguments difficult to grasp; but I should say that it is impossible for anyone seriously interested in the cinema to read through this book without an exceptional amount of pleasure and profit. The long section on Bresson alone, with its brilliant analysis of the director's style, and a most perceptive comparison of the film of *Le Journal d'un Curé de Campagne* with Bernanos's novel, would justify the rest of your trouble.

David Robinson

In *British Film*, 1991

FILM-MAKERS, LIKE MOST ARTISTS, ALMOST ALWAYS DISLIKE THEIR CRITICS. This is not because artists are only interested in praise; it is because they want their work to be examined and interpreted with the same care, the same professionalism as went into its making. Few film critics – and especially those who have to function as journalists – are capable of this. So when I hear that David Robinson is to be honoured for his contribution to the art of film, my first reaction is one of delight that a writer who has functioned for so long and so well as a critic should receive his just recognition.

So many times, over the years, I have been asked by interviewers – who have spoken to me as an artist – if there is any judge or interpreter whose writing I have valued and learned from. My answer has always been the same. First on the *Financial Times*, then as a regular critic of *The Times*: 'There's David Robinson, of course.' And now that *The Times* has shown that it marches to the same beat of opportunism as the rest of our poor epoch, my answer remains the same. Though with pleasure as well as pain, since David Robinson's release from the burden of weekly journalism has meant that he is free to make his contribution in so many of the other ways in which his abilities are outstanding: as chronicler and historian; as interpreter and (certainly not least) as film-maker.

In fact, there are so many reasons why David should be honoured in this way that it is hard to choose one rather than another. For over 30 years he has functioned as a weekly critic – our best, as I hope I have made clear. His papers have, at least until recently, been known for their serious and responsible attitudes towards the arts, and this has suited David very well. For he has never really been a journalist. He has acquired the skill to write about films in a way that will interest and enlighten that mysterious creature 'the general reader', without – and this really is a skill – ever broadening or cheapening his style.

What is his secret? Essentially, I am sure, it lies in that elusive and indispensable quality – enthusiasm. Journalists are very rarely enthusiasts, except for anything beyond their own professional status. It is in this sense that David Robinson has never been 'just' a journalist. He is a historian and an academic. Both of those qualities can make a writer boring and recondite, however authoritative. But David has never been either boring or recondite. As well as anybody, and better than most, he knows the facts. He knows how this wonderful medium was born nearly a hundred years ago and how rapidly and amazingly it has developed. But these facts are never dull, because the cinema – and David has never let us forget this – is the art of the marvellous. His taste is catholic, but it has always inclined towards Méliès rather than Lumière.

Myself (and I am not at all proud of this), I am not at all good at the toys with which the cinema began, the historical development of our medium from those ingenious first steps 150 years ago. But I know that if I want to find out what exactly was Daguerre's Diorama, what would be in a box containing Phenakistiscopes, how the Zoetrope and the Praxinoscope really *worked* – David Robinson is the chap to ask. He will probably have them himself. Posters, too. And photographs and sheet music and gramophone records of the genii of the music hall. For him, their performances still live.

Without doubt, this sense of the life of the past, its inventions and its artists so vividly conjured up, has prevented David Robinson ever declining into a Professor Dryasdust of the cinema. His books on World Cinema, on Keaton and the early funnies are as lively as they are accurate. And of course his life of Chaplin, so brilliantly researched and evoked, became at once a classic of film literature. There would be more books, I suppose, if he had not devoted so much of his time to collecting and to organising exhibitions, on the British cinema in Warsaw, on the history of cinema in Paris and London, regularly at Pordenone where this year his scholarship and his passion will be devoted to the techniques and the aesthetics of the pre-history of cinema. When dramatic cinema was in its infancy, Emile Cohl and his contemporaries were already accomplished artists, whose work can be enjoyed today. And in the 1870s, George Cruickshank turned his hand to animating his drawings. Who but David could tell us that?

There is enough here to justify any award the cinema is likely to make. But I realise that in this emphasis on history I may well have given a wrong impression. Many of David Robinson's enthusiasms carry him into the past; but they have also nourished his care and understanding for the cinema of the present. He is certainly academic; but he is emphatically not an academic. He has made films, very good ones, inspired and warmed by his admiration for performing artists like Hetty King, Elizabeth Welch and Adelaide Hall. And these films, all of which have been shown on television, are not just records, they are works of skill, fondness and charm, which say as much about their author as they do about their subjects. Works of art in fact. And for two years now, David Robinson has been in charge of the International Festival at Edinburgh, which he has devoted to the creative and the new, imbued with the spirit of youth. With the sponsorship of television, the festival will choose from students the Young Film-Maker of the Year. Prizes carry the honoured names of Chaplin and

261

Bill Douglas. The past leads to the present, and the present to the future. This is the achievement of the man whom this festival is honouring.

In the past, as someone who has (perhaps overmuch) embroiled himself in the struggles and controversies of the present, I must admit to having criticised David Robinson. I have criticised him for his liberality, his modesty and his reluctance to polemicise. I have been wrong. For this is a critic who has struggled, with extraordinary integrity, to preserve his enthusiasms and his sympathies, to acknowledge and respect achievement, yet never to sacrifice his principles to the demands of journalism. David is expert about his art, yet never unaware of the world in which films are made, the human and social needs of film-makers and of the people for whom he is writing. He has refused to surrender to contemporary aestheticism (*à la française*), commercialism or artistic non-attachment. He knows that art and morality have never been strangers. He is his own man. He will always be on the right side.

Dilys Powell and C. A. Lejeune

Review of *The Dilys Powell Film Reader* and *The C. A. Lejeune Film Reader* in *The Daily Telegraph*, 4 January 1992

TO JUDGE BY THE AMOUNT THAT IS WRITTEN NOWADAYS ABOUT MOVIES, IN newspapers and magazines, film criticism must be easy to write. Unfortunately this is not true. The profession of film critic, when it is seriously pursued, is an honourable one, as it has been from the start.

The Dilys Powell Film Reader, edited by Christopher Cook, and *The C. A. Lejeune Film Reader*, edited by Anthony Lejeune, celebrate the work of two honourable pioneers. They remind us that it was 20 years after audiences first cried out in alarm as the Lumière brothers filmed a train drawing into a station before a respectable British newspaper (the *Manchester Guardian*) featured an article which took the cinema seriously. Caroline Lejeune, whose mother knew C. P. Scott, wrote a piece called 'The Undiscovered Aesthetic'; and this led, in 1921, to a column signed C. A. L., which covered 'The Week on the Screen'. Five years later, C. A. Lejeune moved to *The Observer* and at the end of the thirties Dilys Powell was appointed film critic of *The Sunday Times*.

There was other writing about cinema, of course. There had been the highbrow *Close Up* and the documentary-makers put forward their Leftish views in *Documentary Film News*. Graham Greene had written about films in the short-lived *Night and Day*. But for many years these ladies, both journalists and very conscious of the fact, dominated middle-class film appreciation.

They were very different. Miss Powell had got her degree at Oxford (Somerville) and had a scholarly and poetic knowledge of Greece. Her first husband, Humphrey Payne, was an archaeologist until his premature death in 1936. She joined *The Sunday Times* three years later. Miss Lejeune on the other hand had early rejected Oxford for journalism. Douglas Fairbanks intoxicated her in *The Mark of Zorro* and she formed the ambition to earn her living by writing about films. She was always a fan.

Indeed they had this in common: they loved going to the cinema. Through the years one has been reassured by the sight of Dilys, isolated far down in the stalls, waiting expectantly for the lights to dim and the curtains to part. Apart from Fairbanks, C. A. Lejeune was early seduced by the 'heart-clutching' serials, John Barrymore and Mary Pickford. The fascination did not leave her until late in life. For Dilys, the cinema has

263

never lost its attraction. Both ladies were very good journalists – Dilys still is. But Caroline Lejeune remained firmly in the English middle-brow tradition from the start ('No nonsense about aesthetics'). *Dr Jekyll and Mr Hyde* was 'a thundering good story' and she kept her readers entertained with three pages of humour about *The Sun Never Sets*: Anthony Asquith praised her for 'that peculiarly English thing, a delicious sense of nonsense'. No doubt this is why she wrote so long on *The Observer*.

Dilys has always been very different. She wanted to – needed to – entertain her readers, but seriousness was always her intention. 'I always wanted to explain,' she wrote, 'why I thought *this* film was good.' The humanistic tone of Somerville never left her. For which, thank God. The gimlet-eyed critic of the dust-cover is quite deceptive. Dilys could be fun, with a most literate, dry tone. Recently, when Greta Scacchi drove over the cliff at the end of *Shattered*, I found myself smiling, remembering Dilys's description of Bette Davis in *In This Our Life* as 'a girl who wrecks lives and, ultimately, cars'.

But Dilys always wrote with conscience and she has always related films to what she holds to be the moral values of living. This is why you will read her for her comments on Jancso and Buñuel, as well as Bette Davis and Greta Garbo ('A great woman and a great actress').

Neither of these books claims to be comprehensive. So we are not given C. A. Lejeune's notice of *Citizen Kane*, or Dilys on *My Darling Clementine*. More significantly, neither of the two writes illuminatingly about the cinema in this country. British documentary comes off badly. Humphrey Jennings does not figure in Miss Powell's index and C. A. Lejeune only talks about Jennings (Talbot) whose pictures included *Mutiny on the Bounty*, *Anna and the King of Siam* and *Across the Wide Missouri*. Anthony Lejeune, who has compiled his mother's collection, thinks that her notice of *Mrs Miniver* shows that the film was not as unrealistic as modern cynicism believes; and as far as British documentary goes, he is of the simple opinion that it has been overpraised.

Christopher Cook, who has edited the Dilys Powell book with higher standards, has at least devoted a section to British cinema: it is good to find here an intelligent, generous welcome to Free Cinema. The general view, though, is a recognisably middle-class one: Dilys Powell was never a politician, nor a sociologue. Yet, however boring it might seem, I doubt whether British cinema can be written about without reference to politics or to class. But, of course, these books are 'readers', not 'histories'. Certainly they are much better for their lack of either semiology or structuralism.

Taking Them All In

Review of *Taking It All In* by Pauline Kael in the *Chicago Tribune*, 15 April 1984

TO ASK AN ARTIST TO COMMENT ON A COLLECTION OF REVIEWS BY A CRITIC who has shown herself especially hostile to his work is to invite trouble. I don't carry Pauline Kael's books around with me, nor are they on my shelves at home. But I remember vividly, as one is apt to, her peculiarly affronted dismissal of my first feature film, *This Sporting Life* – she was on her 'anti-art' kick then – and her equally visceral contempt for *If. . . .* – whose success, such as it was, she attributed wholly to a somehow reprehensible publicity campaign by Paramount Pictures.

I must admit also to a bizarre, though I think revealing, encounter with Kael (she habitually refers to actresses like this) at Downey's restaurant on Eighth Avenue in New York. It was after a preview screening of *If. . . .* The critic led off: 'I was on the Coast when *This Sporting Life* opened in New York, so I didn't realise what a failure it had been.' She followed this up with the advice that a scene in my new film 'could do with some cuts'. A young Canadian film-maker, a friend of her daughter's, was also present; she invoked his professional expertise for support. She only wanted to help, of course.

My inclination then was to write Kael off as a high-pressure bitch. On the evidence of this seventh collection of her reviews I must admit that she is certainly not one of those people whose opinions I would fight my way across a crowded room to hear; but I am not sure that she is simply a bitch. More accurately, perhaps, she is an opinionated obsessive. Certainly she is intensely competitive. She has to be righter than anyone else. She has to win. She is not without knowledge or shrewdness; but these are at the mercy of her emotions rather than at the service of her intelligence. She has to think herself influential, powerful.

Those are all good, traditional American characteristics; which, must, I suppose, account for the extraordinary attention that seems to be paid to Kael in this country. 'She writes so brilliantly,' one is told. I would call her a compulsive chatterbox. The most remarkable thing about her *New Yorker* reviews is their length. In this book, her reactions to films such as *Altered States*, *Dressed to Kill*, and *Melvin and Howard* rattle on over four-and-a-half, five-and-a-half, six-and-a-half pages. These are not pages of sustained or developed argument: Kael seems to prefer to write about Hollywood products that she can patronise. She is generally scornful of what she calls 'tony' pictures. She likes to use no-nonsense epithets such as 'funky', 'spooky', 'trashy' ('trashiness' is a good quality). But essentially, she just loves to bang on about movies. Smartness and paradox rate much higher on her scale than logic or consistency.

One example should suffice to show the quality of Kael's thought. Concerned to put down *Fitzcarraldo* by Werner ('Faker') Herzog, she blasts off some characteristic generalisations: 'Movies are based on illusion – movies are illusion. The sound of Fred Astaire's taps was added to the soundtrack after his dances were shot; Garbo's laugh is said to have been dubbed in *Ninotchka*; when the tiny Yoda stood in the forest advising Luke Skywalker, they were both actually on a platform built a few feet above a studio floor. The magic of movies is in the techniques by which writers and directors put us in imaginary situations and actors convince us that they are what they're not. Then along comes the G. Gordon Liddy of movies, Werner Herzog, who apparently sees the production of a film as a mystic ordeal.'

This specimen of what her publishers call Kael's 'famous style' may pass for wisdom among *New Yorker* editors who know nothing about cinema. It does not, however, take a great deal of knowledge or sense to reveal it as the smart-ass drivel it really is. The first sentence is platitude, not worth saying. The taps on Astaire's dances may have had to be, for technical reasons, post-dubbed: this does not make his talent that of an illusionist. Who is supposed to have dubbed Garbo's laugh; and who 'says' so anyway?

As for the illegitimacy of spectacle, where does that put Griffith, Eisenstein, Kurosawa? How does Kael, in the same volume, manage to be so enthusiastic for the epic staging of Gance's *Napoleon*? Or even, a few weeks earlier, have found that in *Barbarosa* 'the vistas are overwhelming, the landscapes have a near-hallucinatory unspoiled dignity'? Where was G. Gordon Liddy in all that?

Kael's energy is unflagging. And yet she is boring. She is not boring because her tone is spiritless or flat, but because there is just enough spark, perception and paradox in her writing to provide the illusion of originality, of nourishment, but not enough to disguise the fact that what she is dishing up is intellectual junk food.

A few more nuggets of nonsense. This is how Kael evokes the hero of a film called *The Stunt Man*: 'We don't know if he's a perverse, brutal murderer or merely a kid who got into trouble. Railsback . . . manages to suggest a pure, lacerated sensibility that would fit either of those explanations, and many others as well.' Comment on this kind of pure, lacerated gush is surely unnecessary. And when Kael gets on cerebral heat, as she seems to be most of the time, she is capable of even more fetching absurdities. 'Moviemaking is a seedbed of paranoia. On the set, directors, with their feelers out, intuiting what everyone is thinking, are the paranoid kings of backbiting kingdoms. They have to be paranoid to survive . . .' Kael's view of the movies, one realises, is romantic, hot-blooded yearning. 'There's a pecking order in film-making, and the director is at the top. A man who was never particularly attractive to women now finds that he's the *padrone*, everyone is waiting on his word and women are his for the nod.'

Kael is movie-struck, you see; a critical Esther Blodgett. Above all, she wants to be and to show that she is an insider. Sometimes this makes her incomprehensible; 'Cast in the Charles Grodin-Bruce Dern role, Dabney Coleman adds a dash of Paul Lynde's foul-minded relish.' Sometimes it makes her comic: Meryl Streep 'wears a short, straight hairdo – the most disfiguring star coiffure since Mia Farrow's thick wig in *The Great Gatsby*.' She knows what's wrong: 'Movies have gone to hell and ama-teurishness.' She could show them.

But Kael had her Hollywood fling two or three years ago. She took a job at Paramount in an advisory production capacity. She didn't last, and her piece in this book on 'Why Movies Are So Bad', with its odd mixture of perceptiveness and naiveté, shows why. She has very little sense of audi-ence; her responses are subjective and fiercely prejudiced; she is more con-cerned to impose her judgements than to offer understanding.

Her least amiable quality is her self-importance. This must have made her rejection by the industry particularly galling. 'Once when I was at a large party in Los Angeles, a famous director suddenly screamed across an adjoining room at me and another guest, "I know you're talking about me!" He was right.' Ah yes! Roses, roses all the way . . . It is almost sad to reflect that today fewer and fewer people are likely to care whether Pauline Kael is talking about them or not.

Too Much: Art and Society in the Sixties

Review of *Too Much: Art and Society in the Sixties 1960-1975* by Robert Hewison in *Tatler*, September 1986

AS THINGS GET WORSE IT IS INEVITABLE, I SUPPOSE, THAT OUR THOUGHTS TURN to the past. Sometimes to reassure ourselves – we lived through that, we can live through this. And sometimes with nostalgia – things were so much better then. What you feel about the sixties will depend on your age today, and on what you have been prepared to settle for. I have never myself felt the inclination to sneer at the way we were twenty-odd years ago. And it seems to become less fashionable, month by empty month, to do so.

Not that *Too Much*, Robert Hewison's new book on the sixties, is just trendy. It is the long-planned final volume of a trilogy, *The Arts in Britain Since 1939*, which has already covered the War years and the dreary period which followed them. The second of these books, *In Anger*, was subtitled 'Culture in the Cold War, 1945-60'. Perhaps it is this which leads Mr Hewison to define the sixties – 'that form the basis of popular myth'– as lasting only from 1964 to 1967. I find this odd. Certainly the radical impulse in everything, from politics to pop, burst through much earlier. The twin catastrophes of Suez and Budapest, invigorating as well as tragic, had initiated the sixties in 1956. That was *our* Blissful Dawn.

1956 was the year when impatience with the past, boredom with the status quo, produced a New Left, the short-lived illusion of a Popular Front. It was the year when Khrushchev spilt the beans about Stalin and released half a world from a false burden of hero-worship. It was the year when Rock and Roll got going and Bill Haley inspired the slashing of cinema seats. It was the year when the English Stage Company took over the Royal Court and produced *Look Back in Anger*. Angry Young Men, part fact, part invention, hit the scene. Free Cinema got itself a springboard at the National Film Theatre. Our time began.

Robert Hewison has researched all this, nearly all this, with dogged comprehensiveness and a mass of intriguing detail. A specimen chapter will give a pretty good idea of his style: 'Understanding Media' ranges from John Osborne's notorious 'Damn You England' letter in *Tribune*, to a special number of *Encounter* in 1963 (edited by Arthur Koestler) called 'What's Wrong with Britain', to painstaking liberal-left analysts like Leavis, Hoggart and Raymond Williams, to the 'thinkers' of the New Left, all by way of CND and Centre 42, to Hugh Greene and *That Was the Week That Was*, to *The Wednesday Play*, the Satire Boom and Marshall McLuhan. (And did you know that Mary Whitehouse launched her campaign to clean up TV in 1964? She had a long wait for Thatcher's Britain and Winston Churchill II. But of course she had a longer wind and much less flexible conviction than most of her enemies.)

If all this ends in indigestion, there is much fascinating flavour on the way. Mr Hewison evokes the period by quotations, sometimes funny, sometimes sad, often self-important. Arnold Wesker, for example, dear Arnold only wanting the best for us all, describing the cultural ideal of Centre 42: 'Orchestras tucked away in valleys, people stopping Auden in the street to thank him for their favourite poem, teenagers around the juke-box arguing about my latest play . . .' I know it's ridiculous, but touching, too. Who would dare write like that today? And here is Francis Wyndham, with a much smarter accent, celebrating the trend-leaders in David Bailey's *Box of Pin-ups*: 'Many of the people here have gone all out for the immediate rewards of success: quick money, quick fame, quick sex – a brave thing to do . . . His pin-ups have a heroic look: isolated, invulnerable, lost.' The authentic note of seventies corruption creeping in there.

This is an excellent source book, but not as accurate or as comprehensive as it may at first appear. Mr Hewison makes two big mistakes, I think. One affects the general accuracy of his book (and its usefulness); the other betrays, in a more specific way, its most severe limitation. The first is his decision to confine his researches 'entirely to published sources'. Interviews, he admits, are valuable sources of information. Yet he restricts himself to interviews ('testimonies' would be a better word) *which have been published*. Why? It is really not sufficient to plead that talking to witnesses of the period 'would have opened up large questions about selectivity'. All Mr Hewison has done, with his undue respect for literary culture, is to allow his selection to be made by others.

His other error is one that touches me personally, so I hope I will not be thought to be motivated by pique. (It's a long time ago, after all, and I am prepared to claim objectivity.) I find it amazing, having spent a lot of time during these years making films, that a cultural survey of this kind should omit the British cinema almost completely, on the grounds that our cinema in the sixties was 'mainly American and continental'. This is startlingly untrue. In fact, from their modest *putsch* in 1956, the Free Cinema group, plus the Royal Court, plus directors like Jack Clayton, John Schlesinger and Ken Loach, were responsible for a body of indigenous films which, for a little while, revived our cinema by exploring British themes and liberating British talent in a completely new way.

And a significant way, which demands examination both for its achievement and its consequences. By what standards are films like *Saturday Night and Sunday Morning*, *Tom Jones* or *This Sporting Life* less relevant to British 'culture' than Bailey's *Box of Pin-ups* or Peter Brook's

Theatre of Cruelty? Does a characteristically rueful Philip Larkin poem like 'Going, Going' really say more about its and our time than *If. . . .*? Is it because one is a poem and one is (only) a film? Mr Hewison talks quite a lot about McLuhan, but he remains imprisoned within the idea of 'culture' that is essentially literary, claustrophobically 'intellectual'.

This kind of culture is more concerned with ideas than with experience: it is a critic's, not an artist's culture. There is a great difference between art and 'The Arts'. 'The Arts' are about local councils and subsidies and prestige. They are about making money for Britain and satisfying upper-class audiences; they are about bums on seats and the Royal Shakespeare Company triumphing on Broadway. Art is unexpected, uncomfortable, illuminating. 'The Arts' are 'culture'; people write books on them, academics make money out of them, institutions of Higher Education thrive on them. Art is not 'culture': it is Life. That, no doubt, is why we haven't got a lot of it.

Critical Betrayal

Review of *Cinema: A Critical Dictionary* edited by Richard Roud, *How to Read a Film* by James Monaco and *Realism and the Cinema* edited by Christopher Williams, in *The Guardian*, 2 March 1981

ON THE VEXED SUBJECT OF CINEMA IN BRITAIN, TWO THINGS CAN BE SAID WITH certainty. There is not enough creation, and there is too much criticism. Newspaper, radio and television all have to have their 'critic' – usually a journalist, speaking with jokey conceit out of confident ignorance. And on a more elevated intellectual level there are the theorists and aestheticians who reflect the recent acceptance of cinema as a subject for academic study. Ironically, these latter, usually dependent on public funds, tend to be hostile to the native tradition, scornful of its past and dismissive of its present. They constitute, in fact, a *Trahison des Clercs*.

Readers of *Time Out* may have been puzzled some months ago by a review of a film to be shown on television. *Man's Favourite Sport*, directed by Howard Hawks, was described as 'in many ways the quintessential Hollywood *auteur* movie'. This statement is amplified: 'Seen in isolation from the rest of Hawks' work it seems to be merely an out of time slapstick comedy. Seen in context it effortlessly demonstrates the auteur's ability to stamp his artistic identity on anything.' The review ends predictably (to steal a favourite *Time Out* adverb) with the verdict: 'A marvellous film.'

In other words, if you are ignorant or unsmart enough not to be familiar with the Hawksian *oeuvre*, and just switch on for *Man's Favourite Sport* in pursuit of entertainment, you will find it crude. But if you are aware of Hawks as an auteur, you will know better. You will know that *Man's Favourite Sport* is marvellous. It must be. Hawks is an *auteur*.

The idea that the director of a film should be described as its 'author' was first formulated by François Truffaut over 25 years ago in 'La Politique des Auteurs'; an article in *Cahiers du Cinéma*, house magazine of the French New Wave. This was the opening shot in a campaign by the young French would-be directors (Truffaut, Godard, Chabrol, Rivette and co.) to demolish the established tradition of literary art-cinema and to clear the way for themselves as film-makers.

The aim was two-fold. First, to re-assert the primacy of the director as the creative agent in a specifically *cinematic* aesthetic. And second, to reveal consistencies of personality and theme in the films of directors who had hitherto been written off as purely commercial practitioners (Hitchcock, Hawks, etc).

None of this was essentially original, but the approach soon hardened into theory. Auteurist schools sprang up in England (the Movie group) and in New York (Andrew Sarris and friends). The theory soon ceased to perform its intended function. It became a pseudo-aesthetic enabling highbrow critics to demonstrate their expertise by discovering auteurs, generally among the ranks of less reputable American directors (Preminger, Boetticher, Sam Fuller) and by tracing thematic patterns in films – patterns which, even if they really existed, had nothing to do with artistic excellence. An *auteur*, it was discovered, could not by definition make a bad film. Hence the 'marvellous' *Man's Favourite Sport*.

Richard Roud introduces his *Critical Dictionary* by writing 'This is not the place to reopen the dreaded *auteur* controversy' – but then proceeds, rather scrappily, to do so. Auteurism, he makes plain, is his creed. So this extravagant work does not include many of the names which might reasonably be expected to figure in a dictionary of cinema. There is no Lumière, no Friese Green, no Edison. Look not here for Laemmle of Universal, Mayer and Thalberg of Metro, Goldwyn, Korda or Rank. There are a few actors, arbitrarily chosen – Garbo but not Gish, Dietrich but not Asta Nielsen or Magnani, Fairbanks and Pickford but not Cherkassov, Brando or Gabin. So what are there? There are directors. *Auteurs*.

Mr Roud is aware that he is on shaky ground. 'An objective, scientific aura still surrounds the word dictionary . . .' he begins. 'Scientific' is questionable, but 'objective' is surely correct: that is what the word means. 'Book explaining, usu. in alphabetical order, the words of a language or words and topics of some special subject . . .' (*Concise Oxford Dictionary*).

To give this work the sub-sub-title of 'The Major Film Makers' does not justify the use of 'Dictionary', any more than the qualifying adjective 'critical' properly supports Mr Roud's claim to be providing 'a covert statement, a normative view of the art of the film'.

More mystery. 'Covert' means 'secret' or 'disguised'. 'Normative' means 'of or establishing a norm'. So have we here a secret attempt to establish a contemporary critical norm? Yet we learn, the critical bias of the work is 'eclectic', and 'many varieties of critical approach have been used'. An odd way to establish a 'normative view'.

Mr Roud's *Critical Dictionary* is, in fact, no such thing. It is an anthology of film critics, writing about directors (mostly) without the disciplines of objectivity or of any definable critical method. Dates are given irregularly: full filmographies are not provided. The only consistent factor seems to be the editor's whim: Mr Roud adds a postscript of his own to each contributor's piece. Opinionated, courteous, sometimes patronising in his disagreement.

'Opinionated' is the key word. And opinions are so much less interesting than facts. The impression is of an overcrowded, ill-composed cocktail party at which all the guests are holding forth, confidently and loudly at the same time.

'There has been no attempt,' Mr Roud emphasises, 'to impose a monolithic point of view.' So you may find yourself receiving a studious, accurate and informative account of, say, Kozintsev and Trauberg from David Robinson; or you may bypass the over-allusive, slap-dash chatter of Andrew Sarris ('Rock Hudson had reached that dangerous period in an actor's career when a few mannerisms had hardened into a style') to run full tilt into the host, busily making the rounds with a dish of lightweight critical canapes: 'My own preferences go to Ozu rather than Mizoguchi; but it is only fair to say that this is very much a minority view, and one which probably says more about me than about Ozu and Mizoguchi.'

Most disastrous of all, however, will be your encounters with a small, but infernally loquacious bunch of high-brow extremists. Jean André Fieschi, for instance, (b. 1942, France) in his piece on Jean Epstein: 'The broken linearity of the narrative permits the proliferation of formal variation, with microforms and macroforms leading incessantly back to each other on their spatio-temporal plane.'

Or Noel Burch, apparently a leading film theorist (b. USA, French citizen), on *Ivan The Terrible*: 'Cross-cutting and axial matches again predominate, with an almost total respect for screen orientation (the bad matches in screen position which do occur . . . are due to quite fortuitous incompatibilities between Eisenstein's totalitarian conception of composition and the narrow margin allowed for "cheating" by the principle of continuity).' Such quotations, I would stress, are only the tip of a very large iceberg.

You might think that there is nothing worse than an auteurist; James Monaco's and Christopher Williams' books, frankly offered to readers interested in film 'as a serious subject of study', will teach you better. Comprehensiveness is the aim of *How to Read a Film*, with technological sections on cameras, lenses, filmstock, with diagrams, consideration of other media influences (radio, records, TV), a glossary and a bibliography. All capably executed. So far so good.

But there are also chapters on 'Film as Art', including a section on 'The Structure of Art' and on 'The Language of Film: Signs and Syntax'. These plunge us, through sections on 'The Physiology of Perception' and 'Denotative and Connotative Meaning', directly into the airless world of Saussure, Metz ('Film is too intelligible: that is what makes it difficult to analyse'), and Raymond Bellour, author of a hundred-page analysis of the oedipal content and structure of Hitchcock's *North by Northwest*.

Realism and the Cinema is the forerunner of a series of six books inspired by the Education Advisory Service of the BFI; we are later promised *Theories of Authorship*, *Semiotics of Film*, and *Cinema and Ideology*. This is the world of fashionable Higher Education; for Christopher Williams, the editor, is Senior Lecturer in Film, and Course Leader in Film and Photographic Arts, in the School of Communication at the Polytechnic of Central London. His book is designed as a sort of anthology-aid to study, reprinting texts of varying importance and familiarity round and about the issues of film realism, aesthetics and theoretical ideology. Rossellini, Helen Van Dongen, Eisenstein are here among the filmmakers, the turgid Bazin, the Cahierist Jean-Louis Comolli and the semiotician Bettetini among the theoreticians. Mr Williams contributes a confused and ill-expressed commentary. The contributions are poorly listed and indexed.

To explain the background to all this 'intellectual' activity would be much more difficult than to place Mr Roud's auteurists. Fortunately the recent row in Cambridge's English Faculty has somewhat familiarised newspaper readers with structuralism and semiology as disciplines purporting to facilitate and enrich the study of art. The likening of film to language, the attempt to examine and interpret it by methods derived from linguistic analysis – these are part of a general movement inspired (as so often) by the French, towards a 'scientific' or 'logical' consideration of art, an intellectualising of what used to be known as liberal studies, an attempt to substitute rule for taste, formula for intuition.

If I call the whole movement frivolous, it is not to impute to it any kind of lightness or gaiety.

It is to recall that the most graceless intellectual is as capable of elitist self-indulgence, of evading the essential challenge of criticism (i.e. to discover and explore the relevance of art to experience) as is the most irresponsible of traditional aesthetes. It is impossible to be ungrammatical in film. And it is not necessary to learn a vocabulary. Infants appear to understand television images, for example, months before they begin to develop a facility with spoken language. Even cats watch television . . . It is writing like this (in which every sentence is disputable) that makes one suspect the intellectual qualifications, the power of communication, the sense of logic of these critics who are so determined that art and its criticism should be reduced to a logical structure of codes and signs, to be only *intellectually* apprehended.

In what sense and on what evidence, we must ask Mr Monaco, can infants be said to 'understand' television images? What images? Why is it better to write 'develop a facility with spoken language' rather than 'talk'? What does it *mean* to say that cats watch television?

Mr Williams writes even worse, and more pretentiously. This is how he kicks off: 'Discussion of realism, in film as in other art forms, tends to be tortuous or circular. Does the real world exist? Most (though not all) think that it does . . .' There is a fine sense of the unconscious comic here. 'If in doubt as to whether a writer is physically alive or dead, the reader should consult the brief biographies at the end of the book.'

To quote more fully the pretentious, inward-turning convolutions of these books would take too long. Every sentence needs to be examined and queried. They are stuffed with jargon, their 'logic' is illogical and their abstractions confused as only French habits of speculation transposed into English can be. (It took an André Bazin to base an entire theory about William Wyler on a mistranslation of one of the director's statements. 'I try always to work *out* of my own experience,' said Wyler. Bazin translated 'out of' into *hors de* – 'outside' – and went on to misrepresent the artist's intentions absolutely.)

The structuralist movement in film criticism (and in the criticism of any other art, presumably) is harmful because it attempts to substitute stylistic analysis – as if a film were some kind of chemical compound – for interpretation, for examination of meaning, for human implication.

There is, of course, some attempt by these writers to suggest that their methods illuminate the objects of their study. 'Semiology . . . is a logical, often illuminating system that helps to describe how a film does what it does' (Monaco). But the emphasis invariably shifts so that the description *becomes* what the film does. 'Movies are about movies.' Or – to quote Bazin again, a favourite with this school: 'Cinema . . . is an aesthetic state of matter. A modality of the narrative-spectacle.' And so art is emasculated as questions of *value*, human and moral as well as 'artistic', are bypassed, written off as naive, irrelevant or old-fashioned. It is important to realise, and cannot be too strongly stressed, that all this has as little to do with art as moral philosophy commonly has to do with behaviour.

How has all this come about? For part of the explanation we must look, I fear, at the indiscriminate proliferation of 'higher education', generously funded and inadequately supervised, which has resulted in the foundation of departments, lectureships (and degrees, I suppose) in cinema; in the maintenance, far beyond public use or demand, of subsidised magazines like *Sight and Sound* and *Screen*; in schools and Educational Advisory Services – all forming considerable vested interest in something called 'film studies', which, to be justified, must relate to some specialised intellectual discipline. Hence the development of an 'academic' tradition, functionless except as an end in itself, using language, arguing theories, reaching conclusions incomprehensible and valueless except to the initiated: a parody of 'pure knowledge'. Studies are about studies. Semiology is about semiology.

Apart from a spectacular misapplication of public money, does it all matter? As evidence of further retreat from reality and meaning, further enfeeblement of the humanist tradition, and the substitution of only another form of elitism for the old snobberies – I think that it does.

It is significant that there should be a close link between Marxism and this new aesthetic party line. Whatever the claims of each, the results in practice are remarkably similar: depersonalisation; pretension and platitude in place of meaning; self-righteous dictation in place of argument. It is not enough, in the face of all this, for the liberally-minded to heave yet another weary and dispirited sigh. The stables need a good cleaning-out. Sooner rather than later.

Clockwise from centre: Lindsay, author David Storey, musical composer Alan Price, lighting designer Andy Phillips and set designer Jocelyn Herbert on the set of Home *at the Royal Court.*

THE THEATRE

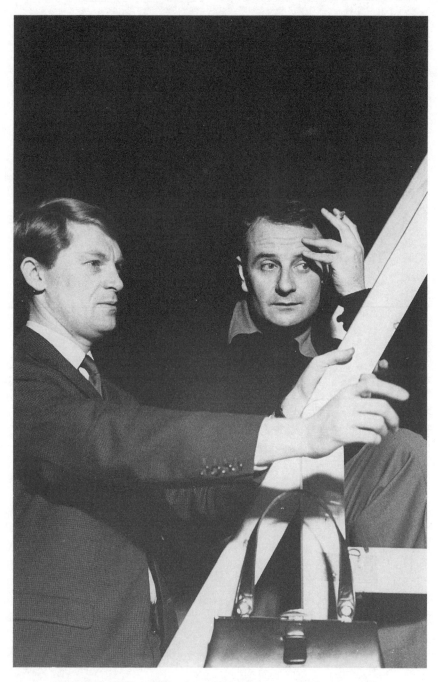

Playwright Willis Hall and Lindsay on the set of Billy Liar, *1960.
Cambridge Theatre, London.*

Vital Theatre

Encore, November-December 1957

I START THIS ARTICLE WITH HESITATION. TRY AS I MAY, I CANNOT HELP FEELING that for me to write anything about the theatre at this stage – as a director anyway – is rather absurd and even impertinent. One Sunday night 'Production without Decor' at the Royal Court does not constitute a very large body of experience on which to construct generalisations. And to write as a critic is likely to be even less rewarding. It has all been said. Yes, of course our theatre is moribund – like our cinema. For a variety of reasons – social, economic, and just through plain lack of vitality. But there's no point in going on sneering at Shaftesbury Avenue (or Pinewood) for ever. Only two courses are honourable: shut up – or do something.

And here you seem to me to have a distinct advantage in the theatre. With all the difficulties of costs, materials, premises, etc., it is still easier to put on a stage production than it is to make a film. Take the Free Cinema films, for instance. They look simple enough, I know: some people even call them primitive. In only one of them (*Every Day Except Christmas*, where we had sponsorship from the Ford Motor Company) is there any direct sound recording. And even there we didn't have enough money for a blimped camera: if you listen hard enough, you'll hear the camera noise. For the rest (*O Dreamland, Together, Momma Don't Allow, Nice Time, Wakefield Express*), the sound was all recorded separately, and laid afterwards. No dialogue. Yet a twenty-minute film of this kind, shot on 16mm, will cost you between four and five hundred pounds. And if you make it in your spare time – as you'll have to, since no one will pay you for it – it's likely to take you between eight months and a year. And all to what purpose? So that a National Film Theatre audience can come in, and sit down, and then go out again saying: 'What interesting faces' . . . Tomorrow night a Japanese version of *Macbeth*. What a rich cultural life we're leading.

In the theatre surely the business is a bit easier, or so I'd have thought. It can't cost so very much to put on a play at the Theatre in the Round. *The Waiting of Lester Abbs* cost the English Stage Society about a hundred and fifty pounds. And quite a lot of that was presumably recovered from the receipts of the audience. But even more encouraging than the number of people who turned up to see the play, was the number of people ready to act in it. And delighted to find they were going to get even a couple of guineas for their trouble. When I started casting the play, I was distinctly timid. It seemed outrageous to be asking people to work for a fortnight for virtually nothing. Yet I found that, in general, they were happy to be asked; and to do it if they could. They even volunteered. And what a pleasure they were to work with! With so much idealistic talent around (and don't let anyone tell me that actors are *all* opportunistic ego-tists), why isn't more of it used? Why doesn't it flower in odd places, in lit-tle theatres, jabbing and stimulating?

This is the fundamental question. But before I attempt to pursue it, let me say just a few words about my experience in producing a play instead of making a film. 'How did I adapt,' I am asked, 'what I had learned in film-making for the theatre?' Now this – as I was forced to reply to that nice young Moscow girl who asked me what the British People are doing for Peace – now this is rather a naive question. I associate it in fact with the disapproving comment of Mr Henry Adler, in the last issue of *Encore*, who remarked that 'Mr Lindsay Anderson did not use his film experience to employ the kind of rhythmic cross-cutting and use of fades which this sort of theatre calls for.' This, to be honest, is the sort of thing that makes you see purple. Such references to 'cross-cutting', to begin with, imply a conception of the cinema that has congealed after an early, traumatic experience with *The Battleship Potemkin*. I should be distinctly sceptical of any director who approached a film with this type of superficial, 'applied' idea of technique. To try to impose it on a play would be ruinous. It is not the 'sort of theatre' that is important – this is the cliché idea of 'Production without Decor', which brings with it Mr Adler's hankering for Vilar-type lighting and 'lozenges of colour'.

As I say, though, what is important is not the 'sort of theatre' – but the *play*. (It seems odd to me that a film director should have to say this to a theatre critic.) *The Waiting of Lester Abbs* may have been Mrs Sully's first work for the stage, but there is nothing tentative or uncertain about it. As in her books, she knows exactly what she is doing, and the effect she requires. The mixture of simplicity and sophistication is perfectly calcu-lated, and there is only one possible style in which it can be played. I mean with directness, austerity, and an utter rejection of conventional methods of 'dramatising'. From the actors, humility before the words, truthfulness to character, complete purity of feeling. This is what we worked for; and I don't think we did badly. But it was what I felt about the play, and not any previous experience with the cinema, that guided me.

And yet – I won't pretend that, as we worked, cinematic parallels didn't present themselves to me. It is perhaps even true that at times the tensions I tried to create derived consciously from films – not the conventional, film-society 'montage' idea of cinema, but the anti-dramatic poetic concentra-tion on the everyday which has characterised some of the later develop-ments of neo-realism. Lester comes into the pub, orders a glass of beer, makes a remark to nobody in general, drinks his half-pint, orders another

Albert Finney in the title role of Billy Liar.

one, drinks again . . . all this before there is any real action, any real dialogue even. Now what do you do with a scene like that? Jog it along with a lot of irrelevant business? 'Cross-cut' with some fatuous piece of character-play in a corner? Or just cut it short? I preferred to take my cue from *Umberto D.*, from that sequence where the little serving-maid gets up in the morning, wanders blankly round the kitchen, sprays some ants off the wall, and sits down, and starts grinding the coffee . . . Can't we try, in the theatre too, to break away from the tyranny of words occasionally? From the tyranny of 'construction' and 'technique'? *The Waiting of Lester Abbs* is a poetic play, as for instance *Together* is a poetic film (the themes, indeed, are related; and I wonder if anyone noticed that the music we used between the scenes was in fact from the soundtrack of *Together*). I wanted the pace to be equally deliberate. I remembered how Lorenza Mazzetti used to insist, when we were editing *Together*, that she wanted it to be the most *boring* film ever made. Of course she meant she wanted it to be a film whose beauty and significance would be expressed precisely in those elements of style (extreme slowness and austerity) which the desensitised, conventionalised audience would fail to understand – and therefore be bored by. This was the kind of lingering, poetic concentration I tried to create on the stage.

'The play was directed with extreme sluggishness . . . ' When an intelligent critic makes a comment like that, I don't feel – 'Oh what a pity, it didn't come off, I should have made the whole thing brisker . . . ' On the contrary, I feel I should have made the whole thing really slow – caricatured the effect I was after – ruined the play, perhaps, but at least in the process boring the audience into a realisation of what they were seeing – into an acknowledgement that they come to the theatre to work – not just to sit, and be 'absorbed', made to laugh or cry by an expert machine, being 'entertained' . . . Not school of Vilar, you see, but school of Brecht. The same attitude towards construction (story-telling rather than play-making); the same shifts in style of dialogue (between semi-formal and naturalistic); and above all the same relationship between audience and play, the same objectivity, the rejection of 'identification'.

This question of the audience is perhaps the most important; and it returns us to the fundamental point I mentioned earlier – that of the overall deadness of our theatrical atmosphere. In nothing is this more apparent, or more depressive, than in the prevailing conception of the passive audience, the audience as sheep, hungry for 'entertainment' or vicarious emotion, or the audience as amateur, Third Programme critics, which conceives of its superior function as being one of 'judgement' – and whose only standards are subjectively emotional, or platitudinously 'literary': i.e., 'profoundly moving' – 'curiously unmoving' – 'witty, compassionate' – 'too episodic' – 'the second half isn't as good as the first' – 'the characters don't develop' – etc., etc. Success, according to this view, is more important than significance; manner provides a richer (certainly an easier) topic of discussion than meaning. This is where I join issue with my friend Kenneth Tynan, when he writes a 'selling' notice of *The Chalk Garden*, and a distinctly chilling one of *The Good Woman of Setzuan*. All right – so the first London production of a straight Brecht play didn't have the high polish of the Berliner Ensemble. All right – so the leading lady was not in all respects successful. But let's keep our eye on the ball.

For effort to be creative, response must be creative too. The development of a new kind of theatre (what Brecht calls 'vital theatre') is intimately bound up with the development of a new kind of audience. But this, of course, cannot just be achieved by slanging existing audiences and critics, and telling them to pull their socks up. It carries us further – to the need for a new conception of the relationship between art and audience, a total change of cultural atmosphere. And in this respect particularly, to produce a play for the English Stage Society gave one food for thought. For these are supposed to be laboratory productions. They can only fulfil their function with audiences who come, not with the passive expectation of 'entertainment', nor just with mouths wide open for another slab of minority culture, but themselves prepared to give something, to work, with minds open and alert, themselves creative. (*Judge Not* should be inscribed on the programme.) But this kind of audience – I am driven to conclude – does not exist in London.

If it did exist, you would surely expect to find it at, or around, the Royal Court. No single management (nor all the others put together, for that matter) has given us such intelligent stimulus in the last eighteen months as the English Stage Company. Yet it remains a significant fact that instead of being able to develop as a theatre with a permanent company, in pursuit of a definable and consistent tradition, the Royal Court has become (or been forced to become) just a theatre run by the most progressive management in London. There is an essential difference. An 'intelligent' theatre, which chooses its presentations on a basis of 'quality' is one thing (and a thing for which one is grateful) – but what we need now are *ideas* even more urgently than 'quality', and a theatre which relates itself to life rather than to culture.

In other words, what we run up against is the economic and social framework within which we have to practise our various arts. Working within the established framework of the West End, upper-class theatre, the English Stage Company has accomplished wonders. Yet this framework is also a prison. Theatre workshop tries to work outside it: yet the penalty they have to pay, of exclusion, of an audience just as ungrateful, of finally a certain inverted snobbery, is equally frustrating. The framework, the system, remains, corrupt and killing; and I doubt whether within it, the vital theatre for which *Encore* wishes to speak, or the lively and aspiring talent which I encountered in my brief experience, will ever be able to find a satisfying means of expression. Is an alternative tradition possible? What ideas are the ones which will revitalise our theatre? Is there a new public that could be attracted to, or reached by, a progressive theatrical company? What do we mean when we talk about a relationship between theatre and life? These fundamental questions are, it seems to me, the ones which should be engaging us at the moment, the ones which young writers should be discussing instead of pulling *Lucky Jim* faces at themselves in the Beaverbrook press. Only criticism written in this perspective is going to be of any value to us. To this extent my experience of the theatre leads me to precisely the same conclusions as my experience of the cinema.

And may I make a final, specific point? I notice that the last issue of *Encore* was praised by one critic for 'not being afraid of letting every side have its angry say . . . ' I believe that this is precisely the attitude we need to escape from – the assumption that all ideas are equally valuable, that intellectual discussion is an end in itself, a superior diversion for the cultured, instead of being a hunt for the useful truth. The opposition has plenty of organs of its own: *Encore* should not be expressing every point of view, but the right one. You see – the question of commitment raises its obstinate, contemporary head. You can't get away from it.

Replying to Critics

Encore, March-April 1958

The Editor, *Encore*

SIR, THE COMMENT AROUSED BY MY PIECE 'VITAL THEATRE' (WHICH I NOTE you have retitled for me – rather well – 'On Being Right') is encouraging. Some of the discord obviously results from conflicting beliefs, uncompromisingly held. But there seems a good deal of misunderstanding in the air – the result, no doubt, of over-compression on my part. May I try to dispel some of this? It seems clear at least, from the emotion generated and the space devoted to it, that we are stumbling here on a problem that is basic.

The problem, as I see it, is not merely one of ideas – of 'what should we believe?' It is equally a question of the *effectiveness* of those ideas – of their 'reality' in a practical as well as a philosophical sense. Part of my contention is that, in the cultural sphere at least, ideas have pretty well ceased to have this kind of reality. Hence the artificial, inbred, hot-house (pick what metaphor you please) atmosphere of our Sunday Paper, Weekend Review, Third Programme culture of the moment. The pseudo-liberal tradition, which abstracts art and culture from their economic and political environment, which accepts the social status quo, and restricts itself almost entirely to formal and aesthetic criticisim, has gone a good way to deprive art of any contemporary function at all. Our problem is to reassert that function. And this means not merely finding some new ideas, but making them effective. Now is it possible to be effective, and to be undiscriminatingly tolerant at the same time?

This, I guess, is where trouble begins. For in this age of fugitive and cloistered virtue, tolerance has become the one absolute, unqualified value, and any suggestion that other people's ideas are not as good as one's own lays one open immediately to charges of fascism, communism, bestiality, or what-have-you . . . Mr Worsley sees me hunting him down with a pack of police dogs, and Groundling shrinks from the 'massive limitations', the 'blinding conformity' which he supposes I wish to impose on *Encore*. Surely the confusion here is obvious? I believe in freedom (which I think is a more positive concept than tolerance); but I also believe in responsibility. And this implies the responsibility to analyse one's situation, come to conclusions, and to act according to those conclusions. Other people may come to different conclusions, and will so be led to different actions. The conflict of such actions, under law, is democracy.

Nobody need be ashamed of believing he is right, or of trying, as force-fully as he can, to convince other people of the rightness of his views – of trying in other words, to make them *effective*. It is a very recent heresy to suppose that either democracy or true liberalism oblige one to allow that the ideas of people who oppose one are as 'right' as one's own.

This attitude does not seem to me to justify accusations of political intolerance. Of course, we all have every reason to be aware of the evils of political authoritarianism; but if as a result we allow ourselves to become too scared to express our own convictions without compromise, we will find ourselves speedily reduced to ineffectiveness. Which is, in fact, pre-cisely what has happened to cultural intellectuals in this country. Mr Worsley says that I am 'mad' if I think that I, or anyone else, am 'in pos-session of the one and only right view' about anything. This kind of scep-ticism makes it impossible for anyone ever to act on right principle. It is on principles, for instance, that I consider that *Encore* is right, and the Treasury is wrong, about the National Theatre. And I deny that there is any true democratic or liberal principle which can require me to accept the equal validity of the Treasury view.

Mr Jerome Clegg of Brooklyn says that 'the world just isn't built this way' – i.e. by people formulating their beliefs in an uncompromising way, and by acting according to them. How else has the world been built then, or any of the enlightened institutions we enjoy today? Not, you may be sure, by people who felt it safer to sneer at belief than to subscribe to it. 'Truth, One and Indivisible, revealed in that Immaculate Entirety to Certain Persons (according to themselves).'

Of course, I do not suggest that the 'right' viewpoint – a viewpoint that an adequate number of us can subscribe to and effectively campaign for – has yet been formulated. What I hope very much is that people are begin-ning to think in these terms, and to understand that solidarity is not mere-ly a polite way of disguising the horrors of conformity. Don't think that I underestimate the difficulties either. As an illustration, we have only to examine Groundling's attempt to define the position (or the objective) of *Encore* in your last issue. The heart is evidently there, the tentative ideal-ism and the liberal aspirations: but how little courage – and how little *thought*! You can see his essential lack of conviction in the way he con-tinually falls back on what he obviously intends to be the style of the detached sophisticated *littérateur*. 'Mr Anderson in characteristic punch-ing form' . . . 'A commitment is a sometime thing' . . . 'There are indeed, more things in heaven and earth than are dreamt of in his philology.' This sort of thing is not merely tiresome; it is positively damaging, because it evokes the atmosphere of smartness and sceptical flippancy which is exactly what we need to escape from. And what conclusion is reached? Is that quotation from Harold Clurman expressive of anything beyond a familiar, innocuous, eye-washy idealism which we can all say yes to easily enough, but which is quite incapable of actively inspiring anybody? Groundling thanks God that he and you are 'Young and unresolved.' But is irresolution really such a wonderful quality? I would thank God for you with much greater fervour if you could announce yourselves 'Young and resolved' – or at least bent on resolution. That young character whose portrait appears at the end of Groundling's article – is he just exhausted? Or is he praying for strength? That would be good. But I like to imagine that he is *thinking* too.

And finally, in case I have still not made myself clear, let me end with a specific illustration. There was once a magazine called *Scrutiny* which, operating in the field of literary criticism, set itself to oppose contemporary fashion, and to stand for certain clear, consistent and defined principles. The magazine ran for some 25 years and exercised a great and salutary influence. Now would *Scrutiny* have achieved as much, and would Dr Leavis have achieved the eminence that he has, if he had printed articles from every point of view – if, in other words, he had been intimidated by the accusations which were continuously levelled at him from Right and Left, of arrogance, intolerance and illiberalism? As Eric Bentley has remarked (and Messrs Spelvin and Clegg might return with profit to the earlier work of their distinguished fellow-countryman): 'The uniformity of attitude which some object to is the defect of a quality without which there could not be such a magazine at all: unity of purpose. If it is to have character a literary review has to stand for something. It has to fight.' I believe this to be true.

Yours sincerely,

Lindsay Anderson

Pre-Renaissance: Is the Left Going in the Right Direction?

International Theatre Annual, 1961

NOT LONG AGO, WHEN WE WERE CASTING A SATIRICAL PLAY-WITH-SONGS FOR the Royal Court, an interesting young performer turned up for audition. I say 'performer' because he had acted only twice in his life, once in a television play and once in a film. His accent was strong, working-class Cockney; his articulation was bad; his vocal projection was non-existent. He was in fact one of the new generation of pop-singers, useless without a microphone, and practically incomprehensible with one – though obviously effective, in his own very personal style. His first disc had just been issued, and was moving rapidly up towards the Top Ten. (It got there very shortly after, and so did his next. He is now earning some thousands of pounds a week.)

I am not trying to poke fun at this boy. Although it was clear soon enough that he did not carry the guns for the part in question, it was equally clear that he had a lively and powerful personality, a lot of courage, and an original intelligence. In short: he had talent. I was interested enough anyway to ask him how he had come to have the idea of being an actor.

'Well . . . ' he said, 'I suppose it was when I saw James Dean in a film.'

What other actors did he admire? Stage actors, for instance . . . Oh, he didn't know much about *them*. No use asking him about Laurence Olivier and all that lot, because he'd never seen them. He didn't go to the theatre – none of his friends did either. Never? Only once. He'd been to a play from which he'd seen a half-hour extract on television. A thriller. But he'd been disappointed when he saw the whole thing. He hadn't gone again.

'But you want to be an actor?'

'Oh, yeah . . . I'd like to have a go at it. I'd like to learn. I think I've got a feeling for it.' Yet he'd always felt that theatres were not for him – not for his friends – not for people of his class. 'I mean you get the feeling it's fundamentally snobbish. They expect you to dress up for it and go in a taxi. If you just go in to buy a ticket they look at you as though you're something the cat brought in . . . No, the theatre definitely isn't for us.'

I suppose the automatic reaction of many people would be to dismiss this boy as an angry young yahoo with a 'chip on his shoulder'. I think this would be foolish. Most of what he said is true. I certainly know exactly what he meant about the attitude of box- office managers. And it is not,

Serjeant Musgrave's Dance: *Lindsay directs Alan Dobie and Patsy Byrne at the Royal Court.*

after all, so long since the entrance to every Underground station in London sported a poster which expressed, in graphic terms, much the same point of view. Four sour-looking swells, ageing and evening-dressed, sat frozenly in a theatre box, waiting for the performance to start and underneath, in dreadful London Transport prose-poetry, ran the appropriate legend: 'Magic hour of curtain rise . . . Hearts beat a little faster . . . Dull would he be of soul . . . ' etc., etc. Whether the purpose of this poster was to lure users of the Underground into the theatres or to warn them off, it was difficult to tell. Plainly however, the patrons in the picture had not arrived by tube train. Plainly also nobody thought that this was an extraordinary or a damaging way to advertise the living theatre. It was a very fair comment.

By tradition, by its own attitude and organisation, the English theatre is almost exclusively an upper- (or at least upper-and-middle-) class pursuit. Also its audiences are diminishing. These two facts raise problems which must concern anyone seriously interested or involved in the theatre today. There are plenty of people, of course, who will deprecate such concern (people with toothache often flinch at the mention of a dentist), and hasten to the defence of the status quo. Show business, they tell us, is thriving: a successful West End play is today liable to run longer, make more money, dispose of its screen rights for a higher figure than ever before. And the tastes of audiences are broadening, changing for the better: look at *The Caretaker*, the Wesker trilogy, *Fings Ain't Wot They Used T'Be* . . . Look at the New Critics, whose explosive writing has again made the theatre newsworthy in the popular press, and who have fought so doughtily for plays like *Ross*, *Make Me an Offer* and *The Wrong Side of the Park*. Look at Joan Littlewood; look at the Royal Court; look at the Mermaid . . .

All this is true, and undoubtedly British drama is from many points of view more vigorous today than it was five years ago. But such facts are arguments for action, not complacency. They show that there is something worth struggling for – which is almost more than might have seemed the case in 1955, before such names as Osborne, Behan, Arden, Wesker, Simpson, Delaney, Pinter, Hall or Logue had ever been heard of. Certainly these authors – together with the actors, directors and designers associated with their plays – suggest a revolution. But it is a revolution that has had to take place inside a system of theatre that remains antiquated and wasteful, which modifies itself only with the extremist reluctance, and which (like so many other of our institutions), relates to a society of twenty or thirty years back rather than ours of today and tomorrow.

Let us consider the characteristics of this system. First, as I have already suggested, it is one that is designed to appeal to the upper and middle layers of our society rather than to everyone. It is therefore strongly conservative – artistically as well as politically. There has been a good deal of jubilation recently (from some who would claim the title of 'progressive') over the speedy collapse of a number of productions which, a few years back, one can imagine running comfortably and dispiritingly in the West End. Personally I also am cheered by such evidence of changing taste: but I am disinclined to imagine we have already one foot in the promised land when I see the enthusiasm aroused by plays like *The Grass is Greener*, *The Pleasure of His Company*, *The Amorous Prawn* and *Oliver!* On the BBC *Critics* programme recently, Mr David Sylvester was heaping reproaches on the English Stage Company for their initial lack of confidence in the plays of Arnold Wesker, and pointing to the success of *Roots* at the Royal Court and in the West End. What Mr Sylvester does not realise (and there are many like him) is that *Roots* actually failed on transfer to the Duke of York's Theatre. In spite of the encouragement of a number of critics, and the enthusiasm of the few, there was not a public for it. Money was lost. Productions like *The Long and the Short and the Tall* and *One Way Pendulum* did, it is true, manage to make a small profit on transfer – but when you compare their runs with plays like *Watch it Sailor or Not in the Book*, their success can hardly be said to be triumphant.

The profitable run of *Rosmersholm*, the Sloane Square triumph of the Wesker trilogy, the crowded West End houses for Miss Littlewood's end-of-the pier musicals – these should not blind us to the fact that neither the English Stage Company nor Theatre Workshop has managed to build up a regular audience that gives them the least degree of security. Surely no director in the history of the English theatre has won such universal acclaim as Joan Littlewood in 1959. Yet she has only to return to Stratford East, to her company and her essential method of working, for the public to stay away in droves. The same public which night after night crammed the Royal Court to capacity for *Rosmersholm* and *One Way Pendulum*, would not even give *The Naming of Murderer's Rock* – a most interesting production by a new, young director, of a play by a new, young dramatist, with a starless cast – a decent fortnight's run. The losses sustained by *Theatre '59* at the Lyric Hammersmith tell the same story. Theatre may have become journalistically 'à la mode': there is still no assured, serious public for the serious venture. (In this sense, I should say the 'serious' the-atre-going public in London numbers about six or seven hundred people.)

And if this is the situation in London, how much worse in the provinces? There is no need at this stage to repeat the dismal catalogue of theatres closed and closing. Television has proved a deadly competitor to repertory – and who can be surprised? – while the financially practical touring dates for productions (unless heavily starred) grow fewer and fewer. The result is that policies – except in rare instances – become less rather than more venturesome. Witness the recent announcement by the new director of the Belgrade Theatre, Coventry, that he would not aim at the production of 'the kind of plays put on at the Royal Court'. What, one wonders, are these weird, avante-garde works which would prove too strong for the burghers of Coventry? *Epitaph for George Dillon? Cock-a-Doodle-Dandy? Live Like Pigs?* In how many theatres in Britain, then, can plays like this hope to be produced?

The point I am concerned to make – and I am aware it is not a partic-ularly comfortable one – is that, in spite of all the cheerful progress of the past few years, there are still fundamental changes that need to be made before our theatre can begin to fulfil its potential. These changes are eco-nomic. To understand them it is worth examining briefly the factors which have got us where we are today.

Probably no one will deny that the chief instrument in the present ren-aissance (pre-renaissance?) of the British theatre has been the English Stage Company – and through the English Stage Company, John Osborne. As every schoolboy now knows, when *Look Back in Anger* was present-ed in the first season at the Royal Court, one period came to an end and another began. This revolution was not effected by any of the traditional or established managements – all of whom had rejected the play. It was effected by a management which did not set itself the primary object of making a profit, but rather of revitalising the theatre; by discovering, supporting and developing new writers; by running plays in repertory: by subsidising a permanent company of actors. The venture was underwritten by a group of private, disinterested sponsors, and aided by a minuscule grant from the Arts Council.

The success of the experiment is well known. Unfortunately its failures are at least as significant. Apart from a brief period in its second year, the schemes both of running plays in repertory, and of running a company of actors, had to be abandoned. The losses were too great. Indeed, these ambitions apart, it has only been the immense success of John Osborne's plays that has enabled the experiment to survive to the present day. An author like John Arden, for instance, is generally regarded as one of the most talented and promising dramatists we have: he has even been prized as such by the *Evening Standard*. Yet how many people (let alone critics) realise that both *Live Like Pigs* and *Serjeant Musgrave's Dance* cost the English Stage Company the equivalent of their Arts Council subsidy for a whole year?

As Osborne has been to the Court, Behan and Delaney have been to Theatre Workshop – though let it never be forgotten that in this case, where the Arts Council record has been for years peculiarly disgraceful, the theatre has been essentially subsidised by its actors. And in spite of all apparent recent success, the real situation of each has not changed. To paraphrase Brecht: unhappy the theatre that has need of great dramatists . . .

For this focusing of attention on the individual success of particular new writers, though valuable up to a point, leads finally to a distorted, unbalanced kind of theatre. To be truly creative, truly satisfying, a theatre needs above all to be an ensemble. And this ensemble needs to be secure – to work towards its own tradition of playing and writing and direction and design, and to be able to attempt those experiments that may be wrong, or may be ahead of both the public and critics, and yet which are essential if real progress, real discoveries are to be made. It needs a continuity which commercialism cannot give.

It is the lack of this kind of security, this kind of continuity, together with the abundance of talent and promise around one, that makes work in the London theatre (I speak personally of course) at the same time so exciting and so frustrating. Try as one may, scorn success as one will, it is almost impossible to remain unaffected by the climate of competition and speculation in which every production is born.

Everyone suffers. The actors who may be at the start of a decent period of employment, or who may find that they have rehearsed for four weeks (at an insultingly low wage) in order to play for a fortnight. The director who may be conscious that the style he is working for is directly opposed to a fashion and therefore bound to prejudice the chances of the venture commercially. The management who want to be both good and successful. What could be less healthy than the atmosphere of a London first-night – riddled with nerves, and strained with that sickening anticipation of success or disaster? Which way will the critics jump? Are we going to be acclaimed tomorrow, or just savaged to make a splashy column?

To some people, I know, all this seems the very essence of 'theatre': the hectic see-saw game of what failed last week, and what will succeed next. But I am sure the resulting fears, tensions, insecurities and egotisms are far more damaging than creative. And even when productions 'succeed' there is an overriding sense of waste. The working relationships that have been established through four weeks of rehearsal and which must now be abruptly terminated. The actors who must be shut up within a single part for six months, nine months or a year. The knowledge that one must now retrace one's footsteps, start again from scratch. It is a barbarous system.

By now perhaps some readers will be wondering what relevance all this has to the point at which I started this piece? Am I suggesting that it is the bourgeois audience that is responsible for these ills? Am I under the impression that an immense other audience already exists, teenage and/or proletarian, hungry for the delights of good drama, capable of offering a progressive theatre company the support and security it needs?

The answer is no.

I think that by clinging so tenaciously to habits and attitudes of the past, by doing so little to attract a new, more recently moneyed public, the theatre is making a mistake. But the concern of the West End managers above all to keep their present patrons sweet is perhaps understandable. Better one middle-class bird in the stalls than 50 proletarian fledglings who might or might not be induced to leave their television sets. The issue is not one of immediate, practical commercialism. It is one of principle, or vision.

It is the bourgeois (or capitalist) principle of theatre that is no longer adequate – this conception of it as an entertainment whose existence is only justified so long as it can succeed as a profit-making speculation. The events of the past five years have shown that there is an immense creative potential in our theatre, which the present system is unable (even unwilling) fully to exploit. This is partly because, in sheer market terms, this creativity could only be developed at a loss (like the Health Service). But it is also, I suspect, because it seems to be inescapably linked to progressive social attitudes – to an assault, for instance, on the traditional carriers of class, to a contemporary relevance of subject, and to a freedom of expression quite alien to the established right-wing theatre of living-rooms (prose) or fastidious metaphysics (verse).

This problem is not, of course, peculiar to the theatre, it is a commonplace to all artists today – to those, at least, who see that creative freedom and social responsibility are not opposing but complementary allegiances. (This was the real point of that debate about 'commitment' which some of us tried to initiate a few years back. And the fact that the word was so immediately and crassly abused, by dogmatists of both Right and Left, does not invalidate the principle.) This is not the place to argue the social value of art, but it is always worth affirming one's belief that as societies, of whatever political colouring, become more conformist, more monolithic, more depersonalised, the genuine, intransigent artist becomes more precious, more necessary. And, inevitably, more resented (the dentist again). We have all seen what the press, that faithful watchdog of conformism, has tried to do to John Osborne . . . Conversely it is not surprising that the arts which benefit most generously from State aid are those which are safest, least relevant – above all those which can be comfortably pigeon-holed as prestige relaxations for the well-educated. No one is liable to be made dissatisfied with his own (or anyone else's) condition by seeing the Royal Ballet dance *Swan Lake* or *Pineapple Poll*; or by hearing a performance of Verdi's *Macbeth*; or by visiting the National Gallery. Arden is difficult (when not sordid); Osborne lets the side down; and Pinter disturbs. When the British Council plan to wave our cultural flag on a European drama tour, they pick *Venus Observ'd* and *The Importance of Being Earnest*.

But it would be wrong, I am afraid, to suggest that the only, or even the chief obstacle in the way of a flourishing, well-nourished British drama is social prejudice or fear. This exists, and it is a factor – and all the more difficult to counter because those who are affected by it are generally unconscious, or self-deluding about their motives. But even more firmly settled, and more impregnable, is the English tradition of philistinism which either dismisses art as valueless altogether or denies it the dignity of proper seriousness. (Is there any other country in the world where critics so frequently use 'solemn' as a pejorative term, or imagine that they are scoring a point off an artist when they describe him as 'taking himself seriously'?) It is a tradition that cuts across class and creed, and it is just as powerful on the Left as on the Right. Art is the icing on the cake; and if people want it they should pay for it. If they don't want it – why then, there is no good reason why it should exist at all. Covent Garden serves a function, since it is convenient for Her Majesty to be able to entertain visiting presidents at the ballet. And the Old Vic and Stratford-upon-Avon are indispensable to the tourist traffic. Otherwise let each man's culture be his own affair. And this (plus snobbism) is why Theatre Workshop's subsidy remains one thousand pounds a year. And why the English Stage Company has had to be content with five – munificently raised this year to eight. And why the total sum spent by the British treasury on art each year compares unfavourably with the subsidy awarded by a single German city to its theatre. The foundation stone of our National Theatre still sits dishonoured on the South Bank, ugly as a broken promise, and a more eloquent monument to English philistinism than the Albert Memorial.

Theatre is not expensive – not compared with a film (anything from 80 to 300 thousand), an RAF bomber (a million or so), or an H-Bomb (anybody's guess). Why, only yesterday the Treasury put up sixteen thousand to help the Tate buy a Matisse nude. Thirty thousand a year (there would be returns of course) would finance a first-class company of actors, with writers, directors and designers to work with them. It takes such conditions to support really good drama – the Moscow Art, the Berliner Ensemble, the TNP. If we could work in this way in Britain, I think miracles might be performed. I am quite sure we could produce a generation of actors second to none in the world: and we have seen with how little encouragement young authors are prepared to write.

We would be working for a minority? Very well then. What artists need to begin with is the opportunity to work at all: the work creates the audience. And in time so will a theatre. I do not believe that the young pop-singer, and the millions he represents, are lost to the living theatre – or not irrevocably so. It might take them some time to find it. But create something vital, something relevant to them, and they would respond. They would have to – that is what vitality means. Would they respond as readily as they respond now to the Pink Camay commercials, to *Sunday Night at the London Palladium* and 'What Do You Want if You Don't Want Money'? Who knows? It doesn't really matter. If the response was a hundred times less, it would still be a thousand times healthier for all us happy participants in the Affluent Society.

Nor would it only work one way. Audiences play an active not a passive part in the theatre, and they could help recreate us, just as much perhaps as we them. It would certainly be marvellous to feel one was working for an *audience*, not just for an assembly of professional and amateur assessors.

No Nonsense About Shakespeare

The Daily Telegraph, 15 December 1964

FIRST OF ALL ONE IS ASTONISHED HOW MANY PEOPLE ASK – 'WHY Shakespeare?' Perhaps one is naïve to be astonished. At best the English attitude towards their national genius seems to be one of love-hate. Pride, certainly, in possession of the world's top dramatist; but filial resentment as well. Familiarity has bred boredom. The English feel they know the plays (as one discovers they do not). Only some eccentric brilliance of conception or some startling virtuosity in performance can justify their production now – at least outside such subsidised shrines as Stratford-upon-Avon or the National Theatre. Why on earth, people ask, do *Julius Caesar* at the Royal Court?

My approach was admittedly subjective. Never having directed anything but new plays – or at least plays new to London – it was exciting to tackle a classic in the same spirit. With a spirit of discovery, that is to say, rather than reverence. And having been generally bored by Shakespeare on the stage, I want to find out for myself if his writing has really become as unmeaning as it often seems. Does his verse demand a special style of rhetorical delivery? Is Joan Littlewood right in her violent attempts to disrupt convention? Above all, is there still a richness in the characterisation, a sinew in the thought, which can make a play like *Julius Caesar* as stimulating for us as a new work by the most brilliant of new dramatists? Does he, in fact, deserve something more than lip-service?

If he does, it is surely no use being reverent. In the controversy threatened by Robert Graves's rewrites for *Much Ado About Nothing*, I side firmly with the National Theatre. *The Times* correspondent who evoked the shade of Dr Bowdler is wide of the mark. No one is suppressing or censoring Shakespeare: the texts are freely available to students and readers. But in the theatre the plays must live: which means they must be understood. When Shakespeare's humour is incomprehensible, it should be elucidated. And when it is not funny, it should be cut. Can anyone feel a sincere pang at the loss of that comic shoemaker at the start of *Julius Caesar* ('Truly, sir, I live by my awl')? Or at the abridgement of passages of fashionable rhetoric? In Shakespeare's text, Brutus heralds the midnight entrance of the conspirators to his orchard with nine lines of rhetorical embroidery. At the Royal Court he says: 'This is the faction.' The result is a clear gain in dramatic tension.

The question of actually rewriting Shakespeare, or of inserting passages of one's own composition, is of course more ticklish. But here the chief point of interest seems to me how few – even among the most pedantic – ever realise what is being done . . . Actors, of course, know well that the insertion of two or three lines of gibberish into a Shakespearian speech will always pass unremarked. But how many spectators (let alone critics) have noticed the 600 lines of blank verse by John Barton which ornament the Stratford version of the Histories? Our contribution to *Caesar*, though far more modest, has equally escaped attention.

It is well known that the last third of the play presents a grave dramatic problem. Once Brutus and Cassius have said farewell, each heavy with the premonition of disaster, there is nothing for them to do but die. The battles today are boring; and Shakespeare's slavish cribbing from Plutarch is mere padding. And what can an audience make of all those new characters who suddenly crop up – Varo, Volumnius, Clitus, and the rest? At the Court we have eliminated them completely, and substituted in their place the junior conspirators (who in Shakespeare disappear mysteriously after the death of Caesar). A far greater cohesion is the result: as well as more enjoyment for the actors. Most radically, though, we have eliminated three pages of text and linked the deaths of Cassius and Brutus with an entrance and a speech of our own composition, spoken by young Metellus Cimber with the accents of a messenger of fate. 'Brutus, the day is lost . . . ' Dare one suggest that this is a vast improvement on the original? At least no one seems to have found it un-Shakespearian.

There remains the problem of the verse. And this, most surprisingly, turns out not to be a problem at all. Cast the play for character, and the verse will follow – not rhetorically, but with the music of intelligence and truth. The young actors of today – and this shows already a significant change from five or six years back – can sense it. The era of provincial realism is over: or at least relegated to its proper territory, on the television screen.

Classics, after all, are not musty. They are endlessly exhilarating and alive. There is one conclusion, I think, we have all come to. There is no more exciting and contemporary writer now represented on the London stage than William Shakespeare.

The Playboy in Edinburgh

Direct, 15 June 1984

To do 'serious' theatre today which aims at something more ambitious than a fringe production, but doesn't have the benefit of protection from one of our over-subsidised, feather-bedded theatrical institutions – it's an adventurous business, challenging and often frustrating. Dispiriting, too, in the way it reflects the current state of our theatre culture.

Nowadays no independent producer is prepared to tour a production out of town, through our culture-starved (but necessarily hungry) big provincial cities, without some kind of a guarantee from the theatre managers. But the theatre managers are unanimous in their cry: 'No TV names, no guarantee.' Yet when you try to cast your production, you are driven sadly to reflect that television must surely be the most destructive influence on acting ability and style in Britain today. And as for the big TV names – most likely they are busy becoming bigger TV names by doing more TV series. Or (even more likely) they are unknown to one because one has better things to do with one's time than to watch TV series, or even one-off plays.

Frank Grimes as Christy Mahon in Lindsay's production of
The Playboy of the Western World.

The Playboy of the Western World has been curiously set up. It's a co-production between the British American Drama Academy, which will be running an ambitious summer school at Oxford this summer, and the intriguing United British Artists, which gathers under its prestigious umbrella some of the most celebrated performing talents on the market. None of these celebrated performing talents will be appearing in our production, though. Instead we have a fine cast of talented actors who I'm sure are going to give (I write before rehearsals start) an exciting version of a marvellously original and poetic play. Whether it will create the same scandal and outrage as it did in Dublin in 1907 is doubtful: to do that it would have to attract the attention of Mary Whitehouse. *Tempora mutantur . . .*

In Edinburgh we will be performing in the Assembly Rooms, which will certainly add an additional spice to the adventure. I'm told that the set will have to be erected and dismantled every time we play – since our performances of *The Playboy* will be preceded by another theatrical company doing something original and followed by a pop group.

And, of course, the actors' need to find food and lodging on their Equity allowance of £40 a week will challenge their resources even further. Fortunately there are still some gypsies in our midst. Especially among the Irish.

A French Hamlet

The Observer, 1954

AN ANGRY, DRAMATIC SKY THREATENS RAIN. NIGHT IS ALMOST UPON US. THE looming tower, the terraced wall confront us, unlit. Two thousand people assembled in the courtyard of the thirteenth-century Chateau of the Roi René at Angers are waiting patiently for the day to die, for *Hamlet* to begin.

Or rather, as it will be pronounced this evening, 'Amlé'. The title, in its French pronunciation, arouses foreboding in the English mind. Art, we all know, is international; but suspicion persists. Hamlet is ours; what tricks will these foreigners be up to? And the language? Odd phrases haunt the memory: 'This bird of dawning singeth all night long.' 'I see a cherub that sees them.' 'There on the pendant boughs her coronet weeds Clamb'ring to hang.' What will be left of *Hamlet* in an alien tongue, stripped of its proper, familiar music?

Floodlights wink on and off – the open-air equivalent of that monitory rapping which announces every French theatrical performance – and fanfares sound from the tower. A cold blue light creeps over the scene. Enter Francisco; and above him, a dim figure on the battlements, Bernardo. '*Qui est là?*' '*A toi de répondre . . .* ' *Hamlet*, by William Shakespeare, translated into French by Marcel Pagnol, produced by Serge Reggiani for Angers' third festival of dramatic art, is on its way.

And, after all, it proves to be an exciting, a refreshing experience. Oddly enough, to one who knows his text well, the language is hardly disconcerting at all. The outstanding virtue of Pagnol's translation (which has never been played before) is its directness, its lucidity, its consistent sense of the dramatic. Less strenuously poetic than most of his predecessors, warmer, more vital than Gide, the author of *Marius* has given his version the impact of contemporary theatrical speech. One or two vulgarisms (French critics are particularly shocked that *Hamlet* should call his uncle *salaud*) are pardonable, against such merits.

The known music vanishes, of course; but for once the shock is salutary. In its new language, the lyric drama seems to reveal its contours afresh. This sense of revelation at Angers – of shape, of proportion – was emphasised by the producer's brilliant use of his huge setting. On the wide stone levels, a Gordon Craig vision comes to life; the scenes were not blurred by superimposition: the lights dimmed on the battlements, to rise in the throne room 30 feet below. Like some enormous, grim doll's-house, the Castle of

The programme for Serge Reggiani's Hamlet *at Angers.*

Elsinore was laid open before us: it was better than Cinema Scope. If Mr Eliot had seen a production like this, he could never have written that notorious essay. '*C'est impeccable,*' whispered an awe-struck Angevin, '*Il n'y a pas de faiblesses.*'

The acting was splendid in its attack; a vigorous, sensual Claudius; a jealous Gertrude; an athletic Laertes; a sturdy Horatio; and an Ophelia (Dominique Blanchar) more poetic than any I have seen in English. And in spite of its austere concentration on the dramatic essentials, the production yet let slip no opportunity for the valid spectacular effect – a giant, luminous ghost, overpowering symbol of instinct – mad Ophelia, wandering out of darkness to the head of the huge staircase, her veils blowing forlornly in the night wind; a magnificent final cortège, with Hamlet, a black moth caught and pinned down at last, borne slowly up the stairway on the crossed lances of Fortinbras's captains. No theatre could hold such effects.

Was Hamlet himself a little diminished in all this space? Perhaps. But Reggiani justified his audacity in combining his first essay in production with his first attempt at the part. Underplayed on the frantic side, this was a Hamlet of great poetic dignity; of emotions torn and confused; of intelligence and passion all the way. From his acting in the cinema – most strikingly in *Casque d'Or* – one already knew this actor's intensity of nerves and spirit. What comes as a surprise is the generosity and authority of his theatrical presence. This Hamlet shared his drama with us, with open heart.

Prefacing this production, Reggiani defined his aim in Hamlet's own words: 'to tell my story'. Fidelity proved its own reward. To feel the rapt attention with which that French audience, 2000 strong, followed the whole course of the tragedy, was in itself a memorable experience. Art may not always be international; but *Hamlet*, on this occasion at least, most certainly was.

At the Court of King George

Review of *The Theatres of George Devine* by Irving Wardle
in *The Guardian*, 7 June 1978

WHAT EXACTLY DO THE WORDS ROYAL COURT MEAN TO ANYBODY TODAY? A
theatre in Sloane Square – home of Shaw and Granville Barker – base of
the English Stage Company since 1956 – a Theatre of George Devine . . .
Even the old labels have the quaint appeal of dated slang: 'The Angries',
'Kitchen Sink', 'The Dustbin Theatre'. Ah, the battles long ago!

Myself, I remember vividly the shock, of freshness and of recognition,
of my first visit to the Court: to George Devine's production of Angus
Wilson's *The Mulberry Bush*, the first play in the English Stage Company's
first season, April 1956. Kenneth Tynan didn't see much in it, I remember.
He spent most of his *Sunday Observer* piece trilling over the merits of *The
Chalk Garden*, which he said evoked 'the spirited elegance of a Mozart
Quintet'. But the Sloane Square ensemble proved more resonant.

At that time I knew very little about George Devine except as a friendly, purposeful presence, the boss of my Oxford friend Tony Richardson. I
wish I had known more, and particularly when in 1957 I did my first stage
production for the Court and then, a year later, joined John Dexter and
Bill Gaskill as an 'Assistant to the Artistic Director'.

I wish that Irving Wardle's book – the first half of it, that is – had existed then, so that we could have appreciated more gratefully the remarkable
qualities and the remarkable range of experiences of the man who, more
than any other, was responsible for the Royal Court phenomenon.

George never – hardly ever – talked about his past. Of course at the
Court he was fully occupied with a risky, strenuous present, a future full
of possibility; that is what made the late fifties so much more lively than
the congealed, over-institutionalised seventies. All the same, it is strange
that he never spoke much of his theatre experience, because it was so rich,
so glamorous.

As a pushy Oxford undergraduate, one of a long tradition of ambitious
flamboyants (did he recognise something of himself in the young Tony
Richardson?), he had captured the presidency of the OUDS, invited the rising Old Vic star Gielgud down to direct *Romeo and Juliet*, got the lovely
young Peggy Ashcroft for Juliet, and landed Mercutio for himself. This got
him his first professional acting job under the legendary Komisarjevsky.

In London, George struck up a friendship with the three spirited girls
who designed under the name of Motley (he married Sophie Harris), and

became part of that glittering circle of talent which it is impossible to read of today without an acute nostalgic envy. The Motleys' studio ('a barn with great oak beams' at 67 St Martin's Lane – what is it now? A hamburger joint? An ice-cream parlour?) became an unofficial club for the acting profession. Gielgud, whose flat was at 7 Upper St Martins Lane (known to friends as Seven Upper) was one regular visitor . . . For meals they went over the road to a pub where they took a regular table which 'got longer and longer. Guinness and Ashcroft and Guthrie used to turn up, they knew they'd always find us there . . . You could get a very good dinner for 1s 6d (seven-and-a-half pence), so what the hell?'

George was never firstly an actor, though he enjoyed doing it – up to a point. (I don't think he ever relished having to take a leading role. It tensed him and made his acting heavy. But he could be wonderful in an ensemble.) He had a gift for organisation, and he was soon managing the Motleys.

But his strongest instinct was for theatre as a total, complex means of expression, that unity of text, staging, performance and design which can alone claim the dignity of art. This made him a director, and (most important of all) a teacher. And it led him to teachers. To his long and devoted association with Michel Saint-Denis.

Saint-Denis, nephew and student of the French theatre-master, Jacques Copeau, director of the highly-admired *Compagnie des Quinze*, never became an integral force in the British theatre. Yet from 1935, when he came to direct Gielgud in the English version of Obey's *Noah*, he was for 20 years a figure of huge repute in the profession, as director, theorist and teacher. Only one of his productions achieved huge and historic success – his *Three Sisters* for Gielgud in 1938 (with Gielgud, Redgrave, Ashcroft, Gwen Ffrangeon-Davies, Glen Byam Shaw and George Devine).

But he did manage somehow to get backing for two schools: the London Theatre Studio before the war, and the Old Vic School with its associated Young Vic Theatre after it. In both those vital, seminal, un-English ventures (masks, improvisations, exercises in style), George, together with Glen Byam Shaw, was Saint-Denis's disciple, adjutant and indefatigable co-worker.

To read about these dreams, struggles, desperate campaigns (about which George, as I say, hardly ever spoke) is fascinating. Irving Wardle has researched them with tremendous care and written about them in vivid, gossipy detail. Their conclusion is bitter.

After the hiatus of war, the Three Boys (as Saint-Denis, Byam Shaw and George were known in jolly English fashion at the Vic) managed to get backing for a revived school and a theatre of their own. A whole generation of young artists was trained: and the theatre toured with internation-

'George was Army.' George Devine holding the Royal Court banner on a CND march.

al acclaim. But the heady days of Olivier-Richardson success did not last. The resentment and triumph of the philistines, the meanness of spirit with which the Old Vic governors turned on the enterprise and destroyed it – and the wretched irony that it should be Tyrone Guthrie, at his most bitchy-autocratic, who put in the boot – all this makes absorbing and instructive reading.

There is no doubt that the harsh experience taught George Devine lessons in policy, scepticism and endurance which he never forgot. He smiled again: but not jovially. 'Never resign,' he said.

George was Army. He had many of the qualities of a good Commanding Officer and he enjoyed exercising them. His Royal Court was a properly run, efficient and professional theatre, about as democratic as a Greenjacket battalion. Yet in certain areas he craved reassurances. He needed to admire; to sense the authority of an intelligence he could respect.

One of the essential factors in the success of the Court was undoubtedly the flair which George spotted in the young Tony Richardson, and his insistence that Tony should rank as his associate. It was a typically modest decision, and a typically realistic one, however painful in its severing of ties – for Tony couldn't bear all that 'mime and sub-Copeau jumping about'. But then a Saint-Denis theatre would not have presented *Look Back in Anger.*

So, with a courage and instinct that were a special kind of genius, George Devine threw in his lot with a younger generation – the new lot who came barging in with ignorance and nerve, with precious little respect for their elders and betters, and none at all for critics and audiences who would not accept them on their own terms. For a few years at least the collaboration worked brilliantly – for longer if we count the Court's extraordinary second wind in the late sixties and early seventies, all entirely the fruit of George's labour. History and the man had come together.

Curiously, Irving Wardle's account of George Devine's Royal Court – indisputably the most important of his theatres – is rather less satisfactory than the first half of his book. There are signs of fatigue, lapses into journalism and too many omissions. The discovery of John Osborne and the production of *Look Back in Anger*, for instance, were crucial, both for the theatre and for George personally. It is hardly satisfying to be told that the story 'no more needs retelling than the fable of David and Goliath'.

Of course the Royal Court chronicles are extraordinarily complex, with personalities, economics, aesthetics and social history conflicting and combining in endlessly varying combinations. Wardle tracks Devine doggedly through the maze. But it is rather a grinding, nose-to-the-treadmill picture that results: the sort of impression you might have got if you asked George your questions at the end of a long day, after a tough committee meeting, when he was longing for a drink. Irving Wardle is stronger, perhaps, on analysis than empathy; and so a lot of these incidents were funnier, their humour more appreciated, than he seems to realise.

At times, even, one gets the impression from these pages that George's Associates and Assistants resembled nothing so much as a bunch of troublesome young priests, jockeying egotistically for position, using the Court chiefly to promote lucrative careers in the world outside. I think Mr Wardle is over-defensive for his hero. We were troublesome, certainly, and we did not respond kindly to Father (and favourite Son) making all the decisions behind closed doors. But these frictions kept the place alive, and they did not affect the basic loyalties. Families are like that.

One vital factor in the Royal Court's success was the coincidence of its birth with that final flicker of vitality in the English soul – the crack-up of the post-war freeze, the new radicalism of post-Suez, post-Hungary, the last, too-brief reanimation of the social democratic ideal in 1956 and the few years that followed.

This perspective, essential I think to an understanding of the achievement, is inadequately, even somewhat sniffily rendered by Irving Wardle: I suspect he would find it distasteful, even sentimental. But like it or not, an aggressive, liberal humanism (not the soppy, conformist kind) was always the basis of Royal Court personality, and of the Royal Court choice of authors.

For there was, of course, a Royal Court choice of authors – has Mr Wardle noticed that George's admiration of Beckett did not extend to Pinter? – just as there were Royal Court actors and Royal Court directors. This is why the theatre was so widely resented; but it is also what gave it a unique character. And it is also why, although sometimes successful, the Royal Court was never fashionable.

One thing this book does convey – it is probably the most important thing – is the richness and the scope of George Devine's vision of theatre. He believed intensely in its importance; he wished ardently that it should relate and contribute to the movement of ideas in the national consciousness, that it should act as a moral stimulant, an imaginative challenge. But he was not a propagandist. And when he wrote that 'the basis of everything in the theatre is the dramatist,' he was not pleading the cause of 'literary' theatre.

He was equally far from subscribing to the sentimentalism of new-writing-at-all-costs, which has become the cant of today. The cry of 1956 was 'We must find new writers'; the whimper of 1978 is 'We have to do new plays, or we'll lose our Arts Council grant.' If George had ever found himself reduced to this kind of snivel, he'd have known it was time to move on. To a new theatre. Would that he were here to show us the way!

Jocelyn Herbert

Introductory words to an exhibition of Jocelyn Herbert's
work at the National Theatre, 14 September 1993

I'M REALLY SORRY THAT THIS THIRD WEEK OF SEPTEMBER SEEMS TO BE THE ONE
chosen for so many occasions one would dearly love to attend. First and
foremost, of course, the opening of this exhibition of the work of Jocelyn
Herbert, artist and friend extraordinary. As fate decrees, I have to be
across the Atlantic, at Bowling Green University, and that is the only reason I am not speaking these words myself. All the same, as you know and
as Jocelyn knows, they come from the heart.

Just the other day, as you may have heard, Jocelyn Herbert joined the
merry party who made up Ned Sherrin's *Loose Ends* radio programme on
Saturday morning. This seemed very unlike Jocelyn, who has always been
an artist of the theatre and nothing at all to do with show business. She
did it, in fact, because she had promised her publisher to take part in at
least two chat shows if she was permitted the cover picture of her choice
for the book which is shortly to be published about her work. This was
like Jocelyn, to whom promises are to be kept. Also, she can't stand anything to be wrong, or contrary to what her taste and her artistic intuition
tell her to be right. And she was quite right about the cover of her book,
as you will see for yourselves. Anyway, we needn't have worried. Jocelyn
didn't seem at all out of place on *Loose Ends*. She talked straight and told
the truth. Her directness and her truthfulness protected her. Her innocence, you might say. These are the very qualities that have always distinguished her as an artist. That have made her work so special, so immediately recognisable.

This distinction really makes any words of introduction to this exhibition quite unnecessary. As she says herself, not absolutely without pride,
she has always stuck to the principles in which she believed and which
informed her theatre work from its start at the Royal Court. George
Devine believed in a theatre which drew inspiration directly from the work
of its writers. Everything – the choice of play, the director's conception, the
selection and the work of the actors, the music, the lighting and the design
– must reflect the personality and the intention of the author. You might
think that this would result in a style more literary than theatrical. But this
would be to mistake the whole nature of theatre and of the creative elements which make it up. Especially design. Of course the author, who is
not a design artist, may sometimes not know exactly how his or her work

Jocelyn Herbert: 'essentially and compulsively creative.'

may best be visualised or set. This is where the designer must be creative as well as interpretive. And Jocelyn has always been essentially and compulsively creative, which in no way implies a conflict with her skill and intuition as an interpreter. What it does imply is always a personal choice of material and of collaborators. You will see the continuity as you look round this exhibition.

It is this continuity that gives the homogeneity of style to Jocelyn's work, however varied its inspiration may have seemed to be. From Arden to Ionesco to Wesker to Beckett to Osborne to Aeschylus to Orton. From Shakespeare to Shaw, Tony Harrison and David Storey – to name but a few, and off the top of my head. And note that all these authors are, each in his own way, moralists. Jocelyn has always been something of an aesthetic Puritan, as she has always been an inflexible moralist when it comes to conduct. This does not, I hasten to say, imply any lack of humour. Her design for *What the Butler Saw* was as bold and as witty as her set for *Home*.

When there is so much talk of creativity, intuition, morality and all the rest of it, there is one aspect of Jocelyn Herbert's work which I think must be emphasised. This is its essential and rigorous professionalism, its necessary grounding in models and drawings and mathematical calculation. I remember very well being invited to the Contemporary Theatre in Warsaw in the sixties, to direct – in Polish – the premiere in Poland of John Osborne's *Inadmissible Evidence*. Jocelyn, of course, had designed the play when Anthony Page first directed it at the Royal Court. I had thought, not wishing to be over-influenced by that fine original production, that I should get a Polish designer to set the play at the Contemporary Theatre. I encountered disaster. The Polish artist produced some rather vague, impressionistic sketches which absolutely evaded the practical – which is to say also the creative – challenge of the play. I seem to remember a glass floor. 'This is what we're used to getting,' they told me at the theatre. 'Then we have to create a set as best as we can.' Apologetically, I called Jocelyn and begged for help. She was in the middle of a production at the Court, and could only spare me a weekend; but thank God she came to Warsaw with her drawings, her instruments and the model which, happily, was still in existence. The director of the theatre and the stage staff were all amazed. It was unheard of to them that an acknowledged artist should present a set precisely measured, calculated and drawn. Of course it worked perfectly. This is what we have learned to expect from Jocelyn.

A few introductory words like this can no more cover the life work of an artist than an exhibition in a limited space like this can represent her varied and venturesome time in the theatre. The operas she designed for John Dexter, for instance, as well as the plays in this country, from Wesker to Sartre. The bold experiments of Harrison Birtwhistle and Tony Harrison. And you will understand if I cannot altogether leave out her contributions to the films of her friends, although there has not been space to feature them here. From *Tom Jones* and *Ned Kelly* and *The Hotel New Hampshire* with Tony Richardson, with whom she worked so closely at the Court. *Isadora* with Karel Reisz. And the three films I have been lucky enough to have designed by Jocelyn: *If . . . .*, *O Lucky Man!* and *The Whales of August*. I know that Jocelyn has never liked the cinema very much. I think she has been alienated by the size of the machine, and the sometimes agonising demands of collaboration. For she has always been a completely, intensely personal artist, even in some respect a private one. That is why we have all quite often had to accept her decision to say No.

That is the price you have to pay in media like theatre and cinema for the work of an artist who has always felt the need of a personal commitment. That is the price we have had to pay for the artistry of Jocelyn Herbert. Look around and see if you don't think it has been worth it. Cheap at the price, I'd say.

Tony Richardson

Introduction to *The Long Distance Runner* by Tony
Richardson, 1993

I HAVE ALWAYS THOUGHT, AND OFTEN SAID, THAT TONY RICHARDSON WAS THE
most remarkable by far of the young artists who battled for change in the
heady days of confidence and enterprise which were the late fifties and the
early sixties in Britain. He did not talk much – less and less, actually – about
the struggles and victories of those days, but at least they were days of hope.
I remember one hot afternoon in Los Angeles when he and Joan Plowright
and I unusually gossiped and reminisced over white wine about the triumphs
and disasters of the English Stage Company in Sloane Square. We had a great
deal to remember and to laugh about. I know I asked Tony more than once,
since the story of the Royal Court was so often and so inaccurately told, if he
had thought of writing his autobiography. As a matter of fact, he replied, very
much as he told his daughter Natasha, he had once started to do just that.
But what he had written was no good, he said, and he had scrapped it.

So it was a surprise to learn that when Tony died so prematurely, he had
left a manuscript behind him, by no means a brief one, which no one
seemed to have read. And it was a surprise, too, to find that these memories were certainly not 'no good', but vivid and unsparing and forceful, full
of things which only Tony could know, humorous, impetuous and intelligent. Just like Tony talking.

It is important to realise that these are memories set down with frankness and impatience. Tony could never see the point of dissembling, except
perhaps sometimes for effect. They certainly do not add up to an autobiography in any strict sense. Tony was writing chiefly for his daughters,
whom he loved and admired without reservation. He wrote about himself
and his experiences, by no means telling everything, but only the things he
wanted his girls – and us – to know. Tony enjoyed gossip; but he had no
time for the kind of journalistic sensationalism which has become more
prevalent as the media pursue, ever more ruthlessly, circulation and success. He chose to tell what he chose to tell. As his daughter says, his recall
(mostly extremely precise) is 'sometimes factually inaccurate and frequently embellished'. Often Tony remembered wrongly; he was not
always concerned with objective truth. His memoirs reflect his ambition,
his preoccupation with himself. But they are rarely ungenerous.

He came from the North, and his memories of childhood, of family and
youth, are among his most vivid. He seldom, if ever, spoke about them in

311

London. This surely accounts for an intimidating, often abrasive direct-ness in the way he talked and wrote. And perhaps also worked. Always a realist, he had little time for sentiment. If I wanted to irritate him, I knew I had only to thank him for the way he had precipitated my career in the theatre. This was true, but it was a responsibility he refused to accept: each man's destiny is his own affair. I remember warning Tony over din-ner one evening that if he insisted on trying to shape policies and decisions to his own ambitions, he might easily bring the whole Royal Court enter-prise to an end. 'Everything comes to an end,' answered Tony, without apology. There was a ruthlessness and determination there which were always a part of him, for good and for ill.

The phenomenon of the Royal Court was the result of an extraordinary partnership of talent, of George Devine and Tony Richardson. It was also the result of George's recognition that Tony's intelligence and conviction, above all his sense of the historic moment, fitted him perfectly to act as Associate. Perhaps this was Tony's great contribution. But his description and his expla-nation of the end of the Royal Court experiment is untrue. His production of *The Seagull* at the Queen's, and the memorable *St Joan of the Stockyards* with which he followed it, were his last really successful productions in London – successful artistically that is: Brecht was as decisively rejected then by upper-class critics as he had always been, and the public followed their lead. But it is fanciful to suggest that George's line at the end of *The Seagull* – 'Konstantin Gavrilovich has shot himself' – prophesied the end of his Royal Court: the historic role of the Court was by no means played out. Tony's thoughts about the possible continuance of the theatre are, of course, interesting. But he was too much of an egoist to care much about the activ-ities of his juniors – the 'tit-swingers' as John Osborne uncharitably labelled us. That Queen's Theatre Season took place without us, except when Tony got into difficulties with *St Joan of the Stockyards* and put out a call for help.

The truth is surely in Tony's own words, not as prominently featured here as perhaps they should be. 'My own future,' he writes, 'was elsewhere.' Like so may Britons (and who can blame them?), he felt that his Destiny lay away from London, far removed from the critics, both of theatre and of film, whom he always felt were hostile to him, in the more challenging, more ful-filling world of the United States. Absolutely characteristic, and significant, is the lack of interest that Tony seemed to feel in what he had left behind him.

It was not 'a very minor theatre' that presented the plays of Edward Bond, directed by Bill Gaskill; or Anthony Page's productions of John Osborne's *Inadmissible Evidence* and the plays that followed it; Peter Gill's discovery of the plays of D. H. Lawrence; and David Storey's plays, from *In Celebration* to *Life Class*, which I was fortunate enough to direct. The same is true of the films which followed the successes of Woodfall. But Tony had moved on, to

Broadway and Hollywood, as George Devine had always known, without resentment, that he would.

From the start, the cinema was Tony's enthusiasm. In the months that led up to our first Free Cinema show at the National Film Theatre, he had collaborated with Karel Reisz on a 16mm film about the Jazz Club at Wood Green, *Momma Don't Allow*, which featured Chris Barber's band and a membership of working-class boys and girls – very different territory from that usually explored by British documentaries. If the cinema (and television) had then been more open to new talent and new ideas, perhaps Tony would have been directing films rather than plays. As it was, the shot that revitalised British cinema in the late fifties came chiefly through his work at the Royal Court and his friendship and partnership with John Osborne. They

Oscar Lewenstein and Tony Richardson during the Royal Court's visit to the Soviet Union, 1957.

formed Woodfall Films with *Look Back in Anger* and *The Entertainer*, which they followed with the ground-breaking production of *Saturday Night and Sunday Morning*, which Karel directed for Woodfall. After that, I well remember how Tony's decision to shoot *A Taste of Honey* entirely on a Northern location was regarded as a foolhardy innovation by the British industry. Together with *The Loneliness of the Long Distance Runner* and the hugely successful *Tom Jones* (which Michael Balcon had turned down for Bryanston), those were films which changed the face of the British cinema.

Tony was certainly not content to remain a 'kitchen sink' director, which was the label used by British upper-class critics to discredit films which explored hitherto disregarded worlds; his work in cinema was venturesome and eclectic. *Tom Jones* defied tradition in its realistic use of colour (it was designed by Jocelyn Herbert from the Court and photographed by Walter Lassally from Free Cinema); and *The Charge of the Light Brigade* determinedly set itself against the tradition of romantic spectacle which the title seemed to suggest. Typically, Tony refused to launch the film with a special showing for the press, a gesture of independence which was fiercely attacked. No doubt the critical rejection, which he could only regard as mean-spirited, helped to turn him away, across the Atlantic. He left London for Los Angeles. Decisively this time.

There is a certain irony about Tony's enthusiasm for the United States and for things American. He escaped gratefully from the cramping confines of the English class system, which he always loathed; he escaped from the tyranny of the past, by which he felt oppressed in London; and he escaped from the carping and the lack of generosity which he had grown to expect from West End audiences and critics. But his wit and his critical sense were too sharp to allow him ever to become part of the establishment of American showbusiness, and there was a dangerous willfulness about the scorn with which he derided Hollywood's studio system. He was respected (and feared?) for his wit, but he remained an outsider there as he had been here. Nonetheless, he remained true to himself and his beliefs. Films like *The Loved One, The Border, The Hotel New Hampshire* (especially) and his last work *Blue Sky* were uneven. But they bore the unmistakable imprint of his personality and his convictions. And this was more important to him than popularity or professional acclaim.

It would be a mistake to think that Tony's decision to leave London for Los Angeles was a wrong one, as many English critics (the BBC, for instance) have assumed. The life-style offered to him by the United States was of the first importance. He writes glowingly of his travels, which were a part of that life-style; and also of the happiness he found among family and friends at Le Nid du Duc in the South of France. He was a genial host, always responsive, in a most attractive way, to people and to places, both well-known to him and unfamiliar. This is why most actors and collaborators liked working for him, even if his decisions might be erratic. An eager relish and an appetite for life were always part of Tony, and always gave an endearing vibrancy to his presence. It was a vibrancy which London seemed sadly to lack after his departure.

Tony's last project was a stage production of *The Cherry Orchard*, which he intended to direct in London and to take on a European tour. He was working on the casting and on the design, and he had the backing of an English producer. Increasingly, it seemed obvious to everyone but Tony himself that he did not have the strength to pull the whole thing off. But his determination was phenomenal and so was his refusal to admit defeat. Success was never important, only the energy and intention which must inspire every enterprise in art, every life worth living. A disrespectful energy informs these pages and makes the story unique. Everything did not happen exactly like this, but this is how Tony chose to remember it. He recognised the truth of Sam Beckett's advice, given to an actor in rehearsal at the Royal Court, with which he ends his book. Perhaps the words will not be understood by a world obsessed with success. But they surely sum up his achievement. He failed better.

John Dexter

Review of *The Honourable Beast*: *A Posthumous Autobiography* by John Dexter, in *The Spectator*, 6 July 1993

SURELY WE, THE 'ANGRY YOUNG MEN' OF THE ROYAL COURT THEATRE 30-odd years ago, were a remarkable bunch. Certainly we were very lucky. George Devine, our unique leader, was at the head of it; and with extraordinary prescience he chose Tony Richardson to be his Associate. As their assistants there were John Dexter, Bill Gaskill and myself. Anthony Page and Peter Gill joined a little later. Jocelyn Herbert was painting scenery in the workshops before she started designing. Alan Tagg did many of the early sets. Joan Plowright, Robert Stephens, Frank Finlay and Alan Bates were junior members of the Company. John Osborne acted and wrote plays . . .

Now come the reminiscences. Bill Gaskill has produced his book. Tony Richardson's memoirs will appear shortly. And here is John Dexter's 'autobiography', put together by his friend Riggs O'Hara from notes, letters and diary records which John left behind when he died three years ago. They are vivid reminders of a better time than this, when we all subscribed to George's slogan of 'the Right to Fail' rather than join the dreary pursuit of 'Bums on Seats'. The attitude stayed with us, which is one reason, no doubt, why we have been so disliked. But arrogance suits an artist better than conformism.

This book is subtitled *A Posthumous Autobiography*, but it is not really John Dexter's story of his life. Riggs O'Hara, who lived with John for many years, has been over-modest in his editorship. His introduction starts with the words: 'A book about John Dexter had to be a book about work.' This is true, but it need not have ruled out the editorial presence altogether, informing us of the facts behind each situation. The tone of voice is certainly John's, very personal and completely frank. But the course of events is not always clearly charted.

Just how, for instance, did John Dexter become part of the Royal Court team? He came from Derby. As a boy, he played with a toy theatre, accompanied on the piano by his father, who had been wounded in the First World War. He thought he was going to be an actor, and indeed he did act in the Army (where he suffered for a time from polio) and in Civvy Street after his release. He got to know John Osborne when they were both playing in rep in Derby. Somehow he got to be interviewed by George Devine and invited to work at the Royal Court. At first he seems to have been chiefly occupied in reading scripts. Then he was assigned a Sunday Night 'production without decor' (Michael Hastings' first play, *Yes and After*), and became Arnold Wesker's first director with *Chicken Soup with Barley*, followed by *The Kitchen* and *Roots*. From the start he was closely concerned with text. 'If you don't shut up, Arnold,' he was heard to shout at one rehearsal, 'I'll direct this the way you wrote it.'

In those early days the Royal Court was very 'Oxford', by which I mean 'empirical', in its approach to theatre, while the Royal Shakespeare Company was emphatically 'Cambridge' (theoretical). Both theatres were inevitably upper-middle-class. John was sharply aware of such characteristics – as he was all his life – and resentful of the fact that his origins were lower-middle and he had never attended either of the major universities. From the start, I think, he felt in some way excluded, though the idea never occurred to any of the rest of us. John was one of us, yet very much on his own. He was an intellectual and a powerfully self-assertive one.

There is not a great deal about the Court in this book, but enough to make it obvious that the experience of Sloane Square was for John Dexter, as it was for all of us, both liberating and formative. George Devine, whom John well described as 'the only man I know who could help without interfering,' was a key, paternal figure; and the importance of Jocelyn Herbert ('the designer who has always guided my best work') is very clear. It is not explained, though, how Laurence Olivier, struggling to crew his National Theatre in the late fifties, got John and his friend and colleague William Gaskill to join him at the Old Vic. This anyway is how, in 1963, John directed Joan Plowright as St Joan and the next year Olivier as Othello, with decor and costumes by Jocelyn Herbert.

The National brought John Dexter together with Peter Shaffer for the first time, for his spectacular *Royal Hunt of the Sun*. Other new plays followed: Arden's *Armstrong's Last Goodnight* (co-directed with Bill Gaskill), Shaffer's *Black Comedy* and Osborne's *A Bond Honoured*. Then he was sacked. Was this because Laurence Olivier, always ambivalent about John's homosexuality, regarded him with suspicion? We are left to guess. But after directing his first film *The Virgin Soldiers* (not exactly a success), John returned to the National for *A Woman Killed with Kindness*. Then more Wesker at the Court. He had always loved and understood music: with Berlioz and Verdi he started to direct opera, at Covent Garden and Hamburg.

It was a tenuous, intense and varied career. Perhaps this caused John Dexter to be looked at askance in his own country, where artists are preferably respectable (his homosexuality and outspokenness deprived him and deprived Chichester of the possibility of his directing the theatre festival there). And in England one is supposed to stick to what one has been seen to do well. So it was somehow inevitable that in 1974 John should be invited to become Director of Productions at New York's Metropolitan Opera. He accepted. But it was probably also inevitable that seven years later conflict with the management and particularly with the Musical Director James Levine, just as wilful as John, should lead to his dismissal.

Mozart, Weill, Verdi, Berg, Satie, Ravel and Stravinsky were among John Dexter's composers at the Met. His productions had been designed by Jocelyn Herbert, Svoboda, Bill Dudley and David Hockney among others. It was a record he could be proud of. And when one remembers that during this operatic career, he found time also for theatre productions like *Pygmalion* and *Phaedra Britannicus*, *As You Like It* and *Galileo* at the National, one can see how he thrived on activity. Neither ill-health, of which he had more than his share, nor opposition seemed ever to make him pause.

The title of this book came to Riggs O'Hara when he remembered John calling his godson, who was always late, 'a beast'. 'You're a beast too,' said Riggs, truthfully. 'But an honourable one.' Perhaps this meant that John's beastliness was always – or so he would claim – in the name of principle. I am not quite sure about this. Although he soon dismissed his early ambition to be an actor, there was something histrionic about his personality as a collaborator and as a director. John enjoyed demonstrating his authority in rehearsal, which too often meant unkindness to one member at least of his cast. Though himself strongly emotional, he seemed scared of emotion, of sentiment. His judgement of character and relationship could sometimes be criticised, though never his sense of *mise-en-scène*. He was always an outstanding theatrical director, with a brilliant sense of staging – as witness the disciplined choreography of *The Kitchen*, the crossing of the Andes in *The Royal Hunt*, the whole conception of *Equus*, which was largely responsible for the play's worldwide success. Such *tours-de-force* were always more striking than the emotional truth of John's work.

Perhaps this is the reason why so many of his collaborative plans came to nothing. After the Met, John tried many times to form a company of his own, to perpetuate a style. But his production of *The Glass Menagerie* in New York, which should have started things off, was not a success. Back in London, he talked with Peter Hall about the possibility of their assuming joint responsibility, each with his own company, for the Olivier and the Cottesloe at the National Theatre; but in the end the appointment went to Peter Gill (and John commented bitterly that he was left to find this out by reading the announcement in the press). He was a loner as well as an egoist, which always made collaborations difficult. What this book makes very clear is his consistency of aim and his refusal to compromise. He was often uncomfortably frank and always impatient with anything he considered second-rate. No wonder the Royal Court rejected him, like Chichester. His diary entry for 4 August 1986 read: 'Hang out the Flags for the New Theatre Company this week.' Unhappily, the breeze did not blow and the flags did not flutter.

John Dexter died in 1990, prematurely (he was born in 1925) and unexpectedly (his heart operation was judged a minor one, not risky). He was still full of plans: Alec McCowen as Othello, Joan Plowright as Cleopatra. He was excited at the prospect of working with Tariq Ali and Howard Brenton on their satire *Moscow Gold*. Ten days before he died he had noted 'Consider Jacobi, Thaw, Woodward, Finney. Phone RSC re. their list of "stars".' The flow of ideas never dried up. Some of them would have come to nothing, but some would have materialised, to jolt, disappoint or stimulate. To lose and to win. No one has replaced John. No one could. This book explains why.

John Osborne

Review of *Almost a Gentleman* by John Osborne, in *The Spectator*, 9 November 1991

SO HERE IT IS AT LAST, THE BOOK WE HAVE AWAITED WITH MUTUAL GRIMACES of trepidation: the second instalment of John Osborne's autobiography. By 'we', I mean, of course, those of us who shared, in sometimes uneasy com-radeship, the years of challenge and risk and heedless optimism which made Sloane Square, from the mid-fifties to the mid-seventies, a more exciting place than you are likely to find anywhere in the theatre today. It began in 1956, with the inception of the English Stage Company at the Royal Court and the opening, on 8 May, of *Look Back in Anger*.

The Court was George Devine's theatre, with Tony Richardson as his bright, fearless adjutant. And John Osborne certainly helped to keep the place going, with *Look Back* and Laurence Olivier in *The Entertainer* (plays and films), then *Inadmissible Evidence* and *A Patriot for Me*. These three dominated the place, until Tony took off to become a film director in Hollywood. We juniors – Dexter, Gaskill, Anderson, Page and Gill – were never quite their intimates. John calls us tit-swingers, which I don't exactly understand, but which does not sound complimentary. We knew him well enough, anyway, to anticipate a good few nasty jibes.

The jibes are certainly here, unbridled and all over the place. But then, at the Court, we always spoke our minds. We were quite sure we were right. This gave the place an atmosphere quite different from the darling-ridden West End. As John says, he was unused to George Devine's 'throwaway vehemence', having grown used to expecting this kind of thing only for him-self. Fry, Ustinov and Whiting – 'They're all absolute shit.' That was the kind of aggressive anti-philistinism with which George led the Court. No wonder *Look Back in Anger*, having been (in Osborne's words) rejected by 'every theatrical management or agent I could find listed in *The Writers' and Artists' Yearbook,*' was taken up only by the English Stage Company. John was paid £25 for a year's option and a £50 renewal clause. And no wonder we all, like-minded egotists, gladly accepted the chance of working in that theatre for very little money. In those days the establishment seemed firmly entrenched and healthily reactionary. We had something to fight against.

This is not, as John Osborne makes quite clear, a book about the Royal Court. It is about John Osborne, only to some degree a representative, rebellious 'angry young man' (a slogan invented by George Fearon, the theatre publicist, doing his best for *Look Back in Anger*). Even more sure-

319

From left: Lady Birkett, E. A. (Ted) Whitehead,
John Osborne and Anthony Page
backstage at the Royal Court.

ly it is about a writer advancing to fame without compromise, hopping from affairs to marriages and back, without much care or logic, only marginally concerned with society or politics.

The late fifties were a time of change, of apparent revolt. *Look Back in Anger*, misinterpreted as a revolutionary statement, gave some people an impression of John Osborne as a leader of the angries. This was never true. John was always, and certainly in that play, firstly and ferociously concerned with himself. At Suez he gave vent to his irritation and wrote 'Damn You, England', which was printed in the *Tribune*. He walked up and down Whitehall with his wife Mary Ure, carrying an antinuclear placard. And he was carried off by the police at a disarmament demonstration in Trafalgar Square, to spend a night in gaol. All the same, his commitment was not full-hearted. It is important to understand that John Osborne looks back on his life with essential and self-absorbed subjectivity.

The same goes for people – unless they happened to engage his fancy or to have become fortuitously a part of his life. His likes and dislikes are entirely personal; facts are of little interest. If the history of the Royal Court ever comes to be written – as it has not been, and as it should be – this book will be quite unreliable as source-material.

It was hugely fortunate that John Osborne found George Devine so sympathetic, and that this sympathy ripened into devotion, 'passionate friendship' as he puts it. Differently, but similarly, he saw Tony Richardson, daring and unscrupulous, pretty clearly; and clarity grew into a kind of love – 'a chaste, severe love circumscribed by some mutually agreed attachment of alienation'. George and Tony gave John his start, and I would certainly not suggest that he did not handsomely pay them back. The price to be paid, though – and paid consistently in this book – is a quite horrid unfairness to many people who were certainly friends, or thought themselves friends, at one time, and who certainly helped John on his way forward. There is scant acknowledgment to collaborators.

For instance: did John Osborne consciously decide to dislike Jocelyn Herbert because of her relationship with George Devine? After all, she designed (brilliantly) *Luther* and *Inadmissible Evidence* and *A Patriot for Me*. But 'Brown' he says she was called, 'because of her addiction to dun-coloured sets.' Nonsense of course, and since Jocelyn, most imaginative and scrupulous of artists, designed my productions of *Serjeant Musgrave's Dance*, *Home* and *What the Butler Saw*, I know exactly how nonsensical this is. And what of Anthony Page, who took over as John's director when Tony Richardson went to Hollywood? He directed *Patriot* and *Inadmissible Evidence*, *Hedda Gabler* and *West of Suez*. John spent a lot of time with him, 'none of it very enjoyable, spitting food all over me.' More nonsense, absolutely.

John Osborne has almost always written extremely well. His rhetoric is irresistible, his aperçus witty and very often just. But the style is not sustained. There are too many quotations, with too many smart comments. Too often the confident glibness of the writing is indistinguishable from the journalism which interrupts it. Towards the end, the book collapses into diary form. '17th February, Old Vic, *Much Ado*. Zeffirelli's, with Robert and Margaret Stephens. Loved all this wog nonsense. He's a clever bugger.' This is not writing: it is just gossip.

On the jacket of *Almost a Gentleman* a photograph by Lord Snowdon shows a worn, quizzical Osborne, tweed-capped, in a dark jacket, black waistcoat, with fob and chain, foulard scarf negligently draped. His right hand, with heavy signet ring, rests on a furled umbrella. He is wearing a large purple (velvet?) bow tie. The picture suggests the performer as much as the writer, standing perhaps on the stage at a dress parade, presenting the costume which the part has been judged to demand. John Osborne, we are reminded, for all his writer's skill, is an actor. This should be borne in mind by anyone who reads this book. Also, he has given us plenty of pointers. 'I am alone, I am alone and against myself,' a chapter-heading quotes from *Luther*. And at the head of another chapter, John quotes appositely from a review he wrote himself. 'How much do we believe of these memories? How much does it matter? All autobiography is fiction to a great extent.'

A final comment. John Osborne writes about his wives with a venom that makes one wonder why he ever married them, and whether he ever experienced contentment except with a mistress. (He is now living with his fifth wife, we must hope more successfully.) Two of his wives, Mary Ure and Jill Bennett, died tragically. Inexplicably, John writes hatefully about them both. He has inserted a chapter on Jill's suicide that says nothing illuminating about his relationship with her, indulges in abuse of the most puerile kind and communicates only a superficial, false and absolutely subjective idea of her personality. The whole wretched chapter anyway falls outside the date-span (1955-66) which the publisher has attached to the book. Faber and Faber, who are publishers of some repute, should have refused to include this chapter. And the posh Sunday which ran it as part of its serialisation deal has reason to be thoroughly ashamed. To quote from John Osborne himself: 'Fuck *The Observer*.'

Jill Bennett

The Independent, 7 October 1990

SOME PEOPLE – VERY FEW – HAVE A STYLE SO PERSONAL, AN INDIVIDUALITY SO absolute that it is with a terrible pang that we realise we will never see them again, never again hear their disrespectful laughter, never find ourselves challenged by that larky voice at the other end of the telephone. Jill Bennett was one of these, and all her many friends knew it.

She was an actress of unique, unmistakable distinction; but it is as a friend I think of her. She gave a colour to life, a zest and a humour, an unflinching directness. But she was not as she seemed. Yes, she was honest; but she was vulnerable and sensitive, too often wrongly doubtful of herself. She was glamorous, but she did not like herself all that much, and she was a Puritan.

She was too intelligent, too clear-sighted to be an actress – not in the theatre as it should be, of course, but in this silly, hurried, pretence-world in which we do our best to create. As she always did.

Jill seemed mistress of herself, because she always talked with such amused self-knowledge. But she was tremendously emotional, passionate under that apparent control. Life, other people, could hurt her. In the end unbearably. It is terrible to think of. Dearest Jill. Who do we know now with such honesty, gaiety and loyalty? No one.

Lindsay and Jill Bennett on the set of The Old Crowd.

Rachel Roberts

Double Exposure, 27 June 1990

I FIRST MET RACHEL WHEN HER THEN HUSBAND, ALAN DOBIE, WAS ACTING IN my production of *Serjeant Musgrave's Dance* at the Royal Court. In the programme notes about the cast, I had written that Alan was married to 'the actress, Rachel Roberts'. Rachel was outside the theatre before the first preview, leafing through the programme. She shrieked delightedly when she saw her name. 'The actress, Rachel Roberts! . . . *the* actress! . . . ' I recognised and immediately warmed to her joyous mixture of send-up, self send-up and huge, astonished pleasure. That was Rachel, ardent and outrageous, in the days before awards and fame and recognition by taxi-drivers. She was simpler then, and happier.

That was also before my friend Karel Reisz, with such brilliant perception, cast her as the discontented, passionate, thwarted Brenda in *Saturday Night and Sunday Morning*. Rachel showed in that how she could respond when her material and her direction were first-class. She was a terrific actress: she would dare anything. Her emotional power could be frightening, self-lacerating. At first, I admit, I doubted that she was right for bitter, walled-up Mrs Hammond in *This Sporting Life*. But it was

Lindsay directing Rachel Roberts in This Sporting Life: *'violent temperament under implacible control'.*

exactly the pressure of violent temperament under implacable control that created that unforgettable performance.

Rachel, of course, was not English: she was a Celt, totally Welsh. And of all the Celts, it is the Welsh who find it most difficult to deal with the cool of the Anglo-Saxons, their unquestioning assumption of superiority, their distaste for temperament. The English theatre could not accommodate Rachel, nor could the English cinema. She scared them. And then she had to fall for Rex [Harrison], who brought with him all that establishment charm and class, all that champagne and caviar and shirts from Jermyn Street. Everything that wasn't Rachel, but to which she obstinately insisted on aspiring.

When she was young she wanted to look like Hedy Lamarr. She had such distinction in the little black dress I would try to make her wear, but she never lost her yearning for fish-net tights. She knew her weaknesses and she laughed at them, but she would still surrender to them. Perhaps she never quite believed in her success; or it was not the kind of success she longed for. We tried to stop her. 'Rachel . . . !' But we couldn't.

She would sometimes say, 'I wish you'd known me earlier. I was good fun then. Not all messed up, the way I am now.' She was messed up, and none of us, friends and hangers-on and foolish doctors alike, could pull her out of it. And yet – what laughs we had! She was one of life's incandescents. Irreplaceable.

John Haynes

Introduction to *Taking the Stage* by John Haynes, 1986

I LIKE VERY MUCH A STORY WHICH JOHN HAYNES HAS OFTEN TOLD ME ABOUT himself and the Royal Court Theatre. It has nothing to do with theatre photographs, but it says a lot about the Royal Court – and himself. It happened in January 1962. John was 'on the board' (operating the lighting) during a technical rehearsal for Tony Richardson's production of *A Midsummer Night's Dream*; on the stage or sitting waiting in the stalls was the typical young Royal Court company of those days: Colin Blakely (playing Bottom), Alfie Lynch (Puck), Lynn Redgrave, Rita Tushingham, David Warner, Ronnie Barker, Nicol Williamson, Samantha Eggar, Corin Redgrave . . . (How the names recall the epoch!) Jocelyn Herbert, no doubt, was wandering around with a paintbrush, touching up bits of the set. Suddenly Tony's voice rang out. 'John Osborne's being interviewed on television: we must see it. Who wants to come?' He wasn't just talking to the actors or to his friends; he was talking to everybody. 'Come back to Woodfall: we can watch it there.' And off they all trooped to the offices of Woodfall Films in Curzon Street and watched with great amusement while John Osborne elaborated the theme of 'Damn You, England!' or some other outrageous, witty, 'angry' anti-establishment declaration. 'I knew I'd found a home,' says John Haynes.

The Royal Court, you will soon see, bulks large in this book; and not just because it is where John Haynes first started taking pictures of plays. It must bulk large in the life and work of anyone who was lucky enough to work there in its golden age – the late fifties, the sixties, the early seventies. For it was a theatre unlike any other, not just in its abundance of talent, but in its unique freedom from the triviality, the competitiveness, the camp and deprecating cynicism which, alas, ran through so much London theatre. Joan Littlewood's Theatre Workshop out at Stratford was of course another dissident group, but of quite a different character. Joan was defiantly proletarian, unliterary, 'socialist'. By contrast the Royal Court of George Devine and Tony Richardson was middle-class (not 'bourgeois'), respectful of tradition, radical rather than revolutionary, 'humanist'. And perhaps even more strongly resented. Certainly just as many seats were noisily vacated, just as many exit doors slammed during first nights in Sloane Square as at Stratford East.

Young John Haynes was not around for those first heady days at the Court: almost certainly he was unaware of them. There was nothing theatrical – or photographic – about his background. His father had driven a bus for London Transport and retired to St Leonards; John discovered the theatre through the weekly rep performance by the Penguin Players at the Bexhill Pavilion. A play which struck him particularly was Priestley's *Mr Kettle and Mrs Moon* – whose London premiere, oddly enough, had been directed by the young Tony Richardson. Its theme of an impetuous rejection of suburban life perhaps influenced John: he came to London and worked for three years in offices. He saw *The Mousetrap*.

He did his National Service as a dog-handler with the RAF Police. In Singapore he started to read plays: *The Importance of Being Earnest*, Shaw, Noel Coward, things like that. Demobbed in London, he got himself taken on – still without any conscious intention – as a stage hand at the Palace Theatre. He shifted scenery for musicals; he trained a follow-spot on Benny Hill. But something told him that this was not the kind of theatre in which he could happily spend his life. What he had read or heard about the Royal Court stirred his interest. He wrote and asked for a job. He got one. It meant demoting from 'first dayman' to 'second dayman' and it meant a drop in salary. But he took it.

And about this time something else happened, just as crucial. He was given a book of photographs by Cartier-Bresson, *The Europeans*, and his eyes were opened. He decided to be a photographer. His father gave him a Leica and he started roaming the streets, trying to capture significant fragments of living. To make some extra money, he took portraits of actors; but that he did not enjoy. Then Keith Johnstone, who ran a mime class at the Court, suggested he take a few pictures of that. George Devine came along sometimes to talk about a subject dear to his heart: the use of the mask. And so the first picture in this book was taken, a touching and characteristic portrait of the man to whom we owe, more than to anyone else, the achievement of the Royal Court. The man to whom (as he put it) the theatre was a temple, not a whorehouse. It is the kind of portrait John Haynes takes best: a personality revealed in action, the artist exposed.

The conjunction of his two prime influences did not, however, lead John directly to taking pictures of plays. He got married – he met his wife Jane, an actress, when she was attending Keith Johnstone's class – and he had to earn a living. He decided to try journalism. For two years he worked as a staff photographer for *The Sunday Times*, where you were (in his words) 'out there in the front line, living on your nerves.' But the pursuit of politicians, strikers and headline personalities proved not much more congenial than the follow-spot at the Palace: John is neither a thruster nor a manipulator. There are times, though, when the theatre calls for persistence, insistence and a tough hide, so probably the experience was good for him. Anyway, when the Royal Court decided in 1971 to appoint a regular theatre photographer, he had enough confidence to

One of John Haynes' photographs of Ralph Richardson and John Gielgud in
David Storey's Home, *directed by Lindsay at the Royal Court in 1970.*

apply for the job. He got it. His first assignment was David Storey's *Home*,
which I was directing with that unequalled cast, a play with almost no
action and a great deal of poetry. John's pictures were simple, responsive,
unerring – the theatrical experience exactly. He had found his *métier*.

Photographers have a hard time in the theatre. Their opportunities, you
may think, are rich. What effects of lighting and decor offer themselves!
What expressive plasticity! What personalities, what emotions, what
moments of gaiety, pathos, violence! . . . Alas, all too often these apparently limitless possibilities create only frustration for the photographers of
theatre. They are there, and they must never forget it, for a practical purpose, generally one sufficiently defined by the word 'publicity'. Pictures
are wanted for the press – and will the artistes please stand a bit closer
together, otherwise those on the edges are likely to find themselves
cropped out of the group. Pictures are wanted for display outside the the-

atre, to entice passing trade. Pictures are wanted to satisfy the players, who naturally want to look good. Whether directors or managements value the photographer's contribution depends on how much they care about permanence in this most transient of the arts. Generally they don't care very much. (And they don't pay very much either.)

Time is the photographer's worst enemy. Usually they have to work in those tense, crowded hours between dress rehearsal and first performance, when tempers are short and nerves are strained. Nowadays they will be lucky if they are given a session to themselves on stage and with the actors, and if they are it will be too short – particularly if the production involves changes of scene and costume. No wonder the custom has grown more prevalent for the pictures to be taken during dress rehearsals, from the auditorium. This at least ensures authenticity, spontaneity. But there are dangers, too. More than one star has broken suddenly in the middle of a scene, peered angrily into the darkness where the photographer is busily clicking away, and shouted: 'Get that damned cameraman out of here!'

Most theatre photographers now – and John Haynes is no exception – work with 35mm cameras, hand-held most of the time, and with available light, i.e. the lighting designed for the production. They will very likely persuade the chief electrician to bump up his levels a bit, but gone are the days when every shot was carefully composed and specially lit. This is another aspect of the freedom won by the 1956 revolution, pioneered like so much else by the Royal Court. I remember vividly Julie Hamilton's pictures, daring now, of Angus Wilson's *The Mulberry Bush*, which opened the Court's first season. Full of life, informal and unposed, they were the first professional theatre pictures taken on 35mm I had ever seen – quite possibly they were the first altogether. They reflected brilliantly and refreshingly the new styles of writing and playing, direct, contemporary, unglossed, which were invading the stage. Gone was the shop-window elegance of grouping and posture which had come to reflect an, in the main, snobby and artificial West End style. This was a theatre in which a young photographer with Cartier-Bresson leanings could feel he had a place.

Admittedly there has been a small loss with the huge gain. We don't often get full-stage shots of contemporary productions, with the characters in their settings, as you would see them from a centre stall or the front of the circle. (There are only two, I think, in this book.) Today's photographers are not interested in such pictures, chiefly I suppose because newspapers would not print them. And it is worth remembering the special effect on theatre pictures of the general use of available light. Fast film can capture the actors satisfactorily enough; but there is rarely enough light on decor to record the stage picture as the audience sees it. Low-key images are the result, with the actors highlit in a more dramatic way than they are in performance. What we see is a concentration, an intensification of the theatrical moment.

The photographer's role in the theatre has, in fact, become more personal, more creative, less that of a recorder or a glamoriser. For *The Sunday Times* John Haynes worked as a journalist: he went out to find the pictures he had been ordered to get. When he returned to the Court he found himself expected to function as an artist, which fortunately he had been without exactly knowing it. From the start he was encouraged to take time, and he was lucky enough to be photographing the work of an author to whom he responded so deeply. The 'still, sad' (sometimes raucous) 'music of humanity' which is what makes *Home* such a great play, as well as the special genius of its performers, struck a chord in John which resounds in his photographs: and I would say the same of his pictures of *The Changing Room*, *Life Class* and *Early Days*. Indeed, his imagination was so stirred by this contact with David Storey's peculiarly Northern world of poetry that he set off north himself and made a lovely set of pictures which he showed in an exhibition at the Court. Nothing – and everything – to do with the theatre. Perhaps one day he will make a book of them.

John Haynes' photographs show, as any collection of stage pictures must, an extraordinary and attractive variety. But in the best of them there is always this acute, tender human response: he is not a pictorialist or a publicist, he is an artist. Of course this book is an anthology. John has enough pictures to fill these pages many times over; and there are many theatres in London where he did not work, many productions over these years which he was not invited to photograph. But not many of our finest players have escaped him. Here they nearly all are, holding the mirror up to our time and our nature with the accuracy and courage with which actors and actresses are so generously gifted. God bless them!

I have often wondered at the different images people have of the theatre, and the difference of their experience of it. It can speak with so many voices, such different accents. It can be trivial and it can be wise; it can soothe and it can disturb; it can flatter and it can teach. To one distinguished director, who was not speaking in anger, it is a 'whorehouse'. To George Devine it was a 'temple' – remembering that a temple is a place for joy as well as reverence. In all its variety, the London theatre seems to me to embody most distinctly these two traditions: the tradition of show and the tradition of truth. Some productions illustrate; critics call this 'conceptual theatre' and they like it because they find it easy to write about, bright pupils sitting down before exam papers. But some productions offer the challenge of feeling, of involvement. This is the theatre of experience, and it is not easy to write about. It is a theatre I recognise and honour. These pictures make me glad to have been a part of it.

John Gielgud

In *John Gielgud, a Celebration* by Robert Tanitch, 1987

NOTHING IN JOHN GIELGUD'S WONDERFUL CAREER IS MORE WONDERFUL, IT seems to me, or more exemplary, than his sanguine acceptance of the passing of time and his coming to friendly terms with whole new generations of writers, directors and fellow artists. Once I (strange to think) represented a young and impatiently critical new generation in the theatre. I had met John several times socially – and had always, I imagined, behaved with a modest discretion, calculated to show the great respect I felt for him. I had failed to understand that every actor, no matter how eminent, needs the reassurance of expressed approval: John, who has pride but no arrogance, was no exception. So I was astonished to be told by Grigori Kozintsev, the Russian director of *Hamlet* and *Lear* on film, of John's reaction on being shown the record of *The Ages of Man*, which I had given Kozintsev on a visit to Moscow. 'How extraordinary,' had been John's comment. 'He hates me.'

Of course I never hated John. I thought of him as a remote, distinguished planet, circling with a certain *hauteur*, above the contemporary struggle. At that time, I think it's fair to say, he regarded our Royal Court activities with suspicion. Nonetheless, I asked him to play Caesar at the Court, and I distinctly remember walking down Cowley Street on a dark evening and putting my carefully phrased invitation through his letterbox. I never received an answer. At the time I put this down to *his* reciprocal dislike of *me*, though John has since denied that he ever received my letter. On reflection, I have to believe him: no one could be more scrupulously courteous about correspondence than John. Anyway, I was in no way deterred from sending him *Home* when David Storey delivered his lovely play to the Royal Court.

Looking back, I realise that asking John to play in *Home* was an inspiration – not a calculation. David had specified two leading men in their late forties. But I felt that *Home* would only be understood and recognised if it was performed by actors of the greatest skill and stature. 'Let's try John Gielgud,' I said, and so we did. I shall never forget the smile, equally delighted and amazed, on the face of Gillian Diamond, when she strode into the directors' office the next day. 'Gielgud wants to do it! His agent says he loves the play, and he thinks it's terribly funny.'

John took it, just like that. He was by now completely transformed from the careful conservative who had advised Ralph Richardson not to do *Waiting for Godot*. In fact it was he who suggested Ralph Richardson.

'But do you think he will want to be directed?' I asked apprehensively. 'Oh yes,' John replied. 'He loves direction. As long as he can respect it.' Well, Ralph and I had a big drink and a convivial chat, and he agreed to do it. So did Dandy and Mona. And so began one of those uniquely happy, harmonious and fulfilling theatre experiences that happen, if one is lucky, once in a lifetime. The kind that forge friendships which last the rest of one's life.

We started with an extra week (beyond the statutory four) with John and Ralph alone on the Royal Court stage. We were joined by David Storey and we had a marvellous time, exploring the long dialogue, apparently so inconsequential but profoundly revealing, comic yet suggestive, with which the play begins. No working method could have been freer, more sensitive or imaginative, less affected by convention or technique than John's and Ralph's. Ralph would discuss perceptively with David, I would contribute on a more superficial level of theatrical effectiveness – and John would listen, suggest, and wait for the cuts. He did not mark these as most of us do, with pencil or crayon: he would call for a pair of scissors and cut them out. So that by the end of the week his script was in shreds and had to be reprinted. With rare wisdom – sometimes perhaps even rashly – John never seemed to mind losing a line. If anything, he is too respectful of his collaborators, too trusting. In the case of David Storey, of course, his respect was justified; his gracious confidence was lovely to see.

I remember an early run-through of *Home*. I was sitting in the Circle. John made his entrance, looked around, appreciated the day, sat down and crossed his legs. He noticed a piece of fluff on his trousers. Carefully he removed it. I caught my breath. I wish I could convey the absolute reality – and at the same time the supreme, musical elegance of that moment. I am sure he had done it before in rehearsal; but this was a run-through, and John had suddenly begun to act, or found himself acting. I looked down at my script: the direction was there: I had never particularly noticed it.

It is hard to express the sheer and absolute actor's genius of John Gielgud. Not his lyrical voice and perfection of phrasing – which became a trap of which he was very well aware. Not his great, inherited actor's intelligence (not intellect – John himself is always amused at the thought that he had been considered an intellectual actor. Intellectual actors are almost always bad actors.) John Gielgud is an actor of instinct, sensibility, emotion. His rhetoric is impeccable; but his moments of pure, exposed emotion are inexpressibly touching. In this, for me, lies the unique poetry of his playing.

David Storey

For a brochure on *In Celebration*, 1974

I HAVE ALWAYS BELIEVED IN LUCK. NOT GOOD LUCK OR BAD LUCK, ESPECIALLY, but Destiny. The 'Divinity which shapes our ends . . . ' It was certainly some Divinity of this kind which arranged my meeting with David Storey, the many effortless collaborations that have followed, my happy association with one of the most profound, poetic and feeling writers of our time.

I read about his first novel, *This Sporting Life*, before it was published – a description of its subject appeared in the literary section of a Sunday newspaper. I thought it sounded as though it would make a good film, and one which I might be able to direct. I missed out, because the rights were bought by the Rank Organisation, who offered it to my friend Karel Reisz to direct. But Karel (and here came the luck) decided that he didn't want to direct anything at that particular moment. He suggested that he should produce *This Sporting Life*, with myself as director. To my astonishment the Rank Organisation agreed. We met David Storey to ask him if he would write the film script.

The extraordinary, often contradictory qualities of this man and artist made themselves immediately felt. He seemed very large and bulky (after all, he had played professional Rugby League), but also very gentle and rather shy. His diffidence went with an immense and effortless authority. He theorised eloquently about almost everything with apparent confidence; yet he was really sceptical of theories, most of all his own. He had the continual humour of the essentially serious man.

During the time of *This Sporting Life* (this was before he was a playwright), David used to theorise and discuss very much more than he will now. I learned a great deal from him. He had never written a film before, but he had an instinctive wisdom about the nature of the medium, its artistic laws. (He was a painter, of course, before he was a novelist; and he wrote poems

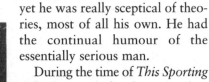

David Storey: 'An immense and effortless authority'.

as well as novels.) His sense of style was always completely integrated with his sense of what had to be expressed. The film, he insisted, must always be an experience for the audience, not an artifice or a construction, however brilliant, which they could stand outside of and admire. The feeling and the ideas, the technique and the content, could never be separated.

It was the same when David started writing plays. *In Celebration*, which was the first I directed, is a deeply felt, deeply understanding drama of family relationships. It is also a comedy, full of the kind of laughter that comes when we recognise the frailties and absurdities of our common humanity played out before us. It is also a play of ideas, rooted in its time, agonised with the problems which afflict all modern societies in which children have been educated beyond their parents, in which traditional ways and faiths have been destroyed, in which the generations find themselves locked in conflict, torn by conflicting urges of rejection and love.

I think that David Storey is unique among contemporary playwrights in this combination of intelligence and feeling. Sometimes the strength of his feeling, and its essential simplicity, has baffled intellectual critics, who feel safer with word-play than with poetry. But it does not baffle audiences. They respond with laughter and with tears to the truth of his vision, the pain of his insights. This is a deeply human art, one that questions and consoles. It is in the great tradition, very rare today.

Lindsay discussing the set of Stages *with playwright David Storey and designer Jocelyn Herbert.*

Lindsay 'flying the flag' on the set of Britannia Hospital, *1981.*

BRITISH CINEMA

A Possible Solution

Sequence 3, Spring 1948

TO VISIT A BRITISH FILM STUDIO TODAY – EVEN SO MODERN AND 'PROGRESSIVE' a studio as Pinewood – is a depressing experience. The organisation is very good: there is a superbly-indexed Art department, two big restaurants, capacious workshops in which plaster reproductions of various portions of Covent Garden Opera House are always being either erected or dismantled; and the stages are occupied by huge atmospheric sets in cunningly false perspective, on which are ceaselessly enacted scenes from the novels of Charles Dickens. Where, one asks, do the ideas come from? But the script department is represented only by Mr Gordon Wellesley, and by a filing cabinet with drawers marked 'Blanche Fury', 'The Blue Lagoon', 'London Belongs to Me', 'The Snow Goose' and 'Esther Waters'.

Various reasons for this stagnation, and for the deficiencies in even the best British films of the last few years, have been suggested: too much money, too much studio work, too many adaptations from novels. Yet none of these is satisfactory as a prime cause. It is true that films which cost a lot of money are not generally very good, but they are not always bad; to shoot in a studio can give a director immense advantages; some of the best, as well as some of the worst, films have been adapted from novels. The deficiencies are too fundamental to be explained by any reasons so superficial, or so particular; it is the attitude of film-makers generally that is responsible. Their films, despite many good intentions, obstinately remain factory products. This is largely because they are produced in factories.

Artists find it difficult to survive in large organisations, especially in large organisations which exist for the purpose of making money. The usual method in the cinema, however, is that the artist works as the salaried employee of a large corporation. This is the Hollywood system; and the most extraordinary thing about it is that a handful of great films has actually emerged from it, amongst fistfuls of tripe and a considerable quantity of good entertainment. But it is no wonder that directors have felt themselves fettered by the machine; some of them, as a result, have set up as independent producers, relying on the big corporations only to distribute their films. These director-producers have not, however, escaped; they have only staked out a claim for themselves inside the factory premises. They are allowed latitude, but they dare not assume too much. In England the experiment of Independent Producers has been an artistic, if not a commercial failure. Launder and Gilliatt, who reached the top through their brilliant script-writing, started with some fresh, really individual pictures – *Millions Like Us, Waterloo Road, The Rake's Progress* – but the killing pace of a non-stop assembly line has forced them to surrender. Their new films are both best-seller adaptations. Similarly Cineguild: *Take My Life* and *Blanche Fury* are both let-downs. There is every hope of *Oliver Twist*, but what of David Lean's future? After a long and apparently unsuccessful search for a good subject, he has chosen *The Snow Goose* as his next film. Second-rate novels can make first-rate films, but it is difficult to imagine this third-rate novelette emerging from Pinewood as anything but a highly proficient piece of hokum.

Nor have directors who have remained unassociated with any particular group been much luckier: Anthony Asquith has gone down in a bog of Rattigan, without so much as a cry for help; Thorold Dickinson has made nothing since *Men of Two Worlds*; the Boultings are at work on Chetham Strode (*The Guinea-Pig*). Of serious directors the only one still seriously at work seems to be Carol Reed.

From this generally unfavourable survey of the contemporary scene, certain exceptions must be made. Peter Ustinov has redeemed the errors of *School for Secrets* with a delightful version of *Vice Versa*; Charles Frank's gothic *Uncle Silas* was an enterprising, largely successful attempt to do something elegant and new. More seriously, Michael Balcon continues to produce one excellent film for every four or five mediocrities. But Ealing achieves its successes by aiming relatively low, and by eschewing experiment; on more ambitious subjects – *They Came to a City, Frieda* – it tends to fail. Sir Michael is not a M. Paulvé.

There is one way of making films which has not yet been mentioned – the way of independent, small-scale production. On occasions in the history of the cinema people who have wanted very much to make films of a certain kind have set out on their own, or with a few fellow-enthusiasts, and made them. When artists behave like this, they are known as avant-garde. The term tends to mislead. To most people avant-garde is synonymous with 'surrealist' – surrealist meaning something odd, fantastic, provoking usually the doubtful comment, 'well, it was different.' This is an inheritance from the French experimental productions of the twenties, the Freudian *Seashell and the Clergyman*, Cocteau's *Le Sang d'un Poète*, Buñuel's *Chien Andalou*. In the British cinema, there has been comparatively little activity in this direction. Our avant-garde was supplied in the thirties by the documentarians; Grierson's motives were formidably sociological, but many of his disciples showed themselves as stimulated by the purely aesthetic potentialities of the medium as by its propagandist power. They experimented, unpretentiously but successfully with new subjects, new techniques; poets wrote commentaries for them, real musicians composed their music. Experiments in feature films were far fewer:

337

Surprise: Harold Wilson, then president of the Board of Trade, visits Jean Simmons and Donald Houston on the set of The Blue Lagoon.

in 1938 James Mason with Roy and Pamela Kellino went on location with some film-stock and a silent camera and shot *I Met a Murderer* – an ordinary enough story with not a few crudities, but a worthwhile experiment all the same, which might have led to more than it did. More recently there was Clive Brook's delightful *On Approval*, the funniest British comedy ever made.

These films form an avant-garde in the widest sense; they are parallel with the Vigo films in France, with *La Maternelle*, which Jean Benoit-Levy and Marie Epstein made for almost nothing at a nursery school in a working-class district of Paris, with *Farrébique* (financed by *L'Ecran Français*, the French film magazine), and with the fine Italian films of the present day. Their limitations are obvious: they lack polish, film-stock is often bad, lighting variable, sets (where used) unconvincing. Yet they date less, or less damagingly, than more elaborate productions, because they have not compromised with the fashions and prejudices of their time; execution has followed from conception, not from the demands of box-office. They remain fresh, spontaneous, individual.

The problem is in a sense economic rather than artistic. It is today impossible to make films which will appeal to a moronic mass-audience (critics should be compelled to spend their Sunday evenings sitting in front of cinema queues, just looking at them), and at the same time be good. The best films of the commercial cinema, whose excellence is limited enough anyway, are not generally popular. If artists are to be free to make films about what they like, as they like, they must make them cheaply. It is hardly the critic's job to consider just what sort of films should be made under these circumstances. We may feel that experiments in surrealism, expressionism and all the rest of it are not exactly what is needed; we may feel that film-makers should get out of the studios and into the lives of the people. But it is idle to specify, and dangerous at this stage to discourage, experiment in any direction. What is required is a cinema in which people can make films with as much freedom as if they were writing poems, painting pictures or composing string quartets. Our avant-garde must number amongst its influences films as various as *L'Idée*, *The Seashell and the Clergyman*, *Song of Ceylon*, *L'Atalante*, *The Plow that Broke the Plains*, *Sciuscia*.

Granted the need, how far are we justified in hoping that films like this will or can be made? That the talent and the ambition is not there it is impossible to believe. During the thirties young people who were seriously interested in the cinema tended to go into documentaries, and since documentary-makers believed in the importance of their job and were on the whole given a great deal of freedom, the results were very good. But today things are not the same. Fewer of us are any longer able to summon up that ardent, proselytising enthusiasm for social democracy which was the inspiration of the documentary movement. 'It is worth recalling,' writes Grierson, 'that the British documentary movement began not so much in affection for film *per se* as in affection for national education. If I am to be counted as the founder and leader of the movement, its origins certainly lay in sociological rather than aesthetic aims.' Again, rather gruesomely (he approves the attitude he is describing), 'you may not be so interested in the individual. You may think that the individual life is no longer capable of cross-sectioning reality. You may believe that its particular belly-aches are of no consequence in a world which complex and impersonal forces command, and conclude that the individual as a self-sufficient dramatic figure is outmoded.'

Against this attitude most (though not all) of us have reacted, and have come to realise more and more that the particular belly-aches of the individual life remain of the extremist importance, that they affect society as much as society influences them. Add to this the disillusion which it is impossible not to feel when we look back on many of those films made so earnestly, with such high hopes (*World of Plenty? Land of Promise?*), and the lessened enthusiasm for documentary becomes understandable enough. Also, of course, documentarians are now civil servants: as a result good scripts are pigeon-holed for years before they are made, and films are held up for years before they are seen. The urgency as well as the enthusiasm has gone out of things.

Enthusiasts today, then, aspire to features. But, as we have seen, the big producers do not want young people with fresh ideas, they want middle-aged hacks who can do a slick job of adaptation at short notice. Art comes in with the trimmings (music by William Walton, cobwebs by Cecil Beaton).

There is no safe and easy way out of this dilemma. There is only the impossibly difficult way of independent, small-scale production. Just how far it will be possible for starless, avant-garde films to recover their costs it is difficult to say. The threatened shortage of American features may help – British quickie production is already booming, and although distributors generally prefer bad films, there is always the possibility that a few good ones might slip in by mistake, especially those like *I Met a Murderer* whose subject and approach is relatively conventional. 'Specialist' cinemas might book more experimental productions; film societies might even be persuaded to take a day off from appreciating the long-canonised masters of the past to encourage aspirants of the present. All these sources of support are of course problematical. But they are all susceptible to exploitation; and if we are ever to have a good, live, serious cinema, the attempt will have to be made.

British Cinema: The Descending Spiral

Sequence 7, Spring 1949

PERHAPS THE TENDENCY IS TO TREAT THE FILMS OF ONE'S OWN COUNTRY LIKE its prophets – with less than justice. We are so close to them as, week by week, they churn out of the studios for our inspection; and now that their excellence has become almost an economic and political necessity (so that film criticism is regarded by many as a form of national service), the temptation to slash, to sneer rebelliously, is almost irresistible. This impulse to generalise hysterically from every boring quickie is one to be resisted. Although the highbrow critic may feel it his duty to attack these films as a dreary procession of lost opportunities (for inside every bad film there is a good one wildly signalling to be let out), he runs the risk of being confronted with the irrefutable argument that they make money, they fulfil their function.

There are, however, British film-makers who take a relatively dignified view of their vocation, and at the failure of their films, anyway, it is legitimate for the critic to express disappointment. And to survey the principal British films which have appeared during the past three months is to find them dispiritingly representative of the present state of the industry – at its most ambitious.

One of the chief disappointments has been the discovery that the impact of the documentary school on feature films has resulted in nothing more than a string of well-intentioned failures. Talk of schools and influences may be suspect as critical jargon; so indeed may the use of the word 'documentary' itself. It is a term that has been grossly overworked, and very often abused, ever since realism made its way cautiously into the British feature film in the early years of the War. It was not long before any director who shot outside the walls of a studio found himself labelled as 'documentary-influenced'. In some cases, perhaps, this was justifiable, in many others not. Launder and Gilliat, for instance, when they took scenes for *Millions Like Us* in a real factory, and partially deglamorised their leading players, were almost certainly not influenced by Grierson. It was inevitable that British features should become more realistic as a result of the War, but whether as a result it is legitimate to associate them with the movement which started with *Drifters*, and during the War gave us many feature-influenced documentaries, is questionable.

Nevertheless the movement existed, and exists; and there are a number of directors at work on feature films today who have sprung from it, or who testify their allegiance to it. Ian Dalrymple, Harry Watt, Jack Lee all produced or directed films for the Crown Film Unit; Charles Frend and Charles Crichton, although not raised in documentary, have made their sympathies clear in the films which they have so far directed for Ealing Studios. From such men we may expect films realistic in style, shot to a large extent on location, and with that awareness of social issues – the social-democratic bias – which has always been the inspiration of the documentary movement. One can think of many subjects on these lines which would afford exciting, stimulating material for the screen, especially today.

Yet somehow the exciting, stimulating films fail to materialise. In the last three months we have had three new films from Ealing: Crichton's *Another Shore*, Frend's *Scott of the Antarctic*, Watt's *Eureka Stockade*. None of them conforms to the pattern set by the wartime 'semi-documentaries'. The first is a contemporary whimsy, the second and third laborious historical reconstructions. They are alike, however, in their use – wherever possible – of actual locations, in their studious avoidance of the conventional vulgarities, in their painstaking surface realism. Less happily, they are alike also in their limitations.

Another Shore is an Irish comedy. A likeable, lethargic young Irishman (Robert Beatty, playing with charm, although miscast) dreams romantically of life on a South Sea Island, without work, without responsibilities. He spends his mornings in bed, and his days in the park, waiting for a rich old lady whom he can rescue from a heart attack. He falls in with a wealthy, toping eccentric, almost achieves his ambition, and ends up in the arms of a predatory blonde, betrayed to domesticity at the last. The film is not in any way an exercise in social morality, yet the flavour of documentary remains. It is full of romantically framed views of Dublin, statues low-angled against a filtered sky: these are echoes of the 'symphonic' films – the first sequence introduces us to Dublin early in the morning, gulls fluttering over the Liffey, clocks and statues silhouetted against the dawn. Rather abruptly we cut to the inevitable milk-delivery: doors open; feet hurry to work. Perhaps all this was intended as a humorous contrast to Gulliver-Shiels lying in bed, reading travel brochures. This is not the effect; the sequence merely appears pretty, self-conscious, irrelevant. After this false start, the film never really comes to life. Battling with an ill-contrived script, the characters are dutifully quaint but seldom funny; the emotional pitch of the film wavers, from satirical to sentimental. It is as though Crichton were inhibited from throwing himself unreservedly into his material; without finesse or true gaiety the picture proceeds with a sort of slogging conscientiousness – not the stuff of which fantasy is made.

Conscientiousness is again the keynote, of *Scott of the Antarctic* – a formidable subject, which Ealing has tackled with, as usual, the best of intentions. In the true spirit of semi-documentary, diaries were read, experts consulted, survivors and relatives interviewed. Actors were chosen who bore close physical resemblances to the members of Scott's expedition; Walter Meade, assigned to the script, had served for some time as H.M. Consul at Shiraz. Yet, as so often, conscientiousness turns out to be an insufficient virtue, and in every other respect the film is deficient. Technically it fails to convince; the early sequences are marred by ugly colour, bad sets and some unfortunate process shots. As the Discovery gets under way, atmosphere is continually broken by wild variations in colour as we cut from studio to location and back: the scenes in the New Zealand

dock – which have to be played without long shots – are similarly unconvincing. (It is only fair to mention that the last half of the film is technically far superior, with some superb matching of studio and location
scenes once the march to the Pole has begun.)

These defects are remedied by nothing in the script or the direction. The
script sticks as closely as possible to 'what actually happened', is too
episodic and very unimaginative. None of the characters is really established, though doubtless the façade of each is sufficiently authentic. Scott
himself, for example, is sketched as a man of charm, good natured, a reli-
able leader, a good platoon commander – not reconcilable with the austere, complex figure conjured up by the diaries. Each of the other members of his team is given a little scene in which to establish himself – Oates
with his horses, Wilson with his gramophone – but so conventionally are
these written that none of them, with the possible exception of Reginald
Beckwith as Bowers, emerges as a three-dimensional character. In the closing scenes the script relies more and more heavily on overlaid passages
from Scott's diary, a device which further lessens the immediacy of the
drama. Vitalised by no touch of imagination or poetry, no inherent sympathy in the handling, the dry bones of the epic remain skeletal.

An effect even more horribly dull is the sole achievement of *Eureka
Stockade*. It would be tedious to catalogue the faults of Harry Watt's second Australian film, since they are largely those already noted. The acting
is worse; less competent players are further handicapped by a worse written script, and negligible guidance from the director. Opening pompously
with the declaration that the history of mankind is the history of the struggle for freedom, the film's intentions are plainly inspirational. Purporting
to be a monument to the struggle for equality waged by the diggers in the
Australian goldfields, it presents a confused narrative of violence, agita-
tion and oppression. Obviously if such a story is to live, it must be given
humanity. Watt's film, partly through his direction, partly through the
script by himself and Walter Greenwood, is devoid of drama and characterisation. Technically also it is shaky, with toneless post-synchronising of
dialogue and photography only passable.

Like Harry Watt, Jack Lee also served his apprenticeship in documentary. His second feature film, *Once a Jolly Swagman*, bears witness to this
background. It follows the career of a young man from obscure tedium at
a factory bench to success on the speedway; his marriage to a nice girl, his
affair with a ritzy ex-fascist blonde, separation, the War, the return and the
final choice between a resumption of his career as a rider and a second
attempt to make a success of his marriage. This spread of years and events,
possible in a novel, does not suit the cinema. To cover it successfully would
demand a speed, grasp and conciseness that are beyond the capacities of

William Rose and Lee himself, who are together responsible for the script.

To his credit, Lee has taken evident pains to give authenticity to his film, and a genuine relation to the period in which it is set. Undoubtedly its best moments are more impressive than anything in the preceding films. The dirt-track scenes (excellently shot and edited) are exciting, and at moments even savage – the crowd shrieking for the blood of its favourites, vicariously stimulated by their danger. The handling, in the first half particularly, is not uninteresting: the lower-middle-class family is faithfully and sympathetically presented, much of the acting is excellent, some of the incidental detail shows intelligent observation – a queer figure jigging past the camera at a Mayfair party, a bored bureaucrat behind the desk of a Labour Exchange. But as the film proceeds, the lack of structure in the script becomes more apparent; the more controversial issues (the speedway racket, trade unionism, the Spanish Civil War) are dropped, and with feebler material Lee's lack of experience with dramatic narrative betrays itself. The War comes, with the usual newsreel shots; the War ends, but the film does not. The central character, despite good acting by Dirk Bogarde, ceases to make anything but a superficial impression, and the final return to speedway thrills is too late to revive interest more than momentarily. Lack of style, lack of shape has killed our belief; reality has been lost.

It is ironic that, for all their determination to avoid hokum, their sense of social and artistic responsibility, these directors end up making films whose predominant characteristic is their unreality. It is not that they lack an eye for realism, but that through inexperience or incapacity each shows inadequate grasp of what is even more important – the technique of drama. In varying degrees, particularly, their ability to characterise is weak. None of these three serious films is able to establish a convincing relationship between a man and a woman. Scott and his wife; Rafferty and the unhappy Miss Barrett: Bogarde and the sweetly, hopelessly refined Renée Asherson – these are novelette relationships, devoid of subtlety, or any feeling but a rosy-hued sentimentality.

Turning from these films to the most recent productions of our seasoned feature directors is like turning from the work of earnest amateurs to that of hardened professionals – the advantage being by no means wholly to the latter. David Lean's new film for Cineguild, for instance, has all the smooth ease, assurance and gloss of a first-class professional job; impeccably lit, luxuriously mounted, *The Passionate Friends* is glossed with as expensive a veneer as any MGM or Warner heavy. The direction, so explicit, so crisp, carves its way straight through an unnecessarily intricate script with a drive that it is impossible not to admire. Yet ultimately there is less interest, and certainly less charm, in Lean's picture than in either *Once a Jolly Swagman* or *Another Shore*. For a director who has announced that the creation of character is his primary aim, *The Passionate Friends* is indeed a deplorable piece of work. Its conventional story, of the girl who rejects her poor but honest lover for a sympathetic but unattractive moneybags, and then keeps wishing she hadn't, eliminates the only interesting features of the novel by H. G. Wells; even so, this need not have been an insuperable barrier to sensitive direction and playing. Yet none of the leading characters has any inner life, the dialogue abounds in bloodless clichés ('I'm sorry, I shouldn't have said that,' etc.) and though the handling is full of tricks, it is as lacking in genuine dramatic power as it is in emotion. The stars shine coldly: no minor character is allowed to excite our interest for a moment.

This is certainly not the case with *The Small Back Room*, in which there is hardly a bit-player without his close-up and his sharply revealing line. With this adaptation of Nigel Balchin's novel, Powell and Pressburger have produced their first work for London Films, and their best, in fact their only tolerable film since *I Know Where I'm Going*. Whatever one's estimate of Balchin as a novelist, the cinematic potentialities of his first two books are hardly contestable. In *The Small Back Room* he created with acidity and wit the tensions, corruptions, fatigues and excitements of secret research work in wartime; the story of the neurotic, self-torturing hero culminates in an episode of great excitement – the dismantling of an unknown German booby-trap, with the imminent expectation of death. Enough of all this is preserved to make the film version interesting – unfortunately one cannot use a more enthusiastic epithet. It is not merely that the Archers have watered down the book and changed its ending, releasing the squirrel from his cage; they spoil their film, disrupting the illusion, by over-emphasis, self-conscious indulgence in bright ideas. This applies not only to the unhappy essay in expressionism, in which Powell strives unsuccessfully to communicate the agonies of alcoholic craving with the aid of 'delirium'; music by Brian Easdale and a twenty-foot high whisky bottle designed by Hein Heckroth: other false touches abound. A Welsh doctor at the bedside of a dying soldier exhibits the quaint humour of the traditional stage Welshman; the young RE officer eyes the heroine with elephantine suggestiveness; an ATS girl emotes like a RADA student; close-ups constantly loom too large, humour is over-stressed and realism jerks sharply into caricature.

Nevertheless there are good things in the film – brilliant performances in supporting parts by Jack Hawkins, Cyril Cusack and Geoffrey Keene; several scenes are handled with imagination and excellently written; the climax is exciting. Most remarkable of all, the film succeeds in establishing a relationship between its hero and heroine (played with satisfying adequacy by David Farrar and Kathleen Byron) which is recognisably one between a man and a woman.

With one exception (*The History of Mr Polly* apart), the other recent British features have included nothing worth even adverse criticism. This is a state of affairs which cannot be relished by anybody, certainly not by critics, who are left with no alternative to sustained disparagement except constructive criticism.

The short-sighted policy which dictates short schedules, standardised sets, lighting and camerawork, standardised handling, overlooks the fact that good pictures – pictures which win the approval of the discriminating – are in the long run not only beneficial but necessary to the industry. Just as British films in the past have had to live down the reputation earned by their execrable predecessors, so the poor output of today is getting by largely on the prestige earned by films of the War period and the first year or so of peace. And unfortunately the fallacy has come to be generally accepted that 'prestige' (i.e. good) pictures must cost, and lose, millions.

That this is not so is proved by *The Small Voice*, directed by Fergus McDonnell for Anthony Havelock-Allan's new company, Constellation: Here is a British melodrama which avoids nearly all the usual pitfalls. There is no overplaying of minor parts, no cockney or regional 'humour', no slushy background music. On the positive side the film has excitement, atmosphere, interesting characterisation and good craftsmanship. Its central situation occurs when a playwright and his wife, an actress, return home after the last performance of one of his plays, in which she has been appearing; their marriage is on the rocks – the lame husband is hypersensitive, self-pitying, unreasonable, the wife tired and exasperated. Their home is chosen by three escaping convicts as a hide-out. The complexities of the situation are increased when a child in the house develops meningitis, and the leader of the convicts refuses to allow a doctor to be sent for.

One would not claim that the film extracts all possible tension from its subject. At times it seems almost to lean over backwards in its determination to avoid the crude and the obvious, and so to miss some of the excitement proper in what is after all a fundamentally melodramatic story. The climax is mishandled, with the emphasis suddenly switching from character to the familiar mechanics of suspense, and the end lapses rather sadly into cliché. In general, though, the screenplay (from Robert Westerby's novel) by Derek Neame and Julian Orde is well written, with good dialogue and no time wasted; the acting is of a high standard, particularly by James Donald as the playwright, and Harold Keel as the leader of the convicts – a firm, unsentimental performance of great promise. Camerawork (Stan Pavey) and editing are both admirable; the film moves slowly but always purposefully, with excellent grouping and some striking, not too ostentatious, use of deep focus. The credit for much of this is due, no doubt, to Fergus McDonnell, whose first picture this is after long experience in the cutting-room (he edited *The Way Ahead* and *Odd Man Out*). It is an auspicious debut: the lapses in tension are, one feels, due more to lack of experience than to lack of ability. And at least one scene in *The Small Voice*, where the playwright, intent on cracking the convict's nerve, plays him an ironically appropriate record ('The Gallows Song') on the gramophone, achieves considerable dramatic intensity.

Craftsmanship in British films today has come to be regarded as applying chiefly to set design, lighting and camerawork, slightly to direction, and not at all to writing. A justly proportioned film like *The Small Voice* emphasises the falsity of this view, which is responsible for the generally low quality of contemporary output. Young directors, young writers who might make the pictures which would win back the industry its reputation, are not being tried. Producers on the whole have neither the desire nor the capacity to pick fresh talent; preferring to play safe, they hasten British films on their way down the descending spiral.

There is need for new directors, but a far greater one for new writers. Although there are a few exceptional directors working in Britain today, and not a few promising or capable ones, time.and again their films break down, through clumsy dialogue, poverty of invention, lack of dramatic structure. It is creditable that directors should feel it necessary to participate in the scripting of their films, but useless if they are not writers themselves, or have no competent scriptwriters with whom to collaborate. *Eureka Stockade*, *The Passionate Friends*, *Once a Jolly Swagman*, were all written in part by their directors. Of the seven films discussed in this article, five were maimed from the start by their scripts.

With the business of making films as it is at present, a healthy art presupposes a healthy industry; and a healthy industry can only exist on producers of enterprise and foresight, on technicians (notice we forebear even to call them artists) who know their jobs, who can make films forcefully, concisely and entertainingly. Grant us this: then we can begin to ask for more.

The Studio That Begs to Differ

Film and Theatre Today: The European Scene, 1949

HOW MANY FILM-GOERS, IT WOULD BE INTERESTING TO KNOW, ARE AT ALL conscious of the studios which make the films they see; who watch with any interest for the trade-mark of the production company as it flashes on to the screen after the censor's certificate? American trade-marks are familiar to us all – Leo, the MGM lion, promising high-grade gloss and heavy production values; the Warner Brothers shield with its assurance that our more superficial emotions are about to undergo a tousing. In Britain, where production policies are less consistent, these insignia are apt to mean less. But there is at least one trade-mark, lettered and garlanded with austere good taste, which heralds films of a certain, fairly predictable quality.

Adapting the slogan coined for one of their films, Ealing may well be called 'the studio that begs to differ'. Of course, like any other producing organisation, Ealing aims first of all to make films which will pay their way; with this proviso, however, they tend to go further than some, and aim to produce films which are also good. In this they are not always successful, but at least there are certain temptations to which they do not succumb; the temptation, for instance, to appeal to the lowest common denominator, to cheapen and sensationalise. Respectable, responsible, cautiously enterprising, their films hang together, and invite survey as the fruit of a conscious, long-term policy.

Every plan presupposes a planner: an Ealing production, as we know it today, presupposes Sir Michael Balcon. It was through his arrival at Ealing in 1938 that the present policy of the studio became possible. Not that in 1938 films were a new thing at Ealing. Throughout the thirties it was the home of Basil Dean's ATP, where Victoria Hopper starred in *The Mill on the Floss* and *Lorna Doone*, and stage directors dabbled uninventively in a foreign medium. Farther back still, it was the site of one of the first glass-roofed studios in the country.

Balcon came to Ealing a veteran (though still a young) producer. Entering the industry after the First World War, he produced his first picture, *Woman to Woman*, in 1922; he founded Gainsborough Pictures and throughout the twenties and thirties was responsible for an enormous number of widely popular films – Ivor Novello in *The Rat* and *The Lodger*; *Journey's End*; *Sunshine Susie*; *Rome Express*; *I Was a Spy*; *Man of Aran*; vehicles for Jack Hulbert and Cicely Courtneidge, Jessie Matthews, George Arliss. As head of production at Gainsborough, and later at Gaumont-British as well, he became the most successful producer in the industry, if not the most celebrated. In 1936 he took charge of Metro-Goldwyn-Mayer production in Britain, and made *A Yank at Oxford*, after which he quarrelled violently with Louis B. Mayer and resigned. Factory methods of production, together with the hierarchic structure of the MGM organisation, made no appeal to Balcon's enterprising, candid and generally unassuming temperament.

Balcon's first production at his new studio was *The Gaunt Stranger*, a heavy-handed melodrama made on the cheap with Wilfrid Lawson and

'The studio that begs to differ': Ealing Studios in the 1950s.

Patricia Roc. But in 1939 there appeared a film which in many ways broke new ground. Produced on a budget which would nowadays be considered microscopic (well under £20,000) *There Ain't No Justice* dealt realistically and straightforwardly with the rackets and corruptions of professional boxing. Though the film made no money, it was a great critical success; and Balcon gave its young director, Pen Tennyson, another, similarly realistic subject to make. This was *The Proud Valley*, a film set in the Welsh coalfields. Neither *There Ain't No Justice* nor *The Proud Valley* could be called outstanding in themselves; but they showed a seriousness and a sincerity encouraging when viewed against the general background of hokum which was the British cinema of the thirties.

When the War came it was chiefly in this tradition of sentimental realism that Ealing advanced and flourished. Escapist entertainment was provided by a series of George Formby and Will Hay comedies, amusing on the whole though Will Hay at least never quite recaptured the robust vulgarity of those early masterpieces with Graham Moffatt and Moore Marriott. But the field which Ealing made peculiarly its own was the war film – the personal drama set against a faithfully recreated contemporary background. 'Semi-Documentary' became the slogan of the day. From the Documentary movement came Cavalcanti and Harry Watt (whose *Target for Tonight* made so great an impression in the early days of the War); from the cutting-rooms three young men graduated to directorship –

Robert Hamer, Charles Crichton and Charles Frend. A fourth, Basil Dearden, graduated from scriptwriting.

The tradition took a little time to develop. Ealing's first few war pictures – *Convoy* (Tennyson's last picture; he died on active service), *Ships with Wings*, *The Big Blockade* – failed to achieve any very satisfactory blend of fact with fiction. The first film to do this was *Next of Kin*, made by Thorold Dickinson; it was followed by *The Foreman Went to France*, the first really successful film in this genre to be directed by one of Balcon's 'discoveries' – in this case, Charles Frend. There followed, in rapid succession, films set against almost every kind of wartime background: the NFS. (*The Bells Go Down*), Desert Fighting (*Nine Men*), Invasion (*Went the Day Well?*), the campaign in Greece (*Greek Testament*), the Merchant Navy (*San Demetrio, London*), Air-Sea Rescue (*For Those in Peril*). But however varied their subjects, these films were all marked by certain similarities; by a relatively high standard of intelligence and taste in their writing, by the concern for realism and probability, and the general modesty of their approach. Perhaps the very limitations of resources (for Ealing is not a large studio) told in their favour, precluding ostentation and making craftsmanship always of prime importance.

In the later years of the War Ealing films became more varied in subject. *Fiddlers Three* (a peculiar comedy which transported three sailors to the Imperial Rome of Francis L. Sullivan and Frances Day); *Pink String and Sealing Wax*, and *Champagne Charlie* escaped with notable elegance to periods other than our own: *Dead of Night*, the 'portmanteau' ghost film (four directors, six stories in one) was another enterprising experiment in escapism. Apart from *The Overlanders*, made by Harry Watt for Ealing in Australia, whose connection with war was only indirect, Ealing's sole venture into contemporary realism in 1945 was the prisoner-of-war film, *The Captive Heart*.

To list the films produced by Ealing since the War is to be reminded of some of the British cinema's most enterprising (not always most successful) attempts to escape the vulgar and pedestrian. *Hue and Cry* and, more recently, *Another Shore*, deserted realism for fantasy; *Nicholas Nickleby*, *The Loves of Joanna Godden*, *Saraband for Dead Lovers*, were further tasteful excursions into period: *Frieda*, *It Always Rains on Sunday*, and *Against the Wind* were contemporary subjects, the first tentative efforts to tackle the 'good German' problem; the second, a lower-middle-class 'slice of life'; the third, a Resistance melodrama. Lately, with *Eureka Stockade* and *Scott of the Antarctic*, Ealing has been out amongst the Pioneers-O! celebrating deeds of enterprise and endurance which made the British Empire what it was. But it is some minor films – two comedies, *Whisky*

Galore and *Passport to Pimlico* (both making extensive use of locations), and a clever, gruesome fantasy, Hamer's *Kind Hearts and Coronets* – all characteristically enterprising, that promise more for the future.

It is a list remarkable first of all for its diversity; then also as testimony to the technical assurance which the studio has gained in the last ten years. Ealing films today are craftsmanlike and generally good to look at – the standard of camerawork and art direction is high, of direction and writing proficient. Partly this is due to the care and flair with which Balcon has encouraged new talent; partly also, no doubt, to the general atmosphere of co-operation, the sense of community which has somehow grown up at Ealing.

'The Studio with the Team Spirit.' One sees it written in huge capitals on one of the walls and though the inscription is a relic from the days of Basil Dean, it appears still to retain its justification. There is an active atmosphere about the place which makes it pleasanter to visit than most film studios; people there are ready and (more surprisingly) *able* to talk about the films they make as though they are the product of a policy, a conscious attitude towards the art and craft of cinema.

The almost universal slogan is 'semi-documentary'. 'Strictly speaking,' says Monja Danischewsky, once head of Ealing's publicity and now one of Balcon's associate producers, 'we've made only two films you could call pure documentaries – *San Demetrio, London* and *Scott of the Antarctic*. Both of these were founded on fact, and stick as closely as possible to actual incidents, actual words. But all our films tend to be realistic; even a romance like *Saraband for Dead Lovers* was founded on an authentic historical episode.' Associate producers and directors at Ealing are allowed a pretty free hand. 'Balcon relies on the enthusiasm of a director and associate producer to start a picture off. What other guarantee can there be, anyway, for a successful picture? There are no box-office formulae. Make the film you want to make, and trust to God that the public will like it.'

To any but the hypercritic, the bird's-eye view of Ealing, juxtaposed with any equivalent British production company, can hardly fail to be favourable. One would say that the people at Ealing are themselves conscious of this; it makes them, perhaps, a little too prone to congratulate themselves that they are not as other studios are.

For films, after all, have ultimately to be seen and judged one by one, each on its own merits, for what it sets out to do and for what it achieves. From this point of view strangely few of Ealing films – creditable tries though they usually are – are really successful. Perhaps this is the fate which is bound to overtake a studio which tries to have the best of both worlds: ultimately its films are liable to be neither debased enough to sat-

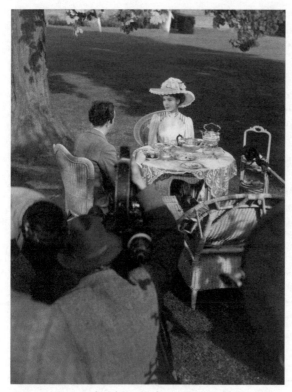

Dennis Price and Valerie Hobson during filming of Robert Hamer's Kind Hearts and Coronets.

isfy the cretin-millions, nor honest enough to satisfy the highly critical few. Ealing's biggest successes are achieved with the middle-brow audiences, who accept *The Captive Heart* as a faithful study of a prisoner-of-war camp, who find in a fundamentally dishonest picture like *Frieda* a courageous treatment of a contemporary problem. Intelligence and taste are Ealing virtues, but not passion. *Saraband for Dead Lovers* (a film generally underrated by the press) had much to commend it, yet its tragic, passionate story never came to life. To aim merely at *not* making a *Wicked Lady* is surely insufficiently ambitious.

'The best,' Sir Michael Balcon might reply, 'is the enemy of the good.' Perhaps. But then the good must also be the enemy of the best. Ultimately the negative virtues of good taste, bright posters and unvulgarity become even more annoying than a blatant and unapologetic commercialism; Richard Winnington's outburst in the *News Chronicle* against 'Ealing good taste' after the premiere of *Eureka Stockade* may well have surprised Sir Michael. It should not have, for it was inevitable. An alternative title to this survey might have been drawn, not from the slogan coined by Ealing to advertise *Hue and Cry*, but from the title of another of their films: *The Halfway House*. One hopes this will not be a final verdict.

Going It Alone: The British Documentarists

IT IS TEMPTING TO SEE THE BRITISH DOCUMENTARY FILM-MAKERS OF THE thirties as a tight little group of pioneers, a family almost, working together on common principles under the stern paternal guidance of John Grierson, believing in cinema not as entertainment or distraction, but as the 'creative treatment of actuality'. Grierson himself wrote in 1937: 'It is worth recalling that the British documentary group began not so much in affection for film *per se* as in affection for national education.' In other words, no fiction and no actors, but the romance of social advance, the inspiration of community and the technological society.

The truth is different. By the time War broke out, Grierson had vanished from the scene to Canada, where he conceived, founded and guided a whole new national cinema, through his invention of the Canadian National Film Board. The GPO Film Unit was now being run by the French-Brazilian Cavalcanti, much less of an idealogue, much more of an artist than Grierson, with a group of talented young men including the turbulent, rough-edged Harry Watt. Watt, a Scotsman, had already distinguished himself with the classic *Nightmail*, on which he collaborated with Basil Wright, and *North Sea*, a vivid and exciting picture of fishermen out in the Atlantic from Aberdeen. He didn't have much time for Grierson or his theories: his instinct was for drama. Humphrey Jennings and Pat Jackson were his young colleagues, chafing for chances.

Britain was at war, but nothing much happened. A Ministry of Information was formed and clearly had no idea how to use the film-makers, beyond changing the GPO into the Crown Film Unit. In fact, the first wartime 'documentary' came from the feature industry – a propaganda piece called *The Lion Has Wings*, flung together by Alexander Korda, in a rush of patriotism. This featured a prestigious cluster of actors, and some appalling dialogue. (Merle Oberon to Ralph Richardson: 'We must keep our land, darling – we must keep our freedom. We must fight for the things we believe in – truth and beauty . . . and kindness.') Grierson, perhaps feeling guilty from afar, spoke respectfully of *The Lion Has Wings* – 'This work of film documentation was Britain actually at war, zooming and roaring above the clouds.' But the intemperate Harry Watt called it 'a ghastly, bloody film', more accurately.

'Nothing happened for six weeks,' Watt told Elizabeth Sussex.* 'We sat on our backsides looking out of the window, watching the tarts in

353

Savile Row . . . Then Cavalcanti took it upon himself to send us out . . .'
They went out and shot a record film called *The First Days*, a kind of cinematic scrap-book of London at the beginning of the War. They all shot
material, and although there is no real shape, there is charm and wit and
feeling in the picture of evacuees and young recruits: Londoners in their
braces, filling sandbags: a little group on a suburban street, gathered
round a car-radio to hear Chamberlain announce the outbreak of War:
the poetry and pathos of plain, ordinary faces confronting catastrophe
that Jennings particularly was to make memorable in later work.

The same humane, characteristically English accent distinguishes further early war films from Crown: *Squadron 992* (about the barrage balloon units*), Dover Frontline* and *Christmas Under Fire*. The Blitz came,
and the whole unit collaborated on another picture under Watt's overall
direction: *Britain Can Take It*. This moving account of a night of raids,
from sunset to sunrise, with its theme of endurance and resilience, was
given a commentary by the American journalist Quentin Reynolds, and
proved extremely successful in exciting sympathy and support in the
USA. Here again there is a sharpness and sensitivity of observation, as
well as humour and understatement, far more effective than rhetoric,
which often take the picture beyond record into poetry.

The Crown Film Unit was soon going out beyond the home front, to
bring to people at home the feel of the shooting war. *Merchant Seamen*,
Men of the Lightship, *Coastal Command* – the titles tell the stories.
Particularly stirring was Harry Watt's *Target for Tonight* in 1941. 'We
were getting very tired of the "taking it" angle,' Watt has recalled, so it
was decided to make a film about the war which Bomber Command was
taking into the heartland of Germany. Simple, unpretentious and dramatic, this tells the story of a typical night raid, from the photo-recon-
naissance which provides the planners with the necessary information, to
the return of 'F' for Freddie, limping home injured to land in heavy fog.

Watt did not use actors. A preface announces: 'Each part is played by
the actual man or woman who does the job.' But sets were constructed,
the pilots' changing room was 'in a little subsidiary studio in Elstree', and
the huge Bomber Command control was designed by Edward Carrick,
and built at Denham. A model was used to show the bombs landing on
railway stockyards; and actors (or soldiers) played German anti-aircraft
gunners. Dialogue was written, and generally played with great natural-
ness and modesty by the airmen. The result was a film which caught most
powerfully the courage and undemonstrative resolution of the RAF.
Making his report at the end, pipe in mouth, the pilot apologises with the
lightest of ironies, 'I'm afraid I didn't see very much. I was rather busy at
the time.' There is nothing affected about the understatement: it has the

dignity of truth, and it still has the power to move.

Target for Tonight, dramatically constructed, shows how far Crown – and particularly Harry Watt – had diverged from Griersonian principle. Pat Jackson showed a similar inclination towards the fictional with *Western Approaches* in 1944. This was the ambitious story of an Atlantic convoy, and a boat-load of survivors from a torpedoed merchantman. Perhaps it was too ambitious, for the result somehow lacks the simple conviction of Watt's picture. Again the characters are played by 'real' seamen, but the story, involving staged scenes on a U-boat, a melodramatic climax and a last-minute rescue, smacks too strongly of artifice. And Jack Cardiff's accomplished colour photography lacks the simple black-and-white authenticity of *Target for Tonight*. Perhaps here documentary was edging too close to the theatrical.

The third of these young men who sat watching the tarts in Savile Row in September 1939 had little in common with the fictional bent of Watt and Pat Jackson. Humphrey Jennings had an approach entirely his own, and one which he developed through a series of wartime films, until he had become by far the most individual and the most imaginatively powerful of the documentary directors. *Heart of Britain* was the first of these in 1940, a somewhat tentative portrait-in-miniature of the North of England at war, lyrical in feeling, personal in style. The same could be said of *Words for Battle*, which followed, in which Jennings used a collection of literary texts, complemented by images of great beauty and originality, to celebrate the national theme. *Listen to Britain* (1941) developed the style with sounds and images alone, wonderfully evocative in its impression of a Britain at war. This, perhaps Jennings' most completely successful work, got him into trouble with his colleagues, suspicious of the 'arty' and the 'intellectual'. (Reviewing it in *The Spectator*, Edgar Anstey wrote, 'the rarest piece of fiddling since the days of Nero. It will be a disaster if this film is sent overseas.') *Fires Were Started* was more safely recognisable in genre (though no less original) – a masterly tribute to London's Fire Service, strongly affectionate, intensely poetic, the 'public film' at its most creative. And the lovely sequence closes with *A Diary for Timothy*, a tender, closely-wrought impressionist chronicle of the last year of the War.

Humphrey Jennings made more films before his tragic death in 1950 at the age of 43, but none of them really achieved the intensity of his wartime work. His colleagues were perhaps right to suspect him of aestheticism: he was certainly an intellectual. But in his war films at least he proved himself an artist, with a power of communication that has survived undiminished and which has won a place for him in the history of the British cinema (and not just the documentary cinema) all his own.

Of course, to pick out a few titles like this is to give a misleading impression of the documentary movement's contribution to Britain's wartime effort. Of great practical value, for instance, and certainly closer to Grierson's ideas, were the torrent of films produced by Basil Wright (who unfortunately spent the war years producing instead of directing) and Edgar Anstey at Film Centre – which Grierson himself had set up when he left the GPO in 1937. There were instructional films for Civil Defence, for the Fire Service, for agriculture, for the Ministry of Labour. Other units produced films for the forces, for the hospital services, for the Ministry of Information. The MOI distributed free to cinemas a new five-minute subject every week, which meant that documentaries were now reaching audiences of over twenty million people. So a vast new public was introduced and accustomed to the idea of a cinema of fact rather than of fantasy.

So did another highly successful genre: the compilation film. One of the first of these, *Wavell's 30,000* showed the British advance into Libya in 1942. Cavalcanti (now at Ealing as a feature producer) supervised a satirical demolition of Mussolini, *Yellow Caesar* (1941). And the victorious campaigns from Africa to the Far East to the Second Front were celebrated in a series of fine compilations: *Desert Victory, Tunisian Victory, Burma Victory* and *The True Glory*. Photographed with skill and daring, edited with outstanding craftmanship, these productions of the Service Film Units showed classic documentary techniques spreading beyond Crown to inspire a whole new generation of film-makers.

Compilation provided a basis of method for another highly individual film-maker, one of the most talented mavericks of the British documentary movement. Paul Rotha was an early member of the Grierson group, but his style and viewpoint were always firmly his own. Rotha set up his own unit in 1941 with the resolution not to try to compete with Crown on battlefield subjects but to 'make films about what was happening in Britain under the influence of a World War'. This resulted in a flow of films about public health, schools, day nurseries, education. Then came a larger inspiration. Together with the writer Eric Knight, Rotha conceived the idea of a film about the problem of world food – a brave attempt to initiate debate and spread knowledge on a subject which was going to be a matter of life or death to millions in the post-War world. It was partly the nature of the subject, and partly the need for economy in time and money, that dictated the style of *The World of Plenty*. A hard-hitting script, uncompromising in its argument, as well as in its statistics, was the blueprint for a powerfully effective montage of library material: a commentary of argument was provided by actors' voices, as well as interviews with authorities of the distinction of Sir John Boyd-Orr, the nutritionist. If Rotha's plea for a world food plan, based on the right of man to eat, failed to achieve its object, the fault was certainly not in *The World of*

Plenty. Documentary could lead, enlighten, even inspire. It could not work miracles.

What did it all mean?

It was Rotha – often prickly, always outspoken – who said of the documentary movement generally: 'I don't think the films themselves are the least bit important. What is important is the sort of spirit which lay behind them.' Perhaps this reflects the anti-art impatience which, from Grierson down, seemed so often and so unnecessarily to reflect documentary thinking. In any case, it plays down the achievement unnecessarily. It is true that not too much of the documentary output survives today on its own terms – *Song of Ceylon, Nightmail, London Can Take It*, perhaps *Target for Tonight*, Jennings from *Words for Battle* to *A Diary for Timothy*, probably a handful more – but this was work that fulfilled an honourable function in its day, and that still illuminates the moment of history that produced it.

Just how influential these films were on the other British cinema is another question. During the War days there were certainly instances where feature film-makers profited from the experience and the understanding of the documentarists. Rotha claims that *Night Shift*, made by his Unit about women working in a Welsh factory, inspired the Launder-Gilliat *Millions Like Us*; Carol Reed's *The Way Ahead* was developed out of an army training film called *The New Lot*; and Basil Wright remembers how Noel Coward studied wartime documentaries when he was scripting *In Which We Serve*. Films like *San Demetrio, London,* too, and Asquith's *We Dive at Dawn*, were certainly affected by the documentary tradition.

But it was not a lasting influence. Documentary directors like Harry Watt, Pat Jackson and Jack Lee, who went across to features, hardly managed to make much of a dint in established tradition; and Paul Rotha had a hard time as an independent producer of his own features. Jennings never made a fiction film, and on the evidence of dramatised documentaries like *The Silent Village* and *The Cumberland Story*, would not have been very successful if he had. Cavalcanti claimed to Elizabeth Sussex that 'perhaps the most important result of the documentary movement' was the imposition of workers 'as dignified human beings' on a British cinema in which the working classes had traditionally been considered as fit for nothing more than comic relief. But it is interesting to find exactly the same charge being levelled, ten years after the end of the War, by the Free Cinema group.

The documentary achievement in wartime was to perform a worthy service and to make some fine films, not to change things. Nor did the movement go forward into peace-time with much vitality. Perhaps one reason was that, having spent the thirties as anti-establishment dissidents,

357

the survivors found that the War had turned them into propagandists for tradition. They were certainly no longer in any sense radical. Perhaps, too, the scorn for 'intellect' and 'art', which had once signified a healthy impatience with pretension, had become too much of an excuse for complacency. When Churchill's Conservative government ungratefully and unimaginatively disbanded the Crown Film Unit in January 1952, no one seemed to really care. Perhaps the chapter had already ended.

The Rise and Fall of British Documentary by Elizabeth Sussex (University of California Press). I have taken most of my quotations from this invaluable compilation.

Only Connect: Some Aspects of the Work of Humphrey Jennings

Sight and Sound, April-June 1953

IT IS DIFFICULT TO WRITE ANYTHING BUT PERSONALLY ABOUT THE FILMS OF Humphrey Jennings. This is not, of course, to say that a full and documented account of his work in the cinema would not be of the greatest interest: anyone who undertook such a study would certainly merit our gratitude. But the sources are diffuse. Friends and colleagues would have to be sought out and questioned; poems and paintings tracked down; and, above all, the close texture of the films themselves would have to be exhaustively examined. My aim must be more modest, merely hoping to stimulate by offering some quite personal reactions, and by trying to explain why I think these pictures are so good.

Jennings' films are all documentaries, all made firmly within the framework of the British documentary movement. This fact ought not to strike a chill, for surely 'the creative interpretation of actuality' should suggest an exciting, endlessly intriguing use of the cinema; and yet it must be admitted that the overtones of the term are not immediately attractive. Indeed, it comes as something of a surprise to learn that this unique and fascinating artist was from the beginning of his career in films an inside member of Grierson's GPO Unit (with which he first worked in 1934), and made all his best films as official, sponsored propaganda during the Second World War. His subjects were thus, at least on the surface, the common ones, yet his manner of expression was always individual, and became more and more so. It was a style that bore the closest possible relationship to his theme – to that aspect of his subjects which his particular vision caused him consistently to stress. It was, that is to say, a poetic style. In fact it might reasonably be contended that Humphrey Jennings is the only real poet the British cinema has yet produced.

He started directing films in 1939 (we may leave out of account an insignificant experiment in 1935, in collaboration with Len Lye); and the date is significant, for it was the War that fertilised his talent and created the conditions in which his best work was produced. Watching one of Jennings' early pictures, *Speaking from America*, which was made to explain the workings of the transatlantic radio-telephone system, one would hardly suspect the personal qualities that characterise the pictures he was making only a short while later. There seemed to have been more evidence of these in *Spare Time*, a film on the use of leisure among industrial workers: a mordant sequence of a carnival procession, drab and shoddy, in a Northern city aroused the wrath of more orthodox documentarians, and Basil Wright has mentioned other scenes more sympathetically shot – 'the pigeon-fancier, the "lurcher"-loving collier and the choir rehearsal are all important clues to Humphrey's development.' Certainly such an affectionate response to simple pleasure is more characteristic of Jennings' later work than any emphasis of satire.

If there had been no War, though, could that development ever have taken place? Humphrey Jennings was never happy with narrowly propagandist subjects, any more than he was with the technical exposition of *Speaking from America*. But in wartime people become important, and observation of them is regarded in itself as a justifiable subject for filming, without any more specific 'selling angle' than their sturdiness of spirit. Happily, this was the right subject for Jennings. With Cavalcanti, Harry Watt and Pat Jackson he made *The First Days*, a picture of life on the home front in the early months of the War. On his own, he then directed *Spring Offensive*, about farming and the new development of agricultural land in the Eastern counties; in 1940 he worked again with Harry Watt on *London Can Take It*, another picture of the home front; and in 1942, with *Heart of Britain*, he showed something of the way in which the people of Northern industrial Britain were meeting the challenge of war.

These films did their jobs well, and social historians of the future will find in them much that makes vivid the atmosphere and manners of their period. Ordinary people are sharply glimpsed in them, and the ordinary sounds that were part of the fabric of their lives reinforce the glimpses and sometimes comment on them: a lorry-load of youthful conscripts speeds down the road in blessed ignorance of the future, as a jaunty singer gives out 'We're going to hang out our washing on the Siegfried line.' In the films which Jennings made in collaboration, it is risky, of course, to draw attention too certainly to any particular feature as being his: yet here and there are images and effects which unmistakably betray his sensibility. Immense women knitting furiously for the troops; a couple of cockney mothers commenting to each other on the quietness of the streets now that the children have gone; the King and Queen unostentatiously shown inspecting the air raid damage in their own back garden. *Spring Offensive* is less sure in its touch, rather awkward in its staged conversations and rather over-elaborate in its images. *Heart of Britain* plainly offered a subject that Jennings found more congenial. Again the sense of human contact is direct: a steel-worker discussing his ARP duty with his mate, a sturdy matron of the WVS looking straight at us through the camera as she touchingly describes her pride at being able to help the rescue workers, if only by serving cups of tea. And along with these plain, spontaneous encounters came telling shots of landscape and background, amplifying and reinforcing. A style, in fact, is being hammered out in these films; a style based on a peculiar intimacy of observation, a fascination with the commonplace thing or person that is significant precisely because it is commonplace, and with the whole pattern that can emerge when such commonplace, significant things and people are fitted together in the right order.

Although it is evident that the imagination at work in all these early pictures is instinctively a cinematic one, in none of them does one feel that the imagination is working with absolute freedom. All the films are accompanied by commentaries, in some cases crudely propagandist, in others serviceable and decent enough, but almost consistently these off-screen words clog and impede the progress of the picture. The images are so justly chosen, and so explicitly assembled, that there is nothing for the commentator to say. The effect – particularly if we have Jennings' later achievements in mind – is cramped. The material is there, the elements are assembled; but the fusion does not take place that alone can create the poetic whole that is greater than the sum of its parts. And then comes the last sequence of *Heart of Britain*. The Huddersfield Choral Society rises before Malcolm Sargent, and the homely, buxom housewives, the black-coated workers, and the men from the mills burst into the 'Hallelujah Chorus'. The sound of their singing continues, and we see landscapes and noble buildings, and then a factory where bombers are being built. Back and forth go these contrasting, conjunctive images, until the music broadens out to its conclusion, the roar of engines joins in, and the bombers take off. The sequence is not a long one, and there are unfortunate intrusions from the commentator, but the effect is extraordinary, and the implications obvious. Jennings has found his style.

Words for Battle, Listen to Britain, Fires Were Started, A Diary for Timothy. To the enthusiast for Jennings these titles have a ring which makes it a pleasure simply to speak them, or to set them down in writing: for these are the films in which, between 1941 and 1945, we can see that completely individual style developing from tentative discovery and experiment to mature certainty. They are all films of Britain at war, and yet their feeling is never, or almost never, warlike. They are committed to the War – for all his sensibility there does not seem to have been anything of the pacifist about Jennings – but their real inspiration is pride, an unaggressive pride in the courage and doggedness of ordinary British people. Kathleen Raine, a friend of Jennings and his contemporary at Cambridge, has written: 'What counted for Humphrey was the expression, by certain people, of the ever-growing spirit of man; and, in particular, of the spirit of England.' It is easy to see how the atmosphere of the country at war could stimulate and inspire an artist so bent. For it is at such a time that the spirit of a country becomes manifest, the sense of tradition and community sharpened as (alas) it rarely is in time of peace. 'He sought therefore for a public imagery, a public poetry.' In a country at war we are all members one of another, in a sense that is obvious to the least spiritually minded.

'Only connect.' It is surely no coincidence that Jennings chose for his writer on *A Diary for Timothy* the wise and kindly humanist who had placed that epigraph on the title page of his best novel. The phrase at any rate is apt to describe not merely the film on which Jennings worked with E. M. Forster, but this whole series of pictures which he made during the War. He had a mind that delighted in simile and the unexpected relationship. ('It was he,' wrote Grierson, 'who discovered the Louis Quinze properties of a Lyons' swiss roll.') On a deeper level, he loved to link one event with another, the past with the present, person to person. Thus the theme of *Words for Battle* is the interpretation of great poems of the past through events of the present – a somewhat artificial idea, though brilliantly executed. It is perhaps significant, though, that the film springs to a new kind of life altogether in its last sequence, as the words of Lincoln at Gettysburg are followed by the clatter of tanks driving into Parliament Square past the Lincoln statue; the sound of the tanks merges in turn into the grand music of Handel, and suddenly the camera is following a succession of men and women in uniform, striding along the pavement cheery and casual, endowed by the music, by the urgent rhythm of the cutting, and by the solemnity of what has gone before (to which we feel they are heirs) with an astonishing and breathtaking dignity, a mortal splendour.

As if taking its cue from the success of this wonderful passage, *Listen to Britain* dispenses with commentary altogether. Here the subject is simply the sights and sound of wartime Britain over a period of some 24 hours. To people who have seen the film it is difficult to describe its fascination – something quite apart from its purely nostalgic appeal to anyone who lived through those years in this country. The picture is a stylistic triumph (Jennings shared the credit with his editor, Steward McAllister), a succession of marvellously evocative images freely linked by contrasting and complementary sounds; and yet it is not for its quality of form that one remembers it most warmly, but for the continuous sensitivity of its human regard. It is a fresh and loving eye that Jennings turns on to those Canadian soldiers, singing to an accordion while away a long train journey; or on to that jolly factory girl singing 'Yes, My Darling Daughter' at her machine; or on to the crowded floor of the Blackpool Tower Ballroom; or the beautiful, sad-faced woman who is singing 'The Ash Grove' at an ambulance station piano. Emotion in fact (it is something one often forgets) can be conveyed as unmistakably through the working of a film camera as by the manipulation of pen or paint brush. To Jennings this was a transfigured landscape, and he recorded its transfiguration on film.

The latter two of these four films, *Fires Were Started* and *A Diary for Timothy*, are more ambitious in conception; the second runs for about 40 minutes, and the first is a full-length 'feature-documentary'. One's opinion as to which of them is Jennings' masterpiece is likely to vary according to which of them one has most recently seen. *Fires Were Started* (made in 1943) is a story of one particular unit of the National Fire Service during one particular day and night in the middle of the London Blitz: in the morning the men leave their homes and civil occupations, their taxi-cabs, newspaper shops, advertising agencies, to start their tour of duty; a new recruit arrives and is shown the ropes; warning comes in that a heavy attack is expected; night falls and the alarms begin to wail; the unit is called out to action at a riverside warehouse, where fire threatens an ammunition ship drawn up at the wharf; the fire is mastered; a man is lost; the ship sails with the morning tide. In outline it is the simplest of pictures; in treatment it is of the greatest subtlety, richly poetic in feeling, intense with tenderness and admiration for the unassuming heroes whom it honours. Yet it is not merely the members of the unit who are given this depth and dignity of treatment. Somehow every character we see, however briefly, is made to stand out sharply and memorably in his or her own right: the brisk and cheery girl who arrives with the dawn on the site of the fire to serve tea to the men from her mobile canteen; a girl in the control room forced under her desk by a near-miss, and apologising down the telephone which she still holds in her hand as she picks herself up; two iso-

Fires Were Started: *'intense with tenderness and admiration for its heroes.'*

lated aircraft-spotters watching the flames of London miles away through the darkness. No other British film made during the War, documentary or feature, achieved such a continuous and poignant truthfulness, or treated the subject of men at war with such a sense of its incidental glories and its essential tragedy.

The idea of connection, by contrast and juxtaposition, is always present in *Fires Were Started* – never more powerfully than in the beautiful closing sequence, where the fireman's sad funeral is intercut against the ammunition ship moving off down the river – but its general movement necessarily conforms to the basis of narrative. *A Diary for Timothy*, on the other hand, is constructed entirely to a pattern of relationships and contrasts, endlessly varying, yet each one contributing to the rounded poetic statement of the whole. It is a picture of the last year of the War, as it was lived through by people in Britain; at the start a baby, Timothy, is born, and it is to him that the film is directed. Four representative characters are picked out (if we except Tim himself and his mother, to both of whom we periodically return); an engine driver, a farmer, a Welsh miner and a wounded fighter pilot. But the story is by no means restricted to scenes involving these; with dazzling virtuosity, linking detail to detail by continuously striking associations of image, sound, music and comment, the film ranges freely over the life of the nation, connecting and connecting. National tragedies and personal tragedies, individual happinesses and particular beauties are woven together in a design of the utmost complexity: the miner is injured in a fall at the coal face, the fighter pilot gets better and goes back to his unit, the Arnhem strike fails, Myra Hess plays Beethoven at the National Gallery, bombs fall over Germany, and Tim yawns in his cot.

Such an apparently haphazard selection of details could mean nothing or everything. Some idea of the poetic method by which Jennings gave the whole picture its continual sense of emotion and significance may perhaps be given by the sequence analysed and illustrated here, but of course only the film can really speak for itself. The difficulty of writing about such a film, of disengaging in the memory the particular images and sounds (sounds moreover which are constantly overlapping and mixing with each other) from the overall design has been remarked on by Dilys Powell: 'It is the general impression which remains; only with an effort do you separate the part from the whole . . . the communication is always through a multitude of tiny impressions, none in isolation particularly memorable.' Only with the last point would one disagree. *A Diary for Timothy* is so tensely constructed, its progression is so swift and compulsive, its associations and implications so multifarious, that it is almost impossible, at least for the first few viewings, to catch and hold on to particular impressions. Yet the impressions themselves are rarely unmemorable, not merely for their splendid pictorial quality, but for the intimate and loving observation of people, the devoted concentration on the gestures and expressions, the details of dress or behaviour that distinguish each unique human being from another. Not least among the virtues that distinguish Jennings from almost all British film-makers is his respect for personality, his freedom from the inhibitions of class-consciousness, his inability to patronise or merely to use the people in his films. Jennings' people are ends in themselves.

Other films were made by Jennings during the War, and more after it, up to his tragic death in 1950; but I have chosen to concentrate on what I feel to be his best work, most valuable to us. He had his theme, which was Britain; and nothing else could stir him to quite the same response. With more conventional subjects – *The Story of Lili Marlene*, *A Defeated People*, *The Cumberland Story* – he was obviously unhappy, and, despite his brilliance at capturing the drama of real life, the staged sequences in these films do not suggest that he would have been at ease in the direction of features. *The Silent Village* – his reconstruction of the story of Lidice in a Welsh mining village – bears this out; for all the fond simplicity with which he sets his scene, the necessary sense of conflict and suffering is missed in his over-refined, under-dramatised treatment of the essential situation. It may be maintained that Jennings' peacetime return to the theme

of Britain (*Dim Little Island* in 1949, and *Family Portrait* in 1950) produced work that can stand beside his wartime achievement, and certainly
neither of these two beautifully finished films is to be dismissed. But they
lack passion.

By temperament Jennings was an intellectual artist, perhaps too intellectual for the cinema. (It is interesting to find Miss Raine reporting that
'Julian Trevelyan used to say that Humphrey's intellect was too brilliant
for a painter.') It needed the hot blast of war to warm him to passion, to
quicken his symbols to emotional as well as intellectual significance. His
symbols in *Family Portrait* – the Long Man of Wilmington, Beachy Head,
the mythical horse of Newmarket – what do they really mean to us?
Exquisitely presented though it is, the England of those films is nearer the
'This England' of the pre-war beer advertisements and Mr Castleton
Knight's coronation film than to the murky and undecided realities of
today. For reality, his wartime films stand alone; and they are sufficient
achievement. They will last because they are true to their time, and
because the depth of feeling in them can never fail to communicate itself.
They will speak for us to posterity, saying: 'This is what it was like. This
is what we were like, the best of us.'

Listen to Britain was shown on BBC television in 1946.

Postscript to 'Only Connect'

From the exhibition catalogue, 'Humphrey Jennings: Film
Maker, Poet, Painter' (British Film Institute/Riverside
Studios), 1982

SINCE 'ONLY CONNECT' WAS PUBLISHED IN *SIGHT AND SOUND* IN 1954, I
have written several times about Humphrey Jennings. One always hopes
– without too much presumption – that one is helping to keep the work
alive. Yet as the years pass these films, which should be familiar to every
schoolboy and girl in the country, seem to be seen and known by fewer
people. As far as I know, BBC Television, which in recent years has shown
films like *The Foreman Went to France*, *Angels One Five*, *The Way to the
Stars* etc., has practically never shown a film by Humphrey Jennings in its
entirety. (They commissioned Robert Vas to make a film about him but the
result was, as usual with Robert's films, as much about Robert himself as

about Jennings. And the extracts from Jennings' work could surely not mean a great deal to people who were not already familiar with it.) Recently perched on a camera crane waiting for clouds to pass, I asked the crew how many of them heard of Humphrey Jennings. One had. But he could not remember the name of any of his films.

So I am happy that Riverside Studios are mounting this exhibition; that this book is being prepared; and that 'Only Connect' has been chosen for reprinting. Although it was written nearly 30 years ago, it still reflects pretty faithfully what I feel. I got into trouble when it was first published, for saying that Jennings was 'the only real poet the British cinema has yet produced'. Lady Elton was particularly annoyed – though, with the exception of Basil Wright, I cannot see that the British documentary movement produced any other director who could be called a poet. But then (again with the exception of Basil) I don't think the British documentarists ever really approved of Jennings; certainly they never expressed any enthusiasm for his work until it was too late. The Griersonian tradition – into which Jennings only fitted uneasily – was always more preachy and sociological than it was either political or poetic.

One aspect of Humphrey Jennings' work I would have to be stricter about if I were writing today: its last phase. My allusion in this piece to *Dim Little Island* and *Family Portrait* is pussy-footing and unilluminating. Of course, there is distinctive and distinguished compositional style to these films. But in the end they can be dismissed. In fact they must be. They demonstrate only too sadly how the traditionalist spirit was unable to adjust itself to the changed circumstances of Britain after the War. By the time Jennings made *Family Portrait* for the 1951 Festival of Britain, the 'family' could only be a sentimental fiction, inhabiting a Britain dedicated to the status quo. I don't know whether Jennings thought of himself as a 'Leftist' in the old Mass Observation days. Traditionalism, after all, does not always have to be equated with conservatism. But somehow by the end of the War, Jennings' traditionalism had lost any touch of the radical: *Spare Time* (which is a beautiful, sharp, bitter-sweet and touching picture) is infinitely more alive than his academic *Family Portrait*. He found himself invoking great names of the past (Darwin, Newton, Faraday and Watt) in an attempt to exorcise the demons of the present. Even the fantasy of Empire persists ('The crack of the village bat is heard on Australian plains . . .'). The symbol at the end of the film is the mace of Authority, and its last image is a preposterous procession of ancient and bewigged dignitaries. The Past is no longer an inspiration: it is a refuge.

But of course whether Humphrey Jennings was able to find the inspiration in peace that he had in war does not matter. That particular problem has been ours rather than his for some time now: and we can hardly claim to have solved it much better. There remain his precious hand-ful of films. They may not seem directly dedicated to our dilemmas; but they can still stir and inspire us with their imaginative and moral impulse, they are still alive (for those who have eyes to see and ears to hear) with that mysterious oracular power which is the magic property of art. The poetry survives.

Lucky Jim

New Statesman, 5 October 1957

WHATEVER VICES THE BRITISH CINEMA CAN BE ACCUSED OF, NO ONE CAN call it over-anxious to exploit other people's successes – in the vulgar fashion of, say, Hollywood. The film version of *Look Back in Anger*, though announced many months ago, still remains but a tantalising promise; and producers seem unaccountably slow in bidding for the screen rights of *The Colin Wilson Story*. Perhaps the general favour shown to the film of *Lucky Jim*, which has just torn into the Gaumont, only a trifle over three-and-a-half years after the publication of the novel, will make film people more aware of the commercial possibilities of an angry young cinema?

Kingsley Amis fans must be warned, however, not to pitch their hopes too high: the translation is rough rather than scrupulous. Not that a real-ist could have expected much else. After all, bearing in mind the standard requirements of a British film subject, just look at *Lucky Jim*. It has, to begin with, distinct contemporary relevance. The milieu is academic, and the wit intelligent. The hero is a lower-crust university lecturer; and he is an intellectual – tirelessly self-aware, self-examining, self-obsessed. Worst of all, there is an edge on the whole thing; the characterisation is sharp, and the observation generally malicious. If it had got on the screen even approximately as it stood, *Lucky Jim* would have represented a revolution in the British cinema.

The revolution, I need hardly add, has not taken place. And it is only fair to say that the film-makers are quite honest about what they are giv-ing us instead. The script is credited to Patrick Campbell, 'with addi-tional scenes and dialogue by Jeffrey Dell'; and we are expressly informed that the picture comes 'from the same kennel as *Private's Progress* and *Brothers-in-Law*'. What exactly does this mean, the unini-tiated may ask? It means quite simply that original comedy has been transformed into conventional farce. The characters have been flattened, simplified and vulgarised. The temptations of realist shooting have been conscientiously resisted, and the story has been wholly abstracted from reality. And, inevitably, Jim Dixon himself has been stripped of personality, and turned into a farcical lay-figure. He emerges as our old favourite, the College Idiot, who does everything wrong but gets the girl in the end – the traditional George Formby formula in fact, even down to the speeded-up chase in the last reel. Ian Carmichael does not *act* Jim; he does him as a turn, with comic grimaces and an intermittent North Country accent.

It is a long-standing fallacy that this kind of simplification does no harm, is indeed made inevitable by some mysterious law of 'Cinema'. Thus, in a revealing discussion of this very film on the BBC programme *Talking of Films* the other Sunday, Mr Anthony Quinton (a Fellow of All Souls I believe) approvingly noted the 'strong element of farce in the film – though not unwelcome in any way, not out of tune, out of harmony in any respect . . .' And Kingsley Amis too submitted to the change as 'inevitable' – 'the machinery of oppression and domination, and so on, is so much more – can be so much more – subtle in a book than it could possibly be in a film.' Presumably he picked this idea up from the Boulting Brothers, for anything more intrusive and obvious than the gimmicks stuffed into *Lucky Jim* it would be difficult to imagine: the bottle of Cherry Brandy which plays a tune when you lift it up; the whimsical boxer terrier; the water splashes and the disturbed lovers in the chase at the end. The direction, too, is continuously over-emphatic, stressing every raised eyebrow, every comic footfall, with a thumping close-up. But this is not 'Cinema'. It is the desperate result of not believing in your subject, not feeling that the situations and characters are comic in themselves, of falling back on artifice instead of observation. *Lucky Jim* could have made a good film; even an important one. Imagine it done with the zest, the wit, the adult intelligence which Castellani gave *E Primavera* or *Two Pennyworth of Hope*, or with the vivacity and social accuracy of Becker's *Antoine et Antoinette* or *Rendezvous de Juillet*. We'd never get away with anything as good as that in Britain? Well, we won't know till we try – will we now?

Come to think of it, another director who might have made a sparkling go of *Lucky Jim* is Michael Cacoyannis, the young Greek director whose three films to date have shown such liveliness and versatility. From next Monday, the Everyman are running an enterprising, three-week season of them – *Windfall in Athens*, *Stella*, and *The Girl in Black*. This is the kind of thing we need at home.

The Films of Carol Reed

Review of *The Films of Carol Reed* by Robert F. Moss in the *Times Literary Supplement*, 8 January 1988

THIS IS A BOOK OF TWO MYSTERIES. FIRST THE MYSTERY OF CAROL REED, ONE of the most deservedly respected of British film-makers, leader of the renaissance – birth, even – of British cinema in its great time of success after the Second World War, the first director to be knighted. Yet today? We need not go as far as Robert E. Moss's blurb, which describes Sir Carol as 'long since banished to a musty corner of film history'. But undoubtedly the once brilliant reputation has dimmed, as it did mysteriously through the last dismal years of his career.

The other mystery is the British cinema itself: 'The falling house that never falls . . .' Periods, movements of creativity recur, only to fail against the opposition of financial crisis and national indifference. Our film-makers have worked perpetually in the shadow of Hollywood, economically disadvantaged, feebly supported, never able to capture the firm allegiance either of the necessary mass audience, or of the sophisticated minority whose enthusiasm has always gone across the Channel to Europe, or across the Atlantic to the more vigorous popular artists of the United States. Is the problem, as Moss implies, purely one of the lack of 'a dependable infrastructure'? Or do we have to admit, however reluctantly, that François Truffaut was right when he suggested to Alfred Hitchcock that 'there is a certain incompatibility between the terms "British" and "Cinema"'? Hitchcock thought he had a point: at all events, he got out. Reed never quite made the break.

Robert Moss, an American academic, has previously written on Boris Karloff, Charlie Chaplin and *Rudyard Kipling and the Fiction of Adolescence*. His examination of Carol Reed's work is detailed, if somewhat pedestrian, and has the merit of whole-hearted enthusiasm. (His publishers, unfortunately, have served him badly with a book that is poorly edited, illustrated without flair, and outrageously priced.) He goes further, as far as I know, than any English critic in claiming a place for Reed 'in the ranks of the world's greatest directors'. At the same time he is aware of the importance of context: he starts his book with a 65-page history of British cinema from 1895 to 1939. This is rather a trudge, with the emphasis chiefly on 'economic realities' and perceptions somewhat shallow. But Dr Moss's application is dogged, right up to his gloomy assessment of present-day prospects: 'In the foreseeable future, a true English national cinema . . . seems an all-but unreachable goal.'

There have been times when optimism seemed more possible. One of these was that ten-year period when the War provided the British cinema with both economic and imaginative protection. We had our own national epic to inspire us, and for a time the British seemed to enjoy – in some cases even to prefer – films made about themselves, by their own countrymen. And after the War, before the floodgates opened and the American log-jam of product which had been held up for the past five years poured in, British films enjoyed top prestige almost for the first time. Carol Reed, just like David Lean and Michael Powell, was just of an age to profit from this afflu-ence. Born in 1906, he started working in the theatre, first as an actor then as stage manager of Edgar Wallace productions, at the age of eighteen. In 1932 he joined Basil Dean's company at Associated Talking Pictures (the first owners of Ealing Studios), to start directing three years later.

Reed's first solo directing credit was for *Midshipman Easy*, starring a youthful Hughie Green. At once he showed himself a capable technician, more than usually bright and more than usually vigorous. (Graham Greene, writing film criticism in *The Spectator*, discerned in Reed 'more sense of the cinema than most veteran British directors'.) By the outbreak of war he had made seven more pictures, none quite outstanding but all creditable examples of their varied genres. Some of them still entertain: *Bank Holiday*, with its lively vignettes of Londoners on a Brighton week-end; *Penny Paradise*, a jovial Northern comedy of the Pools; *A Girl Must Live*, a wisecracking comedy, somewhat American in style, of go-getting London chorus girls. None of these stories – including the petit-bourgeois *Laburnum Grove* – was moneyed or upper-class in its settings. Yet Reed had been, as Moss puts it, 'raised in bourgeois comfort'. His background in fact was an odd mixture of the conventional and the unorthodox. He lived his upper-middle-class boyhood in Putney and was educated at King's School, Canterbury. But his father, 'Mr Reed', was in fact Sir Herbert Beerbohm Tree, actor-manager of distinction, who maintained, apparently with a front of great respectability, a second household (as well as numer-ous extra-marital affairs) along with his official marriage to Lady Tree.

It is a pity that Moss's account of all this is sketchy in the extreme: he seems to have conducted his research at a distance, and mostly at second or third hand. For there seems no doubt that Carol Reed's life, and to some degree his work, were coloured by these family circumstances. He had, we read, five brothers and/or sisters: his father died when he was eleven. He wanted to follow in Tree's footsteps on the stage. 'Mrs Reed', whose real name was May Pinney, objected, and Carol was sent to America to learn chicken farming from an elder brother. Reed had no feelings for chickens, however, and came back. He overcame his mother's objections and managed to join a theatre company headed by Sybil Thorndike: this was followed by small parts in a succession of thrillers by Edgar Wallace. While with Wallace, Reed gave up acting for stage management: it was as an assistant director and dialogue coach that he started to work for Basil Dean at Ealing. This was an unusual background among British film directors,

*Joseph Cotten and Orson Welles in Carol Reed's
The Third Man.*

most of whom graduated from the floor or from the cutting-room.

Like many film-makers, at least of the good old, pre-auteurist days, Carol Reed was always anxious to deny any personal vision or thematic commitment in his films. Significantly, like David Lean, his preferred fellow-artist (five years his senior) was William Wyler, a fine stylist with nothing much beyond that and a certain intelligence of sentiment to distinguish his pictures. After Reed had made *The Stars Look Down*, a decent but not exactly impassioned version of A. J. Cronin's sentimental-radical novel urging the nationalisation of the mines, he took pains to disclaim any special sympathy with the subject of the film. He would make a picture tomorrow, he said, arguing the reverse of nationalisation, 'if the story were valid enough'. There is a certain naivety, even a superficiality here. 'I believe in the story itself, in sincerity and in transmitting a feeling about people.' This kind of evasion is dangerous for an artist who takes himself, or wishes to be taken, seriously.

But consciously or unconsciously, Reed was not telling the whole truth. Of the films he made up to the end of the War, it might be said that they progressed in quality and finish without achieving any marked originality or personal statement. His *Kipps* is decorative, humorous, charming; *Young Mr Pitt* is well staged, conventional and cumbersome; *The Way Ahead* is an outstanding recruiting film, comic and stirring in the English style; *The True Glory*, a documentary compilation on which Reed shared credit with the American Garson Kanin, is forceful, craftsmanlike and properly 'inspirational'. The work is civilised, elegant, well performed: British mainstream film-making at its most respectable.

War breathed new life into British cinema; and for a few post-war years

British film-makers seemed to have entered a period of vigorous maturity. Their work showed the dynamic of confident ambition. Olivier followed *Henry V* with *Hamlet*; David Lean went from *Brief Encounter* to *Great Expectations* to *Oliver Twist*; Powell and Pressburger astonished their audiences with the extravagances of *The Red Shoes* and *A Matter of Life and Death*. And suddenly Carol Reed shot forward into first place with three films which for three years running won him the accolade of Best British Film, international prestige and a knighthood. Whatever may have been Reed's protestations to the contrary, each of these films carried the stamp of personal commitment; and each drew its strength from it. Each, it is surely not going too far to suggest, drew its imaginative nourishment from a sense of failure of relationship, a sense of exclusion, the deprivation of a fatherless childhood.

Moss awards the first of these films, *Odd Man Out*, the palm as 'Reed's masterpiece'. In certain ways it is the most ambitious, a fatalistic tragedy played against the background of Northern Irish politics. But there is a weakness in the abstraction of its hero's long crucifixion from any concrete or specific political circumstances. And finally *Odd Man Out* falls victim to an inflation of style that puts it on a lower level than its successors, Reed's two superb films from scripts by Graham Greene, *The Fallen Idol* and *The Third Man*. Here are two immaculate, ironic, wholly achieved works, beautifully written but in no way literary, promising no more than they can deliver, as shrewd and witty in their disenchanted observation as they are satisfying in their brilliance of style.

Then – mystery again. If Reed's progress to mastery was a steady one, his decline was precipitous. Moss puts *An Outcast of the Islands*, the Conrad adaption with which he followed *The Third Man*, alongside its three outstanding predecessors. But in truth it was a failure, artistically as well as commercially. Reed was not the first, nor the last film-maker to find Conrad's rich, essentially literary texture of character and philosophy 'intractable' (the word was his own); and *Outcast* wholly lacks the crispness, the wry, concise scepticism of the work with Greene. Nor, tragically, was he ever to find those qualities again. Two more British films followed. One, *The Man Between*, was a pale echo of *The Third Man* set in Berlin; and the other was an inept East End whimsy, *A Kid for Two Farthings*.

Worse was to come. Reed fell among Americans, and produced *Trapeze*, a lavish circus vehicle for Burt Lancaster and Gina Lollobrigida, followed by a pretentious, pseudo-poetic romance, *The Key*, with William Holden and Sophia Loren. His patron, Alexander Korda, was dead and Reed found himself directionless. For the rest of his career, he lurched from one mistaken choice to another: even his one further version of a Greene script, *Our Man in Havana*, was disappointing. In 1961 he touched bottom when he rashly undertook (before the script had been finished) the Hollywood remake of *Mutiny on the Bounty*, and found himself crushed between the mighty opposites of Marlon Brando and MGM. Seven years later his film of Lionel Bart's *Oliver!* won him an Oscar; but this was not the kind of prestige one wished for him. Nor did it save his career. His last two films were mistakes, best forgotten.

With all the evidence before us, there is still something mysterious about the achievement and the failure of Carol Reed. As there is something mysterious about the British cinema, with its constant recurrence of talent which it can somehow never sustain. Reed was not just British: he was English. He was very English in his refusal to admit, or consciously to use, the complexities of his own nature. He was very English also in his determination to abstract his work from contemporary social reality. Moss claims Reed as a 'champion of realism'; but the realism of *The Stars Look Down*, of *The Way Ahead* or *A Kid for Two Farthings*, is partial to say the least. In the last ten years of his life a New Wave swelled up and broke, with films that treated working-class life, with scripts by working-class writers, and actors genuinely of the working-class – as opposed to, say, Michael Redgrave's tentatively accented Northern miner in *The Stars Look Down*. Would Reed's talent have proved more lasting if he had been able to make closer contact with the life and experience of classes other than his own? Would he have been wiser to avoid American patronage, with all the compromises and falsities that went with the lavish financing?

These are hypothetical questions. The dependence, with very few exceptions, of British film-makers on American finance is one of the facts of our cinema; and, after all, most of the British New Wave have ended up, at least intermittently, in Hollywood. The British cinema, too, is as much a prisoner of the British class system as any of our arts or institutions: there was no way Carol Reed could have escaped the middle- (or upper-) class prison and remained himself. Perhaps he would have survived longer as an artist if, like his colleague David Lean, he had been able to escape from Britain altogether – without falling into the American trap. But Lean made his choices wisely, and Reed was not good at choices.

So we are left with a talent, a personality, and a unique nucleus of memorable work. Who will ever forget the last shot of *The Third Man*: the bare trees, the last leaves falling, the plangent zither that accompanies the woman walking expressionlessly away past the man, the cigarette thrown with casual finality to the ground, the implacable statements of separation? Graham Greene had thought the long-drawn walk too portentous to end a story which he had seen merely as a diversion, an entertainment. But Reed insisted; and (as Greene admitted) he was right. The image has the enduring, unanalysable eloquence of poetry: Carol Reed is here, his mystery unsolved.

A Prophet without Honour

Review of *A Life in Movies*, Volume One, by Michael Powell, in the *Chicago Tribune*, 22 March 1987

MANY AMERICANS MAY NOT HAVE REALISED THAT LAST YEAR WAS BRITISH Film Year. This minor godsend to the media was a true event of the eighties – not celebrating British achievement in the cinema, so much as dedicated to the ambition of getting 'bums on seats' again in British theatres. The ambition has been partially realised, chiefly by the release of *Ghostbusters*, the Stallone and Schwarzenegger toughies, the Spielberg epics for children, etc. One nice thing happened to a British film-maker, however. In a publication sponsored by British Film Year, 21 critics listed their choice of the ten best British pictures ever. Michael Powell's *Peeping Tom* appeared in nine of the lists. And various productions of the Archers (Powell in collaboration with the writer Emeric Pressburger) gave him no less than 18 further mentions. Do you remember – or have you heard of – *The Red Shoes*, *The Life and Death of Colonel Blimp*, *Black Narcissus*, *A Matter of Life and Death*? Powell directed (and Pressburger wrote) all these.

This book must have been written before Powell received this remarkable accolade, for in it he mentions quite often his soreness at his countrymen's rejection of his contribution to British cinema. Two or three years ago, when he received from Orson Welles his Fellowship of the British Film Institute, he could not restrain an allusion to Prophets being Not Without Honour etc. One could only sympathise with this naughtiness (spoken with a characteristic twinkle in the eye), remembering Powell's 20 years in the wilderness since the Archers split up, with his only significant work, the perverse *Peeping Tom* in 1960, rejected by the critics with scorn and vituperation.

Happily, Michael Powell has been rediscovered – by Americans, of course. It was the Movie Brats of Hollywood who did it. The Show Biz auteurists Scorsese, Lucas and Coppola recognised his rare and extraordinary talent, and sensed their affinity with it and with him. They discovered *Peeping Tom*. They admired and generously proclaimed the combination of skill and originality which makes the Archers' films still unique. Francis Ford Coppola even engaged Powell, youthful in his late seventies, as Senior Director in Residence at his Zoetrope Studios. (The Studios went bust, but that could have been in no way the responsibility of Powell. He always has been a professional to his fingertips.)

Michael Powell has always had a special relationship with Americans,

Wendy Hiller and Pamela Brown in I Know Where I'm Going, *directed by Michael Powell.*

and with the American cinema. As a middle-class schoolboy – he was educated at King's School Canterbury and sang in the Cathedral choir – he saw
D. W. Griffith's *Intolerance*, learned what a film director was, and decided
to be one. He was working in a bank when he had the amazing luck to be
introduced to Rex Ingram, then a refugee from Hollywood when he had
just hit the jackpot and launched Rudolph Valentino with *Four Horsemen
of the Apocalypse.* (Ingram was making huge, romantic epics at the
Victorine studios in Nice, near the hotel owned by young Powell's father.)
Anyone with enough cheek, ambition and persistence could get into movies
in those days. Powell did every kind of job for Ingram: stills cameraman,
movie camera assistant, assistant editor, title writer . . . The golden days of
silent film-making inspire some of the most captivating pages of this book.

Powell has three invaluable gifts for a writer of autobiography. His
experience is rich; his recall is astonishing; and a never-failing enthusiasm
makes him a terrific story-teller. Also he seems honest, sometimes painfully so. He thinks highly of himself and (particularly) his work. But he does
not attempt to disguise the egoism and the impatience which have often
made him as much disliked as admired in his profession.

He has always been paradoxical, as a man and as a movie-maker. By
birth and by temperament he is English: 'I never wanted to go to America
and make their pictures for them. I wanted to make English ones. I was

375

English to the core, as English as a Cox's Orange Pippin . . .' And yet his inspiration came from the international masterpieces of silent cinema, from Germany, France, Scandinavia . . . And of course his talent and his skill were nourished by American example. Like his slightly senior colleague Alfred Hitchcock, he was impatient with English coldness, provincialism and miserable class-consciousness. He was not drawn to America like the English film-makers of today – for money, for work opportunities, for the fleshpots of Beverly Hills. He just loved and admired America and the Americans, 'their generosity and their success in creating a real democracy, owned by the people themselves.' Yes, Powell belongs to the honourable tradition of English eccentricity.

And he does somewhat exaggerate his rejection by the British. In the forties and fifties, the Archers worked with remarkable independence for Rank and for Korda. It was after their collaborations ended that Powell experienced failure – and it has, with respect, to be admitted that neither he nor Pressburger on their own were able to make films which even approached the quality of their work together.

History moved on, and the cinema of image and effect became unfashionable. The generation which – however briefly – attempted to make British films more closely, more directly related to contemporary realities, did not rate the Archers' achievement as highly as Powell does himself. There was always, we felt, an element of kitsch about it, of eccentric fancy rather than true imagination. We had all made documentaries. But when Powell made his first really personal film, *The Edge of the World*, he declared: 'I don't want to make a documentary. Documentaries are for disappointed film-makers.' He always remained like the young man of whom he wrote: 'He stands about dreaming . . . He sees what is going on, but he makes no attempt to change things.' We were not like that.

Well, the whirligig of Time has brought its revenge. It is exactly this quality that appeals to the Movie Brats of Hollywood: they don't want to change things either. Martin Scorsese discovers 'real film magic' in the Archers, and wants to redistribute *Peeping Tom*. Coppola brings Michael Powell to Zoetrope. And the films enjoy fashionable critical prestige. Bravo! Obstinate, uncompromising talent is not always so happily rewarded.

A Life in Movies covers only the first half of Michael Powell's life, and the first two thirds of his career. I hope very much he completes the story. His writing is vivid and vigorous, fascinating and revealing. This is the real stuff of cinema, worth over a thousand pretentious works of 'academic' criticism. The publishers have not done as well as their author: the production is clumsy, and as a film-maker Powell would surely have appreciated the services of a good editor. Also, as an artist who has lived by the image, he deserved pictures.

A Matter of Life and Death

Review of *Million-Dollar Movie: A Life in Movies,*Volume
Two by Michael Powell in *The Daily Telegraph*, 26
September 1992

THIS BOOK COMES AS A SURPRISE, AND A VERY WELCOME ONE. MICHAEL
Powell published his first volume of autobiography in 1986. He died in
1990 and one feared that he had not written a sequel. *A Life in Movies*
took him halfway through his career. It was an outstanding piece of writing, enthusiastic, cantankerous and frank. *Million-Dollar Movie*, much of
which he had to dictate, completes the story. It is just as good.

As a young man, Powell was lucky enough to work for Rex Ingram,
the great and intransigent director of silent films (*Four Horsemen of the
Apocalypse*, *Mare Nostrum*). In Britain in the thirties, he became a film
director himself, battling through a succession of 'quickies', learning the
craft. In 1937 a maverick producer, Joe Rock, backed him in an adventure
on Foula in the Shetlands; *The Edge of the World* impressed Alexander
Korda, who gave him *The Spy in Black* and introduced him to Emeric
Pressburger, a writer from Hungary. They became collaborators and called
themselves the Archers.

Powell and Pressburger were surely the most extraordinary partnership ever to come out of the British cinema. *A Matter of Life and Death*,
The Life and Death of Colonel Blimp and *The Red Shoes* were brilliant,
wilful and idiosyncratic films. They were produced by the Rank
Organisation in its palmy days, and they went about as far as Rank and
its homely English (philistine, complacent, businessman) managing director, John Davis, could go. Powell's first book ended with *The Red Shoes*,
a huge success at home and abroad despite the incomprehension of its
Rank distributors. So the Archers left Rank for Korda, and their long run
of successes came to an end.

Powell is completely frank about Korda, about his machinations and
his attempts to collaborate with the ruthless men of Hollywood, which
involved the Archers with Goldwyn (*The Elusive Pimpernel*) and
Selznick (*Gone to Earth*). Yet Powell could not help respecting Korda,
whom he felt to have size and class, as opposed to the 'bourgeois
tantrums' of John Davis.

All the same, Korda precipitated the end of the Archers: 'He had coat-
ed his web with sugary promises and we had got stuck with them.' *Gone
to Earth* was messed up in America by Selznick, who ordered Rouben

Julian Craster (Marius Goring), Victoria Page (Moira Shearer) and Boris Lermontov (Anton Walbrook) in Powell and Pressburger's The Red Shoes *(1948).*

Mamoulian to put more sex into it. Powell and Pressburger spun off to make *The Tales of Hoffman,* an experiment in filmed opera, which Korda tried to truncate by cutting out the last third. He failed, but it was the end of the relationship. Korda turned out to be more of a politician than an artist, in spite of the Monets in his office at 148 Piccadilly.

The Archers split up. Powell was always puzzled, though he is never less than honest about it, and their friendship survived. Pressburger directed a film, a remake of an Austrian picture for Korda. Powell floundered. As he wrote, his ambitions had only won him a reputation for unpredictability. From expressionism to high drama, to filmed opera to adventure, there seemed no consistency to his enthusiasms.

The sad truth is that, even if the cinema is the director's medium, directors need producers. Films are so horribly expensive, and their organisation so complicated, that artists need the backing of financiers and of those industry politicians we call producers. Powell was a terrible businessman, and he knew it. But if he had been blessed with an understanding producer, would he have listened to him? Or did understanding mean acceptance? He knew himself well, and he seems to have been satisfied with what he was and what he wanted to do. Some artists function like that; they pay the penalty.

Pressburger was very much a European intellectual. He subscribed to *Time* magazine, and he 'worried for hours when he missed the six o'clock news'. Whereas Powell read the *Times Literary Supplement* and 'couldn't have cared less what had happened, so long as they didn't tell me about it.' He cared about art, even if his taste was erratic. He scorned Davis and his Rank nonentities. 'As for tact . . . a bull in a pasture has more tact, but at least I have learned to hold my tongue.' It took a long time, though, and over the years Powell's caustic expression of convictions cost him dear.

He never gave up. In 1952, sitting on a New York hotel bed, Powell compiled two lists, of features he was contemplating (there were twelve) and of tales from which he hoped to make a portmanteau film (eleven). He made none of them. Interestingly, one of his feature ideas was *The Charge of the Light Brigade* (from 'The Reason Why'), which Tony Richardson made many years later. There is no indication that Powell even saw Tony's film, or even heard of it. Indeed he never mentions any of the films which seemed to revive, if only temporarily, the British cinema in the late fifties and early sixties. When Tony Richardson and Karel Reisz made *Look Back in Anger* and *Saturday Night and Sunday Morning*, Powell made *Peeping Tom*. It does not seem likely that the hysterical condemnation of his film by the London critics really 'prematurely ended his career' (as the publishers make out), but it is unfortunate that his temperament led Powell to cut himself off so decisively from the present.

And yet . . . Probably it is exactly Powell's preoccupation with style – too often at the expense of content – that has won him the admiration of the younger generation. It was certainly his cinematic daring that fascinated the young Martin Scorsese, glued to his television for the Archers' revivals on *Million Dollar Movie*. Whether his enthusiasm is exaggerated hardly matters: Ian Christie is surely going a bit far when he describes Powell and Scorsese as 'two of the greatest film-makers of all time'.

But we can only be glad that acclaim came in time to solace the wounded feeling of rejection that Michael Powell undeniably felt. This book tells us so, and a lot more. It tells about a whole life in movies, about the many good and the many awful people whom Powell encountered and insulted, disliked and loved. Very few film directors, very few men, have written as honestly, as entertainingly and as well.

Recollections of a Full Life

Review of *A Divided Life: Memoirs* by Bryan Forbes in *The Daily Telegraph*, 16 May 1992

THE TITLE SUGGESTS A LIFE SPLIT IN TWO, BUT THIS CERTAINLY DOES NOT APPLY to Bryan Forbes. The dictionary definition is more apt: 'separated into parts.' Bryan Forbes has not only acted in and directed films, he is also a writer – of scripts and novels and *belles letters*. He has been a theatre director and has run a film studio. He has a passion for books, owns a bookshop, and is a lover of exceptional personality wherever he has found it (especially among the famous).

All these enthusiasms are featured in these chatty reminiscences, not set down chronologically but seemingly at random. Bryan Forbes has also been the victim of multiple sclerosis, intelligently and courageously defeated. He has been many things, but he is not by nature a victim.

He was born John Clarke, at Forest Gate in the East End. His early concentration was on books and reading; he began his career as a broadcaster. This sounds quite orderly, but that is not how the story is told. It is not until page 244 that we hear about the sympathetic response of Lionel Gamlin (who was the declamatory voice of *Movietone News*) to Bryan's letter asking for advice and enclosing the 'ludicrous rave review' of his Shylock in his school play. It was Gamlin who gave him his name and steered him into RADA. He also warned him, from his own experience, of the perils of homosexuality.

When young, Bryan was something called 'a contract script doctor'. One of his first adventures was to rewrite scenes from a dreadful Alan Ladd epic in this country, about Saracens disguised as Vikings. From this we move on to his obsessive passion for the written word; his appearance as Hitler at a ball, not fancy dress, organised by a Jewish charity; his appearance in Carol Reed's *The Key*; and his friendship with William Holden.

The book is, in fact, a higgledy-piggledy collection of stories, which the author accurately describes as 'the tumbled recollections of a full life'. This has the advantage of giving the whole thing a relaxed tone, rather like a comfortable, slippered conversation, skipping from film to friendship, from domesticity to the hazards of a professional life. But we would perhaps have learned more from a more ordered progression. This would not necessarily have been dull, but it would have made it easier to follow a tremendously busy career.

Bryan Forbes does not write much in this book about the films he has directed, which make up a remarkably catholic lot. He formed a company with Richard Attenborough and they produced *The Angry Silence* (1960). He wrote and acted in *League of Gentlemen*; he directed *Whistle Down the Wind*. His films were always professional; *The L-Shaped Room*, *King Rat*, *The Wrong Box*, *The Whisperers*, to name only a few.

But he says a great deal more about one of the most extraordinary episodes in his life, when he was unexpectedly appointed, in 1970, to be Head of Production and Managing Director of Elstree Studios. Elstree was a large outfit where many British films had been made through the years, with home-grown stars like Anna Neagle and Jack Buchanan, Michael Denison and Dulcie Gray, Owen Nares and Lupino Lane. It became known as 'the British Hollywood', with all that that implies.

The studios had been largely run by John Maxwell, followed by Robert Clarke, hard-headed Scotsmen both. Elstree had always been provincial, with no soft or ambitious ideas about 'art', lacking altogether the cachet of Pinewood and Denham. Workers were liable to be searched at the gate when they left for home. Bryan Forbes' awful failure there was inevitable from the start, and especially because he went in believing 'Bernie' (Bernard, now Lord) Delfont, when he said it was his intention 'to revitalise the British film industry'. The task was beyond either of them.

Bryan Forbes was a fighter, and he did his best to discipline the old-fashioned, small-minded labour force. But the penny-pinching, unimaginative management was just as bad. The £4,000,000 'revolving production fund' was never forthcoming. Worst of all was the 'respectable' taste which dictated the choice of projects. However urgent the pressure, the new Elstree should not have kicked off with duds like *The Man Who Haunted Himself* (Roger Moore) or *Hoffman* (Peter Sellers). Most horribly significant was the grudging, purblind treatment of Bryan's own excellent *The Raging Moon*, which made only too clear the intransigent mediocrity of the people in key positions. Thus, what was probably the last chance of saving the British film industry was lost.

Bryan Forbes has always been critical and enthusiastic, but never a radical. One of the well-chosen pictures in *A Divided Life* shows him strolling with Margaret Thatcher 'in the garden of Seven Pines while shooting a Party Political'. The story would surely have been a more vibrant one if the author's conformism had been tempered with some non-conformism, some spirit of dissidence, some malice even. But of course that would not have been Bryan. He has been trustful rather than suspicious. He has liked most of the people he has met. Artists like Graham Greene, Edith Evans, Peter O'Toole, Katharine Hepburn, Groucho Marx have captivated him and he writes glowingly about them. His are the cheerful memories of a multi-talented, surely likeable man.

The Short Flight of a Golden Bird

Review of *My Indecision is Final: the Rise and Fall of Goldcrest Films* by Jake Eberts and Terry Ilott in *The Sunday Telegraph*, 17 June 1990

IS THERE SUCH A THING AS A BRITISH CINEMA? HAS THERE EVER BEEN? CAN there ever be? British critics – more especially journalists – love asking questions like these. Generally, they smilingly imply that the answer is 'no', sounding the note of mockery which must be expected by any repeatedly failing enterprise in an era which worships success.

Of course British films sometimes 'succeed' – which more and more comes to mean 'make money in America'. The last ten years have seen some notable winners, as well as some equally notable losers. The greatest winners were produced by a company called Goldcrest. So were the most catastrophic losers.

This book gives us – in unsparing detail – the story of Goldcrest from its modest start to its amazing (and quite short) period of triumph, and on to its complete and ignominious failure. All in ten years.

The company was started by Jake Eberts, a chemical engineer from Canada. Bored with designing and installing gas liquefaction plants, he got himself enrolled in the Harvard Business School. He graduated and became something mysterious called a financial analyst and consultant, managing the London office of Oppenheimer and Co, investment bankers. Bored again, he wanted 'to take risks and make money'. When the chance came to raise cash for an animated film called *Watership Down*, he seized it.

Watership Down was a success and Eberts decided to start a company which would finance film development – not making films, but scripting and preparing them for production. He got his principal backing from Pearsons, the British conglomerate which owned, among many concerns, Penguin Books and the Merchant bank Lazard, Martin and Roger. Most of the Pearson publishing subsidiaries (Pearson Longman) were named after birds; so they called the company Goldcrest.

Eberts' ambition was to marry his ability to make money with 'the filmmaker's passion to make pictures, *making a clear distinction between the two functions*'. I italicise the reservation, because Eberts is always so anxious to present himself 'as a financier, not as a film-maker'. He insists on his lack of interest in cinema. 'I knew absolutely nothing about the film business. I had never read about films and *still don't . . .*' (my italics again). 'I couldn't read a book about old movies now even if I had no other book in the house.'

Truly, these shrewd businessmen can show themselves very naive when they stray outside their area of expertise. In Eberts' case, this naivety put him dangerously in the hands of spellbinding film-makers when he had to make decisions which inevitably touched on the creative.

Fortunately, Eberts' intuition was not at fault when he chose his spellbinders. They both deserved (and still do) the title. David Puttnam is described accurately as 'a brilliant salesman and wonderfully perceptive: he knows what you want to hear.' Puttnam, a producer of unrivalled energy and ambition, persuaded Eberts to put up development money for a story called *Chariots of Fire*. Association with this legendary success gave Goldcrest a tremendous boost. 'The British are coming!' famously proclaimed its writer, Cohn Welland, as he brandished his Oscar.

Only a year later, Goldcrest's other spellbinder, Richard Attenborough, stunned Eberts with his project to film the life of Gandhi: 'To this day, it is the only script I have ever read that made me cry.' James Lee, Pearson's representative on the Goldcrest board, went even further. 'We all thought "What a wonderful human being . . ." We'd have got down and felt the hem of his jacket.'

For once, naivety paid off. Goldcrest backed *Gandhi* with courage and generosity. In 1983 Attenborough stormed the Hollywood Academy and carried away eight of its golden grails. This should have have confirmed the company as the flagship of the British cinema. Instead it proved to be Goldcrest's apotheosis – and the prelude to disaster. Three-quarters of this book tells the painful chronicle of ensuing blunders, miscalculations and personality conflicts of the kind that afflict enterprises which succeed unexpectedly and expand too fast.

It is a story from the horse's mouth, told alternatively by Jake Eberts himself and by Terry Ilott, a knowledgeable film-industry journalist. They write with candour, in meticulous detail. The characters are evoked vividly, and remarkably without malice, though the temptation must have been great. Insiders will find it all fascinating; but for the general reader, it may prove hard going. There are 650 pages of text, and we are told awfully little about the films and projects which were the object of all the obsessive wheeling and dealing. It does not seem to have occurred to the authors that readers may not have seen *The Mission* or *Revolution* or *Absolute Beginners*. An explanatory appendix would have helped.

In essence, what happened was simple. Goldcrest was built on one man's vision and intuition. But Jake Eberts did not get on with James Lee, another management consultant virtuoso, whom Pearsons brought in as chief executive. Nor would Pearson pay him what he felt he deserved. Wooed by Americans with lavish promises, he quit and went to Hollywood. Lee (also a graduate of the Harvard Business School) was charming and ambitious, but he did not have flair. Nor did the lawyers and accountants who made up the Goldcrest board. Puttnam and Attenborough were supposed to give expert advice, but inevitably they were too concerned with their own film-making careers to provide close or adequate supervision.

An American production chief was brought in, the amiable Sandy Lieberson, but he was not the man to captain such a crew. Goldcrest embarked on two hugely ambitious, wastefully executed productions: the American *Revolution*, enacted on English locations by expensive American stars, and a misconceived pop version of Colin MacInnes's novel about London in the fifties, *Absolute Beginners*. The latter lost nearly £3 million, the former close to £10 million. David Puttman went to California and Richard Attenborough made *A Chorus Line* in New York. The flagship went down with all hands.

Was this a particularly British disaster? Significantly, Jake Eberts found that neither of the principal British companies, Rank and EMI, would ever invest in his projects. He was 'dismissed with ill-disguised contempt by both'. The London banks were not just wary, they were ignorant – and similarly dismissive.

British goverments do not think films deserve support. Provincialism and arrogant inertia have long characterised the English attitude to cinema. America has the glamour of vitality as well as money. No wonder Alan Parker is more excited by Mississippi than by Ulster burning. No wonder our young Turks (Stephen Frears, Neil Jordan, Mike Figgis . . .) find greater stimulus and more opportunity in Hollywood than in our own dim industry.

David Puttnam resigned from the Goldcrest board to run Columbia Pictures for Coca-Cola at Burbank. He lasted a year. Now he has $50 million from Warner Brothers and Fuji-Sankei of Japan. His latest production, made in Britain, is *Memphis Belle*, the story of an American bomber crew in the Second World War. 'The film,' he explains, 'is only commercially viable because it's about Americans.' If it had been about the RAF, he could never have raised the money. Ah yes . . .

Next year it will be half a century since a British film-maker was able to make *Target for Tonight*.

Bill Douglas

Introduction to *Bill Douglas: A Lanternist's Account*, edited by Eddie Dick, Andrew Noble and Duncan Petrie (1993)

BILL DOUGLAS WAS – IS – THE KIND OF FILM-MAKER WHO HAS ALWAYS BEEN rare in this country. He was not attracted to cinema because he wanted to make a career for himself, nor because he wanted to please an audience. He made films from the heart, and from his experience of life. His work, like that of all good artists, was didactic. By which I mean he wanted his audience to know more about life and to understand it better.

I first talked with him many years ago. We met at a coffee bar called Act One, Scene One, a friendly meeting place in Old Compton Street in the good old days. Bill had sent me a script about his childhood, and he wanted advice about how he could make a film of it. Thank God I immediately understood that he was an artist, and I advised him strongly not to reshape or rewrite his script with the hope of attracting finance. Above all, he should not try to turn it into 'a British film'. Happily, about this time the British Film Institute was starting to back production. Mamoun Hassan became secretary of the Production Fund, and proved himself the kind of patron whom every artist needs. He and his committee backed Bill Douglas, and so *My Childhood* and *My Ain Folk* and *My Way Home* were made.

Film-making was a kind of agony for Bill because, particularly at the start, they were torn out of himself. And helping to make his films was a kind of agony for his collaborators too. But there were people around who knew that his talent, his genius was unique. This is how the films were made. After the trilogy, he only managed to make one feature film; and the existence of *Comrades* is miraculous. It would never have been made if Bill had not had the determination, the doggedness, the unreasonableness that every film-maker needs. He worked out further scripts; but, of course, no one could turn them into the films that he would have made.

Poetry – and these are poetic films – is always a matter of purity and intensity, never of mass. Bill Douglas shot far less footage than many other film-makers. But everything he made showed passionate feeling, as well as a beautiful developing artistry. He was one of the very few. He always will be.

The Lost Past of British Cinema

Review of *Sixty Voices* edited by Brian McFarlane and
Missing Believed Lost edited by Allen Eyles and David
Meeker in *The Daily Telegraph*, 13 March 1993

IT ALWAYS SEEMS HARD THAT THE BRITISH FILM INSTITUTE (MORE POPULARLY
known as 'the BFI') should be saddled with that ominous institutional label.
'Institute' implies something official, academically strict. In fact, the Film
Institute really aims to further the cause of cinema, to give people who love
films the chance of reading about them in its publications, of seeing them (the
Institute runs MOMI and the National Film Theatre), and even of making
them (Terence Davies' films have been produced and distributed by the BFI).

Unfortunately, bureaucracies tend to become bureaucratic. And today, in
the backwash of Thatcherism, profit-making seems to have become an
important function of the Institute. The National Film Theatre is under fire
for seeking to attract rather than to inform; and *Sight and Sound*, the BFI's
quarterly magazine, strives for glossy acceptability. Take these two books,
the latest from BFI Publishing. Brian McFarlane's *Sixty Voices*, a fascinating
collection of interviews, is given the subtitle *Celebrities Recall the Golden
Age of British Cinema* and *Missing Believed Lost* is described as 'The Great
British Film Search'. The plugs are unnecessary as they are inaccurate.

Sixty Voices is the work of an obvious enthusiast. Brian McFarlane, a
Professor of Cinema at Monash University, Melbourne, describes how he
grew up in rural Victoria and came to think of British films as 'exotic'.
What this means is that the essential *decency* of the British middle-class
view of life, its habitual understatement and refinement, its 'inhibiting
gentility' made, as he puts it, 'indelible impressions' on this son of the out-
back. Class is an essential part of this period, when British cinema was
essentially middle-class, which Brian McFarlane very fairly admits
'embraces weakness as well as strength: the inherently class-bound attitudes, the sometimes over-decorous treatment of literary and theatrical
sources . . .' No doubt it really was a 'key period'.

Even if you don't share Professor McFarlane's enthusiasm, I don't see
how you could find this book less than a compulsive read. It is limited
only by the sad disappearance of many of British cinema's practitioners.
So there is no word from Jennings, from Hamer, Lean, Dearden or Harry
Watt. No Wilcox or Neagle. But there are invaluable contributions from
Phyllis Calvert and Jean Kent, Ronald Neame, Alec Guinness and Bernard
Miles. Cherished memories are evoked of the pseudo-Gothic absurdities of

Gainsborough, the pleasant surburbanism of Ealing, the emotional restraint which long characterised the British film – 'I'll just put these flowers in water,' spoken so many times by Gladys Henson on hearing of the death of her husband, usually a policeman.

Sixty Voices is a revealing book, with a rich cast list. The introduction is by Googie Withers and there is a delightful shared interview with Michael Denison and Dulcie Gray. By contrast, Lewis Gilbert, who has won some deserved successes in recent years, evokes the tradition sharply. '*Look Back in Anger* showed that working people could have lives of their own . . . prior to then, working-class people just didn't exist in the West End or the cinema.' We have advanced in some ways. 'I was a sergeant,' says that fine actor Bill Owen, 'and I never played anything higher.' Everybody loved 'Puffin' [Anthony] Asquith. Brian McFarlane even loves Lawrence Huntington. *Sixty Voices* is not exactly exhilarating, but it is spell-binding. It supplies essential evidence.

So does *Missing Believed Lost*, perhaps less entertainingly. On the cover, Eric Blore, Hollywood's quintessential 'Gentleman's Gentleman' leers round a door-frame, clutching a bottle of Haig's whisky. Blore only made one British talkie, and it is lost. So is Alfred Hitchcock's second feature *The Mountain Eagle*, an Anglo-German production shot in Munich. So are no fewer than twelve early 'quickies' made by Michael Powell.

Very few of these one hundred British features missing from the National Film Archive seem to be 'good' – or even worth seeing. But loss is always deplorable, and one must hope that this book will lead to rediscoveries. The films are illustrated, with synopses and credits and (mostly) naïf reports from the trade press and the *Monthly Film Bulletin*. J. Paul Getty, who has been such a supporter of the National Film Archive, contributes a foreword. Like him, we must wonder what has happened to Jack Hulbert and Cicely Courtneidge in Walter Forde's *The Ghost Train* and to Max Miller in *Educated Evans*. And what about so much of the output of Teddington Studios? Are these films on a laboratory shelf somewhere, or in some cob-webbed vault? What a lot of bad cinema has been made in England!

The Lights That Failed

Review of *British Cinema: The Lights That Failed* by James Park in *Screen International*, 1 February 1991

GEORGE ORWELL'S OBSERVATION OF THE FONDNESS OF ENGLISH INTELLECTUALS for celebrating European culture at the expense of their own remains horribly true of the cinema. There seems in fact – and this book is an example – to be nothing that the film intellectuals of the UK enjoy more than slagging off their own cinema, emphasising its limitations and denying its virtues.

James Park is one of these 'intellectuals', which means that he operates, or claims to operate, in the realm of ideas. Once a *Variety* reporter on British film activity, he was the author a few years back of a misguided little book on 'The New British Cinema' called *Learning to Dream*.

Now Park has produced a more substantial survey of British Cinema, tendentiously subtitled *The Lights That Failed*. From this title and the following, Park's pronouncement, that '. . . the British can write novels and plays, even produce an occasional world-class painter but, when it comes to cinema they might as well forget it,' we are left in no doubt as to where the author stands.

In spite of its title, this book is not a comprehensive or historical survey of the British cinema. It is emphatically a work *à thèse* , even if the thesis is often confused. There is a lot of waffle here that seems to have become inseparable from 'film studies'. For instance: 'So strong was the film-makers' infatuation with Hollywood that they were unable to work from an understanding of the situation that faced them, and develop British cinema according to its own economic and cultural realities.' These 'realities' remain undefined.

No account of film-making in this country will be worth anything which does not start with an admission of the inevitable superiority, in terms of market and consequent finance, of the American industry. Even Park admits this: 'The US had 20,000 cinemas, the UK only 4,000: 80 million people a week went to the cinema in the US, against only 20 million in the UK.' And this was at the end of the twenties, before sound came in and American advantage was further strengthened by community of language.

The economic advantage of Hollywood, as well as our common language, is only part of the story. We cannot write about British films without reference to British social tradition and the resistant social structure that is part of Britain's imperial inheritance. I know this is not a pleasant thought, particularly to those who automatically accept the idea that art has no connection with either finance or history.

But in no other way can we explain the domination of our screens and our popular audiences by Hollywood. The US has its class structure, of course; but it is very different from the system that affects everything that happens in this country.

The British cinema has always been a middle-class preserve: and even if working-class heroes are now two-a-penny, the standards by which they are judged remain mostly bourgeois. It is no wonder if, during the first half-century of cinema, the British popular audience preferred the 'classless' (to them) ethos of Hollywood, as opposed to the class-conscious values of Islington and Shepherd's Bush, Elstree, Pinewood, Denham and Ealing.

American pictures were not only more luxurious: they were smarter and relatively classless. The US has been a dynamic, pushy, expanding society, dedicated (however questionably) to the values of democracy and classless wealth.

Jews from central Europe created Hollywood, entertained the immigrant masses and even gave employment to artists. They still do. The Jews of Birmingham produced Oscar Deutsch, who founded the Odeon circuit; Victor Saville, who graduated to Hollywood; and Sir Michael Balcon, who achieved his apotheosis on Ealing Green.

When a true history of British cinema comes to be written it will surely feature a proper assessment of the careers of these men and of Balcon in particular. Middle-class and middle-brow, amiable and ruthless, Balcon is a key figure in the story of British cinema.

This is a poor book and a mistaken one. Far from seeing the British cinema in the perspective I consider necessary, Park deplores 'the failure of the production machine to push directors towards projects that would tap their potential and excite audiences'. Just what these grandiose phrases mean is not clear. Park apparently believes in a 'national film-making tradition', though he is unaware of the realism that is essential to that tradition, which informs our best feature films as well as Grierson's documentary movement and the poetic masterpieces of Humphrey Jennings.

Park's final solution is to advocate the foundation of 'script factories' which would employ screenwriters 'willing to work consistently in a stimulating creative environment . . . likely to miss out on the occasional big deal, but always working at developing first-class scripts.' This is nothing more than question-begging hot air, I am afraid.

In case anyone is misled by its very decent production into thinking that *British Cinema* presents any kind of a valid survey, let me list some of the films that are not mentioned, in no particular order: *Journey's End, Sunshine Susie, Song of Ceylon, Man of Aran, South Riding, Gaslight, The Way Ahead, Henry V, Western Approaches, A Diary for Timothy, The Queen of Spades, Chance of a Lifetime, Every Day Except Christmas, We are the Lambeth Boys, The Naked Civil Servant, O Lucky Man!* . . . There is no mention of Karl Francis, whom we should know more about, or of Amber Films, of which any book with this title should take account.

Realism and morality, as well as social stagnation and economic disadvantage, are traditions which any critic of the British cinema cannot afford to neglect.

British Cinema: The Historical Imperative

International Film Guide, 1984

I AM NOT – AND I REGRET IT – REALLY THE RIGHT PERSON TO WRITE ABOUT THE British cinema in 1983. I regret it because it is a subject that has concerned me, plagued me, haunted me for a long time, and about which I have felt deeply. It has been indeed more than a 'subject': it has been a cause. But a defeated rather than a triumphant cause. And defeat is never pleasant to face.

Also, even as a mere subject, there is the challenge of complexity. The sheer statistical complexity: the dates and details of Quota acts, of Eady acts, of legislation and recommendation and subsidy: the endlessly quoted, endlessly forgotten facts of the long, hard-fought, hard-disputed campaign to protect the British cinema, to nurture it, to save it. And the *facts* of the failure of the campaign: the losses, the closures, the defections and the betrayals. Korda bankrupt, Ealing gone, Denham gone; the American occupation; the steady flow of emigration; our own failure of vitality and nerve and belief in ourselves. Cinemas boarded up, smashed, no longer useful even for Bingo. British film-makers wearing bare the path to the Beverly Hills Hotel, the Beverly Wilshire, to Burbank, Melrose and Universal City in search of finance for British movies, justification by American acclaim. 'The Brits are coming!' – that craven cry of pseudo-victory . . .

I must admit to a temperamental weakness. I cannot rid myself of the feeling that to make the case absolutely water-tight, the conclusions inescapable, statistics, dates, figures all need to be marshalled, quoted, accurately set out. This I cannot bring myself to do. It is probably unnecessary anyway. The statistics, after all, have been endlessly quoted, whether in White Papers, in union demands for nationalisation, or in 'objective' (i.e. sitting-on-the-fence) articles in *Sight and Sound*. And it hasn't made an atom of difference. The essentials are well known. Let us recapitulate. The motion picture as entertainment was developed simultaneously in a number of different countries (France, Britain, the United States) as the nineteenth century came to an end. It was an 'industrial' entertainment, relatively expensive to produce. From the start the American industry had the advantage of huge home markets, of huge, unsophisticated audiences avid for entertainment, of huge potential investment in an expanding economy. Hollywood (the place that soon became synonymous with American cinema) did not suffer from the dislocation which weakened its European rivals in the First World War. By comparison the British cinema was puny, ill-nourished, despised, with an envious but confident eye fixed on the American market. Producers in Britain who needed some guarantee of profitability for their product (Michael Balcon, for instance making his first independent film in 1922) had to import American stars, Alfred Hitchcock's first picture was shot for Balcon's company in a German studio with two American leading ladies.

The thirties
The sound cinema of the thirties only confirmed these melancholy truths. It hit Britain hardest of all. European film industries had at least the protection of language: their audiences liked, from time to time, to hear movies spoken in French, German, Italian, Spanish . . . Audiences in Britain, on the other hand, were just as happy with English accents. (Working-class audiences, in fact, were probably happier to hear dialogue spoken with the accent of Brooklyn or the Western Territories than with the posh affectation of 'Mayfair'.) Attempts to protect the British industry by legally requiring cinemas to screen a certain amount of native product resulted in cheap, 'quickie' productions by American companies, usually starring one or more Hollywood players on the skids, offering employment to British craftsmen, but further lowering the creative reputation of British cinema. Popular comedy with the likes of Gracie Fields, Jessie Matthews, George Formby, represented the strength of native tradition. There was a documentary movement which made films that relatively few people saw.

It is a familiar story, and it is only partially true. Or rather it only offers a partial explanation for the defeat of our own cinema, in our own country, at the hands of the American industry. Just as important as these basic economic facts are the historic and social realities which the British cinema has always reflected – the reality of a nation past its prime: an Empire still nominally the greatest the world had ever known, yet already, in the first half of this century, carrying the fatal infection of decline, and of which the majority of intelligent and imaginative Britons were already less proud than ashamed; a society educated (by a system admirably devised for the administration of Empire) into snobbery and philistinism, deeply divided into mutually contemptuous classes. Not necessarily creatively, but certainly industrially, the cinema is a mass medium. One of the great strengths of the American cinema has always been its freedom from the petrification of class, the limitations of accent. Of course, like every nation, America has its class system: but it is a system based on money, not on inherited position. As a result, it is stimulating rather than paralysing. Few British films of the thirties crossed the barriers of class: most film-makers remained implacably surburban: very few drew anything at all either from British popular tradition or from the world around them.

Most characteristic, and probably most fatal of all, was the *gentility* of the British film tradition; its cosiness, whether bourgeois or working class; its essential conformism to class and cultural norms. Even *South Riding*, one of the films of the thirties that came nearest to themes of class as well as personal conflict, and that dared to portray a regional society, had to end with the celebration of the Silver Jubilee of King George V. Films were made in London: Scotland, Ireland, Wales were not explored. History was not explored. Even the Empire was not explored. Vitality, the essential ingredient of art as of entertainment, was absent, whether of theme or of treatment. No wonder the mass audience preferred Hollywood. And no wonder the 'intelligentsia' sneered – it was the habitual refuge of their impotence – and shopped abroad for their movie entertainment: the France of Pagnol, Duvivier, Carné – Russian revivals of Eisenstein and Pudovkin – the documentarists – even sometimes the Americans.

There were a few British exceptions. Hitchcock, Victor Saville – both, of course, to end up in Hollywod. And one, the most significant, who was not British at all – or rather a great deal more British than the British. Alexander Korda achieved his first truly international success with a film about a British monarch (Henry VIII), played by a brilliant English actor at the head of a talented English cast. Of course, the cameraman was French, the story and dialogues were by a Hungarian, and so was the direction. But the picture counted as British and it impressed the world. Korda, however, was alone in following his own example. He made historical romances (*Fire Over England, The Scarlet Pimpernel*); he made fantasies (*The Man Who Could Work Miracles, Things to Come*); he made modern stories (*Farewell Again, Storm in a Teacup, South Riding*); and even – again alone – celebrated the myth of Empire: *Sanders of the River, The Four Feathers, The Drum*. Korda was significant, even more for his uniqueness than for his achievement. Perhaps by the thirties only a foreigner could believe strongly enough in Britain and could care enough about it in the right way to create a distinctive and *vital* tradition for British films.

Wartime cinema

Or it took a war. The 1939-1945 war is chiefly thought of now, I suppose, as having inspired a great number of propagandist works celebrating, in the most conventional way, the dedication and bravery of British soldiers, sailors and airmen, as well as their womenfolk and families on the Home Front. And incidentally, the very first of these, a dreadful film but still the first, was produced by Korda: *The Lion Has Wings*. It is true that most of these films, particularly in the early years of the war, were astonishingly naïf, melodramatic, and narrowly bourgeois in their class attitudes. But then so was Britain. And there is something which, in spite of their schoolboy level of imagination and their emotional platitudes, gave them and gives them still a dignity and warmth of emotion which demands respect. They were *about* something. And here and there, even, there were films which, almost for the first time in British film-making, showed the originality and the grasp of film form which can produce true master-pieces. I am thinking, of course, first of Humphrey Jennings and his imper-ishable *Listen to Britain, Fires Were Started* and *Diary for Timothy*. But also of Carol Reed edging towards maturity, and David Lean edging towards authority.

So the British cinema arrived, for the first time in its existence, with confidence and a sense of identity in the post-war period. It will be very difficult for people who were not aware (or alive) in the late forties to imagine that climate of optimism and vigour. David Lean followed *Brief Encounter* with *Great Expectations*; Carol Reed followed *The Third Man* with *The Fallen Idol*; Powell and Pressburger, weird and wonderful, pro-duced *A Matter of Life and Death*; at Ealing, Balcon and Cavalcanti, Danishewski, Hamer and Mackendrick discovered comedy . . . But once again the old truth was proved, of the dependency of the cinema on national morale. Or to put it another way, that the cinema can reflect, can even stimulate the vitality of a nation, but it cannot *create* that vitality. Britain in the fifties fell back into a kind of torpor, an exhaustion perhaps: the flare-up of radicalism and progressive fervour which resulted from the war did not survive the first years of peace. The Labour government nationalised coal and steel and transport and health; but they did not dare to (or care to?) nationalise education, and the class system remained intact. The Americans returned and the audience received them with open arms. Even when, for a short while, the flow of Hollywood films checked (by a regulation from the Exchequer), the Rank Organisation's stepped-up production programme, supervised by Sydney Box, only resulted in a flow of mediocre pictures which nobody wanted to see. And who today recalls the unique attempt at government sponsorship of feature film-making, 'Group Three' Productions, supervised by John Grierson (of all people) and John Baxter at Beaconsfield Studios? No, we just couldn't keep it up.

Free cinema

1956, however, was a year of stimulus and change. Suez, Hungary: the end of sentimental communism and the birth of a 'New Left': commercial tel-evision: the English Stage Company at the Royal Court: Free Cinema at the National Film Theatre . . . Here is another time of aggression, opti-mism and amusement, which must be unimaginable to the under-forties of today. It led to the sixties, but it was better than the sixties, which already carried the seeds of the smart opportunism which has characterised the last, say, fifteen years. Free Cinema has, of course, been largely forgotten, but it was a phenomenon worthy of recall. Half a dozen would-be film-makers combined to present work (two 16mm documentaries and one poetic fiction on 35mm) at the National Film Theatre, coined a provocative title and wrote a coat-trailing manifesto – film-makers against a constipated, classbound British cinema which in no way reflected the realities of today, etc, etc. The shows were quite successful, attracted far more publicity than would be possible today, and aroused a lot of hostility. The National Film Theatre soon found the tone of the presentations too tendentious and withdrew its facilities. The Ford Motor Company terminated their sponsorship after their first two films won Grands Prix at international festivals. And the rising generation was more interested in working for television than in asserting the liberty of the artist in shoe-string independent production.

The Free Cinema shows only took place for two or three years. But indirectly they led (via the Royal Court Theatre, in fact) to a new British wave in the sixties, a succession of films characterised first by what might be called 'working-class realism' (*Saturday Night and Sunday Morning*, *A Taste of Honey*, *This Sporting Life*), but extending in style and subject matter to films as various as *Morgan* and *Isadora*, *Tom Jones* and *The Charge of the Light Brigade*, *If. . . .* and *0 Lucky Man!* It is not an unimpressive list. Yet as a movement, a propagating influence, Free Cinema failed. It was a failure of significance, I think, and in some ways a final one.

Perhaps I need to explain just what I mean by 'failure' in this context. I do not mean that the achievement was inconsiderable, that the films themselves were creatively unsuccessful. But the movement, insofar as it began with certain general principles, failed to generate support or acceptance. The effort was not sustained. After *Isadora*, Karel Reisz went to Hollywood, where he made *The Gambler* and *Dog Soldiers*; Tony Richardson has lived in Los Angeles for over ten rather unproductive years; other contemporaries (Schlesinger, Clayton, Boorman, Yates) became as much American as British film-makers. In the late sixties the British cinema itself followed the lead of Dick Lester and produced a succession of swingin' comedies, few of which proved successful either artistically or at the box-office. And inevitably, following the time-honoured snobbery of their class, British critics and film 'intellectuals' failed to support either the effort of Free Cinema or its result. For them this was the era of Godard and Jean-Marie Straub: at home Joe Losey was about the only reputable name. *Cahiers du Cinéma* had taught the English intelligentsia to admire Hawks, Preminger and Samuel Fuller. When François Truffaut suggested to Alfred Hitchcock that the words 'British cinema' constituted a contradiction in terms, the English applauded his cleverness.

It is interesting to consider just why, and how, the 'Free Cinema' new wave failed. It was the last movement – and the last possible movement probably – which aimed to reanimate, to *take over* the mainstream of British cinema. We believed that there was a right British film tradition (however meagre) and a wrong one (firmly established). We believed that we could find enough popular support from British audiences, or create it, to make a healthy and British industry possible. Or at least that this was worth trying. We had about eighteen months of success. Our aims were not supported, partly because the American tradition of popular entertainment cinema was too deeply established: and partly because, amongst the British themselves, resistance to change, acceptance of the straitjacket of middle-class social-artistic conformism, was too strong. I still have a cutting from the *Evening Standard* at the end of the year, in which the paper's film critic announced, with unmistakable relish, that 1963 had been 'the Year the Kitchen Sink Went Down the Drain'. (This was apropos a speech in which John Davis, as head of the Rank Organisation, attacked such gloomy working-class fantasies as *This Sporting Life*, and announced that in future his company would devote itself to the provision of family entertainment.)

The younger generation
But there was failure within Free Cinema too: the commitment was simply not strong enough, and unequally held. Tony Richardson got fed up with the English and went to Los Angeles, where he says he enjoys life a great deal more. Karel Reisz abandoned the social for other, more personal preoccupations, and also preferred to operate where opportunities were less grudgingly offered. My own contribution has perhaps been too intermittent, certainly too idiosyncratic and unconforming to have much influence. Supporters have been few. The younger generation in particular were bored and frustrated by Britain: they found stimulation as well as opportunity and reward in America. This is not to criticise them. It is to state a simple, significant fact of history.

The Free Cinema ethos, you might say, was Social Democratic: radical, moral and reformist, rather than revolutionary, theoretical and intellectual. We were succeeded, as I have described, by the 'swingers', the would-be sophisticated mannerists whose image of Britain derived from journalists and media-fantasy rather than from experience. They failed. And they in turn have been succeeded by the self-regarding theoreticians of 'Alternative Cinema' – Marxists, Trots, semiologists etc, who have substituted a Red Brick puritanism for the old Oxbridge camp, without influencing anything more important than a handful of critics, certain departments of the British Film Institute, and the specialised film programmes on Channel 4. Alternative Cinema has not aimed to transform or take over the British cinema: it has been content to establish a ghetto of the self-righteous, just as snobbish in its admiration of Wim Wenders and the intellectual criticism of France as were their bourgeois predecessors in their preoccupation with Duvivier or Bergman.

It must now be clear why I do not consider myself really an appropriate – certainly not an objective – assessor of the British cinema in 1983. Experience has made me pessimistic, even gloomy. The cinema, I have always believed, gives a clear indication of a nation's morale, vitality, creativity. The British cinema has reflected only too clearly a nation lacking in energy and the valuable kind of pride – the pride which cherishes its own traditions without chauvinism, and will scorn foreign domination either in terms of money or ideas. In nothing is this clearer than in the attitude of today's film-makers, audiences and media towards America. The American cinema, as we know, has always dominated; but hardly in the unquestioned way it does today. Take note, for a couple of days, of how many times you see or hear the phrase 'Oscar-winning' used in the press, on the radio or TV. Success for a British film is now most convincingly represented by a hyped-up accolade bestowed by a self-appointed jury of American film technicians. Of course, British film-makers are not to be blamed for going where the work and the money and the appreciation are. It is Britain, not America, which does not value or support what they have to contribute: and in Britain they will gain only respect and glamour from success in the Hollywood adventure.

At home, meanwhile, the little world of cinema shrinks, as the public grows less and less inclined to pay high prices for the shoddy presentation of movies in (mostly) badly run theatres. For how many years now have Sir Harold Wilson and Lady Falkender presided over their committee of whatever-it-is, investigating or advocating the institution of a British Film Authority? Are they still sitting? Who knows or cares? Critics in the national papers continue to review the films presented to them each week by distributors for presentation in the West End, or perhaps as far afield as the Fulham Road. The appearance of the old system must be preserved: although the truth is the historical truth – that it is already extinct. 'Men are we, and must grieve . . .' Yes, history – unless we are very lucky – conquers us all in the end.

These reflections may seem unduly mournful, even perverse, when it is considered that they are penned in June 1983, at the very centre (if not yet the climax) of the British Film Renaissance. For the British cinema is on the move again, with David Puttnam, tycoon Jake Eberts of Goldcrest, and Sir Richard Attenborough in the van, the Oscars won by *Chariots of*

Fire and *Gandhi* borne along behind them, like the Ark of the Covenant, as assurance that British enterprise, technical know-how, middle-class and middle-brow-humanistic appeal can capture the screens and video-recorders of the world.

Well, let me make it clear that I have never doubted our ability in this country to make films which entertainingly and stimulatingly reflect our own ways of life. We still can, and sometimes do. Consider the achievement of *The Boys from the Blackstuff*, *Octopussy*, *Local Hero*, *The Meaning of Life*, *The Draughtsman's Contract*, *The Ploughman's Lunch* . . . It is an uneven achievement, of course; and it is ironic that the only one of these with the kind urgency, moral passion and imaginative concern a film needs if it is to move mountains – which is after all the highest function of art – was made for television. (Of course, if our film industry was not moribund, Alan Bleasdale and Philip Saville would already have completed a movie successor to their TV series.) But there is enough creativity there to make it clear that a British film industry is not going to fall back through lack of talent.

Through lack of what, then? Through lack of what we seem always to have lacked – and I am not speaking just of film-makers but of critics, 'intellectuals' and the whole useless army of institutional, over-subsidised academics. What we lack is a proper understanding of our own traditions, a proper pride in our own achievement. And, based on such pride and understanding, the will and the vitality to support our own talent, the imagination to nurture it, the determination to sustain it. All we need, in other words, is a reversal of history. That's not much to ask. Is it?

They Were Expendable *(1945). John Ford and his unit.*

AMERICAN CINEMA

Inventing Hollywood

Review of *An Empire of Their Own: How the Jews Invented Hollywood* by Neal Gabler and *Goldwyn: A Biography* by A. Scott Berg in the *Times Literary Supplement*, 15 December 1989

IT IS ONLY 80 YEARS SINCE THE FIRST FILM STUDIO WAS BUILT. BEFORE THAT, American movies were shot in New York – and ten years earlier such things did not exist. Film producers moved to the West Coast partly to escape the prosecuting Trust of Thomas Edison, who claimed the patents to movie cameras and projectors, and partly to profit from the wonderful constant sunshine of California. Growth was phenomenal, keeping pace with the demand for this new entertainment, which required no knowledge of language. It was all part of a cataclysmic national expansion, promising not just shelter but opportunity and the possibility of wealth to countless victims of European poverty and oppression. By 1918, Neal Gabler writes in *An Empire of Their Own*, 'there were well over seventy production companies in Los Angeles, and over 80 per cent of the world's movies were made there.'

It is well known, of course, that the early American film industry was Jewish in ownership and authority, but I doubt if the phenomenon of its genesis and astonishing growth has been described as clearly, with such a wealth of factual and personal detail, as in *An Empire of Their Own* and A. Scott Berg's biography of Samuel Goldwyn. Together they give a comprehensive and graphic account of Hollywood's dream factories. These are not critical books – judgements and descriptions of particular films are conventional, often perfunctory. The originality of *An Empire of Their Own* is to show how the Hollywood studios came to exist through the unstoppable ambition – and the entrepreneurial flair – of a small group of Jewish immigrants from Eastern Europe. They were colleagues, they intermarried, they were even sometimes friends. But they were above all competitors (this was, after all, America), and always ruthless.

It is one of this group who is the subject of Berg's biography. His original name was Schmuel Gelbfisz. In 1895, at the age of sixteen, he set out from Warsaw to walk to Hamburg. He took ship to London, then walked to Birmingham, where he stayed with relatives and sold sponges. Later, he walked across the Canadian-US border, worked in the glove trade till he found himself obsessed by the flickering images of the Nickelodeon, and produced the first full-length western to come out of California (*The Squaw Man*, directed by Cecil B. de Mille). He ended up with a studio of his own and universal respect for his personally supervised, 'quality' productions, one of Hollywood's most idiosyncratic, most tenacious tycoons, Samuel Goldwyn.

Few of Goldwyn's peers, the men who were to become the dictators of Hollywood's major studios, could rival his epic journey, but all started with similar disadvantages. Their backgrounds were orthodoxly Jewish, they spoke no English, but to them all America was the land of promise. Scott Berg groups the future masters of Metro-Goldwyn-Mayer, Fox, Warner Brothers, Paramount and Universal in their remarkable historic context:

> Between 1880 and 1910, one and a half million Jews joined wagon trains of pushcarts leaving Eastern Europe. In the 1880s alone, the family of Louis B. Mayer left Demre, near Vilna, in Lithuania; Lewis Zeleznick (later Selznick) ran away from Kiev; William Fuchs (later Fox) emigrated from Tulcheva, Hungary; the Warner family uprooted itself from Krasnashiltz, Poland, near the Russian border; Adolph Zukor abandoned Ricse, Hungary; and Carl Laemmle left Wurttemberg, Germany – gamblers with nothing to lose, all from within a five hundred-mile radius of Warsaw.

None of these men came from theatrical backgrounds or from the business of entertainment (the cinema, of course, did not yet exist). Most of them were raised in matriarchal families, with ineffective or shiftless fathers, and mothers who kept things going and looked to their sons to succeed. The immigrants burrowed their way as tradesmen into the expanding American markets: clothing, furs, gloves, jewellery. Harry Cohn (King Cohn of Columbia) was successively a shipping clerk, a trolley conductor and a song plugger. Jack Warner toured as a boy soprano. Perhaps the greatest potential for expansion was offered by the entertainment industry, stimulated by the inventions of Thomas Edison. The appeal of his Penny Arcades and primitive movies to the illiterate working populations of America's industrial cities was instant and overwhelming. Also the source of seemingly unlimited profit. It was their recognition of this that brought these men to their vocation, running arcades, then theatres, then stockpiling and distributing films, then going into production themselves – inventing Hollywood.

Profit was the lure. Even as a child, Agnes de Mille told Scott Berg, she felt that what fired her uncle Cecil and Sam Goldfish (as he then translated himself) when they set out for California to make *The Squaw Man*, was unmitigated greed, 'pure lust for money and power'. But there is romance

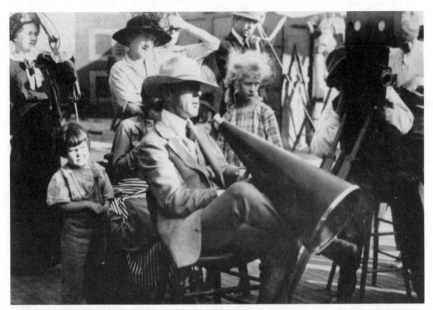

D. W. Griffith (with megaphone) on the set of The Birth of a Nation.

in show business, too. Adolph Zukor, the most cold-blooded of the tycoons, was doing well with his Novelty Fur Company when, in 1897, he took his fiancée to an evening of Vaudeville where they saw a brief film of stage stars exchanging kisses in a Broadway hit: 'It ran maybe a minute . . . but it made an indelible impression on my mind.'

Respectability was also a motive. These men were Jewish, but they were determined to be Americans first, accepted by a society which, for all its youthful dynamic, already had a Protestant establishment with its own hierarchy, its own snobbism of wealth and culture. The immigrants knew they had to build an American Empire, and the result was the golden era of American cinema.

In its early years, Hollywood produced classic silent films whose artistry soared far beyond commercialism. The studios survived the invention of sound. By the end of the 1930s they were manufacturing wonderful pictures which combined with a skill that now seems lost, a popular, classless, international appeal with emotion and wit and a naïf humanity that is distinctly American. Mickey Rooney and Judy Garland (in *Babes in Arms*, filmed 50 years ago) often reappear on our television screens, hymning the praise of 'God's Country', marching to the drum beat of Louis B. Mayer,

We've got no Duce – we've got no Führer –

We've got Garbo and Norma Shearer . . .

The optimism and assurance still amaze.

The Second World War was a time of prosperity for Hollywood, but its aftermath brought slow death to pioneers. Neal Gabler painstakingly, painfully charts their decline. It began most decisively with the divorce, by anti-Trust legislation, of film production and distribution from exhibition. Stripped of their theatre chains, the studios found themselves without a guaranteed market for their product. Television, at first despised (as sound had been), became a lethal competitor. Morale was shaken and creative talent lost by the attacks of Senator Joe McCarthy (ardently supported by Louis B. Mayer, who even suggested to John Huston that he make a documentary tribute to him) and the Un-American Activities Committee. Defensively 'American' now, the Moguls lacked the confidence or the courage to withstand. Instead they heeded the counsel of Rabbi Edgar Maguin, their spiritual leader. 'You are a very small minority,' he warned them. 'You can't do things that other people can do and get away with them . . . You see what happened in Germany. It can happen here.'

Monsters they undoubtedly were. Jewish-European they were born; American they made themselves. And of them all Schmuel-Samuel Gelbfisz-Goldwyn (Scott Berg's biography is as exhaustively researched, as richly detailed, as his life of Maxwell Perkins) became one of the most American and the most successful. He was never, though, quite one of the most powerful. He was too compulsive an egoist, too jealous of anyone who might threaten his predominance, ever to be a top politician or a trusted collaborator. He never became head of a Hollywood studio, and was never responsible for a film he did not produce himself.

The 'Goldwyn Touch' became a synonym for 'Quality'. Even if William Wyler, his preferred director, remarked sarcastically that the films he made for Goldwyn – among them *Dodsworth, Dead End, Wuthering Heights, The Little Foxes, The Best Years of Our Lives* – constituted the chief evidence for the 'Touch', there is no doubt that Goldwyn had a special feeling for, and was determined to employ, outstanding creative talent. His famous 'Goldwynisms' ('Include me out,' etc) were usually shrewd and often the invention of an expert publicity department. He might always insist on calling it 'Withering Heights' – but he made the picture. Hollywood's greatest cameraman, Gregg Toland, developed his style and his technique under contract to Goldwyn. Richard Day designed his sets and Alfred Newman headed his music department. Robert Sherwood, Lillian Hellman, Ben Hecht wrote scripts for him – all talents which could give distinction even to mediocre pictures.

He could make horrendous mistakes, of course, like his stubborn attempts to make a Goldwyn Garbo out of poor Anna Sten. But that is the privilege of a master showman. It does not detract from his fascination, or his significance, that on close inspection Goldwyn turns out to be a pretty monotonously odious character. Much of the same could be said of most of his peers. Perhaps it is the price that has to be paid for the kind of success they lived for. He married twice, both times without love. His first wife left him quite soon: he refused to pay her the alimony he owed, and he felt sorry for himself when his neglected daughter refused him the love he could never feel for her. His second wife said of herself that she had a cash register where she should have a heart. They made a good team.

His emotional shallowness together with his prodigious energy made Goldwyn a master-manufacturer of the kind of popular entertainment with which Hollywood captured the world. Energy without depth: it is the American formula for success. His daughter understood him best: 'He'd cry at corn and laugh at pratfalls – the perfect audience. But those feelings were only skin deep, because when it came to people – to real emotions – he knew nothing.' There was nothing, in other words, to deflect his ambition.

By one of history's suggestive coincidences, the year (1896) that Schmuel Gelbfisz arrived in Birmingham, England, on his way to the United States, was the year of the birth in that same Midland city of Michael Balcon (also Jewish), who was to become the most affectionately respected of English film producers. It is a telling juxtaposition: the bourgeois gentility of Ealing against the populist dynamic of Hollywood. No wonder, in the fierce competition of entertainment industries, the British cinema has always gone to the wall. Energy without depth may not produce film art of the highest creative quality; but it will certainly achieve better results than a cinema without either.

Charlie Chaplin

Review of *Chaplin: His Life and Art* by David Robinson in *The Tatler*, 4 March 1985

FASHION IS A MYSTERIOUS BUSINESS. UNPREDICTABLE, APPARENTLY WHIMSICAL, its reversals as capricious as its enthusiasms. Why should Charlie Chaplin, yesterday the whole world's favourite, become *démodé* in only a few years? Today it seems fashionable to deny the genius once universally acclaimed.

Yet how instantly once, how irresistibly he triumphed! In 1914 Chaplin was a 25-year-old English music-hall performer touring the United States as a member of Fred Karno's company of mime-comedians. Just how the telegram came inviting him to Hollywood is disputed. Was it Mack Sennett, monarch of the Keystone Comics, on holiday with his girlfriend Mabel Normand in New York, who discovered him? Sennett claimed it was. '"Feller's pretty funny," Mabel said. "Think he'd be good enough for pictures?" I said, "He might be," Mabel said . . .'

On the other hand Kim Peters, engaged on adding veils to the big semi-nude Mucha-style murals he had painted at the Pantages Theatre in Los Angeles, maintained it was Harry Aitken, a major stockholder in Keystone, who spotted Charlie's picture in the foyer and got him hired. Anyway, Chaplin signed with the Americans, left the Karno troupe and arrived on the Coast in December 1914. A year later he had made 35 comedies, discovered his archetypal costume (invented for his second Keystone film: he thought it up, he said, 'on the way to the wardrobe'), had become his own director and was already, as we say today, a Superstar.

See these films today, scratched, familiar and probably mutilated, and they look – like old movies. To the audiences of 1914, as David Robinson puts it, 'they arrived like rockets'. Chaplin had only been in movies for six months when Keystone were proclaiming 'The Chaplin Boom'. The British trade paper, *The Cinema*, greeted his first film in release as 'about the funniest film we have seen' and called Chaplin 'a born screen comedian; he does things we have never seen on the screen before.' Four years later he had his own studio and created the character who had become (again to quote Robinson), 'the most universally recognised representation of a human being in the history of mankind,' and if we except Jesus and the Buddha as being gods, I suppose he is right.

There have been any number of books about Charlie, including his own autobiography; and I must admit to having read none of them. Still, I am quite sure that this is the best. There are a number of reasons why David Robinson should be Chaplin's ideal biographer. He is our best film critic, both knowledgeable and responsive, and blessedly free from that ingratiating journalistic style which afflicts so many of his colleagues. He is a devoted authority on music-hall: his film of Hetty King in performance uniquely preserves the spirit of that vanished art. And he has the loving investigative zeal of the born historian. Given the freedom of Chaplin's archives – letters, contracts, cuttings, all the scrupulously preserved records of his productions, as well as reel upon reel of rejected or reshot film – he used this treasure to produce a classic piece of film biography which is also the fascinating story of a brilliant, perverse, courageous man, indisputably one of the great artists of the twentieth century.

Charlie Chaplin eating 'bootlace spaghetti' in a scene from The Gold Rush *(1922).*

David Robinson's first intention, he says, was to deal only with Chaplin's work; fortunately he changed his mind. Most artists' lives, after all, are inseparable from their art, and Chaplin's especially, from his yeoman English antecedents, his impoverished, adventurous south London childhood (which inspired the settings of so many of his movies), his long apprenticeship in the halls and theatres of the English provinces. David Robinson is exactly the writer for all this: 'The Chaplin family lived for generations in Suffolk . . . Chaplin's great-great-grandfather, Shadrach Chaplin, was born in 1786 and became the village bootmaker in Great Finborough, Suffolk.' So the story begins, with the calm solidity and texture of some monumental Victorian novel.

With a father who was a successful music-hall singer and a mother who had her little hour of performing success, it is no wonder that the child Charlie wanted to act. From the start his talent was outstanding. He was nine years old when he got his first job as one of the Eight Lancashire Lads ('who treat the audience to some of the finest clog dancing it is possible to imagine'). Between 1903 and 1906 he played Billy the Pageboy in a dramatised version of *Sherlock Holmes* on no fewer than 70 touring dates (including the Duke of York's in St Martin's Lane). And in 1908 he joined Fred Karno's troupe, in which his brilliant miming soon made him a leading player. The path of destiny was straight before him.

Genius is not much value unless it is accompanied by the capacity for hard labour. Chaplin had that kind of genius. The speed and fertility with which the early films poured out is amazing. After the 35 Keystone comedies in 1914, there were fourteen for Essanay and twelve for Mutual: this got him to 1917. Inevitably the pace slowed as new ideas and techniques developed. The virtuosity and wit which had entranced a whole world came to serve conceptions more personal, a vision more poetic. And always the search for perfection was compulsive. By the time he made *The Gold Rush* in 1922, Charlie was working in his own studio, distributing (as a co-founder of United Artists) his own films, and taking over a year to produce a 90-minute movie.

Not only film-makers, surely, will find themselves absorbed by these pages in which David Robinson describes, in meticulous detail, the making of masterpieces like *The Kid, The Gold Rush, The Circus, City Lights*. Here is Chaplin putting his universal popularity to work to buy him the total creative freedom of painter or poet, taking his time, owing no authority but his own. When inspiration didn't come, production would be halted. When perfection was not achieved, a scene would be retaken, or scrapped. *The Gold Rush* was started with one leading lady: Chaplin married her (she was found to be pregnant), retook her scenes and finished the picture with another. He tried to replace Virginia Cherrill in *City Lights*, shot some sequences with a replacement, then brought her back again (and had to pay for it). The evolution of that last, classic scene in *City Lights*, achieving its perfect form through take after take, is described in rare and absorbing detail; this is the best, most illuminating kind of writing about cinema.

Genius can be attractive – sometimes fatally so: it is often formidable, rarely 'nice'. David Robinson, with his fair and very full account of Chaplin's life outside his film-making, gives us a completely recognisable portrait of the artist as a man of charm, generosity and egoism; ruthlessly determined, snobbish and sensitive; also a man of principle and courage. (It is interesting to find him, even in his Keystone days, being described as 'a bit off-colour in his politics'.) Perhaps partly because of his debt of honour to the Chaplin family, more likely because of his own essential decorum, Robinson mostly refrains from psychological speculation and from judgement; I think his book is the stronger for this. But he calls convincing witnesses. Ivor Montagu, for instance, in his book *With Eisenstein in Hollywood*, retelling a conversation between himself and two great friends of Charlie's, Georgia Hale, his leading lady from *The Gold Rush*, and Henry Bergman, actor and devoted colleague. 'Ah,' said Georgia, 'three hearts that beat as one – yours, mine and Charlie's. 'Yes,' replied Henry. 'And they're all thinking of the same thing: Charlie.' When we retold the tale to Charlie in Georgia's presence, Charlie considered, then admitted: 'Yes, it's true.'

Chaplin inspired loyalty and affection as well as the disappointment and even bitterness inevitable when people expect consistency from a temperament of this creative kind. 'A brilliant diamond is the apt simile,' wrote Thomas Burke. 'He's as hard and bright at that, and his lustre is as erratic. And if you split him, you would find – that there was no personal source of those changing lights; they were only the flashings of genius.' Burke, storyteller and essayist, was a south Londoner like Charlie, and a contemporary. His summing-up of Chaplin is absolutely convincing:

'Whatever he is, generous, cold, capricious, he calls out all my affection as a man, and all my admiration as an artist.' And as for his selfishness: 'Charlie lives as most of us would if we had the necessary nerve to face ourselves as we really are.'

Like many artists who start with a tremendous burst of creativity and success, Chaplin suffered from time's changes. His genius was in mime, and his heaven-sent medium was the silent film. 'For myself,' he told an interviewer in 1931, 'I know that I cannot use dialogue.' He was right, but although he resisted obstinately for another five years (*Modern Times* appeared in 1936), he had to give in. There are brilliant things in the later films, but when sound broke in to disrupt the purity of the style, a certain clumsy didacticism came in too – as well as a certain self-consciousness, even a smugness. Chaplin was not an actor: his weak voice and an ineradicable habit of playing to the camera make his performances in films like *The Great Dictator*, *Monsieur Verdoux* and *A King in New York* often painfully amateurish. *Limelight* is another matter: you may, like Picasso, detest its sentimentalism: or you may surrender to its self-absorption. It must be the most purely *auteurist* film ever made.

David Robinson is too discreet, perhaps too kindly, to dwell on the creative decline of Chaplin's later career. And he is right. We don't after all read Wordsworth's later poems, and we don't need to watch *A King in New York*. (We can be glad, though, that those years brought Chaplin his marriage to Oona O'Neill, and a personal happiness he had never known before.) There has been a danger that the late productions might cast a shadow over Chaplin's twenty-odd years of supreme achievement. This book dispels that shadow. I don't know if this was David Robinson's ambition; but this is what he has done. Chaplin's genius is reinstated.

Mary Pickford

Review of *Mary Pickford* by Scott Eyman, in *The Spectator*, 25 April 1992

IT WAS NOEL COWARD, I BELIEVE, WHO SAID THAT HIS FAME, IN THE EARLY days of his success, equalled that of the Beatles 40 years later. This was not exactly true. Coward was a star of the theatre, and so of no interest to the working class. He never received the adulation lavished by their fans on popular musicians. For that we have to go back to the huge popularity of the heroes and heroines of the silent cinema.

Mary Pickford was a stupendous star. Her films, and the lively, childlike character she played so consistently (and so well) made her immensely rich and beloved of the most rapidly growing nation in the world.

She was born in Toronto, and she lived and died a Canadian. Her real name was Gladys Smith. She began acting in stage melodramas at the age of six, possibly five. She supported her widowed mother, her sister and her brother. Scott Eyman has researched her life story with great care; his book is authoritative as well as gripping. Clearly Gladys had exceptional, instinctive talent. David Belasco, producer, writer and actor of great renown, took her on and gave her the name of Mary Pickford. She went into films, under D. W. Griffith in his Biograph period, because they paid better.

Mary Pickford.

Mary Pickford never forgot that, like her friend Lillian Gish, she started in the theatre. She was a real actress. But her aim was also to give pleasure, and she knew she depended on the approval of her public. She learned a great deal from Griffith and understood that he was better than the others. She left him, though, because Carl Laemmle at least named his artistes. Then she signed with the business-like Adolf Zukor and his fast-growing Paramount Pictures. So began her great period of fame.

As this book makes clear, Mary Pickford was quite different from the darling with the rosebud mouth and the corkscrew curls whom everybody loved. 'A miserable nuisance,' she called the curls, which were reinforced by George Westmore, who manufactured artificial pieces from hair bought from Big Susy's French Whorehouse in Los Angeles. Tutored by a fiercely solicitous mother, she showed herself to be a determined, demanding businesswoman. In this she was quite unlike the swashbuckling performer who became her second husband. (Her first, a precipitate mistake, was the alcoholic actor Owen Moore.) Undoubtedly Douglas Fairbanks was the love of her life, and for a time his popularity equalled hers. Their divorce, after thirteen years of marriage, brought happiness to neither of them.

Together with Fairbanks, with Chaplin and with Griffith, Mary

Pickford was one of the founders of United Artists, the distribution company which was designed to give the partners maximum control over their work, and maximum profit from it. In this area, too, she never let sentiment interfere with her exercise of power. It was Ernst Lubitsch – whom she brought from Germany to the United States – who would joke about the 'vast gulf' (Scott Eyman's words) 'between Mary's dainty looks and her tough sensibility.' She never unlearned the lessons of her childhood.

Mary Pickford could not, and nor could her husband, make the transition from silent to sound cinema. She grew too old to continue to play the girl of spirited innocence, which was how the world wanted to see her. She never made a film which, in these days of auteurist fallacy, has become known as 'great'. But she knew good from bad, and she knew what happened. She told Kevin Brownlow: 'I left the screen because I didn't want what happened to Chaplin to happen to me. When he discarded the little tramp, the little tramp turned round and killed him.' She grew to dislike Chaplin, whose avarice was too close to hers. And she was jealous of him.

Scott Eyman has written a remarkable book and a valuable one. He has restored to life a woman who was full of contradictions, of genuine innocence and of ruthless determination. Irish, she refused ever to conform; and finally she turned to alcohol, became a drinker and in the end a recluse.

The life finishes sadly, but then so do most stories of Hollywood success. Perhaps Scott Eyman's greatest achievement is to make us want very much to see the films which he calls her best: *Suds* and *Sparrows* and *My Best Girl*, *Little Lord Fauntleroy*, *Little Annie Rooney* and *Rosita*. Once they delighted the whole world. Will our National Film Theatre please bring Mary Pickford back to life? Her films will surely help us to understand the roots from which modern America has sprung. And perhaps also to understand better our grandparents, and their fathers and mothers, who loved them.

The Films of Alfred Hitchcock

Sequence 9, Autumn 1949

As, GEOGRAPHICALLY, BRITAIN IS POISED BETWEEN CONTINENTS, NOT QUITE Europe, and very far from America, so from certain points of view the British cinema seems to hover between the opposite poles of France and Hollywood. Our directors and producers never – or rarely – have the courage to tackle, in an adult manner, the completely adult subject; yet they lack also the flair for popular showmanship that is characteristic of the American cinema. It is significant that the most widely celebrated of all British directors should be remarkable for just this quality. So much so indeed that, when his powers were at their prime, he emigrated to Hollywood; and today, when he returns to work again in a British studio, he carries with him the pervasive aura of Hollywood success, and stays at the Savoy Hotel.

Alfred Hitchcock's long career has been intimately bound up with the history of the cinema. He began in the early twenties, title writing, then joined Michael Balcon's first production company, first as assistant and art director, then directing on his own. Between 1925 and 1929 he made nine pictures, and established himself as the foremost British director of the day. His *Blackmail* was the first British sound film. During the thirties he went on to perfect his grasp of technique, win a Hollywood contract and the opportunity to exploit the finest technical resources in the world. Essentially he is a man of the cinema – one who has approached the film as an art through the film as an industry.

His first two films are remarkable for their evidence of an immediate ease, an instinctive facility in the medium. *The Pleasure Garden* (1925) is a novelettish story – a good-hearted chorus girl befriends a vixenish dancer, and ends up eight reels later menaced by her drunken husband who believes himself incited to murder her by the ghost of his native mistress (whom he has drowned in the lagoon). The most enjoyable passages are at the start: the first shots of chorus girls hurrying down a circular iron stair, then out on to the stage, gyrating enthusiastically in the abandoned fashion of the period. *The Mountain Eagle*, another romantic melodrama, was set equally far from home, among the hillbillies of Kentucky; one is not surprised to find *The Bioscope* commenting that 'in spite of skilful and at times brilliant direction, the story has an air of unreality.'

Both these films were produced by Balcon in Munich; in 1926 Hitchcock returned to Islington to make his first picture in Britain, and the first opportunity to work on the sort of subject most congenial to him – the story of uncertainty, suspense and horror amid humdrum surroundings. *The Lodger* was again a melodrama, but biased this time towards violence rather than romance. One winter evening, in a London terrorised by a homicidal maniac known as The Avenger, a handsome stranger arrives at a Bloomsbury lodging-house. He behaves strangely, creeping from the house at night, removing from his wall the portrait of a beautiful fair-haired girl (The Avenger attacks only blondes), and gradually the suspicion is built up that he is The Avenger himself. *The Lodger* is by no means a perfect thriller; it creates its suspense too often illegitimately: the innocent young man behaves like a stage villain, arriving out of the night heavily muffled and mysteriously silent. Playing chess before the fire with the landlady's attractive (blonde) daughter, he remarks with sinister

411

emphasis, 'Be careful, I'll get you yet,' and picks up the poker – only to poke the fire vigorously on the entrance of a third person into the room.

This improbable development of the plot is partially disguised by the conscientious realism of its locales and characters: the authentic middle-class decors and homely atmosphere of the Buntings' house in Bloomsbury, the mannequins' dressing-room at the couturier's where Daisy works, the flirtatious progress of Daisy's affair with Joe, the detective in charge of the case. Most remarkable, though, is the rapid, ingenious style of narration. From the opening – the close-up of a man's pale hand sliding down the bannister-rail as he slips quietly out of a dark house – the camera seizes on the significant details which convey the narrative point of the scene. The result is a compression which gives the film continuous excitement.

For this compression, some credit is evidently due to Ivor Montagu, who was called in by the distributors when they found themselves dissat-isfied with the first copy of the film. After specifying certain re-takes, which Hitchcock shot, Montagu re-edited the film, and produced a version which the distributors accepted with delight. In view of later develop-ments, however, there is no mistaking Hitchcock's primary responsibility for *The Lodger*, and for the ingenuity of its 'Style' in particular: a series of rapidly super-imposed close-ups show alarm spreading as a new murder is reported; as the Buntings listen suspiciously to their lodger walking up and down in his room above them, we see a shot of the ceiling with his feet superimposed walking to and fro, as though the floor were made of glass.

This inventiveness and visual dexterity were to form the basis of Hitchcock's style; they are the characteristics of a born story-teller, of one who delights to surprise and confound expectation, to build up suspense to a climax of violence and excitement. Strangely enough, though, the suc-cess of *The Lodger* did not lead Hitchcock to concentrate on this kind of film. He followed it with a return to romance, *Downhill*, which again starred Ivor Novello, as a noble boy who takes the blame for a chum's offence, is expelled from school ('Does this mean, sir, that I shall not be able to play for the Old Boys?') and progresses downhill to the docks of Marseilles. There are interesting patches of technique: a delirium sequence as the hero is carried home on a cargo boat – scenes from his past super-imposing and dissolving over shots of a gramophone playing in his cabin, the ships' engines turning over, the whole a powerful visual equivalent of discordant sound; and a daring subjective sequence as he lurches through the streets on his way home, the camera tracking and panning unsteadily to recreate his feverish impressions.

Three years and six pictures passed before, with *Blackmail* (1929), Hitchcock was able to find a story which suited as happily as *The Lodger*; in between there came a version of Noel Coward's *Easy Virtue* (which must have been almost as prodigious an achievement as Lubitsch's silent *Lady Windermere's Fan*), a boxing melodrama, a version of *The Farmer's Wife* and a couple of novelettes. Then at last Hitchcock hit on Charles Bennett's play, prepared a screenplay of it in collaboration with the author and Benn Levy, and shot it as a silent film. It was released, however, as Britain's first sound film, in part re-shot and in part dubbed; it is thus of double interest – both for Hitchcock's uninhibited ingenuity in dealing with a new medium, and as a second example of his primary excellence in melodrama.

Blackmail is not as satisfactory as *The Lodger*; in construction it is less concise, less inevitable in progression. The connection of the first reel (the police at work) with the rest of the film is not well established; the scene in the artist's studio, in which Cyril Richard sings sub-Coward songs and attempts to seduce Anny Ondra is ludicrous in writing, setting and handling; the famous chase, ending up with the blackmailer's fall through the dome of the British Museum, is too obviously tacked on to provide a spectacular climax. Also the film is weakened by the happy ending Hitchcock was forced (not for the last time) to substitute for the ironic fade-out he had planned.

Much of *Blackmail*, though, is excellent and survives in its own right. The everyday locales – a Corner-House restaurant, the police station, the little tobacconist's shop where the heroine lives with her parents, empty London streets at dawn – are authentic; the characters are believable; and at least one scene, between the blackmailer, the girl and the detective, in which the detective does not know the guilt of the girl, the girl is too frightened to confess to it, and the blackmailer tries to play on the nerves of each, is worked up to a most successful tension. As in *The Lodger*, Hitchcock develops his story with a succession of felicitous, striking or revealing touches, particularly remarkable in this instance for the ingenuity with which they exploit the new dimension of sound. The portrait in the artist's studio, for instance, of a malevolently smiling jester is used as a sort of dumb commentator on the story – the last shot shows the picture carried away down the passage of the police station while the walls re-echo to the sound of ironic laughter. Sound is used throughout with extraordinary freedom, for the period: to support continuity, as where the heroine, wandering in the streets after knifing her seducer, sees a man lying in a doorway, his hand angling like the dead artist's; she opens her mouth to scream, and we cut to the scream of the landlady discovering the body of the murdered man. Two famous, and very effective, examples of the distortion of sound to convey a subjective impression of tension and near-hysteria occur as the girl sits miserably over breakfast the next morning. A garrulous neighbour is discussing the news: 'I don't hold with knives . . . No,

knives isn't right . . . now, mind you, a knife's a difficult thing . . .'
Gradually all other words are mixed together in a monotonous blur, the
word 'knife' alone stabbing clearly out of the soundtrack over a close-up
of the girl. 'Cut us a bit of bread,' says her father. The camera tilts down
to a close-up of the knife; the girl's hand reaches out. Suddenly 'KNIFE!'
screams the voice, the hand jerks sharply up, and the bread knife flies into
the corner of the room. A similar use of distortion and sudden crescendo
conveys the girl's alarm at the sudden ringing of the shop-bell; instead of
dying swiftly away, the sound of the bell is held for some four seconds,
swelling up to a startling intensity.

Again like *The Lodger*, the films which followed *Blackmail* presented
in the main a series of disappointments. *Juno and the Paycock* is straightforward filmed theatre, well and respectfully handled; it is memorable
however not so much for Hitchcock's contributions as for its perpetuation
of some fine performances – in particular Sara Allgood's Juno, a figure
that one sets beside Jane Darwell's Ma Joad for its grandeur and humanity. *Murder*, which followed it, is an odd mixture, with some effective
sequences – a midnight murder in a sleepy village, an exciting climax in a
circus tent, with the murderer (Esmé Percy as an epicene trapeze artist)
hanging himself from the big top. Amongst the enterprising uses of sound
are one of the first uses of an overlaid track representing the thoughts running through a character's head while he shaves, and a not altogether successful experiment in expressionism – an impatient jury chanting in chorus against its one dissenting member. Long stretches of the film, though,
are theatrical in the extreme, clogged with dialogue and dominated by an
excessively stagey performance by Herbert Marshall.

None of Hitchcock's remaining films for British International (the producers of *Blackmail*) achieved much success. In 1933 he left to direct an
unhappy excursion into musical comedy, *Waltzes from Vienna*. His career
seemed to have reached its nadir when, with his infinite capacity for surprise, he rejoined Balcon at Gaumont British, renewed his association with
Ivor Montagu (associate producer) and Charles Bennett (scriptwriter) and
directed in a row a series of films which were to mark his most memorable
and enjoyable contribution to the cinema.

The team of Hitchcock, Bennett and Montagu remained in collaboration for three years, during which, with Balcon as producer, it was responsible for *The Man Who Knew Too Much*, *The Thirty-Nine Steps*, *The
Secret Agent* and *Sabotage*. In 1937 Balcon and Montagu left Gaumont
British, but Bennett remained to write *Young and Innocent*: in 1938
Hitchcock made his last good British film, *The Lady Vanishes*, from a
script by Launder and Gilliat. All these films are melodramas – stories of
violence and adventure in which the emphasis is on incident rather than

on characters or ideas. Hitchcock had himself come to realise that this was the form ideally suited to his talent and his temperament. In his autobiography, Esmond Knight quotes an illuminating *cri-de-coeur* on the set of *Waltzes from Vienna*: 'I hate this sort of stuff,' groaned Hitchcock, 'melodrama is the only thing I can do.'

Melodrama does not, of course, preclude commonsense; with the exception of *The Lady Vanishes*, with its Ruritanian locale and its deliberate light comedy accent, these films gain a particular excitement from their concern with ordinary people (or ordinary-looking people) who are plunged into extraordinary happenings in the most ordinary places. This gives them immense conviction, and enables Hitchcock to exploit to the utmost his flair for the dramatic value of contrast. Instead of dressing-up the Temple of Sun Worshippers – which covers the headquarters of the gang in *The Man Who Knew Too Much* – he presents it as a drab little non-conformist chapel, bare and chilly, with a typically shabby congregation of elderly eccentrics. In *The Thirty-Nine Steps*, the head of the organisation lives in a solidly respectable country house, and entertains the County to cocktails after Sunday morning service. Verloc, the secret agent of *Sabotage*, runs an unpretentious suburban cinema: the pursuit in *Young and Innocent* winds up at a *thé dansant* at a seaside hotel. Similarly the people are conceived in commonsense, unglamorised terms; the leading players (one hardly thinks of them as stars) dress with credible lack of extravagance, get dirty, behave like average human beings – neither brilliant nor foolishly muddled. And supporting them are a multitude of equally authentic minor characters, maids, policemen, shopkeepers and commercial travellers. This overall realism makes it all the more thrilling when the unexpected occurs – as it inevitably does: pretty maids lie to the police without blinking an eyelid, harmless old bird-fanciers are revealed as sabotage-agents, old ladies who are playing the harmonium one minute are whipping little revolvers from their handbags the next.

The plots of these films are less important for themselves than for the way they are unfolded. They are all stories of violence and suspense, five exploiting in one way or another the excitement of espionage and political assassination (of these *The Thirty-Nine Steps* and *The Man Who Knew Too Much* are perhaps the most completely successful and continuously exciting), the sixth (*Young and Innocent*) centring on the pursuit of a murderer by the young man accused of his crime. In most of them the tensions of mystery and intrigue erupt in a climax of public violence: the agents in *The Man Who Knew Too Much* are exterminated in a street-battle which recalls the historic battle of Sidney Street; *The Thirty-Nine Steps* winds up with a shooting during a Crazy Gang show at the Palladium; *The Secret*

Agent has a train crash, *Sabotage* a time-bomb exploding in a crowded bus, and *The Lady Vanishes* another gun-fight, between the agents of a foreign power and a party of Britons stranded in a railway carriage in a central European forest.

These set-pieces are not, however, isolated delights; the films are continuously enjoyable for the brilliance and consistency of their narration – a technique which shows the value of experience with the silent cinema and the necessity of unfolding a story in visual terms. Hitchcock has freely acknowledged his debt to Griffith; his own style, at its best, has always been firmly based on cutting. In a famous article on his methods of direction, published in *Footnotes to the Film*, he states his credo specifically: 'What I like to do always is to photograph just the little bits of a scene that I really need for building up a visual sequence. I want to put my film together on the screen, not simply to photograph something that has been put together already in the form of a long piece of stage acting . . .' Besides being an admirable instrument for the building-up of tension within the scene, Hitchcock's cutting contributes to the boldness and ingenuity with which his plots are developed, with continuous speed and surprise. (His scripts are pre-planned, his films edited in the camera rather than the cutting-room.) We are precipitated at once into the middle of events – *Young and Innocent*, for instance, starts brilliantly, at the climax of a murderous quarrel. With a few happy strokes a locale is sketched in, an atmosphere established; the stories proceed with a succession of ingenious visual, or sound-and-visual effects (the Hitchcock touch), as a celebrated continuity from *The Thirty-Nine Steps*; or the ominously sustained organ note in *The Secret Agent* (a film packed with ingenious touches, and Hitchcock's favourite of the series) which announces the death of the Allied agent, strangled in the lonely Swiss church.

Hitchcock's best films are in many ways very English, in their humour, lack of sentimentality, their avoidance of the grandiose and the elaborately fake. And these qualities were threatened when, in 1939, he succumbed to temptation and signed a contract to work in Hollywood for David Selznick. He was ambitious to make films for the vast international audience which only Hollywood could tap; also no doubt he was eager to work with the technical facilities which only Hollywood studios could provide. It was particularly unfortunate, however, that Hitchcock chose the producer he did; for Selznick is a producer who has always relied on pretentiousness, the huge gesture, the imposing facade, to win success (*Gone with the Wind*, *Since You Went Away*, *Duel in the Sun*). Almost in advance Hitchcock was committed to all that is worst in Hollywood – to size for its own sake (his first picture for Selznick was 2,000 feet longer than any he had directed previously), to the star system for its own sake, to glossy photography, high-toned settings, lushly hypnotic musical scores.

The negotiations with Selznick were carried on while Hitchcock was working on his last British film, *Jamaica Inn*, a dully boisterous smuggling adventure with Charles Laughton. It was curious and unhappily prophetic that his first film in Hollywood should also be an adaptation from a Daphne du Maurier bestseller, *Rebecca* – a less boring book, but equally Boots Library in its level of appeal. *Rebecca* is a very skilful and competently acted film: numerous imitations employing the same theatricalities of suspense – the great house dominated by a mysterious figure, the frightened girl, the sinister housekeeper – emphasise the smooth plausibility of Hitchcock's handling. But the film as a whole is not recognisable as the work of the Hitchcock of, say, *The Thirty-Nine Steps*; it is at once bigger and less considerable.

The films which followed it in the next four years are of uneven quality, and represent no progression, no real acclimatisation. *Suspicion* (the next-but-two) was an attempt to reproduce the high-class tension of *Rebecca*, again with Joan Fontaine; it succeeds only in ruining a fine thriller by Francis Iles, the story of a sensitive, unattractive girl married and murdered for her money by a handsome wastrel. By dressing her hair with severity and intermittently fondling a pair of horn-rims and a book on child psychology, Joan effected the conventional compromise between glamour and realism successfully enough to filch an Academy Award; but the film lacks excitement or conviction. The English backgrounds (Hunting, Church) are pure Burbank; and the ludicrous happy ending – neither written by Iles nor desired by Hitchcock – sets the seal of failure on the film.

Suspicion was preceded by a comedy, *Mr and Mrs Smith* (of which one would welcome a revival), and a thriller, *Foreign Correspondent*; after it came another reminiscence of the Gaumont-British period, *Saboteur*. The earlier of these, written by Charles Bennett in collaboration with Joan Harrison, has excellent sequences embedded in a diffuse and vexatious story. The assassination of an elderly statesman in Amsterdam is brilliantly staged: rain drizzling, the square thronged with umbrellas, the news-camera which fires a bullet, the assassin's escape through the crowd of bobbing umbrellas. There is a pleasantly sordid scene many reels later in which the kidnapped diplomat is grilled in a Charlotte Street garret, while a terrified German girl (in thick-lensed spectacles) sobs in terror by the wall; and the climax is worth waiting for – a transatlantic airliner shelled and nose-diving into the sea (entirely from within the plane), water crashing through the pilot's window, passengers fighting hysterically, and finally a handful of survivors clinging exhaustively to a floating raft.

Saboteur is even more an affair of sequences, and is remarkable for its barefaced pilfering from almost every film Hitchcock had ever made. Its handcuffed hero and heroine (limp derivatives from *The Thirty-Nine Steps*) are pitched from one exotic location to another, individual episodes are directed with enjoyable virtuosity – the aircraft factory fire at the start, a gunfight in a cinema, the final megalomaniac climax on the Statue of Liberty – but the film as a whole has the over-emphasis of parody.

It was not until 1943 that Hitchcock made a film which might be construed as an attempt – his last – to justify himself as a serious director. Before writing the screenplay of *Shadow of a Doubt* he and Thornton Wilder went to live for two months in the little Californian town of Santa Rosa, where their story was to take place. Most of the film was shot there. As a result it had an everyday realism that is reminiscent of earlier days; and in its opening stages, a subtlety of characterisation distinctly superior to them. Its central character is Charlie Newton, handsome and debonair, who lives by marrying and killing rich widows. Hard pressed by the police, he comes to Santa Rosa to stay with his sister (who idolises him), and her family: her quiet, respectable husband, her beautiful adolescent daughter, who feels that there is some special, secret bond between her and her uncle, and two smaller children. The film is at its best in its first half, establishing the family and their town, the impact of Uncle Charlie's arrival on each of them; experimenting once again with sound, Hitchcock adopted for these scenes a technique similar to Orson Welles in *The Magnificent Ambersons*, superimposing one conversation over another, dovetailing, naturalistically blurring and distorting. The strange bond which seems to unite Young Charlie (the niece) with her uncle is subtly conveyed; the acting is excellent: Joseph Cotten as Charlie, bitter, arrogant, his smooth charm concealing a spirit wounded and festering, the exquisite Patricia Collinge, his sensitive, over-strung sister, Teresa Wright as Young Charlie, youthful and mercurial, waiting for love. In its later reels the film falls away; there is not the progression and development necessary to a serious study, and as a simple thriller (which is all perhaps Hitchcock would claim for it) it fails to sustain excitement and surprise. It remains, all the same, his best American film.

After *Shadow of a Doubt* Hitchcock completed one more picture in Hollywood, then ventured across the Atlantic to make his contribution to the Allied war effort. This came in the form of two short French-speaking films for the British Ministry of Information, *Aventure Malagache* and *Bon Voyage*. Each tells its story – the former of resistance activity in Vichy-dominated Madagascar, the latter of underground work in France – economically (most scenes are played in a single set-up), tastefully and not very excitingly. A project for Hitchcock to direct a film about German concentration camps, for which he viewed a large quantity of documentary material, eventually came to nothing. This visit to Britain inspired no renaissance of style, no return of reality.

Almost, in fact, it appears to have precipitated his flight from it. From 1945 onwards the quality one associates with Hitchcock films is neither their excitement, nor their power to entertain, but their technical virtuosity. The trend had indeed already started in 1943, when he followed up *Shadow of a Doubt* with *Lifeboat*. For an hour and a half the camera remains in a lifeboat carrying eight survivors from a sunken Allied ship, and one German who turns out to be the captain of the U-boat which attacked it. The virtuosity of the direction is undeniable, and in a theatrical way the film is effective; but the attempts to build the story into a propagandist allegory, stressing the feebleness of a democracy in comparison with a dictatorship, were as unconvincing as (at this stage of the war) they were unnecessary. One remembers *Lifeboat* chiefly for its reintroduction of Tallulah Bankhead, and for some suspenseful episodes – a grim amputation carried out by the German with a clasp-knife, a realistically contrived storm.

Spellbound, with which Hitchcock returned to Selznick in 1945, also contains its entertaining passages of exhibitionism; its psychiatric background is futile and its Dali dream-sequence merely pretentious, but one can enjoy the acid observation of the psychiatrists' common-room, and some facile patches of melodrama revolving around razors, glasses of milk and the like.

It is unfortunate that even these are marred by a tendency to overplay, to inflate, a tendency which in *Notorious* swelled to an obsession and produced a film which shares with its successors, *The Paradine Case* and *Rope*, the distinction of being the worst of his career. In these films technique – lighting, ability to manoeuvre the camera in hitherto unimaginable ways, angles – ceases to be a means and becomes an end in itself; *Notorious* is full of large and boring close-ups. For hundreds of feet Ingrid Bergman and Cary Grant nuzzle each other in medium close-up, a sequence of embarrassing (because so thoroughly fake) intimacy. *The Paradine Case*, maimed from the start by Selznick's creaking script and a heavy roster of stars, is lit with magnificent but inexpressive artifice, contains further nuzzling by Ann Todd and Gregory Peck, and moves at a pace slower even than that of *Notorious*. And with *Rope*, a debilitated version of Patrick Hamilton's play, which abandons all the resources of cutting and lighting on the pretext of an experiment in technique, we come pretty well to a full-stop.

Different though the results are, the experiment of *Rope* resembles the stylistic elephantiasis of *Notorious* and *Spellbound* in its preoccupation with technique, to the detriment of the material. The films, as a result, are neither good nor entertaining. To such highbrow accusations Hitchcock has a ready answer. To quote from an acutely critical article by Lawrence Kane (*Theatre Arts*, May 1949): '*Spellbound* cost $1,700,000 and grossed $8,000,000. *Notorious* cost $2,000,000 and had enough love in it to take in $9,000,000 . . .' 'Beyond that,' said Alfred Hitchcock in a 1946 interview, 'there's the constant pressure. You know – people asking, "Do you want to reach only the audiences at the Little Carnegie or to have your pictures play at the Music Hall?" So you compromise. You can't avoid it. You do the commercial thing, but you try to do it without lowering your standards. It isn't easy. Actually the commercial thing is much harder to do than the other.'

Disregarding the latter irrelevant (and untrue) argument, the critic can only comment that Hitchcock's career in America has suffered from more than compromise with commercialism. (A compromise to which he has been no more exposed than any other director of equivalent status.) He is a director, in the first place, who depends considerably on his scripts; in the last ten years he has found no writer to give him what Bennett gave him at Gaumont British. It is not a coincidence that his collaboration with Thornton Wilder resulted in his best Hollywood film.

But *Shadow of a Doubt* hints at a more crippling limitation. When Hitchcock left Britain, it was, at least in part, because he felt that a chapter in his career was ended, and he was ripe for further development. And in certain directions, it is true, Hollywood has offered him vastly greater opportunities than Shepherd's Bush; there are sequences in *Foreign Correspondent* and *Saboteur*, *Shadow of a Doubt* and *Lifeboat* which outstrip anything in his earlier pictures for virtuosity and excitement. What these films lack is the wholeness of their predecessors. The Gaumont British melodramas succeed as works of art (however minor) because they attain a perfect, satisfying balance between content and style; the enlargement which Hitchcock's style has undergone in Hollywood has been accompanied by no equivalent intensifying or deepening of sensibility or subject matter.

Hitchcock has never been a serious director. His films are interesting neither for their ideas nor for their characters. None of the early melodramas can be said to carry any sort of a 'message'; when one does appear, as in *Foreign Correspondent* and *Lifeboat*, it is banal in the extreme – 'You'll never conquer them,' Albert Basserman wheezes on his bed of torture, 'the little people who feed the birds.' In the same way, Hitchcock's characterisation has never achieved – or aimed at – anything more than a surface verisimilitude; which in a film where incident and narrative are what matters, is perfectly proper.

The method, though appropriate to *The Thirty-Nine Steps* and *The Lady Vanishes*, is inappropriate to *Suspicion* and *Shadow of a Doubt*. In these the more deliberate pace, the constant emphasis on the players (dictated by the star-system) directs our attention to the characters; their emptiness becomes apparent, and the dramas fall apart. *Suspicion* is not a failure simply because of its outrageous *volte-face* at the end; the characters have never begun to live, so there is nothing really to destroy. In *Shadow of a Doubt* an atmosphere and a complex of relationships of some subtlety is established – only to dwindle conventionally instead of developing. *Notorious* presents an unpleasant but by no means uninteresting situation, which is thrown away largely because characterisation is sacrificed to a succession of vulgar, superficial effects. In films like these, in *Rope* and *The Paradine Case*, even the old skin-deep truthfulness has been lost; Hitchcock's attitude towards his characters (as towards his audience) would seem to have hardened into one of settled contempt.

Hitchcock's progression from *The Pleasure Garden* to *Rope* is aesthetically pleasing; on the graph it would appear a well-proportioned parabola. But he does not oblige us by bringing his career to so satisfyingly geometric a close ('I am interested only in the future,' he says). At the time of writing he has a period barnstormer, *Under Capricorn*, already completed, and a modern thriller, *Stage Fright*, almost finished. What is to be expected from these? Prophecy is always rash, but it is safe to assume that neither will present a dramatic reaction from the standards of showmanship which he has set himself in his 'International' period; at their worst they will be heavy, tedious, glossed, at their best, ingenious, expert, synthetically entertaining. They will make a lot of money. Which, Hitchcock would reply, 'is why they were made!' But at this point the wise critic resists the temptation to enter once again the vicious circle, and withdraws.

Return of the Prodigal: Von Stroheim

The Observer, 10 January 1953

'A FILM GROWS OLD AND DIES,' SAID RENÉ CLAIR RECENTLY. 'WHOEVER HAS attended the performance of a film 20 or 30 years old will have been amazed by what he saw.' Amazed, he meant, in the sense of shocked or amused by the crudity of what so lately passed for art, or at least for sophisticated entertainment. And it is true that one is too liable to think now of the silent screen chiefly as something to giggle at. Fashions in romance have changed violently in the past thirty years, and Valentino, Gloria Swanson and Theda Bara have become less erotic than ludicrous in their appeal. But not all screen masterpieces fade with the rapidity of *A Fool There Was*. The season of films by Erich von Stroheim, which opened last week at the

National Film Theatre, and which the Master himself came to inaugurate, may well leave its audiences amazed – but in the dictionary sense, surely, rather than M. Clair's: 'Confounded or stunned, with fear, surprise or wonder.'

To this generation of film-goers, von Stroheim is, of course, familiar only as an actor. English-speaking audiences last saw him in *Sunset Boulevard*, as the mysterious Max von Mayerling, first husband of the faded star (played by Miss Swanson) and the director responsible for her earliest successes. Recalling the twenties, this character remarked: 'In those days, there were three directors of promise – Griffith, De Mille and I.' The words were near enough to the truth about von Stroheim himself to have strange overtones for those who remembered him not merely as Hollywood's Rommel (pre-James Mason), or as 'The Man You Love to Hate', but also as one of the great directors of the silent cinema, the creator of *Blind Husbands* and *Foolish Wives*, of *The Merry Widow* and the monumental *Greed*.

Almost as remarkable as these films themselves is the story of von Stroheim's stormy passage through Hollywood. Like many of America's great men of the cinema, he came to films from a European background. An ex-officer of the Austrian Imperial Guard, he landed in New York, penniless, in 1909, aged 24. Five years, and a variety of jobs, later he was in Hollywood, assistant to Griffith on *Birth of a Nation* and *Intolerance*. In 1918 he directed his first film, *Blind Husbands*, a triangle drama of an American couple on holiday in Tyrol, and their disastrous encounter with a libertine Austrian Army officer.

The success of von Stroheim's first film was, in every sense of the word, sensational. It established at once the style in which he was to excel, the harsh and cynical comedy of sexual manners. The frankness of von Stroheim's analysis of such a situation was something new in the American cinema, and his own performance as the debonair Lieutenant von Steuben aroused in audiences fascinating complexities of attraction and detestation. The genre attained perhaps its most potent expression in *Foolish Wives*, a film whose essence is contained in von Stroheim's portrait of Count Wladislas Sergius Karamzin, a professional Monte Carlo adventurer who is shown in successful commission of blackmail, rape and (above all) seduction, before justice catches up with him. He is murdered by the father of one of his victims, and his body stuffed into a sewer, to drift out into the bay in the closing shots of the film, together with all the other debris of the corrupt and tawdry city. (Happily, *Foolish Wives* is amongst the films which will be revived in the present season.)

Like many moralists who are also artists, von Stroheim was fascinated by excess and perversity, at the same time as he was appalled by it. The cruelty and disillusion, you might say, were European, but the exuberance and vitality seem wholly American. And though in other films he harked back to Europe and the decadence of the Austrian Court, his master-piece is wholly of America. 'I consider that I have made only one real picture in my life,' von Stroheim said of *Greed*, his adaptation of Frank Norris's novel, *McTeague*; and the emphasis is on the word real. Not a single scene in this film (made in 1923) was shot in the studio. The insistence every-where is on utter realism, of setting, feeling and behaviour. Again the underlying theme is sexual: it is the timid heroine's frustration that turns her into a fanatical miser, that poisons her relationship with her stu-pid, genial husband, and makes a murderer of him. The daring of this film, the sharpness of its

Director and actor Erich von Stroheim.

satire, its vividness of performance, and the dreadful truth of its images made immediate and lasting effect.

But, like other great film-makers, von Stroheim had conceptions that were too grand and revolutionary for the cinema of his day. He started modestly enough, shooting his first film in seven weeks; but the possibili-ties of the medium were too much for him. *Foolish Wives* was designed to run for three hours: the studio became nervous, and cut it from 21 reels to fourteen. Nothing daunted von Stroheim, he launched recklessly into *Greed*, and emerged after two years with a colossus of 42 reels (roughly seven hours' running time). After an agonising struggle, he reduced this to eighteen. But it was still too much for the studio, and *Greed* was taken away from von Stroheim and butchered down to ten reels by a studio cut-ter. This is all that remains: the rest of the negative they burned.

He could not tolerate an incorrect detail, and he could not bear to leave anything out. This, and a temperament incapable of compromise, was von Stroheim's undoing. He made three silent films after *Greed*, but each entailed the same extravagance and the same disputes. It is not really surprising that in the end no producer would employ him as a director and he was forced to fall back on acting for his living. He has given some memorable performances: opposite Garbo in *As You Desire Me*, and in France in Renoir's *La Grande Illusion*: but his personality is too distinctive to make him easy casting. There have been projects from time to time for new von Stroheim films, but none have ever materialised. So he lingers on in our midst, appearing at festivals here and there, or at these scarce revivals of his work, his great talent unused for the last 25 years.

Yet there is something of the miraculous as well as of the tragic story. Thirty years ago the movies were in many respects infantile, yet the opportunities von Stroheim enjoyed before disaster overtook him would be unthinkable in the Hollywood we know. Techniques have developed, of course, but as von Stroheim himself once declared: 'I detest technique whose subject is his own display.' In his films style has no existence, except in so far as every image is expressive of an intense, personal vision of the world. By comparison many of today's triumphs look pallid, for all their, colour: flat, for all their extra dimensions; and for all their inflated size, terribly small.

Garbo and Shearer

Review of *Garbo: Her Story* by Antoni Gronowicz, *The Legend of Garbo* by Peter Haining, and *Norma Shearer: a Life* by Gavin Lambert in *The Sunday Telegraph*, 19 August 1990

NEARLY 50 YEARS AGO, IN 1942, TWO OF HOLLYWOOD'S MOST FAMOUS actresses – which means two of the most famous actresses in the world – bade an unepected farewell to the screen. They were not old; in fact, they were much of an age. Norma Shearer was born in Montreal in 1902 (possibly 1900), while Greta Garbo (née Gustafsson) was born in Stockholm three years later. These remarkable books tell us a lot about their remarkable lives.

Garbo: Her Story, which purports to be mostly in her own words, is the work of Antoni Gronowicz, a Polish *littérateur* and poet, now dead. He claims to have been her lover, then her friend, to whom she confided many of the closest secrets of her youth and career. *The Legend of Garbo*, by Peter Haining, is a sort of scrapbook, full of excellent photographs and a jumble of pieces, some good and some probably whipped up by the studio publicity department.

The third is by Gavin Lambert, novelist, screenwriter and critic, as experienced in the achievements as in the absurdities of this art that fascinates us all. Mr Lambert knew his subject personally, which gives him the advantage; certainly his knowledge of the political and financial background of MGM has helped fill out the picture. His *Norma Shearer* is the best of these three books.

Garbo and Shearer – 'The Divine' and 'The First Lady of the Screen' – worked all their lives for MGM, arguably Hollywood's greatest studio, certainly its most glamorous. Both came to Hollywood as the art was developing from promise to fulfilment; both achieved pre-eminence when sound joined the black-and-white image to yield a dramatic medium which seduced the world.

Their origins could hardly have been more different. Norma Shearer was a middle-class Canadian girl with grace, a handsome profile and a sense of humour; but she had bad legs, her arms were a bit stubby and she suffered from a cast in her right eye which needed care and exercise if it was not to develop into a squint. When her friend Margery Cohen pointed this out, Norma laughed. 'Oh,' she said, 'I can take care of that!' Determination was always her middle name.

Greta Gustafsson, by contrast, was a working-class girl from Sweden. Her mother, like Mrs Shearer, was the dominant partner in the marriage; and like Mrs Shearer she had two daughters and a son. There the resemblance ended. Mrs Gustafsson did not favour Greta. She was actively hostile to her husband who drank, and she carried on a liaison with the hypocritical pastor for whom she worked. With a resolution as firm as Norma's, Greta decided to be an actress.

Unlike Norma, Greta seems to have been born with some kind of magic which reinforced her resolution. In pictures this is not immediately apparent. Miss Gustafsson was plump, her hair piled unbecomingly on her head, her style distinctly more European than American. But there was something about her that men found peculiarly attractive. The *coup de foudre* came from Mauritz Stiller, the celebrated film and theatre director, who watched her audition for the Royal Academy Dramatic School. 'He whispered in my ear, "I would like to see you in Svensk Filmindustri". . . I almost fainted.'

Greta did not faint, but at that moment the die was cast for both of them. Svengali had found his Trilby. Greta Gustafsson became Greta Garbo (Stiller's invention, from a Polish derivation); and when Louis B. Mayer signed Stiller to direct Metro pictures in Hollywood he had to take her (of whom, says Gronowicz-Garbo, he had never heard) as part of the package.

It was in August 1925 that SS *Drottningholm* carried Mauritz Stiller and Greta Garbo into New York harbour. Greta had made only two movies, but she does not seem to have been pleased when MGM's Hubert Voight described her as the 'Swedish Norma Shearer'. He meant it as a compliment.

Within two years at MGM, Norma had overcome the gloomy prognostications of experts like Griffith ('Eyes too blue and too small') and Ziegfeld ('Limbs too thick for authentic beauty') and by sheer hard work had established herself as one of the studio's most versatile and profitable stars.

It was Irving Thalberg, Metro's pocket genius, who had first spotted her potential and removed her from her New York struggles, playing second-leads and appearing on billboards advertising bicycle tyres as Miss Lotta Miles. At first Thalberg's interest does not seem to have been romantic; it took time and patience for Norma to discover that it could be. Constance Talmadge was not interested. Norma Shearer was. In 1928 she became Mrs Irving Thalberg. This did not mean she could now play what she wanted; but it helped.

Greta presented her employers with a quite different source of profit. Her forte was not versatility but intensity. Her first film for Metro, *The Torrent*, was not directed by Stiller but by Monta Bell. It does not seem to have been outstanding, but the studio's Swedish discovery, smouldering with a mysterious European sensuality, certainly was. Garbo was able to insist that her next picture be given to Stiller. Alas, though he was able to take Greta through her role, movement by movement, syllable by syllable, his extravagance and irritability did not avail him on the floor. Within 10 days, Stiller found himself replaced by the ordinary but amenable Fred Niblo. For Garbo-Stiller this was the beginning of the end. Garbo's next picture was *Flesh and the Devil*, which plunged her into a violent romance with John Gilbert, the American housewife's dream of dark-moustached, flashing-eyed passion.

Stiller achieved one great success at Paramount; but Pola Negri was not Garbo, and within a year he had returned, defeated, to Stockholm. On the railroad station, Greta wept at his departure with warm, torrential tears. No doubt she was sincere. But she did not follow. She would not – could not? – surrender her beloved, closely-guarded self. She had affairs – with both sexes – but she never married.

Acting is a strange business. We are apt nowadays to think that what we respect most is truthfulness, that the artists we most admire are those who penetrate most deeply, most sincerely, the essential, feeling reality of the characters they play. This is only partially true. The element of personality is strong, as strong as truth and often stronger. (That is why Brecht, for all his apparent respectability, is so generally disliked.) Norma Shearer acted as much from personality as truth, and this is what brought her such success. She knew what the public wanted, and she knew that, if she worked hard enough, she could give it to them. Whatever Joan Crawford said, it was not just Norma's position as Mrs Thalberg that made her, as the Metro publicist put it, 'Queen of the Lot'.

In Garbo, the element of personality was also strong, but she was a far finer actress. To be fair also, she did her best to satisfy her masters' bidding. Throughout the thirties the balance was held. As she had learned from Stiller, she used her passionate, self-absorbed personality in a succession of passionate, self-absorbed roles. Then came the War, and the loss of the public (European) most faithful to her.

Greta Garbo and John Gilbert in
Flesh and the Devil.

One comedy, *Ninotchka*, showed that with the guidance of a master-director she was as able to make audiences laugh as to cry. But the ill-fated *Two-Faced Woman* told Garbo that the Americans were too shallow to comprehend her talent. They were wrong, of course. But American comedy rarely gets beyond the flippant; and flippancy was the one quality Garbo could not manage. It was an enormous denial, but perhaps an inevitable one. Garbo stopped acting for the Americans.

So did Shearer. Throughout the thirties, she too had continued to perform, with distinction rather than depth, but always with intelligence and style. She had two children, whom she did not want, and a sister she suspected of schizophrenia; but she behaved as though her family problems did not exist. All the same, it was her husband, with his yen for gentility, who won in the end. Irving saw Norma play the Juliet he had planned (well, but too old); and after his premature death she plunged on into *Marie Antoinette* (a high-class if determined performance). She became sexually charged; Gavin Lambert recounts, with frankness as well as discretion, her affairs with Mickey Rooney, James Stewart and George Raft (almost her second husband, but too common).

The years crept on and so did her resolve to stay young and beautiful. She wisely turned down *Gone with the Wind* and foolishly refused to play a woman with a grown-up son in *Mrs Miniver*. Instead she chose two dated comedies. 'On those two,' she said later, 'nobody but myself was trying to do me in.' By a strange coincidence, both her last comedy, *Her Cardboard Lover*, and Garbo's 'all-American' *Two-Faced Woman* were

427

directed by the American master of sophistication, George Cukor. Both failed at the box-office. Neither star acted again.

These two biographies – and Garbo's, for all its first-person narration, is best described as such – do not end with abrupt termination of their subjects' careers. True to her decision of 1942, Greta changed her life, lived in New York and internationally, solitary among friends. These later years are spasmodically chronicled by Gronowicz-Garbo and there is rather a censorious afterword by Richard Schickel. But she was an actress, after all, and a narcissist; she is hardly to be blamed for being nothing else. And we are familiar enough with those pictures of the long-haired, unkempt old lady who spent her last weeks on the dialysis machine and who died in hospital attended only by her niece. That was her choice.

Norma Shearer had perhaps a happier life, for a time. Mr Lambert does not let us shirk its sad finale. Towards the end, her wits failed her. Not only her devoted ski-instructor second husband but friendly visitors would find their wrists gripped tightly and themselves addressed as 'Irving'. For both, the sun had shone too brightly.

If you want to know what it took to become one of MGM's most incandescent stars in its time of glory; what strength of character and power of will it demanded; and what price had eventually to be paid – these books will tell you as much of the truth as you need to know.

Shirley Temple

Review of *Child Star: An Autobiography* by Shirley Temple Black, in *The Daily Telegraph*, 23 November 1989

ONCE, ON AN AMERICAN TALK SHOW, RALPH RICHARDSON WAS ASKED HIS definition of a star. He answered briskly: 'Ethel Merman.' If he had been asked the same question 40 years before, he might with equal accuracy have answered: 'Shirley Temple.' Both these ladies had the gift for what Kenneth Tynan liked to call 'High Definition Performance'. Performance, that is, of powerful and indisputable impact; of unique individuality; of the clarity that comes from total conviction.

Shirley Temple's autobiography is perfectly titled. She was certainly a child – in spite of people who tried to make out she was a middle-aged dwarf. In fact she must have been the most popular performer in the history of showbusiness. And her star quality was unmistakable from the start. Standing on the set when she made her first appearance for Fox

Pictures, Harold Lloyd was heard to murmur: 'Good Lord! A feminine Jackie Coogan!' A year later Adolphe Menjou, playing opposite her, groaned: 'An Ethel Barrymore at six!'

At five, her only experience a series of cheap burlesque shorts, she was signed to an exclusive contract at Fox. The publicity department immediately knocked a year off her age. Within six months she had completed four feature films. Within two years the *Motion Picture Herald* was reporting that Shirley was the biggest money-spinner of the year.

What did Shirley have?

Lindsay sits with Shirley Temple at the Berlin Film Festival, 1990.

She had *sparkle*. This was Mrs Temple's famous last-moment instruction to her daughter before a take – and a good one. Happily, it was also one that Shirley found no difficulty in following. She had more than natural performing skill, natural rhythm. Blessed with the gift of enjoyment, of energy, of zest, she would have found it more difficult not to sparkle.

I have often thought that 'star quality' is more a sickness than a gift – an elephantiasis of the ego – whose sufferers are to be pitied rather than envied. But probably this is truer of actors and actresses than performers. Like Ethel Merman, Shirley was essentially a performer. None of that psychological stuff, delving into one's own personality. It was a game; and she loved playing it. 'You sure do like to dance,' said 'uncle' Bill Robinson, her much-loved best partner (you can still see them dancing up the stairs together in *The Little Colonel*). 'You'll never peter out. Guess you'll just grow up.' A wise perception. 'I'd much rather dance than act,' said Shirley.

This is where clever Graham Greene got it all wrong – and got (I have always thought) the come-uppance he deserved. *Night and Day* was an English attempt to do a London *New Yorker*. Elizabeth Bowen reviewed theatre and Evelyn Waugh books. Superior stuff. Graham Greene was the

429

superior film critic ('The idea came to me at a cocktail party after the dangerous third martini'). Reviewing *Wee Willie Winkie* (directed by John Ford of all people), he had sophisticated fun with Shirley's 'mature suggestiveness' and 'dimpled depravity'. 'Her admirers,' he explained, 'middle-aged men and clergymen, respond to her dubious coquetry, to the sight of her well-shaped and desirable little body . . .' (Was Greene himself responding, one can't help wondering?) Fox sued and the piece was judged a 'gross outrage'; $5,250 punitive damages were awarded to Fox and $7,000 to Shirley. Serves them all right.

Shirley never indulged in this kind of suggestive hanky-panky; not at least after her first appearances at the age of three in a series of 'Baby Burlesks'. She triumphed through innocence, or candour. Talent, she reminds us, will get you nowhere without energy: enthusiasm is infectious. You can feel it today as fresh as ever, as her films come up on television. Of course, they are sentimental. But Shirley is never soppy: she is having too much fun. You can't be soppy and sparkle.

Child Star is dedicated to Mrs Temple. Showbusiness mothers can, we all know, be dangerous wreckers of their children's lives. Shirley was lucky. She had a devoted, dedicated mother, whose ambition for her was that she should dance, not act. She nourished and protected her daughter, but she did not try to live through her success.

She did her best to get Zanuck, the tyrant of 20th Century-Fox, to develop Shirley's career, and when he wouldn't (or couldn't) she disliked him and made no bones about it. Later, at Metro, she had, in a different way, to fight Louis B. Mayer. 'He grasped her hand, pulling her toward him': but Mrs Temple 'retreated out of the door, walking backwards'. Like mother, like daughter. During Shirley's brief sojourn at MGM, she was 'flashed' by Arthur Freed. Metro's master-producer of musicals executed 'a bizarre flourish of clothing': Shirley, astonished, reacted with 'nervous laughter'. 'Get out!' shouted Freed. 'Go on, get out!'

Of course, the image of Shirley that has stamped itself on the world's memory is the curly-headed tot of the Fox musicals: *Baby Take a Bow*, *Little Miss Broadway*, *The Littlest Rebel*, *Heidi*, etc. There were 22 of these, all loved by a world that could still respond to innocence. But adolescence brought thirteen more, contracts with Metro and Selznick, a mistaken marriage and more than $3 million in earnings that shrank, through chicanery and mismanagement, to $44,000.

Thank goodness the story ends happily, with a successful marriage that has lasted nearly 40 years and survival from a near-fatal delivery. The amazing diplomatic career (US Ambassador to Ghana, representative to the UN) awaits another volume.

Shirley's recall is phenomenal. She writes with understanding, but without sentimentalism. Her tone is candid, shrewd – and sometimes tart. She never suffered fools gladly. As, for instance, poor Dickie Moore, who had to give Shirley her first screen kiss in *Miss Annie Rooney*. A handsome boy, with big dark eyes and cherubic features, he was also terribly shy. He had been in pictures since he was 11 months old, but was terrified of the historic moment. Shirley grew impatient: ' the director asked him if he had inhibitions. "What are inhibitions?" Moore asked. "If you knew what they are, you wouldn't have any," I interjected . . . weary of his ineptness.'

Dickie and Shirley met again some 40 years later, when Dick Moore was researching his book about Hollywood juveniles, *Twinkle, Twinkle Little Star – But Don't Have Sex, or Take the Car* (a fascinating book, which has never found a British publisher). Dickie said to Shirley: 'You were really isolated, weren't you? Far more than any of us.'

'Shirley was silent for a minute. Then the hazel eyes sparkled . . ."Yes," she said finally. "But I turned out all right."'

She did turn out all right.

Mary Astor

Sight and Sound, Autumn 1990

WHEN I THINK OF MARY ASTOR, WHICH IS QUITE OFTEN, THAT PRAYER THAT was recited over our heads at college comes into my mind. 'Lord,' (or some such) 'who has granted that when two or three are gathered together in Thy Name, Thou wilt grant their requests . . .' And I have thought how strange it is, and how indisputable that when two or three who love the cinema are gathered together, the name of Mary Astor always comes up, and everybody agrees that she was an actress of special attraction, whose qualities of depth and reality always seemed to illuminate the parts she played. And all this in spite of – or because of – the fact that she was never exactly a star.

I suppose the parts for which she was most famous came from the thirties and forties. And of these, the most celebrated was undoubtedly John Huston's debut picture, *The Maltese Falcon*. She herself wrote of Brigid O'Shaughnessy: 'First of all, she was a congenital liar ("I am a liar. I've always been a liar") and slightly psychopathic. And that kind of liar wears the face of truth, although they send out all sorts of signals that they are lying . . . One of the tip-offs is that they can't help breathing rather rapidly. So I hyperventilated before going into most scenes.'

The analysis and the solution are typical of Mary Astor. More impor-

Walter Huston and Mary Astor in William Wyler's Dodsworth.

tantly, they are typical of a good actress. An actress, that is, who conceives of her performance from the start in the terms the author has laid down, not in terms of her own personality. This is why every performance she gave has the ring of truthfulness and the depth of reality. She was never a good liar.

The extraordinary thing is that Mary Astor started, at the age of eleven, by sending her photograph to Brewster Publications, who promised Fame and Fortune to eight youngsters every month: one a year would receive the opportunity of a Film Test. Eleven-year-old Lucile Langhanke sent in her picture without her parents' knowledge – about the last thing she did without her father's domination and her mother's close attendance. She made the Eight, but she was not picked as the One. (Anyway, as her father said, the winner was probably Mr Brewster's girlfriend.) And two years later she was in New York, closely guarded by father and mother, now a photographic model and a bit player.

Several things happened. First of all, the photographer Charles Albin took a series of Madonna-like stills that won her a contract with Harry Durant, of the Famous Players-Lasky Corporation. Then Jesse Lasky, Louella Parsons and Walter Wanger decreed that the name of Lucile Langhanke should be replaced by the more manageable Mary Astor. And then there was an encounter with Lillian Gish, who arranged a test for her by D. W. Griffith at his Mamaroneck Studios. Griffith failed her, as he had, about this time, nixed Norma Shearer: this time, though, as she learned later, it was because D. W. had glimpsed her father and noted his rapacity. 'The man's a walking cash-register. I could never mould this child into an actress with him on my neck all the time.' But this did not, unhappily, prevent Otto from clinging round Mary's neck for a long, long time.

Then came a stroke of luck. After a spate of quite ordinary roles, carrying her from support to leads, Mary found herself starring as Lady Margery Alvanley opposite John Barrymore in *Beau Brummel*. This brought her two things, both important: a lover and a teacher. With characteristic reserve, Miss Astor says little about John Barrymore as a lover, except to wonder what her mother and father actually thought she was doing during those long afternoon sessions when she and John were supposed to be working on their art. (I am quoting from Miss Astor's *A Life on Film*, which must surely be the most suggestive and the most intelligent autobiography ever written by a film actress.) John Barrymore opened doors for her. For him, acting was never 'self-expression'; it was the duty of the actor to be 'the expresser' of the writer. From this simple truth, quite apart from her native ability, came Mary Astor's later greatness as a screen actress.

One is tempted to wonder what would have happened to Mary Astor if she had never met John Barrymore. Surely she would have been successful, and surely her intuitive taste and talent would have led her to discover these truths that made her acting so exceptional. As it was, the challenge came too soon. Jack Barrymore wanted her to be great; but Mary knew, or thought she knew, that to be great demanded more bravery than she possessed. 'I was not to learn the simple ingredients of courage for some time.' So she gave in to Dolores Costello. She was not anyway allowed to play Ophelia in Barrymore's London company of *Hamlet*; nor could she be his Lady Anne in *Richard III*. There was no money in it. Otto remained her mentor.

Perhaps all this explains how Mary Astor was a fine actress – who played lots and lots of parts in lots and lots of indifferent films. Her screen personality was very different from her personality in life: cool, she seemed, always a touch superior, witty, wise and distinguished. In fact she was uncertain, longing for the certainties of family, deprived always by the cupidity of father and mother of the warmth and security she longed for.

It was this, surely, which accounted for the extraordinary charm she gave to Edith Cortright, Walter Huston's lover in *Dodsworth*. Here is a woman who had truly loved and truly suffered. She had learned what life is about, what can be expected and what one has to put up with. 'She walked tall,' (the words are hers). 'She made no unnecessary gestures or movements. She was cool.' Could there be any advice more sensible, yet more understanding and more warm, than Mary Astor manages to put into the three words with which she warns the scatterbrained Ruth Chatterton when she is about to make a fool of herself with Paul Lukas – 'My dear, don't'? There is magic here, of course, not to be analysed.

It was at the time of *Dodsworth* that Mary Astor became famous as the author of a Diary (largely, she says, apocryphal), in which she is supposed to have recounted, with the frankness we would expect, her love life. And particularly her passionate affair with the author, George Kauffman. What is really interesting about this – more interesting even than the vain supervisory meeting at the Goldwyn Studios of Goidwyn, Harry Cohn, Jack Warner, Irving Thalberg, Louis B. Mayer and Jesse Lasky – was Mary Astor's survival through the trial really by playing the part of Edith Cortright. 'She was three-dimensional in my mind, and I knew all about her.' Even more revealing is the comment: 'She had complete confidence in herself, and I had very little.' This terrific effort of compensation is one of the keys to Mary Astor's great distinction.

Try as she might, she could never play a completely commonplace woman. If you saw, out of curiosity, *Page Miss Glory*, a Marion Davies vehicle directed for Warners by Mervyn LeRoy, you will have seen Mary Astor as Frank McHugh's wife. Well, she couldn't play that. Or at least, if she did, you kept wanting the film to cut back to her, and show what she was thinking. *The Maltese Falcon* was quite different – and one can only thank God for the good fortune that caused the leading roles to be turned down by George Raft and Geraldine Fitzgerald.

Yet even here – and I must admit that the thought only occurred to me after seeing the film three or four times – it is difficult to be sure that Sam Spade and Brigid O'Shaughnessy have actually slept together. Perhaps this is due to the relationship between Huston and Mary Astor (which she herself never mentioned); perhaps to the innate puritanism of both Astor and Bogart. The film, you may say, doesn't need it; and as it was made, it doesn't. Yet a certain unbridled sensuality should be there. It isn't; and that is another fact about Mary Astor.

Before *The Falcon* came *The Great Lie*, for which, amazingly, she had to test. This was a slice of hokum if ever there was one. 'Hey, Astor,' called Bette Davis. 'Let's go talk a minute.' The result of their talk was a uniquely pointed and amusing relationship – and, to emphasise another fine point about Mary Astor's acting, an extraordinarily intelligent succession of scenes. She played Tchaikovsky marvellously, like a steam engine; but the interesting part – in her words, 'the fun part' – was the contrast between the two women, the goody-goody (Davis for a change) and the hard-working, egotistical professional artist. Their scenes have a wit and an edge unique in movies. You see how Mary's comedy, always strong, had to come out of character, out of truthfulness to situation, which makes

Brigid O'Shaughnessy's sudden attack on Joel Cairo funny as well as shocking.

It is astonishing indeed to hear that Preston Sturges was dissatisfied with her lovely, dizzy millionairess in *The Palm Beach Story*. Sturges must have had, fixed firmly in his mind, the actual style of those crazy ladies who used to accompany his mother, Mary D'Este, with Isadora Duncan round the South of France. Mary had to be true to herself, and to give his dialogue an accent quite different – but just as funny. There is a lesson here for all directors.

After her long spell of freelancing, Mary Astor settled for an MGM contract and (much too young) a string of 'Mom' parts. Most of these, quite properly, she despised. But it is impossible to think of the best of them, *Meet Me in St Louis*, without remembering Mary Astor, endlessly capable, deeply feeling, as mistress of the family. On Christmas Eve, Father announces that there will be no move to New York: there is laughter and relief and an opening of presents: Mother turns away from her family, giving way at last to tears of thankfulness and love. It is a moment of private joy, expressed at last by one who has believed in keeping her feelings to herself, exquisitely played. Only a wonderful actress, as sure of her technique as of her emotion, could have brought it off.

Films need stars, or at least audiences do. But stars cannot always act; and some actresses reject stardom. Mary Astor lacked the vulgarity, the elephantiasis of the ego, that almost always goes with stardom; and she refused the responsibility that goes with it too. She was never ambitious – perhaps to a fault. When she got tired with playing Marmee in LeRoy's indifferent, over-upholstered remake of *Little Women*, she went across to a neighbouring stage, put on a two-bit dress bought at a cheap department store, and played – brilliantly – a sleazy, getting-on whore in *Act of Violence*. She loved to act.

Mary Astor was always more of a pro than an *aficionado*. She left Hollywood to concentrate on TV, on the stage, and finally writing. She came back to films for *Hush, Hush Sweet Charlotte*, an inflated horrifier with Bette Davis and Olivia de Havilland. As Bette said to her director, Robert Aldrich: 'Turn her loose, Robert, you might learn something.' She only had two short scenes as the ageing murderess, waiting over her teacups to die; but they are scenes worth waiting for when the old clinker comes up on television. When all the tributes to truthfulness have been paid, I still don't know quite what it is that makes the woman so instantly real. It must be what she herself said: the character is three-dimensional, and Miss Astor knows all about her.

One should not ask for more, but one does. What a pity, one cannot help reflecting, her matchless ability, in comedy and in tragedy but best of all in both, seems never to have tackled the sharp, compassionate observation of Chekhov. I think particularly of *The Cherry Orchard*, which Garbo turned down. The mythic Swede would have been marvellous, but top-heavy. Bette Davis would have done splendid things with Ranevskaya. But best, most spell-binding of all, would have been Mary Astor. She would have given the character its enchanting fickleness, its absurdity; but also its heart-wrenching poetry, its sense of the passing of time. She acted (as she would have been the first to admit) in some dogs; but she left us a collection of performances of complete authority, sad as well as funny. I wish I had been privileged to direct her. I should have learned a lot.

Katharine Hepburn

Review of *Me: Stories of My Life* by Katharine Hepburn in *The Spectator*, 21 September 1991

IF YOU WERE ASKED TO DESCRIBE IN A SINGLE WORD THE UNIQUE QUALITY OF Katharine Hepburn, as a personality as well as an actress, what would you say? 'Candid', perhaps? Or 'forthright'? Something stronger, anyway, than 'honest', though she has always been that. You need a word that is more challenging, more abrasive. Americans of whom I asked the question – all admirers – suggested 'tough' or 'aggressive'. That is how she has long appeared to her fellow countrymen. She still does.

You could have said, until now, 'private'. Much interviewed and much written about, Katharine Hepburn has firmly refused to feed the media with details of her personal life. Since Spencer Tracy's death 24 years ago, it became well known that for many years she shared the life of one of Hollywood's most respected actors. But she never discussed their relationship; and with rare consideration (for Tracy was a Catholic and a married man), journalists didn't write about it during his lifetime. The publishers of *Me* are surely wrong to call these memoirs 'eagerly awaited', for we had grown to accept that Katharine Hepburn would not talk about personal things. Now she has changed her mind.

Age has made her decide to write about herself. Katharine Hepburn has been part of our lives for so long that it is difficult to realise that she is 84. There are not many parts now, in theatre or film, that she will be asked or willing to play. But she is irrepressibly active; she had to do something. And she has found herself more and more obsessed by the question that must nag at us all as we get old. What made us what we are? And what gave her particularly the strength to combat and survive opposition and hostility? What made her so strong to grasp and hold on to the stardom for which she has always hungered?

Katharine Hepburn has dedicated her book 'to Mother and Dad', which one well understands from the warmth and admiration with which she has written about her parents. Her father was a doctor, vigorous, sensible and courageous. And her mother partnered him with an equally active sense of responsibility: she fought for women's suffrage and against the evils of prostitution and disease. At the age of eight, her daughter Katharine was handing out gas-filled balloons carrying the slogan VOTES FOR WOMEN. She could also dive, play tennis, play golf and walk on her hands.

Katharine Hepburn's parents were New Englanders, which means they were energetic, daring, somewhat puritanical and quite without pretension. They had six children over a period of 15 years. The family was close-knit, made secure by love. So Katharine was lucky in her formation, and she has always known it: 'What luck to be born out of love and live in an atmosphere of warmth and interest.'

There is a glow about her memories of childhood which tell us what they have meant to her, though she is not sentimental about them. By tragic accident, her elder brother died when he was only sixteen, inexplicably by his own hand. That was the only time Kate saw her mother cry, and only once. Her father did not cry. Both parents believed that life is to be taken and used; one must never be dominated by it: 'They took what life had to offer and gobbled it up.' The inspiration of her whole life is here. It is enviable; and of course it can be formidable too.

Just what made Katharine Hepburn decide to be an actress is not clear. Her father thought it was a rubbishy occupation, but he did not try to stop her. Her mother was glad that her daughter had an ambition which would take her beyond the domestic, child-bearing functions of a woman in those days. Katharine was lucky from the start, but she was also determined not to be put down. She had, she knew, a 'too vivid personality', which got her parts but also got her fired. From a play by Philip Barry, for instance, in which she was playing opposite Leslie Howard. She tried to conform. 'What would you like me to do here, Mr Howard?' she asked. And he answered, 'I really don't give a damn what you do, my dear.' The next day she was sacked. But nothing discouraged her. She tested for films and won the lead opposite John Barrymore in *A Bill of Divorcement*. She was a success overnight.

Me is not the work of a practised writer. It is written colloquially, at times stridently, at times breathlessly. All the time one feels the earnest, jokey presence of the author beside one. And because Katharine Hepburn has respected most of the people she has worked with, from her friend George Cukor to Louis B. Mayer to David Lean (she seems only to have disliked the theatre director Jed Harris, who did his best to destroy her in *The Lake*) she is never offensive or indiscreet. It is the same with the men she lived with, from the agent Leland Hayward to Howard Hughes. None was inconsiderable.

Katharine Hepburn seems always candid. She knows well that her drive has always been to have her own way. 'Usually I'm a bit push-push,' she admits, putting it mildly. She married once, early, a devoted, helpful man: 'All he wanted was me, and of course all I wanted was to be a great star in the movies.'

Even at the start, she could only imagine herself in all the leading parts. An exhibitor once famously attacked her (together with Joan Crawford and Marlene Dietrich, both strong women) as 'Box-Office Poison'. Her reply was to return to the theatre, appear in *The Philadelphia Story*, sell it to Louis B. Mayer and star in it herself. Sometimes she acted brilliantly, sometimes not so well. But her personality has always made her a star.

Inevitably, the chapters about her long and close relationship with Spencer Tracy have attracted most journalistic attention. She writes admirably about him, with frankness and discretion. He was, it is clear, a private and complicated man, with his problems of guilt (his son, one of the two children of his marriage, was born deaf), his seriousness as an actor and his refusal to theorise or discuss, his drinking, his Irishness . . . Katharine knew that she was wholly attracted to him, but she never knew what he found in her. She was much too wise to ask. She knew that for her, love was more in giving than in getting, and she was ready to give anything. Enormously egotistical, she was yet prepared to sacrifice her career to his needs.

For Katharine Hepburn, Spencer Tracy was the perfect actor: 'He is simple and totally honest. He makes you believe what he is saying.' Only one other performer seems to have had the same quality, which won her complete admiration – Laurette Taylor, Irish, like Tracy, 'both troubled ones'. Katharine found her 'effortless, easy . . . one could never see the wheels go round. It was always a happening.' This is how she tried to act. In acting, of course, the relationship between art and personality is never easy to define: it is a mystery. And so is the appetite for success, which seems to be part of it. Katharine Hepburn has always been compulsively ambitious, as well as a dedicated actress.

There may seem to be a paradox here. But the combination of driving ambition and straightforward common sense has always been a part of Katharine Hepburn. She is very American. There is a great deal of self-knowledge in this book; yet sometimes one wonders if she fully realises the impression she has made on others, and the world. But then, which of us does?

George Cukor

Review of *George Cukor: A Double Life* by Patrick McGilligan in *The Daily Telegraph*, 20 June 1992

AMERICAN FILMS ARE SO AMERICAN, SO GENERALLY FORCEFUL AND DIS-respectful, that it is difficult to realise how many of their makers came – especially in the Golden Age – from Europe. Hollywood itself was mostly the creation of Eastern European Jews. Rex Ingram and John Ford were Irish; William Wyler was born in Alsace. And George Cukor's parents were Hungarian, his mother an immigrant. Also they were Jewish. Perhaps it was this that made him, as well as enormously talented, such a determined survivor. (A Hungarian, remember, has been defined as the only man on earth who can enter a revolving door behind you, and come out first.)

A survivor he certainly was. He directed his last film, *Rich and Famous*, in 1981, when he was 82 years old. He had made his first, *Tarnished Lady*, with Tallulah Bankhead, 50 years before. In the years between, movies like *Dinner at Eight, Little Women, David Copperfield* (all pro-duced by David Selznick), *Camille, The Philadelphia Story, Adam's Rib* and the Judy Garland remake of *A Star is Born* had ensured his position as one of Hollywood's perennially top directors.

His work was praised for its professionalism, its style, its habitual sophistication. Above all, he was publicised by MGM, the studio for which he most often worked, as a 'woman's director', which implied a particular understanding of women's psychology and the needs and prob-lems of actresses. No-one was surprised when Cukor, fired by his friend Selznick from *Gone with the Wind* (reputedly at the insistence of Clark Gable), returned immediately to MGM and one of his greatest successes, *The Women*, with its brilliant all-female cast.

Unlike many of America's great directors, George Cukor came from the theatre. Patrick McGilligan, who has researched his book extremely well, records how Cukor went regularly to see the woman stars who reigned on Broadway when he was young. He ran his own company in Rochester (from which Bette Davis would never forget she was fired) and directed plays in New York. These included Laurette Taylor in *Coquette* and Ethel Barrymore (his idol) in *The Constant Wife*. Then, in 1929, he went into films.

In 1932 Cukor directed Katharine Hepburn, his great find and his favourite actress, in her film debut, *A Bill of Divorcement*. She became his great friend. She is quoted as admiring the 'tremendous continuity' Cukor built into his life. This is certainly true as far as his relationships, loving and friendly and professional, were concerned. Hepburn made ten films with him; Spencer Tracy made five. George Hoyningen-Heune, the photographer, worked often as his colour consultant. Donald Ogden Stewart wrote seven of his films. Seven others were scripted by Garson Kanin and Ruth Gordon. Artistically, though, Katharine Hepburn's remark was less true.

Like many theatre directors, Cukor would all his life take subjects that were offered, as long as they satisfied (usually) his standards of taste, intelligence and importance. Otherwise there was no need for them to conform to any particular philosophy or point of view. Cukor had rules of proper behaviour, but he had no interest in politics. Primarily he was a professional. He did not refuse the last films of Greta Garbo and Norma Shearer (both of whom he had directed successfully before) when it was clear the scripts were impossibly weak; but it took the right actress or the right actor (Ronald Colman won the Academy Award for *A Double Life*) in the right script to make his work as brilliant as it could be.

This book is subtitled *A Double Life*, which does not seem very appropriate. George Cukor did not make a great secret of his homosexuality and, not being an actor, he did not have to present a false front to the world. The attention (considerable) that Patrick McGilligan pays to his private life, to the 'chief unit' of friends who would gather round his pool on Sundays, does not really pay off. Perhaps Garson Kanin was right when he said: 'I don't think there is a book in George.'

This one has certainly been hard for Mr McGilligan to put together. The closest friend of Cukor's later years refused to talk to him. Katharine Hepburn met him once and gave him 'exquisite Borscht and cold sandwiches', but would not otherwise assist. Cukor's films are all chronicled, but it has to be said that the judgements are often erratic. There are a lot of interesting facts in the book, but it is chiefly successful as gossip.

George Cukor fascinated and charmed many people. He was witty and generous. He lived the life of the wealthy and successful man he was. Did lasting happiness elude him? It is impossible to know, but one suspects so. At least it can be said that he left many wonderfully crafted, wonderfully entertaining films behind him – is there a more perfect American comedy than *The Philadelphia Story*?

Pragmatic to the end, Cukor hated to be called an artist; the term, he said, did not apply to him. But many artists have left a far less diverting legacy behind them.

David O. Selznick

Review of *Showman: The Life of David O. Selznick* by
David Thomson in *The Daily Telegraph*, 26 January 1993

DISCUSSING OVER AND OVER AN ASSEMBLY OF *DUEL IN THE SUN*, THE MON-
umental Western which he made to celebrate his obsession with Jennifer
Jones, David Selznick complained, 'I know when I die the obituaries will
begin, "David O. Selznick, producer of *Gone with the Wind*, died today."'
He was right. The day after his death, *The New York Times* ran the headline, 'David O. Selznick, 63, Producer of *Gone With the Wind*, Dies'. And
even the blurb on the jacket of this book starts with the claim that 'The
legendary producer and maker of *Gone with the Wind* is brilliantly portrayed in this full-scale biography.' David Thomson's biography is certainly 'full-scale'. It is 700 pages long, and the author has been able to consult letters, memos, production reports, gambling accounts, the exhaustive
documentation of the most compulsive memo-writer and correspondent of
any of Hollywood's great producers.

Many books have told us recently how the American cinema was largely created and developed by Eastern European immigrants, mostly Jewish.
David Selznick and his brother Myron were the sons and the tempera-
mental heirs of one of these. Lewis Selznick may have walked out of
Russia when he was twelve; he arrived in the US in 1888 and became an
American citizen six years later. From being a 'diamond expert', Lewis
moved into the film business. He could sell almost anything, so naturally
he became a movie producer. For a while he was one of the richest men in
America. His son David inherited his gift for enterprise and fast-talking.
He never lost it.

The affairs of the Selznicks were always complicated, partly because of
their continuous and fearless drive, and partly because of the ceaseless way
they would bounce back from failure. David Thomson's book is
researched in extraordinary, even impeccable detail. It communicates the
personality of a remarkable family: if 'Pop' Selznick's ventures into film
production failed, he spent two hours with the president of Standard Oil,
outlining a brilliant but impossible scheme. His son Myron, a victim of
alcoholism, became the first and outstandingly successful Hollywood
agent, the scourge of the studios.

Early on, David O. Selznick (the 'O' was an invention of his own, added
as 'a measure of rhythm, gravity and business ambition') devoted himself
to his father's company – the Selznick Picture Corporation. This failed,

Lewis became bankrupt, and David spent time under the influence of his friend Ben Hecht, planning to become a writer and publisher. He started a book of his own (never finished) about the movie business. The Selznicks embarked on a large-scale promotion in Florida. Failure again, then David fled to California and the film industry. He landed a job with MGM, then went on to Paramount, as assistant to B. P. Schulberg. The helter-skelter of movies in the early days of sound suited him. He loved and married Irene Mayer, Louis B.'s younger daughter, which confirmed his position among the young up-and-coming of Hollywood. He was bought by RKO to take charge of production, and in 1932 he personally produced *What Price Hollywood?* Six years later as an independent producer, he bought and began shooting *Gone with the Wind*.

Hollywood has always boasted film directors of outstanding talent and reputation. But the studio system, on which its greatness was founded, relied on executives (they were very rarely artists) called 'producers', who were primarily responsible for the flow of product which kept the studios rich. David Selznick was this kind of film-maker, not without his own kind of taste and judgement, but never himself undertaking the responsibility of direction. After RKO, he spent two years at MGM, where his early reading bore fruit in films of *David Copperfield* and *A Tale of Two Cities*. But he craved independence. He shrugged off the patronage of his father-in-law (which had given rise to the Hollywood joke of 'The Son-in-Law Also Rises') and left to found Selznick International. For his own company he made *Gone with the Wind*. It was a project which, for once, matched his own obsessive concern with perfection and size. No film has been more successful.

Selznick felt that he instinctively understood what the movie-going public wanted, what made 'hits'. For a time this coincided with his own passion for significant narrative, for 'quality'. *Gone with the Wind* was followed by *Rebecca*, for which Selznick had brought Hitchcock to Hollywood, then by his own wartime family epic, *Since You Went Away*, much of which he wrote himself, a film which reflected his own infatuation with women – and his obsession, which took hold of him about this time and which dominated the rest of his life, with the dark beauty of Jennifer Jones.

David Selznick was possessed by an unceasing drive for 'quality' and success in the movie business. He was convinced, always, that he was right. In the war, James Forrestal, then Under Secretary for the Navy, received a letter from him compounded of 'eagerness and panic, modesty and big-shot' (Thomson's words). Not surprisingly, he wrote Selznick off as an egomaniac, which was surely the truth. He was also, and significantly, a persistent gambler (not a successful one) and an inveterate womaniser. His marriage disintegrated, apparently because Irene could no longer bear his unceasing falsehoods, his manic obsessions and his escapades. She was no fool and went on alone to produce several successful plays on Broadway, most notably *A Streetcar Named Desire*. Selznick could never quite abandon her but found himself obliged to marry Jennifer Jones, who became another obsession and his victim. One is not surprised that she refused to be interviewed by his biographer.

As time went by, Selznick lost his popular touch. The catastrophes of *Portrait of Jenny* and *The Paradine Case* brought his Hollywood pre-eminence to an end. He entered into partnership with Alexander Korda, but co-produced only one successful film, *The Third Man*, on which he harassed the director with an endless torrent of know-all memos. By the finish of the picture there had been 72 of these, most of which Carol Reed fortunately consigned to the wastepaper basket. Selznick's last film for Jennifer Jones, a remake of *A Farewell to Arms*, failed badly. But he could never give up his ambition to try again.

The twists and turns of this hypertense man and his incredibly complex life are scrupulously chronicled in this biography with repeated columns of income and debt, detailed until one's head spins. 'He was at times,' the author concludes, 'a fool, a coward, a liar, a scoundrel and a bore – he was just like us.' But in truth, he was not like us. Katharine Hepburn, whose first film Selznick produced, was nearer the mark when she wrote of 'the big, individual driving force – extraordinary people – in this age they seem a kind of fairy tale.' I am reminded of Ranevskaya's words: 'Giants? They're all right in fairy stories. But I wouldn't like to meet one.' If you read this book from beginning to end, you will have met one, certainly.

Meeting in Dublin with John Ford: *The Quiet Man*

Sequence 14, 1952

'I'm a quiet, gentle person.'
John Ford

IT IS FUTILE TO ATTEMPT TO ENVISAGE BEFOREHAND WHAT PLACES, PEOPLE will be like. Inevitably, though, images form in the mind. They certainly had plenty of time to form in mine, for by the time I actually got to see John Ford I had crossed Ireland twice, trusting the telegram I had received to say that the *Quiet Man* unit would be shooting in Cong (in Ford's – or rather his father's – native Galway) till the end of the week. By the time I had got there the unit had left. So back I crawled to Dublin, hoping to catch Ford before he flew off to America the next day.

A succession of slowly moving trains and buses had by this time lent to the journey a dream-like quality, not inappropriate to a pilgrimage to the source of a well-loved myth. About Ford himself I felt no temptation to speculate; as my last bus stopped and started its way through the Dublin suburbs I found that I almost ceased to believe in his existence. What of the setting in which I should find him? I imagined something large, rather formidable; an aloof Georgian or nineteenth-century mansion staffed with a squad of retainers, furnished in mahogany, with soft carpets and tall, dark rooms. I was, anyway, quite unprepared for the trim, very contemporary little surburan home in front of which the conductor set me down; neat front lawn, paved path from the gate; aproned parlourmaid to open the front door. Voices and the clink of knives made it clear that supper was still in progress; I was shown into the front room. But I had scarcely time to sink into a chair and look around me when footsteps sounded outside, the door opened and Ford came in with a rush.

Bypassing the stage of first impressions, we seemed to be plunged straight into familiarity. But let me try. A bulky man, craggy as you would expect, sandy hair thinned and face deeply lined. Eyes hidden behind dark-lensed spectacles. Informal in clothes as in manner; he wore an old sports coat and a pair of grubby grey flannels, his shirt was open at the neck. He flopped into an armchair, in which, as we talked, he shifted from position to position of relaxed comfort – legs crossed, then one up over the arm of the chair, then both. Speech forthright, with a matching ruggedness of vocabulary. Frank; responsive to frankness; a bit impatient, but ready to listen.

He was sorry to have missed me in Galway; they were behind schedule on the picture and, once finished, had no thought but to get away at once, back to Hollywood to polish off the interiors. He did not seem altogether happy about the experience. 'Something seemed to get into people down there. I guess it must have been the climate.' Had the rain held up shooting? 'No, the weather was all right – that softness is fine with Technicolor. But the unit seemed to go soft too; they started standing about looking at the scenery. I had to start watching for points of continuity – people looking out of windows, that sort of thing, which no one else noticed. Then, of course, our technicians work a lot faster than yours. It was really too big a job for one man to tackle on his own . . . I'm just going back to making Westerns.' He looked at me. 'Of course, you're one of those people who think it's a disgrace the way I keep turning out these Westerns.' I protested. 'Yes, you do. You've written that, haven't you? I'm sure I read that somewhere.' One other thing from that article had caught in his memory. 'And what was that you said about me being anti-British?' I told him. ('*A true Irishman, Ford has no time for the English.*') He laughed, but took pains to deny it. 'I've got more British than I have American friends . . . Of course, you must remember I'm Irish – we have a reputation to keep up.'

About here I made an attempt to pull myself together and be businesslike. I asked if I might get my notebook (which I had left in the hall) and ask some questions. 'Carry on,' said Ford, but with a slight unease. 'I'm not a career man, you know,' he announced defensively. 'I don't suppose I've given more than four interviews in my whole life. And now two in an evening . . .' He didn't speak as if the prospect attracted him. 'Christ,' he said, 'I hate pictures. When people ask me if I've seen some actress or another, I say, "Not unless she was in *The Great Train Robbery* or *Birth of a Nation*. Then perhaps I've seen her. Otherwise, no."' I said: 'Why do you go on with them?' 'Well, I like *making* them of course . . . But it's no use asking me to talk about art . . .'

We chatted for a bit about Ford's early days in the cinema. How had he started directing? 'I just started,' he explained. (He had gone out to California at the age of nineteen, after three unprofitable weeks at the University of Maine, to work for his brother Francis – at that time an established star and director.) He began making Westerns in 1917, when he was twenty-two. 'I can't remember much about them now,' he said. 'We made one about every week. I directed them and Harry Carey acted them. All those early ones were written by Carey and me – or stolen. We didn't really have scripts, just a rough continuity . . .' But he well remembered the making of *The Iron Horse*, his railroad epic of 1924. 'We went up there prepared for routine Hollywood weather – all sunshine and blue skies. We got out of the train in a blizzard and nearly froze to death . . . We lived in a circus train, had to dig our own latrines, build up a whole town around us. Saloons opened up; the saloon-girls moved in . . . The whole thing was very exciting.'

Suddenly we had skipped twenty years and were talking about *They Were Expendable*. Perhaps Ford's attitude towards this film so dumb-founded me that a whole tract of conversation was wiped from my memory. As a matter of fact, we were both dumbfounded. He was looking at me in extreme surprise. 'You really think that's a good picture?' He was amazed: 'I just can't believe that film's any good.' I was amazed. 'But – didn't you want to make it?' Ford snorted. 'I was ordered to do it. I wouldn't have done it at all if they hadn't agreed to make over my salary to the men in the unit.' (Naval, not film.) He added: 'I have never *actually* seen a goddamned foot of that film.' I told him that horrified me. 'I'll use the same word,' he said, 'I was horrified to have to make it . . .' Didn't you feel at least that you were getting something into it even though you hadn't wanted to take it on?' He scorned the idea. 'Not a goddamned thing,' he said, 'I didn't put a goddamned thing into that picture.' He had been pulled out of the front line to make it, had just lost thirteen men from his unit, and had to go back to Hollywood to direct a lot of actors who wouldn't even cut their hair to look like sailors. I said I found this partic-ularly extraordinary because the film contains so much that needn't have been there if it had been made just as a chore. 'What, for instance?' I made example of the old boat-builder (played by Russell Simpson), who appears only in a few shots, yet emerges as a fully, and affectionately, conceived person. Ford relented slightly: 'Yes, I liked that . . .' He shifted his ground: 'The trouble was, they cut the only bits I liked . . . Is that scene in the shell-hole still there, between the priest and the boy who says he's an atheist?' 'What priest?' I asked. 'Played by Wallace Ford.' 'There's no priest in the film at all.' This surprised him. I said I found it extraordinary that one could cut a whole (presumably integral) character from a story without leaving any trace. 'MGM could,' said Ford. I said: 'But *Expendable* runs two and a quarter hours as it is . . .' Ford said: 'I shot the picture to run an hour and forty minutes – it should have been cut down to that.' I said that this could not be done without ruining the film. 'I think I know more about making pictures than you do,' said Ford.

He asked me what the music was like; he said he had fierce arguments when the MGM music department had shown him the score they intend-ed to put over it. 'But surely – it's full of just the tunes you always like to use in your pictures.' But Ford had found it too thickly orchestrated, too symphonic. 'I wanted almost no music in it at all – just in a very few places like "Red River Valley" over Russell Simpson's last scene. We played and recorded that as we shot it. Otherwise I didn't want any music; the picture was shot as a documentary, you know. No reflectors were used at any

John Ford, 'old father, old artificer', on location in Ireland for The Quiet Man.

time, and we kept the interiors dark and realistic.' He asked if that last shot was still in, with the aeroplane flying out, and the Spanish rower silhouetted against the sky; and what music was over it. He seemed satisfied when I told him it was 'The Battle Hymn of the Republic'.

But chiefly Ford was amazed at the thought that anyone could find *They Were Expendable* an even tolerable picture. 'John Wayne had it run for him just recently – before he went to the States. And afterwards he said to me: "You know, that's still a great picture." I thought he was just trying to say something nice about it; but perhaps he really meant it.'

I asked him about the music in his pictures generally; how close was the relationship between himself and the musical director on the pictures he had made at Fox? 'Very close – we knew each other very well. I think you can say that I'm responsible for the faults or the qualities of the music we

447

used in those pictures.' (Films like *Young Mr Lincoln*, *The Grapes of Wrath*, *My Darling Clementine*.)

I tried to switch from the particular to a more general view: what was Ford's bird's-eye view of his career; of that astonishing trail? Looking back, did he trace periods of exploration and discovery; the series of pictures he had made with Dudley Nichols, for instance, how did he now feel about them? Ford countered: 'What pictures did I make with Nichols?' 'Well . . . *The Long Voyage Home* – *The Fugitive* – *The Informer*.' 'Oh,' said Ford, 'so Nichols wrote *The Informer*, did he?' He resisted implacably, in fact, any attempt to analyse his motives in picking subjects. 'I take a script and I just do it.' Even when I suggested that there were some films (apart from *They Were Expendable*) that he must have undertaken with reluctance, I got nowhere. He had *enjoyed* making *Wee Willie Winkie*, and was charmed by Shirley Temple, now as then. The nearest he would come to discrimination was: 'Sometimes I get a story that interests me more than others . . .' Such as *The Quiet Man*, which he had wanted to do for ten years. 'It's the first love story I've ever tried. A mature love story.'

Singly, he would comment on films I mentioned. How did he feel now about *The Informer*? 'I don't think that's one of my best,' said Ford. 'It's full of tricks. No, I think that comes quite a long way down the list.' His favourite is *Young Mr Lincoln*: 'I've got a copy of that at home, on 16mm. I run that quite often . . .' He thought. 'Now let me see . . . What other pictures have I got copies of? Not many . . . *The Lost Patrol* – I still enjoy that one; and I think I may have a copy of *Yellow Ribbon*.' He is fond of *How Green Was My Valley* and *The Fugitive*. ('I just enjoy myself looking at it.') With some trepidation I asked about a personal favourite – *My Darling Clementine*. 'I never saw it,' said Ford.

We talked for a bit about the Westerns to which he has devoted himself since *The Fugitive*. I asked if they had been undertaken primarily to make money. 'Oh, yes. I had to do something to put my company back on its feet after what we lost on that. And they've done it.' All these films, apparently, from *Apache* to *Rio Grande* have achieved commercial success – particularly (which surprised me) *The Three Godfathers*. Since Ford gave the impression of anticipating attack about them, I made the point that the objection was less to the fact that they were 'just Westerns', than to the carelessness with which, too often, they seemed to have been put together. I asked if it wasn't true that *Fort Apache* was shot deliberately in a hurry and under budget, as it appeared to be. 'Yes, it was,' Ford admitted; then scratched his head. 'Now what was that one about? Oh yes; that was a very concocted story. But very good box-office.' *She Wore a Yellow Ribbon*, he said, was made even quicker than *Fort Apache*; though it was a picture he liked. And so was *Wagonmaster*: 'I really tried to do something with that.' When I instanced crudities that seemed to me to disfigure some of these films, Ford countered with the familiar arguments of finance. 'I think you're being too demanding,' he said. 'These refinements cost money – and all the time there's that tremendous pressure of money on top of you. You do the best you can. And remember that with all these pictures I wasn't just working to pay off on *The Fugitive*, but to make enough for *The Quiet Man* as well. Of course, it'll probably lose the lot again; but that's the way it always goes.'

Another point Ford made about his recent Westerns, or rather about his reasons for making them, was more personal. Holding up his left hand he said: 'It looks all right, but it isn't.' Injuries inherited from the war give him, intermittently, a good deal of pain; they had put him out of action for a few days on *The Quiet Man*, and generally made studio shooting – in the glare and oppressive atmosphere of a sound stage – a penance. 'I was out in Korea before coming to Ireland – I made a documentary there called *This is Korea* – and oddly enough I never had a twinge. But out at Cong it really got me down.' He could even, as a result, envisage *The Quiet Man* being his last picture; at any rate, after it, he would have to take a good long rest.

In the end we talked for about an hour and a half, and I forgot all the questions I had meant to ask. I prepared to take my leave. But first Ford had a question he wanted to put to Maureen O'Hara in front of me. (I had not realised before that this was her family's home where Ford was staying.) 'Now, Maureen,' he said, 'have you ever heard me talk of a film called *They Were Expendable* – or have you ever seen it when we have had a show at the house?' 'No,' said Miss O'Hara, 'I haven't.' 'You see?' Ford said. 'But we'll put it on when we get back. The kids will like the boats anyway.'

We shook hands, and Ford went out into the garden to talk. 'He's a great man,' said Miss O'Hara. 'And a wonderful director to work for. In other films you'll be just mediocre; then with him . . .' I asked her how he did it. 'He seems to know just what's necessary to get a good performance from anyone; some people he'll be entirely gentle with, and with others he'll be a brute. But you don't mind because, when you see it on the screen, you realise why.' I asked her about the last scene in *Rio Grande*, Ford's most recent picture. The band plays 'Dixie' as the cavalry rides past – Captain York's olive branch to his Southern wife, received by her not with tears or sentiment, but with mischief and a parasol provocatively twirled. 'Whose idea was that?' I asked. 'Oh, his,' she laughed, 'he told me to do that.'

As the foregoing has probably made plain, Ford is pretty well interview-proof. This is not to say that my hour and a half was not a memorable one, but it was not exactly rich in generalisations, personal pronouncements readily quotable to illustrate the views of John Ford on the film as an art. About other people's films he professed himself uninterested; and certainly it requires a stretch of the imagination to visualise him 'going to the cinema'. Of his own hundred-odd films he was quite willing to talk, or at least to answer questions; but he shied away from any invitation to generalise. They were like, as he spoke of them, stories that he has told, some with more care and enjoyment than others. Some he remembers, some he has all but forgotten, all are of the past. 'The best in this kind are but shadows.' At one point, when I broke off for a moment to refer to William Wootten's index of his films, he reached over and took it from my hand. 'I suppose I ought to have one of these,' he said as he inspected it; but there was no conviction in his tone.

How far this impression of a first meeting corresponds with the truth, I am in no position to say. Any such talk has to be seen in its context: a director in mid-film, at the end of six weeks on location, somewhat wary perhaps at being thus pursued to an interview for the first time for a number of years. And at any time (one senses) Ford is a man who speaks by mood, from impulse rather than reflection and without much concern to qualify – he might very well contradict any of his statements the next day. For instance, it is obvious to everyone who knows his films that his attitude towards his craft has not been always as instinctive, as unconcerned with questions of style and subject, as it pleased him to make out. But in a single interview there was no opportunity of breaking past this firmly held position.

There remained the man. It is natural that anecdotists should concentrate on his wild Irish temper, his fondness for horseplay, the violence of his conflicts with producers and high-stepping actresses; and there is no reason to suppose these stories exaggerated. (Ford has only to protest, 'I'm a quiet, gentle person,' for one to be quite sure they are not.) But besides the stampedes, the war parties, the knock-about fights, there are those quiet moments in his films, equally characteristic, of tenderness and insight; and these too his presence reflects. This was the Ford I found in Dublin – a man of fascinating contradictions; of authority in no way diminished by a complete rejection of apparatus; of instinctive personal warmth as likely to evidence itself in violence as in gentleness; confident of his powers, yet unpretentious about their achievement. A patriarchal figure, sitting among friends; it was easy to understand the devotion he inspires in those who work for him.

When Ford started talking in terms of his 'last picture', I had the impression that this was not necessarily serious – the momentary result of ill-health and fatigue rather than a real determination to bring his career to a close. And perhaps also a sense that yet another turning point had been reached? Today Ford stands apart, an isolated figure as well as a great one – and the isolation is different from the fierce independence which has characterised his whole career. It is not merely the penalty of remaining true to his own, at the moment unfashionable, vision; his recent pictures have not been consistently of the quality he can give us. The argument of commercial necessity in fact sounds in his mouth far more like the uneasy justification of one who feels himself in some degree guilty, than the callous admission of one who has problems of artistic conscience firmly behind him. It is not necessarily a question of subject; the fresh and vigorous poetry which his often repeated themes evoke from him is more to be valued than the artwork which has sometimes resulted from his tackling of more conventionally ambitious material. It is rather a question of seriousness.

A good deal would seem to hang on *The Quiet Man*, for its success or failure must affect Ford's attitude towards film-making in the future. In any event it is difficult to believe that he will not continue at it for a while yet. 'I want to be a tugboat captain,' he says. But God made him a poet, and he must make the best of that.

My Dublin interview with Ford had an epilogue. By the time we had finished talking it was too late to return to London the same day so I took a hotel room for the night: I suppose I gave my telephone number to the publicity man who arranged the interview.

In the morning, as I was packing my bag, there was a knock at my bedroom door. I was wanted on the phone. I was mystified: who on earth knew where I was? I went to the telephone. It was Ford.

'I want to thank you for going to all that trouble to come and see me,' he said. I was touched and amazed: it was for me to thank him. But Ford went on. 'You were quite right with some of those criticisms you made. Some of that stuff isn't up to standard.' I was humbled, as one is apt to be when people readily admit errors one has charged them with. I hoped I hadn't been too impertinent. 'No – no. It's easy to get careless. Particularly when the financial pressure is so great. But that's not a justification. Thank you for reminding me.' (By now I was speechless. Ford went on.) 'I'm going back now to finish *The Quiet Man*, and I promise you I'll do my best. I'll make it as good as I possibly can.'

I wished him good luck, and he thanked me again – then added, before he rang off: 'I'll see *Expendable*, and I'll let you know what I think.'

He kept his word. Some weeks later I received a telegram. It read: HAVE SEEN EXPENDABLE. YOU WERE RIGHT. FORD.

I carried this around with me for a long time, till my wallet was stolen. The police found it, but of course the money in it had gone. So had the telegram.

They Were Expendable and John Ford

Sequence, Summer 1950

> . . . *And since I care*
> *For dear Guercino's fame, to which in power*
> *And glory comes this picture for a dower,*
> *Fraught with a pathos so magnificent;*
> *And since he did not work thus earnestly*
> *At all times, and has else endured some wrong,*
> *I took one thought his picture struck from me*
> *And spread it out . . .*

Robert Browning, 'The Guardian Angel'

TO HIS ADMIRERS, AS TO HIS CRITICS, JOHN FORD HAS ALWAYS PRESENTED something of an enigma. Unquestionably enshrined among the great, it has often seemed that he owes his celebrity rather to his association with a random group of distinguished films, than to any consistent personal quality as an artist. Certain French critics, indeed, with their meaningless battle-cry of '*A bas Ford, vive Wyler!*' have crystallised this misapprehension into heresy – coupling these two directors as impersonal master-craftsmen, neither of whom seeks any form of individual expression in his art. If one had taken this seriously, one would perhaps have been more surprised, on seeking out one of Ford's lesser-known pictures (very few critics appear to have seen it), to find it a work of outstanding quality, one of the few great films to come out of the recent war, and especially remarkable for its combination of the broadest sweep of action with the most delicate strokes of imagination and feeling.

They Were Expendable is the story of a defeat – the rout of the American Forces in the Pacific in the first stage of the war against Japan. Above all, it is a personal film, with the sincerity and purpose of a dedicated work. This, at least, is how one feels it was regarded by its director; the credits carry not merely his name, but also his rank: Captain, USNR. Similarly, with its author (Cmdr Frank Wead, who based his script on W. L. White's factual account of the campaign), cameraman (Lt-Cmdr Joseph August), second unit director (Capt. James Havens) and leading actor (Cmdr Robert Montgomery), all of whom had served with the Navy during the recent war. The impression of dedication is reinforced by two opening titles, both phrased with some solemnity. The first, from a speech by MacArthur, runs: 'Today the guns are silent. A great tragedy has ended. A great victory has been won . . . I speak for the thousands of silent lips, forever stilled among the jungles and in the deep waters of the Pacific, which marked the way.' The second sets the time and the place: 'Manila Bay. In the Year of Our Lord Nineteen Hundred and Forty One.'

The film starts with a sort of prologue, an introduction to the story's protagonist: Motor Torpedo Boat Squadron Three of the US Navy. Led by its Commander, Lieutenant Brickley (Montgomery), the squadron is showing its paces in Manila Bay, before the appraising eye of its Admiral; after the exercise the Admiral makes a perfunctory inspection, and leaves with a few politely disparaging remarks. The sequence closes with Brickley alone on the quay, eyeing his boat with speculation. With a minimum of words the main threads of the story have been drawn: its element, the sea; the PT boats, graceful and dangerous weapons of war; official doubts of their worth (they are 'expendable'): Brickley's quality as an officer, his faith in his boats, his deep and undemonstrative feeling for the Squadron – contrasted with the careless impetuosity of Ryan (John Wayne), his friend and Second-in-Command. That evening the news comes through of the Japanese attack on Pearl Harbor. Later the Admiral announces to his staff that war has been declared.

The war is soon a reality; next day, enemy bombers attack in force and reduce the Squadron's base to a shambles. But in spite of rumours that a Japanese task force is in the vicinity, Brickley is ordered to stand by for messenger trips. It is not till after the fall of Manila that the squadron's first real opportunity comes – an attack on a Japanese cruiser, sunk with the loss of one boat. Further actions follow, and further losses; Ryan is injured and sent, protesting, to the sick-bay, where he meets an Army nurse; with charmingly humorous formality she is entertained to dinner by the officers of the Squadron; the Commander of one of the boats is wounded and dies in hospital. All the time the enemy press nearer. At last, the Admiral sends for Brickley and orders him to stand by: his boats are to carry 'certain key personnel' south to Mindenao, *en route* for Australia; his spare crews must dwindle into soldiers, reinforcing the Army on Bataan. So, with the first of a series of farewells, the break-up of the Squadron begins; carrying their Admiral and his staff, their Commander-in-Chief (MacArthur) and his family, the boats make off for Mindenao, while the two redundant crews stand watching them leave, then form up and march forlornly away to Bataan.

Losing one boat on the way, Brickley arrives at Mindenao with only three; he is refused permission to return to Bataan for his men, and surrendered by his Admiral to the Army. An accident cripples two further boats, which have to be towed to a shipyard on the coast, still working

under the tough old trader who has spent his life building it up. One of
these is ready in time for Brickley and Ryan to go out on a last attack
against a Japanese cruiser. On their return, the boats are separated; Ryan's
is attacked from the air and blows up; two of his crew die with it. As he
and his men sit silently in a bar, after burying their dead, they hear radio
announcements of the fall of Bataan. This presages the ultimate defeat:
making contact again with Brickley, Ryan finds the last boat being hauled
away on a truck, turned over to run errands for the Army. Directionless
and exhausted, what remains of the Squadron marches off, to lose itself in
the confusion of defeat. Brickley, Ryan and two junior officers are ordered
back to Australia in the one plane that remains. As night falls, the remnants of the Squadron straggle away down the deserted beach, while over
their heads the plane soars out to Australia, and MacArthur's words come
up to fill the screen: 'We shall return.'

The sweep is epic, its rhythm cumulative. The three fine battle-scenes
are vigorously cut, but otherwise the story unfolds at an even, leisurely
pace. Ford has shown no great concern for clarity of development; maps
are used only once, to cover the flight south to Mindenao, and the continuity of action is not beyond reproach. Yet the occasional obscurity hardly matters at all. The essential continuity, of approach, is preserved without a lapse. It is based on a uniform authenticity of atmosphere and
behaviour: there is no trace of what the Services know as 'bull'. When war
is announced, the news is taken gravely, but without surprise; there are no
propagandist allusions to its cause, its purpose, or its consequences; the
Japanese are neither discussed nor execrated, they are simply the enemy,
anonymous and invisible. Tensions and relationships within the American
Forces are similarly convincing – between officers and men, between the
Navy and the Army.

'Authenticity' should not be taken to imply a ruthless and objective
realism. *They Were Expendable* is a film with a viewpoint, a purpose; it
sets out not merely to relate, but to pay tribute to the courage and tradition of service in one section of the American Navy. Its theme is, indeed,
put into words by the Admiral when he explains to Brickley the reasons
for their inactivity at the beginning of the campaign: 'Listen, son. You and
I are professionals. If the manager says "Sacrifice!" we lay down the bunt
and let somebody else hit the home runs . . . Our job is to lay down that
sacrifice. That's what we were trained for, and that's what we'll do.' Its
characters are shown in the light of their sacrifice, ennobled by it – not
through words, but through image after image of conscious dignity:
Sandy, the Army nurse, assisting at an endless series of operations as the
casualties pour into the hospital on Corregidor; the men of the Squadron
watching with amazement and pride as their Commander-in-Chief boards

the leading PT boat.

In spite of its emotional unity, the mood of the film is by no means monotonous. It is frequently varied with humour; of a fond, colloquial kind: the young Ensign who finds himself continually carried away by the dignity of his position; the rating who offends every canon of discipline by asking for MacArthur's autograph (one may even sense a further humour in the readiness with which the General grants it); the submarine Captain who is blackmailed into surrendering half his torpedos by allusion to his performance, in former years, as Tess of the d'Urbevilles at the Academy ('And does your crew know?'). Equally true are the moments of serious emotion: Brickley, for instance, saying goodbye to the men who have to go to Bataan, and leaving his speech incomplete, unable to bring himself to utter hopes he knows cannot be fulfilled; or the visit of the officers of the Squadron to their friend whom they know is dying, each side rising to the occasion with pathetic, transparently false jocularity. The film is full of such moments of emotion, expressed in a word or two, an inflexion, a silent pause.

This under-emphasis is saved from any taint of theatricality by the consistent sincerity and power of the feeling which inspires the film. Supported by acting of complete integrity, and by the magisterial technique of realisation, this enables Ford to proceed with absolute freedom. Close-ups, noble or affectionate, are held at leisure; long-shots are sustained long after their narrative function is performed; a marginal figure is suddenly dwelt on, lovingly enlarged to fill the centre of the screen. Informed with this heightened emotion, a single shot, abruptly interposed – a ragged line of men marching into nowhere, one of them playing a jaunty bugle-call on his harmonica – assumes a deeper significance than is given it by its position in the story. This is one of the properties of poetry; *They Were Expendable* is a heroic poem.

II

A pure example of an artist's style, if ever there was one, *They Were Expendable* demands, perhaps, for its full appreciation, a previous acquaintanceship and sympathy with the work of its director. (This, at any rate, would account for its general neglect by the critics.) Conversely, it has that compensating power of any very personal work, to illuminate films which come before it, and reveal qualities in them which may up to now have gone unremarked. In its light recognisable patterns emerge from the rather baffling diversity of Ford's films, so that, even at this late stage, a new attempt to set his career in perspective and his achievement at its proper worth, may not be valueless.

Sean O'Fienne arrived in Hollywood in July 1914, at the age of nineteen. The second son of Irish parents – his father was from Galway, his mother from Aran – he came fresh from Maine University, which he had entered after failing for Annapolis, the Naval training college. Under the name of Francis Ford, his elder brother had established himself as a director and actor in serials, and it was for his company that Sean worked, as a property man, stunt man, actor. Within a year (now Jack Ford) he had graduated to the post of assistant director; in 1917 he directed his first film, *Cactus, My Pal*, a two-reeler western for Bison-Universal, starring Harry Carey.

By 1920 Jack Ford had directed thirty Westerns, hearty adventure stories with titles like *The Range War, Thieves' Gold, A Fight for Love*. Harry Carey starred in all of these except the eighth, *The Scrapper*, in which Ford himself played the battling hero, Buck the Scrapper. With his 31st subject he broke new ground: *The Prince of Avenue A* featured the boxer, Gentleman Jim Corbett, in a comedy of Irish life in New York. There followed a random assortment of thrillers, romances, comedies and Westerns, until in 1923 Ford (now working for Fox) was assigned his first 'A' feature, *Cameo Kirby*, a romance of the South, starring John Gilbert, for which he assumed the new dignity of John Ford. Three pictures later, he celebrated his half-century by directing his first popular success, *The Iron Horse* (1924), an ambitious super-Western, Fox's reply to James Cruze's *The Covered Wagon*, produced by Paramount the year before.

'The Iron Horse,' writes Paul Rotha in *The Film Till Now*, 'was vast in conception, and John Ford, despite the hindrances of a story interest, handled it with a great deal of talent.' No copies of the film appear to have survived in Britain; and this also, unhappily, applies to Ford's two other outstanding silent pictures, *Three Bad Men* (1926) and *Four Sons* (1928). This means that it is impossible today to estimate his achievements in the silent cinema: by the coming of sound he had directed 60 films, and had gained experience in every variety of popular entertainment. How far the best of these would stand on their own merits today one cannot tell; it is obvious from their synopses that the majority would prove too naïve to be of much interest except as period pieces. It is evident, however, from repeated commendations in the trade press that they showed a progressively maturing craftsmanship, with repeated emphasis on their high visual qualities.

It was with his third sound film that Ford entered upon a partnership which was to prove of the greatest importance in his career. His *Men without Women* (1930) was written (from a story on which he had collaborated himself) by Dudley Nichols, one of the many talented journalists who had been drawn to Hollywood by the advent of talkies. The story of fourteen men trapped in a crippled submarine, *Men without Women* became one of Ford's favourite films; as a result the collaboration was continued intermittently until in 1934 it achieved its first *succés d'estime* with *The Lost Patrol*. The favourable reception of this tragic melodrama (the story of a British patrol wiped out in a Mesopotamian desert) induced Ford and Nichols to persuade its producers, RKO, to let them undertake the subject they had planned for several years – an adaption by Nichols of Liam O'Flaherty's novel, *The Informer*.

A flop in New York, *The Informer* (1935) was transformed into an outstanding success by its reception in the provinces and among the critics. In this respect the *Crossfire* of its day, it was a cheap picture, made with great speed, which brought immense prestige to its makers; by it Ford and Nichols were established as two rebels against the Hollywood system, successful protestants against the domination of the American cinema by spectators and businessmen. For the next six years Ford divided his time between deliberately 'artistic' ventures with Nichols – including adaptations from Maxwell Anderson (*Mary of Scotland*), O'Casey again (*The Plough and the Stars*) and O'Neill (*The Long Voyage Home*) – and his routine commercial chores for Fox, out of which grew a series of more ambitious pictures, firmly rooted in the American scene. This period of activity reached its climax with Ford's *annus mirabilis* – the twelve months' span from March 1939 to January 1940, which saw the successive releases of *Stagecoach*, *Young Mr Lincoln*, *Drums Along the Mohawk* and *The Grapes of Wrath*. Three pictures later came the war, and Ford left Hollywood to help supervise the making of films for the Navy. Returning in 1945, he made *They Were Expendable*, which he followed a year later with *My Darling Clementine*, his 100th film. Then, in 1947, Ford ventured into independent production; for his own company, Argosy pictures, he went to Mexico and made *The Fugitive*, from a script by Dudley Nichols, based on Graham Greene's novel, *The Power and the Glory*.

III

Nichols has written fourteen pictures for Ford. It is unfortunate that of the nine that are relatively unassuming, most are now inaccessible – an early assortment of adventure stories and comedies which includes two attractive-sounding regional pictures with Will Rogers, *Judge Priest* and *Steamboat Round the Bend* (both written in collaboration with Lamar Trotti). Of this group there now survive only three celebrated melodramas, *The Lost Patrol*, *The Hurricane* and *Stagecoach*. The last alone can claim the epithet 'classic'. *The Lost Patrol* has dated badly, craftsmanlike in direction but embarrassingly theatrical in writing and performance. *The Hurricane*, remarkable chiefly for its final cataclysm (astonishingly staged by Basevi), is otherwise very patchy. *Stagecoach*, though, very nearly pulls it off. The first four-fifths, economically scripted, and propelled along with irresistible urgency and drive, constitute perhaps the best chase film ever made – certainly the climactic pursuit of the Stage across the salt flats by a party of whooping Apaches, the last-minute rescue by the Cavalry, bugles sounding and pennants flying, could not be done better. One regrets only the faulty construction which tacks on a two-reel anti-climax after the film has reached its natural end, and a certain banality of characterisation, not wholly compensated by the sympathy and tact of the handling.

But it is on his more pretentious scripts that Nichols' reputations has been chiefly based; and it is on these, too, that critics have tended to concentrate in their estimations of Ford – *The Grapes of Wrath* is usually set apart, as though a miraculous and inexplicable sport. The most renowned is *The Informer*, almost invariably classed among the 'great' American films; others that may be grouped with it are *The Long Voyage Home* and *The Fugitive*. They are all adaptations: *The Informer* from Liam O'Flaherty's terse, objective account of an Irish hoodlum, giant in size and strength but infantile in brain, who betrays his Communist friend to the authorities and is hounded down and shot by the party; *The Long Voyage Home* is out of a collection of playlets by Eugene O'Neill set in the fo'c'sle of a British merchantman in time of war; *The Fugitive* is based on Greene's realist, tendentious study of the last priest to survive in the atheist totalitarian state of Mexico. Widely different though these originals are, Nichols has managed to imbue them all with characteristics of his own: with a sentimental simplification of issues and characters, a highly self-conscious striving for significance, and a fundamental unreality.

In degree of failure they are unequal. *The Long Voyage Home*, for instance, is an uneven work with whole stretches (particularly in the first half) of great power and success. As long, in fact, as the literary content is kept to a minimum, as long as the sailors are allowed to be themselves and the camera to speak for them, the film realises its poetic intention. In the last half, however, it falls victim to O'Neill's sentimentality (in the mawkish episode of the English gent turned alcoholic), and to Nichols' eternal pursuit of the Universal. Once off the ship, we are plunged into a symbolic no-man's-land, the sailors dogged by a bowler-hatted Cockney – an unhappy cross between a pimp and a fate-symbol – through the incredible Wapping mists. Nothing points Nichols' wrong-headedness more clearly than the ease and beauty with which, in the last, silent sequence of the men's slow return to their ship, Ford and Toland convey the sad sense of impermanence, which the script, with its literary symbolism, has strained after so hard and missed so completely.

With *The Informer* and *The Fugitive* Nichols has lighted on excellent material (greatly superior to O'Neill) which he has cheapened and debased. He has his apologists. Thus Theodore Huff (of N.Y. University Motion Picture Dept) on *The Informer*: 'Nichols . . . took a rather second-rate novel and by removing the extreme sectionalism and more unsavoury elements, transmuted the story into a psychological study of Man's Conscience, giving the film a larger and more dramatic conflict with universal meaning.' This means that the organisation which Gypo betrays is no longer the Communist but the Irish Nationalist Party; this less sectional and more savoury change enables Nichols to substitute for the ruthless, twisted leader of the book, a featureless, sympathetic Nationalist (Preston Foster) whose conversations with the betrayed man's sister are conducted with such lines such as: 'I love you Dan; I'll always love you. No matter what happens, there'll never be anyone else.' So that Gypo may adequately represent Man's Conscience, he is given an appreciable motive for his crime; but since he is played and presented throughout as the brutish creature of O'Flaherty's imagination, incapable of reasoned thought or planned action, no psychological conflict can emerge. The only successful sections of the film are those which remain true to the original.

The same would no doubt be true of *The Fugitive* had not Nichols in this case jettisoned his original completely. Universality (that quality best left to develop by itself) is again the object of urgent seeking. Gone is Greene's 'whisky priest', and in his place an indeterminate wraith, wandering uneasily through a maze of religious symbols: he makes his first appearance riding on an ass, and is harried constantly by a Judas-figure, and a Holy Mother-figure. Wholly without vitality, Nichols' conception is remarkable for a sickly dishonesty, which finds its typical expression in the Sign of the Cross which the principal and most determined enemy of God is shown to make as he hears the shot which signifies the death of the priest.

The tragedy of these films is less Nichols' than Ford's – that he should have devoted his great talent to material often meretricious, and foreign to the true source of his inspiration. He is, perhaps, an artist who has never realised where his real strength lies; it is characteristic that he should have disowned the films he made for Fox before 1940. Yet it is these which point on to his later poetic masterpieces.

IV

It is no easier to define poetry in the cinema than in literature, if only because – granted the common factor of intensity – it can be so various in style and method. The artist's way of reaching, or suggesting, truths behind appearances, it may apprehend these realities through fantasy or myth, derive from inventions peculiar to his own temperament, or from the common inheritance of feeling and tradition. Ford has always found his true image of reality in this world, not in the deliberately fashioned symbolism of a literary invention; his symbols arise naturally out of the ordinary, the everyday; it is by familiar places, traditions and themes that his imagination is most happily stimulated. There is a sort of strain, apt to evidence itself in pretentiousness of style, about his attempts with material outside his personal experience or sympathy. It is significant that, in contrast to his success with American actors, he rarely succeeds in getting a good performance from a foreigner: *How Green Was My Valley*, in which the only satisfactory acting came from an Irishwoman, Sara Algood, is a case in point. One remembers also the stagey Britishers in *The Lost Patrol* (a true Irishman, Ford has no time for the English), Wallace Ford and Heather Angel in *The Informer*, Ian Hunter in *The Long Voyage Home*, and the startling crudity of the British Admiralty official in the same film.

The films which, of those that can still be seen, one would select as Ford's most completely successful are all distinctively American in theme; and the majority are set in periods other than our own: *Drums Along the Mohawk* takes us back to the days of the War of Independence, in a series of scenes from Frontier life affectionately and excitingly sketched; *Young Mr Lincoln* is a story of Abraham Lincoln as a young hick lawyer, how his common sense and sheer moral power saved two innocent boys from lynching and a trumped-up charge of murder; *The Prisoner of Shark Island* is Dr Mudd, one of several innocent people accused of complicity in the murder of Lincoln; *My Darling Clementine*, a history of murder and retribution in the primitive West, is more essentially a gentle and loving exploration of a pioneering township.

All these manage with remarkable success to revive the manners and appearances of past times. Designed with obvious care, they show a keen pleasure in their period appurtenances, in dresses and uniforms, furniture and decoration. Delighting in dances and communal celebrations of a long-forgotten style, there is a sense about them of regret for ways of living at once simpler and more colourful than those of today. This implied lack of concern with contemporary issues is evident also in Ford's present-day films. *They Were Expendable* is hardly, in the modern sense, a film about war, but rather a film about a species now almost extinct – the professional, dedicated warrior. In *Tobacco Road*, that strange mixture of the grotesquely humorous and the nostalgically sentimental, the emphasis is less social than human; the derelict share-croppers, withering away on the burnt-out tobacco lands of the South, are presented for themselves rather than for the economic moral their predicament might suggest. Even of *The Grapes of Wrath*, justly described by Roger Manvell as 'the most courageous social film Hollywood has ever produced', it may be observed that its greatness comes less from its significance as propaganda, than from its profound, uncircumstantial humanity.

The films all start with the advantage of a good story. Further, they are the work of expert writers – Nunnally Johnson (*Shark Island*, *Tobacco Road*, *The Grapes of Wrath*), Lamar Trotti (*Lincoln*, *Drums Along the Mohawk*), Samuel G. Engel and Winston Miller (*My Darling Clementine*) – experienced story-tellers with no pretentious ambitions to transcend the natural bounds of their subjects. As a result their scripts leave Ford free to tell stories at his leisure, to enrich and enliven them through his own humane inspiration. This is everywhere apparent. Sometimes it is explicit: the indignant trial scene in *Shark Island*, where the bewildered victims of expediency are herded into court to hear with terror and incomprehension the fantastic charges levelled against them; Abe Lincoln's sad rebuke to the lynch-mob in *Young Mr Lincoln*; Tom Joad's fumbling intuitions of human solidarity and social justice in *The Grapes of Wrath*. More often – continually, rather – it is evident in the whole approach, the texture of the films: in odd, unscripted actions and gestures; in the robust humour which runs through them all, simple and genial, of character rather than incident; in the consistent dignity (rising at times to grandeur) with which the human figure is presented.

This has resulted in a gallery of memorable portraits – not, of course, confined to these particular films: Jane Darwell and John Carradine as Ma Joad and Casey in *The Grapes of Wrath*; Carradine again as the Southern gambler in *Stagecoach*; Claire Trevor as the prostitute in the same film; a procession of lovable wrecks in the person of Francis Ford; Ward Bond as Chief Bosun's Mate Mulcahy in *They Were Expendable* or as Yank in *The Long Voyage Home*; Ernest Whitman as Mudd's faithful Negro servant *(Shark Island)*; the self-possessed simplicity of Cathy Downs' Clementine . . . The reponse to life which finds its expression in these films is crystallised in the composite figure of their hero – the character who appears, with variations, in them all except *Tobacco Road*. (Even Tom Joad comes to approximate to it through his playing by Henry Fonda.) Lieut. Brickley, who ruthlessly subordinates his personal feelings to the job in hand; Dr Mudd, who stands by his duty to heal and minister in spite of the wrongs he has suffered; the young Lincoln who undertakes what seems a hopeless case and sees it through to the end; Wyatt Earp, the mild-mannered avenger of his brother in *My Darling Clementine*: all men of purpose, of principles unostentatiously but firmly held. Skilful and courageous in action, they combine their hardihood with a personal gentleness and moral grace; hesitant and tender in love, resolute against injustice. Owing the traditional reverences to God and to his fellow men, the Ford hero – particularly as personified by Fonda –

is the cinema's most convincing representation of the righteous man.

V

The control of the medium which is evident in these films bears witness to the value of those long unpublicised years of Ford's apprenticeship in the silent cinema. It is a technique which has gained in expressiveness as it has gained in assurance – utterly distinct from the soulless craftmanship of a Curtiz, or from the virtuosity of a Wyler, to whom the visual image is a means to an end, rarely the end itself. Its basis is a firm and comprehensive photographic skill. Though he has worked with many different cameramen, Ford's films are remarkable for their consistent pictorial flair – most obviously, of course, in the spacious landscapes of his open-air pictures. A rare adjunct to this is his effective manipulation of artificial light; a typical example is the fade-out of *The Long Voyage Home*, in which a lonely figure on the deck of the S.S. *Glencairn* is brought up into silhouette by a slow darkening of the foreground which powerfully accentuates its bowed and silent isolation. Similarly, in *Young Mr Lincoln*, one of the film's most striking intimations is effected silently by a shift in lighting between long and mid-shot; with its emphasis on the noble structure of the face, the piercing eyes gleaming from under the suddenly prominent stovepipe hat, the nearer shot brings an unexpected awareness of the formidable qualities implicit in the awkward, drily humorous young lawyer.

Closely allied to this skilful use of light is Ford's gift for composition. It is by a combination of the two that he achieves those close-ups which, in their power to confer dignity without diminution of humanity, have become almost the hallmark of his style. Varying in key from the bold chiaroscuro effects of *Young Mr Lincoln* to the common-daylight tones of *The Grapes of Wrath*, the heroic portraits of *They Were Expendable*, they are the poetic (and philosophic) complement to those solemn long-shots which set man in his mortal perspective, lonely in silhouette against an early morning skyline, dwarfed by the vast panoramas of the natural scene.

His fine plastic sense enables Ford to develop his stories in a continuous succession of telling compositions. (It is worth noting that when Welles and Toland caused such a stir with their use of ceilings in *Citizen Kane*, Ford and Glennon had been using them without ostentation for years – in *Stagecoach*, *Lincoln* and *Drums Along the Mohawk*.) His camera moves comparatively rarely, but so strong is his sense of the essential dynamism of the film that, even where movement within the frame is at a minimum, his films are never static. Ford's action sequences are justly famous for their vigour and grasp, their unrivalled ability to build and sustain tension; less often remarked, but perhaps even more to be admired is his power to slow the pace almost to a standstill, to elaborate (and intensify) apparently insignificant moments of pause and silence – young Abraham Lincoln standing in reverie by the river bank, the youngest Earp Boy (in *My Darling Clementine*) watching his brothers ride off into Tombstone, the old trader in *They Were Expendable* sitting alone on the steps of his shack, a jar of whisky beside him and his shotgun across his knees, waiting for the arrival of the enemy.

In part this command of sustained movement in the slowest of rhythms result from Ford's ability to draw from his performers acting of extraordinary naturalism and relaxation. The same familiar faces appear again and again in his pictures, actors of tried worth both in leading parts, and giving solidity to marginal characterisations. But fundamentally this power to sustain is the result of absolute integrity of feeling; it is not only on faces and discernible expressions that the camera lingers, but on long-shots also, on arrivals from a distance, departures deliberate and prolonged.

Where such integrity is not preserved, where Ford's true sympathy is not with his material, or the material itself is counterfeit, this visual opulence can become overblown. This objection may be made to *The Informer* – a brilliant but sometimes showy exercise in the sort of expressionism one has come to associate rather with the German cinema, with its use of heavy-contrast lighting, studied grouping, and deliberate non-realism. Equally it is possible to criticise the last section of *The Long Voyage Home*, where the visual pretentiousness stems directly from the script; portions of *Tobacco Road*, in which Ford's tendency to idealise is not really in tune with the writing; or all of *The Fugitive*, where Figueroa has been given unfortunate licence to reinforce Nichols' vulgarity with his own. But when the material is genuine, and Ford's response to it a spontaneous one, his technique is characterised by its extreme simplicity. Seldom indulging in the sophistications of camera movement, his films proceed in a series of visual statements – they are as sparing in their use of natural sound as a dialogue. Rich in phrasing, simple in structure, it is a style which expresses a sure, affirmative response to life – the equivalent to that Biblical prose which, today, it takes greatness of spirit to sustain.

VI

Choosing for his theme 'traditional sanctity and loveliness', Ford is, by Yeats' definition, also one of the last Romantics. Nothing is more typical of his films than the traditional songs, the popular tunes and marches which accompany them: 'Red River Valley', 'Rally Round the Flag' 'The

Battle Hymn of the Republic'; revivalist hymns like 'Shall We Gather at the River?' and 'Bringing in the Sheaves'; the Naval marches and bugle calls which echo through *They Were Expendable* – all in significant contrast to the pretentious symphonic scores by Steiner and Hageman for *The Informer* and *The Fugitive*. Heavily charged with emotion and nostalgic associations, this music carries us back to another, simpler world of clear-cut judgements, of established and unquestioned values.

With the collapse of its popular traditions, Western art has become increasingly sophisticated and eclectic; the popular themes are in general left to be exploited, and degraded, by opportunists. Ford's films, in this context, seem hardly to belong to our time at all. His art is not intellectual; his impulse is intuitive, not analytical. Unsophisticated and direct, his work can be enjoyed by anyone, regardless of cultural level, who has retained his sensitivity and subscribes to values primarily humane. He applies himself to traditional themes, and is happiest when his story is set in the settled society of another era – typically, Ford's is a man's world, one in which woman's function is largely domestic, to build the home and bear children, to sympathise and support. Relationships in these films are never complex (which does not mean that they are not subtle). Ford's heroes do not analyse themselves into negation; uncomplicated and instinctive they realise themselves in action; and they win. Even the defeated heroes of *They Were Expendable* are indomitable in disaster, and Ford ends his film with a positive symbol, a presage of the ultimate victory.

Whether the word 'romantic', unqualified, adequately defines this attitude is questionable. It is typical of our sloppy habits of criticism that we tend to use 'romantic' to express 'poetic' – 'romanticised' usually means little more than a view or a style not strictly realistic. Certainly Ford's art is inspired by an optimistic faith in man's nature, a reverence for the human creature which is evident always in choice of subject and manner of treatment; but this is combined with a firm emphasis on discipline, an implicit stress on moral and social duties which may properly be described as classical, and which are matched by a sympathetic decorum of style. The poetry which, at their most intense, the films attain, approximates more closely to the Johnsonian 'grandeur of generality' than to the romantic's glorification of the particular.

But what ever the label, it is obvious that films of this kind are likely to be received with great favour by a public, the majority of which has had its taste debased by years of commercialised cinema, while the minority finds its state of mind most satisfyingly mirrored in the elegant despair of *The Third Man*, or in the compassionate defeatism of *The Bicycle Thieves*. *They Were Expendable*, which represents an extraordinary revitalising of a tradition one might have thought dead, runs the risk of being unpopular with the many, for not being like *To the Shores of Tripoli*, and dismissed by the few, for being like *To the Shores of Tripoli* (and *not* like *The Naked and the Dead*). More serious is the possible effect of such isolation on the artist. It is possible, no doubt, to overestimate the importance of being fashionable, but an artist who cuts himself off – or finds himself cut off – from the thought and feeling of the world he lives in, is in danger of emasculating, even finally denying his talent.

From his record over the past five years one fears that this may indeed be the case with Ford: since the disappointment of *The Fugitive* – received well neither by the critics nor the public – he has devoted himself to a series of potboilers, varying in quality (the best, *She Wore a Yellow Ribbon*, has much of the old sweep and strength of sentiment), but realised generally with sadly wasteful impatience and lack of care. But whatever the cause of this decline – and the temptation to speculate and hope is irresistible – it cannot affect the validity of the contribution he has already made. How we regard his films, as manifestations of a still valid faith or merely as nostalgic reminders of a lost state of grace, will depend on the state of mind and heart in which we approach them. It is not in either case to be denied that they stand among the few truly noble works of art of our time.

Last Meeting: Palm Desert

From *About John Ford*, 1981

IN THE SUMMER OF 1973 I WAS IN LOS ANGELES FOR A FEW DAYS IN THE middle of a publicity tour talking to journalists, disc jockeys, and Dial-a-Dollar show presenters about my film *O Lucky Man!* The Warner Bros. publicity department (who clearly had no very precise idea what to do with me) asked me if there was anything I particularly wanted to do in Hollywood. When I said I would like to call on John Ford, I sensed a certain unease: he was not in Los Angeles anymore, he was a very sick man. People must have looked like this, I couldn't help reflecting, in the forties if anyone was tactless enough to mention the name of D.W. Griffith. I said I knew Ford wasn't well, and I knew he had moved out to Palm Desert: but I wanted to call him. His telephone number was produced. To my surprise it was the correct one.

My friend Marion Billings, who was shepherding me on my tour, put the call through from my room at the Beverly Hills Hotel. We both felt rather strange about it. I remember how she went pale and tottered slightly when she found out she was talking to John Ford. I took the phone. His voice was vigorous and welcoming, as though we had met a month or two ago. 'Hello – Lindsay! What are you doing in L.A.?' I explained, and said I'd like to come and see him, if that was possible. 'Yeah . . . Come on out – it'll be good to see you.' I told him I was only in town over the weekend.

'I've got my lawyer coming out tomorrow – I've got some business to talk over with him. Can you make it Sunday? Anytime: come out in the afternoon. You've got the address?'

It was difficult to believe he was dying of cancer.

I drove out on Sunday afternoon in the large limousine provided by the studio. Palm Desert is well into the San Fernando Valley, beyond Palm Springs, where the landscape is flat and featureless and the air very dry. It didn't seem much of a township. Just a spatter of houses, and the usual restaurants and drive-ins lining the highway. We stopped at a garage and asked the way to Old Prospector Trail. That was where Ford had come to make his last home.

We drove down a dusty road and stopped outside a sizeable bungalow, shuttered against the sun. I got out of the air-conditioned limousine into intense heat. At the gate I turned back, realising I had left my shoes in the car. I slipped them on and suggested to the driver he come back in an hour. I rang the bell at the front door. There was no immediate answer. My black limousine sat waiting to make sure I was taken in. No sound, no breath of air broke the intense heat of the desert afternoon. Then there was the sound of unlocking and the door opened a little way, cautiously. I made out a middle-aged lady, standing in some kind of shift or housedress, barefoot. I explained that I'd come to see Mr Ford, at his invitation. The lady hesitated, then asked me to wait. She closed the door again. The silence reasserted itself. I signalled to my driver and the limousine glided away. A minute or so and the door opened again, and I was asked in.

The bungalow was cool, air-conditioned and shaded. We went through a small hall into a spacious living-room. Barbara Ford, who had greeted me, introduced herself as Ford's daughter and asked me who I was. Her father had mentioned that a friend would be coming to see him, but had given her no details. I realised that my name meant nothing to her, but she was very friendly. There were two other ladies in the room, one middle-aged and one old. The old lady, delicately handsome, moved laboriously, using one of those tubular framed devices which enable the arthritic to walk. Barbara introduced me to her mother, Mary Ford. I was acknowledged graciously, then Mrs Ford made her way to her room. Barbara left me to go and see if her father was ready to receive me.

I made small talk with the other lady, who seemed to be some kind of cousin. As we talked, I glanced round the large, homely, well-ordered room. The furniture was comfortable, substantial. It was a room full of the past: pictures, photographs, groups and signed portraits. The odd framed document: naval appointments, citations. There was an Admiral's sword on the wall. Oscars and other awards. Tradition, pride in achievement was all around me. I found myself consciously resisting the temptation to examine, to list, to think, 'I will write about this.' Barbara Ford padded back in her slippers and told me that her father was ready to see me. 'Excuse me,' she said, 'but could you tell me your name again . . . Daddy only said he had an old friend from England coming.' I told her. 'Are you a film maker?' I said, sometimes. 'Daddy didn't tell me anything about you, but he was determined to look smart.' We were on our way out of the drawing room, down a passage to a room at the back of the house, when she stopped.

'It's the big one, you know,' she said, and I knew she meant cancer. 'It's only a matter of time. He's had the last rites: and last week we thought he'd gone. He had a giant haemorrhage and they rushed him into hospital in the middle of the night, but he fought his way out of it. He insisted on coming home.' 'Who is that lady I was talking to?' 'She's my cousin,' Barbara told me. 'She's come to help. We have a nurse too, who comes in part-time.' She talked familiarly: I felt no constraint.

'What shall I call him?' I asked. 'What does he like to be called?' Like Robert Parrish, only, of course, Bob had served under him, I had always found it impossible to address Ford as anything but 'Mr Ford' or 'Sir'. Barbara seemed surprised. 'Who, Daddy? Call him Jack. That's what he likes to be called.'

We went down the passage and into a light, quite small room, mostly occupied by a bed. Ford lay there, propped up on pillows, smoking a cigar and drinking brandy. Revolver shots rang out from a portable TV set by his bed. Figures on the screen were chasing each other up and down a ship's gangway. 'Hello, Lindsay,' he said warmly. 'Hello, Jack – it's good to see you.'

He looked gaunt and old. It was easy to see how disease had eaten into him. But the pugnacious, commanding spirit was still strong. It only took a moment to get used to his appearance, and then he looked much the same. It was easy to forget that he was fatally ill. I glanced at the TV screen: a bulky figure came clattering down a stairway, firing back at the deck above.

'Is that Victor McLagen?' 'No, Tommy Mitchell.' Ford leaned across and switched off the set. 'Some rubbish.' Ford asked me what I was doing in L.A. and I gave him a copy of the book we'd produced of the *O Lucky Man!* script. It would mean nothing to him, I knew, but I thought he might appreciate the gesture. He looked at it a moment and put it on the table beside his bed.

'I missed that one of yours,' he said. 'But I enjoyed that football picture you did.'

'Did you see it?' I said, surprised.

'Of course I did,' he said. 'Good picture.'

I couldn't help wondering if he'd really seen *This Sporting Life*. I couldn't think of any good reason why he should have. Not that it mattered. I asked him if he'd been working on any projects, knowing there had been several in the last few years.

'Oh, I had a couple of scripts,' he said, 'but I'm beyond that now. This has put a stop to all that. Haven't got the strength for it.'

He didn't say it bitterly. It was almost as though it was a truth he had long avoided and now was glad to face.

We chatted in a relaxed way. The send-up tone had gone. No need for that now. We had no great store of common experience, and not much old acquaintance: but I knew that in a strange way the fact of my visit mattered to him, and I was glad. We talked a bit about picture-making now and in the old days. He talked contemptuously as ever about producers. I asked him if there was anyone he liked working with.

'Oh, Zanuck. He knew the business. When I'd finished a picture I could go off to Catalina on my boat and fish. Didn't have to hang around. I could leave the editing to him. None of the others knew anything.'

I congratulated him on his award from the American Film Institute. The ceremony had been a few months back; the presentation had been made by Richard Nixon, and Jane Fonda had protested outside against his presence. 'Did they do it well?' I asked. 'Oh, it was fine,' he said. 'A great occasion. The President made a speech. Of course he didn't know much about it, but he did it very well. I was very touched.'

People had been to see him. 'Hawks has been over a couple of times. He was here last week. And Hank Fonda – he's a nice man, Hank.' Maureen O'Hara was on an island somewhere in the Pacific. He reserved his familiar caustic tone for John Wayne. 'Duke's up in Seattle shooting some rubbish. Playing a goddam policeman . . .'

After twenty minutes or so, Barbara came back. 'Well Jack, it was a piece of great luck that brought me out to California now. I'm glad I could see you.' His hand lay on the bedcover, freckled with age. I held it for a moment, then kissed it goodbye. 'Thanks for coming,' said Ford. 'It's a long drive out. It was good of you to come.'

I turned at the door. 'Anything I can do for you in England?' 'Oh, give

Brian Hurst a call. Tell him you saw me.' 'Is there anything else you want?' 'Only your friendship.' 'You have that.'

I left him with his brandy glass and cigar stub. I called Barbara a couple of times during my American tour. And from Washington I sent him a postcard of Lincoln with his son Thad. Six weeks later, back in London, I switched on the radio one morning and heard that he was dead.

The Hustons

Review of *The Hustons* by Laurence Grobel in *The Daily Telegraph*, 12 May 1990

THE HUSTONS, FOR THE UNINITIATED, ARE THE NOTABLE AMERICAN THEATRE-and-film family whose record begins with the actor Walter Huston and is now strikingly represented by his granddaughter Angelica, who achieved stardom in her father's *Prizzi's Honor* and his last, much appreciated version of James Joyce's story *The Dead*. Angelica has two brothers, writer Tony and director Danny, whose talents are still in the 'promising' stage.

These four Hustons are pictured in postage-stamp portraits on the wrapper of this bulky book. Behind them, wearing a smile that suggests a benign, quizzical understanding, looms a grizzled, sepia-tinted John, the undisputed star of the show.

John Huston, of course, is best known as a film director – 'one of the greatest ever,' according to the blurb, 'a man of vast imagination and supreme artistry.' This is the kind of exaggeration one would not be surprised to find on the jacket of a cheaper book than this, but objectionable in one with more serious pretensions (particularly when printed within).

Huston was an exceptional film-maker, a teller of tales often recognisable for their vigorous, intelligent craftsmanship and disabused, if not cynical, tone. He was a man's director: Humphrey Bogart was his ideal interpreter. Often his films achieved popular success as well as critical respect. *The Maltese Falcon* would be found on many lists of Desert Island films. *The Treasure of the Sierra Madre*, *The Asphalt Jungle*, *The African Queen* are as famous today as when they were new. After a prolific, uneven career, he made *Under the Volcano* and *Prizzi's Honor* in his late seventies and when he brought his career to a respected close with *The Dead*, he was over 80.

All his life, Huston was a man of compulsive energy. From the age of

469

Humphrey Bogart, Mary Astor, Barton Maclane, Peter Lorre and Ward Bond in John Huston's The Maltese Falcon.

ten, he spent two years in bed, suspected of 'an enlarged heart' and Bright's (kidney) Disease. It was a wrong diagnosis. On his feet again, he boxed (Jack Dempsey was 'a god') and indulged in explosive practical jokes. He discovered painting, and then, through his father's influence, theatre and writing. He spent a couple of years on the loose in Mexico. In the early thirties he got to Hollywood and wrote scripts. He enjoyed cutting a roistering figure and fought Errol Flynn over Olivia de Havilland.

From early on he was a rampant womaniser. (One of his mistresses described him as 'probably the most prolific man sexually I ever knew.') He was married five times. He drank, rode, hunted, gambled and assumed Hemingway postures. His generosity was spasmodic, not to be relied on. He lived for a while in Ireland, where he enjoyed playing the role of Master of Fox Hounds. Most people found him charismatic.

Lawrence Grobel certainly did. In 1984, he was flown to Puerto Vallarta in Mexico to interview 'the great man' for *Playboy* magazine. Grobel fell victim to the charm.

Two years later Scribners suggested he should write a book about the Huston family. John and his children agreed: they all enjoyed talking about themselves – and each other. Friends, relations, colleagues, ex-wives and lovers were exhaustively interviewed. John answered questions for 'over a hundred hours'. As Grobel listened, captivated, he came to realise 'how much of a father-figure John had become . . . we all wanted to make him proud. We were all John's children.' These are dangerous sentiments for a biographer.

The book that has come out of this devotion is not uninteresting. Grobel's tireless research tells us a great deal about John Huston, both as a man and as an artist. His special parentage: his mother's father was a drinker and a rover; her mother was a newspaper editor, and she herself a journalist and would-be writer. Walter Huston (from whom she separated when her son was three) was a fine Scottish-Irish character actor: excellent in O'Neill, a brilliant Dodsworth, a failure as Othello.

John's career is minutely traced. An intelligent writer with a flair for narrative. As a director, a fluent, sometimes masterly stylist. Brilliant with actors he liked; uncaring, even brutal, with those he did not – he mishandled Montgomery Clift horribly in *Freud*; he made Paul Newman feel 'bourgeois'; he could do nothing with John Wayne. The genesis of films, including the many he undertook simply to make money, is doggedly described.

But if ever there was a book that needed the shaping hand of an editor, it is (at close to 800 pages) *The Hustons*. The facts are not sifted or proportioned, and the gossip is endless. Gossip can be enticing, but after a time it becomes boring, reducing everything to the same significance – or lack of it.

All right, so Huston slept with Mary Astor during the shooting of *The Maltese Falcon* . . . So Marlon Brando was 'interested' in Victoria Principal when he visited the set of *Judge Roy Bean* . . . So when Jack (Nicholson) first caught sight of Angelica (Huston) he saw (as he told a reporter) 'cla-a-ass' . . .

All this is pure *People* magazine stuff. And so mostly is Lawrence Grobel's writing on the films. Success is measured in terms of Oscar nominations: judgement and interpretation are supplied by quotations from Pauline Kael in *The New Yorker*, from *The New York Times*, or the *Village Voice*. The clichés are abundant and discretion absent.

He was not a great director, though he had remarkable talents. At its best, the cinema is a poetic medium, and Huston was not a poet: his style was lucid, intelligent, prosaic: when he attempted the epic of the lyric, he failed. Some depth of commitment was missing; perhaps his self-indulgence was too great. His relationships were intense, but unstable. And is it not strange that an artist to whom women were so important never made a film in which that relationship was central, or fulfilled?

John Huston said that his mother 'had the good sense to understand that one should first hear about sex in the gutter'. When she died, she left him the journals in which she had chronicled her life and her feelings and ambitions for him. He never could bring himself to read them. When he died, he asked to be buried not with his father, his pal, but with his mother, whom he often accused of 'stifling' him.

Yes, there is material here for a good biography.

Orson Welles

Review of *Orson Welles: The Rise and Fall of an American Genius* by Charles Higham in The *Spectator*, 9 August 1986

WHAT EXACTLY DID MARLENE DIETRICH MEAN WHEN SHE TOLD MAXIMILIAN Schell (he was making her film biography) that 'people should cross themselves when they see Orson Welles'? In this absorbing life of the man he calls an American genius, Charles Higham refers to this as 'an unfortunate gaffe'. Surely it was not that. But was it a tribute, or an exasperated comment on her brilliant friend's egoism, unreliability and capacity for betrayal? Like all Welles' colleagues, she must have had many moments of such exasperation – as, for instance, when she organised, at Welles' insistence, a lavish, high-society dinner party for a scene in one of his late, unfinished films, only to receive at the last minute a telegram informing her that he had left for abroad and could not be there to shoot it. (She later found out that he had not left for abroad.)

Charles Higham tells this story slightly differently: but then every story about Welles seems to exist in at least three versions. More likely anyway, since Miss Dietrich has an artist's comprehension of her kind, she meant that Welles was a creative Holy Man, one of those uncomfortable, self-destroying gift-bearers the world is often happy to leave singing in the gutter.

Mr Higham subtitles his book *The Rise and Fall of an American Genius*. American certainly; not for just his impeccable bourgeois antecedents (here painstakingly traced back to the *Mayflower*), but for the special kind of dynamic, more energetic than profound, that distinguished all his life and work. And genius too, with the unceasing inventiveness, the dazzling confidence that seems almost to define the word.

But Orson Welles seems never to have risen: he was there from the start. A prodigious infant talent, driving the servants mad with his compulsive story-telling, entertaining the children of Grand Detour, Illinois (where his alcoholic father ran a hotel) with puppet shows and plays. And at school in his teens, appearing in musical shows, directing and performing Shakespeare and Shaw. He was sixteen when, motherless and fatherless, he took off for Ireland, determined to prove himself a painter, or an actor.

What radiant allure young Welles must have projected in that bright and breezy morning of his talent! In Dublin he swept Michael McLiammoir and Hilton Edwards off their feet and they recruited him immediately into their Gate Theatre Company. The sixteen-year-old amateur impressed the critics as Duke Karl Alexander, the 'brutally anti-Semitic, bullying nobleman who dominated *Jew Suss'*, and went on to double as the Ghost and Fortinbras to McLiammoir's Hamlet. Back in the States, he easily persuaded his Irish patrons to join him in a provincial repertory season (in which he played Svengali and Claudius), wrote a play, got married and joined a Kathleen Cornell tour of *Romeo and Juliet* as Mercutio. He had moved down to Tybalt when he was spotted in New York by the young director-producer John Houseman. Mr Higham describes *the coup de foudre*: 'Houseman had a compulsion, equivalent to desire for a woman, to work with this man.'

Everyone knows that Orson Welles made *Citizen Kane* at the age of 25. Most people know that he had already caused nation-wide panic with a radio version of H. G. Wells' *The War of the Worlds*. The theatre, though, is transient, and the sensational career which launched Welles as the young genius of American show-business is largely forgotten. He and Houseman began with an all-black voodoo *Macbeth*, which premiered in Harlem and put a spell on the New York theatre. There was a *Dr Faustus,* all magic and lurid melodrama – all his life Welles was a gifted, fascinated magician. There was a Brechtian operetta, *The Cradle Will Rock*, which their sponsors, the Federal Theatre Project, tried to suppress as being too radical. And a modern-dress *Julius Caesar* made headlines by parallelling the European dictatorships. All this time Welles was running off to act in other theatres, creating the deep-voiced 'Shadow' in a spoof thriller serial for radio, producing, directing and performing in a series of prestige dramatic adaptations, also for radio. It was the most notorious of these, *The War of the Worlds*, which won him the unprecedented offer from RKO Radio Pictures in Hollywood: to write and direct a movie from any subject of his choice. Years later Welles would speculate ruefully that he might have done better to stick with the theatre. In 1939 there seemed no choice.

Energy created *Citizen Kane*. A phenomenal, American energy. The giant creative energy of Orson Welles, channelled, disciplined. It was not an instant birth. Two subjects, Conrad's *Heart of Darkness*, C. Day Lewis's *The Smiler with the Knife*, were envisaged, worked at, discarded. Welles ran out of money, got divorced and fought with Houseman. Then they heard that the screenwriter Herman Mankiewicz was planning a script based on

Orson Welles and Rita Hayworth in The Lady from Shanghai.

the life of William Randolph Hearst. They met and decided to collaborate. Probably fortunately, Welles was still short of cash: he embarked on a lecture tour. Mankiewicz and Houseman hammered away at the script. Welles had to be content with supervising, criticising and contributing.

Critical pygmies, most notoriously *The New Yorker*'s over-indulged Pauline Kael, have tried to question or at least diminish Welles' authorship of *Kane*. But his achievement was no less for having been able, once at least, to accept and use contributing talents. That is how films are made. Mankiewicz contributed. So did Houseman. So, most crucially, did the cameraman Gregg Toland, who offered his services to Welles. One of

Hollywood's most brilliant and respected artists, Toland had been waiting impatiently for the chance to practise the techniques of deep focus photography he had been developing in his spare time at the Goldwyn Studio: the look of *Kane* was largely his invention. Welles brought in his favoured actors from the theatre and played the autocratic lead himself (ideal casting). He viewed John Ford's *Stagecoach* many times over, determined to assimilate the style and tempo of a master. And he felt free. Out of that perfect freedom, enjoyed by no Hollywood director since Griffith, a masterpiece was born.

Citizen Kane was not a box-office success, but it was received with huge, almost unanimous acclaim. Another big theatre success, a provocative version of Richard Wright's black autobiography *Native Son*, confirmed Welles' pre-eminence. He returned to Hollywood, dangerously confident, to tackle a successor to Kane. And now, with awful suddenness, things started to go wrong. It was not bad luck, it was tragedy, according to which classical definition you prefer. The Aristotelian flaw? The precipitate fall of a great man? Most accurately perhaps the traditional tragic nexus: from too much, to hubris, to nemesis – to destruction.

Riding high the tide to success, Welles rapidly involved himself in a jumble of projects. A Mexican 'political' thriller, soon censored for anti-Nazi bias; a version of Eric Ambler's *Journey into Fear*; a portmanteau subject called *It's All True* which was to cover aspects of life, fictional and documentary, in North and South America, supposedly to the advantage of US policies. And as if those were not enough, Welles plunged into work on his second film, *The Magnificent Ambersons*, an adaptation of the Booth Tarkington novel he had already directed for radio – and ironically itself a sad chronicle of hubris. Here was a fine subject with which Welles identified personally. He had his own script, his own players, brilliant designers and a virtuoso (though slow) cameraman. What could go wrong?

What went wrong was that Welles never finished his film. Even before shooting was completed, he was off to Rio to record the carnival for *It's All True*, leaving *Ambersons* behind to be put together by others. Afterwards he tried to put the blame on studio politics. A new management at RKO took fright at disastrous preview reactions to the picture and demanded cuts and retakes. The end was reshot to provide a lamely conciliatory 'happy ending'. Welles tried to deal with the crisis (or to run away from it?) by sending long cables from Rio. The result was inevitable. *The Magnificent Ambersons* was destroyed – not wholly, but essentially – and still lost money. Perhaps it was only later that Welles knew he had allowed a masterpiece to be wrecked.

It was not a single catastrophe. *Journey into Fear*, which Welles had assigned to another director, was no more than mediocre; and *It's All True* lurched from mishap to mishap and was never completed. Charles Higham tells the painful story in gripping, closely researched detail, as he does the remainder of Welles' career – over 40 years of it. Assiduously, he tracks the wounded monster, from Hollywood to Europe and back, from theatre to cinema, from mostly rubbishy acting roles (for money) to desperate struggles to finance and complete his own films. All this wins him no praise from the Wellesian idolators. In *Sight and Sound* the critic-director Gavin Millar even brackets Higham with Kael and dismisses them both as 'debunkers'. This is quite misleading. Charles Higham may not be a distinguished interpretive critic (thank God), but he tells the extraordinary story fairly well. And sympathy cannot be withheld, as the ruthlessly egomaniac artist manages somehow, anyhow, to keep going, energy unfailing, leaving a unique testament of films. He never made another masterpiece; yet everything he made was recognisably the work of a master.

To be born with genius, but without the character to support it, is a harsh fate. Orson Welles had genius: incandescent rather than deep, but always humane in its concerns. He was a master of his craft. Himself he could not master. Success and the intoxicating exercise of stupendous ego were his undoing. To see him in the last years of his life, sitting at his regular lunch table at Hollywood's Ma Maison, surrounded by the uncaring business crowd (studio executives, agents, stars and would-be anythings) was a sad, strange sight. That huge body contained the author of *Kane* and *Ambersons*: and now there issued from it, with rich authority, the voice that commended Paul Masson wines and Carlsberg lager in a steady stream of television commercials. Welles would be surrounded by disciples, and he would laugh a lot. But behind the laughter there was something watchful and unappeased, a bitterness, an anger.

Welles died with much work unfinished, many frustrated projects, works 'in progress'. His *Don Quixote*, which he had been making for years, was never completed. Nor was a thriller called *The Deep*. Plans for a *King Lear*, to be financed by the French government, and a film about the production of *The Cradle Will Rock*, had fallen through. There is an incomplete version of a Karen Blixen short story; and when he died of a heart attack, he was working on a television special about magic. Ownership of the unseen material is apparently disputed between Welles' third wife the Countess Mori and a Yugoslav sculptress called Oja Kodar.

One is eager, of course, to disinter these *disiecta membra*; to see, speculate, regret and hopefully to admire. But one is apprehensive also. Perhaps it is safer to let them lie, in the darkness to which their author consigned them. I think again of Marlene's oracular command. When we invoke the name of Orson Welles, we should cross ourselves, with awe and a certain dread, thanking God that he has not burdened us with such a talent, such a fate.

Joseph Losey

Review of *Joseph Losey* by Edith de Rham in *The Independent*, 24 November 1991

THE AMERICANS, AND THE HOLLYWOOD ESTABLISHMENT PARTICULARLY, gained nothing by their respect for the House Un-American Activities Committee. Under its nefarious Chairman J. Parnell Thomas (who ended up in prison, condemned for claiming the wages of a phantom staff), this turned its red-baiting attention on the American film industry in the late forties, branding as 'Communists' many artists who could at the most be described as strong-minded liberals. Writers were arraigned and imprisoned; actors and actresses were deprived of their livelihoods; directors took flight. One of these was the promising Joseph Losey, who had only made five feature films when disaster became imminent.

Unlike most American directors, Joe Losey was born into a relatively moneyed middle-class family, in the little Midwest town of La Crosse, Wisconsin. Strangely enough Nicholas Ray (born Ray Kienzle) came from the same town, though from the wrong side of the tracks. As boys, the two knew each other.

The schoolboy Losey was (according to a friend) 'very, very smart'. He read a lot and was 'fascinated by the theatre'. His father, an amiable unambitious businessman, died when quite young; it was his wife who was the arty one, playing the piano and drinking bootleg liquor. Losey left home for university (Dartmouth) where he spent most of his time acting, attending rehearsals and directing plays. When he was twenty, he joined a repertory company. In New York, he managed to apprentice himself to the legendary Jed Harris, hugely successful at the age of 28. Harris, a brilliant monster, directed the young Laurence Olivier as a callow homosexual in *The Green Bay Tree*; later Olivier vowed that he used Harris as the model for his Richard III.

It is generally, if rather vaguely known that Losey worked as director on the first production (in Hollywood and in New York) of Brecht's *Galileo* – which probably meant that he slaved away as assistant to that peculiar partnership of Brecht and Charles Laughton. He was a youthful radical, which is why he had to leave America. First in Europe, then in Britain, he found work with difficulty and had to work anonymously. It took him nearly ten years before he landed a contract with the Rank Organisation and made *The Gipsy and the Gentleman*. Better subjects followed, more ambitious (*The Criminal, Eve*). Losey became known, a leader of his profession, a favourite of the French cinematic intelligentsia. Edith de Rham claims that her book celebrates 'the long and productive life of a great film director'.

But was Losey a great film director? Miss de Rham (she is the great-granddaughter, by the way, of the poet Longfellow) seems to be in no doubt about it, though the judgement is disputable. Of course, it is never easy to convey in words just what it is that makes an artist 'great'. Some sort of originality, I suppose, and depth of insight. Vitality? Consistency? Something more, surely, than technical invention and stylistic prowess. These, certainly, were an important part of Joe's gift.

He was also, and permanently, ambitious. John Houseman, always a shrewd observer, made a comment on Joe Losey's early, Leftist years that sounds accurate. 'Joe was a very bright young man, very ambitious. He was a real operator, with one eye always on the main chance. He was habitually suspicious and quarrelsome. He loved feuds . . .' This seems to be borne out by Joe's later career in Britain. He worked his way to prominence with intelligence and determination: *The Servant* and *Accident* with Pinter; *Eve* and *The Go-Between*. Radicalism, be it noted, seemed to be largely left behind. There followed films with the Burtons which were undertaken primarily for commercial gain and professional prestige. Losey began to drink too much and got dangerously fat. He became famous in France and among film intellectuals who rated style above content. His output, from *A Doll's House* with Jane Fonda to an operatic *Don Giovanni*, from *Galileo* for the American Film Theatre to a final clutch of films made in Paris, did not exactly add up.

I have often thought that the political pressure that impelled American film artists to flee to Europe did them no good – just as they certainly weakened the American cinema. Hollywood style at its best is assured, dramatic, camera-wise, strong in effect and in the presentation of actors. It is seldom profound or consistent or (except in rare instances) poetic. Joe Losey aimed for profundity; but he was always an American. Perhaps this is why it is difficult to think of him, for all his skill, as one of the 'greats'. This book, excellently researched as it is, though only part perceptive, will hardly persuade its readers otherwise.

Edith de Rham tells a sadly revealing anecdote. At a party thrown by Dirk Bogarde at the Connaught Hotel, to celebrate the successful opening of *The Servant*, the British director Basil Dearden sank theatrically to his knees. 'How,' he asked Losey, 'does one make a masterpiece?' Losey told him to take his son away from Eton, to sell his wife's furs, his house, his pool and his cars, to move into a small flat and think things over. 'No overheads, Basil. Just the films.' It was nonsense, of course; and tragically Losey was quite unable to live up to his own advice.

What about Joe Losey the man? There is plenty of evidence here that he was inconsistent, jealous, spiteful and ambitious in the wrong way. He was four times married, never really happy. Let us not forget, though, that he could also be charming, inspiring and appealing. Edith de Rham dedicates her book to the memory of Jill Bennett, with whom Joe was in love early on, who refused to marry him, and with whom he spent much time in his last illness. Jill was a fine friend. Stanley Baker said that working with Losey changed his acting – and his life. Dirk Bogarde counted him always, in spite of everything, a valued friend. These fond memories say a great deal about the people involved. And about Joe Losey too.

Nicholas Ray

Review of *Nicholas Ray: An American Journey* by Bernard Eisenschitz in *The Daily Telegraph*, 27 April 1993

SOME TIME IN 1949 THE ACADEMY CINEMA IN OXFORD STREET, WHICH usually showed exceptional films from Europe, programmed two American films. Top of the bill was *They Live by Night*, a sensitive and poetic adaptation of Edward Anderson's novel *Thieves Like Us*. The director, new to the cinema, was Nicholas Ray. The film was produced by John Houseman, who had worked with Orson Welles on his Mercury Theatre productions and on *Citizen Kane*; he had also engaged Ray for the radio programmes, *The Voice of America*. Much later Houseman was to write that of the many people with whom he had collaborated over the years, Nicholas Ray was one of the five who gave him more than he gave them. *They Live by Night* began a film career which was to bring fame if not always fortune to a distinctive American talent.

The author of this biography, Bernard Eisenschitz, is described by the publishers as 'a writer, film critic and cinema historian . . . a member of the editorial board *of Cahiers du Cinéma*'. You have been warned. His book is essentially for the cinema cognoscenti. It assumes that the reader already knows who Nicholas Ray is, admires him and does not need his pre-eminence to be argued or described. The 'celebrated dictum' of Jean-Luc Godard (the hyphen is misplaced on the jacket) is quoted with apparent approval: 'The cinema is Nicholas Ray.' To the French of the New Wave, manner was always more important than matter.

Eisenschitz's aesthetic is questionable, but he has researched his subject exhaustively. Nicholas Ray was born in Wisconsin in 1911 (so was Joe Losey, in the same town, two years earlier). His father, of German extraction, was an architect. Nick (he was born Raymond Nicholas Kienzle, Jnr) went to university in Chicago, where he knew Thornton Wilder. He spent time studying under Frank Lloyd Wright. He joined the Theatre of Action, a revolutionary theatre group, and was for a while a Communist. An early friend was Elia Kazan.

By the time Ray got to Hollywood as Kazan's assistant on *A Tree Grows in Brooklyn*, he had worked in Roosevelt's Works Progress Administration as a theatre director, then collecting and recording folk songs, then producing on radio. He had married, had a son, and separated from his first wife. When America came into the War, he was enlisted by John Houseman to produce (in 26 languages) programmes for *The Voice of America*. Then Houseman got him his first picture to direct.

They Live by Night did not make money, but it – and especially the acting – was noticeably well directed. In the ten years that followed Ray directed twenty films, ranging from *In a Lonely Place* (Humphrey Bogart valued his talent) to the weird *Johnny Guitar* (Joan Crawford as hero) and *Rebel without a Cause*, which was probably James Dean's most famous role. His choices were usually intelligent, though he was at first anxious, in a very American way, for acceptance and success. He once asked Buñuel the secret of making a good film. Buñuel advised him, instead of making a three-, five- or ten-million dollar film, to make a picture for $200,000. Ray protested that if he did that in Hollywood, he would be finished as a director. But that is how he ended up none the less, scraping the barrel for cash.

Eisenschitz charts Ray's career in detail, but he seems much less concerned with his personality and the instability which constantly betrayed the talent. From the start, Ray drank and gambled compulsively; his emotional relationships almost always end up in a mess. Eisenschitz says 'The psychological explanation – Ray being a manic depressive, an inherited family trait – is obvious but not very helpful.' On the contrary, I would say it is very helpful indeed. Surely this is the explanation of Ray's decline from eminence to the eccentric progress – from director to teacher to erratic avant-gardist – of his later years.

Talking of Ray's marriage to the actress Gloria Grahame (who later married his son by his first marriage), John Houseman said that the truth was 'they were both a bit loony'. Which is a shorthand way of explaining Ray's last years as a film-maker, after his contract with the monstrous Sam

Bronston in Spain terminated with the unfortunate *King of Kings* and half of *55 Days at Peking*. A lone, mesmeric figure, Ray devoted himself to teaching and to efforts to produce independent, autobiographical films without relation to the industry or the mass public. 'Nick could create a sucking vacuum,' said his fourth wife, 'like a black hole. This enormous energy that was desperate and would just suck you up. It was also extremely creative.'

Well, was it? It certainly exercised a powerful attraction. Young people surrendered eagerly to his charm, his extravagant theorising. European *cinéastes* gladly became his disciples. But the films were never really formed or finished. And his last picture was not one he himself directed. It was made by Wim Wenders and devoted to Ray in person, dying of cancer even as the film was shot. The journey from *They Live by Night* had been a long one. As told in this book the story does not make easy or comfortable reading. But the facts are all here. It is a sobering tale.

Don Siegel

Review of *A Siegel Film* by Don Siegel in *The Daily Telegraph*, 25 September 1993

WITH AUTHORS LIKE EISENSTEIN, KIESLOWSKI AND TARKOVSKY (ALL LISTED ON the jacket of this book), Faber and Faber have established themselves as publishers for the knowledgeable film enthusiast. So it comes as a surprise to find them producing this 'autobiography' of Don Siegel, the director of hard and fast American crime films, and the mentor of Clint Eastwood. 'He encouraged me to direct . . .' Eastwood writes in his pithy, accurate introduction. Don Siegel made five films with him, after a long career of the varied, mostly successful pictures that established him as a film storyteller of exceptional talent and dynamic. He was not, he admitted, a writer; he was, or he became, a director/producer. His book was written for 'lovers of film, for would-be directors'. And he writes with complete honesty, telling the truth. Many truths, in fact, of a kind often not told.

This is the story of a career rather than a life. Don Siegel was Jewish: he married Viveca Lindfors, whom he met on one of his pictures and later divorced; he married again and had two or three children. That is about all we get to know about his private life. His professional relationships, though, are sharply evoked and defined. On the whole he admired and understood actors; some writers he liked and respected, some he didn't; he regarded producers as usually his antagonists. He liked Walter Wanger and felt that *Riot in Cell Block Eleven* (which he directed for Wanger) was one of his best pictures.

Don Siegel started in pictures in 1934, when his Uncle Jack fixed an appointment for him to see Hal Wallis, then producing at Warner Bros. He was completely without experience, knew nothing about movies and seemed to have no ambition to make them. He was given the job of an assistant in the studio film library, which he thought would be full of books (it wasn't). He learned how to carry cans, and survived the absurd trial of being sent round the studio to collect sprocket-holes. He was pushed on to be an assistant editor, then graduated to shooting inserts, about which he knew nothing. But he learned.

From the start, this was Don Siegel's great gift. He had an active, disrespectful intelligence and a terrific self-confidence. From shooting inserts (Bette Davis' eyeline on her diagnosis in *Dark Victory*, for instance) he became expert at designing and making montage sequences: *Confessions of a Nazi Spy, They Died with Their Boots On, Yankee Doodle Dandy* and so on . . . He was happy to learn from Thomas Mitchell (who passed on a tip Ford had given him on *The Long Voyage Home*), from Jimmy Cagney (who set him right on a camera set-up on *Yankee Doodle Dandy*) and from Walter Huston (whom he provided with 'idiot-boards' on *Mission to Moscow*). All those stories are recounted in graphic, idiomatic dialogues, like most of the book. Siegel's recall is extraordinary.

Inevitably his experiences inspired Siegel with the desire to direct a film himself. Warners offered him a contract with terms laughably low. He refused to sign and characteristically spent six months on suspension. It was 1946 before he got his first picture to direct, *The Verdict* with Sidney Greenstreet and Peter Lorre. Siegel felt he had done a good job on it, until Jack Warner made nonsense of the story by pronouncing, when he saw the final cut, that 'Greenstreet can't be a murderer.' 'Of course it made no sense,' Siegel writes, though he had to submit. Such clashes between Don Siegel and his producers were to be a feature of his career.

The films with Clint Eastwood, whose forceful, no-nonsense style obviously fitted perfectly with Siegel's own, were to come much later. By the time they made *Coogan's Bluff* together, pictures like *Invasion of the Body Snatchers* (the original version), *The Killers* (the remake for television) and *Madigan* had made it clear that Don Siegel was an outstanding narrative director who would bring incisive craftsmanship as well as continual invention to any decent story. 'I think,' Eastwood writes in his introduction, 'you will be extremely entertained by his droll, acidic humour and the constant fight against the bureaucracy of studio mechanics.' This evokes exactly the personality of a vivid, hard-hitting book. Siegel admits to being 'feisty', which gives his accounts of conflict, his often commonsense collisions with actors and producers, a continuously comic accent.

I was lucky enough to meet Don Siegel once. It was at the 1987 Telluride Festival, that famous gathering in the Rockies which is dedicated to the cinema as art and highly esteemed by its artists. So it was not surprising that the Festival's chief accolade went to Stephen Frears, for his 'lifetime achievement'. Don Siegel was there to present a selection of his early montages. He got no medal to hang round his neck and it was with a certain irony that he looked around at the assembled film buffs who seemed rather patronising (perhaps puzzled) in their attitude towards him. By then, of course, he was well established as a brilliant and very personal stylist; his amused, sceptical attitude showed an irony not often found in America.

It is never easy, as every author must know, to write as one talks, but this is what Don Siegel has achieved in this book. His publishers call him 'controversial', which he surely was not – unless his intelligent, disabused attitude be taken to imply such a thing. He was a loner in his work, obstinate in his convictions, with a special sympathy for the outsider, the impenitently individual. He was also extremely professional. Perhaps Faber are a bit defensively conscious of his 'popular' status: the jacket information is skimpy, and most certainly he did *not* direct *Magnum Force*. The book has no index and no filmography; it has no need of Clint Eastwood (whom Siegel greatly liked and worked well with) to act as its passport. *A Siegel Film* is full of information, of good stories and wry truths. It is enlightening as well as entertaining.

Martin Scorsese

Review of *Martin Scorsese: A Journey* by Mary Pat Kelly in *The Daily Telegraph*, 11 April 1992

WITH THE RELEASE OF HIS MOST COMMERCIAL FILM, A REMAKE OF THE 1960s thriller *Cape Fear*, Martin Scorsese's is a name that is being buzzed around the media. Here is the story of his life and of the succession of movies, remarkably similar in tone and most of them featuring actors like Robert de Niro and Harvey Keitel, which have raised him to the status of (perhaps) the world's most famous film director.

From *Mean Streets* to *Goodfellas*, his films have consistently shown a preoccupation with the macho qualities of violence and the Roman Catholic conception of guilt. They have also shown an increasing technical, or stylistic skill. And yet it still seems questionable whether Scorsese's work has the range and the depth which would properly carry him beyond celebrity to 'greatness'. A question like this would surely not occur to Mary Pat Kelly.

She is a terrific admirer of Martin Scorsese. That is why her biography, which she describes as 'an oral history', including interviews with his collaborators, actors, writers, cinematographers, parents, and so on, does not try to interest readers, but takes all that for granted. 'If you are reading this,' she says in her introduction, 'I am sure that Scorsese's films have inspired animated discussion for you . . . I hope so because that is the premise of this book. The movies, of course, speak powerfully for themselves.' That 'of course' is not the language of a critic.

Early on, Mary Pat Kelly became fascinated by what she read about the film which Scorsese made when he was still a student. She wrote to him and he sent her a 16mm print, together with letters twelve and fifteen pages long, 'jammed with such enthusiasm for movies that words ran together and the pressure he applied to the keys left the paper riddled with holes.'

That is the way Scorsese talks. And also the way he makes films. Mary Pat Kelly met him first in the mop room of the convent where she was studying to be a nun. As a student, her favourite subjects were James Joyce and the movies. Fellini, Antonioni and Bergman used, she says, the cinematic equivalent of Joyce's stream-of-consciousness, non-linear narrative. And Scorsese, presumably, is of the company. The parallels are stated, not reasoned. This is that kind of book.

The 'journey' that Martin Scorsese took started on New York's Lower East Side, and proceeded through the Catholic Church (his early ambition was to enter the priesthood), via New York University, where he majored in movies. He was intoxicated by cinema from the start, and his films came directly out of his own experiences and from a total dedication. He emigrated to Hollywood, worked as an editor and made *Boxcar Bertha* for Roger Corman. Since then, he has made a succession of movies, from *Mean Streets* and *Alice Doesn't Live Here Any More* to *Raging Bull* and *Goodfellas*. All are hot-blooded, hectic and recognisably personal.

Martin Scorsese is a very subjective artist, if not one with much sense of perspective. He has made comedies, but seems quite without the vision that elevates humour to satire. Perhaps this is why his films and his personality are so emphatically of today. He is a 'movie' man; and nothing does him greater credit than his energetic campaign to get Kodak to mend their stock, so that colour films of the past do not automatically fade and turn green. His own work certainly deserves to survive. Try to get his movies from your local video store, and you will find that they will tell you as much as this book.

Behind the Mask of Innocence

Review of *Behind the Mask of Innocence* by Kevin
Brownlow in *The Daily Telegraph*, 15 June 1991

KEVIN BROWNLOW IS OUR BEST ACADEMIC CRITIC OF CINEMA. IF THIS SOUNDS
musty, it should not. For his academicism is based on enthusiasm, which
is rare. It is also based on rare experience in editing and making films.
How many lecturers are as much at home behind a Movieola as in their
study with a copy of *Cahiers du Cinéma*?

In his early teens Brownlow, already a crazy collector of silents,
embarked on *It Happened Here*, a story of Britain invaded and conquered
by the Germans. Somehow this most professional of amateur films was
completed, and he wrote about it in *How It Happened Here*. Then there
was *Winstanley*, an Eisenstein-influenced film of the English Shaker revo-
lutionaries. And the revised re-edited restoration of Gance's *Napoleon*.
Then the brilliant compilations for television (with David Gill) and the Live
Cinema shows they both presented at the Dominion. And more books.

Behind the Mask of Innocence is Brownlow's third book in a masterly trilogy. This started 25 years ago with his celebration of great films and directors of the silent cinema, *The Parade's Gone By*. With that pioneering work,
he fired his first shot in a battle which has now surely been won. Silent films
were at one time thought of as 'crude, fumbling, naive' (Brownlow's words).
Whereas, as he was at pains to establish, Hollywood's silent era was 'the
richest in the cinema's history' with photography that 'glistened and
gleamed', lights and gauzes that fused with magical effect until 'the art of
lighting reached its zenith'. As you can tell from his language, Brownlow had
fallen in love with the American silent cinema. Love, as we know, can be
blind; but it can also see the truth of things. As it did here.

The Parade's Gone By was followed some twelve years later by *The
War, the West and the Wilderness*, another celebration, this time of the
stories filmed by Hollywood directors far from their studios. Memorable
films like Cruze's *The Covered Wagon*, Ford's *The Iron Horse*, Vidor's *The
Big Parade*. Classics like Flaherty's *Nanook* and *Moana*, pioneers like
Merian C. Copper and Ernest Schoedsack (to whom the book was dedicated). It was clear that Kevin Brownlow was not simply a connoisseur of
brilliant design, gauzes and filters; he was also fascinated by history.

History is the inspiration of his new book. Its title is clumsy but apt.
The conventional idea of silent American cinema is that it was dedicated
to the idea of innocence – to a life 'quieter . . . gentler, more civilised' than

ours. We think of Mary Pickford and her corkscrew curls, of the delicate beauty of Lillian Gish. Or there were the brilliant comedians, Chaplin, Keaton, Lloyd and their colleagues, who made a whole world laugh. Or the high-spirited antics of Fairbanks and the lavish emotionalism of the vamps. But of course life in the USA was not really like that, and from the start many American film-makers were eager to exploit the violence, scandal and corruption of their society.

Headlines have always been a prime source of drama for the American cinema. Brownlow shows that it was not just Warner Brothers in the thirties, or the smattering of progressive independents, who took their stories from the press. American movies have never been intimidated by the truth or felt much was at stake in the status quo. Commercialism was not always an excuse for conservatism. It was Brownlow's discovery of *The Passaic Textile Strike*, made in 1926 and financed by the striking workers themselves, that led to the writing of this book.

Many of these films have perished. Sound made silent pictures seem out of date, and only television proved that old films might still be valuable. This means that much of this book is about films which can no longer be seen. So it is not exactly a comfortable read; but every page is fascinating. And it gives a comprehensive view of the silent American cinema's portrait of a burgeoning urban society. Methods of censorship are detailed; also films whose subjects were sex, drugs, prohibition and crime; political corruption and women's suffrage; prisons and poverty; and finally industry – child labour, socialism and populism, the red scare, capital versus labour. Could such a list be compiled of social subjects treated by the early British cinema? I think not.

Here then are facts about *Traffic in Souls*, 1913 (white slavery), *Where Are My Children?*, 1916 (pro-birth control, anti-abortion), Lois Weber (early woman director), *Human Wreckage*, 1923 (the anti-drug picture produced by the widow of Wallace Reid, who died of morphine addiction), *Twelve Miles Out*, 1927 (John Gilbert in a story of alcohol smuggling). Read further for Griffith's *Broken Blossoms*, Von Sternberg's *Underworld*, DeMille's *The Godless Girl* – and you will still only scratch the surface of the subject.

This is a heavy, substantial book. It is beautifully printed on art paper, and splendidly illustrated, a credit to its publishers. It may seem expensive, but it is nearly 600 pages long and extremely well written. Listening to a programme on BBC Radio recently, I heard how suitable people may be recommended for Honours. Apparently you only have to write to the Honours Department, 10 Downing Street, with a sensible suggestion. After reading this book, and seeing compilations on television and silent films (with orchestra) at the Dominion, I have one. Sir Kevin Brownlow – and Sir David Gill. They both deserve it.

The Birth of a Nation

Sight and Sound, January-March 1953

As every Film Appreciator knows, *The Birth of a Nation* is the earliest surviving example of the Film as an Art. Or at least, of all the contestants to that title, the most readily available: film societies have long used it to study Griffith's pioneering use of close-up and long-shot, his fiercely dynamic editing, his exploitation of the tracking camera, his fine casting sense and brilliant handling of players, his experiments in parallel cutting which led him on to the magnificent folly of *Intolerance*. Now the film has been re-released as a commercial feature, and we gain the rather extraordinary experience of seeing the picture once more, not merely as an object of historical and academic interest, but performing the function for which it was created – that is to say, the entertainment and edification of popular audiences. Does it survive?

Before that question can be answered, there is another point to consider. Does the new version adequately represent Griffith's work of nearly 40 years ago? In the first place it has been shortened: the original silent film ran about 12,500 feet, this one is nearly 3,000 feet less. A soundtrack has been added, carrying crowd noises and battle effects, with here and there an occasional shriek, as well as the original score by Joseph Breil, part composed for the film and part arranged from already existing music (songs and marches of the Civil War, Grieg, Wagner, etc). and since the negative has not been 'stretched', projection of the film at sound speed involves the acceleration of movement on the screen by about 50 per cent.

Not all these alterations are serious. The cuts do not seem savage: apart from the loss of the allegorical conclusion (depicting 'The coming of the Prince of Peace, the free intermingling of the world's peoples, and the victory of love in Christ'), whereby the film's close is both lamed and distorted, the gaps are not obtrusive, and all the scenes which have remained in the memory though a four-year interval reappear. The sound effects help rather than hinder and the music is excellent. The change in projection speed, however, is highly regrettable. It is ironic to recall Bitzer's description of 'the tremendous zeal, energy and genius Griffith put into having its timing just so, its tempo right to a hair. I remember how hard he worked through the day, and then far into the night . . .' What would he have said to this speeding-up, severely impairing its spectacle and many of its most sensitive moments? The appreciation of silent screen acting, with its generally accentuated style, usually requires some adjustments on the part of a contemporary audience; the principal performances here are extraordinarily good, but it would be unreasonable to expect them to stand up wholly to this treatment. Particularly sad is the effect on Mae Marsh's beautiful performance as Flora Cameron, vivid and mercurial, with the thoughtless innocence of a bird: the touching figure becomes a silly puppet, the eager movements distorted into frenetic parody. One can hardly blame the audience for laughing.

Adjustment, therefore, has to be made; and it is worth making because the vitality of the creation still persists. By the standards of developed cinema (which this film, of course, helped to establish) the rhythm is rather distractingly discontinuous. One sees how the use of titles – instead of a pre-planned visual continuity – made it possible for Griffith to carry a whole film in his head, dispensing with a finely organised script, and shooting to a great extent off the cuff. Inevitably the result now seems choppy; and particularly where the dramatic continuity is interrupted for the insertion of a *tableau vivant* representation of some historical event (generally 'after' a well-known painting of the scene). It is futile, too, to claim that Griffith's staging and handling remains unsurpassed: compare, for instance, the assassination of Lincoln here with its representation – very similarly done – in *The Prisoner of Shark Island*. Perhaps Ford did it better than Griffith because Griffith had done it first; it does the more primitive work no favour to claim for it a supremacy it no longer possesses. Particularly when there is still much in it to astonish and entertain. The battle scenes are magnificent: the wonderful pan from the refugees sheltering on the hillside to the valley below where Sherman's columns are on the march 'from Atlanta to the sea'; the excitement and ferocity of the fighting; the sombre silence of the battlefield after the cease-fire has blown – 'War's Peace'. Best of all are the episodes which give most scope to Griffith's response to the tender human affections, never more memorably than in the return from war of the only surviving Cameron son: the shabby, hesitating figure at the gate, his naively happy sister on the steps, pathetic in her mock finery, the look between them which suddenly brings home to her all that they have lost, and the final exquisite reticence of the boy's entry into the house, welcomed in by his mother's arms.

But *The Birth of a Nation*, like another celebrated epic of the American Civil War, has a second part; and, again like *Gone with the Wind*, this latter half is a let-down. (For different reasons certainly.) There is no point in re-flogging the old controversy of Griffith's racial prejudices: he was a Southerner by birth and conviction, as traditional in his hates as in his loves. His picture of the South after the war is an inflamed and a bitter one; however sincere his theoretical belief in tolerance and equality, he is unable to regard the Negro with anything but the eye of an overlord. Even his 'Old Faithfuls' (the name given to the Camerons' loyal Negro servants) are white actors in blackface, and the approval accorded to their behaviour on the titles is not reflected in any real respect or affection in their presentation. The climax of the film is a stylistic *tour de force*, but its amalgam of traditional, stagey melodramatics and hysterical racialism is extremely distasteful. The camera is tracking for the first (or the second) time in the history of the cinema; but where to? These hooded figures, whose actions we are so brilliantly being urged to approve; who are they, and what are they doing? Griffith is cross-cutting marvellously; but from what to what, and why? These questions are all part of film appreciation too.

Louisiana Story

Sequence 6, Winter 1949

> *A Stranger here*
> *Strange things doth meet, Strange Glories see . . .*

AT A TIME WHEN SO MUCH MAGIC HAS GONE OUT OF THE WORLD, WHEN THE faculty of wonder seems likely to disappear altogether, it is not surprising that the innocent eye of childhood should commend itself more strongly than ever as a subject for the artist. In very different styles we see the tendency reflected in painting, by the naivety of a Klee or a Chagall; by films like *La Maternelle* or (with different emphasis) *Sciuscia*; by novels like *Le Grand Meaulnes* or Forrest Reid's trilogy about Young Tom. The same feeling informs Robert Flaherty's *Louisiana Story* – to which Traherne's lines seem especially applicable, chiefly perhaps because of the unfamiliar loveliness of its setting in the Bayou marshlands of Louisiana. The hero of the film – a thirteen-year-old French-Canadian boy – has indeed a great deal in common with Reid's Tom; both are sturdy boys, self-reliant, unsentimental, instinctively at one with the animal world; and each has the rapt, creative imagination of a poet, Tom with his dreams of Greece, and Alexander Napoleon Ulyssess Latour with his magic bag of salt and his belief in fairies and mermaids with green hair.

It is an enchanted world. Lilies float on the surface of the water; air bubbles ominously up from the depth. Down the river there glides a little boat: as he paddles, the graceful, dark-eyed boy glances cautiously about him, as though everywhere there lurk mysterious, hidden enemies. He brings his boat to the bank and steps ashore. The sun filters down through the great trees and their long, leafy drapery. With this boy, equally at home on or in the

Robert Flaherty's Louisiana Story.

water, or up a tree, we explore the river and the forest; we watch him fishing, playing with his pet racoon, filching eggs from an alligator's nest. And with him we watch the arrival of the crew who have come to drill for oil in the bed of the river – fascinating intruders with their motorboats, their huge structure of floating steel, their crashing, terrifying, absorbing machinery.

Here one might expect conflict; but with his constant respect for human nature, his optimistic belief that, with all their differences, people can live together, Flaherty has preferred to show us harmony rather than discord. At first Alexander is shy; but soon he is persuaded aboard the oil-rig, to sit for hours fascinated (as we are) by the great shafts of steel, racketing from side to side, plunging deep into the river-bed. The incursions of the oil company means a new gun for Alexander, money and extra comfort for his father and mother; in return they give their help, his father with a pen, Alexander with his magic. Here in fact are two ways of living, the Latours who live by shooting and trapping on their own land, and the oil-men who are also masters of a craft and as such worthy of respect. Having a skill, that is the important thing; that, and due respect for the skill of your neighbour. In this sort of productive cooperation rests our only hope: it is absurd to write Flaherty off as an escapist.

All this is, of course, implicit in the film, which is not a sermon, but a story (Flaherty calls it a 'dramatic fantasy') of great beauty and many excitements. Theme and incident are preserved in perfect balance, with just enough story to give shape and direction, and as much as possible of incident to fill in the background: Alexander's feud with the alligator he believes has eaten his racoon, culminating in a very frightening struggle in the water; the oil-men chatting with each other, or fishing from the rig; Alexander's father setting his traps among the reeds.

'Since we do not use professional actors,' Flaherty has written, 'it is necessary to find people who will fit the parts that are called for in the picture, and who can live their roles. If you are careful and get people to perform what they have done all their lives, they can do it better than actors.' Of this use of 'natural' actors, *Louisiana Story* is one of the few completely successful examples. It took three months to find the perfect Alexander (Joseph

Boudreaux), which does not, considering his absolute *rightness*, seem very long. By his solemn beauty, his spontaneous alternations of intentness and gaiety, the impression in him of a courageous, imaginative spirit, the film is incalculably enriched. The other characters, also handled with humour and affection, are less important, but they fill in the picture: the grand, rugged figure of Alexander's father; the casual, friendly men on the rig.

Flaherty has been well served also by the other members of his team. Richard Leacock's photography captures the contrasting qualities of the film's two worlds, and Virgil Thompson's lovely score reinforces the visual enchantment of the marshland and the forest. Helen van Dongen has edited, one feels, with loving respect, giving the film a deliberate, unhurried movement, letting the story grow as Flaherty wanted it to grow – out of the people and the place. It is a fine conception, beautifully executed. Once seen, *Louisiana Story* is not to be forgotten.

Guys and Dolls, A Hill in Korea and Smiles of a Summer Night

New Statesman, 1956

IT IS A PITY, BUT SAM GOLDWYN HAS NOT SUCCEEDED IN MAKING A GOOD FILM out of *Guys and Dolls*. The reason is obvious enough in the film's trailer: in large, Technicolor close-up Mr Goldwyn's hand signs the million-dollar cheque he gave for the screen rights to the play. To ensure a return on this investment, it was necessary to spend four and a half million dollars more on the production. The result probably cannot lose money; but it has certainly spoiled the fun.

Over-produced, over-dressed and over-crowded, *Guys and Dolls* is the biggest of the current crop of CinemaScope musicals – there are two hours and 29 minutes of it. This, to begin with, is a mistaken inflation of the racy 'Broadway fable' which was Frank Loesser's description of his original, Runyon-inspired show. But probably Goldwyn's cardinal error was to hire Joseph L. Mankiewicz to write and direct it. On the stage, *Guys and Dolls* was Loesser's musical comedy, with a book by Jo Swerling and Abe Burrows. It has been turned into a film 'written and directed by Joseph L. Mankiewicz' (large letters), with music and lyrics by Frank Loesser. The difference is profound. From *All About Eve* to *The Barefoot Contessa*,

Mankiewicz's pretensions to 'make with the words' have grown steadily more tiresome. Turned loose on *Guys and Dolls*, he has expanded the narrative scenes quite unnecessarily, over-plugged the Runyonisms, and got everything (actors included) bogged down in otiose passages of dialogue. Fortunately most of Loesser's marvellous numbers turn up in the end: brilliantly witty and well performed, they are worth waiting for. The cast is excellent. Marlon Brando does not take to song-and-dance exactly like a duck to water, but he has a good and engaging go at it. Jean Simmons is fresh and very winning as the Salvation Army heroine, and Sinatra and Vivian Blaine need no commendation from me. It is Mankiewicz's direction that sorely lacks the lyric impulse, and I do not think that his film's deficiency in charm is merely because (in the words of *The Times* critic) 'the majority of its characters are the kind of men who would take part in a crap game in a sewer at midnight'.

Whatever one's reservations about a film like *Guys and Dolls*, there is no denying its supreme professionalism. The vitality of its dancing, the effectiveness of its orchestration, its superb technical qualities, the enormous, gorgeous Goldwyn girls – these represent Hollywood at its still unbeatable best. Beside such showmanship, our native entertainments cannot help looking a bit amateurish. But perhaps *A Hill in Korea* is aimed at doing something more than senselessly divert? If so, what? A poster describes this as 'The very first film dedicated to National Servicemen and drafted men of the free nations, past and present.' But a limp posy of screenwriter's clichés seems a poor offering with which to reward these honourable sufferers. *A Hill in Korea* is far from being a realistic film about modern war. It is not about its futility; and it says nothing very convincing about courage. It is not about why we were right to send these men to fight in Korea, and it is not about why we might have been wrong, either. Presented with a certain, ineffective good taste, it is a pointless reworking of stale conventions: the isolated patrol, the inexperienced lieutenant, the fatherly sergeant, the coward – and, of course, the inevitable chorus of indomitable Cockney wit. The Bren guns blaze away; the British infantrymen grit their teeth in close-up; the Chink Commies are mown down. 'Honest,' as one of the characters remarks, 'it binds you rigid.' Its supporting role actors like Ronald Lewis, Michael Medwin, Victor Maddern and Harry Landis give honest and impressive performances.

The new film at the Academy is a Festival discovery: Ingmar Bergman's *Smiles of a Summer Night* caused rapture among the French at Cannes this year, and was given a prize for *'L'Humour Poétique'*. Its theme is love and licence among a group of *fin-de-siècle* Swedes: heavily frolicsome, emphatically sensual, and beautifully photographed in that hygienic, refrigerated style the Swedes are so good at. A French critic caught the personality of this film perfectly when he called it 'a film for adults, made by a man who knows that love is a very serious matter, which should never be talked about except with a smile.' If you like that sort of thing, go to it.

The Big Heat

Sight and Sound, July-September 1954

IT SEEMS A LONG TIME SINCE FRITZ LANG GAVE US A GOOD FILM: IN FACT, THE sense of strain and stylistic pretentiousness in his recent work – when it has not been mere commercial hokum – had almost made one abandon hope. This makes it the more unfortunate that his latest film should have passed almost unnoticed. For it is an extremely good thriller, distinguished by precisely those virtues which Lang's pictures have in the past few years so painfully lacked: tautness and speed; modesty of intention; intelligent, craftsman-like writing. Above all, it is directed with a dramatic incisiveness, a sharp-edged observation that keeps the pitch of interest and excitement continuously high.

Adapted from a novel by William McGivern, *The Big Heat* is scripted by Sidney Boehm. He has not done so well since *Union Station* – a film which this rather recalls in its ingenious construction and clever, likely motivation. The handling here, however, is more frankly melodramatic, and the world evoked nearer to that of Raymond Chandler. The situation is classic: the unassuming crusader versus the high-class racketeer; the crusader operating alone; the racketeer manoeuvring his thugs (inside and outside the city police) from his guarded mansion in the snob section of town. Unlike Marlowe, Dave Bannion is a professional cop; but his disrespect of persons soon gets him suspended, and his conduct shows the same doggedness, the same human fallibility, the same hunger after righteousness as the Chandler hero's. He challenges the racketeer, and pays for it: his wife is murdered; bitterly he dedicates himself to vengeance. Glenn Ford plays this part with a deceptively casual charm that covers without concealing a real inward intensity. (This admirable actor is one of the few surviving in Hollywood who are able convincingly to convey any moral awareness or conflict.) As the gay, incautious girl friend of a vicious hoodlum, Gloria Grahame acts with brilliant wit and considerable subtlety; and all the way down the cast – of generally unfamiliar faces – the characterisations have a welcome individuality of line.

The Big Heat is one of those enjoyable films which make no great claims for themselves, yet which so balance style and intention (like the early Hitchcocks, for instance) that they are finally more satisfying than many more ambitious works. The film lacks the density of a *Maltese Falcon*; one or two of its elements are over-conventional; Lang's viewpoint remains exterior. All the same, it creates its world, and proves that, when his interest is engaged, this director still has at his control the technique of a master. Contributory skills that also deserve praise are Charles Lang's, whose lighting powerfully contributes to the atmosphere of tension and incipient violence, and Charles Nelson's, whose editing is immaculate. The timing of the end-title, in its relation to soundtrack as well as image, is a little triumph in itself.

Them!

Monthly Film Bulletin, September 1954

ACTING ON A REPORT RECEIVED BY THE NEW MEXICO POLICE, SERGEANT Ben Peterson sets out to find a little girl wandering through the desert in a state of shock. Nearby he comes upon a car and trailer, mysteriously wrecked. A general store a few miles down the road has been smashed up, and the storekeeper crushed. What can be the explanation? The only clues are the theft of sugar from the trailer and store – and a number of weird, huge foot- or paw-prints. Dr Harold Medford, one of the world's most distinguished entomologists, and his attractive scientist-daughter are assigned to the case by the FBI. It is not long before the problem is solved – a giant species of ant, 'a giant mutation . . . engendered by lingering radiation from the explosion of the first atomic bomb'. The nest of these ants is located and fumigated with poisonous gas. A search reveals, however, that two queen ants have hatched and escaped, together with a number of winged males. Efforts must be made to locate these queens and destroy them before they can breed further. Prolonged search locates the surviving ants in the sewer system of Los Angeles. The army moves in, and they are destroyed. The film ends, however, with the ominous suggestion that further horrors may at this moment be breeding as a result of the succeeding atomic experiments.

The science-fiction film has not been with us very long, yet already the genre has its recognisable sub-divisions: the other-worldly, the primeval-monstrous, the neo-monstrous, the planetary-visitant, etc. *Them!,* a well-built example of the neo-monstrous, is less absurdly sensational than most, quite persuasively documented, and pleasantly traditional in trimmings (brilliant fuddy-duddy scientist and attractive daughter) and development (up to the final sewer battle, the rescue of two kiddies, and the death of the less personable of the two leading men). The ants themselves are reasonably horrible – they do not entirely avoid the impression of mock-up that is almost inevitable when over-lifesize creatures have to be constructed and moved, but they are considerably more conceivable than those prehistoric remnants that have recently been emerging from bog and iceberg.

Again like most science-fiction, *Them!* is on the whole serviceably rather than excitingly cast. But Edmund Gwenn is quite acceptable as the entomologist, and there is nothing much wrong with any of the other performances. The direction is smoothly machined, and the writing decent; though more short cuts might have been taken. The start especially is too slow.

Giant

New Statesman, 12 January 1957

WHETHER THROUGH SHEER SIZE, OR FOR THE LAST APPEARANCE OF JAMES Dean, or for its apposite concern with Texas oil, *Giant* commands attention. Here at least is a mammoth (about three and a quarter hours) which isn't just another film record of a Broadway musical, and which aims to be something more than a gaudy and expensive spectacle. Expensive it must have been: but in taking Edna Ferber's long chronicle of Texas cattle-barons and oil-men as his first subject since *Shane,* George Stevens had something to say as well.

What he has to say is often interesting, pregnant, and worth hearing. The first hour of *Giant,* centred on a vast Texas cattle ranch in the twenties, is full of good scenes, memorable vistas: the nineteenth-century Gothic mansion starting up like a mirage in the arid waste; the coarse, friendly, materialistic community of cattlemen and their dowdy wives, clannish and racially intolerant; the decrepit shanty town to which their Mexican servants ('waterbacks';) are condemned. It is all internally reminiscent of what one reads of South African society today; and Stevens, who is a liberal without being quite a radical (he is too fascinated by wealth for that), shows it vividly, with honesty and edge.

There is a story, of course. Bick Benedict, owner of the fabulous Reatta ranch (595,000 acres) brings a wife to Texas from the East, and it is through her eyes that we see this strange, feudal, epic world. Her impulses are more civilised than her husband's. She wants to share his life; and she finds herself excluded from most of it. She wants to heal and help the poor; and her husband tells her she should be unaware of their existence. But Benedict's complacent conservatism does not have the last word; odd-job man around the ranch, befriended only by Bick's sister, is young Jett Rink. Jett is a bitter-friendly, mercurial character (you will readily guess who plays him), despised by the prosperous cattlemen, yet not to be classed with the Mexicans, a poor white, a trouble-maker. But it is Jett who strikes oil.

It is Jett's oil, rather than Benedict's children and grandchildren, that powers the second half of *Giant*. But the transmission is faulty, and there are times when the film slows perilously near to a standstill, before the theme of racial tolerance is revived, and the story ends with a good and valuable gesture. The reasons for this loss of grip are worth pondering. Is it just a question of length? Are these long chronicle films just too demanding in a medium as intense and concentrated as the cinema? I do not think so. It is the scenario of *Giant* that falters; and I think the way it falters is inevitable in a film which costs as much money to make as this one – and which therefore has to *make* as much money as this one. For how can interest be sustained? The people must develop, the relationships deepen and progress. And themes (of money, power, etc.) must develop too. Stevens, alas, is able to do neither of these things. The characterisation remains *Saturday Evening Post* – indeed, with Bick and his wife declining into a gracious, greying hero and heroine, and their children multiplying, growing up and marrying, it becomes more rather than less superficial. And, for obvious reasons, the criticism of Texas capitalism has to be implicit rather than explicit, hinted in ironic touches rather than plainly exposed. However, even at this diminished strength, Stevens' achievement deserves a salute. Jett Rink's jubilee dinner party, with its fawning politicos and its unabashed worship of cash, is a remarkable satirical set-piece; and the last two reels – a sort of *Gentleman's Agreement* in miniature – take us back to those post-War days when Hollywood had more courage and vitality to the foot than it has now to a couple of miles of film. As the American friend with whom I saw *Giant* remarked, respectfully: 'Nobody's dared do a thing like that since they kicked the Communists out of Hollywood.'

Deeper considerations apart, this is an exceptionally handsome film, and a fine piece of craftsmanship. Only the music is trite (Dimitri Tiomkin). The settings have attentive feeling for period and social level, and Stevens' direction, if only intermittently really eloquent, has a rare solidity and sobriety throughout. The acting is modestly adequate by Rock Hudson, good by Elizabeth Taylor and virtuoso by James Dean, whose Jett Rink is a wilful and brilliant variation on the character he made his own, and died for – the baffled, tender, violent adolescent, rejected by the world which he rejects. The middle-aged Jett Rink he could not manage: a matured, hopelessly corrupt character was beyond him. And there is one other player I would like to mention: that frumpish, well-meaning girl-next-door, who develops so splendidly into a roaring, red-haired middle-aged Texas hoyden. Who is this but Jane Withers, once the plumper, more rumbustious rival of Shirley Temple?

The Girl Can't Help It

New Statesman, 23 February 1956

FILM CRITICS THINK THEY HAVE A HARD TIME; AND THEY ARE RIGHT. BUT, BY restricting their viewing to the official press shows, they miss an unfair number of the trials their readers are liable to fall victim to. At the Canton, for instance, with *The Girl Can't Help It*, is a CinemaScope short about Esquimaux (ten minutes of snow and cliché), and another short subject in which Mr Derek Bond explains how fearfully complicated and expensive ('without a penny being wasted') the process of film-making must be. To exemplify, we are privileged to watch some scrappily assembled shots taken during the filming of *Anastasia*. 'The cameraman takes endless trouble, even personally adjusting the shadows on Ingrid Bergman's face.' Well – who ever would have thought it!

There is also, of course, a newsreel. Solemn tones for the enthronement of a new Roman Catholic Archbishop, and jocular stuff about Cruft's ('Not a tree in sight!') and the Duke's Tour ('Piccaninnies on Parade! Swing dose arms! Stamp dose feet!') The *pièce de résistance* here is a heart-rending appeal to the public to support the film industry's campaign for the easing of Entertainment Tax. 'The lights are going out' – grim images of shuttered cinemas – a civic dignitary with a face like doom bewails the plight of his now cinema-less town – a manager's farewell to his staff, like Noel Coward in *In Which We Serve*, only more *sincere*.

This sort of spiritless whine is no way to defend the cinema: but I suppose we must not be surprised if the System can produce nothing better. In this context, the main feature at the Carlton (it is also on at the Rialto) is particularly revealing. *The Girl Can't Help It* is the first rock 'n' roll film I have seen. I approached it in friendship, ever on the side of the socially underprivileged; but, I admit frankly, I recoiled pretty sharply as it hit me. Is this what they're asking us to fight for? Cheaply prefabricated and carelessly assembled, *The Girl Can't Help It* is a juke-box thrown into the face of the public with a great blare of ugly, debilitated music. Seeing it is like being shut up for a couple of hours *inside* one of those huge, booming machines, all pink, green and mauve lights, gobbling up the small change of the ignorant. I suppose that Jayne Mansfield, 'launched' in this film, is human: but she so resembles a strip-cartoon parody of the Monroe-Dors figure that she might very well have been fashioned out of some disturbing new plastic substance. The 'comedy' is provided chiefly by Tom Ewell and Edmond O'Brien: two desperate, disillusioned performances, whose scenes have the fragrance of stale cigarette smoke and whisky bottles all but emptied. The music is jazz under neon lights, commercialised, devitalised, put across with the kind of showmanship in which hysteria and cynicism are most distastefully blended.

You can see, from a few snide touches, that Frank Tashlin, who wrote and directed this film, is no rock 'n' roller. But this only deprives the whole affair of the vitality it might have possessed if he had been. He can have a few laughs, but finally he must capitulate to commerce and subscribe to the publicist's lie. Fifteen years ago, made by the same studio, *The Girl Can't Help It* would have been either a conventional, but bright and well-turned musical, with artists like Betty Grable, Charlotte Greenwood and Carmen Miranda; or an intelligent, hard-boiled satire – remember Ginger Rogers in *Roxie Hart*? But today . . . This is Hollywood on its knees.

Minnelli, Kelly and *An American in Paris*

Sequence 14, 1952

RARELY, IN THE FIELD OF PURE ENTERTAINMENT AT LEAST, CAN THERE HAVE been a film awaited with greater expectation than *An American in Paris*. 'Gene Kelly in . . .' 'Directed by 'Vincente Minnelli . . .' These were the key phrases; and what a cluster of memories they conjured up. *On the Town* and *The Pirate*. And, further back, *Cabin in the Sky* and *Meet Me in St Louis*. And, in between, *The Ziegfeld Follies* and *Yolanda and the Thief; If You Feel Like Singing* and *Cover Girl*, and *Living in a Big Way*. Continue to reminisce over past pleasures in this genre, and you find other titles cropping up, of films which Minnelli did not direct, and in which

Kelly did not appear. *Summer Holiday*, for instance, that uniquely enjoyable, inexplicably loathed film *maudit*; *Good News*; *State Fair* . . . All these are not just a random group of films with music that happen to have entertained us in the last seven or eight years. Widely though they differ, they all approach the business of putting songs and dancing into cinema from roughly the same angle. *An American in Paris* is a film in a tradition.

Of course, Hollywood, with the lusty troops of American show business to draw on, has had its tradition of musicals ever since the introduction of sound: a tradition of immense professional competence from the start, of numbers put across with unfailing vivacity, staged with an opulence and daring which soon went beyond mere good or bad taste. It is with warmth that one remembers them – these phalanxes of chorines tapping their streamlined limbs through the *Gold Diggers* of the thirties; those mountains of pulchritude piled up into living wedding cakes or battleships or Christmas trees in the *Broadway Melodies* and MGM extravaganzas which followed them; routines which diminished in size, though not in energy, when Technicolor came in and the Grable period began. The Astaire-Rogers series was a lonely exception; as far as the conservative mainstream went, spectacle was the thing – spectacle, that is, in the sense of what went on in front of the camera. The camera recorded. Frequently, it is true, it recorded remarkable things: massed choruses patterned into intricate abstract designs, like snow crystals viewed through the microscope, stage spectacles glossier and more enormous than could be accommodated in any theatre on earth (invariably they danced on glass). But the camera never entered into it, to become part of the pattern. Further, these entertainments, machine-like in their efficiency, were rigidly conventional; personal emotion or sensibility played no part in them.

These were the revelations of Minnelli's first films. *Cabin in the Sky* (1943) and *Meet Me in St Louis* (1944) – the first for the sophisticated *faux-naïveté* of its decors and general style, miles removed from the slick unenterprise of the current musical fashion, and the second for the genuine feeling, for character as well as decoration, with which it managed to tell its story of middle-class American family life in the early days of the century. Undoubtedly these films reflected the developing tradition of American lyric theatre (Minnelli came from Broadway, where he had worked as a designer and director), but they were very far from theatrical in their manner of presentation. From the first Minnelli seems to have seized with joy on the expressive potentialities of the movie camera. These potentialities he has continued to exploit, though never again quite as he did in *Meet Me in St Louis*, for his musical films since have concentrated on style rather than sentiment, on appealing to the eye through a use of colour and design which, if it verges from time to time on the chi-chi, is

Leslie Caron and Gene Kelly in Vincente Minnelli's
An American in Paris.

never less than elegant. This research was brought to a climax in *The Pirate* – Minnelli's last musical film before *An American in Paris* – and his most daring experiment in artifice. Based on a comedy by S. N. Berman (written for the Lunts), it was transformed for the screen into a musical, with a score and lyrics by Cole Porter, and dances by Gene Kelly and Robert Alton. Though not an entire success, the result was a film of unrivalled *chic*: an urbane fairy tale dressed and set with exuberant flair, and studded with numbers of the most polished brilliance. Judy Garland's 'Mac the Black' is strung to an electrifying pitch and filmed at the same intensity, and 'The Pirate Ballet' records a dream-fantasy in colour and movement (scarlet and black, and great sweeping crane shots, all to a bold and brassy orchestration) which demonstrates with what excitement dance and cinema can be mated by a director, a dancer and a designer sensitive to the resources of both mediums.

Where *The Pirate* did not 'come off' was in its novel attempt to mix high comedy with music and dance. Probably Judy Garland and Gene Kelly made a better showing in their dialogues than the Lunts would have done in 'Be a Clown' or 'Nina', but in the scenes where the wit was thin and brittle, and success dependent on a comedy technique of the lightest touch, their playing quite lacked the necessary finesse. They started to shout. In Kelly's case at least this reflected less inexperience than discomfort; such a style of behaviour was not his and never will be.

Gene Kelly also came to Hollywood from the theatre, and at about the same time as Minnelli. Primarily a dancer, he had played the part of the saloon-bar hoofer in the Broadway production of Saroyan's *The Time of Your Life*, and then the lead in the Rodgers and Hart *Pal Joey*. This led to Hollywood in 1942. In 1944 he made his first splash in *Cover Girl*, a musical conventional enough in conception, but distinguished by some good design and colour and by Kelly's dances – one of which (his *alter ego* dance in double exposure) has justly become a classic. Since then, working continuously at MGM, Kelly has developed first as a dancer-actor, then as a choreographer, and most recently as a director, to establish a quite individual style and personality of his own.

It has been said that Kelly 'dances people'. Perhaps it would be truer to say that he dances 'a person' – himself. He is a dramatic dancer, but not a character dancer, in the sense in which that term is generally used. Consistently his dances express attitude, a response: one of humour and humanity, and an abounding vitality. Sometimes the touch is delicate: he dances with children, sings for them, plays their games. The humour is personal, whimsical: he dances with a broom, a statue, makes a partner of a discarded newspaper and his music from a squeaking board. His romantic dances are usually restrained; the emotion is fragile. But in other moods, no dancer can more exhilaratingly communicate gaiety and the joy of living, with a freedom of movement and an appetite for the sheer physical activity of it which is constantly controlled by the discipline of a natural artist – a discipline less strictly exercised by Kelly the actor, who is always liable to launch into vulgarities of which Kelly the dancer would never be guilty. It is not a personality of great sophistication. Unlike Astaire, Kelly seems ill at ease dancing in a top hat and tails; while to Astaire, Kelly's territory is equally foreign – as in his toyshop dance with the bad-tempered little boy in *Easter Parade* (a role he took over from Kelly). Astaire, one felt was not really very fond of little boys.

These two talents of Minnelli and Kelly, alike in brilliance, dissimilar in personality, may be said to have civilised the Hollywood musical. (With a salute in passing to Arthur Freed, who brought Minnelli to Hollywood, and produced nine of the twelve films listed at the beginning of this notice.) In their films standards of design and presentation have been immeasurably raised – the work of designers like Jack Martin Smith, of choreographers like Eugene Loring, Charles Walters, Alton, and Kelly himself has given them a distinction undreamed of in the routine Hollywood musical. In fact, by regarding the film-with-music as something more than a strung-together collection of numbers, or a freakish spectacle, they have made it a genre of drama with subtleties and satisfactions of its own. Thus, when Kelly came to direct a film himself, in collaboration with the dance director Stanley Donen, *On the Town* integrated to a remarkable degree its songs, dances and story. It is not surprising that after it a film choreographed and danced by him and directed by Minnelli should be awaited with eagerness.

Being in a tradition is advantageous in that it implies resources that can be drawn on, and challenging in that it implies expectations to be satisfied, achievements to be advanced from. It must be immediately admitted that *An American in Paris* suffers distinctly if approached with hopes of a crowning achievement or of fresh fields conquered. Its record is, in fact, almost the direct reverse of *The Pirate* – which was a resounding failure commercially and critically, and a highly enjoyable near-success as a musical entertainment. Commercially and critically *An American in Paris* seems to be a resounding success, while as a musical entertainment it provokes considerable disappointment. To work methodically through its various elements would be a depressing business, since from almost every point of view it is inferior to its predecessors. In design the flair of Jack Martin Smith is sadly missed; the script is conventionally conceived, constructed with confusion, and lamely written; and too many of the ideas are derived too directly from previous films. For instance: from *On the Town* comes the prefatory, multi-sided glimpse of the heroine (as gadabout, bookworm, shy young thing, etc). A theft not justified by any improvement on the original; and the ambitious climatic ballet is, in theme and dramatic function, an expansion of the 'Day in New York' ballet in the same film.

This is not to say that *An American in Paris* contains nothing that is enjoyable. The Gershwin songs are as good today as they ever were, and some of them are delightfully staged. The ballet itself is at least something to get your teeth into. But there is an unevenness about the whole entertainment that seems to betray a divided, or at least an incomplete, conception. What were they after? Was it to be a naturalistic, dramatic musical, doing for its American in Paris what *On the Town* did for its sailors in New York? Or a pure confection, with style and design to match a deliberate artificiality of plot? The film falls somewhere between these two stools. Apart from the ballet, the designs are not striking, and the movement is generally rather untidy: thus the clever idea of dressing the Students' Ball (which immediately precedes the ballet) entirely in black and white fails to achieve the effect it should. A lot of footage is given over to the plot, and played by Kelly as though he meant it; but for this the material is simply not good enough, and his 'good guy' with the warm heart and the too-ready grin becomes somewhat irritating. Most disappointing is the relapse into the conventions of old-time musical comedy: this is at bottom a Paris firmly in the Culver City tradition of ebullient, gesticulating bistro-proprietors and their huge wives who love nothing better than to mother these so-gay, so-irresponsible young Americans (Kelly and Oscar Levant, if you please). Of the French members of the cast, Leslie Caron looks charming but is given little to do, and George Guetary exerts the old Gallic magnetism with determination, but the make-up and wardrobe departments have handicapped him fatally.

One is tempted to wonder whether the patchiness of so much of this film is not the result of its makers' preoccupation with their set-piece – the 'American in Paris Ballet'. (There is certainly no attempt, once it is over, to end the story satisfactorily: a mumbled explanation and a couple of shots are enough to sort out the plot and bring up the end titles.) They have been given their heads with it: it runs for about two reels, is photographed by a different cameraman from the rest of the film, and is designed with distinctly more style. Set in decors adventurously derived from Dufy, Renoir, Utrillo, Rousseau (particularly delightful), and Lautrec, it generates an excitement which raises the temperature with a leap. Like 'A Day in New York', its function in the story is to crystallise the moods and confusions of the film's hero, but dramatically it is much weaker, resolving itself into a series of elegant *divertissements* in which the connecting theme is largely sacrificed to a profusion of decorative *tours-de-force*. The performance of these is continuously virtuoso: the episodes have abundant invention and are danced with splendid verve; and Minnelli's camera patterns the whole with that free, invigorating movement which always distinguishes his handling of dance.

Perhaps such success, limited and sporadic, though on a high level, is all that *An American in Paris* was designed to achieve. And it is true that, in the perspective of, say, *On the Riviera* and *Call Me Mister*, *Let's Dance* and *Tea for Two*, the achievement is something to be thankful for. But it was in a different perspective that one looked at this film for the first time, one formed by the completer pleasures its makers have given us in the past. Let us hope that the tradition has been broken, only to be resumed.

Science Fiction Movies

New Statesman, 6 October 1956

SEE: WORLD CONQUERED BY THE HORRIBLE BEAST FROM BEYOND THE Stars!' 'SEE: Terrifying She-Monster who Lures Men with her Unearthly Beauty!' Everyone says that comedy is the thing at the moment; but clearly the desire for shock prevails. Science-fiction cinema is enjoying a new boom. A lot of these films are never shown in the West End, and never get a release on the circuits; but there are over 2,000 independent cinemas in Britain, and films like *It Conquered the World* and *The She-Creature* (from whose advertising I have lifted these alluring phrases) are going to be seen by a lot of people. This is a new double-bill shown to the trade last week by Anglo-Amalgamated Film Distributors, Ltd.

Anglo-Amalgamated are making a good thing of their double-X, all-sensation policy. It started last year, when they put out *The Day the World Ended* with *Phantom from 1,000 Leagues*. Launched without benefit of notice from the critics, this programme did 'fantastic business' (particularly in the industrial north), and even broke house-records at a circuit cinema in Birmingham. Two further low-budget American shockers were hastily coupled and hurled into the thrill-hungry provinces: *The Beast with a Million Eyes* and *The Mystery of the Black Jungle*. 'Of course,' Anglo-Amalgamated explain frankly, 'some people just enjoy taking the mickey out of them . . . We play them on the exploitation value.' It is the promise of sensationalism that counts. In fact the current programme in this series, released last month, is not science fiction at all (and one of the pictures even suffered the indignity of a U Certificate), but the exploitation technique is the same. 'Double Sock Rock and Thrill Show!' proclaim the advertisements for *Girls in Prison* ('What Happens to Girls Without Men?') and *Hot-Rod Girl* ('Youth on the Loose! Speed Crazy Rock'n'Roll Rampage!'). Social historians please note.

Of course, the trouble is that films on this level are more remarkable to hear about than to see. The publicity hugely inflates their interest. Made quickly and cheaply (they are all from America), they are apt to resemble television plays in style, and their monsters, when finally disclosed after much screaming, are frequently ludicrous. *The She-Creature*, for instance, is a sort of Pantomime Demon Queen, emerging from primeval ooze without a drip or a trace of slime; and the Thing from Venus in *It Conquered the World* (it didn't) resembles nothing so much as an inverted carrot, with a large, fanged mouth in its stomach, and stubby claws that wave with a certain pathos. To be fair though, we must note that we are shielded from the most gruesome moments in even the X-certificate films by the ministrations of our kindly censor.

Two more ambitious ventures in this genre are worth recording. *Invasion of the Body Snatchers* is made by the team responsible for *Riot in Cell Block 11*; which means that it is intelligent, craftsmanlike and decent. But I could not really surrender credulity to those giant pods (whence? and why?) which bud out so nastily into replicas of human bodies. After a good first half this loses grip. *X – The Unknown* (now at the London Pavilion) seems to me better thought-out, more sustained, and altogether a pretty upsetting hour-and-a-half. This is a British picture, admirably directed by Leslie Norman, and produced by Anthony (*Quatermass*) Hinds. Its monster is not out of time or space, but a terrifying emanation of energy from the centre of the earth, and the film plays very effectively on one's mistrust of all this fooling about with atoms and hydrogen. Not poetic exactly, but a valid exploitation of our contemporary nightmare.

The Last Sequence of *On the Waterfront*

Sight and Sound, January-March 1955

FIRST, AND SPECIFICALLY, THE DATA. TERRY MALLOY, THE SENSIBLE BRUISER who is the principal character of the film, has given evidence against Johnny Friendly, the crooked Union Boss. As a result he has found himself cold-shouldered by his mates. But he has regained his pride. 'I ain't a bum,' he tells his girl. 'I'm just going down there, and get my rights.' The last sequence of *On the Waterfront* is as follows:

> The dockers are on the quay, waiting for the call to work. When Terry arrives, they ignore him. There is work for them all – except him. Left alone there, he turns and makes for the hut that is Friendly's dockside headquarters. At an interval, the dockers follow him.
>
> Terry strides down the gangway between the hut and the quay-side, and shouts a challenge to Friendly. (The dockers line the quay, looking silently down on the hut.) Friendly comes out with a bunch of his thugs. 'You're nothing!' shouts Terry. 'I was ratting on myself all those years and didn't know it. I'm glad what I done!' Friendly challenges him to fight, Terry accepts; and he and Friendly set to on the raft. The dockers watch.
>
> Friendly gets the worst of the fight; he calls in his men to deal with Terry. They start to beat him up. The dockers move tentatively to his assistance, but are halted by two of Friendly's men at the bottom of the gangway. They turn away, cowed.
>
> The dockers are starting to move away when Father Barry arrives with Edie, Terry's girl. Terry is now stretched out still on the planks; Friendly and his men march up the gangway. 'The little rat's yours,' he shouts. The work whistle blows. The dockers turn their backs on Friendly. One of them says: 'How about Terry? He don't work, we don't work . . .' Friendly lays hands on an old workman, who shakes himself free with a shove. Friendly overbalances into the water. The dockers cheer.
>
> Father Barry and Edie are with Terry; he is bruised and bleeding and all but unconscious. One of the dockers runs up. 'If Terry walks in, we walk with him.' Father Barry turns to Terry: 'You hear that, Terry?' Terry nods dazedly. The priest continues: 'You lost the battle, but you have a chance to win the war.' Terry mumbles; the priest

hauls him to his feet. 'Finish what you started . . . You can – you can!'

With a terrible effort Terry summons his strength to stand and walk alone. Someone stretches out a helping hand. The priest shouts: 'Take your hands off him! Leave him alone!' Terry lurches through the crowd of dockers, followed by the priest, still warding off any helping hands. Terry staggers on towards the shed, his face bloody and agonised, his feet dragging through the dust. The dockers stand and watch as he passes them. The overseer stands in the doorway of the shed.

Terry gets to the doorway; he totters but remains on his feet. The overseer regards him impassively, then shouts: 'All to work.' The dockers stream forward into the shed; Terry vanishes with them. The priest and the girl stand together, smiling. Friendly appears among the dockers; they stream past, heedless of him. As they pass into the dark shed, the iron door starts to descend. The priest and the girl continue to smile. The workmen have all vanished into the darkness; the iron door closes behind them. The End.

Suppose now that we were presented with this curious sequence in isolation, divorced from the film of which it forms the climax. What would we legitimately conclude its attitude and its import to be? First of all we would presume, I think, that on a superficial level at least, the episode is intended to present some sort of conflict between good and bad. Terry Malloy is obviously 'better' than Johnny Friendly – the film, that is to say, is 'on his side'. Certainly he is more courageous, since he fights his battle himself; and the ordeal of his final, unaided walk reveals a capacity for physical endurance of no mean order. And in some vague way, there is a suggestion that this ordeal is undertaken by him for a principle, selflessly.

On closer examination, however, the principle proves difficult to define. Terry is an individualist; his opposition to Friendly is personal; his concern is with himself. 'I was ratting *on myself* all those years.' Why then the ordeal? A desire to gain leadership through an impressive display of strength? Or, more charitably, perhaps merely because he is persuasively urged into it by someone whose opinion he respects, little as he himself may understand its necessity.

For the truth is that this agonised pilgrimage down the quay is pointless. The mob has been discredited; Friendly's hold is broken; the dockers have it in their power to be their own master. Yet, instead of rising to the occasion, they turn like leaderless sheep in search of a new master. 'If Terry walks, we walk in with him.' If there is any principle expounded here, it is surely not that of democracy. Men collectively – 'the people' – are shown as incapable of either self-government or mutual aid. The dockers are craven: at first they shun the man who has delivered their enemy to justice; they follow him tentatively; they look on passively while he takes a beating. Even Friendly's ignominy is half-accidental; he overbalances into the water. And when their oppressor is vanished, the dockers apparently find themselves lost. To whom are they to turn? To the new strong man, bruised and bleeding though he may be. First, though, he must perform a ritual demonstration of superiority. 'If Terry walks in . . .'

The conception of this sequence seems to me implicitly (if unconsciously) Fascist; the impression is further emphasised by the behaviour of the Catholic priest and of the girl. If one were considering the events, and the behaviour of the participants, realistically, one might be tempted to suppose that in Father Barry the film is concerned to present a particular, rather hysterical priest with a taste for engineering vulgar theatrical effects in real life. (Karl Maiden's playing of the role provides convincing support for this impression.) Plainly, though, the intention is not realistic but symbolic. 'Leave him alone! Take your hands off him!' Such good Samaritans as there may be in the crowd (and we do not see many) get short shrift from Father Barry; and the blessing of the Christian Church is invoked on Terry's suffering. The girl is used to perform an equivalent function. For all her fragile appearance, there is the spirit of a Spartan mother within the breast of Edie; seeing her lover disappear, battered almost out of recognition and hardly able to stand, to perform a day's labour in the dockyard – she smiles contentedly.

With the climax, the social moral seems to become almost overt. In the doorway of the shed stands the overseer; Terry lurches to a stop before him. Authority, well dressed, paunchy, complacently in control, confronts its weary, pain-racked subject. It opens its mouth, to shout an order: 'All to work!' In this relationship, we can only suppose, the ordinary human impulses of generosity and compassion are irrelevant. To pity sheep on their way to the slaughter-house would be the merest simple-minded sentimentalism. It is with this charitable thought that the film comes to an end. The dockers stream out of the daylight into the dark. The priest and the girl smile. The last image, powerful and grim, is of the iron portcullis, descending to shut the workers away in a shadowy and remote world of toil.

Whether intentional or not, the symbolism is unmistakable. There is, it is true, a shot of Friendly, vainly trying to assert his authority again, jostled aside by the dockers as they move forward to work; but there is not much that is positive in the image; it is almost an aside. Nothing expresses a sense of liberation. The impact is made by Terry's battered face, the overseer, the priest and the girl, the expressionless dockers, the portcullis . . . It is a conclusion that can only be taken in two ways: as hopeless, savagely ironic; or as fundamentally contemptuous, pretending to idealism, but in reality without either grace, or joy, or love.

It has been remarked that the success this year of three films like *From Here to Eternity*, *The Caine Mutiny* and *On the Waterfront* is a hopeful sign, demonstrating that inflationary techniques are not essential to the seduction of mass audiences. All we need are good films. It is true that these films share the negative merit of not being in CinemaScope; but in view of the basic corruption of each of them, it is depressing to find that they represent so many people's idea of a 'good film'. *On the Waterfront* is a bad film. Unfortunately, bad films are important too. This one is important because of its special kind of badness, and because of the enormous degree of acceptance it has won.

It has first of all been accepted commercially; turn up any trade paper of the last few months, and you will find a paragraph somewhere rejoicing at its triumphant progress from the West End round the country. Even more remarkable has been its acceptance by the intelligentsia generally, and by the critics in particular. In November it was easily the favourite selection in the Film Institute's publication *Critics' Choice*. For once the panel seemed unanimous. '*On the Waterfront* is good, very good.' 'A haunting film, superbly made . . . grey with pity and terror, it contrives to put in a word for the indestructibility of the human soul . . . the film grinds with the majestic inevitability of a Beethoven symphony to a final chord of hope.' Nor were William Whitebait, Paul Dehn and Fred Majdalany alone in their enthusiasm. *The Financial Times* noted that 'neither the anger nor the indignation has a trace of insincerity.' *The Times* called it 'a grim film which pulls no punches and makes no concessions', and even *Tribune*, where one might have expected some awareness of the social issues involved, found itself carried away: 'His slow-burning and soul breaking into intense but short-lived flame, Marlon Brando – it could be no one but the superb Marlon Brando – is on the screen again.'

The film, in fact, has been accepted at its face value; or, more correctly perhaps, at its *sensation* value – as if it were a strong drink or an electric shock – and liked to a greater or lesser degree, according to individual taste. Here and there objections are made that the last sequence is 'theatrical' or 'melodramatic'; but this is mentioned as a regrettable blot, not as a possible indication of intentions and motives which may have been present all along, though less obvious at first sight.

Yet a preliminary title to the film is quite specific in its claims. The story will show how 'self-appointed tyrants can be defeated by right-thinking people in a vital democracy.' We are entitled, even invited, then, to examine closely the social implications of what we are shown.

The first thing revealed is the virtual absence of at least half the elements necessary to make the situation convincing. A social problem of this kind needs to be placed in a context, shown with a certain fullness, in the round. Rackets like Johnny Friendly's do not spring up out of the ground; they are not the productions of one wicked man. We know that the story of *On the Waterfront* is taken from actuality; yet, as it reaches the screen, the drama is played out in a vacuum. The locations are real, yet the action which takes place on them is as isolated from life as though it were all happening on a succession of stage sets. We are expected to accept Friendly's position and his domination over the waterfront through the agency of (apparently) half a dozen picturesque thugs. The means by which he has achieved his power – through negotiations with ship-owners, on the one hand, through exploiting the dockers' fear of unemployment, on the other – are not clearly shown. Only two episodes hint at the extent of corruption: the very skimped scene at the inquiry (where the emphasis is almost entirely on the personal conflict between Friendly and Terry), and the single shot of one of Friendly's highly placed sponsors watching the proceedings on a television set. This last incident is so elliptically presented, anyway, that one doubts whether most audiences will grasp its meaning. What, meanwhile, of the police? Our sole contact with these is through the two avuncular plainclothes-men who try to persuade Terry to give evidence. And, most significantly, the principle of concerted action (i.e., unionism) is referred to once or twice, but all the emphasis is on the individual gesture. As we have seen, the film's climax evades, or rather perverts this essential issue.

To such criticism it may be objected that the makers of *On the Waterfront* have purposely chosen to dramatise the problem through one particular case: the moral awakening of Terry Malloy. There is nothing to be said against such an approach, so long as its limits are clearly defined. The vital question then arises: what exactly does Terry awake to? Over her first beer-and-chaser, Edie is not slow to remind him that no man is an island; but after this promising start, the subject is dropped. Terry finds his dignity – that is to say, he develops a capacity for individual action; but what he does, he does for himself, to avenge his brother's murder, and for the *beaux yeux* of Edie. All of which has little relevance to the duties of 'right-thinking people in a vital democracy'. In fact, *On the Waterfront* is essentially an extremely artful conjuring trick; underneath its brilliant technical surface, essential conclusions are evaded and replaced by a personal drama whose implications are entirely different. Put another way, one might say that the potency of Marlon Brando – physical, emotional and romantic – is effectively employed to palm off a number of political assertions, all of them spurious and many of them pernicious.

The dishonesty of method becomes clear when we compare *On the Waterfront* with one of America's really great social films. *The Grapes of Wrath* provided its adaptors with a similarly radical subject, where a general social (or political) problem is approached through the sufferings of a handful of selected individuals. Also, as a film *The Grapes of Wrath* owes its greatness to its affirmation of human dignity (as *On the Waterfront* seeks to do), rather than to any factual indictment of the society in which its disasters take place. But it does this without evasions. The background is there; the corruption in the police; the economic pressure which forces the Joads into their hopeless odyssey; the inhumanity of ordinary man to man, and his humanity too. When Tom Joad awakes, it is to the slow realisation that individuality is somehow not enough; that perhaps all men are his brothers. It is no disparagement of Brando to say that he fails where Fonda succeeds, for Brando too is an actor of rare poetic power. In spite of an over-free indulgence of his genius for naturalistic mannerism (and here one suspects the misguiding influence of his director), the enormous passionate honesty he puts into Terry Malloy, his beautiful sensitivity, shines out like truth itself in all this falsity. At times it almost seems as if he is going to save the picture. But no actor can give a film poetic validity on his own; and while Ford's images of human dignity have faith in them to make them true, Kazan's ingenious lip-service reduces all aspiration to a platitude.

An article in the last issue of *Sight and Sound*, 'The *Metteur-en-Scène*', raised some questions which relate interestingly to this one, of Kazan and *On the Waterfront*, and the currently fashionable estimate of each. But Tony Richardson seems to me to have blurred his argument by basing it on a most dubious theoretical premise. He categorises directors according to the relationship he discovers between them and their subject – those who 'dominate' their material; those who 'translate' without 'transforming' it and a third group, the *metteurs-en-scène*, who work in a somewhat shadowy no-man's-land between these two extremes. This does not seem very helpful as a basis for analysis; particularly if it leads us to class Carné and Becker with Kazan, Reed and Orson Welles as directors in whose work 'it is too easy critically to expose the bare and creaky structure behind the façade.'

Some directors create their own world; some do not: here is a valid distinction. Of those who do, some are more successful than others, some greater, some lesser. Of those who do not, some have still something to give of themselves; some have almost nothing, but work honestly and with professional skill (which we should respect) on whatever material comes to their hand. The directors whom Tony Richardson would be more justified in castigating are surely those false creators, with professional talent beyond the ordinary, with heavy-weight pretensions, but without equivalent honesty, insight or sensibility, who undertake significant subjects only to betray them. It is less a question of 'dominating' one's material, than of being truthful about it.

The brilliance with which a film is realised is not sufficient to compensate for emptiness, or fundamental falsity of conception. If we praise a film like *On the Waterfront* for the 'mastery' (etc., etc.) of its direction, we are attaching considerable over-importance to skill on a very superficial, not to say dubious level. One of the few perceptive reviews that this film found in the British press (in the *Daily Worker*) remarked that it was directed 'with every dramatic device except sincerity', and referred to 'a noisy collection of

The last sequence of On the Waterfront: *Terry Malloy's showdown with Johnny Friendly (Marlon Brando and Lee J. Cobb).*

emotional tricks'. This is hysterical film-making, every incident whipped up by tricks to a quite spurious dramatic intensity: music to shock and scare, effects that boom, dialogue incomprehensibly shouted or mumbled in a theatrical affectation of realism, looming close-ups that seek to impose their mood on us by sheer size, jazzed-up cutting and compositions meaninglessly bold. A style, in short, of horrid vulgarity; to which the notion of *decorum* is unknown; using every possible device to batter and bemuse.

The cinema is a hypnotic medium, we know. An audience surrenders easily to a skilfully directed barrage of sounds and images and the allure of an attractive and potent personality. All the more urgent that those who have intelligence to use, should use it, to scrutinise and question, to explore for themselves what may be concealed behind the imposing façade. As I have said, *On the Waterfront* is a political film, and should be considered as such. (Interesting, by the way, is the parallel of another director who now finds himself in the same political position as Kazan – the progression of Edward Dmytryk from the apparent revolt of *Give Us This Day*, to the conformist *Caine Mutiny*, to the Catholicism of Graham Greene's *End of*

511

the Affair.) Lest it be thought by this that I am advocating judgement of films according to any narrow set of specific political principles, let me stress that I am not. I prefer to condemn *On the Waterfront* because analysis reveals a deep human falsity, a demagogic dishonesty of argument; not because it fails to conform to any particular political creed. Here, through the human falsity, one detects the social falsity. *The Daily Worker* was right about *On the Waterfront* but merely fatuous about (for instance) *The Quiet Man.* The true critic will preserve his standards independently; and their application must be as impartial as it must be strict.

Time was . . . But perhaps you say that it is too easy to discountenance *On the Waterfront* by going back fifteen years to compare it with a film so generally acknowledged to be a masterpiece as *The Grapes of Wrath.* I will conclude, then, with a word about another film, which shows that younger talents exist which can undertake themes of this importance with integrity and a true passion. Only five years ago Abraham Polonsky, a writer, directed his first film in Hollywood – *Force Of Evil,* the story of two brothers, one sharp and one stupid, caught in a situation of civic and political corruption. Here the outcome was reversed: the dumb brother is killed, the shyster is brought by tragedy and by love (the girl in this case no shy wallflower, thank heavens, but a proud and morally pugnacious innocent) to a sense of shame, and an acknowledgment of moral responsibility. A film without tricks, but highly individual in writing and direction; with enough genuine human feeling in it to allow for a sense of humour; finely acted, with a most sensitive study by John Garfield of the central character; a last sequence which enclosed and expressed the essential significance of the fable in a series of stern, forlorn, authentically poetic images. A film which attracted little attention, and less favour.

And where is the director of *Force of Evil* today? It remains his only film. He has been banished from Hollywood for his political sympathies. Abraham Polonsky is not working in the American cinema just now.

Hooray for Hollywood

Review of *Jane Fonda* by Thomas Kiernan, *The Unquiet Man: The Life of John Ford* by William Kimber, *Hawks on Hawks* by Joseph McBride, *Moving Pictures: The Memories of a Hollywood Prince* by Budd Schulberg and *Running Time* by Gavin Lambert in *The Guardian*, 19 March 1983

AM I ALONE IN FINDING MYSELF DRIVEN TO EXTREME IRRITATION RECENTLY BY the English infatuation with those damned Oscars? A film director dies and the BBC spouts endlessly about the five Oscars he won, the Oscar Nominations he achieved or the Oscar he was never awarded.

The current poster for *Gandhi* carries four commendations by British critics who can only convey the film's greatness by the certainty that Ben Kingsley merits the Oscar, will be short-listed for the Oscar, must win the Oscar. And if I am ever asked again whether last year's Oscar for *Chariots of Fire* was not 'a shot in the arm' for British cinema, I will answer with a short, sharp shot somewhere quite else.

How many Oscar winners did the Queen patronise at her Twentieth Century-Fox banquet? I know the British emigrés were up at the long table with her, and Tony Richardson (look back, comrades, with a wry smile) was at her left hand. Favoured slaves – of whom?

The American cinema has, of course, always won; and never more decisively than now, when it holds us more firmly captive than ever. 'Hollywood' is the word that works the spell, the talisman, and no present-day corruption or vulgarity can tarnish it.

History did it. A vast expanding nation, markets and money did it. And most of all energy did it, that one indispensable quality. Energy to give greed and ruthlessness and creativity their reward. Some new books that I have read recently, each throwing a different light on the myth, will surely fascinate those who are fascinated by the whole fascinating phenomenon.

Jane Fonda first, because she personifies, crystallises so many themes. The pictures on the jacket tell the story. Not just her story, but the essential story of Hollywood. The compulsive dynamic, the ruthless confidence which have enthralled the world for over 70 years. On the front cover of Thomas Kiernan's *Jane Fonda*, Jane smiles an exhilarated, wide-mouthed, voracious smile, eyes sparkling, expensively capped teeth gleaming. And on the back, still smiling, she reclines on the floor of (I assume) her Jane Fonda Workout Salon, lissom in leotard and black tights, one long, well-shaped leg pointing triumphant to the skies. No wonder the American cinema has had us licked from the start.

Jane Fonda is a star. She is also an actress of great talent, an intelligent, enthusiastic woman who manages to combine genuine concern for people and causes with the inviolable egoism which is the essence of star-quality. She had a privileged start, but not an easy one. Her father, Henry Fonda, was one of America's finest actors; but he was emotionally recessive, dutiful rather than warm in family relationships, often moody and inclined to be more demanding than sympathetic. Her parents separated when Jane was twelve and her mother, depressed and mentally disturbed, killed herself. No wonder the girl grew into an erratic, undisciplined adolescent, then into an autocratic, uncertain and rebellious young woman.

Thomas Kiernan's biography is an odd mixture. At times it is shrewd, in patches well researched. It gives the facts of Jane Fonda's developing social, radical conscience, her growth as a woman and her astonishing progress from dedicated discipleship at Lee Strasberg's Actors' Studio (derided and resented by her father) to Hollywood stardom on pretty much her own terms.

'An American Original' George Cukor called her, and it is true. Idealistic and courageous Jane Fonda has certainly been, flying to Hanoi, flying to India, speaking out for the American Indians, for the Black Panthers and many other causes. Plainly she has a God-given capacity to rationalise her own compulsions into apparently disinterested action.

As a radical colleague put it, 'For some strange reason, her sincerity drives her into obsessive, compulsive behaviour.' Often admirable, often absurd and maddening, never mean-spirited, she seems to have found with her present husband a relationship that can satisfy both her need (paradoxical for such an unswerving feminist) for male sanction and her driving spirit of revolt.

With all this, it is unfortunate that Mr Kiernan lets his subject down by too much slap-happy journalism. When Jane arrives at the Actors' Studio we are told 'even the most celebrity-jaded class members were aquiver with anticipation' – that sort of thing. And he is infuriatingly vague about his sources – 'A friend of hers told me . . .', 'Says another friend . . .' etc., etc. The book has no index, and in spite of being labelled 'a new biography', with a 1982 publication date, does not include (though it illustrates) *On Golden Pond* and Jane's final reconciliation with her father. A pity, because they suffered much from each other, yet persevered, and duty and fondness won – as is not always the case.

Did Jane Fonda ever meet John Ford? I seem to remember (or did I imagine it?) a story of Jane and her anti-war demonstrators picketing the Beverly Hilton Hotel when her father's greatest director and sometime friend was presented with the Medal of Freedom by Richard Nixon, only a few months before Ford died of cancer in 1973.

Dan Ford's biography of his grandfather *Pappy* has been re-titled *The Unquiet Man: The Life of John Ford* for British readership, and contributes quite another, broader and further-reaching view of the Hollywood phenomenon. Sean Feaney, the son of an Irish immigrant, was born in Maine in 1895. He became John Ford only when he arrived in Hollywood at the age of nineteen to act as propman and assistant to his elder brother, who as Francis Ford had become a successful leading man and director of serials for Carl Laemmle's Universal Pictures.

Jack worked for Griffith and rode (he claimed) as a Klansman in *Birth of a Nation*. He started directing two-reeler Westerns in 1917: he matured slowly through the silent twenties (*The Iron Horse, Three Bad Men, Four Sons*) and the talkie thirties: he reached greatness (*Young Mr Lincoln, The Grapes of Wrath*) in 1939, and maintained an extraordinary level of achievement through the late forties, fifties and sixties. It is a record which offers a unique bird's-eye-view of the development of an industry and a popular consciousness.

Dan Ford is not an academic, nor (thank God) a critic. What he has produced in *The Unquiet Man* is a full-length portrait, understanding but not sentimental, of a genius. Ford was a dreadful, lovable man, an uncomfortable, ambiguous, self-torturing man, 'black Irish', one of the few great poets produced by this purely twentieth-century medium, something new in the experience of mankind.

Built by individualists, the film industry has never been indulgent to individual artists; and though Ford made a huge number of popular, successful films, he had to struggle and sacrifice to make many of his greatest successes – *The Informer, The Quiet Man, Stagecoach*. There was an honesty about him too, a truth-to-himself even at his most disgraceful or devious, that made him beloved. This book brings him to life and a whole intensive era with him.

Howard Hawks was a quite different kind of director from his friend John Ford and *Hawks on Hawks* by Joseph McBride is a quite different kind of book. Hawks was a romantic in his own way, but he was not a poet. His films were literal, dramatic, quite without the 'grandeur of generality' (Ford's forte). He was also genially if craftily communicative, unlike Ford who treated questioners like idiot interlopers and amused himself mightily by baffling them with lies.

Howard Hawks started in Hollywood a little later than Ford. He also started as a prop-man (for De Mille, whom he despised). He wrote and produced pictures before he started directing in the mid-twenties. Like Ford he was a 'mainstream' film maker all his life, with successes in every genre from *Scarface* in 1932 to comedies like *Bringing Up Baby* (1938) and *His Girl Friday* (1940), to thrillers, *The Big Sleep* (1946), and Westerns like *Red River* (1948) and such late Wayne adventures as *Rio Bravo* (1959) and *El Dorado* (1967). Incisive, tough and masculine, he shunned pretension. 'All I'm doing is telling a story. I don't analyse or do a lot of thinking about it . . . I think our job is to make entertainment.'

Critics, of course, tend to disapprove of statements as direct (and defensive) as this. Joseph McBride, who has made his book out of a series of conversations he had with Hawks, regrets his 'disinclination to expand on the thematic intentions of his world'. He quotes Truffaut, inflationary in the usual French style: 'In my opinion he is one of the most intellectual film-makers in America'; and Molly Haskell who defines the 'guiding principle' of Hawks as 'the picture of a man poised comically or heroical-ly against an antagonistic nature, a nothingness as devoid of meaning as Samuel Beckett's . . .'

These European – or Europeanised – critics mistake completely the characteristic virtue of American cinema. It is not necessary to place Hawks 'alongside Ozu, McCarey and Rohmer' to value or understand him. Nor should 'intellectualism' be confounded with intelligence. Hawks was a highly intelligent and skilful director. He certainly had his charac-teristic way of looking at the world, and that can be deduced from his films; but he did not feel the need to intellectualise. He was American. Fortunately, Mr McBride, once his sententious introduction is over, reports his conversations excellently. They are stuffed with revealing sto-ries, funny, specific and informative. This book is well worth having.

Ford and Hawks were both second generation men in the American cinema. To me, the chief fascination of Budd Schulberg's *Moving Pictures: The Memories of a Hollywood Prince* is its spritely, anecdotal, absolutely convincing account of the amazing start of the whole business. Here are the Jewish immigrants Zukor, Lasky and Goldfish, Zelezinek, Mayer and Loew, whose indomitable drive to survive and to succeed created the American film industry. Schulberg himself became a writer (*On the Waterfront*, *A Face in the Crowd*): his father was B. P. Schulberg, early publicist and writer for Zukor, later producer, gambler, studio head of Paramount in the days of Dietrich and Sternberg, Jeanette McDonald and Maurice Chevalier.

Schulberg has many good tales to tell about his growing-up years as son of the studio chief: early encounters with the vibrant, unblushing Clara Bow ('an easy winner of the Dumb-bell Award') throwing squashy figs at John Gilbert, Greta Garbo and Norma Shearer from the shelter of a large fig tree on the MGM lot; righteously insulting Sylvia Sidney, his father's protegee and mis-tress. These memories of growing up in Hollywood have irresistible glamour and pathos. But I still return to those earlier sagas of enterprise and intrigue by which the merchants from Dvisnk and Pinsk, from Hungary, Poland, Latvia fought each other and the world to create and control this new medi-um of entertainment for a huge, growing, greedy and classless public.

Moving Pictures is factual, its facts made vivid by the glow of Budd Schulberg's personal recollection and writer's imagination. *Running Time* by Gavin Lambert is imaginary but nourished by the writer's own intimate experience of Hollywood. He escaped from the British Film Institute, where he had created the modern *Sight and Sound*, to Santa Monica to assist Nicholas Ray nearly 30 years ago: and before that, from schooldays and earlier, he was in love with movies.

His novel returns, but in a major key and with far wider ambition, to the territory of his first classic collection of stories, *The Slide Area*. *Running Time* is more genial, more wise: it is epic.

The book has two heroines. Elva Kay, widowed, sharp and determined to survive, arrives in Hollywood in 1919 with her precocious seven-year-old daughter. It is the daughter who becomes the actress, first as Baby Jewell, the infant Sherlock of a serial which the nation takes to its heart: then at Metro, where she graduates to *The Secret Garden* and (as a feminine version of Jim Hawkins) *Treasure Island*. She impresses Mayer and Thalberg (though Louis B. fancies Elva more) and leaps effortlessly into sound with *Freckles*, meets Lon Chaney and Charlestons with Ramon Novarro.

The integration of history and fiction is brilliant, witty and absolutely convincing. Elva, who developed genius as a real estate operator, is revealed as the key to the mysterious (real life) murder of the director William Desmond Taylor, has a long and passionate affair with Bugsy Siegel and ends up a coke-sniffing (but never depraved) fantasist, dedicated to the mythic Hollywood of the past. Her daughter, also a survivor, has a fling with Warren William and a longer-running marriage and affair with a delightful, erratic, irredeemable performer with some of the manic characteristics of Mickey Rooney. The vitality of the whole thing is amazing. No such story could be inspired, I'm afraid, by Elstree, Denham and Pinewood.

Running Time is a comic *tour de force* with a relish and an authority that prevent the story ever slipping into caricature. It proves that for this larger-than-life subject facts are not enough. It takes the shaping spirit of the novelist's imagination to complete the whole picture. Hooray – for the Hollywood that was!

Hype vs. Old Lies

Review of *Hollywood vs. America: Popular Culture and the War on Traditional Values* by Michael Medved and *The Oscars: The Secret History of Hollywood's Academy Awards* by Anthony Holden in *The Daily Telegraph*, 27 March 1993

UNTIL RECENTLY, PUBLISHERS SHRANK FROM BOOKS ABOUT CINEMA. THEY were reckoned to be of minority interest and certain to be remaindered.

But the flourishing of the media has changed everything: technology has revolutionised printing and culture has become a staple. Now books about film come thick and fast. Every week produces a new biography, most of them (especially from the USA) terribly thick. The cinema has become invaluable media-fodder. These two books are horrid examples.

On the dust jacket of *Hollywood vs. America* Michael Medved is described by Jim Svedja, film critic of CBS Radio, as 'not only the most perceptive and persuasive of the major American film critics, but . . . also the most courageous.' This is a surprising label to find attached to the co-author of *The Golden Turkey Awards* and *The Hollywood Hall of Shame*. Medved, in truth, seems to be less a critic than an expert in journalistic hype. He does not examine: he passes judgement. He is much better at research than at either moral or aesthetic analysis. This suits the media very well.

His book has been widely publicised, but it does not contribute much to our appreciation of film either as art or as entertainment. Essentially it is a ferocious attack on libertarian (which too often means sensational) trends in recent American films and television programmes. Its condemnation of sex, violence, bad language and the attack on established values has provided material for many newspaper and television features. It has been serialised by *The Sunday Times*. It has inspired a massive meeting and discussion at the Dominion Cinema, with the author supported by authorities no less distinguished than David Puttnam, Michael Winner, Barry Norman and Josephine (*Damage*) Hart. Supposedly Medved, like a latter-day John Knox, had Hollywood shaking in its shoes.

But this book is not so much about American cinema as it is a work of strongly biased social research. Its bias comes from Medved's preference for 'the old lies' over the 'frankness' of today. But whether it is a symptom of decadence that Meryl Streep and Sissy Spacek have both vomited on screen, or that Alan Rickman forced Madeleine Stowe to drink his urine in *Closet Land*, depends on a much closer exegesis than that provided here under the heading of 'The Urge to Offend'. We have to accept that most films (not all) are produced in order to make money; and as long as profit-making is held to be the chief end of existence – and as long as journalists and their editors continue to give publicity to outrage – things are not likely to improve.

I must not give the impression that Michael Medved's research is altogether valueless, or his strictures quite without foundation. There is no doubt that American TV, particularly in its soaps, has exploited the possibilities of licence and fashionable immoralities. So have many movies, particularly from the independents who reject traditional shibboleths in favour of contemporary freedoms of language and action. But this does not mean we should pine, as apparently Medved pines, for the good old days of Louis B. Mayer and his belief in 'God's Country', hymned with such dutiful conviction by Judy Garland and Mickey Rooney in *Babes in Arms*, still to be wondered at quite frequently on television. The humbug of the past was not much better than the disorder of the present.

Further evidence of the baleful power of the media is provided by *The Oscars*, an exhaustive and exhausting history of Hollywood's Academy Awards by Anthony Holden, himself once, we are told by his publishers, 'an award-winning newspaper columnist and editor'. Prizes and presentations, we are reminded, make good copy and save journalists and advertisers the trouble of actually having to think. They also provide excellent free material for TV programmes. Most artists despise them – and this includes actors and actresses – but are human enough to be glad when they win.

One can only deplore the way the media now make use of awards – in the case of the Oscars, the voted opinions of American film-makers and technicians. For instance, on a BBC radio programme the other day *Rain Man* was described as 'The Oscar-winning Buddy-movie.' And *Howards End* is now advertised as 'Nominated for nine Oscars, including Best Picture' and for 'eleven BAFTA Awards, including Best Film.' Even the National Film Theatre announces its Treasures from the National Film Archive with clichés like 'Oscar-winning success' (*Annie Hall*) and 'Oscar-winner for Best Foreign Film' (*Day for Night*).

Are these vulgarities effective? It is certainly depressing to reflect that all the world loves a prizewinner, especially when we all know that awards are almost always given for reasons quite other than excellence.

I have to admit that I was unable to get through all the 477 pages of this book, which chronicle Oscar competition over the 67 years since the Hollywood Academy was founded. Almost 200 more pages list 'Winners and Losers' and 'Oscar facts and figures', such as 'The only Oscar ever to win an Oscar' (Oscar Hammerstein). The subtitle of the whole cumbersome volume is misleading because the book consists mostly of verifiable facts, padded out with recognisable journalistic gossip. Thus: 'As Cruise lay low at the Bel Air, eating in the solitude of his room rather than joining his co-nominee Robin Williams and show host Billy Crystal in the hotel restaurant, his chances of a win still seemed tantalisingly stronger . . .' If this wets your appetite, you may enjoy this book. The best place for it, I think, is the bathroom.

Lindsay directing Tadeusz Lomnicki as Bill Maitland in John Osborne's
Inadmissible Evidence *at the Contemporary Theatre,*
Warsaw, Poland, 1966.

An International View

Sergei Eisenstein

Review of *Immoral Memories: An Autobiography* by Sergei
Eisenstein and *Nonindifferent Nature: Film and the
Structure of Things* by Sergei Eisenstein in the *Times
Literary Supplement*, March 31–April 6 1989

ON 2 FEBRUARY 1946 SERGEI ESENSTEIN, AGED 48, WAS CELEBRATING THE
award of a Stalin Prize, First Class, for his film *Ivan the Terrible (Part
One)*. His sixth completed film, it had been passed for release by the
Committee for Cinema Affairs over a year before; Eisenstein had just finished editing its sequel, the second part of his planned trilogy – another reason for celebration. Sergei Mikhailovich was not a great dancer, but he was
proud of his way with a foxtrot, which he claimed to have performed 'with
great success even in Harlem'. That night he overdid it. Dancing wildly
with the actress Vera Maretskaya, he felt a sudden intense pain shoot
across his chest. He fell to the floor, the victim of a shattering heart attack.

A doctor ordered Eisenstein to be carried to an ambulance. He refused
to be lifted. He managed to get to his feet and walk steadily from the
room. His friend Grigori Alexandrov drove him to the Kremlin Hospital.
He was Russia's greatest, most innovative, most internationally celebrated, film director; he had known triumph, disgrace and triumph; he was a
brilliant theorist, an outstanding teacher. His personality was warm, jovial
– yet elusive. He was a lonely man. Fatally ill now, he had two more years
to live. In hospital, then at the sanatorium to which he was moved, he
began to write his memoirs.

'Notes', he called them, with a typical lack of pretension; or 'Immoral
Memories'. Not, he stressed, 'Immoral' in the manner of Frank Harris
(whom he dismissed as 'unpleasant, importunate'). He would eschew
morality and moralising altogether. For once, he was not setting out to
teach anyone anything. Like a dying man, Eisenstein saw the image of his
crowded, enthusiastic, perpetually enquiring life flash across his memory.
These are the stuff of his 'Autobiography'.

It was not written for publication in his lifetime – or in Stalin's.
Sometimes one feels it was not even written with much thought of its readers. 'I began to write these memoirs with the sole purpose of giving myself
free rein to drift in the vortices and whirlpools of free association.' This
gives the book a great liveliness, an engaging frankness, glimpses of friends
and fellow-artists by a perceptive, humorous observer. James Joyce auto-
graphing *Ulysses* ('some almost indecipherable marks and the date . . .

obviously drawn from memory'); a visit to Windsor and Eton ('which by its regimen, discipline and spirit, moulds frail, degenerate and overfed boys into soulless and cruel gentlemen'); Paul Eluard breaking up the premiere of Cocteau's *La Voix Humaine* ('like blows of a hammer, he rhythmically intoned the classic *"Merde! Merde! Merde!"'*); André Malraux proving by recitation that he knew by heart the whole of Dostoevesky.

Memories of youthful theatre escapades, of travels in Europe, the United States, Mexico, bulk large. These were Eisenstein's sunshine years, when the young Russian prodigy-genius (he was 23 when he started directing in the theatre, 27 when he made *Battleship Potemkin*) was feted in France, Germany and Britain, signed a contract with Paramount which took him to Hollywood, where he prepared three subjects, all rejected by the studio, and spent an unforgettable year in Mexico. There his tragedy began.

For Eisenstein's life, in spite of his monumental achievements, was a tragedy. His Mexican film was stolen and despoiled. Back in Russia, he found himself in a changed climate, in which revolutionary freedom to experiment had been stamped out under the heavy boot of Socialist Realism. Eisenstein became a lecturer at the Film Institute. It took three years for him to find an acceptable film project: he worked on it for another two years and started shooting – only to have it cancelled (for 'subjectivism', 'formalism' and 'Biblical emphasis'), and his material destroyed. Personally he drifted into isolation, made a companionate marriage and devoted himself to teaching and aesthetic studies as a substitute for creative work. Only with *Alexander Nevsky* (1938) did he return to favour.

Very little of all this figures in Eisenstein's *Immoral Memories*, which leave almost all the big questions unanswered. There is little about his domineering father, little about his possessive mother, who broke up the marriage and the family. There is nothing about his sexual problem, his research in Germany at the Magnus Hirschfeld Institute where he investigated the possibility that he was homosexual (he decided he was not). Politics are scarcely discussed. But what kind of a Marxist was Eisenstein? In his youth he was certainly a revolutionary. Speaking at the Sorbonne in 1930, he subscribed in a naïf way to the ideas and ideals that would later characterise Stalinist cinema. 'The idea that governs our cinema is that same idea that not long ago governed our Revolution. It is the predominance of the collective element over the individual element . . . All film production and distribution is the monopoly of the state. This greatly facilitates the achievement of our educational and cultural aims,' etc., etc.

Did Eisenstein change his mind as the terrible thirties took their victims? The theatre director Meierhold, whom he revered – the writer Babel, with whom he worked – so many of his fellow artists denied, like him, the

Sergei Eisenstein's Ivan the Terrible.

right to work . . . Eisenstein accepted his fate (through fear? through cunning?) and devoted himself more and more obsessively to speculation and aesthetic research, to his compulsive need to propound an all-embracing theory of art. But his avoidance or evasion of so many fundamental issues makes his memoirs a lightweight book, good for the bedside, more diverting than illuminating.

It is tempting to suggest that Eisenstein's increasing labour of writing and lecturing, speculation and philosophising on the subject of art, was essentially the sublimation of a frustrated creative ambition. But this would be to simplify his complex nature. 'In my creative work throughout my life,' he wrote, explaining what his *Immoral Memories* would *not* consist of, 'I have been occupied with composing *à thèse*. I have proved, I have explained, I have taught . . .' His reading was as exhaustive as it was enthusiastic, from Agatha Christie to Goethe, Lewis Carroll to James Joyce. He could derive stimulus from Japanese and Chinese art and Piranesi, from El Greco and the popular art of Mexico. From the start (he was educated as an engineer) he talked, lectured and wrote energetically, compulsively, idiosyncratically. His first essay, 'On Expressionism, America and of course Chaplin' appeared in 1922. A year later came 'The Montage of Attractions', followed by a succession of essays in which he expanded his particular conception of film style. These appeared later in English in translations by his pupil Jay Leyda, and would be found at any time over the last 40 years, ornamenting the bookshelves of every serious student of film: *The Film Sense, Film Essays, Film Form.*

I say 'ornamenting' because I do not believe that many (any?) of these serious film students – and I was one of them – were ever able to read their way profitably through the dense pages of these books. Aesthetics, it is generally acknowledged, have practically nothing to do with the practice of art, or with the enjoyment and understanding of it. And this is certainly true of the theoretical works of Eisenstein. Strangely, they are written not by a remote and ineffectual academic, as is usually the case, but by a film-maker. A film-maker, though, of a unique and sometimes baffling intelligence. As Marie Seton, who loved him and wrote about him, put it: 'In any one meeting he would talk about such a variety of subjects and spin such fine webs of speculative thought, that it was almost impossible to retain with any clarity more than a fraction of the conversation.' And as he spoke, so he wrote.

There are plenty of fine webs of speculative thought in *Nonindifferent Nature*. This is Eisenstein's last theoretical work; he was writing it when he died, and here it is translated (like the memoirs) by another of his pupils, Herbert Marshall. The Cambridge University Press, in its jacket blurb, gives a pretty fair idea of this 'engaging but difficult work', which it describes as 'the most advanced stage of Eisenstein's thinking on the structure of film', which 'reveals dramatically the "second Eisenstein" after his shift from a Pavlovian to an organic viewpoint.'

Eisenstein in this late work went beyond his early theories of the 'montage of attractions' – film construction as the piece-by-piece assembly of colliding images – to develop a theory of pathos, 'the heightened emotional states produced by works of art'. (I am quoting from Herbert Eagle's useful introduction to this volume.) Such a state of heightened emotion, he believed, could only occur through 'a compositional structure identical with human behaviour in the grip of *pathos*'. ('*Pathos*' is used by Eisenstein to signify inspiration or ecstasy – artistic creation at its most intense.) 'The organic unity of a work,' (this is Eisenstein) 'as well as the sense of organic unity received from the work, arises when the law of the construction of this work corresponds to the laws of *the structure of organic phenomena of nature.*'

The second half of *Nonindifferent Nature* develops an argument along different lines. This is described by Mr Eagle – and I have no reason to doubt him – as 'the culmination of Eisenstein's work on the subject of "vertical montage" and "polyphonic structure" first investigated in *Film Form.*' The fragmented montage of *Potemkin* gives place to a 'systematic unity of diverse components'. Those whose interest is in aesthetics rather than cinema will be able to judge from this just what intellectual stimulus and nourishment they can expect from those final essays of Eisenstein.

And the rest of us?

It was Dovzhenko, the great Ukrainian poet-film-maker and Eisenstein's contemporary, who said, 'I'm convinced in more ways than one that his erudition is killing him.' He also said that one can burst from too much knowledge, and he feared that this would happen to Eisenstein. And did it? He was labouring at an essay on colour in cinema when he died: the black handwriting of the manuscript broke off abruptly, followed by a red scrawl . . . A last, fatal heart attack had cut him short.

Questions remain. What influence did Eisenstein exercise with all this thought, all this speculation, all this writing? Not, surely, a great deal. Intellectual cinema, with its self-consciousness of style, its impersonality, its dialectical ambition, has not flourished. Eisenstein himself abandoned his bizarre idea of filming *Das Kapital*. Today the 'intellectual montage' of *October* seems an obvious manipulation of symbols that fails to persuade; in *Ivan the Terrible* it is the magnificent acting of Cherkassov (never acknowledged by Eisenstein) which goes some way to atone for the alienating coldness of the style.

Another question. Would Eisenstein have so immersed himself in theory if his creative gift had not been stifled by the oppression of politics? How did those dreadful years of enforced silence, of self-suppression, affect him? Of course, we can never know. We can only remember the perilous conditions under which he produced his work, and which partly shaped it. And remember too the lonely, laughing artist who died at his desk, with no companion. Marie Seton describes how the margins of his books were pencilled with his personal, intimate comments. In *Idols Behind Altars* by Anita Brenner, he had marked a line: 'Laugh thereafter though they speak in much solemnity.' Beside it Sergei Mikhailovich had written one word – '*Me!*'

Theoretical Writings of Eisenstein

Review of *On the Composition of the Short Fiction Scenario, A Premature Celebration of Eisenstein's Centenary* and *Eisenstein on Disney* by Sergei Eisenstein in *The Sunday Telegraph*, 19 March 1988

WE HAVE HAD A LOT OF SERGEI MIKHAILOVICH EISENSTEIN DURING THIS PAST year – the ninetieth since his birth and the forty-first since his death. There was an exhibition, 'Eisenstein at Ninety' at the Hayward Gallery. The British Film Institute started publishing a series of his selected writings. There has been a season of his films at the National Film Theatre, most of them also shown on BBC2. An American entrepreneur has presented *Alexander Nevsky* at the Festival Hall, with full, live orchestral accompaniment. It has been something of a renaissance for one of the cinema's greatest, most ill-used artists.

Has any film-maker achieved a reputation so overwhelming from such a relatively small body of work? Or suffered worse frustration? His career went off like a rocket. His first film, *Strike*, showed brilliant originality; his second, *Battleship Potemkin*, swept the world. Still in his twenties, Eisenstein was handling film with an experimental mastery which put him up there with D. W. Griffith as one of the masters of the twentieth century's new art.

Unfortunately Eisenstein was not just an artist: he was a compulsive intellectual. Not only did he make films, he could not stop writing about them, talking about them, speculating and theorising. Selections of his essays translated (usually with awful clumsiness) into English have achieved classic status. I am not sure this means they are still much read. Today's film students, when they bother to listen or to think, are more likely to find themselves subjected to auteurist, structuralist or semiological discourse – though I understand that these Frenchified fashions are now on their way out. Eisenstein's theory of the 'montage of attractions', his claim that the organic unity of a movie 'corresponds to the laws of the structure of organic phenomena of nature' – one cannot imagine this kind of stuff cutting much ice at the National Film School or at Robert Redford's Sundance Institute. Has the new edition of selected writings, published under the aegis of the BFI, really 'revolutionised knowledge of Eisenstein as a writer and thinker'? I haven't noticed it.

Here are three little books which at least have the merit of brevity, and of containing material new in English, some of it quite comprehensible. They are nicely produced, if rather expensive, and the result of a happy collaboration between Methuen and Seagull Books of Calcutta. The sources are various and sometimes unexpected. *On the Composition of the Short Fiction Scenario* dates from the German invasion of Russia in 1941. Eisenstein had the idea that at a time when the production of full-scale features had become impossible, Russian film-makers should collaborate on a series of 'Fighting Film Albums' (a more likely translation would surely be 'Anthologies'). These would group short stories or documentaries together for distribution instead of full-length features. Eisenstein gave two lectures. The first analyses a story by Ambrose Bierce as a possible subject; the second examines two alternative versions of an original script. (The second and demonstrably better of these was filmed by Pudovkin.) Here Eisenstein's writing is concrete, sensible and helpful. It is a pity that none of the resulting films has ever been shown outside Russia.

The second book in the series calls itself *A Premature Celebration of Eisenstein's Centenary*. It is an odd sort of celebration, a bit of a ragbag, starting with an angry, confused exchange between the young director and his sponsors at the Moscow Proletkult ExecBureau, disputing the script credit for *Strike*. This resulted in Eisenstein's resignation (expulsion?) from the Proletkult, who objected to his 'formalistic and psychoanalytic twistings' – the first but by no means the last of his conflicts with cultural bureaucracy.

Other letters follow: 'To Japanese Colleagues', 'To a Latin-American Poet', and to his friend, the documentary film editor Esther Shub. Some of these are personal, some perfunctory. They could certainly have done with better explanatory editing and more colloquial translation. So could a dense section 'On Imagery'. ('Impressionism as a *method of cognizance* of concrete reality warrants unconditional condemnation . . .' etc.) Finally there is an application from Samuel Beckett (writing from Dublin in 1936) for admission to the Moscow State School of Cinematography. This seems to have gone unanswered.

With the third and most ambitious of these pamphlets we are back, I am afraid, with Eisenstein the wild and whirling polymath. A light-hearted title, *Eisenstein on Disney*, promises some fun; and a jovial photograph on the cover shows a beaming Sergei Mikhailovich shaking hands with his 'best friend in the USA' – Mickey Mouse.

But, as always when Eisenstein gets serious, his writing loses humour and clarity. He has – let it at last be admitted – no gift for exposition. The surrender to intellectual subjectivism is complete. The best things in the book are his drawings, witty, grotesque and suggestive. Otherwise there is little either to entertain or to enlighten. There are certainly no concessions to the common reader. Here, in a single chapter, are the references we are invited to digest: Victor Hugo, Chaplin, Darwin, Lewis Carroll, Walter Trier (remember those *Lilliput* covers?) and Hokusai. Mary Baker Eddy and Aimee Semple MacPherson. Dr Erich Wulffen (author of *Der Sexualverbrecher*), Bloch and Näcke (sexologists?). Wagner and Rachilde (pseudonym of Marguerite Vallette Eymery, French writer closely associated with the Symbolists). Moses, Zoroaster and Buddha. Napoleon and Gorky. Mallarmé and the Russian fabulist Krylov. Taine, Grandville (French satirical artist who drew animals as human types), La Fontaine and Buffon (naturalist, 1707-88). Shakespeare, Aristophanes and Ovid.

A fourth paperback is promised in the Methuen-Seagull series, *The Psychology of Composition*. And British Film Institute Publishing (in collaboration with the Indiana University Press) announce two more volumes of *Selected Works: Towards a Theory of Montage* and *Writings 1935-1947*. More formalistic and psychoanalytic twistings may be anticipated. Sometimes, in spite of our necessary respect for the great, put-upon artist, our sympathy goes out to the Moscow Proletkult ExecBureau.

Kozintsev's *Lear*

Review of *King Lear: The Space of Tragedy* by Grigori Kozintsev in *The Guardian*, 4 April 1977

IT WAS ALWAYS A PLEASURE TO MEET GRIGORI KOZINTSEV AND HERE, IN THIS journal of the making of his last film *King Lear*, it still is. In the fifties and sixties he was often to be found at film festivals, at Cannes or at Venice, when those occasions still had some style to them, representing his country or showing one of his civilised, distinguished films. Gentle, wistfully smiling, endlessly discursive – it was always difficult to remember that in the exciting, iconoclastic days of early Soviet cinema he had been an exuberant experimentalist, a founding father of Eccentric Cinema.

In the twenties Kozintsev and his creative twin, Leonid Trauberg, moved from irreverent anti-naturalism to the eloquent expressionism of *The New Babylon*, one of the classics of silent Russian cinema. In the thirties, the tandem progressed to poetic realism with their beautiful *Maxim* trilogy, the education of a Communist. Then Stalinism weighed down, and Trauberg, being Jewish, was barred from direction. Kozintsev's fate was not so tragic; he was never crushed like Eisenstein or Dovzhenko. All the same, the biographical and literary subjects he devoted himself to for the rest of his life somehow inspired respect rather than excitement. Even those who survived Stalinism had a price to pay.

Kozintsev was, or became, an amateur in the most refined sense of the word. He loved Shakespeare and this diary is his tribute. It is not a detailed, or even comprehensive, account of the making of his *King Lear* (his last film and the successor to his more widely celebrated *Hamlet*).

The 'diary' is really a sequence of ideas, reminiscences and experiences, set down at odd intervals by the director during the long travail of preparation, shooting and completion. It is friendly, speculative, far-ranging, from its reflective start in Soami's Stone Garden in Kyoto to its final vivid glimpses of Shostakovitch at work on the score.

In print (as he was in life) Kozintsev is an artist of extraordinary charm and intelligence, sometimes rather maddening. He corresponded regularly with Peter Brook, another brilliant eclectic, who was filming *Lear* too at about the same time. 'What interested Brook most of all was the delocalisation of space', he notes, and he calls his own book *The Space of Tragedy*. I prefer his warmer, simpler side. For instance: 'Art is a reflection of life, of course. But how does this reflection come about? Only by the power of the awakened response, by suffering and by sympathy.' There speaks the Russian poet.

L'Atalante, the Forgotten Masterpiece

Independent on Sunday, 13 July 1990

I WAS TALKING THE OTHER DAY TO A YOUNG FILM-MAKER, A GRADUATE OF our National Film School and already the author of two reputable features. I mentioned the name of John Garfield. 'Who's John Garfield?' He had never heard of Jean Arthur either and had no idea what films Capra had made. I was startled. I began to wonder how many distinguished names, knowledge of whom one would assume to be an essential for cinematic literacy, were unknown to the talented young of today. 'Have you ever,' I asked, 'heard of Jean Vigo?' 'Jean who?' he asked.

I know we have to accept that today nobody knows anything, and is quite happy that way. Plainly it is no use writing about 'Vigo and his lovely *L'Atalante*, as though one's readers know who he is, or what it is. So take note. Jean Vigo was a French film-maker who died in 1934, at the age of 29. He had made only four films; but two of them were (are) masterpieces. Few artists in the history of cinema have won a reputation so high by achievement so modest. If, that is, works of genius can be described as modest.

Vigo's father was an anarchist, who adopted the name of Almereyda – an anagram of '*Y'a la merde*', or 'there is shit'. A militant, he was imprisoned and murdered by the authorities in jail. Jean inherited the same violent moral sense, the same responsible disrespect, though he was not a militant. When he was 24 he made his first film, a satirical documentary called *À Propos de Nice*, which he subtitled '*point de vue documentée*'. About this witty, indignant work he said: 'I don't know whether the result will be a work of art, but I am sure it will be cinema.' In other words, he was an artist, not a critic.

Vigo's second film was one of a series of shorts about sport, an inventive portrait of the swimming champion Tans. Then he had one of those strokes of luck which all artists need. He met an agreeable businessman who had the idea of producing medium-length films – and had the good taste and the courage to commission one from Vigo. The subject they chose was derived from his traumatic experience of boarding school. Vigo called it *Zéro de Conduite: Nought for Conduct*. This is one of his two films which every schoolboy should know.

There is something portentous about the word 'masterpiece'; and nothing could be less portentous than *Zéro de Conduite*. Its tone is light, lyric, personal and completely original. It is ferocious in its satire of the grotesque teachers who persecute the schoolboys (all except the young master who likes to impersonate Chaplin); but it is a comic ferocity, the spirit is never heavy, always resilient. A picture I myself directed has sometimes been described as plagiarised from it. I am happy to admit that *If. . . .* was influenced by it. When David Sherwin and I were starting on the script, we screened *Zéro de Conduite*, not to purloin its anarchistic spirit (of which we had plenty of our own), but to learn from what we called its 'epic' structure. Like Vigo, we were setting out to make a film in which the theme was the story.

This is Vigo's poetic method, episodic, fragmentary, charged. Interestingly, both *Zéro de Conduite* and *If. . . .* end with an outbreak of violence, both comic, mischievous in Vigo's case, lethal in ours. But our climax of violence in the quad was not just a transposition of Vigo's barrage of books, shoes and stones from the rooftop. Our Mick Travis is left firing desperately, trapped by the massed fire power of the establishment. Vigo's children escape joyfully along the skyline, singing their Maurice Jaubert song of liberty.

Innocence did not save *Zéro de Conduite* from the outrage of authority. Audiences demonstrated, for and against, and the film was soon banned from public exhibition. But Vigo's luck held. His patron kept faith and confidence in him, and he was able to go on to the production of his second masterpiece. This was a love story, adapted from an original script about which Vigo was not greatly enthusiastic, but which he felt he could make his own. This he did.

'*L'Atalante*' is the name of a barge, working the canals between Paris and the sea. There are three in the crew: Jean, the young captain; Père Jules, the grizzled seadog, with his collection of exotic souvenirs and his gramophone with the enormous horn; the cabin boy, a rather mysterious, observing presence. Also many cats. The start of the film is the marriage of Jean to Juliette, a delicate yet sturdy country girl. The little crowd of guests follows the idyllic couple walking alone except for each other, down village streets, round haystacks and through fields . . . The cabin boy's bouquet falls in the river and he runs off to search for more flowers,

Jean Dasté (back to camera) with Jean Vigo and Dita Parlo on the set of Vigo's L'Atalante.

returning hugely garlanded with leaves, just in time to retrieve his bouquet from the water, and thrust it dripping into the bride's arms . . . Night falls and Juliette stands dreamlike in white at the prow of the barge. Jean comes to take her and gets scratched by the cats . . . He carries her into the cabin; they embrace and she kisses his bleeding face.

The story of *L'Atalante* is like the *prétexte* of a ballet. Life is strange for the young bride with Père Jules and his cats and the enticement of the bright lights of the city. Juliette runs off and gets lost. Jean surrenders to despair. Père Jules brings her back. Romance is restored. The magic is not in the story, but in the continuous flow of poetic invention, the intensity of romantic feeling, the subtleties and richness of the characters. Vigo was fortunate in the stars which commerce demanded. Michel Simon, most idiosyncratic of great character actors, is an unforgettable Père Jules, the ambiguous guardian of a storehouse of memories and mementoes. (Simon was completely sympathetic to Vigo. 'What's he done?' he asked when it was suggested he should work with him. 'A film banned by the Censor.' 'Ah – bravo! I like that . . .') Dita Parlo (Juliette) had been a silent star in Germany; a fragile but strong-willed beauty, she went on to work for Renoir in *La Grande Illusion*. Jean Dasté and Louis Lefèbvre were old comrades from *Zéro de Conduite*. So was the cameraman Boris Kaufman, brother of the explosive Russian documentarist Dziga Vertov, who later went to America and shot *On the Waterfront*.

Narrative always presents a problem for the poetic film-maker, and no one would claim for *L'Atalante* the virtues of shapeliness or smoothness of construction. Additionally, it was chopped about by the distributors, who thought they could make it more commercial by imposing a hit song, 'Le Chaland Qui Passe', and making that the title of the film. Here it is, devotedly restored. This *L'Atalante* is as true to Vigo as any version we are ever likely to see.

If ever an artist sacrificed himself to his work, that artist was Jean Vigo. He suffered from a fatal lung infection, its progress undoubtedly hastened by his persistence in the shooting of *L'Atalante* through a damp, cold winter. He died shortly after the film opened. He left a film which opposes, more wholly and more beautifully than any I can think of, the conception of cinema that largely obtains today – a cinema of sensation, of technical display, of coarse (however sophisticated) commercialism. Vigo's cinema is intimate and personal, its ideas always poetic. The only violence is that of truthful, whole-hearted feeling.

May I suggest that the National Film School hire a bus or two and drive its students up to the Lumière. Attendance compulsory. The experience may not bring them nearer an award-winning music video, or a *Film on Four*; but it will do them a lot of good in other ways.

Leni Riefenstahl

Review of *The Sieve of Time: The Memoirs of Leni Riefenstahl* in *The European*, 1994

ONE JUNE AFTERNOON IN 1924 AN EXCEPTIONALLY BEAUTIFUL YOUNG woman was standing on a subway platform in Berlin, on her way to see the doctor who would, she hoped, cure the pain in her knee which threatened to end her meteoric career as a solo dancer. This was Leni Riefenstahi. On the wall opposite her, as she waited for her train, a highly-coloured poster first attracted, then fascinated her. It advertised *Mountain of Destiny*, 'a film about the Dolomites by Dr Arnold Franck.' Leni let her train come and go, then hobbled out across the square (she could only walk with a stick) and found the cinema, where she was entranced by Franck's film, all clouds, mountains, alpine slopes and peaks. Her life changed. With characteristic determination she arranged a meeting with Franck at the Rumpelmeyer pastry shop on Kurfürstendam (of course he fell violently in love with her) and became an actress and a climber – and later, under Franck's influence, a film-maker.

The incident was typical of the impulse, passion and conviction which had marked – and have marked ever since – the life and work of Leni Riefenstahi. She has often changed direction, always with enthusiasm and, against all odds, outstanding success. At the age of 22 she had achieved fame as a dancer. Her father had been much against this. A successful middle-class businessman, he gave his daughter a disciplined, very German upbringing. He kept her away from men (or tried to), sent her to domestic science college and denied her ambitions to act, or to dance. Or tried to. From the start, Leni was an enthusiast and an obsessive, determined on some kind of artistic career and on independence. Her father was forced to give way and she became a dancer, with immediate success performing throughout Europe, in Berlin, Paris and London. She broke bones in her feet three times, then tore the muscle in her knee, which caused a growth of cartilage 'the size of a walnut'. An operation was successful. But by that time she had met Franck, and switched to a new career.

The spectacular mountain films which Leni Riefenstahl made, first as an actress with Franck, then by herself as actress and director [*The Blue Light*], were hugely applauded. In the first half of the thirties, she was a leading figure in European cinema. Sternberg, who became her friend, wanted to take her to Hollywood; but she refused to go. Her real fame, though, and later her notoriety, came as a result of her meeting and relationship with Hitler, and her tremendously impressive documentary of the Nazi Party rally at Nuremberg in 1934, *The Triumph of the Will*. Even more memorable was *Olympiad*, her film of the Berlin Olympics in 1936, whose power and poetry have never been surpassed.

Olympiad remains a wonderful film, and Leni Riefenstahl's account here of its preparation, its shooting and (above all) its editing shows the meticulous concentration of the true film artist. It won the Grand Prix at Venice at the last festival before the War. But its identification with the Nazi myth cast a shadow over its director for the rest of her life. And it put an end to her career as a film-maker.

One cannot help feeling that this condemnation, and the continual repression that went with it, has been largely unjustified. Leni Riefenstahl was naive, and certainly unwise in accepting the patronage of Hitler and the party. But she is by no means the only artist to have sacrificed her good name to the possibility of practising her art. Films are expensive; they demand organisation and sponsorship. 'You can and you will do this project,' Hitler had insisted, when the idea was proposed of a film about the Nuremberg rally. 'It sounded almost like an order.' The alternative was inactivity. Also, Leni was fascinated by Hitler: 'I had never met anyone with such powers of persuasion.' She denies that she was ever his mistress, though the accusation was often made. She probably tells the truth. But no wonder she obeyed him, and no wonder she went on to film the Olympics in 1936. In a political world, though, there is no such thing as an unpolitical documentary. Such can be the cost of a masterpiece.

Dedication implies disproportion and even a kind of fanaticism. And often a lack of humour. These are all a part of Leni Riefenstahl's personality, which is faithfully reflected in her memoirs. They are extraordinarily detailed, always subjective and absolutely truthful, I am sure, in their account of the penance which her acceptance of Hitler's patronage brought with it. But of course the Nazi connection is only part of the story. Her book is over 600 pages long and plunges forward into the four hundreds when she leaves Europe for America in 1956 and attempts once again (and again unsuccessfully) to make a film about the still-flourishing slave trade. She turned to photography, lived with, and produced a fine book about the Nuba, then turned to underwater exploration and produced another splendid book of photographs.

Add to this a long succession, of course, of sexual encounters and adventures. Leni spurned Dr Goebbels, with unfortunate results, and seems to have ended up in bed with most of her cameramen. She made one tempestuous experiment in matrimony. 'I knew,' she writes, remembering her childhood, 'that no matter what might happen to me, as long as I lived, I would say "Yes" to life.' She was 90 last August; she is saying it still.

Encounter with Prévert

Sight and Sound, July-September 1953

ST PAUL, ONE OF THOSE LITTLE, WALLED TOWNS PERCHED ON A ROCKY eminence, about 30 miles inland from Cannes, is a place that has managed to remain remarkably itself in spite of its cultivation by a number of French artists and film people, and its consequent attraction of tourists, buses and souvenir shops. Jacques Prévert has lived there for some years now, in a little, plain, pink, pleasant house just up the road from the Colombe d'Or – the wonderfully situated hotel, decorated all over with paintings by contemporary French masters, which is where St Paul's habitués are apt to gather. This is where I met him.

It was almost a disaster. I happened to be carrying, or had just put down on a table, a book called *Dieu au Cinéma*, which I was reading for review. Prévert looked at it. 'It's rather good,' I said, in a tone which nicely implied (or was meant to imply) that I knew quite well what his *a priori* attitude towards such a book would be, that to a considerable extent I sympathised with him, but that in all honesty M. Amedée Ayfre had written a creditable book. Prévert was intransigent. '*Livre imbécile,*' he remarked, smacking it down on the table. But a little later he took it up again and began peering inside the uncut pages. At last he found what he was looking for – the particular reference to his films with Carné. '*Voila!*' he exclaimed, and quoted with scorn, '"*Mais toutes ces histoires méritent une étude particulière. Laissons les pour l'instant . . .*"' And he chuckled over what evidently struck him as fresh proof of Catholic evasion.

Well, it was no good trying to get Prévert to be fair to M. Ayfre, though M. Ayfre writes very fairly of him. For instance, he says of the Carné-Prévert films amongst others: 'If, in such works, there is no reference to "religion", it is because religion would be incompatible with their particular climate; because there is no room to spare for it in this world already full, already "significant" in itself. A religious sense could only be imposed on it from the outside . . .' If the word 'religion' were not such a red rag to Prévert (as he says, that and 'war' are the two things in the world for which he has no patience whatever), he would surely be pleased to be so well understood. You do not need to be long in his company to know that he does indeed find himself in a significant world. His distastes are not based intellectually (at least that was my impression); they are rather the violent emotional obverse of his loves. He loves women, children, animals, and men – in that order.

But this may wrongly give the impression of someone testy or self-important. Paradoxically, I think his vehemence is the result of his utter lack of the latter quality. He is grey-haired but smooth-faced; half cherub, half satyr. He bubbles over with youthful enthusiasm, intolerance, and a continuous play of whimsical, disrespectful humour. A cigarette droops habitually from his lips, through which there flows in conversation a staccato torrent of words – difficult for even many a Frenchman to follow precisely. An extremely fascinating position to be in, it may be imagined, for even without understanding a word you would perceive that an endless succession of witty and piercing and challenging things were being said.

I didn't 'interview' him, of course; so these are only a few sniffs of personality. He likes England, that is to say London, which is all he knows of it. (*'J'adore surtout Limehouse.'*) He does not read English, but in translation loves de Quincey and Blake. Also Hogarth, particularly for what he describes as his masterly *theatrical* staging. Modern English writing doesn't mean much to him: Graham Greene, of course, is out of it, and anyway he greatly prefers our women writers. Virginia Woolf: *'Les Vagues – vous avez lu ça? – c'est magnifique!'* As usual with foreigners, he admires our cinema but for its *unreality*. *Kind Hearts*, of course, and *Dead of Night*, and *Henry V*. Realism, of course, is not his cup of tea; *Bicycle Thieves* doesn't interest him much, though *Sciuscia* is a different matter. He has no time for *The Third Man* (Greene again), but he found *The Rake's Progress* extraordinary . . .

Bergman's Reticent Confessional

Review of *The Magic Lantern* by Ingmar Bergman in *The Spectator*, 4 June 1988

WHEN INGMAR BERGMAN WAS BORN, HIS MOTHER WAS SUFFERING FROM Spanish influenza. Perhaps this affected the baby; it certainly affected his mother's ability to feed him. His grandmother took him out of hospital and found him a wet nurse who saved his life. But he remained a sickly child, who was 'always vomiting and had constant stomach aches'.

Here at the start are two constant, surely related themes in this autobiography. The theme of family and the theme of recurrent (psychosomatic? neurasthenic?) illness. So influential does Bergman feel those early days to be, that he writes as though he was already fully conscious. 'I suffered from several indefinable illnesses and could never really decide whether I wanted to live at all.' Of course, he cannot really know his mental state in infancy, but his first conscious memory ('suddenly I vomit over everything') is characteristic. And the recurrence of such memories is constant in this life-story which is, above all, or certainly seems to be, honest, unflinching.

> I have always suffered from what is called a nervous stomach, a calamity as foolish as it is humiliating . . . It is like housing an evil demon in the most sensitive core of your body . . . In all the theatres I have worked in for any length of time, I have been given my own lavatory. These conveniences are probably my most lasting contribution to the history of the theatre.

There are smiles in this book, but they are generally sardonic.

Most readers will be attracted to this autobiography by its author's great reputation and achievement as a film-maker. They will not be disappointed, as long as they do not expect an account of his career that is detailed or comprehensive. Bergman's relationship with his readers is rather a strange one; sometimes he seems to be writing more for himself than for them. At times he tells his story in a direct, objective way, so that we know where he is and why. But more often we are not told very much about why a particular film was written, or exactly why Bergman feels what he does about it. He describes *The Seventh Seal*, for instance, as 'an uneven film which lies close to my heart, because it was made under diffi-

Victor Sjostrom in Ingmar Bergman's Wild Strawberries.

cult circumstances in a surge of vitality and delight.' That is about all. But we are given a glimpse, worth more perhaps than any critical exposition, of the shooting of the unforgettable Dance of Death which is the climax of the film, achieved at hectic speed because most of the actors had finished for the day. Assistants, electricians, a make-up man and two summer visitors, who never knew what it was all about, had to dress up in the costumes of those condemned to death. A mute camera was set up and the image captured before the cloud dissolved.

Bergman is highly intelligent; but he writes as a practising artist, not a critic. His obsession with cinema started early. As a little boy, he was taken to see a film of *Black Beauty* and was 'overcome by a fever that has never left me.' Next Christmas he swapped a hundred of his tin soldiers for the Magic Lantern which was his brother's present. You turned a handle and the people on the screen moved; from that moment he was a film-maker. Yet it was in the theatre that his career began, first as an assistant at the Stockholm Opera, then in charge of a huge, decrepit provincial theatre, which he took over at the age of 25. These chapters of early theatre work are among the most likeable in Bergman's story. It was a time of learning and discovery, with a sense of busy enjoyment, of comradeship in creativity which contrasts attractively with the often painful chronicles of his film-making, his marriages, his affairs and his guilty self-involvement. Bergman's theatrical career climaxed with his three-and-a-half years as director of the Swedish Royal Dramatic Theatre – a time which exemplifies the extraordinary energy which seems to have characterised his whole life. 'During my 42 months as director, I did seven productions, two films and wrote four scripts.' He writes more about his time in the theatre than in the cinema; but few of his productions are fully described. What, one cannot help wondering, were they like? Probably uneven. Bergman's *Hamlet*, which our National Theatre presented last year, was dreadfully silly; his *Miss Julie* was a great deal better. But he is neither pretentious nor defensive about his work. 'From a strictly professional point of view, my years as a theatre director were wasted.' One knows how he feels.

Bergman has constructed his book in a subjective, associative way, not necessarily chronological or always clear. The result is poetic, confessional. There are brief, expressive sketches of artists he has encountered: Garbo, Olivier, Ingrid Bergman. He talks illuminatingly of his professional methods, creative beliefs. Continually, though, and compulsively he returns to the traumatic experiences of childhood and family: his father, the puritanical pastor whom he hated and tried to love; his mother, whom he loved but could never understand or come near to; the elder brother he would like to have murdered; the younger sister 'crushed into a scream'. All of them somehow more real, more vividly described than the many wives, children, beautiful mistresses who come and go, often vaguely, through the years.

The book ends where it begins, with Mother. Only after her death does Bergman seem to approach understanding. He searches in her diary for July 1918 – the month of his birth. She writes what would be an appropriate epigraph to this unique, reticent, revealing portrait of an artist. 'One will probably have to manage alone as best one can.' Like mother, like son.

Satyajit Ray, Commitment to Humanity

Review of *Satyajit Ray, The Inner Eye* by Andrew Robinson in *The Spectator*, 7 April 1990

BEFORE DAVID LEAN STARTED SHOOTING *A PASSAGE TO INDIA*, HE TOLD AN interviewer, 'I don't think anyone has really captured India on the screen, with the possible exception of parts of Renoir's *The River*.' Obviously Lean's acquaintance with Indian-language cinema was minimal, or he could not have so confidently dismissed the extraordinary fresco of Bengali life, historical as well as contemporary, documentary as well as fictional, intelligent as well as poetic, which is the life achievement of the great film-maker Satyajit Ray. (Ray, I'm glad to say, got his own back when he described Lean's film, not unjustly, as of 'some professional competence but not Forster at all'.)

Of course, there were Indian films which broke the crude conventions of popular cinema before Ray – mostly films of protest, influenced by European neorealism – but not very many, and none with his distinction. At the Cannes Festival in 1956 journalists were happy to learn that the competition entry which clashed with the Japanese reception was a new film by an unknown director from Bengal. Everyone wanted to go to the Japanese party where there were sake and (sometimes) free umbrellas; and here was a programme that could be safely skipped. Which is why the showing of *Pather Panchali* was attended by only a few critics; and when it won its prize, most of the Western journalists knew nothing about it.

Yet Satyajit Ray's first film was – and still is – one of those inspired works that announce the arrival of a fresh, wholehearted, masterly talent. It is a lyric work, as intelligent as it is poetic, a story of peasant life and childhood, its material the happiness and sorrow common to all humanity except the very rich or the hopelessly poor. Andrew Robinson quotes Kurosawa's description of his feelings after repeated viewings of the film: 'Each time I feel more overwhelmed. It is the kind of cinema that flows with the serenity and the nobility of a great river.' *Pather Panchali* was immediately recognisable as a classic work, in the cinema's great humanist tradition.

Like Mark Donskoi's fine (now unfashionable) *Childhood of Gorki*, the film expands into a trilogy which shows, less lyrically but with hardly less poetry of style, its small hero's growth to manhood and maturity. But Ray has never been a revolutionary. Social themes have always given richness and validity to his work, but the films are never specifically political. In early days he was criticised by his contemporaries and by youthful radicals for a lack of political commitment. But look back on the 30 or so films of his career, on his stories of middle-class struggle in Calcutta, his adaptations from Tagore (which produced at least one masterpiece, *Charulata*) and from other Bengali writers, his ironic historical fables like *The Music Room* and *The Chess Players* . . . In retrospect it is clear that this is an artist who has stubbornly maintained a proper commitment – to his art and to humanity. Wisdom has always protected him from idealism.

Andrew Robinson did not set himself an easy task when he undertook a biography of Satyajit Ray. Born into a Bengali family of intellectual and creative as well as social distinction, Ray is both reticent and proud. He does not easily accept the inaccuracies and vulgarities of publicity. 'I don't want another foreigner writing a book about me without learning Bengali', was his response to the idea of this book. Whether Mr Robinson now speaks Bengali is left doubtful; but he has done very well for a foreigner. Ray's background, his life and his films are carefully and illuminatingly researched. The book is rather hero-worshipping – but then Ray is an authentic hero. Heroic in the elevation and consistency of his aim and heroic to have survived so obstinately and so long in the jungle world of cinema.

Ray comes from a family of artists and craftsmen. His grandfather was a writer and a musician who set up a printing firm and became expert in the science of graphic and photographic reproduction. His son carried on the tradition and became famous for his children's stories and nonsense rhymes. Satyajit himself was trained as a graphic artist; but from early on it was the cinema that fascinated him.

'A rare combination of East and West' is how Satyajit Ray describes his grandfather. It is a description that applies as well to him. Amongst his favourite painters are Giorgione and Cézanne; but his art teacher was Binode Mukherjee (as well as Tagore), himself influenced by Chinese art and calligraphy. As a graphic artist working for a British advertising agency in Calcutta, he drew equally on Eastern and Western examples. He has composed the 'Indian' music for his own films; but as a young man his enthusiasm was for Bach and Beethoven. When he began to take cinema seriously, his most important influences were the de Sica of *Bicycle Thieves* and Jean Renoir (whom he considered his 'principal mentor'). But Ray has always had too much taste and intelligence to follow Western fashion. His previous biographer, Marie Seton, quoted revealingly from a letter he wrote to the Singhalese director, Lester Peries:

> The exterior of a film is beginning to count for more than ever before. People don't seem to bother about what you say, so long as you say it in a sufficiently oblique and unconventional manner . . . As if being modern for a film-maker consisted solely in how he juggles with his visuals and not in his attitude to life as he expresses it through the film.

This has only become truer as the years have passed – and it is a trend that has affected critics as well as artists. But it has never affected Ray.

In spite of his complete fluency in English, written as well as spoken, Satyajit Ray has never made an English-language film. He was probably lucky that his early project to film *A Passage to India* failed to win Forster's approval. He was certainly right to disentangle himself from an American-financed fantasy (of his own invention) which would have starred Peter Sellers and a small humanoid who may well have inspired Spielberg's *E.T.* (Ray, like Eisenstein before him, was utterly unequipped to deal with the ruthless falsities of Hollywood.)

Not that survival in Calcutta has been easy: it has been, in fact, heroic. The perpetual struggle for finance where audiences are comparatively small; the primitive shooting conditions, with ancient equipment that should be resting in a Museum of the Moving Image, inadequate air-conditioning, inadequate sound-proofing and perpetual cuts and fluctuations of power. But Ray has always been among friends, and largely protected from the 'feverish contact' of Western cinema. I have often been reminded of another mythic hero when I have seen Ray among his Western admirers. 'Fly our greetings!' I have wanted to call, 'Fly our speech and smiles!'

Satyajit Ray is not exactly a Scholar Gipsy; but he is a Scholar Film-Maker who could hardly have existed, and certainly could not have survived in our Anglo-American cinema of sick hurry and divided aims ('Its heads o'er-taxed, its palsied hearts . . .') and its pretentious celebrations of the mediocre. Here is an artist who has been, and who continues to be, inflexibly true to himself. Amongst other things, Andrew Robinson's book is a signal salute to integrity.

Roman Polanski

Review of *Roman* by Roman Polanski in the *Tatler*, January 1980

LIFE STORIES – OR THOSE CELEBRATIONS OF PERSONALITY YOU FIND IN THE Sunday magazines – are always irritating when you know their subjects well. But reading about acquaintances is usually interesting, or so my experience has been. I certainly wish I had been able to read the early chapters of this book about Roman Polanski before the two or three times our paths have crossed. I would surely have been able to get more from our brief encounters. Or would I?

I first met Polanski in Paris in 1960. I had gone over to see the Berliner Ensemble playing Brecht, because we were going to do a Brechtian-style musical at the Royal Court. I went to a party at an apartment on the Left Bank one evening, and there was a young Polish film-maker, author of a brilliantly original short, *Two Men and a Wardrobe*, which we had shown at our Free Cinema programmes at the National Film Theatre. Roman Polanski was small, voluble and intelligent; conspicuously lively, but over-conscious of his cleverness, infantile in his demand for attention, his sulk-iness when anyone else threatened to hold the floor for more than fifteen seconds. I found him quite a pain.

Reading now about the experiences which had formed, or profoundly affected that irritating young Pole, I am sorry for my impatience. After all, I had been raised in a comfortable secure upper-middle-class England; I had been in the War, though not really uncomfortably; and I was well insured by an Oxford degree and a good accent. Polanski had been brought up a Jew in perilous, divided Poland (Europe's Ireland); he was six when the Germans invaded and he and his family had to wear 'strange white armbands with the Star stencilled on them in blue'. His parents were both deported: his father returned at the end of the War: his mother per-ished. Polanski's childhood was passed in continual struggle for survival, by evasion and masquerade, sheltered by friends or by impoverished Polish families who protected him for payment or through pity. After the War he felt as oppressed by the Communists as he had been by the Germans. He soon found he was a performer and became quite famous in a children's radio serial. He was obsessed by movies, hated the Russian imports, and saw *The Adventures of Robin Hood* again and again. By toughness and ingenuity he hacked his way through the Polish jungle, escaped military service and got into film school. He acted in Wajda's first film, *A Generation*. He tried to escape to the West by hiding above a false ceiling in the lavatory of a railway train. He got to Paris eventually as the husband of a young Polish star who had landed the lead in a French pic-ture in spite of being unable to speak a word of the language.

Was it that early fight to survive that gave Polanski his extraordinary dynamic, the ceaseless energy that seems to have characterised his life ever since? Or is it something you're born with? Cosmopolitan though his career has been for the last twenty-odd years, he has never ceased to be a Pole. This book, he tells us, was partly inspired by memories awoken when he returned to Warsaw in 1980 to direct and play the lead in *Amadeus*. There is a spunky resilience, an epic vigour about this self-por-trait of the artist as a young survivor that makes these chapters the most vivid and the most sympathetic in the book.

Polanski gives another, sadder reason for writing this early autobiogra-phy. His years in the West can be divided into four main periods: London – success in Hollywood leading to tragedy – life as a top director leading to catastrophe – refuge in France. The tragedy was the murder of his wife and three of his friends in Los Angeles at the hands of maniacal hippies; and catastrophe came with the charge of raping a minor, persecution by

Polanski's 'brilliantly original' short film Two Men and a Wardrobe.

the media and by the law, and flight to Europe. He now has to live in France, from which he cannot be extradited.

Energy, a voracious appetite, these are the keynotes of the story; and I doubt whether they are in any way due to the experiences of his youth. (Though without them he might well not have survived.) His egotism remains exceptional, and he is clearly much more concerned with his own susceptibilities than he is with other people's. With this reservation, he is truthful and sure enough of himself to stand by his own truth. He is sharp-edged, like the films which won him his escape from Warsaw to the wonderworld of the West. *Knife in the Water, Repulsion, Cul-de-Sac* – these are tremendously lively, inventive pictures, ironic and effective, with no time for sentimental illusions. I have never found a very significant core to them, but I suppose that is not their kind of virtue. If you are interested in the way cinema works, you will appreciate the detail with which Polanski chronicles the setting-up of his films and their making. He is frank about personalities, and unsparing in his judgements.

Sex is also a constant theme. Clearly Polanski's sex drive is as powerful as his artistic creative energy; and he is at no pains to conceal the fact. He is more a realist than a cynic, and there seems no doubt that when Filmways Inc pressed Sharon Tate on him to play the heroine in *Vampire*

544

Killers, he fell really and truly in love with her. And her horrible death threw him violently off course. His principal achievements since then have been *Macbeth*, *Chinatown*, and *Tess*, of which only one can be accounted (my personal judgement, of course) exactly a success. And although one can never imagine Polanski as anything but an impenitent philanderer, one feels equally sure that his priapic obsession with teenagers would never have got out of control as it did if fate had not so dreadfully deprived him of happiness as a husband and a father. There was surely desperation behind those amoral escapades with the girls at the Swiss finishing school near his chalet – as there certainly was behind the grubby goings-on with a thirteen-year-old photographic 'model' up in Jack Nicholson's pad which smashed his Hollywood career.

This last episode, with its attendant betrayals, his shabby treatment at the hands of the American legal system and his understandable flight into exile, is fully and fairly frankly covered in this book. Perhaps too fully and not quite frankly enough: the excuse of a feature article for *Vogue* does not quite explain how Polanski found himself in that shady house at the far end of the San Fernando Valley, or why he fell so eagerly into the horrid trap. No matter. He was tempted, he fell and he paid a very high price. It is a sternly moral story.

I hope I have made it clear that the stuff of *Roman* is fascinating. Some of it is amusing, some of it enlightening and a lot of it depressing. It would have been less depressing if Polanski's helpers in putting it together had not so often fallen into a style of shallow journalism which suggests a vulgarity and even a snobbery which I don't think is really characteristic of its author. 'That night I went to Victor Lownes' place and wished I hadn't. Simon Hesseri and I sat chatting with some girls we didn't know while Victor banged some chick in his bedroom. Conversation languished. One of Victor's horrible pekinese had diarrhoea on the drawing-room carpet . . .' 'One day on the ski slopes I said to Andy Braunsberg, "Why don't I do *Macbeth*?" He loved the idea. We packed up at once and left for London.' This sort of thing. The reputable firm of Wm. Heinemann should edit better than this.

But you end up, in spite of everything, respecting Polanski. There is an honest, indignant impulse behind his book which (for me anyway) excuses the lapses of taste. He is an artist, after all, and we can only regret that a certain weakness, which plays straight into the rapacious hands of the media, has so often been his undoing. I am glad to know that he is filming again, and on a subject he has long pursued through the shark-infested Hollywood seas: *Pirates* it is appropriately titled.

I echo the farewell of that decent guard who escorted Roman out of the main gate of Chino prison. 'Take it easy, Tiger.'

Paisà

Sequence 2, Winter 1947

PAISÀ, ROBERTO ROSSELLINI'S FIRST FILM SINCE *OPEN CITY*, HAD ITS FIRST British showing at the Edinburgh Festival of Documentary in September. This is interesting chiefly because *Paisà* is not, strictly speaking, a documentary at all: it is a fictional film, though its stories spring out of recent history; its chief parts are acted by professionals. Like *Carnet de Bal* or *Dead of Night*, *Paisà* tells not one but many stories; as in *Tales of Manhattan* each story is enacted by different characters, in a different setting. The common factor in this case, however, is war; the theme common to each episode is the effect, direct or indirect, of war on people – sometimes people taken individually, sometimes in a group. As the war moves north, so does the film; though only three of its six episodes actually deal with the fighting.

The stories themselves range from the sentimental to the tragic; they are all pessimistic, if not defeatist, in feeling, and each ends with an unexpected twist. But despite Basil Wright's claim that the theme of the film, which it is the function of these stories to illustrate, includes 'the paradoxical co-existence of absolute good and absolute evil in human relationships' and 'the fact that the human spirit in all circumstances, and never more so than when tragically defeated, is imperishably triumphant,' it is difficult to feel that they have much importance in themselves. They serve, in fact, rather as a pretext for taking us on a journey through Italy at war, so that we may look around and see the sort of things that happen. An Italian girl gives her life to save an American patrol from ambush (the Allies are throughout represented by the Americans, apart from the fleeting appearance of two disgruntled RAF men in the last episode); a Neapolitan shoeshine boy makes friends with a Negro MP and steals his boots; an American soldier is picked up by a prostitute in Rome and fails to recognise in her the gay, attractive girl he had met on the first day of Rome's liberation; a small, isolated group of partisans, villagers and soldiers are annihilated by German forces in the Northern marshes.

In the telling of these stories the qualities which Rossellini showed in *Open City* are again apparent. Most striking is the tremendous sense of reality – actuality is perhaps the better word. The film was shot, we are told – and we need no persuading – in every case on the actual location of whatever events are represented; and in every case, whether it is a brothel-cum-night club in Rome, a tart's bedroom, a street in Florence under fire, a monastery, or a sandbank in the Northern marshes, we know that this is exactly what it is like, and that we are really there. Rossellini can handle people, whether individually or *en masse*, with absolute certainty, and he helps his actors by giving them consistently good, likely dialogue, by a cunningly naturalistic use of sound, and by his never-failing sense of how people actually do behave in circumstances of stress and danger.

Paisà moves almost throughout with great speed and urgency. Like *The Last Chance* and the much older *War is Hell* it is multilingual; but this does not obviate the necessity of sub-titles – the lack of titles on the copy shown at Edinburgh rendered the point of at least two of the episodes incomprehensible to members of the audience who could not speak Italian. Rossellini's editing may be described as ruthless; when it is successful this makes for speed, but sometimes it gets out of hand, to break the rhythm of the film and result in confusion. The acting varies from the sincere but amateurish to the sincere and accomplished. Dots Johnson does a delightfully comic sketch of the Negro soldier, and Maria Michi, who played Marina in *Open City*, reappears, very movingly, as the prostitute. All the small parts are played faultlessly.

All the same, in spite of all the realism, all the sincerity, all the truthfulness of *Paisà*, I cannot help feeling that it lacks something. At the end of both these films of Rossellini's I have found myself wishing that he would now step forward and, so to speak, gather the whole film together, present it to us as a unity, make a statement. That he could not do this in *Open City* was understandable enough; he was too close to the events he was depicting. But in *Paisà*, made after the War, the attempt might have been made. As it is, the film comes to an abrupt (almost self-consciously so) conclusion. Certainly this last episode, the best of the lot, is superbly filmed. There is an excitement, an immediacy about it which is typical of Rossellini's direction at its best. One remembers the partisan's body floating silently down the broad river, the disgust of the over-tired soldiers at the fatuous orders they receive from Headquarters, the child left crying in terror and bewilderment amongst a backyard full of dead bodies; and then, on a note of sudden, hurried, almost insignificant defeat . . . it just stops.

The so-called 'documentary approach' has no doubt its very considerable virtues. It makes for realism, for authenticity of atmosphere, for sincere if unpolished acting. But to the extent that it inhibits the artist (in this case the director) from imposing his ideas on his raw material, from exercising his right to shape and to exclude, it is not conducive to the making of masterpieces. Most directors would be all the better for a spell in the open-air (provided it didn't kill them); Rossellini one would like to see take an enforced vacation in a studio.

547

Sciuscia

Sequence 4, Summer 1948

WHAT IS IT ABOUT THESE ITALIAN PICTURES WHICH MAKES THE IMPRESSION they create so overwhelming? First, their tremendous actuality, second, their honesty, and third, their passionate pleading for what we have come to term the humane values. The uses of adversity are once again demonstrated: lack of money has made it necessary to shoot on real locations, against backgrounds which themselves forbid the phoney and the fake. But it is chiefly the impulse of generous and uncompromising emotion which gives to *Sciuscia*, as to the Rossellini films, a force unknown to the Warner heavy, or the tasteful problem picture from Ealing (or the distasteful one from Shepherd's Bush). Like *Open City* and *Paisà*, the setting of *Sciuscia* is contemporary, and – also like them – it has no respect for the old lies, the safe conventions. It is the story of two shoeshine boys loose in 'liberated' Rome – Rome liberated not only from fascism but also from order and security. It is the boys' highest ambition to own a horse of their own; in contriving to get hold of enough money, they become party, all but innocently, to a black market deal. They are caught by the police and, since they refuse to implicate their friends, sent to prison as juvenile delinquents.

The atmosphere of the exhausted, disintegrated city is superbly conveyed; the rough, newsreel quality of Brizzi's photography, the sharp cutting, the abrupt naturalism of the acting persuade us that we are watching scenes as they actually take place, people as they actually are. This in itself is enough to make *Sciuscia* an exceptional film. But with the story's development it seems to attain another degree of excellence; the film acquires a real significance. The friendship of Giuseppe and Pasquale is an affair of innocence – the boys are never sentimentalised, but they are shown, for all their acuteness, as innocents, with innocent love, candour and trust. By contact with the world we see these qualities perverted and finally destroyed. When the boys are sent to prison by the harassed, overworked official who is trying desperately to organise chaos, we are sickened but not horrified. It is when the casual brutality of a warder separates them, when one hand gropes vainly for another, that we perceive the inevitability of disaster. At this point *Sciuscia* becomes a tragedy.

The prison scenes, persuasively detailed, are austere and horrifying; but the agony is never piled on – the director has rightly felt that the thing in itself is agonising enough. The authorities are not condemned, they are shown as merely human – fallible, weary, losing hope. The conditions which lead to this warping of young lives seem inevitable: so much so, indeed, that the story becomes not merely an account of some tragic happenings in post-war Rome, but universal in its implications. The climax may be described as symbolic (Giuseppe dies by the hand of his friend, whom he realises too late has not betrayed him after all, as the horse they both loved gallops away into the darkness), but it is the true kind of symbolism, implicit in the material, growing naturally out of what has gone before.

Comparison with the other Italian pictures is inevitable. *Sciuscia* is as good as either of the two Rossellini films, perhaps better: it is tighter, firmer in structure, with no less honesty, but more courage. Unlike *Vivere in Pace* (a more polished production) it has not a single element of *kitsch*. Vittorio de Sica's direction is sensitive and straightforward, with some charmingly lyrical touches at the beginning, where they are not out of place. The acting throughout, but especially of Rinaldi Smordoni and Franco Interlenghi as the two boys, is marvellous.

Casque d'Or

Sight and Sound, October-December 1952

JACQUES BECKER'S FILMS SEEM ALL TO RECEIVE THEIR PECULIAR IMPETUS (THEY are nothing if not highly charged) from a searching, sympathetic fascination with doing and being. It is never a question of people in isolation. The Goupis' farm and countryside; the salons and workrooms of the couturiers in *Falbalas*; the Metros, Bon Marchés and bistros of *Antoine et Antoinette*, and the hectic Left Bank locations of *Rendezvous de Juillet* – none of these backgrounds have been merely incidental. Instead, reflecting personality and influencing behaviour, they are assimilated into the stories, as much a part of the whole film as the characters or the incidents. Nor does Becker ever seem exposed to the opposite temptation – the exploitation of decor for its own effect. The elements are all fused (this at least is his intention) to form a unified, concentrated dramatic whole.

To have effected this fusion with *Casque d'Or* (English title: *Golden Marie*), is more than ever a proof of Becker's strictness of control; for this is his first 'period' film, and in certain respects an avowed venture into the picturesque. The world that has excited his imagination is that of Paris 50 years ago – Paris of *La Belle Epoque*, with all its attendant decorative charm. The social level of the story is low, its tone violent. Marie, its heroine, is a beautiful gigolette, nicknamed 'Casque d'Or' from her glorious crown of golden hair which she wears dressed *'en casque'*; she is the mistress of Roland, one of a gang of cut-throats who operate under the orders of Léca – who himself desires Marie. But the rivalry which motivates the plot is not between Léca and Roland. Herself tiring of her lover, Marie's eye falls on Manda, a friend of one of the gang, an ex-convict now working as a carpenter at the riverside café which the apaches and their girls are visiting in the course of a Sunday outing to Joinville. Marie gives Manda a lead, to which he instantly responds. From then on, his road leads precipitately to tragedy: the murder of Roland in a knife-duel; separation from Marie when Léca has his friend Raymond arrested for the murder, and Manda has no alternative but to give himself up; the death of Raymond when the two make a break from custody; Manda's vengeful murder of Léca, and his final ignominious death on the scaffold.

Becker is reported to have described the effect he has striven for as 'something between the painter Renoir and Eugène Sue': an illuminating statement, if not one to be pressed too literally. The spirit of Renoir is present chiefly in the portrait of Casque d'Or herself, most obviously in her coiffure and dress, but also in her generous and challenging sensuality, her delighted response to the physical joy of love; and it is there as well in the presentation of the happier phases of the story – the slow procession of boats, oars dipping and voices singing, laden with apaches and their *'filles'*, down the river at Joinville; and the pastoral idyll, with its blowing grass and trees, which is Marie's and Manda's short experience of life together. It is the other side of the drama, presumably, that Becker wishes to evoke by his mention of Sue: the narrarive of plotting and intrigue; Léca's gang with its code of 'honour' and violence; the ruthless fights-to-the-death. But although there are conventional thriller elements here, all this is a far cry from *Les Mystères de Paris*. Sue's celebrated melodrama, chockful of the traditional apparatus of its genre – fair innocents, disguised monarchs, exuberantly coincidental encounters – is the sort of material that would justify an approach far less serious, and decoration far more wild (something like John Bryan's for *Oliver Twist*, perhaps). D'Eaubonne's sets for *Casque d'Or* and Robert Le Febvre's straight-forward photography eschew the Gothic for a natural, though continuously atmospheric visual style; and this is matched by a *découpage* of corresponding sobriety. The story unfolds evenly, in a steady march of gradual, overpowering effectiveness.

Firstly, it is a love story. His acute sensibility to what one may call the emotional geography, the varying currents and strange depths which characterise the most intimate human relations, has always been one of Becker's strengths; and just as this made of *Antoine et Antoinette* some-

Simone Signoret and Serge Reggiani in Jacques Becker's Casque d'Or.

thing more than a light comedy, so it lifts *Casque d'Or* from the category of melodrama, or merely another essay in the romantic-pathetic, to tragedy. Marie and Manda are characters vividly and roundly presented; their relationship changes and progresses, and as it progresses our insight into their situation deepens. This is not the director's achievement alone; he owes a great deal to his actors. The performances of Simone Signoret as Marie and Serge Reggiani as Manda are remarkable above all for their complete fusion, at a level of great intensity, of their own personalities and acting styles into a shared conception. The effect of unity makes it as impossible to imagine the film without these players, as to imagine it directed by anyone but Becker. Signoret's Marie, in particular, shows a radiant blossoming of talent: a creation entrancingly feminine, with a range of intuition that compasses the arrogant (and irresistible) willfulness of the earlier sequences as persuasively as the later warmth of a woman passionately and constantly in love. Superbly confident in her power of attraction, it is she who dominates the first half of the film: her reckless provocation of Roland, her summons of Manda, her impertinent encouragement of Léca's advances. Manda, seduced by a glance, fatally allows himself to be led back to the world of crime which he had resolved to put behind him. Once the two have become lovers, however, the balance shifts, to reveal the basis of truth in a relationship so doubtfully entered into.

Manda has been shown from the first as a secret man, driven in upon himself by harsh experience, inflexibly self-reliant. (Reggiani's performance, with its banked interior fire and its almost heroic renunciation of display, communicates exactly the strength and the weakness of this fine-tempered pride. This is resolutely interior acting, with the strength in it to afford the sacrifice of certain immediate effects, to achieve moments of subtle and startling revelation.) With intimacy, it is Manda's influence that becomes dominant, his love for Marie still combined with an unswerving pursuit of his self-chosen course of action. Marie loses her stridency (with her *casque*); devotion replaces appetite and the cocotte becomes a wife. When the couple eavesdrop on a bourgeois marriage in the village church, it is she who finds herself affected by the solemn symbolism of the ceremony; Manda, a tender but unsentimental lover, is impatiently indulgent. And when Léca has his friend Raymond arrested for the murder of Roland, the same pride that won Manda his happiness with Marie forces him to sacrifice it. 'N'y penses plus,' says Marie as she lies beside him in bed, knowing that he is thinking of his friend, 'Penses a moi.' 'Je pense toujours a toi, Marie,' he replies; but in the morning he has gone. It is the perfect harmony of these scenes between Marie and Manda, very soft and quiet (there are no dwelt-on passages of love-making), and above all their sense of promise as well as fulfilment, that give the end of the film, and their long tearing-apart, its peculiar quality of pain. The intimacy and intensity of the two leading performances proves also an essential element in the style of *Casque d'Or*.

Equally, Becker has been able to present the scenes between Marie and Manda with absolute directness and simplicity. Dialogue between them is pared to a minimum; all but the barely essential has been excluded. Marie's seduction of Manda is told in three long panning shots as she waltzes across the room in front of him, cutting from her glowing self-display to his guarded eyes as they follow her past. When she has pursued him to his lodgings, his acceptance and their mutual desire are established without a word: one charged close-up on each, and an embrace. By contrast, it must be admitted that other passages in the film – the Eugène Sue element – lack this extreme clarity and subtle emphasis. Some of the plot manoeuvres (the events, for instance, after the duel between Manda and Roland, and the rather confusing glimpes of the informer) would benefit from a sharper exposition: in plot construction one feels that Becker and Jacques Companeez, as authors, have not always equalled the achievement of Becker the director. In part a certain lowering of the tension is due also to the shallower presentation (in comparison with Marie and Manda) of Léca. Claude Dauphin's performance is an admirably competent essay in callousness and vanity; but it lacks the extra dimension of personality.

Writing of Becker in 1947, on the strength of his first three films alone, the French critic Roger Regent remarked on the singular purity of his style, and on its power to build sequences to an extreme degree of tension. In *Casque d'Or* this style is more strikingly than ever in evidence. The movement of the whole picture shows a highly developed command of tempo, a rhythm which can accommodate the long, sustained look at a scene (the first set-up of all, for instance), as well as the series of swift, detailed glances. The images are of continuous but simple richness – in particular a poetic use of close-up such as is possible only to an artist who has achieved great sureness of his attitude, as of his metier. I shall, no doubt, be mocked if I find some of these reminiscent of Ford, but it is so; here is the touching-point of two quite different worlds. I would hesitate to call Becker a romantic; but he is very powerfully a humanist.

Powerfully, and also sternly: *Casque d'Or* grimly accepts.

While the outcome of the love between Marie and Manda lacks nothing in terror and pity, it provokes no protesting cry against society or destiny: the human responsibility is grimly accepted. This is in interesting contrast to the films of Carné and Prévert, and the impression is one of greater maturity. Manda is master of his fate as the Gabin-hero of *Quai des Brumes* or *Le Jour Se Léve* is not; and at his death there is no cutting away to ship's siren or to unheeded alarm clock. From beginning to end, in fact, the focus of the story is human: the procession of minor characters is socially as well as individually pin-pointed – the members of Léca's gang, each acutely differentiated; the undemonstrative loyalty of Bussières' Raymond; Dominique Davray as Marie's admiring girlfriend: the crone at whose cottage the lovers take shelter (herself a grim *memento mori*); the anonymous wedding group at the village church. This last episode, with its perfect social and human observation, bears witness to Becker's admiration (lately admitted) of Stroheim, elsewhere evident in the fullness and accuracy of background detail.

But unlike Stroheim, Becker does not make use of caricature: the result is no realism with a capital 'R', but rather a pervasive sense of *reality*, potent enough to assimilate into a scene of great dramatic urgency – a tragic crisis, in fact, in the protagonists' lives – a minor character who shuffles away from the point of action to piss against a wall: a corner-eye glimpse that completely avoids the eccentric, to add an enriching element of irony, and a conviction all the completer.

Of this conviction perhaps the most striking instance in the film is the marvellous sequence with which it ends, of Manda's execution. Photographed in drab and chilling tones, this is shot with an unflinching precision, a masterly selection from the event of its most significant elements – the pale, tottering figure that expresses the brave man's agony and fear; the straps that bind him, and the dark figures that walk at his side through the hideous prison courtyard; the shining blade that descends; and, repeatedly, the sick face of Marie at her window – all these are seen with open eyes, not lingered over, but put there before us as facts from which there is no turning away. There are many chords of experience, beyond the common one of horror, set vibrating by the scene: separation and irrecoverable loss; the strength and the fragility of love; the futile human protest against mortality. From Marie's bowed head the scene dissolves: ghosts from the past, the figures of the lovers, tightly clasped, waltz away down the bistro where they first met (the floor strangely distended and empty) into limbo.

Madame de. . .

Sight and Sound, April-June 1954

TWO OR THREE YEARS AGO, AT A PROGRAMME ORGANISED BY THE LONDON Film Club in honour of Max Ophuls, James Mason introduced the director to his admirers with a little poem. I forget exactly how this went, but I am sure of one thing: 'Max' rhymed with 'tracks'. The appositeness of the joke was obvious even then, from the films Ophuls had made in Hollywood which, culminating in *Letter from an Unknown Woman*, had won him the unquestioned status of *petit maître*. Even less successful pictures like *Caught* and *The Reckless Moment* have a finesse and a style unique in the American cinema of that (or this) time. In all these films, Ophuls' virtuosity with the travelling camera was obvious to the trained eye; but it was a legitimate virtuosity, not merely pleasing in its skill, but expressive, too, of this artist's characteristic, nimble shrewdness. As his camera swooped and glided round sets and actors, so Ophuls himself skimmed over the landscape of his stories, uncommitted, unconcerned with profundities, but clear-sighted, sharp to analyse and observe.

Perhaps it was unfortunate that he had to return to Europe with a subject that put so high a premium on virtuosity. In Ophuls' *La Ronde*, decoration and wit triumphed over the harsher cynicism of Schnitzler; but the camera moved more brilliantly than ever and – apart from the errors in casting which weakened its second half – the film seemed a wonderfully successful *tour-de-force*. The same good fortune, however, did not attend *Le Plaisir*; Maupassant proved less easy to take over than Schnitzler, and for the first time one felt a sense of strain, of style exaggerating itself into mannerism. Like the little girl in Grimm's story who put her feet into the magic shoes (except that in this case the damage must have been done one day when he eased himself on to the boom of a crane in some marvellously equipped Hollywood studio), Max Ophuls could not stop travelling.

These remarks may seem an oblique approach to *Madame de. . .* but here, more than ever, the style of the film is its essence. Take the start: a long wardrobe, full of expensive clothes – a woman's hand passes tentatively down the row, inspecting, rejecting, finally selecting. This is Madame de. . . , preparing to visit her jeweller. She picks out a pair of earrings, sits down at her dressing table, puts them on, admires herself in the mirror. She leaves the room. All this quite intricate action is caught, with breathtaking precision, in a single, continuous shot. And so onward: the camera is never still; every shot has the tension of a conjuring trick. The sleight of hand is dazzling, but fatally distracting.

Louise de Vilmorin's book has perhaps been over-praised. ('*Madame de. . .* must be taken very seriously indeed, as seriously as a flawless lyric, or an epigram from the Greek Anthology' – Vita Sackville West in *The Observer*). It is a long short story, the ironic history of a romance that starts as sophisticated intrigue, and ends as tragedy. The beautiful Madame de. . . sells her diamond earrings to pay some debts that she has incurred without her husband's knowledge; the jeweller informs Monsieur de. . . who buys the earrings back and presents them to his departing mistress. The jewels are again sold, to a foreign diplomat who is posted to Paris as Ambassador, falls in love with Madame de. . . and gives her the earrings as a token. This neat figure is only the preface to the essential conflict of the story. Madame de. . . accepts the Ambassador's gift without revealing the truth. When he discovers her duplicity, the blow to his pride is so great that he breaks off their relationship to the despair of Madame de. . . , who now finds that what she had started as a diverting flirtation has taken a ferocious hold on her heart. And the earrings, which have become the symbol of her pride, without which she cannot live, are removed by Monsieur de. . . The dénouement is fatal.

If this bitter little fable lacks quite the passion and penetration claimed for it by Miss Sackville West, it is nevertheless a most satisfying piece of work, exquisitely constructed and balanced, dignified by a classical austerity of style. So bare is its narrative, in fact, and so uncompromising its exclusion of the picturesque and the emotional, that it would seem impossible to adapt for the cinema without either gratuitous expansion, or the substitution of an altogether more detailed and seductive style. Ophuls has chosen the latter solution. With a supple, ingenious, glittering flow of images that is aesthetically the diametrical opposite of Mme de Vilmorin's chaste prose, he has made the story an excuse for a succession of rich decorative displays. Christian Matras's lighting has his usual sophisticated gloss, and the settings by d'Eautonne exploit to the full the habitual charms of period decor. In all this visual *frou-frou*, it is not surprising that the characters become lost, and the interior development of their drama (discrete enough in the original) is almost completely unobserved. This is the more regrettable, since the actors (Danielle Darrieux as Madame de..., Charles Boyer as the husband, and Vittorio de Sica as the Ambassador) present their exteriors remarkably well. Without exploration of these relationships, however, and a more serious irony, the story is reduced to a series of adroit, finally rather tedious manoeuvres round the persistent earrings. I, for one, have to admit a sharply sympathetic response to the remark with which Madame de... greets the jeweller, returning to re-sell him the earrings for the fourth or fifth time: *'Fichez-moi le camp* [or something equivalent] *avec ces bouclets d'oreille!'*

One is accustomed to commiserating with European directors who have gone astray in Hollywood. The uneasy progress of Ophuls since his return to Europe is less easy to explain. Perhaps the success of *La Ronde* was too heady. Certainly both *The Reckless Moment* and *Letter from an Unknown Woman* are better films than *Le Plaisir* or *Madame de...* A less sophisticated climate might perhaps help: what a pity he is not, after all, coming to make a film in England.

The Adventures of Robinson Crusoe

Sight and Sound, October-December 1954

THE EMERGENCE – OR THE RE-EMERGENCE – OF LUIS BUÑUEL IN THESE LAST two years or so has been a strange and wonderful thing. Not that it is unknown for names of bygone celebrity to pop up as if from nowhere, but generally these resurrections have been more sad than joyful: Dupont is rediscovered in Hollywood as director of *The Scarf*; Von Sternberg suddenly reappears directing Jane Russell in *Macao*; Boris Kaufman, whose name will shine for ever on the credits of *Zéro de Conduite* and *L'Atalante*, shoots *On the Waterfront* for Kazan. But Buñuel surprises us the other way, with continual revelation. *The Adventures of Robinson Crusoe* is a film by an artist of fresh, still developing talent, a poetic film with a purity of style that marks it as the statement of a man of integrity, direct, uncompromised.

It is particularly marvellous because, though the film is a wholly personal work, Buñuel did not himself want to make it; or rather it was not his original idea to make it. 'I didn't like the book; but I liked the character. I accepted it because there is a certain purity about him. Above all this is man face to face with nature: nothing romantic about it, no facile novelettish love scenes, no plot . . .' Readers of *Sight and Sound* will remember Tony Richardson's revealing article in the January issue: further light on Buñuel is shed by the long and delightful interview with him in the June issue of *Cahiers du Cinéma*, from which I quote. 'There's simply a chap who arrives, finds himself face to face with nature, and has to feed himself. Well, I liked the subject, I took it on, and I tried to do something that might be interesting . . .' The approach could not be better described. In fact so simple, so inevitable are the images, that you have to imagine what the conventional film treatment of the story would be to appreciate quite how daring – and how masterly – is Buñuel's naked, unadorned presentation of the simple facts. No jolly establishing sequences at Plymouth, no sentimental farewells, no pretty Polly waving a handkerchief from the jetty, not even a smashing storm sequence: just long waves rolling in to a deserted beach, and a man staggering up out of the water.

'*Simply a chap* . . .' This precisely is the impression we first get of Crusoe as Dan O'Herlihy presents him. A good-looking chap, rather than strikingly handsome; alert, clear-eyed, ordinarily pleasant rather than obviously heroic. At first we wonder whether he is going to be able to sustain this taxing role. But soon we forget our doubts, forget even to admire; plainly, unheroically, ingeniously he sets to work – builds his stockade, grows his corn, goes hunting with his beloved dog, makes pottery, wins his battle against nature. This just *is* Crusoe.

The first reels of the film are like the best kind of documentary – like *Moana*, with its loving, contented observation of the practical details of living. Then comes the second theme, of solitude. 'I also wanted to tackle the subject of Love . . . that's to say the lack of love or friendship: man without the fellowship of man or woman.' Buñuel emphasises the terrible loneliness of his hero with vivid scenes of hallucination – staged with the utmost economy. The flapping of the woman's dress with which Crusoe has clothed his scarecrow becomes a torment to him: he dashes to the hilltop from which he knows his cries will re-echo, a bitter parody of companionship. The build-up to this wonderful scene has apparently been severely cut: it remains a most powerful invention.

If O'Herlihy were not so excellent from the start, one would be tempted to say his performance gets better and better. He manages the transition to the eccentric Crusoe of the goatskin umbrella and the shaggy hat with the greatest skill. (Tony Richardson wrote of Crusoe at this stage as 'a wayward, crazed old man', and others have described his 'degeneration'. I found him most humorously sympathetic.) And further riches follow: excitement with the cannibals, tender comedy with Man Friday.

The scenes with Friday are a development of that second theme, of loneliness. Crusoe and Friday have to learn to live together: Crusoe is suspicious – not unreasonably after all – and Friday frightened and bewildered. (James Fernandez' performance of this noble savage is perfect: funny and beautiful at the same time.) The delicate humour with which these scenes are presented, Friday's dignity and naif wisdom, Crusoe's shame, the warmth of their eventual *'grande fraternité humaine'* (Buñuel's words) – all these must surely astonish those who had docketed this director in their minds as a harsh and cruel experimentalist, fascinated exclusively by the violent and the depraved.

But of course there has never been any doubt of Buñuel's great love of life and the living. It has made him angry in the past; in this film it makes him reflective, observant, gentle, stirring but never inflamed. *'J'ai accepté parce qu'il y a en lui quelque chose de pur Robinson Crusoe'* is a salute from one pure spirit to another.

La Terra Trema and *Baby Doll*

New Statesman, 5 January 1957

THUNDER FROM THE RIGHT, AS WELL AS THE FASHIONABLE *RÉCLAME* OF ITS authors, have made the new Kazan-Tennessee Williams picture the conversation piece of the moment. But there is something more remarkable than *Baby Doll* at hand, at least for London film-goers.

From tomorrow, 5th January, to Wednesday the 9th, the National Film Theatre is showing, for the first time in this country, the full version of Luchino Visconti's *La Terra Trema*. This magnificent film – for two pins I would call it great – was made nine years ago: it is intended as the first part of a trilogy of poverty and struggle among the fishermen and peasants of Sicily. Shooting entirely in the little village of Aci Trezzia, Visconti used no actors: he made actors out of the people on the spot. He scripted no dialogue: all the lines were suggested by the fishermen themselves, from their knowledge of the plot and the characters. The film took six months to shoot, and runs two hours and 40 minutes.

This kind of approach (and this kind of length) is more familiar to us now than it was in 1948. But *La Terra Trema* is unique among neo-realist films in the grand formality of its style, the mastery with which Visconti has fashioned its everyday elements not into a rough, violent and actual picture, but into a meticulous, beautifully proportioned fresco of injustice and exploitation, of natural dignity and baffled revolt. The design is simple. The fishermen of the village are the victims of a system of sale which guarantees them nothing but toil and risk for their bare livelihood: unscrupulous middlemen reap big profits when fishing is good, and sit back comfortably when seas run strong and the catch is scanty. One young fisherman alone realises the basis of inequality and makes a bid for independence: he persuades his family to mortgage their house and buy their own transport. But their resources are too small, and the first run of bad luck reduces Antonio and his people to poverty and submission. The film ends in defeat, with exploitation triumphant, and the fishermen, who have not yet learned the lesson of strength through unity, putting out again on to the dark, dangerous sea.

Visconti's way with this story is original and extraordinary. Unlike most directors using 'natural' actors, he has preserved a formal, almost mandarin style of composition and movement, marvellously controlled, and the lighting (by the late G. R. Aldo) has a perfection of tone surely unique in a film shot under such circumstances. The progression is slow, massive; the cumulative effect immensely powerful. Its aestheticism gives *La Terra Trema* a quality of refinement which at times, perhaps, cuts against the essential nature of the subject, but then realism, in the unadorned sense, is far from being Visconti's aim. And his film is saved from preciousness by the unsparing integrity with which he has told his story and presented his men and women. By, in fact, the frankness and importance of his commitment. This film is a classic work of art of our time; see it if you possibly can.

Swift and steep is the descent to *Baby Doll* (and in this juxtaposition how apt that time seems). For this is another excursion into the airless fantasy world of Tennessee Williams: the grotesque comedy of an infantile girl married to a broken-down Southern cotton miller, and seduced by the vengeful Sicilian rival whose mill he has sabotaged. It is difficult to care much about all this. In the hands of another director, the script might have been translated into a briskly, bitterly funny film, but Kazan's touch is a trifle heavy for comedy. His, indeed, is the cinema of effect: a technician of brilliance and continual ingenuity, he charges every shot, every line and gesture with the greatest possible, immediate potency – to the detriment of any overall conception. (Or rather the conception is simply one of 'effect'.) Perhaps this is the reason why his actors, for all the Stanislavskian fidelity of their 'method', are rarely able to convey much interior life. Their calculated spontaneity is merely a contemporary kind of mannerism, monotonous in its sameness. As for Cardinal Spellman's fuss: *Baby Doll* is decadent, all right, but not for his reasons. It is less odious than *On the Waterfront*, which I suppose the Cardinal liked.

A *Generation* and *Bridge on the River Kwai*

New Statesman, October 1957

THE NEWS FROM WARSAW HAS BROUGHT THE FILMS OF ANDRZEJ WAJDA INTO my mind. These films, *Kanal* and *A Generation*, were shown at Cannes this year, and I was able only briefly to mention them in my *New Statesman* report on the festival. The former (which is in fact the more recent) will be shown in the *Sunday Times* festival at the National Film Theatre next week, and I recommend anyone who can to see it. The latter will, I suppose, not be shown here at all. I saw it again, privately, at the beginning of the week and, as I say, my mind is full of it.

A Generation belongs to a well-established Communist cinema: a young worker, something of a vagabond, comes to understand the nature of the class-struggle and the revolutionary ideal, is transformed by his new understanding, and dedicates himself to the cause. It is a tradition which naturally has produced a quantity of banal film-making, but to which we owe also some of the most memorable achievements of the Soviet cinema – Donskoi's Gorki trilogy, and the *Maxim* films of Kozintsev and Trauberg. But there the theme is varied, enriched by another element: a national pride and a kind of passionate, humane idealism which seems distinctively Polish. As the title tells us, *A Generation* is a picture of Polish youth at a particularly tragic moment of their history, during the German occupation, when all conflicts were simplified by the presence of a foreign enemy. And the Marxist, conformist trimmings obligatory at the time (the film was made two years ago) are insignificant beside the gallant and youthful spirit of the picture, its intense aspiration for liberty, and also a romantic, underlying melancholy totally absent from its Russian equivalent. The light is sunless: there is a grey reality about these Warsaw streets which makes one feel the truth is being told. The close-ups are humanistic, full of dignity. One is reminded of the wonderful pictures Cartier-Bresson took in Poland last year – and in particular that one of an editorial meeting of *Po Prostu*, the students' paper whose suppression touched off the recent trouble. These are Socialists, not Communists, and one trembles for them. They are not unaware that there is a price to pay for liberty. It is significant that the positive symbol with which the story ends – the group of young people who lope awkwardly up to continue the fight – is set against the grief of the young hero who has just seen his girl (and mentor) taken away by the Gestapo. We remember the words with which she sadly ended her vision of the bright future after victory: 'unless it is easier to die for our cause, than to live for it . . .' This was the first full-length film of its young director: his style is already taut, personal and richly expressive. Its sober, powerful images are beautifully photographed. The acting is overwhelmingly sincere; and as the boy, Tadeusz Lomnicki plays with a reserved power, a sensitivity and an intelligence which put him immediately in the class of Fonda or Gabin.

As I say, *A Generation* is unlikely to be shown in this country, the system being what it is. Why, then, am I writing about it? First, because this is only the third week of William Whitebait's holiday – yet I already feel as though I give the impression that I never enjoy a film. Such is the effect of having to attend a succession of West End press shows. And, secondly, because it seems to me important that the existence of films like this should be noticed – trumpeted – by critics, whether commercial showing is planned for them or not. Too many of the good films that are being made in the world are excluded by our present system of distribution and exhibition. To allow oneself to be reduced to carping, week after week, at the shoddy stuff we are given instead, is only another way of conforming.

The week's ration for the public screens may be shortly dealt with. *Bridge on the River Kwai* is a huge, expensive chocolate box of a war picture. Inside it is perhaps a bitter and ironic idea; but it takes more than the word 'madness' repeated three times at the end of a film to justify comparisons with *All Quiet on the Western Front*. They'll be saying that the new Jayne Mansfield is better than Lubitsch next. *Woman in a Dressing Gown* is neo-unrealist; a little suburban story directed with unsuitable gloss, and a kitchen-sink performance by Yvonne Mitchell that reminded me of Hermione Baddeley in one of her turns in an Ambassador's revue. *Robbery Under Arms* is an Australian Western which lacks grasp and tempo, but has some quite vivid stuff towards the end.

Three to Cheer For

International Film Annual Number Two, 1958

WE ARE MUCH GIVEN TO GRUMBLING ABOUT THE CINEMA THESE DAYS: AND certainly there seems enough to complain about. On the one hand, indisputably, extraordinary technical advances. Things are possible today that twenty years ago most cinemagoers had never even dreamed of: panoramic screens, stereophonic sound, refinement of colour and recording. And other improvements, of which audiences may be unaware, have even more valuably increased the possibilities of the art. Ultra-fast film stock means that shooting can be done in conditions of light that would formerly have made a cameraman shake his head in firm refusal. The development of tape-recording and magnetic sound stock has meant an immense increase in the possibilities of direct sound recording, particularly on documentary work. Inventions like these should result in freer, more exciting, more expressive work. And yet . . .

And yet they don't. At least not automatically. The sad truth is that simultaneously with the technical development of the cinema has come its economic inflation. It may be twice as easy to make films these days; but it is also four or five times as expensive. Instead of being liberated, artists are finding themselves imprisoned by the new techniques which a ruthless commercial system forces them to use. As Orson Welles remarks with some bitterness, 'A film is a ribbon of dreams. Sometimes we dream in colours, and sometimes in black and white; but nobody ever dreams in CinemaScope . . .' Forgetful of the fact that it is always the artist who re-invigorates and re-inspires the medium, the commercial cinema of the West seems to be doing its best to eliminate him altogether. The fight against television is too grim, too serious, to permit extravagances like poetry, imagination and intelligence. The situation is too crucial for us to allow young talent to try out new ideas. No wonder golden eggs seem harder to come by now than ever before.

And yet, again . . . the astonishing thing is, that in spite of all discouragement, in spite of repeated assurances that the cinema is dying, and that it is TV or space travel we should be thinking about – young talent keeps on appearing, insisting that the film is its art, the art of our time, proclaiming its faith and refusing to surrender. It is a touching and a fearful sight. Touching because determination in the face of overwhelming odds is always something to stir the beholder. And fearful because . . . well, one is beginning to fear that the odds may in truth be overwhelming.

One can be wrong, though. And certainly it is better to cheer than to deplore, to help rather than discourage. Increasingly, in fact, this seems to me the only really valuable function a critic can perform today – to be the prophet and partisan of those few artists in the cinema with the hardihood or the stamina to resist pressures which would reduce them to conformity, and condemn their work to moulder unseen in the vaults of the distribution companies. On the battlefield of the cinema, the critic also has his place in the line.

Our first cheer then, for an independent. And it is a pleasure to write about Richard Williams, not merely because his film *The Little Island* represents such an extraordinary practical fact (it is surely the longest animated film in the history of the cinema ever to be conceived and drawn by a single man). And not merely because he is an artist of great seriousness and wit, and enormous originality. But also because his film is British: and in the sluggish atmosphere of the British cinema today, experiments as vital and successful as this are as valuable as they are rare.

I use the word 'experiment'; but I should add quickly that Williams does not very much like his film to be called 'experimental'. One understands why: the word has acquired unfortunate connotations, due largely to its appropriation by the narcissistic avant-garde of California. And anyway, every good film is an experiment. Let us call *The Little Island* a pioneer work because its aim is to extend the range of the cartoon film beyond the childish, or the sophisticated gagging which has been its sole function, with very few exceptions, for the last 30-odd years. It is conceived as a comedy, but a philosophic comedy, and in the end a very disturbing one. For what Williams is obsessed with is the apparently ineradicable tendency of human beings to see life in different terms, with different aims and different values, and their equally ineradicable intolerance of any conception that is not their own. In an allegory of extreme simplicity, but also of extreme brilliance, he portrays the obsessions and the disagreement of humanity's three types – the man of Truth, the man of Beauty and the man of Goodness. The start is friendly enough, as they sit together on their little island, with the blue water lapping round them and the sun zooming up and down the sky. But each has his vision. And the visions do not agree. And twenty minutes later there are Beauty and Good, swollen into monstrous, armed giants, locked in deadly combat, while above them Truth, metamorphosed from Yogi into atomic scientist, busies himself with a gigantic bomb . . . Williams calls his film 'a satire on everything', but this makes it sound negative and despairing, which it is not. The humour is sharp, but very sane: it is *a reductio ad absurdum* not of life, but of human folly, which is a very different thing. It is also very funny.

Williams is 25, and it has taken him three years to make *The Little Island*. Before he started it, he was a painter. And before that, he worked

Top: *Andrzej Wajda's* Kanal. Above: *Wajda's* A
Generation.

on cartoon films in America, for Disney and UPA. He made his film because he wanted to, in the way that artists do; and while he was making it he earned his living (and also the technical facilities he needed) by working on TV commercials. To make his soundtrack and his musical score he was lucky enough to find another enthusiast, Tristam Cary – who was likewise able to give time and money to the project, through writing scores for such feature films as *Time without Arty, Town on Trial* and *The Flesh is Weak*.

This is getting to be the only way good films can be made.

Unless, of course, you have money of your own. The strange thing is, though, that people with money of their own seem very rarely to have the talent, or the inclination, to spend it on creative work. This is one respect in which Claude Chabrol is an exceptional person. Twenty-eight years old, a writer and critic on the French film magazine *Cahiers du Cinéma*, he was lucky enough to inherit a fairly substantial sum of money. He did not invest it or buy a house: he decided to make a film. The result is one of the best, and certainly the most promising film to come out of France for a good many years. It is called *Le Beau Serge*.

As another French critic pointed out, if Chabrol had wanted just to make any sort of a film, and to play safe with his money, he could easily have used it to imitate a big-budget production with a popular type of story and familiar stars who would guarantee a substantial return at the box-office. Instead he decided not to borrow further, but to keep the budget of the film entirely within the limits of his own resources. He wanted, in fact, to make a good film; he believed that he could make a good film; and he was prepared to take the risk of it not paying off. He wrote his own script, and cast it with a group of young actors who, though not unknown, were not yet commercially established names. The film was shot with a full professional unit in eight weeks: it was shown out-of-festival at Cannes, and now awaits distribution.

Chabrol is an intellectual (with a strong and personal sense of humour), and he is also a Catholic. Both these characteristics mark *Le Beau Serge*, and for the good. It is the story of two friends in their early twenties, Serge and François. François has left their native village, a forlorn and stagnant place, and gone as a student to Paris. Returning after an illness to rest and regain his strength, he finds his friend in a wretched state of drunkenness, self-hatred and despair. Essentially the film is a study of relationships: of François's love for Serge, which is stronger than he is prepared to acknowledge even to himself, of his resolution to help him, of Serge's love for his wife, and yet his incapacity to live with her in peace, of François's callow lack of understanding, and yet his final justification. And this is most sensitively and intelligently done, with a feeling for the rough little village and the melancholy, decaying landscape that somehow broadens and humanises the whole effect. This is Chabrol's own country, and one feels that his film, like many a good first novel, must spring at many points from his own experience.

But *Le Beau Serge* is more than just a good, or even a remarkably interesting film. The present state of the cinema in France is hardly more sparkling than in Britain (a witty critic there has recently remarked that 'the French cinema is an English cinema that doesn't know it') and although more young directors are getting a chance than in Britain, virtually none of them seems to be interested in making films out of his own feelings, or in tackling subjects of any moral or social importance. *Et Dieu . . . Créa la Femme* may have made more money in America than any foreign film ever shown there before, but it still remains a silly (even if cunning) little film. Vadim's imitators in France are no more interesting; and the senior French directors all seem to have lost their battle to make pictures worthy of their talent. Chabrol, however, has had the courage to make a completely serious film, and one which makes not the smallest concession to the supposed bad taste of the public: the result is, of course, to prove more forcefully than ever just how boring triviality has become.

The case of Andrzej Wajda, the young Pole, is in certain respects different from either of these two gallant independent fighters. For one thing, at the age of 30 he already has two features to his credit, the second of which, *Kanal*, won him a prize at Cannes in 1957 and an immediate reputation as one of the white hopes of the European cinema. But an even more significant difference is that he comes from a country which takes the cinema seriously, which believes in training its film-makers as well as its doctors, its scientists and its soldiers, and where the sole criterion of a film's value is not its success as a commercial speculation.

Of course, perfection is not to be found in this world, particularly not in the cinema, and if the pressures of commerce are removed from a film direc-tor's shoulders, they are more than likely to be replaced by the pressures of something else. Partly it has been Wajda's luck to be starting his career at a time of social movement and excitement: since Gomulka's return to power in October 1956 the creative climate in Poland has been one of comparative freedom, and undoubtedly the style and some of the message of *Kanal* is the result of that freedom. But what Western critics sometimes forget is that young Polish cinema started to stir well before the change in the political sit-uation – as a new note of liberty and lyricism in the Hungarian cinema can be seen now, in the sad perspective of the last two years, to have heralded the rising in Budapest. It is to Wajda's undying credit as an artist that his first film, *A Generation*, though made at a time when Stalinist theories were still in the ascendant, clearly affirmed those principles of idealism and humanity without which revolution inevitably degenerates into bureaucracy.

Apart from a few showings at the National Film Theatre, *A Generation* has never been seen in Britain, and its circulation outside Poland has alto-gether been limited. This is doubly a pity, because besides being a moving and beautiful film, it is one that tells us a great deal about one side at least of the Polish temperament. In theme, it is a mixture of two classical gen-res: the resistance film, with its adventurous story of youthful resistance to the German occupying forces, and the revolutionary biography of the young worker, at first ignorant and irresponsible, who learns to under-stand the social system which penalises him, and becomes an intelligent fighter in the cause of justice. Wajda's great achievement is to have escaped completely from the traditional platitudes of this kind of film, and to have made a picture genuinely youthful in spirit, and one which interprets its social theme in human, individual terms. Stach, its young hero, is a human being, not a symbol, and his playing by Tadeusz Lomnicki has a self-con-tained strength and moral intuition that reminds one of Fonda in the great days of *Young Mr Lincoln* and *The Grapes of Wrath*. His development from the scruffy idler of the first sequences to the responsible leader at the end is conceived in terms of character, of inward development, not just of a thesis demonstrated. And an essential part of this development is his brief love affair with Dorota, the girl who first led him to the movement. The scenes between these two young people, restrained but most lyrical and tender, are in no sense an interlude or an escape (as they would be in a bourgeois version of the same subject). Love, to Wajda, is an essential part of revolution – its real justification in fact.

But what makes Wajda so truly remarkable is his feeling for the *poetry* of film. This is always the great problem for the director of a narrative, dialogue film: to keep the images expressive in their own right, instead of merely a means to the end of telling a story, registering characters while they talk. *A Generation* is full of shots, or whole sequences, whose drama and significance are visual: the blank, dreadful wall of the Warsaw Ghetto, with German soldiers lined before it; a pall of smoke drifting away over a merry-go-round; the Germans in pursuit of a partisan, through desolate backyards and up a high winding staircase where there is only a barred door at the top; and, at the end, the sad isolation of Stach, waiting in sculptured immobility for a bunch of young recruits to join him, knowing that Dorota is in the hands of the Gestapo.

There is the same visual eloquence in *Kanal*, Wajda's second film, which has had a public showing in London. A grim and bitter story of the last Polish attempt to rise against the Germans in Warsaw – with the Russians standing by inactive on the other side of the Vistula, while the Poles were cut to pieces and their city destroyed – this posed problems of style even more difficult than *A Generation*. Driven from their positions by the German tanks and gunfire, the Polish troops take to the sewers beneath the city, hoping to find their way through them to reform and continue the battle. But, in the darkness and stench beneath, all is chaos. The small detachment which is the collective hero of the film loses its way, disintegrates, and in ones and twos its members collapse or die. This is war without sentimentality or glamour: this is catastrophe.

The style again is poetic, at times almost expressionist, so that these dank, interminable corridors, in which lights flicker and echo, filled with the wandering and the lost, become the symbol of a world where confusion reigns and disaster must in the end overtake the most courageous spirit. Here again the greatest, most significant emotion is love: the tortured progress of the young officer, dying slowly of his wounds, and the girl partisan, through the haunted, pestiferous tunnels, until they reach the last ironic grille that cuts them off for ever from the sunshine and the world of living men – this is impassioned romantic poetry, an affirmation of love and an outcry against the monstrous callousness and barbarity of our terrible age. I can think of no literary artist who has been able to do it as powerfully.

To produce work of the originality and significance of these three young men – and particularly in the context of the film today – is proof of integrity as well as talent of no mean order. That is why we cheer them. Unfortunately, though, to cheer is not enough – at least as far as there is something conclusive about the act, something that suggests that the ship is anchored safe and sound, its voyage closed and done. To make good

Gérard Blain and Jean-Claude Brialy in Claude Chabrol's
Le Beau Serge.

films is extraordinari-
ly difficult; but that is
only the start of the
problem. Films have
to be paid for; and
that means they must
be distributed, shown
and seen. We want
these artists to be able
to go on working, but
we must realise that
the fact that they have
already given evidence
of outstanding talent
is bound to count
against them in a
world where medioc-
rity and conformism
are the cardinal virtues. What chances have they of survival? What chance
has their work of being as widely screened as it deserves?

From certain points of view, Wajda's chances are the best. As I have
said, he is working in a society which values the cinema, and which sub-
sidises its artists instead of throwing them on the open market to compete
with the manufacturers of tinned soups and television sets. *Kanal* was chosen to represent Poland at Cannes in 1957, and it has even achieved a fairly good showing abroad. At the same time, the fact must be accepted that
where the State supports its artists, it is liable to expect a return; and
bureaucrats and politicians are not necessarily more enlightened than capitalist traders. Since October 1956 the régime in Poland has been remarkable not merely for its tolerance, but for its positive encouragement of
artistic freedom and experiment; as a result it boasts today the most promising younger generation of film-makers in Europe. Whether, as the political climate changes, this policy will be maintained is anybody's guess. We
can only pray that it will – and at the same time shout as loudly as possible for work as outstanding as Wajda's to be given the circulation and
appreciation it deserves.

Paradoxically, the chaos that is contemporary France may in the long
run provide surer chances for the serious, determined film-maker than the
less flexible structures of better organised societies. Where else in the
world could a film like Bresson's *Un Condamné à Mort s'est Echappé* have
been not merely produced, but actually shown a profit? In spite of the fact
that *Le Beau Serge* was turned down by the French selection committee as

unworthy to represent its country at either the Cannes or the Brussels festivals (in favour, naturally, of distinctly inferior work by better-placed producers), it will benefit from State aid, as a film of exceptional quality, and Claude Chabrol is already able to plan a new film. Apparently phlegmatic, he has a sage and philosophic way of regarding the situation. 'It's good to make commercial pictures,' he has said, 'and it's commercial to make good pictures.' This turns a nice phrase, but of course, as Chabrol knows very well, it depends what you mean by good.

With a heart that sinks, one turns to Britain. When *Kanal* was announced for presentation by the Academy Cinema in London, a member of the staff of that theatre was approached by an apparently intelligent member of the press. 'But surely,' he was asked, 'that's more a National Film Theatre type of film isn't it?' This dreadful attitude, which imagines that out of 50 million or so people in Britain, only a couple of thousand in the capital can possibly be interested to see a really outstanding film, goes far to explain the present lamentable condition of our cinema. 'Stuitable booking for industrial halls' writes the trade press – and you can be sure that the film referred to is a piece of degraded and incompetent rubbish. The result, of course, is to kill off not merely your potential audience, but any film-maker rash enough to produce a work of imagination and artistry. And this is the shortest way to see British cinemas turned either into dance halls, or into exclusive purveyors of American musicals in CinemaScope, Cinemiracle or Todd-AO.

In this situation, a film like *The Little Island* is more than an individually deserving case; it is a symbol. As things stand, its chances of adequate distribution are slim. Yet has not Richard Williams the right to have his work shown? And have audiences not the right to see it? It is worth noting that of the half dozen British short films that have won distinction at international festivals during the last few years, not a single one has been booked for showing by the circuits. Is *The Little Island* likely to fare better? It is a brilliant, funny, serious and important picture. Therefore the odds are against it.

As I said at the start of this piece, it is not enough for the critic today – or for enthusiasts such as I presume the readers of this book will be – passively to accept the system of cinema as it exists at present, with all its attendant frustration and waste. It is not enough for us to confine ourselves to praise or blame of what that system allows us to see. A better system is what we need, in which the good works which somehow continue to be created by the faith and persistence of the few, can achieve the showing they deserve. The films of these three young men are works of this kind. They give us something to fight for. Thank God for them.

Cannes 1955

Sight and Sound, Summer 1955

WRITING ABOUT FESTIVALS IS A PROBLEM. AS EVERY CRITIC KNOWS, NOTHING is harder than to communicate the quality, the precise feel of films that one's readers have never heard of – and may never have a chance to see. 'I read your article,' people say. 'Very interesting. What were the films really like?'

What was Cannes 1955 *really* like? First of all a rich festival, with a good many interesting, stimulating pictures. Much promise, if few revelations. The general impression is still of an interim period, with our few Masters scattered about the world in lonely eminence. And the march of Progress goes on: colour – panoramic screens – stereophonic sound . . .

It is a march that woefully few artists dare publicly to question. Asked (as was inevitable at every Cannes Press conference) what they think about CinemaScope, they shift uneasily and reply that it is right for certain kinds of subject. But in private some of them are franker. Gene Kelly admitted that he found the system unsuitable for musicals, ugly for dancing. 'You want to do a *pas de deux* and you find yourselves in an acre of empty space . . . Widescreen, yes: but CinemaScope, no. And now there's the business of trying to compose for all proportions of screen at the same time. Directors just aren't in control.' From Russia, Serge Youtkevitch said much the same. 'In so far as all these developments extend the creative possibilities of cinema, of course we much welcome them. But they must not be imposed on directors regardless of their fitness to subject. The same is true of colour. We still make black-and-white films in Russia; and we are going to try to make more. I've been asked if I want CinemaScope for the *Othello* which I am going to make next. I've said no. On the other hand, for a big, fresco-style film like my *Scander-Beg*, it might have been interesting.' 'But do you really think,' I asked, 'that the aesthetic effect – as distinct from the purely sensational effect – of CinemaScope, in even a subject like that is likely to be greater?' Youtkevitch thought, smiled, and shook his head. 'No – not really.'*

Were some feelings of this kind responsible for the jury's award of the Grand Prix to the little, unpretentious, black-and-white *Marty*? And the first prize for shorts which went to Norman McLaren's brilliant, idiosyncratic *Blinkety Blank*? Here were two merited victories for the artist's cinema, unswamped by apparatus. *Marty*'s American rival, Kazan's CinemaScope *East of Eden*, only strengthened one's suspicion of panoramic drama: the more the medium is 'used', the more essential conflict there must be between the spectacular and the dramatic. Of course if there are no genuine dramatic qualities, CinemaScope can give a passable illusion of solidity to a film – e.g. *Bad Day at Black Rock*, which was surprisingly well received at the festival.

But the proper function of the panoramic screen was pointed at Cannes by its more successful use in documentaries. (Or at least in films that are conventionally classed as 'documentaries'.) The American short on tuna-fishing (produced by Fox) could not have been more banal in its human observation; but its wide and colourful vistas of tuna-infested ocean, the row of fishermen ceaselessly whipping the fish through the air to land gasping on the deck of their boat, with the vividness of stereophonic sound to replace the subtler rhythms of a cutting-pattern – these scenes certainly achieved a style of their own. The Italian Cinépanoramique short *Island of Fire* had some well-composed, dramatically effective sketches of peasant life on Etna, including some impressive shots of eruption; and the long Italian exploration film, *Lost Continent*, though rightly jeered for one inexcusable error of taste, otherwise earned repeated volleys of applause for its striking CinemaScope scenes of life on the Chinese and Malayan islands. Made by a group of five Italian directors working under Leonardo Bonzi (who was responsible for last year's *Magia Verde*), and including Enrico Gras, *Lost Continent* achieves at times a style distinctly beyond that of a succession of spectacular *camera obscura* views. But it is at best a rhetorical style; journalistic rather than poetic. Size counts. The thing is simply too big for intimacy.

Perhaps significantly, the best national contribution at Cannes came from the cinema whose cultural tradition seems at the moment the purest, most cultivated in the world. Equally significantly, none of these Japanese entries figured in the list of awards. Yet *A Tale from Chikamatsu*, by Kenzo Mizoguchi, was the one film at the festival that had the absolute distinction of style that marked it as the work of a master-director. Films by Mizoguchi have been seen at other European festivals, but none has yet reached Britain, and it is difficult to convey his quality to those whose idea of the Japanese cinema has been formed by the Kurosawa of *Rashomon* and *Seven Samurai*. *A Tale from Chikumatsu*, a tragic love story set in sixteenth-century Japan, is nearer in feeling to *Gate of Hell*; but a *Gate of Hell* still further refined, shorn of its decorative trappings (Mizoguchi's film is in black-and-white), more austere in technique (there is not a single close-up in the picture), with an altogether classical restraint, with which goes a classical, sublime intensity. This intensity was lacking in *Princess Sen*, another historical tragedy, this time in Eastman Colour. Without being as unfailingly felicitous as *Gate of Hell*, *Princess Sen* is still a civilised, immensely satisfying entertainment. The third

Japanese entry, *Five Sisters*, proved little more than a good class commercial film – magazine story level, but of distinct charm, and continually interesting for its pleasant glimpses of contemporary middle-class life.

In comparison with the Japanese films, it must be admitted that most Western film-making seems the work of a band of more or less adept vulgarians. The American contribution, stronger on paper than on the screen, had mostly been seen in this country: its two new offerings, *Marty* and *East of Eden*, are reviewed elsewhere in this issue. It is unnecessary to say more here than that, if the award of the Grand Prix to *Marty* over the head of *Chikamatsu* was absurd, the American film nevertheless remains one of the most likeable, honourable and praiseworthy in the festival. Britain did not shine: *The End of the Affair* and *A Kid for Two Farthings*. (In passing, it may be regretted that the continued ban on the festival by the British Film Producers Association prevented the showing of a film as respectable as *The Dam Busters* – which would almost certainly have been prized.) A more successful childhood fable was the Spanish *Marcellino Pane e Vino* (directed by Ladislas Vadja); the miraculous climax of this, in which a six-year-old orphan is taken into the arms of Jesus, is rather dubiously edifying, but the story that leads up to it is told with a genial and unforced charm, and most winningly played by its small star. The Germans, alas, were as German as ever – chiefly an ornate, ponderous *Ludwig II* by Kautner, which turned out rather surprisingly to have been photographed by Douglas Slocombe. France submitted a new social melodrama by Cayatte, *Le Dossier Noir*, even more muddled and heavy-handed than its predecessors. More interesting was *Du Rififi chez les Hommes*, made in France by Jules Dassin after four years of enforced inactivity. This accomplished thriller, with its central twenty-minute setpiece of a robbery staged with a documentary wealth of detail and without a word of dialogue, shows that Dassin has lost none of his incisive skill; but the film is chiefly to be welcomed as an opportunity for its director to re-establish himself, and to get to work now on projects that may be nearer to his heart.

From Italy the most eagerly-awaited contribution was of course the new de Sica-Zavattini *Oro di Napoli*. This proved disappointing – at least to those who were hoping for a return by the team to their pre-*Indiscretion* style. The film (in the full version shown at Cannes) consists of six episodes of Neapolitan life, adapted from stories by Giuseppe Marotta. The material is promising: the stories are rich in their elemental themes of love, humour and death, and much of the realisation is inventive, full of zestful, ironic detail. Yet there remains something exterior, and even patronising, about the film; it is heavy with stars, finally uneasy in its compromise between art and commerce.

We have had disquieting news lately of the pressures under which serious Italian film-makers now have to work; and no doubt *Oro di Napoli* is at least partly the result of the unsympathetic attitude of their government towards de Sica's and Zavattini's real social sympathies. Conversely, films from the East showed the strength rather than the weakness of a film industry working in complete accord with official policy. *Heroes of Chipka*, directed by the veteran Vassiliev, would make any Hollywood producer of spectacle green with despair: whole armies deploy magnificently in front of the camera, through the mountains and valleys of Bulgaria, re-enacting the Russo-Bulgarian campaign against the Turks in 1877-8. The scenario has little sense of construction, and the overall design (constantly interrupted by static and tendentious scenes of diplomatic intrigue in Western capitals) is very faulty. But the main action scenes have a grandeur, and from time to time a human liveliness, that is irresistible. One fact is certain: if *War and Peace* is ever worthily to be filmed, only the Russians can do it.

From a spectacular point of view, the Russian ballet-film of *Romeo and Juliet* is less successful: too much of it is simply dowdy. But some of the direction – and the dancing – has splendid vigour and precision; and the poetry of Ulanova's interpretation of Juliet is in itself ample justification for the film. The only contemporary feature from Russia, *A Great Family*, was an agreeable, leisurely chronicle of life in a family of Kiev shipbuilders: the old grandfather who becomes too old to work in the yards; the designer who neglects his wife for his work; the boy who falls in love . . . Social responsibilities are, of course, not forgotten – the point is sometimes rather laboured – but there is a generally relaxed note to the film that is perhaps evidence of a more humane, less nervously propagandist trend in Russian cinema. The neglected wife leaves her husband; returns one day, out of the blue, to see him; they talk . . . But it won't work, and she goes on her way alone. There are no recriminations, and no moralising in this sad, sensitively handled little episode. It is good to find once again in a Russian film this willingness to admit that all is not always for the best, in this best of all possible worlds.

Awards, we all know, are nonsense. If good films manage to get them – so much the better: but at festivals, the prizes are bound to be distributed with a heavy political bias. That is part of the price we have to pay for having them at all. Nevertheless, it was particularly disappointing that at Cannes this year all the spoils went to the big battalions; for one of the most encouraging features of the festival was the liveliness, the almost defiant vitality shown by the smaller film-producing nations. Lack of resources, lack of experience: one or the other, or both of these were evident in the entries from Israel, Greece, Yugoslavia, India, Mexico . . . Yet these are just the deficiencies that prove immaterial. Happily, London showings are assured for at least two of these – *Hill 24 Does Not Answer*, directed by Thorold Dickinson for an Israeli production company; and *Stella*, the second film of Michael Yannis, the young Greek director of *Windfall in Athens*. Both these are vibrantly national productions: the Israeli film with three stories set in their war for independence, each inspired by the common, passionate will towards freedom and nation-hood. Independence is also the theme of *Stella* – in this case a craving for personal independence which is the ruin of its heady, temperamental heroine. Yannis' style is less mature than Dickinson's and there are times when he is apt to overplay his hand; but the full-blooded gusto of his film is extremely engaging.

There remain three productions which must be noted. From India, *Boot Polish*, a sort of sentimental neo-realist story of orphan children in the slums of a big Indian city: less successful than *Two Acres of Land*, but vivid, wholehearted, continuously alive. The Mexican *Roots* – four stories of Mexican Indians, made by an independent unit subscribing to allegiances very different from those of Fernandez and Figueroa – is less crude and sentimental: again a fierce national feeling; a strong, poetic irony; and, above all, an intransigent love for the oppressed people who are its subject. This film should certainly be brought to London.

And London should see, too, *La Route Sanglante*, the wartime story of a Nazi concentration camp for Yugoslav partisans in Norway, made in co-production by a Yugoslav and Norwegian company. There was a good deal of war at Cannes; much blood was spilt on the screen of the Palais des Festivals in the name of national pride and independence; and one responded the more deeply gratefully to a film whose values were pacific. Such are the values of *La Route Sanglante*. The slow movement of the film is the mark of its sincerity: the horrors of the camp are flatly, not dramatically, presented, and the dignity of the prisoners, and of the Norwegians who help them, is unconscious, unassumed, innate. Films like these, of such dogged integrity, restore ones faith.

How can the cinema ever be finished'? What nonsense we are sometimes driven to talk!

---

*It is interesting that such misgivings are felt not only by established directors. J. A. Bardem, the very promising young Spanish director of *Comicos*, who served on the jury this year, expressed himself decisively. 'Sound, colour, even 3-D are real expressive extensions of the cinema. CinemaScope – the panoramic screen generally – is an arbitrary development, aesthetically speaking, imposed on us from outside. The true revolution has been caused by the other innovations – they've made the old grammar out of date. We've got to invent a new language, unfortunately, before the old one had by any means fully developed. As for CinemaScope – the only ray of hope is that most European producers won't be able to afford it. I certainly prefer the ordinary screen.' Bardem's latest film, *Death of a Cyclist*, was shown extra-festival at Cannes with great success, and shared this year's critics' prize with *Raices*.

Cannes for the Tenth Time

New Statesman, 25 May 1957

OF COURSE IT IS ALWAYS TEMPTING TO MAKE LIGHT JOURNALISTIC COPY OUT of a film festival. Absurdities abound. This year at Cannes, for instance, there was Mike Todd's balloon riding over the Croisette, and his planeload of tame journalists flown over from Britain to attend the premiere and have dinner with a dozen lions. There was that young French actor who looked something like James Dean, slouching with tinted hair, leather jacket and jeans, before the cameramen in front of the Canton Hotel. There was that jury of gaga Academicians (Jules Romains, it was reported, had not seen a film for twenty years), whose award of the Grand Prix to *Friendly Persuasion* was met with a torrent of very French boos and catcalls and cries of 'Dassin!' And there are always the starlets undressing hopefully on the beach. Since these are the only aspects of a festival which the popular press is prepared to feature, inevitably many people get the impression of a vast, wicked, commercialised junket. But this is only a part – the least significant part – of the truth. The trouble is that the really important aspects of a festival are so much more difficult to make vivid. Titles of films one has not seen, and may never see, are always off-putting, and their excitement is difficult to convey. Besides, people say, the good ones will come to London anyway.

This is not true, though, or not necessarily. In spite of the cinema's apparent internationalism, films today are not circulating anything like as freely as they should, particularly if they are of quality. Festivals provide an invaluable way of easing their passage. They also provide unique opportunities for keeping in touch with the progress of the cinema out in the world – and for bringing grimly home to us how disastrously the British industry is declining into provincialism. (Our feature entries at Cannes this year looked as though they had been made in 1935.) In London or Hollywood it may be possible to believe that the cinema is going under to television. If we want to appreciate how false this is, we have to go abroad. And this is another reason why it is urgently important that Europe's international film festivals – which now include Berlin, Karlovy Vary and Venice as well as Cannes – should have the support of serious papers and critics of conscience. If art is important, they are important.

This was the tenth festival at Cannes, and of the six I have attended it was the best. I do not mean by this that it was all masterpieces. There were a number of new films by established names, all of high quality (Dassin, Fellini, Kozintsev), and at least two of outstanding success (Bresson's *Un Condamné à Mort s'est Echappé*, and Ingmar Bergman's *The Seventh Seal*). But it was the vigour and promise of the younger directors that impressed the most – many of them new on the international scene. In Poland, Russia and East Germany, in America and Argentina, in Finland and Ceylon work is being done of the greatest artistic and social interest. The backgrounds of these directors vary enormously, as do the means at their disposal. Some of them come from film schools (in countries where society acknowledges its responsibility to the cinema); some of them come from television; and some of them have simply fought their way into filmmaking in the traditional style. Their accents vary, but they have vitality in common, and a generally humanist viewpoint. Through them, the cinema is saying many necessary things about our time.

I have never understood why the social significance of cinema is so generally neglected. Last year at Cannes the greatest impression was made by the Hungarian films: in *Merrygoround* and in *Discord* there was an intensity of feeling, a lyricism and a spontaneous humanity that clearly signalled something new. Yet I can think of no political or social commentator who availed himself of this striking evidence. (In that extensive survey of the Peoples' Republics which appeared in the *New Statesman* last summer, no mention was made of the cinema at all.) And this year? The Hungarian offering was dead: conventional, dated, sentimental and poorly made. And instead the exciting contribution came from Poland. We saw two Polish films, both the work of the same young director, Andrzej Wajda, aged 31. They were both war stories; but this does not mean that they were mere nostalgic harkings-back to romanticised values of the past (as was our own *Yangtse Incident*). It was their spirit that mattered. The first, in fact, *A Generation*, was made before the thaw, and now its makers regard this tale of young Communist resistance to the Germans with a certain dissatisfaction. To a foreigner, however, it is not the immediate political significance of the picture that signifies, so much as its intense idealism, its vibrant humanity. The same attitude inspires the more recent of these two films, *Kanal*, a tragic story of the last days of the Warsaw Rising in 1944, centred on the attempt of a partisan detachment to escape through the city sewers, and its final annihilation. You would have to be blind and deaf not to sense here the independence and national pride of the Poles; and at the same time their obsessive need to exorcise the horrors of their recent past by making art out of it.

It was this resurgent liberalism, implicit in so many of the films shown at Cannes, that I, as a Briton, found most heartening. It can be done, you see. It is there, unmistakably, in the films from Russia too. Kozintsev's *Don Quixote* represents to some extent, perhaps, a retreat into the past: but the mature, compassionate irony of that forlorn idealist, impinged absurdly on the windmill-sails of the world, still obstinate in his affirmation – these images are not accidental. And *The Forty-First*, with its love story between the Communist girl partisan and the young White Russian officer, is done with a humour and an understanding which show a real and valuable evolution of attitude. The humanistic note was sounded again and again, not rawly, but with the depth and complexity proper to art. The Argentinian *House of the Angel* (also the work of a new, young director, Torre Nielsson) was a study of adolescence, unusually subtle and acute; and here also social background – the perverting puritanism of its upper-bourgeois milieu – was made to play its important part. The American *Bachelor Party* (from the team responsible for *Marty*) gives a disturbing, sensitive picture of middle-class life in New York; and the East German *Duped till Doomsday* is a powerful, haunting allegory of the corruptions which produced or submitted to Nazism.

It was an extraordinarily rich festival and I have no space to detail the fresh, adventurous work contributed by countries like Ceylon, Finland, Denmark and Norway. Nor to discuss the important new films by Fellini (*The Nights of Cabiria*: Giulietta Masina again, as a Chaplinesque prostitute) and Jules Dassin (*Celui qui Doit Mourir*, a powerful adaptation of Kazantzakis' *Christ Recrucified*). Robert Bresson and Ingmar Bergman have each made superb films which will surely be shown in London. For the moment I will only say that the Bresson is a triumph of poetic concentration, and one of the best pictures made in France since the War; while Bergman's *Seventh Seal* is a marvellous (in every sense of the word) medieval fable. Surely, I say, such films will come to London. But will they?

The cinema, for artists of integrity and ambition, is a battlefield. But you can also imagine it as a witness – one which can testify most eloquently to the struggles, dangers and efforts of men in our time. The tragedy is that this witness is so consistently disregarded, where it is not actually choked. Here in Britain, for instance, not merely is our own cinema (for a complex variety of social and economic reasons) largely stagnant; but the machinery for circulating works of quality from abroad is hopelessly inadequate. London has about half a dozen specialised cinemas: of these only two follow a consistently respectable policy of programme – and this naturally leaves an enormous number of films either

waiting interminably in the queue, or without the possibility of any showing at all. As a specialised distributor said to me at Cannes: 'It's no use my
buying a picture for Britain if I can't get a West End cinema to show it.
The critics won't write about it; film societies won't book it; and the specialised cinemas in the provinces will only take films that have been successful in London.' And so, however enthusiastically I write about these
two Polish pictures, about *The House of the Angel*, and about *Duped till
Doomsday*, I know that their chances of distribution in Britain are not
good. And as a result most intelligent people in this country – whose idea
of an outstanding film remains stuck at *Baby Doll* or *La Strada* – still fail
totally to understand the stimulus that contemporary cinema can give.

But all this only increases the value of the impetus which festivals like
Cannes – in spite of all their commercial trappings and their publicity
gimmicks – can give to the progress of the cinema. Somehow these films
got made. Somehow they got to Cannes, and were seen by critics from 30
or 40 countries, and were written about round the world. Commercialism
has its lackeys in plenty – decent intelligent men, many of them, the victims of our situation – while art has pitifully few partisans. We must seize
all the opportunities we can. These international festivals do not only
demonstrate the strength of the opposition: they also show us what there
is to fight for. We must use them.

Two Inches off the Ground

Sight and Sound, Winter 1957

> After 1930, the Japanese cinema turned to sound, and confined
> itself to the filming of traditional plays or imitations of
> Hollywood. Work of social significance disappeared . . .
> – Georges Sadoul, *History of the Cinema*

WELL WE (AND NO DOUBT M. SADOUL AS WELL) KNOW BETTER NOW. AND NOT
merely as a result of the few Japanese films – all post-war – that have been
commercially distributed in the West; not merely through enthusiastic
reports from festivals, and informative articles in *Sight and Sound* – but
now, at last, from the films themselves. This wonderful season at the

National Film Theatre has been, of course, only a start; but at least 6000 or so people in London have now had the opportunity to see for themselves that Kurosawa has a range that extends far beyond the exotic and the violent; to experience the work of great directors like Mizoguchi, Ozu and Gosho; to become acquainted, in short, with a whole tradition of film-making of which Western historians of the cinema have, up to now, been perfectly ignorant and which must in future basically affect any of those generalisations we are all so fond of making about 'The Cinema'.

For instance: 'Movies have got to *move*.' One of the things these Japanese directors have made clear to us is that our interpretation of this precept has been a great deal too facile. They almost persuade us, in fact, that movies are best when they don't move at all. More seriously, they oblige us to reconsider and re-define what we mean by movement. (And here, it is interesting to note, their calm example seems to confirm the most interesting and daring ventures of Western avant-garde work in recent years.) For in the West, 'cinematic movement' has usually been related to our experience of the theatre, in effect if not in style. 'Cinema is not literature.' And in the name of this principle almost all the world's great novels have found themselves simplified, sharpened, streamlined and betrayed by translation to the screen. Of course, we too have had our anti-theatrical prophets: most consciously, I suppose, Bresson. But it is in the work of these Japanese directors that we see at its richest and most devel-oped a conception of cinema where the relationship of the artist to his public is far nearer that of the novelist to his reader than that of the *met-teur-en-scène* to his audience. This is not quite the same thing as being 'lit-erary'. Imagine when you have seen *Ugetsu Monogatari* or *Chikamatsu Monogatari*, an *Anna Karenina* filmed by Mizoguchi. It is not merely that he is a finer artist than the Western directors who have taken the subject; it is that the method, the *wholeness* of his vision can create a whole world in which detail and atmosphere are as significant (contribute as much to the 'movement') as the characters-in-action, the plot.

Probably of all these directors, Kurosawa is the most Western in his attitude – one might almost say the most modern (without implying that the others are old-fashioned in any pejorative sense). And presumably this is why he has been the first to become anything like a celebrity in Europe. But his *Ikiru*, which we should call *Living* (the proper translation) and not *Doomed* (which is a silly, distributor's title), comes as a fascinating reve-lation after the more brilliantly-surfaced *Rashomon* and *Seven Samurai*. It is a modern story, and we start simply, directly, without dramatisation. The screen is filled with an X-ray photograph of the principal character's chest. He has got cancer, a voice tells us. And we see him, an elderly, des-iccated little man, a civil servant sitting behind his desk, methodically applying his seal to a pile of papers – which obviously arouse in him not the slightest attention or interest. Deliberately and in detail this man's situation and story are explored. He learns that he can expect only six months more to live, and with this discovery comes the realisation of the complete meaninglessness of his life. His work is without purpose; he has sacrificed everything for his son (he is a widower), to whom he is nothing but a nuisance and a potential source of a legacy. Nowhere in his life can he find anything of the slightest significance: a night spent despairingly in pursuit of joy, in bars and brothels, only leaves him sick and exhausted. It is the ebullient, spontaneous office-girl, who has left her job in disgust to go to work in a toy-factory, who gives him his answer. 'Why are you happy?' the wretched man asks, and in her simplicity she tells him. Her toys are a pleasure to make, because she can think of the pleasure they give. And for the last tortured months of his existence, the man finds purpose and fulfilment by accepting the responsibility of his position and forcing through the indolent and corrupt bureaucratic machine a scheme for the construction of a children's playground on a waste area in the city.

Whether there is a deficiency in the central performance of this story, or whether the awakening and change of direction by the principal character is too arbitrary, I am not sure: but I am conscious of (to me) a certain lack of conviction in the total effect. But what is more to the point, and richly suggestive, is the whole method of the film; the bare force of its style, the awareness and relevance of a whole social background, the edge and sharpness of its characterisation. Perhaps most striking is Kurosawa's conception for the last half of the picture. Instead of being recounted as a straight narrative, the process of the parks construction (naturally, once it is completed everyone gets the credit for it except the true originator) is pieced together in flashbacks from the dead man's funeral, where his family, colleagues and superiors sit ceremoniously together, discussing him in varying terms of hypocrisy, misunderstanding or (in one case only) sympathy. Here Kurosawa's clear-sighted, analytical view of human nature is at its most telling, and the deliberate, piecemeal tempo at which the reconstruction is taken is completely at variance with conventional ideas of 'How to Construct a Screenplay'. In comparison with *Living*, in fact, *Umberto D*. seems hardly experimental at all. It is almost incredible that films of this seriousness and weight can be produced within the framework of a commercial industry. Too often, it is clear, the cinema is not credited with limitations of the medium at all, but simply the limitations of the cultures within which Western film-makers have had to work.

In comparison with Kurosawa, both Mizoguchi and Ozu seem traditionalist in feeling and style. Both were famous in the silent cinema of Japan –

Ozu, in fact, fought shy of sound as heroically as Chaplin; his last silent film was made in 1934. But this traditionalism does not make their films inaccessible; though perhaps it does demand slightly greater readjustment from a Western audience. Both are austere directors – in Mizoguchi's case this is less obvious in *Ugetsu*, where the tale itself is so full of marvels, than in *Chikamatsu*, where the restraint of the style is only rarely broken by the exciting use of Kabuki music, or a sudden, eloquent movement of the camera. In *Tokyo Story*, the camera moves only three times from the beginning to the end of the picture, and then with the most gentle discretion; and in this film particularly, the whole concept of 'pace' (with which, significantly, Western film-makers are so apt to be obsessed) is not so much different from ours as irrelevant. This is an extremely important point, and one which must be understood if the best of the Japanese cinema is to be appreciated as it deserves. And so, for the rest of this piece, it is of *Tokyo Story* that I shall write – with no insult intended, of course, to Mizoguchi. But surely both *Ugetsu* and *Chikamatsu* will be shown again, and written about in full.

Tokyo Story is not a good title: the American, *Their First Trip to Tokyo* is better, since it at least manages to suggest the theme and emphasis of the film. The story is not about Tokyo, but about two old people, living a good way from the capital, who come to see their two grown-up children who are now working in the city, as well as the young widow of another of their sons. They spend a few days there, but soon realise that their children have grown away from them, and that they are more tiresome than welcome. Only the daughter-in-law, a sweet, unhappy woman living by herself, receives them with real affection and generosity. On the journey home, the old lady becomes ill, and they stop off for a day with another of their sons, a clerk on the railway. Home again, with their youngest, still unmarried daughter, the illness becomes serious; the children are sent for; the old woman dies. The children return to Tokyo, and the father remains with his daughter . . .

It is a film of relationships, a film about time, and how it affects human beings (particularly parents and children), and how we must reconcile ourselves to its working. Apart from the great fact of death, the incidents are all slight, and there is no chiaroscuro either in characterisation or mood. The tempo is all the way calm, leisurely, inevitable. There is only one element in the style which might seem at first to jar; the sequences do not fade into each other or dissolve. Every transition is effected by a cut, to some view of the new setting, a rooftop, a wall, a harbour vista, which then cuts again directly to the scene where the characters are going on with their living. But this is not jarring; on the contrary it is a way of conveying the essential unity of existence, of matter and spirit, which is intrinsic to the film's philosophy.

> The Taoist mentality makes, or forces nothing, but 'grows' everything. When human reason is seen to be an expression of the same spontaneous balance as the natural universe, man's action upon his environment is not felt as a conflict, an action from outside. Thus the difference between forcing and growing cannot be expressed in terms of specific directions as to what should or should not be done, for the difference lies primarily in the quality and feeling of the action. The difficulty of describing these things for Western ears is that people in a hurry cannot feel.

This quotation from Alan Watts' recent introductory study, *The Way of Zen*, seems to me to describe exactly the feeling of *Tokyo Story* – and the difficulty of explaining it to those who find (like some film society secretaries) that it is 'too long' and 'nothing happens'. For what we have here is a work that expresses in every image, and in the precise *growth* (as opposed to *force*) of its movement, a whole attitude to living, an attitude that comprehends, in the sense both of understanding and embracing, the painful necessities as well as the joys of existence. From our point of view this philosophy can be called, at least partly, humanistic; but this is by no means its essence. And it is here, I think, that even a reviewer as appreciative as John Gillett (in *Film*) is in danger of missing the point. For with all its understanding and compassion, *Tokyo Story* is not a simple humanistic protest against the transience of life and the bitterness of experience. Specifically, in the 'marvellous shot' (which it is) 'of the tottering figure returning to the house and the mourners' it is *not* the 'inner grief' of the old man that is being symbolised, but rather his wisdom and acceptance. For what has he just said to the girl who has just hurried out to be with him? He has remarked placidly: 'It was a beautiful sunrise. I think we're going to have another hot day.' Surely here many people in a Japanese audience would remember Basho's poem:

> How admirable
> He who thinks not 'life is fleeting'
> When he sees the lightning.

Even more than its humane virtues (I know one ought not to attempt the differentiation), it is the directness and clarity with which *Tokyo Story* reflects a whole philosophy of living that makes it so memorable an experience. For this reason I have chosen to illustrate it, not with a dramatic or 'beautiful' shot, but with a sequence which may convey something of its method and its quality. The funeral is over, and the children have gone back to Tokyo. The old man is saying goodbye to his daughter-in-law: he has given her a watch as a memento of his wife. 'It's funny,' he says, 'but though we have children of our own, you are the one who has been kindest. Thank you.' She cries; and we hear the voices of children singing; the song goes to the tune of 'Massa's in the Cold, Cold Ground'. (The overlap of sound is like something out of *Diary for Timothy*, and the poetic implications are the same.) The schoolhouse: a corridor; at the end of which passes a line of children. Then the classroom, where the youngest daughter is teaching. From the window she sees the train go past, carrying the daughter-in-law back to Tokyo. Then just railway lines, empty.

However hard its artists have tried, the cinema has never seemed satisfactory as an intellectual medium. Perhaps Zen Buddhism, anti-conceptual, and as unhesitating in its acceptance of the world as it is basically anti-materialist, has a particular relevance to film-making.

And my title? Alan Watts writes: 'When Professor D. T. Suzuki was once asked how it feels to have attained *satori*, the Zen experience of "awakening", he answered, "just like ordinary, everyday experience, except about two inches off the ground."' Progressive film-makers of the West have always tried to make men feel that, by keeping their feet firmly on the earth, they can still be ten feet tall. This is not, I think, just another way of saying the same thing. Or can we have it both ways? Here is an important question these films invite us to ponder. Its implications spread considerably wider than the screen; but that, after all, is what the cinema is for.

Commitment in a Cold Climate

Review of *Politics, Art and Commitment in the East European Cinema*, edited by David Paul in *The Guardian*, 7 May 1984

THE ENGLISH, IT IS WELL-KNOWN, DO NOT FAVOUR THE IDEA OF ART THAT expresses a social commitment or that seeks to admonish or persuade. This goes for the cinema as much as for literature. Films are chiefly valued for their qualities as diversion: they are likely to be commended in spite of any seriousness of purpose. David Lean's account of a conversation between himself and Noel Coward comes to mind. 'Do your work,' said Noel, 'as well as you can. Do it the way you want it, and pray the public likes it. If they don't – get into another business.'

'Sound advice,' was Lean's comment, quintessentially English. No nonsense about art. No nonsense about reaches exceeding grasps. And no nonsense about society, politics, contemporary relevance and all that sort of thing.

Of course the cinema was born, and not so long ago, in a tradition of mindless, popular entertainment. Goldwyn's aphorism (about Western Union being the proper carrier for messages) crystallises the Hollywood approach. British cinema is characterised either by middle-class humanism (no one would ever accuse *Gandhi* of an ambition to enlighten politically) or by sophisticated or popular jokiness (from *Carry On up the Khyber* to *The Meaning of Life* to *An Englishman Abroad*).

We had our period of 'commitment' in the late fifties and early sixties. For a short while film-makers admitted to concern with social and even political themes. That was when the post-war ice was breaking and it was briefly possible to believe in (or to hope for) the birth of a New Left, an alliance in which artists and intellectuals, people and even politicians might mingle and communicate. This was a European idea.

In Europe, distinctions of artistic function have never been as rigid as they are here. In a discussion with a Frenchman or a German, one does not have to spend time differentiating between 'art' and 'entertainment'. Artists over there do not need to make special claims for the relevance of their work. Is not the very term 'commitment' European in origin, deriving from Sartre's demand for *'engagement'*?

Partly the difference derives from cultural tradition – which comes down to education. The Imperial tradition, the strongest influence on English education during the last hundred years, has encouraged the notion of art as something irrelevant to experience – even if prestigious. A diversion rather than a necessity: cake rather than bread. And there is also the question of history. World wars apart, the English have not (until lately) needed to feel much concern about the tides of history. They have not been invaded; their national identity has never been in jeopardy. In this they are luckier than the Europeans, for whom politics have long been a matter of direct and intimate concern, not separate from private life but conditioning it, usually unpleasantly.

Especially this is true of the East Europeans, those mostly unfortunate people whom history has compelled to live under imposed Communist regimes. This is a point well made by Boleslaw Michalek, a film critic on the board of Poland's most enterprising production group. In an ambitious symposium published under the title of *Politics, Art and Commitment in*

Anglo-Czech Entente, Prague 1965. Left to right: Jerzy Pitterman (film critic), Miriam Brickman (casting director for the Royal Court), Jirina Tvatochova (actress), Ivan Passer (writer and director), Jaromil Jires, Jan Papousek (writer) and centre, Milos Forman and Lindsay Anderson.

the East European Cinema, he writes: 'Successive wars and social and political crises have made the very existence of these countries insecure . . . The preservation of a sense of identity has been crucial to any attempts to recover or sustain independent national existence.'

Here is the essential difference between them and us. For us that national identity has long been defined – strongly enough indeed to promote reaction (especially among the young). East Europeans know that they must still struggle to affirm and maintain it. As a result, 'commitment' in the Russian-dominated societies of East Europe is an ambiguous term. It may imply conformism (whether principled or opportunist) to Marxist ideology. Or it may imply rebellious, nationalistic idealism. Either way, artists can hardly avoid taking positions directly or indirectly political.

When the Communists took over Eastern Europe at the end of the last war they at once applied established socialist principles to all forms of expression. In those days the cinema was still, for Marxists, as Lenin had pronounced it, 'the most important of arts'. It was nurtured by subsidy, with training generously provided for young film-makers: production was controlled strictly according to the rules of socialist realism.

But the policy contained a built-in contradiction. Education stimulates

585

Andrzej Wajda welcoming Lindsay in Poland, 1992.

then liberates. Soon the young socialist directors were displaying the disruptive symptoms of creativity. They began to outpace the politicians and to show themselves far more intelligently attuned to the developing themes of history. I remember the excitement I felt at Cannes in 1957 when at a thinly attended early morning showing I saw Andrzej Wajda's first film, *A Generation*. Here was a work that paid its socialist realist dues but which, by its intense humane lyricism, made clear a commitment far more urgently felt than the usual obligatory dramatisation of party policy. It gave clear indication of political stirrings that were to come.

A Generation is essentially a poetic film. There is no way of telling how far the young worker-hero's naif enthusiasm for a simplified account of Marxist ideology (which today greatly amuses audiences at the National Film Theatre) was imposed or sincere. It is done with such conviction, such magical innocence that it transcends the literal.

Ten years after that Cannes Festival I was in Warsaw, directing John Osborne's *Inadmissible Evidence* at the Contemporary Theatre – with, as it happened, Tadeusz Lomnicki, so brilliant in the leading role of *A Generation*, playing Bill Maitland. Friends at the Documentary Studio suggested I should make a film for them. 'What about?' 'Anything you like.'

So when the play had opened, I made a little Polish film, about the third-year students at Warsaw Dramatic Academy presenting the songs they had prepared for their singing teacher. An innocent enough subject.

But I chose to intercut the songs and the youthful faces of the student audience with glimpses of the grey world which awaited them outside: a Song of Innocence and Experience. And to my astonishment I found myself, at the routine pre-censorship screening of the finished film for the studio head and my fellow directors, under fire for implied criticism of the regime

'Why is nobody smiling?' asked Jerzy Bossak, in charge of production, as preoccupied, harassed faces from the Warsaw streets moved across the screen. There was no point, I realised, in my saying that I had just felt like that. My climactic sequence alternated waltzing, laughing students with the set-faced crowds of everyday. Around me I heard voices whispering that this sequence was surely designed to evoke the finale of Wyspiansky's *The Wedding*, 'The symbol' (this is Michalek quoting Professor Kazimierz Wyka), 'of a society drugged by inertia and incapable of action . . .' Vainly I protested that I had neither seen nor read *The Wedding*. Even if the evocation was unintentional, it would certainly be remarked and condemned by the censorship. Everyone would get into trouble.

These critics were not party diehards. They were artists, intimidated into auto-censorship by experience of the authorities. Bossak, who was also an artist, was a fair man and a courageous one. But he knew himself threatened by the approaching wave of anti-semitism and reaction which was to break over Poland in the late sixties – and swept him away to Denmark. (He later returned, though not to run the Documentary Studio.)

I got away with my sequence, just. When the censor arrived at the studio the next day, it was in the person of a nice, elderly lady. She thought my singing lesson was 'charming'.

The advance of post-war cinema from the approved subjects of conformism – wartime atrocities and suffering, Communist resistance to the Nazis, Socialist harmony and progress – was slower in Czechoslovakia than in Poland. The Czechs are more phlegmatic than the Poles; the Slovaks had no film tradition to build on; and the Russians were genuinely and hopefully welcomed in Czechoslovakia. (Whereas in Poland they were almost as much feared and disliked as the Germans.)

When Czech film-makers began to break through the party orthodoxies in the early sixties, they were not so much attacking Marxism as exposing a corrupt and slothful bureaucracy – always supposing that such a distinction can be made. In fact, long before politicians dared suggest any such thing, they were foreshadowing Dubcek's 'Socialism with a human face'.

The over-concern in this book with the career of Milos Forman is deeply unjust to his predecessors, who were the first to defy Stalinist convention, as well as to his talented contemporaries of the phenomenal Czech New Wave. None of them could be called anti-socialist: if the Russians had not invaded there would have been no need for that brilliant

Vladimir Pucholt and Hana Brejchova in Milos Forman's A Blonde in Love.

group to be split and suppressed by socialist authority.

It was not their commitment which caused these film-makers to fall foul of the neo-Stalinists; it was the fact that they belonged unmistakably to the supra-national brotherhood of artists. I never made a film in Czechoslovakia, but I remember fondly my first meeting with Milos Forman, Ivan Passer and Miroslav Ondricek in the shoe factory in Zrouch where they were shooting *A Blonde in Love*. We were instant colleagues. I was invited to rushes and asked which takes I would use (which made me very nervous).

Later, in a Prague screening room, I met Ewald Schorm, who made *Courage for Every Day*, a true and moving picture of socialist conscience. I was touched as well as flattered when he quoted a phrase I had written in some provoking article: 'The artist must bite the hand that feeds him.' Years later, at a National Film Theatre exhibition where those words were displayed, a yahoo English 'revolutionary' scrawled his comment over them: 'Self-indulgent Bourgeois Shit'. Which proves that cultural Stalinists may lie in wait round any corner.

In the liberal West, we tend to be complacent about our freedoms. And unimaginative too. Western editors and cultural entrepreneurs need to remember that artists and critics from the Eastern block are never 'free'. Even abroad they must conform if they are to survive: certain areas of discussion are best avoided.

Among the Poles not mentioned at all, I particularly regret the omission of Marek Piwowski, whose dangerously satirical short films, comic, humane and impenitently anti-establishment, I recognised in Warsaw as the work of a blood-brother. Piwowski has only made two features, both of which encountered official objections. Michalek could hardly write about him without sticking his own neck out.

The same considerations may have inhibited another contributor, Yvette Biro, 'screenwriter, film theorist and teacher', who presumably still carries a Hungarian passport. Her chapter on 'Pathos and Irony in East European Films' hints at problems of independence, but soon takes shelter behind portentous obscurantism: '. . . We strive to be freed from the dictatorship of belief, be it based on faith or heresy. The consciousness of history, in the old sense, meant a sense of time moving towards a messianic goal where transcendental values were supposed to emerge.'

This kind of writing – and there are many worse examples in this book – is significant in a number of ways. It is unspecific, abstracted from anybody's actual experience. The 'auteurist' vocabulary employed by these hierarchs of 'film culture' is anonymous and alienating. It seeks to display erudition (which is safe) rather than to enlighten (which can be risky). Its essential commitment is to the maintenance of academic reputation. Unhappily, it is not only to be found flourishing in the East.

Commitment is not just an issue for artists. Nor are these relationships, between politics and art, between independence and conformity, more fodder for academic discussion, crucial only in far-off countries. I noticed the other day a statement by my friend Albert Finney, talking with a journalist about his production of *The Biko Inquest* at Riverside Studios.

'I'm not interested in politics,' he said. 'I don't believe in them. I'm interested in people.' Is this wisdom? Or naivety? I know many Eastern Europeans who would applaud – or at least envy – such a rejection of the tendentiousness, the question-begging and the bullying that goes so often with 'political' art.

On the other hand, isn't there a risk of thinness, of provincialism in art from which political awareness is so specifically excluded? Politics without people make sterile art: people without politics are soppy. But what do we mean by 'politics'? Not just futile intrigue between indistinguishable parties. Not only the knock on the door in the small hours and violent death in the prison cell. Nor only the siting of the Cruise missiles or who gets in at a by-election.

'Politics' is an inescapable element in the haunted twentieth-century air we breathe. Nowhere are its agonising paradoxes more pressing, more frustrating, more revealing than in Eastern Europe. Criticism, like art itself, is a function altogether too important to leave to the aestheticians.

Appendix: The Theatre We Deserve

Editor's Note

In 1984, Lindsay Anderson directed the first major American production of David Storey's *In Celebration* at the Manhattan Theatre Club, New York, with a cast that included Malcolm McDowell and Frank Grimes in the roles originally played by Alan Bates and Brian Cox. While in New York, Lindsay agreed to a public interview at the New Dramatists under the title, 'Naturalism and the works of David Storey'. The interview, conducted by Ada Brown Mather, and including questions from the audience, ranged much further than its rather academic title might suggest, and gave Lindsay free rein to express his feelings about British (and American theatre) in the mid-1980s. At that time, the Royal Court had been experimenting with a kind of 'exchange' programme of productions with New York's Public Theater, then run by the late Joseph Papp, so the fact that Lindsay was presenting one of his past Royal Court successes at an entirely different New York theatre had a certain piquancy.

My initial intention with this piece was to extract some of Lindsay's remarks and insert them into the Commentary that accompanies the first section of this book. On reflection, and given that the Commentary is taken from remarks Lindsay made in the last two years of his life, this seemed inappropriate. In 1984, despite the bitter disappointment he felt over the poor reception of *Britannia Hospital,* Lindsay still had a great deal of energy and a measure of (realistic) optimism. He expressed his thoughts on theatre with clarity, wit and not a little mischief (the Ranevskaya who ran around the stage, by the way, was Irene Worth in a production at the Public Theater).

For this reason, I have removed the questions posed by the interviewer and the audience, and radically altered the order of Lindsay's responses (although without making internal changes in them) in order to give the piece a natural, roughly linear flow. The result might easily have gone into the section of this book on Theatre, but I wanted to end the book with a piece in which Lindsay spoke of his own work and of collaborators who were dear to his heart. So it comes here as an Appendix, quietly calling attention to itself, and encouraging us to deserve better of our theatre and of all our arts.

I REMEMBER QUITE CLEARLY READING IN THE BOOK PAGES OF *THE SUNDAY Times* about the forthcoming publication of a book called *This Sporting Life.* I had just finished directing a musical play at the Royal Court called

The Lily White Boys, and I went to Paris for a few days relaxation. I was sitting in a cafe reading the morning paper and was attracted by the sound of the book, although it was really misleadingly reported. The report suggested that this was emphatically a social work, with some kind of connection (to speak in cliché) to the Angry Young Man or 'protest' theme. In fact, *This Sporting Life* turned out not to be like that at all. But I ordered the book and read it. I must have been one of the first people to read it, because it came to me immediately on publication.

To be honest, I cannot remember anything specific about reading *This Sporting Life* for the first time, but I know I liked it and thought that perhaps it was a film I could make. I knew Tony Richardson, who was George Devine's co-director at the Royal Court, where he had directed John Osborne's *Look Back in Anger*. When this finally succeeded, Tony was invited to film it, so he and John Osborne formed a production company, Woodfall Films – Woodfall Street being where John Osborne had his house in Chelsea. The company prospered. Tony had often said to me, 'Why don't you make a film for Woodfall? What would you like to do?' And this was a time, largely through the theatrical renaissance centred on the Royal Court, when the British cinema was beginning to stir after a long period of fossilisation, of quiescence after the war. One of the films that caused the ice to break was Woodfall's *Saturday Night and Sunday Morning* directed by my friend, Karel Reisz. So it was all beginning and young actors were starting to appear in British cinema, which had never till now had much use for new faces – actors like Albert Finney and Peter O'Toole. The prevailing climate can be judged from the fact that the first play I directed at the Royal Court – it was called *The Long and the Short and the Tall*, in which Peter O'Toole acted with great success – was filmed by Ealing Studios and I wasn't allowed to direct it, and Peter O'Toole was not allowed to appear in it. His part was given to Laurence Harvey.

Anyway, the success of *Saturday Night and Sunday Morning*, which by some miracle Woodfall managed to get financed, changed all that. So I put my idea up to Tony Richardson and he said, 'Well, I'll read it.' I spoke to him about a week later and he said, 'I've read *This Sporting Life*, but I don't think it's the right kind of film for you.' I said, 'Oh, all right. Perhaps I'll find something else.' And about a week later I found that Woodfall had in fact put in a bid for *This Sporting Life*, which Tony had decided was a film for him. However, the ways of providence are mysterious: Woodfall didn't have enough money to buy the rights and they were acquired instead by the Rank Organisation, for not a very large sum – but enough. Rank was interested because Joseph Losey wished to direct it and Stanley Baker wanted to play the lead. Then the producer who got the book said to Stanley Baker, 'Well, fine, I'm delighted for you to play this part, but I don't

wish to make another movie with Joseph Losey.' They had worked together once and he didn't want to repeat the experience; I know no more than
that. Anyway, Stanley Baker, in all honour, said, 'Well, I'm committed to
Joe so I'm out.' So then they approached Karel Reisz because he had directed *Saturday Night and Sunday Morning*. But Karel did not want to make
another film with a Northern, working-class milieu, though he did think he
would like the experience of production. So Karel asked me if I would be
prepared to direct the film if he offered to produce it. I said, 'Well, you can
try. I don't see any reason why they should agree, but have a go.' And he
came back the next day and, somewhat to my astonishment and trepidation, said, 'Well, they've agreed.' So I said, 'I suppose I'd better do it then.'

And this is how I got to know David Storey. Karel said, 'I think we
should get the author to write the script,' because he'd worked very successfully with Alan Sillitoe on the adaptation of *Saturday Night and
Sunday Morning*; so we met David Storey. We were both immediately taken
with David, who is a very fine and impressive person besides being a good
writer. When we were making the film, because I'd been at the Court, I did
ask him, 'Have you ever thought of writing a play?' And David said, 'Well,
as a matter of fact, I've got one.' This was *To Die with the Philistines*, and
we planned to do it at the Royal Court with Richard Harris.

But *This Sporting Life* was a success, Richard Harris got an Oscar
nomination, and naturally his American agents got hold of him and told
him he should stop messing about with art and get out to Hollywood and
do a film with Doris Day. So he did that instead. The project to do David's
play fell through, which was probably a very good thing. He had written
the play before we made the film. He'd written it for television, but it was
rejected by the television companies because it contained an episode in
which the hero went to bed with his mother-in-law. In the innocent days
of the early sixties, this was enough to ban a work from television. The
play was eventually staged at the Royal Court after being premiered at the
Traverse Theatre in Edinburgh and it was, as I said, very well received. I
don't think David would disagree with me if I say that it wasn't fully
achieved as a play. It had two relatively realistic acts and then a third act
which went into a sort of subjective extravaganza. In other words, the
hero went mad. It was full of ideas which then preoccupied David – the
myth of the artist as hero-victim, and all sorts of other very personal mythic themes which I found difficult to sort out. The script sat on a shelf, until
an assistant from the Royal Court who was now running the Traverse
Theatre in Edinburgh asked if he could produce it. I really feel that this
was the best thing for the play because, as I said, I never felt it was quite
fully achieved. I was very conscious of what I felt were its faults, whereas
the director in Edinburgh was not impeded by any such doubts and did a

very successful production. As a result, the Royal Court asked the Edinburgh company to come down and show it to them. The Edinburgh company came down guilelessly, thinking they might be invited to present *To Die with the Philistines* at the Royal Court. Of course, what actually happened was that they showed their production and then one of the Court directors decided he would like to do it himself. So he managed to get the play away from the people who had launched it and he directed it. The title was changed to *The Restoration of Arnold Middleton*. Again, it was a good thing it was done by a director who was not particularly aware of the faults of the play, because he just did it. If you do a play feeling it is faulty in certain respects, you are likely to end up not doing it very well. So I'm glad I didn't direct the play. I'm sure it did better than if I had.

It's a great tribute to David's writing that *Arnold Middleton* was so critically successful. It won him an award, the *Evening Standard* 'Most Promising Playwright of the Year', simply by the truth and vivacity and imaginative promise of the writing. Rather to my surprise, I was invited to direct his second play by the Royal Court, from which I had been more or less excluded when William Gaskill took over as artistic director after George Devine retired. Bill wanted to have a clean sweep at the Court, which meant the exclusion of some of the people who had been working there regularly. But he got into trouble, because his new broom fell to pieces rather quickly. Anyway, he invited me to direct *In Celebration*, just when I was finishing my second feature film, *If....* We were very lucky: we had a brilliant cast, the play was very well received, and I was then asked to do *The Contractor*. So it began.

At that time David was producing an extraordinary flow of work. He's always been a writer who just sits down and writes; he doesn't plan. He sits down in the morning and starts writing, like a coal miner who goes down the pit and starts digging out coal and can never be sure what he's going to produce until he's produced it. That was the time he wrote – and I can never be quite sure in what order – *The Contractor* and *In Celebration* and, possibly, *Home*, all in a very short space of time. He has said that he took about three days to write a play, and I think that's more or less true. When he tried to re-write, it was often not very successful. *In Celebration* may have been written after *The Contractor*, which was the second of his plays I directed – in fact David says so. They are certainly very different, with *In Celebration* much more novelistic in style.

As David went on writing his plays and his novels, he developed a much barer and less traditional style. But different as they were, the plays were all well received. Of course they weren't always fully understood, particularly by the people whose job it was to write about them; but that would be asking rather a lot. *In Celebration* did exceptionally good business at the Royal Court – although it was the policy of the theatre to change its programme every five or six weeks, there wasn't another play to follow it and it ran for twelve weeks. It didn't, however, achieve a West End transfer. All the other David Storey plays I directed after that did go on into the West End. *In Celebration* certainly should have, but in London, in the West End in particular, there is a persistent prejudice against what the middle-class audience and critics label 'working-class' plays. I think that's something that does not happen in New York, because the American class system is quite different from ours. Unfortunately, the British remain morbidly fascinated by class and helplessly entrenched in their class system. One of David's difficulties in finding an audience has always been that, although he writes what may be called 'working-class plays', (i.e., they are generally about working-class people and set in the North of England), they aren't what the bourgeoisie – and very often the working class themselves – expect working class plays to be. They're not plays of protest; they're not plays of scandal or squalor; they are subtle, poetic plays. Of course, his style developed from *In Celebration*, he acquired a reputation for naturalism, although I don't think that's a word that accurately describes his writing. He does not really write naturalistic plays. If you want to use that kind of label, I would prefer to say that he writes poetic and realistic plays. He has written plays in other styles, which I haven't directed. He wrote *Cromwell*, which is not a realistic play, and he wrote *Mother's Day*, which is a black, somewhat Ortonian comedy. But the plays I have directed I would call poetic and realistic.

Every play presents its own kind of challenge. The three plays I did after *In Celebration* were interesting because they were autobiographical in a different way from *In Celebration*. This, of course, David had written out of his own emotional family experience. I would say it has the same relationship to him, is as close to him as *Long Day's Journey Into Night* was to O'Neill. In plays like *The Contractor* and *The Changing Room*, he again drew on his own experience, though on a different emotional level. As a schoolboy on vacation, he had worked on the erecting of tents, he had been for a period a professional Rugby League player, and he had studied at art school, where a lot of *Life Class* came from. So these plays were also autobiographical, but in a different way.

For those who don't know it, *The Contractor* is a play of which the central event is a wedding. At the start of the play, five workmen arrive to erect the tent in which the wedding reception is going to be held. The play begins with a bare stage, grass-covered, on which three poles have already been erected. The workmen arrive, with all the impedimenta – the canvas, the ropes – and in the first act, through all the dialogue, they erect the tent. In the second act, they put down a floor and bring in flowers and decorations and chairs and tables. All this action, too, has to be integrated with the dialogue. In the interval before the third act, the wedding has taken place. When the curtain goes up, we see that the beautifully appointed tent has been reduced to a shambles by a riotous celebration. The workmen arrive, look around, find a few bottles with some champagne in them, glasses and furniture scattered around, and proceed to tidy everything up, take out the dressing and the floor, let down the tent, roll up the canvas, until we're left at the end of the play with the empty stage again . . .

Looking back, I'm not sure how we did it. I certainly couldn't have done it if David hadn't been there, because he knew from experience how tents were erected. I had the feeling – I don't really know how correct this was – that the actors needed to discover the play and the physical practical activity at the same time, so we had one preliminary day when a professional came down from the firm who supplied the tent and showed us how it was done. From the start of the play, the actors with their books in their hands had to carry out all the business of erection, furnishing and dismantling. It drove them nearly mad. I really don't know how we did it, but in the end the action and the dialogue were perfectly integrated. Of course, there's a very strong choreographic element in a play like that. There is a choreographic element in every play, except that in a more conventionally structured work the choreographic element is not so observable; actually most audiences and most critics do not see that there is any. They're not receptive to that element in a production. Whereas, if you have something spectacular like the erection of a tent – or a battle or a scene in a crowded street – they begin to see, and to realise that there is some kind of pattern unfolding before them.

In *Home*, which followed *The Contractor*, there were only five characters. In the first act there were only two, sitting on chairs in the middle of the stage. David has described how the initial idea of *Home* was the image at the end of *The Contractor*. The workmen have finished their work: one table is carried back, and their boss brings in some champagne and glasses, pours it out and they all drink a toast before they go home. So there's just this single white table on the stage, and that gave David – who is also an artist and trained as a painter – the image of a man sitting on a chair, with a table, on a bare stage, and another man comes in and they start talking. I quite believe David when he says that initially he didn't know who the men were or why they were there, and it was only when he had reached the end of the first act that he realised they were in a mental hospital. As you can imagine, that situation offered very few moves indeed. There were two actors and two chairs. Of course we were incredibly lucky to have John Gielgud and Ralph Richardson play the two men. I think each of them probably had two moves – they got up, walked around a little bit and sat down again. And that was that. But to do that is just as difficult in its way as to erect a tent – or at least demands just as much precision. The movement is just as important if there are only four moves in the act as if there are three hundred and fifty.

I sent the play first of all to John Gielgud. John Gielgud had, at about that time, allowed himself to become a bit 'elderly', a bit stuffy, frightened of young people and new things. I think this was largely because of the kind of people he was associating with, and had long been associated with, in the West End theatre. Then he changed course and became much more venturesome: he was in Alan Bennett's play, *Forty Years On*, and in Tony Richardson's film, *The Charge of the Light Brigade*. He discovered for the first time that he could play in the cinema – he's a marvellous screen actor, but he never thought he could do it. Changes took place in his personal life as well, and, really, he's been young ever since and getting younger. When we sent him the play, to my amazement, the very next day the casting director at the Court came in with a big grin on her face and said, 'Gielgud wants to do it! We've had a call from his agent and he's said he'd like to do it. He thinks it's terribly funny.' Then David and I met Gielgud and found that he just instinctively wanted to do the play. He did think it was very funny and that's about it. He hadn't really gone into it a great deal or realised how tricky it was – but perhaps that's how the best decisions are always made. It was he who suggested Ralph Richardson, whom I hadn't worked with before. I knew of course that Ralph was a wonderful actor, but I did think that he often gave performances so eccentric that I couldn't really relish them. Ralph's eccentricity was so colourful that people tended to say, 'Isn't he wonderful? Isn't Ralph marvellous?', and the truth is that often he did act badly – as a fine actor can. When he wasn't sure what he was doing, when he felt uncertain about the material or the direction, he'd fall back on tricks, which were to a great extent defensive. Anyway, I went to see him and he was intrigued by it and also by the prospect of working with his admired old friend.

We got on very well together and he said he'd like to do it. And then I remember he said, 'When are we going to start?', and I said, 'About seven weeks ahead.' The Court had a programme and the next play was already scheduled to go into rehearsal. Ralph said, 'Oh, I can't wait that long. If I have to wait that long, I'll take something else because I can't bear to sit around waiting.' So I went back to the Court and we did manage to re-jig the programme. Thank God the other actors were free and we were able to start rehearsing *Home*. It was during rehearsals that both John and Ralph became extremely frightened: they realised what they'd let themselves in for. They were great actors, but this was a new thing and it was naturally scary. I remember Gielgud would suddenly say, 'I just sit here. I say, "Yes,

yes. No, no." What am I supposed to be doing? Aren't they all going to get terribly bored?' And I would say, 'Now John, it's marvellous and it's going to be great. It's perfectly all right. Don't worry.' And he'd say, 'Well, I suppose you know what you're talking about. I'd better leave it to you.' Ralph would come into rehearsal taking off his crash helmet (he rode his motorbike down to the Court) and he would announce, 'Oh, I decided to withdraw from the play. I woke up in the middle of the night, I was having nightmares. I can't possibly do it. But my wife said, "Go on, don't be an old fool. Go on. Get down there." So I'm here.' Their fears were perfectly genuine. It's a great tribute to their instinct, to their great feeling of respect for David – who was there, of course, all the time – that they rehearsed the play without a moment of disharmony or recalcitrance. It was really only in the last week of rehearsals, I think, that they began to believe we might pull it off. We opened the play in Brighton, but in the last week of rehearsals at the Court, we had a run through and I invited the cast of *The Contractor* to come and watch it, and also the cast of the company then performing at the Royal Court, a company from La Mama. I was a bit apprehensive about this, because I thought this American avant-garde company would probably think this a load of old-fashioned rubbish. But fortunately, all the actors, American and British, responded with wonderful enthusiasm. That was the first time that Gielgud and Richardson felt that, 'This can work.' Really, they did it on faith. It was a great act of courage.

It's a common critical cliché and a great fallacy to say that a director *extracts* good performances from his (or her) actors. Really this is nonsense: a director is not a Svengali. It may be that the *actors* have extracted a good production from the director. That can happen just as easily; many an inadequately directed production has been saved by the actors. It is the responsibility of the director, as far as the acting goes, to first of all cast the play correctly, and then to provide an atmosphere in which the actors can be confident and relax and achieve the best performances of which they're capable. Of course he can help by giving them an understanding of the play and of their relationships to each other, and by finding the right choreography and rhythm to express these. And, if you can give them technical guidance along the way, so much the better.

If an audience becomes aware of the rhythmic structure of a dialogue, it usually implies a destructive self-consciousness – they start admiring instead of experiencing. (The famous 'Pinter pauses' for instance.) I think the kind of work that I have tried to do – or the only kind of work I am able to do really – is to discover within the text the rhythms and the movement that is most expressive of that text. If I've been able to bring out those elements in a production, I'm extremely pleased. I'm gratified that it should be recognised, but I think it's very important to realise that the rhythms, patterns, and moves derive from the text – exist, so to speak, within it. If you haven't got a text with the necessary thoughts, feelings, rhythms built into it, of course you can't do this. You can only then trick it. And a great deal of virtuoso direction is trickery. It's something I've never been responsive to, and have never been good at anyway.

During all of that period, I was extremely lucky to have a writer as talented, to put it mildly, as David, and to have the opportunity to direct those plays. From time to time I would make a film and afterwards I could go back to the Royal Court and do a new play by David Storey. That was a great, great stroke of luck.

For me, rhythm of dialogue, rhythm of movement, shape of movement on the stage is very important, very satisfying and very much a part of the expressive quality of a production – a vital part of one's function as a director. As I say, it is an element often not consciously recognised. It is something that audiences are not very aware of, or helped to be aware of, by people who write about the theatre. In general, those people are extremely literary in the way that they experience plays – literary rather than theatrical. The literary person or critic will judge a play primarily in terms of its dialogue, maybe its characterisation, and then in terms of any sort of *coup du théâtre* that the director may produce, which is so striking that even they can't help seeing that something is happening on the stage. Often it's heartbreaking. I remember at the Royal Court, which is a little theatre, one could look down from the side of the Upper Circle and watch, for instance, the venerable Harold Hobson, the influential critic of *The Sunday Times*. So often, in moments which were treasurable and expressive on the stage, he'd be looking down and writing in his program and not seeing them at all. Unaware of the expressive quality of what was being performed in front of him, he was only just listening.

David rewrote a lot of his first play, which I didn't direct, trying to get the last act right. *In Celebration* was considerably cut, and had a little bit of rewriting. I made a suggestion of reconstruction which David carried out with great reluctance. He is very emotional and subjective about this – almost superstitious. He would always feel that rewritten scenes didn't have the validity of the original, which really was not true. Since then I'd say the plays have had very little rewriting. *Home* was considerably cut in rehearsal, because David felt he needed to hear the initial, too-long dialogue before he could be sure where to cut it. *Early Days* was considerably worked over, from the first text which was quite long and not very formed, to the final version as performed by Ralph Richardson, which was concentrated into two acts of about forty minutes each. As a result it became much more poetic and less naturalistic.

When we came to do the film of *In Celebration*, I thought that one of the characters somewhat diluted the concentration – particularly from the point of view of a movie. We weren't adapting or reconstructing the play for the screen, we were filming the text, so I felt that it was extremely important to maintain tension. And it worked so well, the play gained so much in concentration, that I suggested to David that we should use that text for the New York production, and he agreed.

The play had never been presented in New York, though I think there have been quite a few productions around the U.S. I didn't know anything about these; but I did know, from the critical reception of the film version which we made five years after the first production at the Royal Court, that the themes and emotions of the play were perfectly comprehensible, even familiar, to Americans. So I thought it should certainly be done in New York. I was, of course, a bit apprehensive in that, for the first production, we had been extremely lucky with our cast. I don't need to say how important it is to have the right actors for a play like this – especially when you are presenting it for the first time. Casting was always given great importance at the Court, and for *In Celebration* we searched long and hard. We were successful, and we found a group of actors who not only suited the roles perfectly, but worked together most happily. We even had the extraordinary experience, five years after the first production, of filming it, with exactly the company we had in the theatre. This gave the film, I think, a quite unique quality, because the actors knew not only the play, but each other so well. When the opportunity came to do it in New York, I started off thinking, 'Well, I don't suppose I can do it as well as before.' I was also somewhat intimidated by the disadvantage of coming to a country where I don't know the profession, the actors, as well as I do at home. It's more difficult in America, too, because of this terrible split between New York and Los Angeles, the capitals of theatre and television, which of course is something we don't experience in London.

But once again we were lucky. I was particularly lucky in having two actors I had worked with often before. Malcolm McDowell was able to come to New York and do it, and Frank Grimes, whom I've worked with on two other David Storey plays at the Royal Court, is now living in New York. So I began with two familiar talents whom I knew I could work with. I feel I was incredibly lucky with the other casting and I think we have a production that is absolutely as valid and as good as the first one – with inevitably different qualities – but in no way inferior. As a matter of fact, when I've done productions again, I've never found the experience repetitive or boring. It's the actors who recreate the show.

As far as David's plays go, neither *Home* nor *Early Days* really present one with a strong physical world. And even in *The Contractor* or *The Changing Room*, although the physical action gives the plays a strong framework, one must never forget that this framework is poetic rather than purely naturalistic. The action-scenario is rather like the pretexte of a ballet: the staging has to be choreographic rather than simply naturalistic. In fact, I am not too fond of the word 'naturalistic' – or at least as it applys to these plays. I would rather call them 'realist.' Shakespeare is also a realist, particularly in a play like *Hamlet*. I've only directed *Julius Caesar* and *Hamlet* and they are both realist plays in a way that I find congenial – and somehow familiar. Even their rhetoric is dramatic rather than literary. I'd be very Intimidated if I had to stage *Love's Labours Lost*, say, or *Richard II*. I'd be very vary of *Romeo and Juliet* – or of *Coriolanus*, because so much of it is so difficult to understand.

You know, if you get your Ranevskaya to run six times round the stage at the end of *The Cherry Orchard*, you're providing meat and drink for the critics – they've got something they can write about. But if you simply (not that it's simple, of course) put *The Cherry Orchard* on the stage, with the sort of subtlety and immediacy you're talking about, what is the wretched critic to do? *He's got to write about The Cherry Orchard.* They're just not up to it. I remember a reputed critic, Michael Billington of *The Guardian*, saying to me apropos my production of *Hamlet*: 'Yes, it was good. There were some very good things in it – but I really prefer a more conceptual production.' That is what critics want – a conceptual production. In other words, a production in which the director's concept can be seen and discussed, as distinct from the play which the author has written. My formation – apart from any temperamental qualities I may have been born with – was at the Royal Court. At the beginning, when George Devine and Tony Richardson started it in 1956, the Royal Court was called a Writers' Theatre. It wasn't a Writers' Theatre in any literary sense, though; it was a Writers' Theatre in that the aim was to conceive and execute productions which would realise what the author had written. That was very different from the intellectualised theatre that has become the tradition of, say, the Royal Shakespeare Company. The RSC has developed a tradition of intellectual theatre, which often involves, at the beginning of rehearsals, the director sitting with the actors and giving a long talk about the play and then having a long discussion about the play in which the actors all try to behave like intelligent people instead of being content and happy to be intelligent actors. Actors can be very intelligent, but with their own kind of intelligence, which is often, as far as the theatre goes, much more valid than the intelligence of the intellectual. (When they try to be intellectual, the result is usually disastrous.) So, although I have felt frequently that it's a great disadvantage not to be what Michael Billington calls a conceptual director – and it is a particular disadvantage today – I have to accept the fact that I'm just no good at it. I'm unable to form concepts which are distinct from an intuitive, and I hope intelligent, apprehension of the text.

I find it difficult to talk about British theatre today because I'm not a critic, and this means that my opinions are very personal, very subjective. Certainly, since the early days of the Court, it is much, much easier for young and new playwrights to get their work performed. Sometimes it's a bit too easy. Very often the plays are not worked on as carefully as they should be, and as they would have been. New playwrights tend to be over-indulged and over-praised. After the first fifteen years of the Court, I personally found myself out of sympathy with the new young generation of writers. This is the generation of what I call the university wits: intellectual left-wingers, generally university educated, like David Hare, Howard Brenton, Howard Barker. I find their plays much too theoretical, written not with experience but with 'concepts'. Unfortunately this became the ruling fashion in Britain. Of course, critics favour this kind of writing, because (like a 'conceptual' production) it is easy to write about. It's also not emotionally challenging.

So far as the general picture goes, I think the big subsidised companies are pretty disastrous. It's a sad irony that the idea of a National Theatre, which seemed so necessary, which was so tenaciously fought for, should have occasioned such errors. In the euphoria of the sixties, of course, the economic situation was completely misread and, partly as a result of that, the fatal decision was made to go for size. And so, instead of a living National Theatre, we got an oversized, soulless white elephant. Theatre subsidies in Great Britain have been hogged by the National Theatre and the Royal Shakespeare Company to a quite unjustifiable degree. And over-subsidy has resulted in over-expenditure. Scenically, for instance, we are almost back to the era of Beerbohm Tree: the technology may be modern, but the extravagant display and the conspicuous expenditure are fully eighty years old. These productions represent a great waste of resources as well as being bad theatre art; but unfortunately, the public tends to like circuses and so do the critics. Shakespeare said that there were no tricks in 'plain and simple faith', but I'm afraid plainness and simplicity are not popular. They require too much attention. I don't go to the theatre much in London.

I always think of Jonathan Miller as a 'conceptual' director. I believe he has done simple productions, and I've been told they are excellent. But I can find his intellectualising temperament very irritating; intellectuals tend to relate ideas to other ideas, instead of to life. As a result, they offer illustration rather than experience. Of course, Jonathan has been in charge of producing the BBC Shakespeare series for television, which has been an Anglo-American enterprise, part-financed from the States. I personally feel this whole enterprise has been unfortunate, most particularly because of the decision that the productions should be entirely British. It is fallacious to suppose that the English, and no one else, know how to present Shakespeare. I myself

601

find the English way of doing Shakespeare at the moment emotionally inadequate and over-pictorial – technical rather than truthful. I cannot watch those BBC versions even if, certainly through Jonathan's influence, they are more handsome and more intelligent than they were.

Who controls theatre in Britain? Well, Jonathan Miller is paranoid about Peter Hall – even if with some justification. But really, he should have known better. He became one of the artistic directors at the National Theatre when Peter Hall took over, and did some productions there. And then both he and Michael Blakemore had a row and left. It was naïve of Jonathan not to have known what the place would be like – you know the proverb, 'He who sups with the Devil must use a long spoon.' Of course Peter Hall does not control theatre in Britain. As head of the National Theatre, he exerts a powerful influence; he is an accomplished politician and knows how to manipulate the media. But he has been too busy with his own career, making the considerable amount of money he needs, to give the National Theatre a strong sense of style or ensemble. There isn't really a style at the National. You'll see on the back of their programmes a list of 'The National Theatre Company', about ninety names, but this is mostly window-dressing. All it means is that those are the actors who are working at the National Theatre at that particular moment. A lot of them will only have been engaged for one production, and maybe towards the end of that production will only be working once every ten days. There is an unfortunate lack of overall policy at the National Theatre – perhaps the place is just too big.

But after all, you've got the Royal Shakespeare Company too, which is powerful and well-subsidised, and not part of the National Theatre empire. They have their own empire. They have a strong house sense, a marked technical style, and a demand – in a rather schoolmarmish kind of way – for what they like to call 'loyalty.' Loyalty from the actors, that is, which generally means the actors putting themselves at the disposition of the management. Then there is the mini-establishment of the Royal Court, which is conventionally leftish in its policies – the alliance with Joe Papp is significant. And of course there is still what is called the 'commercial theatre,' (which perhaps ought to be known as the 'independent theatre'), West End producers who can do more or less well with more or less conventional work. The West End is going the way of Broadway, though it hasn't gone so far, so fast. There's a flourishing fringe theatre in London of various kinds, performing in clubs, in little theatres, doing lunchtime theatre – a lot of that. There are repertory theatres around the country, which are mostly run (of course there are exceptions) by fairly mediocre directors appointed by the Arts Council. Generally I think the British theatre is probably what Britain deserves, as must be the case of any theatre. I suppose the New York theatre is what New York deserves.

Acknowledgements

Thanks are due to a great many people for their practical and moral help in bringing this book to completion.

After Lindsay Anderson's death, I spent several weeks at his London flat, in the company of Lindsay's long-time friends, David Robinson and the late Jocelyn Herbert, and his tireless secretary Kathy Burke, boxing up the material that would form his archive. David, Jocelyn and Kathy were the first to encourage me to complete this book, and I owe them an immense debt of gratitude. For this reason, I dedicate my work on the book to all three of them.

The archive boxes were held at the British Council offices, under the care of Dr Sean Lewis, Paul Howson and, especially, Paul Cotgrove, and I thank them for the free access they granted me. The archive is now at the University of Stirling, under Dr. Peter Kemp and Professor John Izod, and it has been catalogued by the archivist Karl Magee, who deserves special thanks.

In my researches, I have been aided by a number of books, including Elizabeth Sussex's 1970 monograph, *Lindsay Anderson*; Eric Hedling's *Lindsay Anderson: Maverick Film-maker*, and the work of Charles Loring Silet who was the first to attempt an anthology of the film writings of Lindsay Anderson; and his bibliography of the writings of Lindsay Anderson. Two memoirs have proved invaluable: David Sherwin's *Going Mad in Hollywood* (which is the best record of Lindsay at work), and Gavin Lambert's, *Mainly About Lindsay Anderson*. David and Gavin have also been very generous with their advice in person.

My thanks are also due to Nicky Akehurst, John Berger, Kate Buckland, John Cartwright, Lucian Freud, Kevin Jackson, Herbert Lom, David Lucas, Sarah Martin, Gaz Mayall, Tim Nimmo, Julien Planté, Marzena Pogorzaly, Dr Sarah Wilson, Kevin Jackson, David Thompson, Tim Nimmo, Marzena Pogorzaly, Deidré Wallace, Liz Webber and Sarah Wilson for innumerable kindnesses along the way. I wish also to thank two of Lindsay's favourite theatre photographers, John Haynes and Lewis Morley. Lindsay gave his publishers a number of photographs from which to illustrate the book but often without reference to the photographers, so we would be pleased to hear from any such unacknowledged sources.

For their advice and support on this project, I must thank Sandy Anderson, Stephen Frears, Peter Gill, Frank Grimes, Eric Hedling, Leslie Hardcastle, Mike Kaplan, Malcolm McDowell, David Storey, the late Alexander Walker and, of course, the indefatigable Lois Smith whose long association with Lindsay and his work continues today in her establishment of the Lindsay Anderson Memorial Foundation. The Foundation exists to promote Lindsay's work and to safeguard his legacy, and its committee members – including Graham Crowden, Kevin Brownlow, Anthony Page, Saxon Logan, Charles Drazin, Tom Sutcliffe, Kelly Anne Robinson, Ted Craig and Paul Graham – have been a source of immense support.

This book would never have seen the light of day without the unwavering commitment of Lindsay's long-time friends and publishers, Sandra Wake and Terry Porter of Plexus; I thank them, as I do Nicky Adamson and Steve Adamson, and Rebecca Martin who has designed the book so beautifully.

On a personal level, I offer my loving thanks to Sophie Mortimer who has given me more than she can know.

Of course, I must reserve my deepest thanks for the late Lindsay Anderson whose friendship and advice I will always treasure and sorely miss. He remains the invisible reader over my shoulder at all times, and my work on this book has taught me the true meaning of the phrase 'a labour of love': it is, essentially, his book and his alone.

Some of Lindsay Anderson's writings and pieces collected here originally appeared in books, newspapers, magazines; some were first heard on radio and stage. Acknowledgement is hereby made to the following: My Country Right or Wrong?, *Sunday Telegraph Magazine*, 26 June 1988; The Value of an Oscar, BBC Home Service, 9 September 1956; Bernard Miles, Celebration, Mermaid Theatre, 29 January 1991; Notes from Sherwood, *Sight and Sound*, Winter 1956; Free Cinema, *Universities and Left Review*, Summer 1957; The Court Style, *At the Royal Court*, ed. Richard Findlater, 1981; Glory Days, *Plays and Players*, May 1986; Sport, Life and Art, *Films and Filming*, February 1963; Roberto Gerhardt and the Music for This Sporting Life, *Tempo*, December 1981; School to Screen, *The Observer*, December 1968; Preface to the published script of *If*. . . . by Lindsay Anderson and David Sherwin, 1969; Stripping the Veils Away, *The Times*, 21 April 1973; Introduction to the published script of The Writer in Disguise by Alan Bennett, 1985; Bette Davis, Obituary, *The Guardian*, 11 October 1989; 35 Days in Toronto, Interview with Gerald Pratley, *Sight and Sound*, Spring 1989; The Long Night of the Russian Canapé, *Independent on Sunday*, 25 November 1990; From *Sequence* 2, Winter 1947, 3, Spring 1948, 4, Summer 1948, 5, Autumn 1948, 6, Winter 1949, 7, Spring 1949, 9, Autumn 1949, 12, Autumn 1950, 14, 1952, Angles of Approach, Creative Elements, The Director's Cinema?, A Possible Solution, British Cinema: The Descending Spiral, The Films of Alfred Hitchcock, Meeting in Dublin with John Ford: *The Quiet Man*, *They Were Expendable* and John Ford, *Louisiana Story*, Minnelli, Kelly and An American in Paris, *Paisà*, *Sciuscia*; The Cinema Is . . . , unpublished article written for *The Observer*, 1954; Stand Up! Stand Up!, *Sight and Sound*, Autumn 1956; Get Out and Push!, *Declaration*, edited by Tom Maschler, 1957; French Critical Writing, *Sight and Sound*, October-December 1954; *Positif* and *Cahiers du Cinema*, *Sight and Sound*, January-March 1955; Catholicism and the Cinema, review of *Dieu au Cinéma* by Amedée Ayfre, *Sight and Sound*, January 1954; David Robinson, *British Film*, 1991; Dilys Powell and C. A. Lejeune, *The Daily Telegraph*, 4 January 1992; Taking Them All In, the *Chicago Tribune*, 15 April 1984; *Too Much: Art and Society in the Sixties 1960-1975*, *Tatler*, September 1986; Critical Betrayal, *The Guardian*, 2 March 1981; Vital Theatre, *Encore*, November-December 1957; Replying to Critics, *Encore*, March-April 1958; Pre-Renaissance: Is the Left Going in the Right Direction?, *International Theatre Annual*, 1961; No Nonsense About Shakespeare, *Daily Telegraph*, 15 December 1964; The Playboy in Edinburgh, *Direct*, 15 June 1984; A French Hamlet, *The Observer*, 1954; At the Court of King George, *The Guardian*, 7 June 1978; Jocelyn Herbert, introductory words to an exhibition at the National Theatre, 14 September 1993; Tony Richardson, introduction to *The Long Distance Runner* by Tony Richardson, 1993; John Dexter, *The Spectator*, 6 July 1993; John Osborne, *The Spectator*, 9 November 1991; Jill Bennett, *The Independent*, 7 October 1990; Rachel Roberts, *Double Exposure*, 27 June 1990; John Haynes, introduction to *Taking the Stage* by John Haynes, 1986; John Gielgud, *John Gielgud, A Celebration* by Robert Tanitch, 1987; David Storey, for a brochure on *In Celebration*, 1974; The Studio That Begs to Differ, *Film and Theatre Today: The European Scene*, 1949; Going It Alone: The British Documentarists; Only Connect: Some Aspects of the Work of Humphrey Jennings, *Sight and Sound*, April-June 1953; Postscript to 'Only Connect', (British Film Institute/Riverside Studios), 1982; *Lucky Jim*, *New Statesman*, 5 October 1957; The Films of Carol Reed, *The Times Literary Supplement*, 8 January 1988; A Prophet without Honour, the *Chicago Tribune*, 22 March 1987; A Matter of Life and Death, *The Daily Telegraph*, 26 September 1992; Recollections of a Full Life: Bryan Forbes, *The Daily Telegraph*, 16 May 1992; The Short Flight of a Golden Bird, *The Sunday Telegraph*, 17 June 1990; Bill Douglas, Introduction to *Bill Douglas: A Lanternist's Account*, 1993; The Lost Past of British Cinema, *The Daily Telegraph*, 13 March 1993; The Lights That Failed, *Screen International*, 1 February 1991; British Cinema: The Historical Imperative, *International Film Guide*, 1984; Inventing Hollywood, *Times Literary Supplement*, 15 December 1989; Charlie Chaplin, *Tatler*, 4 March 1985. Mary Pickford, *The Spectator*, 25 April 1992; Return of the Prodigal: Von Stroheim, *The Observer*, 10 January 1953; Garbo and Shearer, *The Sunday Telegraph*, 19 August 1990; Shirley Temple, *The Daily Telegraph*, 23 November 1989; Mary Astor, *Sight and Sound*, Autumn 1990; Katharine Hepburn, *The Spectator*, 21 September 1991; George Cukor, *The Daily Telegraph*, 20 June 1992; David O. Selznick, *The Daily Telegraph*, 26 January 1993; Last Meeting: The Hustons, *The Daily Telegraph*, 12 May 1990; Orson Welles, *The Spectator*, 9 August 1986; Joseph Losey, *The Independent*, 24 November 1991; Nicholas Ray, *The Daily Telegraph*, 27 April 1993; Don Siegel, *The Daily Telegraph*, 25 September 1993; Martin Scorsese, *The Daily Telegraph*, 11 April 1992; Behind the Mask of Innocence, *The Daily Telegraph*, 15 June 1991; The Birth of a Nation, *Sight and Sound*, January-March 1953; *Guys and Dolls*, *A Hill in Korea* and *Smiles of a Summer Night*, *New Statesman*, 1956; *The Big Heat*, *Sight and Sound*, July-September 1954; *Them!*, *Monthly Film Bulletin*, September 1954; *Giant*, *New Statesman*, 12 January 1957; *The Girl Can't Help It*, *New Statesman*, 23 February 1956; Science Fiction Movies, *New Statesman*, 6 October 1956; The Last Sequence of *On the Waterfront*, *Sight and Sound*, January-March 1955; Hooray for Hollywood, *The Guardian*, 19 March 1983; Hype vs. Old Lies, *The Daily Telegraph*, 27 March 1993; Sergei Eisenstein, the *Times Literary Supplement*, March 31-April 6 1989; Theoretical Writings of Eisenstein, *The Sunday Telegraph*, 19 March 1988; Kozintsev's *Lear*, *The Guardian*, 4 April 1977; *L'Atalante*, *Independent on Sunday*, 13 July 1990; Leni Riefenstahl, *The European*, 1994; Encounter with Prévert, *Sight and Sound*, July-September 1953; Bergman's Reticent Confessional, review of *The Magic Lantern* by Ingmar Bergman in *The Spectator*, 4 June 1988; Satyajit Ray, *The Spectator*, 7 April 1990; Roman Polanski, *Tatler*, January 1980; *Casque d'Or*, *Sight and Sound*, October-December 1952; *Madame de . . .*, *Sight and Sound*, April-June 1954; *The Adventures of Robinson Crusoe*, *Sight and Sound*, October-December 1954; *La Terra Trema* and *Baby Doll*, *New Statesman*, 5 January 1957; *A Generation* and *Bridge on the River Kwai*, *New Statesman*, October 1957; Three to Cheer For, *International Film Annual Number Two*, 1958; Cannes 1955, *Sight and Sound*, Summer 1955; Cannes for the Tenth Time, *New Statesman*, 25 May 1957; Two Inches off the Ground, *Sight and Sound*, Winter 1957; Commitment in a Cold Climate, *The Guardian*, 7 May 1984.

Index